Talking About People

A Guide to Fair and Accurate Language

Rosalie Maggio

ORYX PRESS
1997

The rare Arabian oryx is believed to have inspired the myth of the unicorn. This desert antelope became virtually extinct in the early 1960s. At that time several groups of international conservationists arranged to have 9 animals sent to the Phoenix Zoo to be the nucleus of a captive breeding herd. Today the oryx population is over 1,000, and over 500 have been returned to the Middle East.

© 1997 by Rosalie Maggio
Published by The Oryx Press
4041 North Central at Indian School Road
Phoenix, Arizona 85012-3397

Published simultaneously in Canada
Printed and bound in the United States of America

Library of Congress Cataloging-in-Publication Data

Maggio, Rosalie.
    Talking about people : a guide to fair and accurate language / Rosalie Maggio.
        p. cm.
    Includes bibliographical references.
    ISBN 1-57356-069-3 (alk. paper)
    1. Rhetoric. 2. Language and languages—Sex differences. 3. Nonsexist language. I. Title.
    P301.M33 1997
    428—dc21   97-30047
                                                            CIP

To DAVID
Liz, Katie, Matt

Contents

Acknowledgments

The pathbreaking women and men who worked in this area long before I was even aware of it have my respect and gratitude. Casey Miller and Kate Swift, pioneers of nonsexist language and dear friends, have been endlessly inspiring and supportive. Sandy Berman, energetic, compassionate, and encyclopedically knowledgeable, has kept my mailbox full and my questions answered. Through their writings and kindnesses, Cheris Kramarae and Dale Spender have inspired and influenced me.

Nick Levinson, widely read and accomplished wordsmith, contributed hundreds of suggestions, additions, refinements, and citations.

Chris Dodge, Vivian Jenkins Nelsen, Mary Maggio, Bob Epstein, Bonnie Goldsmith, Laura Gintz Jasper, Matthew Windibank, Judy Ryan Haaversen, Susanne Skubik, Mary Kaye Medinger, and Liz Topete-Stonefield were generous with their time and specialized knowledge.

I owe a great deal to the thoughtful people who wrote with comments and useful information, especially John A. Hobson, Ralph P. Boas, Diane Currie-Richardson, Rabbi Cheryl Rosenstein, E. Mendelsohn, Michael Nicholson-Beer, Jennifer Boerio, Janell Joseph Siegfried, Julie Bach, Sandra G. Kramer, Anne R. Carroll, Susan D. Zager, Alan R. Brown, Alicia S. Jamerson, Nancy Marie Robertson, and Jennifer Belyea.

Liz Welsh is the editor every writer hopes for—knowledgeable, professional, and good-humored. Despite hours of discussing commas and other important issues, we still like each other.

A broad thank you to my supportive and charming parents, Irene Nash Maggio and Paul Joseph Maggio, and to my loved and loving siblings, Frank Maggio, Patrick J. Maggio, Kevin Michael Maggio, Mary Maggio, Paul T. Maggio, Mark E. Maggio, and Matthew J. Maggio.

Best of all, I've been blessed with a family—husband and friend David, adult children Liz, Katie, and Matt—that values each other and the work each is doing. I find these congenial and talented people a bottomless source of joy and inspiration.

User's Guide

If words are to change their meanings, as assuredly they are,
let each user of language make such changes as please himself,
put up his own suggestions, and let the best win.

—*Rose Macaulay*

Macaulay's quotation—despite its exclusionary language—should set the tone for an enjoyable and productive use of this guidebook. It is you—each individual user of the language—who will make the choices that you think appropriate in your speech and writing. This guide is no substitute for your own experience, knowledge, and common sense. Language belongs to the people who use it.

This book—and the two previous ones—came out of my own need for it. Like many writers, I enjoy "getting the words right" (Hemingway's explanation for his 39 rewrites of the ending to *A Farewell to Arms*). But my reference shelf—dictionaries, thesaurus, usage books, style manual—wasn't very helpful when it came to "people language" (how we characterize the various ways that you are you, and I am I). I often didn't know if a term was accurate and current or, if I knew the word wasn't a good choice, it took too long to find the best alternative each time I encountered it.

Today it's not only writers who want to "get the words right," but also people in education, government, publishing, business, the nonprofit sector, the arts, the judiciary, social services, and almost every other identifiable group that has a collective pulse.

Why a third book? Like everything else in our speeded-up world, changes in people language occur at unprecedented rates. Never before have so many people had so much to say about the importance of naming and the ways we characterize human differences. In the six years since the publication of the last book, there has been a growing awareness not only of the effects of language on the quality of our lives but of our power to decide for ourselves how we want to be described and to convey this information to others. Much of the material in this book was not generally accessible six years ago.

The organization of the book is fairly simple: the Writing Guidelines give you the rationale for fair and accurate people language, some general guidelines and practical help, and suggestions about handling special situations (letter salutations, for example). There are also sections on who controls the language, on ridiculisms, and on everybody being "so sensitive" these days. People often don't read a book's front matter, but you might like the Writing Guidelines.

The Dictionary of Terms consists of some 8,000 words and phrases that are or may be perceived as problematic. Each entry term is followed by just enough information to allow you to make an informed judgment about its use. Sometimes alternatives are included; sometimes statistics are given to situate the term in time and space; and many quotations are included, especially in cases of controversial words. When alternatives are given (in italics), they are listed in order of presumed usefulness and are separated by semicolons when they are for different meanings of the entry term. Not all alternatives are synonyms for the entry term and not all are equally useful; like a thesaurus, they offer you a number of possibilities. To avoid overwhelming the entries, many of which are very brief, citations are indicated simply by author and title.

And, as Dave Barry would say, we didn't make any of this up. All entry terms and alternatives have been gathered from reference works, from daily newspapers and weekly magazines, from everyday speech and writing. One enjoyable source of information has been feedback from readers of the previous books; by letter, telephone, call-in radio show, and speaking engagement dialogues, people have offered their expertise, anecdotes, reading suggestions, and criticisms.

You will not agree with everything in the book, but the nice part is you don't have to. A range of entry words, alternatives, and information is offered so that most people will find some help in making word choices. At least once as you are looking through the book, you will see something that makes you think, "Now *that* is going too far!" We all reach that point. But we don't have to "buy" everything in here, nor do we have to do everything all at once. Vivian Jenkins Nelsen says, "Guilt is to be tasted, not eaten." The same could be said of this guide.

Using respectful people language can be satisfying and rewarding. It can also be difficult and frustrating, and it is helpful to admit that. However, this makes sense in context: *any* kind of writing can be difficult and frustrating. Verifying that people language is fair and accurate should be as commonplace as checking for spelling, grammar, usage, and style.

By considering the way we talk about people, we may begin to understand the power of word choices and to fashion language that respects our individual and common humanity.

Writing Guidelines

INTRODUCTION

Language both reflects and shapes society. Culture shapes language and then language shapes culture. Little wonder that the words we use to talk to each other, and about each other, are the most important words in our language: they tell us who I am, they tell us who you are, they tell us who "they" are.

Rabbi Donna Berman says, "Language doesn't merely reflect the world, it creates it." She points out that like the eye that can't see itself, we have trouble seeing our language because it is our "eye."

The process of looking at our language, discussing it, debating it, increases our awareness of the social inequities reflected by our word choices. There can certainly be no solution to the problem of discrimination in society on the level of language alone. Replacing *handicap* with *disability* does not mean a person with disabilities will find a job more easily. Using *secretary* inclusively does not change the fact that fewer than 2% of U.S. secretaries are men. Replacing *black-and-white* in our vocabularies will not dislodge racism. However, research indicates that language powerfully influences attitudes, behavior, and perceptions. To ignore this factor in social change would be to hobble all other efforts.

And our biases go deep. A high school student who felt that nonsexist language was disastrous said, "But you don't understand! You're trying to change the English language, which has been around a lot longer than women have!"

The language we need to hone is the language of our differences. We have either insisted that we are all the same here in the United States ("the melting pot") or we have been judgmental about our differences.

Poet Pat Parker ("For the White Person Who Wants to Know How to Be My Friend") said it best: "The first thing you do is to forget that i'm Black. / Second, you must never forget that i'm Black." In the same way, we acknowledge our differences with respect and our samenesses with joy. "Unity, not uniformity, must be our aim. We attain unity only through variety. Differences must be integrated, not annihilated, nor absorbed" (M. P. Follett).

DEFINITION OF TERMS

Bias/Bias-Free

Biased language refers to people in imbalanced or inaccurate ways: (1) It leaves out certain individuals or groups. "Employees are welcome to bring their wives and children" leaves out those employees who might want to bring husbands, friends, or same-sex partners, and it implies at some level that everyone has wives and children. (2) It makes unwarranted assumptions. To write "Anyone can use this fire safety ladder" assumes that all members of the household are able-bodied. "Flesh-colored" assumes everybody's one color. Addressing a sales letter about diapers to the mother assumes that the father won't be diapering the baby. (3) It calls individuals and groups by names or labels that they did not choose for themselves (e.g., *Gypsy, office girl, Eskimo, pygmy, Bushman, the elderly, colored man*) or that are derogatory *(libber, savage, bum, old goat)*. (4) It is based on stereotypes that imply that all lesbians/Chinese/women/people with disabilities/men/teenagers are alike *(adolescent behavior, male ego, hot-blooded Latins)*. (5) It treats groups in nonparallel ways in the same context: *Asian Americans, African Americans, and whites; two men and a female.* (6) It categorizes people when it is unnecessary to do so and when this is not done in similar cases: *the black defendant* when it is never *the white defendant*; *the woman lawyer* when it is never *the man lawyer*. As soon as we mention sex, ethnicity, religion, disability, or other characteristic—without a good reason for doing so—we are on thin ice. Although there may be instances in which a person's sex, for example, is germane ("A recent study showed that female patients do not object to being cared for by male nurses"), most of the time it is not. Nor is a person's race, sexual orientation, disability, age, or belief system.

Jean Gaddy Wilson (in Brooks and Pinson, *Working with Words*) suggests, "Following one simple rule of writing or speaking will eliminate most biases. Ask yourself: Would you say the same thing about an affluent, white man?"

Inclusive/Exclusive

Inclusive language clearly includes everyone it intends to include; exclusive language intentionally or unintentionally excludes some people. The following quotation is inclusive: "The greatest revolution of our generation is the discovery that human beings, by changing the inner attitudes of their minds, can change the outer aspects of their lives" (William James). It is clear that James is speaking of all of us.

Examples of sex-exclusive writing fill most quotation books: "Man is the measure of all things" (Protagoras). "The People, though we think of a great entity when we use the word, means nothing more than so many millions of individual men" (James Bryce). "Man is nature's sole mistake" (W. S. Gilbert).

Sexist/Nonsexist

Sexist language promotes and maintains attitudes that stereotype people according to gender while assuming that the male is the norm—the significant gender. Nonsexist language treats both sexes equally and either does not refer to a person's sex at all when it is irrelevant or refers to men and women and to girls and boys in symmetrical ways.

"A society in which women are taught anything but the management of a family, the care of men, and the creation of the future generation is a society which is on the way out" (L. Ron Hubbard). "Behind every successful man is a woman—with nothing to wear" (L. Grant Glickman). "Nothing makes a man and wife feel closer, these days, than a joint tax return" (Gil Stern). These quotations display various characteristics of sexist writing: (1) stereotyping an entire sex by what might be appropriate for some of it; (2) assuming male superiority; (3) using unparallel terms (e.g., *man and wife* should be either *husband and wife* or *man and woman*).

The following quotations clearly refer to both sexes: "It's really hard to be roommates with people if your suitcases are much better than theirs" (J. D. Salinger). "If people don't want to come out to the ballpark, nobody's going to stop them" (Yogi Berra). "People keep telling us about their love affairs, when what we really want to know is how much money they make and how they manage on it" (Mignon McLaughlin). "I studied the lives of great men and famous women, and I found that the men and women who got to the top were those who did the jobs they had in hand, with everything they had of energy and enthusiasm and hard work" (Harry S. Truman).

Gender-Free/Gender-Fair/Gender-Specific

Gender-free terms do not indicate sex and can be used for either women/girls or men/boys *(teacher, bureaucrat, employee, hiker, operations manager, child, clerk, sales rep, hospital patient, student, grandparent, chief executive officer).*

Gender-fair language involves the symmetrical use of gender-specific words *(Ms. Cortright/Mr. Lopez, councilwoman/councilman, young man/ young woman)* and promotes fairness to both sexes in the larger context. To ensure gender-fairness, ask yourself: Would I write the same thing in the same way about a person of the other sex? Would I mind if this were said of me? If you are describing the behavior of children on the playground, to be gender-fair you will refer to girls and boys an approximately equal number of times, and you will carefully observe what the children do, and not just assume that only the boys will climb to the top of the jungle gym and that only the girls will play quiet games. Researchers studying the same baby described its cries as "anger" when they were told it was a boy and as "fear" when they were told it was a girl (cited in Cheris Kramarae, ed., *The Voices and Words of Women and Men*).

Gender-specific words *(councilwoman, businessman, altar girl)* are neither good nor bad in themselves, but they sometimes identify and even emphasize a person's sex when it is not necessary (and is sometimes even objectionable) to do so. Male and female versions of a root word are also likely to be nonparallel *(governor/governess, master/mistress)*.

One problem with gender-free terms, however, is that they sometimes obscure reality. *Battered spouse* implies that men and women are equally battered; this is far from true. *Parent* is too often taken to mean *mother* and obscures the fact that more and more fathers are involved in parenting; it is better here to use the gender-specific *fathers and mothers* or *mothers and fathers* than the gender-neutral *parents*. Saying *businesswomen* and *businessmen* instead of *business executives* reminds us that there are women involved, whereas *business executives* evokes a picture of men for most of us.

Amanda Smith (in *The Albuquerque Tribune*) writes, "A word like 'legislator' does not exclude women, but neither does it do anything to change the mental picture for some who already see legislators as male." She tells the story of teachers who took two groups of children to opposite ends of the playground: one group was told they were going to build "snowmen"; they made 11 snowmen and 1 snowwoman. The other group was told they were going to build "snow figures"; that group made 5 snowmen, 3 snowwomen, 2 snow dogs, 1 snow horse, and 1 snow spaceship.

Generic/Pseudogeneric

A generic is an all-purpose word that includes everybody (e.g., *workers, people, voters, civilians, elementary school students*). Generic pronouns include *we, you, they*.

A pseudogeneric is a word used as though it includes everybody but that in reality does not. For example, "A Muslim people of the northern Caucasus, the 1.3 million Chechens are dark-haired and tawny skinned, often with lush mustaches" *(The New York Times International)*. Until you get to the "lush mustaches," you assume "Chechens" is generic, including both women and men. Explaining why he felt homeless people who aren't in shelters should be locked up, Patrick Buchanan (cited in *New Woman*) said, "I don't think we should have to have them wandering the streets frightening women and people."

Words like "everybody" are often used as though "everybody" can afford a new television, celebrates Christmas, can walk up stairs, is married or wants to be, can read, gets enough to eat, worries about sunburn, and so on. Pseudogenerics are thought to include everyone because the people who use them are thinking only of themselves and their immediate world.

When someone says, "What a Christian thing to do!" (meaning kind or good-hearted), it leaves out all kind, good-hearted people who are not Christian. The speaker is undoubtedly a Christian and assumes others are too. Similarly, assuming everyone gets rosy-cheeked and goes pale in the same way ignores our diverse skin colors. When words like *mankind, forefathers, brotherhood,* and *alumni* got a foothold in the language, it was because men were visible, men were in power, and that's what their world looked like.

Certain nouns that look generic are often used as though they mean only men *(politicians, lawyers, voters, legislators, clergy, farmers, colonists, immigrants, slaves, pioneers, settlers, members of the armed forces, judges, taxpayers)*. References to "settlers, their wives, and children," or "those clergy permitted to have wives" illustrate this.

See the sections below on the two most damaging pseudogenerics: "man" and "he."

Sex/Gender

Sex is biological: people with male genitals are male, and people with female genitals are female. Although this is an oversimplification, in general, sex may be thought of as a physical, physiological, biological attribute.

Gender is cultural: a society's notions of "masculine" are based on how it expects men to behave, and its notions of "feminine" are based on how it expects women to behave. Words like *womanly/manly, tomboy/sissy, unfeminine/unmasculine* have nothing to do with the person's sex; they are culturally determined, subjective concepts about sex-appropriate traits and behaviors, which vary from one place to another and even from one individual to another within a culture.

It is biologically impossible for a woman to be a sperm donor or for a man to be pregnant. It may be culturally unusual for a man to be a secretary or for a woman to be a miner, but it is not biologically impossible. To say automatically "the secretary . . . she" and "the miner . . . he" assumes all secretaries are women and all miners are men, which is sexist because the basis is gender, not sex. Alleen Pace Nilsen (in Nilsen, Bosmajian, Gershuny, and Stanley, *Sexism and Language*) gives the example of "paternity suit" and "maternity suit"; they are sex-specific but they are not sexist because they involve actual sex-related differences.

Gender is a subjective cultural attitude. Sex is an objective biological fact. Gender concepts vary according to the culture. Sex is, with few exceptions, a constant.

The difference between sex and gender is important because much sexist language arises from cultural determinations of what a female or male "ought" to be. When a society believes, for example, that being a man means to hide one's emotions, bring home a paycheck, and be able to discuss football standings whereas being a woman means to be soft-spoken, "never have anything to wear," and love shopping, babies, and recipes, much of the population becomes a contradiction in terms—unmanly men and unwomanly women. Crying, nagging, gossiping, and shrieking are assumed to be women's lot; rough-housing, beer drinking, telling dirty jokes, and being unable to find one's socks and keys are laid at men's collective door. Lists of stereotypes appear silly because very few people fit them. The best way to ensure unbiased writing and speaking is to describe people as individuals, not as members of a set.

GENERAL GUIDELINES

Pseudogeneric "He"

The use of *he* to mean *he and she* is ambiguous, the grammatical justification for its use is problematic, and it is not perceived as including both women and men. A number of careful studies, beginning with Wendy Martyna's in 1978 ("What Does 'He' Mean?" *Journal of Communication*), have shown that women, men, and children alike picture only males when *he* is used to mean *everybody*. "It is clear that, in spite of the best efforts of prescriptive grammarians, *he* has not come to be either used or understood in the generic sense under most circumstances" (Philip M. Smith, *Language, the Sexes and Society*). Donald G. McKay (in Cheris Kramarae, ed., *The Voices and Words of Women and Men*) says that each of us hears the pseudogeneric *he* over a million times in our lifetime and that the consequences of this kind of repetition are "beyond the ken of present-day psychology." He describes pseudogeneric *he* as having all the characteristics of a highly effective propaganda technique: repetition, covertness/indirectness, early age of acquisition, and association with high-prestige sources; "Although the full impact of the prescriptive *he* remains to be explored, effects on attitudes related to achievement, motivation, perseverance, and level of aspiration seem likely." Linguist Suzette Haden Elgin gives this example of a pseudogeneric *he* with important consequences: "Every American child knows that he may grow up to be President."

Young children, who are unfamiliar with the grammatical rule that says *he* really means *he and she*, and who are also fairly literal-minded, hear *he* thousands of times and come to think of maleness as the general state of being and femaleness as something peripheral. In a study by Steven Gelb of Toronto's York University, young children were asked to describe pictures of sex-indeterminate bunnies, dinosaurs, and babies; 97% of the time boys labeled them male, and 81% of the time the girls also labeled them male.

When parents and teachers use pseudogeneric *he* to refer to people, they inadvertently teach youngsters that maleness and humanness are equivalent.

The ubiquity of *he* is not to be underestimated. When the Minnesota legislature ordered the removal of gender-specific language from state statutes, the Office of the Revisor of Statutes deleted or replaced some 20,000 sex-specific pronouns; only 301 of them were feminine.

Defenders most often claim that *he* as a generic term is a longstanding grammatical convention and that its use is not intended to exclude anyone. But pseudogeneric *he* does, in reality, exclude over half the population, and allusions to some fundamental concept of grammar are on shaky ground. *He* was declared generic and legally inclusive of *she* by an act of the English Parliament, following a rule invented in 1746 by John Kirby, who decreed that the male gender is "more comprehensive" than the female; since then, advocates have been fond of saying "he embraces she." The 19th-century grammarians articulated the policy that between an error of number ("to each their own") and an error of gender ("to each his own"), it was preferable to make an error of gender. Thus this "convention" of grammar is based on the indefensible premise that the category "male" is more comprehensive than the category "female." In fact, it can be argued that the latter is more comprehensive linguistically: *female* contains *male*, *she* contains *he*.

The following, which appeared in the introduction of a recent book, is typical of many such disclaimers: "The pronouns 'he' and 'him' are used in this text to include both males and females. This is for grammatical purposes only. No discrimination is intended." That the usage needs to be explained and defended says it all.

(In a related contemporary story, a female anchor on a television news show was assured that a new male anchor had been hired simply to co-anchor her show, and that they would be equals. But, as a subsequent court case showed, he was in fact the lead or primary anchor. According to the broadcasting company president, a media consultant told him that anchors on a male-female team should be equals. But another anchor was told by the same media consultant that "the male is the first among equals.")

The pronoun *he* (when used in any way except to refer to a specific male person) can be avoided in several ways.

- Rewrite your sentence in the plural: "It's the educated barbarian who is the worst: he knows what to destroy" (Helen MacInnes). Educated barbarians are the worst; they know what to destroy. "When someone sings his own praises, he always gets the tune too high" (Mary H. Waldrip). Those who sing their own praises always get the tune too high.
- Omit the pronoun entirely: "Repartee: What a person thinks of after he becomes a departee" (Dan Bennett). Repartee: What a person thinks of

after becoming a departee. "The American arrives in Paris with a few French phrases he has culled from a conversational guide or picked up from a friend who owns a beret" (Fred Allen). The American arrives in Paris with a few French phrases culled from a conversational guide or picked up from a friend who owns a beret.

- Substitute *we/us/our*: "From each according to his abilities, to each according to his needs" (Karl Marx). From each of us according to our abilities, to each of us according to our needs.
- Use the second person: "No man knows his true character until he has run out of gas, purchased something on the installment plan and raised an adolescent" (Marcelene Cox). You don't know what your true character is until you have run out of gas, purchased something on the installment plan and raised an adolescent.
- Replace the masculine pronoun with an article: "Can't a critic give his opinion of an omelette without being asked to lay an egg?" (Clayton Rawson). Can't a critic give an opinion about an omelette without being asked to lay an egg?
- Replace the pronoun with words like *someone, anyone, one, the one, no one*: "He who cries, 'What do I care about universality? I only know what is in *me*,' does not know even that" (Cynthia Ozick). The one who cries, 'What do I care about universality? I only know what is in *me*,' does not know even that. "He who can take advice is sometimes superior to him who can give it" (Karl von Knebel). One who can take advice is sometimes superior to one who can give it. "Everyone can master a grief but he that has it" (Shakespeare). Everyone can master a grief but the one who has it. Or, as La Rochefoucauld put it: "We all have the strength to endure the misfortunes of others."
- Use genderless nouns *(the average person, workers)* or substitute job titles or other descriptions for the pronoun.
- Replace the pronoun with a noun (or a synonym for a noun used earlier): "He is forced to be literate about the illiterate, witty about the witless and coherent about the incoherent" (John Crosby). The critic is forced to be literate about the illiterate, witty about the witless and coherent about the incoherent. "To find a friend one must close one eye—to keep him, two" (Norman Douglas). To find a friend one must close one eye—to keep a friend, two.
- Use *he and she* or *her and his*, but only if there are not a great many of them. *S/he* is not recommended for anything but memos or notes: "Education is helping the child realize his potentialities" (Erich Fromm). Education is helping the child realize his or her potentialities. There are times when it is better to use *he or she*, for example, when you want to raise consciousness about both sexes being involved in a certain activity: the new parent . . . he or she; the plumber . . . she or he.

- Singular *they* ("to each their own") has strong supporters (see dictionary entry singular "they"). When nothing else works and you need to use it, remember that you can make an error of gender (use *he* when you really mean *he and she*) or you can make an error of number (using plural instead of singular). Choose your error: "Nobody is a good judge in his own cause" (St. Thérèse of Lisieux). Nobody is a good judge in their own cause. "Only a mediocre person is always at his best" (Somerset Maugham). Only a mediocre person is always at their best.
- Recast in the passive voice: "Pessimist: One who, when he has the choice of two evils, chooses both" (Oscar Wilde). Pessimist: One who, when given the choice of two evils, chooses both. (Objections to the passive voice are generally valid, which is why this solution is farther down the list; at the same time, it is sometimes a good choice.)
- Use masculine and feminine pronouns in alternating sentences, para-graphs, examples, or chapters, although this technique should be used sparingly and only as a last resort as it can be annoying to read.
- When referring to animals and nonhuman objects, avoid arbitrarily assigning them a sex. If the sex of an animal is known (and this infor-mation is important to your material), specify it. When the sex is unknown or unimportant, use *it*. Instead of "When you see a snake, never mind where he came from," W. G. Benham could have said: When you see a snake, never mind where it came from. Many writers automatically use *it*: "There is nothing in nature quite so joyful as the very young and silly lamb—odd that it should develop into that dull and sober animal the sheep" (Esther Meynell). Also use *it* instead of *she* to refer to entities such as nature, nations, churches, ships, boats, cars, engines, and gas tanks, and *it* instead of *he* to refer to the enemy, the devil, death, time, etc. (These terms are included as individual entries in the Dictionary of Terms.)

Pseudogeneric "Man/Men/Mankind"

Much of the debate on inclusive language centers on the use of *man*. Some say *man* is defined not only as "an adult male human being" but also as "a human being," "a person," "an individual," or "the whole human race." They claim that the use of *man* does not exclude women but is merely a grammati-cal convention.

There are two problems with this thinking: (1) We are never sure which meaning is intended, so *man* is ambiguous. A columnist expressed his annoyance with "the feminist campaign to eliminate the word 'man' from a lot of common, historic terms." He said women should "accept the fact" that the Founding Fathers meant to include women when they wrote "all men are created equal." He apparently forgot that it took two constitutional amend-ments to give women and people of color the vote, since the men created equal were exclusively and legally white, male men. Susan B. Anthony found herself in the equivocal position of not being "man" enough to vote (per the Constitution) but "man" enough (per the tax and criminal codes) to be prosecuted for trying to vote and then for refusing to pay taxes when she couldn't. (2) Even when used as if intended to be a generic, *man* has often revealed its persistent ambiguity for both writers and readers. Douglas Hofstadter (in *Metamagical Themas*) quotes an example of David Moser's: "Man has traditionally been a hunter, and he has kept his females close to the hearth, where they could tend his children."

Researchers who studied the hypothesis that *man* is generally understood to include women found "rather convincing evidence that when you use *man* generically, people do tend to think male, and tend not to think female" (Joseph Schneider and Sally Hacker, cited in Casey Miller and Kate Swift, *Words and Women*). According to Miller and Swift, that study and others "clearly indicate that *man* in the sense of *male* so overshadows *man* in the sense of *human being* as to make the latter use inaccurate and misleading for purposes both of conceptualizing and communicating."

Few wordsmiths will tolerate an ambiguous word, especially if there is an unambiguous one available. Imagine discussing giraffes and zebras, where sometimes *zebras* is used to include both giraffes and zebras but sometimes it means simply zebras. The audience would never know when it heard *zebras* whether it meant only zebras or whether it meant zebras and giraffes.

A high school honors student explained that the reason his western civilization textbook used only the words *man* and *mankind* was because "women were dogs. You might as well say 'men and their dogs plowed the fields.' Or 'men and their dogs tanned hides.' The reason women aren't mentioned in our book is that women did nothing, contributed nothing, *were* nothing." His startling conclusion shows practically and graphically what happens when a word means one thing *(women and men)* but is heard as another *(men)*. Is it possible to receive 12 years of schooling in this country and not understand that "man" includes women? Quite possible—because it effectively does not.

How people hear a word is far more important than its etymology or dictionary definition. Jeanette Silveira (in Cheris Kramarae, ed., *The Voices and Words of Women and Men*) says "there is ample research evidence that the masculine 'generic' does not really function as a generic. In various studies words like *he* and *man* in generic contexts were presented to people who were asked to indicate their understanding by drawing, bringing in, or pointing out a picture, by describing or writing a story about the person(s) referred to, or by answering yes or no when asked whether a sex-specific word or picture applied to the meaning." In all these studies (14 of them are summarized in *Women's Studies International Quarterly*, vol. 3, no. 2, 1980), women/girls were perceived as being included significantly less often than men/boys. Both women and men reported that they usually pictured men when they read or heard the masculine pseudogeneric.

The justification for *man* becoming the set and *woman* the subset is linguistically, sociologically, philosophically, and psychologically indefensible. *Human beings* clearly includes both men and women. With such a simple, commonsensical alternative available, it seems unnecessary to defend a convention that is almost surely on its last legs.

Finally, Dennis Baron says *(Grammar and Gender)* that attempts today to justify the use of the masculine generic "are but thin masks for the underlying assumption of male superiority in life as well as language; despite the attempts of the wary language commentators to include women under masculine terms, the effect is to render women both invisible and silent."

Not all words containing *man, men,* or *boy* are sexist. When in doubt, see individual entries (e.g., *boycott, highboy, dragoman, menopause*) or the entries *man-, -man/-men.*

We are so used to *-man* compounds that we feel helpless without them. Worse yet, their replacements somehow don't "sound right." However, *-man* nouns are outnumbered by the common and useful *-er* and *-or* words. *Fisher* seems alien to people yet has a far stronger precedent in the language than *fisherman.* The same is true of *waiter* for *waitress, flagger* for *flagman, deliverer* for *deliveryman,* and *repairer* for *repairman.* If we had grown up hearing *shoeman,* would we balk at *shoemaker*? What about *roofman* for *roofer, gardenman* for *gardener,* and *teachman* for *teacher*?

The following sample list may help those alternatives for *-man* words sound a little more "right" to us (and are useful alternatives for some *-man* words): angler, barber, batter, bottler, builder, butcher, buyer, canoer, caregiver, caretaker, carpenter, catcher, commissioner, consumer, customer, dealer, doer, dressmaker, driver, employer, executioner, farmer, fitter, gambler, gamester, gardener, golfer, hairdresser, handler, healer, hunter, insurer, jogger, jokester, laborer, landscaper, leader, lexicographer, lithographer, lover, maker, manager, manufacturer, member, messenger, nurturer, officer, outfielder, owner, painter, performer, pitcher, planner, player, plumber, practitioner, producer, promoter, provider, race-walker, reporter, retailer, retainer, rider, robber, roofer, runner, shoemaker, speaker, speechmaker, storekeeper, striker, subscriber, teacher, trader, treasurer, trucker, waiter, whaler, woodworker, worker, writer; actor, administrator, ambassador, ancestor, arbitrator, auditor, author, benefactor, coadjutor, conqueror, contractor, counselor, director, doctor, editor, executor, facilitator, governor, inspector, instructor, janitor, legislator, liquidator, major, mayor, mediator, navigator, negotiator, operator, professor, proprietor, protector, purveyor, sculptor, surveyor, testator, traitor, vendor, victor.

Parallel Treatment

Parallel treatment of terms is essential when discussing different groups; "white" and "nonwhite" are not parallel; neither are "Jewish persons" and "Protestants." The problems with nonparallel treatment are most easily seen in gender asymmetries.

If you refer to a woman as Margaret Schlegel, refer to a man in the same material as Gavan Huntley. If he is Huntley, she will be Schlegel; if she is Margaret, he will be Gavan; and if she is Ms. Schlegel, he will be Mr. Huntley.

Do not make of one sex a parenthetical expression: "hats off to the postal employees who manned (and womanned) the Olympic stamp cancellation booths"; "each nurse had her (or his) own explanation."

Male-female word pairs are especially troublesome. (1) Certain words are used as parallel pairs, but are in fact asymmetrical, for example, cameragirl/cameraman, man Friday/girl Friday, mermaid/merman, makeup girl/makeup man. The most common offender in this category is man/wife; the correct pairs are man/woman and wife/husband. (2) Other words are so unequivalent that few people confuse them as pairs, but it is revealing to study them, knowing that they were once equals: governor/governess, patron/matron, courtier/courtesan, master/mistress, buddy/sissy, hubby/hussy, dog/bitch, patrimony/matrimony, call boy/call girl, showman/showgirl, Romeo/Juliet. We all know what a Romeo is, but if we didn't we could look it up in the dictionary; this is not true of a Juliet. A call boy is a page; a call girl is a prostitute. Buddy is affectionate; sissy is derogatory. A study of word pairs shows that words associated primarily with women ultimately become discounted and devalued. Muriel Schulz calls it "semantic derogation." (3) Acceptable words and constructions sometimes become unacceptable because of the nonparallel way they are used. For example, a male and three women, aldermen and women, and two girls [referring to women] and a man should read: a man and three women, aldermen and alderwomen, and two women and a man.

Gender Role Words

Sex-linked words like *feminine/masculine, manly/womanly, boyish/girlish, husbandly/wifely, fatherly/motherly, unfeminine/unmasculine,* and *unmanly/unwomanly* depend for their meanings on cultural stereotypes and thus may be grossly inaccurate when applied to individuals. Somewhere, sometime, men and women have said, thought, or done everything the other sex has said, thought, or done except for a very few sex-linked biological activities (e.g., only a woman can give birth or nurse a baby and only a man can provide the sperm needed to fertilize an egg). To describe a woman as unwomanly is a contradiction in terms; if a woman is doing it, saying it, wearing it, thinking it, it must be—by definition—womanly.

Good writers have rarely used such terms—they evoke no sharp images, only fuzzy impressions that vary from culture to culture and from individual to individual. This is not a recommendation to "ban" the terms; nobody can ban words. But you might look further afield for a more precise, fresh way of conveying your meaning. Steven Pinker *(The Language Instinct)* says, "Vehicles for expressing thought are being created far more quickly than they are being lost." This would be a good place to lose a few vehicles and create some new ones.

"Feminine" Word Endings

Suffixes like *-ess*, *-ette*, and *-trix* (1) specify a person's sex when gender is irrelevant; (2) carry a demeaning sense of littleness or triviality; (3) perpetuate the notion that the male is the norm and the female is a subset, a deviation, a secondary classification. A poet is defined as "one who writes poetry" while a poetess is defined as "a female poet"; men are thus "the real thing" and women are sort of like them. Marlis Hellinger (in Cheris Kramarae et al., *Language and Power*) says these suffixes have "a weakening, trivializing or even sexualizing effect on an occupational activity which for a man may connote power and prestige." Even the nonhuman varieties of "feminine" word endings connote a sense of being smaller than and inferior to their "mates": flannelette, novelette, kitchenette, dinette, featurette, luncheonette, sermonette, operetta, lorgnette, cigarette, leopardess, tigress, lioness.

The purpose of a suffix is to qualify the root word. Where is the need to qualify a standard word describing a standard human activity? A poet should be a poet—without qualification. The discounting and devaluation of the female term in a word pair is the best argument against "feminine" endings; invariably the parallelism, if it ever existed, breaks down, and the female word ends up with little of the prestige and acceptability of the male word.

Alleen Pace Nilsen *(Sexism and Language)* says, "the feminine form is used as much to indicate triviality as to indicate sex." A woman conducting high-altitude tests for NASA was referred to as an aviator; a few days later the same newspaper called a woman participating in a small-time air show an aviatrix. Harriet Tubman was a conductor, not a conductress, of the underground railway.

The recommended procedure is to use the base word (thus, "waiter" instead of "waitress," "executor" instead of "executrix"). If the individual's sex is critical to your material, use adjectives ("At a time when male actors played female roles . . .") or pronouns ("The poet interrupted her reading . . .").

The following words with "feminine" endings have all been or currently are part of 20th-century U.S. English. Not included are terms formed to ridicule (Rush Limbaugh derides those women who succeed in traditionally male-dominated professions as "professorettes" and "lawyerettes"). In general, replace the "feminine" ending as shown (but see individual entries in the main text for some of the more problematic terms).

actress/actor
administratrix/administrator
adulteress/adulterer
adventuress/adventurer
ambassadress/ambassador
ancestress/ancestor
anchoress/anchorite
authoress/author
aviatrix, aviatress/aviator
benefactress/benefactor
cadette/cadet
canoness/canon
clairvoyante/clairvoyant
coadjutress/coadjutor
co-heiress/co-heir
comedienne/comedian
conductress/conductor
deaconess/deacon
detectivette/detective
directress/director
doctoress/doctor
Druidess/Druid
drum majorette/drum major
editress/editor
electress/elector
enchantress/enchanter
equestrienne/equestrian
executrix/executor
farmerette/farmer
giantess/giant
goddess/god
governess/governor
heiress/heir
heroine/hero
hostess/host
huntress/hunter
inheritress/inheritor
inspectress/inspector
instructress/instructor
janitress/janitor
Jewess/Jew
judgette/judge

laundress/launderer
majorette/major
manageress/manager
mayoress/mayor
mediatress, mediatrix/mediator
millionairess/millionaire
murderess/murderer
Negress/African American, black
ogress/ogre
peeress/peer
portress/porter
preceptress/preceptor
procuress/procurer
prophetess/prophet
prolocutrix/prolocutor
proprietress/proprietor
protectress/protector
priestess/priest
Quakeress/Quaker
sculptress/sculptor
seamstress/sewer
seductress/seducer
seeress/seer
shepherdess/shepherd
songstress/singer
sorceress/sorcerer
starlet/star
stewardess/steward
suffragette/suffragist
temptress/tempter
testatrix/testator
tragedienne/tragedian
traitress/traitor
tutoress/tutor
undergraduette/undergraduate
usherette/usher
victress/victor
villainess/villain
votaress/votary
waitress/waiter
wardress/warder

-Woman, -Man, -Person

The weak, awkward, and annoying suffix *-person* is not generally recommended. It was useful in making the transition to inclusive language because it was so easy to tack *-person* onto words, but it not only looks contrived, it is contrived. Because the *-person* suffix comes so readily to mind, we don't look any further and thus overlook more dynamic and descriptive words.

Words that end in *-woman* and *-man* are generally listed in this guidebook as a last resort, for three reasons: (1) in most cases it is unnecessary to specify sex; (2) male-female word pairs rarely get equal treatment and thus are better avoided; and (3) the alternatives are almost always a better linguistic choice. "Mail carrier" and "mail handler," for example, are more descriptive than "mailman" and "mailwoman."

Sometimes the *-man* and *-woman* words are preferable in order to emphasize the presence or participation of both sexes in some activity or position: "Local businesswomen and businessmen donated their weekends to do plumbing, electrical, and carpentry work in the new downtown shelter for homeless families."

When using these suffixes, however, be aware of sex symmetry. *Salesmen and women* should be *salesmen and saleswomen*; *layman and layperson* should be *layman and laywoman*.

Word Order

Because the male has been considered more important than the female, the male word has traditionally been placed first. However, this gives the impression that women are not only less important but afterthoughts as well. But, as any five-year-old knows, we should take turns going first. The following list of word pairs is given in their "natural" order (which you are invited to switch half the time): men and women, boys and girls, male and female, M or F, he and she, his and hers, sons and daughters, husbands and wives, brother and sister, Mr. and Mrs., guys and dolls, kings and queens. Francine Frank and Frank Anshen *(Language and the Sexes)* offer Jack and Jill, Romeo and Juliet, Hansel and Gretel, Roy Rogers and Dale Evans, Tristan and Isolde, Abelard and Héloïse, Antony and Cleopatra, Samson and Delilah. Alleen Pace Nilsen *(Sexism and Language)* says we break the pattern only in words relating to the traditional women's domain of family and marriage: bride and groom, mother and father, aunt and uncle, widow and widower. We also do it in the polite but empty convention of "ladies and gentlemen."

The general rule here is to vary the order.

NAMING

Power belongs to those who do the naming, which is why naming is one of the most critical issues for fairness and accuracy in language. We know more about our own lives than others do; we must also assume that other people know more about their lives than we do. As Bill Pensoneau wrote, "If we say that 'Redskins' reminds us of massacres, believe us."

Self-Definition

"One of the most basic ways of showing respect for others is to refer to them by the names with which they have chosen to identify themselves and to avoid using names that they consider offensive" *(American Heritage Book of English Usage)*. The correct names for individuals and groups are always those they have chosen for themselves. "It isn't strange that those persons who insist on defining themselves, who insist on this elemental privilege of self-naming, self-definition, and self-identity encounter vigorous resistance. Predictably, the resistance usually comes from the oppressor or would-be oppressor and is a result of the fact that he or she does not want to relinquish the power which comes from the ability to define others" (Haig Bosmajian, *The Language of Oppression*).

Ian Hancock, linguist and president of the International Roma Federation, uses the term *exonym* for a name applied to a group by outsiders. For example, Romani peoples object to being called by the exonym *Gypsies*; they do not call themselves Gypsies. Among the many other exonyms are: the elderly, colored people, homosexuals, pagans, adolescents, Eskimos, pygmies, savages. The test for an exonym is whether people want others to refer to them with that term—as "redmen," "illegal aliens," "holy rollers," etc.—or whether only outsiders describe them that way.

There is a very small but vocal element today demanding that gay men "give back" the word *gay*—a good example of denying people the right to name themselves. A late-night radio caller said several times that gay men had "stolen" this word from "our" language. It was not clear what language the gay men spoke.

A woman nicknamed "Peg" early in life had always preferred her full name, "Margaret." On her 40th birthday, she reverted to Margaret. An acquaintance who heard about the change said sharply, "I'll call her Peg if I like!"

We can call them Peg if we like, but it's arrogant, insensitive, and uninformed. The only rule we have in this area says we call people what they want to be called.

Relevance

"As a general rule, it is good to remember that . . . you should ordinarily view people as individuals and not mention their racial, ethnic, or other status, unless it is important to your larger purpose in communicating" *(American Heritage Book of English Usage)*.

"People First" Rule

Haim Ginott taught us that labels are disabling; intuitively most of us recognize this and resist being labeled. The disability movement originated the "people first" rule, which says we don't call someone a "diabetic" but rather "a person with diabetes." Saying someone is "an AIDS victim" reduces the person to a disease, a label, a statistic; use instead "a person with/who has/living with AIDS." The 1990 Americans with Disabilities Act is a good example of thoughtful wording. Name the person as a person first, and let qualifiers (age, sex, disability, race) follow, but (and this is crucial) only if they are relevant. Readers of a magazine aimed at an older audience were asked what they wanted to be called (elderly? senior citizens? seniors? golden agers?). They rejected all the terms; one said, "How about just *people*?" When high school students rejected labels like kids, teens, teenagers, youth, adolescents, and juveniles, and were asked in exasperation just what they would like to be called, they said, "Could we just be *people*?"

Women As Separate People

One of the most sexist maneuvers in the language has been the identification of women by their connections to husband, son, or father—often even after he is dead. Women are commonly identified as someone's widow while men are never referred to as anyone's widower. If a connection is relevant, make it mutual. Instead of "Frieda, his wife of 17 years," write "Frieda and Eric, married for 17 years."

Marie Marvingt, a Frenchwoman who lived around the turn of the century, was an inventor, adventurer, stuntwoman, superathlete, aviator, and all-around scholar. She chose to be affianced to neither man (as wife) nor God (as religious), but it was not long before an uneasy male press found her a fit partner. She is still known today by the revealing label "the Fiancée of Danger."

For some people it is difficult to watch women doing unconventional things with their names, especially when they flout the rules that connect them with men in a "readable" way. For years the etiquette books were able to tell us precisely how to address a single woman, a married woman, a divorced woman, or a widowed woman (there was no similar etiquette on men because we have never had a code to signal their marital status). But now some women are Ms. and some are Mrs., some are married but keeping their birth names, others are hyphenating their last name with their husband's, and still others have constructed new names for themselves. Some women—including African American women who were denied this right earlier in our history—take great pride in using their husband's name. All these forms are correct. The same rule of self-definition applies here: call the woman what she wants to be called.

Name-Calling

It's unlikely that people come to this guidebook for help in choosing the most accurate and precise epithets when they need them. However, some are included because not everybody considers them slurs or because alternatives are often needed. See, for example, *animal names for people, ethnic slurs,* and *food names for people,* as well as individual entries (*bastard, bitch,* etc.).

SPECIAL PROBLEMS

Hidden Bias

Writing may be completely free of biased terms yet still carry a biased message. According to a radio news item, "More women than ever before are living with men without being married to them. And more unmarried women than ever before are having babies." An accurate, unbiased report would have said: "More men and women than ever before are living together without being married. And more unmarried couples than ever before are having babies."

Too often, language makes assumptions about people—that everyone is male, heterosexual, able-bodied, white, married, between the ages of 26 and 54, of western European extraction. Until it becomes second nature to write without bias, reread your material as though you were: a gay man, someone who uses a wheelchair, a Japanese American woman, someone over 80 or under 16, or other "individuals" of your own creation. If you do not feel left out, discounted, and ignored, but instead can read without being stopped by some incongruence, you have probably avoided hidden bias. It is also wonderfully helpful to ask someone from a group with which you aren't familiar to read your work; they can quickly spot any irregularity.

Passive Constructions

Most writing style books recommend the active over the passive voice; this is also an important concept in the language of bias. There are important differences between "she was beaten" and "he beat her," between "the first black woman who was admitted to the university" and "the first black woman who entered the university." The active voice is too often reserved for those in power while everyone else is acted upon.

Perspective

We all have our little ways of viewing things, for example, "I am firm. You are obstinate. He is a pig-headed fool" (Katharine Whitehorn). In the same way, men are "cautious" but women are "timid"; some people are "shiftless" while others are "unemployed"; if the Indians won it was a "massacre," if the Cavalry won, it was a "victory." "A man has to be Joe McCarthy to be called ruthless. All a woman has to do is put you on hold" (Marlo Thomas). It is helpful to mentally substitute other groups for the ones you are describing and see if your adjectives are still as precise and accurate.

Fellow, King, Lord, Master

Fellow, king, lord, and *master* have three things in common: (1) Either from definition, derivation, or people's perceptions of them, they are biased: all four are male-oriented; *king, lord,* and *master* are also hierarchical, dominator-society terms; *master* evokes the horrors of slavery. (2) They are root words: many other words, phrases, and expressions are formed from them, thus extending their reach. (3) Not everyone agrees whether all forms of them are biased. Someone who might admit that a *fellow* sitting next to them at lunch can only be a man might see nothing unacceptable in the expression *fellow student*. Those who agree that the *master* of a certain house is a man might believe that *mastering a skill* is fair language. But consider, for example, the cumulative effect on the language when such a masculine and slavery-related word as *master* is encountered in so many everyday ways: *master bedroom, master builder, master class, masterful, master hand, master key, master list, mastermind, masterpiece, master plan, master stroke, master switch, master tape, master teacher, masterwork, mastery, overmaster, past master, postmaster, poundmaster, prizemaster, self-mastery, trickmaster, truckmaster, weighmaster, wharfmaster, yardmaster.*

Those who prefer to use these four words only in their narrowest, male-defined meanings will find alternatives in the main text for all other uses.

Letter Salutations

A state commission on the economic status of women receives a surprising number of letters addressed "Dear Sir" or "Gentlemen." Pueblo to People, a nonprofit organization of craft and agricultural cooperatives run by low-income people in Central America and the Philippines, notes in their catalog under "When Writing to Us": "Please remember we are a cooperative of women and men. We prefer to be addressed in terms that include all of us, such as 'Friends,' 'Folk,' or 'People,' rather than exclusive terms such as 'Gentlemen' and 'Sir.'"

In discussions of language choices, the problem of letter salutations is usually the first one mentioned. The standard "Dear . . ." salutation in business letters seems to be giving way in many cases to the memo format, a subject line instead of a salutation, or beginning the letter directly after the name and address (no salutation). "Dear" is an odd way to begin a letter to those we don't even know; you can always begin "To . . ." Below are some other suggestions for inclusive letter openings.

Dear Agent	Dear Manager
Board Member	Mr./Ms.
Citizen	Neighbor
Colleagues	Owner
Committee Member	Parent/Guardian
Councilor	Permissions Editor

Credit Manager	Personnel Officer
Customer	Publisher
Director	Reader
Editor	Recipient
Employee	Resident
Executive	Subscriber
Friend	Taxpayer
Homeowner	Teacher

Dear Friends of the Library	Dear Ellen Howard-Jeffers
Members of the . . .	Acme Drycleaning
Supporters	L. Koskenmaki
Volunteers	Tiny Tots Toys
Voters	Office of the Bursar

Dear Superintendent Rajanivat
    Vice-President Morris
    Senior Research Specialist Jordan
    Administrative Assistant Chuang

Greetings!
Hello!

To the Chief Sales Agent
To the Consumer Relations Department
To the Freestyle Credit Department
To: Chair, Commission on Language Abuse
To: Parents/guardians of Central High School students
To: J. G. Frimsted

Re: Account # 4865-1809-3333-0101
Subject: Reprints of your article on hearing loss
Please send me a copy of the most recent committee report.
I am ordering six copies of your publication.
Enclosed please find complete payment for . . .

Miscellaneous

Generally, retain familiar names for nonhuman items even if they are sex-linked, for example, *timothy grass, daddy longlegs, alewife, sweet william, myrtle.* (These and similar items are found as entries in the main text.)

Rewriting history is not recommended. *Fathers of the Church* is a historically correct term. But we commonly refer now to the *Founding Fathers* as the *Founders.* It may be uncomfortable or even painful to encounter the word *nigger* in a literary work, but if we erase or forget our historical and literary past, we may be doomed to repeat it. Awareness and discussion of such bias is effective and necessary; replacing biased words without comment is not.

The following words can be used in conjunction with more specific words to arrive at nonsexist phrases: agent, aide, anyone, artisan, artist, assistant, associate, attendant, builder, chief executive, citizen, civilian, clerk, clinician, coach, colleague, commissioner, companion, consultant, consumer, contractor, coordinator, correspondent, counselor, crew, customer, dealer, deputy, employee, engineer, everybody, everyone, executive, expert, fabricant, facilitator, folks, guide, hand, handler, individual, inhabitant, inspector, intermediary, laborer, loader, machinist, maker, manufacturer, mechanic, member, messenger, motorist, nobody, nominal head, no one, notable, officer, one, operator, owner, patriot, performer, person, personnel, planner, politician, practitioner, producer, professional, program director, promoter, proprietor, purveyor, repairer, reporter, representative, retailer, scientist, someone, soul, specialist, student, steward, subscriber, technician, tender, tutor, vendor, worker, writer. (See also the list of -er- and -or words under Pseudogeneric "Man/Men/Mankind," above.)

HOW TO MAKE A FORTUNE WITH FAIR AND ACCURATE LANGUAGE

Actually, there's not a lot of money in this business, and this section just contains some basic understandings about language, which people usually won't read. But stay; it's kind of interesting.

Who Controls the Language?

The correct answer is always: "You do." Language doesn't belong to grammarians, linguists, wordsmiths, writers, or editors. It belongs to the people who use it. It goes where people want it to go, and, like a balky mule, you can't make it go where it doesn't want to go.

Constructions that were once labeled incorrect are now in dictionaries because people persisted in using them. Constructions that were mandated by law (the use of "he" to mean "he and she" by an 1850 Act of Parliament, for example) were ignored by many speakers and writers of English because people wanted to say what they wanted to say. Those who understand language know there's only one reason for it to change: because a critical mass of people want it to.

An often-expressed fear of keep-it-the-way-it-is fans is that they will be forced to use language they don't want to use. And, in fact, many publishing houses, businesses, government offices, churches, mosques, synagogues, universities, and national organizations have policies on the use of respectful language. Are rights being abridged here? Freedoms taken away? Probably not. Absolute freedom doesn't exist and never did. Just as we don't spit on the floor at work, swear at customers, or send out letters full of misspellings, so too we might have to "watch our language." It is odd that the request for unbiased language in schools and workplaces is considered intolerable when other limits on our freedom to do whatever we want are not.

The rigid orthodoxy, the narrowest view of language, belongs not to those who offer 15 ways of dealing with the personal pronoun but to those who insist that the pseudogeneric *he* is right in all cases and tell us to quit "tinkering" with the language.

Tinker away. It's yours. That means you can use this book if you like, but you don't have to if you don't like.

Does It Really Matter?

One objection to people language is that it is really too trivial an issue when there are so many more important ones that need our attention.

First, it is to be hoped that there are enough of us working on issues large and small that the work will all get done someday. Second, the connections between the way we think, speak, and act are by now beyond argument. Language goes hand-in-hand with social change—both shaping it and reflecting it. Sexual harassment was not a term anyone used 20 years ago; today we have laws against it. How could we have the law without the language? In fact, the judicial system is a good argument for the importance of "mere words"; the legal profession devotes great energy to the precise interpretation of words—often with far-reaching and significant consequences.

Words matter terribly. The difference between *fetal tissue* and *unborn baby* (referring to the very same thing) is arguably the most debated issue in the country. The United States changed *The War Department* to *The Department of Defense* because words matter. When President Bush used the word *hostages* for the first time in August 1990, it made headlines; up to that time he had been using *detainees*. The change of terms signaled a change in our posture toward Iraq.

It is ironic that some of the strongest insistence that this issue is "silly" comes from political conservatives. In 1990 a pamphlet titled "Language: A Key Mechanism of Control" was sent to Republican candidates running in state elections by GOPAC, a conservative group headed by House Republican whip Newt Gingrich. One of the key points in it was that "language matters." The pamphlet offered a list of words and phrases "to use in writing literature and letters, in preparing speeches, and in producing material for the electronic media. The words and phrases are powerful. Read them. Memorize as many as possible. . . . Use the list[s] to help define your campaign and your vision of public service." Two basic lists were given, one set of words to use for one's own campaign (e.g., common sense, courage, crusade, dream, duty, peace, pioneer, precious, pride, fair, family, hard work, liberty, moral, pro-environment, prosperity, reform, rights, strength, truth, vision) and another set to use for one's opponent's campaign (e.g., anti-child, anti-flag, betray, cheat, corruption, crisis, decay, devour, disgrace, excuses, failure, greed, hypocrisy, incompetent, liberal, lie, obsolete, pathetic, radical, red tape, self-serving, shallow, shame, sick, taxes, traitors).

Alleen Pace Nilsen (in Nilsen, Bosmajian, Gershuny, and Stanley, *Sexism and Language*) gives the example of the U.S. Marines, who used to guarantee that you would become a man with them; "But this brings up a problem, because much of the work that is necessary to keep a large organization running is what is traditionally thought of as *women's work*. . . . They euphemize and give the jobs titles that either are more prestigious or, at least, don't make people think of females. Waitresses are called *orderlies*, secretaries are called *clerk-typists*, nurses are called *medics*, assistants are called *adjutants*, and cleaning up an area is called *policing* the area."

In the end, then, it appears that our choice of words is not too trivial—not for presidents, for conservatives, for Marines, for any of us.

They've Got to Stop Changing the Language!

Some people are like George Crabbe's friend: "Habit with him was all the test of truth, / it must be right: I've done it from my youth." Having come of age using *handicapped, black-and-white, chairman, leper, mankind,* and the pseudogeneric *he,* they are bewildered and upset by discussions about such terms' correctness.

And yet if there's one thing consistent about language it is that it is constantly changing. The only languages that do not change are those whose speakers are dead. When the *Random House Dictionary of the English Language,* 2nd ed., was published in 1988, it had 50,000 new entries, words that had come into use since 1966, and 75,000 new definitions. Dictionary maven Ken Kister estimates that some 25,000 new words enter the language each year. So it isn't language change alone that frightens and annoys some people, but specifically language change that deals with people.

Anne H. Soukhanov, executive editor of the most excellent and useful *American Heritage Dictionary,* 3rd ed., says in *Word Watch,* "In bringing together into one lexicon diverse linguistic elements from diverse peoples, nations, and cultures, the English language—*the* prime exponent, in fact, of multiculturalism—has been much more accepting of and tolerant to change and new ideas than some of its own speakers and writers have been."

In any case, the "changes" in people language are not so much changes as choices. For example, *firefighter* has been in the language since 1903; using it instead of *fireman* isn't so much a change in the language as a choice to use what some think is a better word. We make these kinds of choices all the time; we call it good writing. Inuits and Roms and the San never did call themselves Eskimos, Gypsies, and Bushmen; the fact that we have finally grasped the terminology is not as much a change as it is a correction or a choice to use the correct words. *Chair* (meaning the person in charge of the meeting) came into the language before *chairman*; people mistakenly think *chair* is a new and strange usage. Actually it's been there all the time.

What Ridiculous Word Will We Have Next?

The most common tactic in trying to unhorse fair and accurate people language—probably because it is assumed to be entertaining—is ridicule. Dozens of syndicated columnists and letter-to-the-editor writers posit some hypothetical endpoint of unbiased language, skillfully show how absurd it is, and retire from the field, victorious. In one case, the writer showed how silly the word "woperson" (for "woman") is. Quite right, too. In another case, "ottoperson" was given as the height of linguistic absurdity. No argument there. Another person wrote, "So I suppose now we're going to say: He/she ain't heavy, Father/Sister; he/she's my brother/sister." In a magazine letters column, a reader complained about the problems we were going to have with pronouns as parts of words: "'Herman was a hermit who had a hernia when climbing the Himalayas' translates to 'Itit was an itmit who had an itnia climbing the Himalayas.'" The magazine editor added: "*It*alayas?" We've also had great fun with—among dozens of others—"follicularly challenged" (bald), "cerebrally challenged" (stupid), "ethically challenged" (criminal), "personipulate," "personperson" (for mailman—William Safire's contribution), "personhole cover," and "chairperdaughter" (for chairperson).

The problem with ridicule (aside from it being the first and last argument of fools, according to an old proverb) is that nobody is asking for such silly language. Those who are serious about writing that is as graceful as it is inclusive can choose from among thousands of standard terms. There is no need to use awkward, contrived, or bizarre terms (unless you want to, of course). Anyone who says we must choose between elegant, standard language and respectful language is stuck in a binary thinking warp. In some of today's best literature you can find poetic, grammatical writing that is free of stereotypes and demeaning language.

This is not to deny that people language isn't occasionally awkward; cutting edges are always a little rough, and we're all still getting used to this. But then there is a great deal of bad writing in this country, and only a small fraction of it can be laid at the door of those who use unbiased language. The myth here is that either you write beautifully or you write respectfully. You *can* do both. It's work, but so is any other good writing.

But Will It Be Better Writing?

One of the rewards of breaking away from traditional, biased language—and, for many people, the most unexpected benefit—is a dramatic improvement in writing style. By replacing fuzzy, over-generalized, cliché-ridden words with explicit, active words and by giving concrete examples and anecdotes instead of one-word-fits-all descriptions you can express yourself more dynamically, convincingly, and memorably.

"If those who have studied the art of writing are in accord on any one point, it is on this: the surest way to arouse and hold the attention of the reader is by being specific, definite, and concrete" (William Strunk and E. B. White, *The Elements of Style*).

Writers who talk about *brotherhood* or *spinsters* or *right-hand man* miss a chance to spark their writing with fresh descriptions; unthinking writing is also less informative. Instead of the unrevealing *adman* there are precise, descriptive, inclusive words like *advertising executive, copywriter, account executive, ad writer*, or *media buyer*.

The word *manmade*, which seems so indispensable to us, doesn't actually say very much. Does it mean artificial? handmade? synthetic? fabricated? machine-made? custom-made? simulated? plastic? imitation? contrived?

Communication is—or ought to be—a two-way street. A speaker or writer who uses *man* to mean *human being* while the audience or reader understands it as *adult male* is an example of communication gone awry. "Meaning is not something that belongs solely to the utterance that is spoken or the piece of writing. Meaning also depends on the person who hears the utterance or reads the text" (Ronald Macaulay, *The Social Art: Language and Its Uses*).

Bias-free language is logical, accurate, and realistic. Biased language is not. How logical is it to speak of the "discovery" of America, a land already inhabited by millions of people? Where is the accuracy in writing "Dear Sir" to a woman? Where is the realism in the full-page automobile advertisement that says in bold letters, "A good driver is a product of his environment," when more women than men influence car-buying decisions? Or how successful is the ad for a dot-matrix printer that says, "In 3,000 years, man's need to present his ideas hasn't changed. But his tools have," when many of these printers are bought and used by women, who also have ideas they need to present? And when we use stereotypes to talk about people ("isn't that just like a welfare mother/Indian/girl/old man"), our speech and writing will be inaccurate and unrealistic most of the time.

Everybody Is Getting So Sensitive!

A common complaint today is, "A person can't say *any*thing anymore!" Actually, a person can. And people do. Although we have anti-disparagement laws for fruits and vegetables (see hate speech), we don't have them for people, which means you can say dreadful things about people, yell insults to their face, and nobody will stop you. You may get dirty looks and criticisms but, hey, you can take it.

Most stories about people failing college classes or losing jobs because "just once" they happened to refer to a woman as a *chick* are apocryphal; the courts have upheld verdicts only in the cases of the most egregious abuses and tend to favor allowing anything short of mayhem. The few stories that have some basis in fact rarely hinge solely on language, but reveal long-term patterns of harassment, discrimination, personality conflicts, or other factors. The fear of saying the wrong thing is the proverbial fear that springs from ignorance. Those who respect other people's realities, who read and listen carefully, and who have some common sense do not walk in fear.

There are complaints that it's hard to remember what you can say and what you can't, which words are "in" for certain groups and which words are not. And yet we started out learning that the "kitty" on the sidewalk was actually a squirrel, we learned to differentiate between fire trucks and school buses, and many people today know the difference between linguini, fettucini, and rotini. The same people who say they can't remember the "right" terms in referring to people are often whizzes at remembering which professional sports teams have moved where and are now called what.

People are tired of having to "watch what they say." But from childhood onward, we all learn to "watch what we say": we don't swear around our parents; we don't bring up certain topics around certain people; we speak differently to friend, boss, cleric, English teacher, lover, radio interviewer, child. Most of us are actually quite skilled at picking and choosing appropriate words; it seems odd that we are "tired" of being expected to be courteous, to call people what they want to be called.

Joan Steinau Lester *(The Future of White Men and Other Diversity Dilemmas)* explains, "The group with the most social power usually doesn't notice its own language; it doesn't have to. So it can feel uncomfortable to suddenly become self-aware. Thus the common complaint, 'I can't say anything anymore. I have to walk on eggshells.' . . . The 'free speech' we may remember wasn't actually there for everyone in the past. The excluded group long felt silenced and invisible."

Judith Martin ("Miss Manners") says, "It's no longer socially acceptable to make bigoted statements and racist remarks. Some people are having an awful time with that: 'I didn't know anybody would be offended!' Well, where have you been? I remember when people got away with it and they don't anymore."

Morris Dees (of the wonderful Southern Poverty Law Center) says, "Claims of moral ignorance ['I didn't know it was wrong'] are among the oldest tricks of bigotry."

"If men and women are temporarily more cautious and self-conscious about what they may say and do, that may not be too high a price to pay for a new understanding of what is appropriate behavior and what is not" (language consultant Kaylene Weiser).

And, as writer and former editor of *Ms.* Robin Morgan once wrote, "P.C. doesn't stand for Political Correctness, it stands for Plain Courtesy."

So instead of wondering why everybody is so sensitive these days, we might wonder about those complaining: are they uninformed about the issues? are they simply discourteous? are they, perhaps, "insensitive"?

Additional Information

In the main body of the book, in addition to entries on specific terms, there are brief guidelines on various topics:

- adjectival forms as nouns
- exclusive language
- "feminine" word endings
- inclusive language
- "insider/outsider" rule
- offensive
- "people-first" rule
- prostitute
- pseudogeneric
- salutations (letters)
- sexist language
- sexist quotations
- sex-linked expressions
- shortened forms of words
- singular "they"
- "the"
- unconventional spellings

YOUR HELP WANTED

Language about people is constantly changing, more especially perhaps in this period than in any other in U.S. history. This book owes a great deal to all those who responded to the "Your Help Wanted" request in the earlier volumes, *The Nonsexist Word Finder* and *The Dictionary of Bias-Free Usage* (also published as *The Bias-Free Word Finder*). If you disagree with something here, if you find biased terms not listed, or if you know of additional alternatives for biased terms, please send your comments to: Rosalie Maggio, The Oryx Press, 4041 North Central, Suite 700, Phoenix, AZ 85012-3397. Thank you!

Dictionary of Terms

A

In every civil rights movement . . . the first battlelines are always drawn around labels. It's far easier to agree on what words should not be used than on what to replace them with.

—*Irving Zola*

Accuracy of language is one of the bulwarks of truth.

—*Anna Jameson*

To speak of "mere words" is much like speaking of "mere dynamite."

—*C. J. Ducasse*

abbess/abbot retain these formal titles for persons holding them. "Abbess" is one of the few exceptions to the rule on avoiding feminine endings; abbesses were generally equal to abbots in power, influence, and respect (seventh-century abbess Hilda of Whitby had both monks and nuns under her authority, and her influence spread throughout England). In the generic sense of "abbess" or "abbot," you might use *religious, superior, administrator, director.*

abigail *See* lady's maid, maid.

able-bodied this term (and its partner "temporarily able-bodied") had its Warholian 15 minutes of fame but has lost ground, probably because of its artificiality and vagueness (very few people are 100% able-bodied, whether a toddler needing help up the stairs, a young person wearing glasses, or an older person with arthritis). Trying to establish a one-size-fits-all term to mean the opposite of "people with disabilities" emphasizes an adversarial and distancing us/them, either/or attitude. If you need a blanket term, circumlocute ("both those who use wheelchairs and those who don't") or, as a last resort, use *non-disabled.*

ableism although this term doesn't appear in most dictionaries (it is, however, in the *Oxford Dictionary of New Words*) and doesn't have wide currency, it is used in some contexts to describe discriminatory actions based upon the belief that people with disabilities are inherently inferior. *See also* able-bodied, handicapism.

abnormal *See* normal. *See also* deviant.

abominable snowman *yeti, the yeti.* "Yeti" is in any case the preferred term.

aboriginalism this term was coined in 1990 by Bob Hodge and Vijay Mishra *(Dark Side of the Dream)* to describe the body of "knowledge" about Australian Aboriginals that has been constructed and continues to be constructed largely by non-Aboriginal people. For example, the terminology "legends," "myths/mythology," and "folklore" has been applied to Aboriginal creation stories. Also disputed is the "settlement" of Australia; "This land was not 'pioneered and settled,' it was invaded and occupied" (Kevin Carmody, in *Social Alternatives*). *See also* aborigine/aboriginal.

aborigine/aboriginal in their general sense of referring to the earliest peoples in an area, these terms are correct. However, to refer to the earliest peoples of Australia, the terms are always capitalized ("Aboriginal peoples") and the nouns "Aboriginal/Aboriginals" are thought to be more respectful than "Aborigine/Aborigines." (The shortened "Abo/abo" is always condescending and pejorative.) "When referring to other native peoples, such as American Indians or the early Kelts of Britain [use] *aboriginal inhabitants* or *indigenous peoples* instead of *aborigines.* While there is nothing offensive in the notion of prior habitation—indeed, it is a point of considerable pride among most native peoples—the lowercase noun *aborigine* may well evoke an unwelcome stereotype" *(American Heritage Book of English Usage). See also* aboriginalism, indigenous peoples, shortened forms of words.

abortion clinic reserve this term for facilities where performing abortions is the principal activity; if abortion is incidental to or a minor part of its main business (counseling, family planning, mammograms, health screening, etc.), it is a *women's clinic.*

abortion debate language some of the bitterness of the abortion debate has focused on the terms "pro-life" and "pro-choice." Alternatives suggested (usually by each group for the other) have been generally rejected. The ambiguity of two opposing groups both being "pro-" something is unusual, but these are the terms the groups prefer to use for themselves. Because of the limitations of labels, avoid them as much as possible. *See also* abortionist, anti-choice, pro-abortion, pro-choice, pro-life.

abortionist "'Abortionist' . . . is a highly charged word that is pejorative, derogatory, and defamatory" (Warren M. Hern, M.D., in the *New York*

Times). In the past, he adds, "abortionist" described illegal providers of abortions "in a sleazy world of avaricious, incompetent criminals." Some dictionaries note that the term is usually offensive and that it often carries the meaning "providing abortions, especially illegally." Alternatives include *physician who performs abortions, abortion doctor, abortion provider* (this might also refer to an organization).

Abraham, Isaac, and Jacob these traditional ancestors of Jews and Christians should be joined by their partners, also authentic and important ancestors: Sarah, Rebecca, Leah, and Rachel. "The God of Abraham" would read "the God of Abraham and Sarah."

absent parent or, use "absent mother"/"absent father." The "absent" terms should be used cautiously, however; a noncustodial parent is generally not "absent." David Levy, president of the Children's Rights Council, an organization that helps children maintain contact with both parents, says (in the periodical *Copy Editor*) that the term "absent parent" dates to the 1935 Social Security Act; "In those days, when welfare was first set up, Social Security was for survivors of the deceased—fathers who were lost at sea or in mine disasters. Now 60 years later the main problem is divorce, and we're still using the same antiquated term to describe parents who are not absent." The federal Office of Child Support Enforcement uses "absent parent" only in references to parents whose whereabouts are unknown; otherwise they use "noncustodial parent." In particular, avoid the nonparallel terms, "mother/maternal deprivation" and "father absence" unless you use their correct equivalents ("mother absence"/"father absence" and "maternal deprivation"/"paternal deprivation"). *See also* broken home, deadbeat dad, noncustodial parent, visitation.

accessible some facilities described as "accessible" are accessible to wheelchair-users, but not particularly accessible to others with disabilities.

according to Hoyle there is nothing wrong with this phrase, but be aware of how many such expressions in the English language are male-based. Balance their use with female-based expressions, creative expressions of your own, or sex-neutral alternatives: *according to/by the book, according to/playing by the rules, absolutely correct, cricket, in point of honor, on the square, proper/correct way to do things. See also* sex-linked expressions.

acculturation *culture change.* Sanford Berman points out (in *Prejudices and Antipathies*) that "acculturation" implies a one-way process, which is seldom the case.

Achilles' heel there is nothing wrong with this phrase—it is useful for both sexes, popular, and irreplaceable by anything nearly as apt—but be aware of how many such expressions in the English language are male-based.

Balance their use with female-based expressions, creative expressions of your own, or sex-neutral alternatives: *vulnerable point/spot, weak spot, vulnerability, only weakness, soft spot, chink in one's armor, where the shoe pinches.* **See also** sex-linked expressions.

acid-conditioning man *acid-conditioner.*

acid-correction man *acid-corrector, acid-correction hand.*

acid man (explosives) *acid-mixer, nitrating-acid mixer.*

acolyte depending on the denomination, this might be a woman or a man. When it means "attendant," it can be either sex. **See also** altar boy.

acquaintance rape *See* date rape.

activist Vivian Jenkins Nelsen *(New Voices in the Media)* points out that "activist" is often "code for busy-body, trouble-maker, radical—someone who courts media attention." If not abused, "activist" is a strong, useful word; reserve it for those who self-identify as activists or when it is not double-talk for something else.

act like a man *See* man, act like a/be a/take it like a.

act one's age it is doubtful whether there exists such a phenomenon as "acting one's age." Replace this vague term with precise descriptions of the behavior.

actress *actor.* Many women call themselves actors, pointing out that they are members of the U.S. Actors' Guild or British Actors' Equity Association. "I think actresses worry about eyelashes and cellulite, and women who are actors worry about the characters we are playing. A separate category is another way of making us a special-interest group" (Alfre Woodard, in the *New York Times*). "Actor" was used for both sexes for about 75 years before the appearance of "actress"—"a woman who is an actor." The specification of gender supports the male-as-norm system ("actor" being the standard and "actress" being the deviation). However, use it for women who so identify themselves. **See also** "feminine" word endings.

A.D. these familiar initials stand for "anno Domini," which means "in the year of the Lord." C.E. (for Common Era) is sometimes used to remove the Christian element from dating, although ironically C.E. has some-times been taken to mean "Christian Era." **See also** B.C.

Adam, don't know from the commonly used partner to this sex-specific expression is *don't know from Adam's aunt.*

Adam's rib the word "adam" means "human"; "adamah" means "earth." In telling how God made the adam from the adamah, the creation story in the Bible says humans are from and of the humus. This "adam" is an earthling who is not yet either male or female (Genesis 2:7). Not until the lines of poetry near the end does the story use the Hebrew words "is" and "issah," expressing male and female sexual difference. In the story, common humanity precedes sexual differentiation. Dennis Baron *(Grammar and Gender)* says that the phrase "Adam's rib" (as womankind's point of origin) should be put in quotation marks to show its dubiousness and reserved for discussions of the term itself. *See also* Eve.

adjectival forms as nouns it is considered unacceptable to use adjectives as nouns when referring to something that describes only a part of a person's or group's existence. Incorrect constructions: the blind, the poor, the learning disabled, the elderly, an amputee, a diabetic, a quadriplegic. In most cases, it doesn't help to simply put a noun after the adjective. The construction itself is usually changed: those who have been blind from birth; poor and low-income renters; children with learning disabilities; older patients; someone with an amputation, with diabetes, with quadriplegia. *See also* disability/disabilities, "people first" rule, "the."

adman *advertising executive, creative/art director, copywriter, ad agent/ writer/creator, account executive/manager/supervisor, media buyer, ad rep, advertising representative.* Generic plurals: *advertising executives, ad agency staff, advertising people.* Or, use specific job titles.

adolescent this term for a person in the period of development between youth and maturity, or from the onset of puberty to maturity, does not indicate a specific span of years. Adolescents' characteristics vary enormously from individual to individual. In addition to being vague, the word has negative connotations (nobody ever self-identifies as an "adolescent") because of its use in terms like "adolescent behavior" and because it defines someone solely in terms of age (much like calling someone "old person" or "fortyish person"). Either refer to a specific age ("Ali, age 16"), or use young person/people, young adult, young man/ young woman. "The teen years" is preferable to "adolescence." *See also* ageism, children, juvenile, teenager, youth.

adopt-a programs ubiquitous for a wide range of temporary or trivial campaigns (adopt-a-highway, adopt-a-wolf, adopt-a-family, adopt-a-pothole), the overused "adopt-a" programs can confuse children— adopted or not—and perpetuate myths and stereotypes that undermine adoption as a real, permanent family relationship. Adoption expert Pat Johnston notes that adoptive families "build their relationships on the powerful notion of *forever.* The 'adopt-a' programs, more accurately described as 'sponsorship' programs with acknowledged short-term commitments, promote misconceptions and a trivialized perception of this family-building method." Consider using instead *sponsor-a, choose-a, embrace-a, opt-for-a, take-up-a, save-a, help-a, be-a-friend-to.*

adoption language many terms used to describe adoption and adopted children—particularly to distinguish adoptive families and adopted children from families and children related genetically—tend to portray adoption as a second-best, even last-resort way to build a family. Calling a biological parent a "real" parent or a "natural" parent implies that adoptive relationships are artificial, tentative, less than complete, and less important than are relationships by birth. The phrase "children of their own," referring to children born into a family, implies that genetic relationships are stronger, closer, and more enduring than adoptive relationships. Birth mothers and birth fathers who choose adoption for their children generally do not "abandon," "surrender," "release," "relinquish," "give up," or "put up for adoption" their children. In most cases it is accurate to say they "made an adoption plan" or "chose adoption." "International adoption" is preferred to "foreign adoption." In addition to the somewhat judgmental-sounding "home study," agencies and prospective parents also work on "parent preparation," "adoption preparation/ study." "Hard-to-place" children can be called "children with special needs" or "waiting children," terms that are less damaging to their self-esteem. When an adopted child meets a birth parent for the first time, it is not a "reunion" but a "meeting" (although for a child adopted at an older age it might truly be a reunion). Avoid the qualifier "adopted" (e.g., "survivors include two sons and an adopted daughter") unless there is a specific reason for mentioning the fact of the adoption. *See also* adopt-a programs, biological father/mother/parent, birth mother/father/parent, illegitimate, "natural" child/parent, "real" father/mother/parent.

advance man *advance agent, publicity/press agent, agent, booker, publicist, promoter, talent coordinator, representative, rep, go-between, negotiator, producer.*

adventuress *adventurer.* Also: *sensation-seeker, explorer, pacesetter, globetrotter, bird of passage, gadabout, vagabond, gambler*—all equally applicable to women or men. "Adventurer" and "adventuress" have different cultural overtones and definitions; the latter seeks to support herself by "questionable means" where the former courts danger and risk. *See also* "feminine" word endings.

advertising advertising creates and reinforces numerous sexist stereotypes: women are sex objects and men are success objects; women live to please men and men live to take care of women; men are hopeless at the simplest household tasks while women are fulfilled doing the simplest household tasks; all women really want is male sexual attention and all men really want is fast cars and cold beer. Women are shown primarily as housewife or sex partner; appear in fewer ads than men; tend to promote beauty, home, food, and clothing products; and are shown primarily at home rather than at work. The most harmful role is that of the pouting, inviting woman who signals very clearly her sexual availability. When real-world women fail to live up to the image, resentment and even rage follow. Men who rape women believe women are teases who try to control them; advertising reinforces the notion. "Advertising seems to encourage and magnify personal dissatisfaction in order to stimulate the demand for products. We already know that sex sells. The question is how long we will consider an increased incidence of rape and other problems of abuse as unavoidable costs of doing business" (Paul Paulos). Advertising doesn't do much better by men, especially in recent years. Joyce Brothers says that now men "are the ones who come off looking like jerks." Partly because of the growing strength of the women's movement and partly because women are major consumers, poking outright fun at women has become financially risky. In a year-long study of over 1,000 print and television ads, Men's Rights Inc. concluded that men are portrayed as ignorant, incompetent, and at the mercy of women. Men's roles as parents and caregivers are largely ignored. In any ad in which a man and a woman appear, if one of them is a jerk, it's the man. Studies show that male-bashing ads are remembered far better than others. In a survey of 18,000 commercials and 70,000 print ads in its New York creative library, ad agency J. Walter Thompson found that the nine basic stereotypes used for men in 1960 are still being used today: the Lone Wolf (the Marlboro man), Mr. Success (the Rolex guy), the Expert, the Lover, the Stud, the Husband, etc. Where are the catchy, memorable ads that don't demean or stereotype either sex? Racist and ethnic stereotypes have also played a prominent part in advertising; today, instead of learning to portray people in diverse, respectful, and real-life ways, some advertisers are opting not to use people at all in case they "offend" someone.

advertising layout man *advertising layout planner/artist.*

adzman *adzer.*

aficionada/aficionado these are good sex-specific and sex-parallel terms. If you need alternatives to include both sexes in the plural consider *fans, enthusiasts, devotees, nuts, hounds, buffs.*

affirmative action coined in 1965 as part of Lyndon Johnson's "Great Society" initiatives, this term refers to efforts to improve the employment and educational opportunities of women and members of minority groups. "To some, the term means only that an employer casts the widest possible net when searching for employees. To others it means that minorities can be preferred over equally 'qualified' whites for the sake of 'diversity,' two other extremely controversial concepts. To some, affirmative action programs ought to be only for blacks as a historical redress for slavery. To others, women and ethnic minorities always may be included, or, in the case of some Asians, excluded. The questions are nearly endless" (Steve Berg in the Minneapolis *Star Tribune*). In response to current opposition (on the grounds of "unfairness," especially to white men) and the dismantling of some affirmative action programs, Julian Bond says, "What they're really complaining about is that they used to have 100% of the slots and now they have to share, and it burns them up." Opponents of affirmative action like to quote Martin Luther King Jr.: "Injustice anywhere is a threat to justice everywhere." But King also said that giving people their "due may often mean giving [them] special treatment. . . . A society that has done something special against [Negroes] for hundreds of years must now do something for [them], in order to equip [them] to compete on a just and equal basis." Tim Wise (in *Blueprint for Social Justice*) says, "Much of the American public has apparently decided that African Americans have had enough time to 'catch up,' politically and economically. We are asked to believe that discrimination against blacks is a thing of the past, and that the new victims are white males, left in the gutter of economic opportunity while unqualified, semi-illiterate blacks take 'their' jobs, 'their' promotions, and 'their' children's scholarships because of affirmative action. We are asked to believe that two-and-a-half decades of remedial politics can erase the legacy of over 300 years of racial oppression against black people in this country. . . . Does it bother any of the bold defenders of the merit system that one-sixth of this year's graduating class at Harvard were 'legacies,' admitted more because of who they knew than what they knew?" Columnist Tom Teepen writes, "It's OK with the Constitution to limit college scholarships, as the Western Golf Association does, to former caddies, but the Constitution apparently is offended beyond endurance by state scholarships for black students. Wasie Foundation of Minneapolis offers scholarships to Christian students of Polish descent, but that's all right because in addition to the foundation being private there's no racial exclusion. All the black Christian Polish kids can apply right along with the white ones." Teepen also lists the United Daughters of the Confederacy with its scholarships to lineal descendants of Confederate soldiers, scholarships designated for descendants of signers of the Declaration of Independence, ones offered by Miss Italian USA for those of Italian descent, by the Sons of Norway, or to students of Huguenot ancestry, scholarships to the University of North Carolina for folks named Gatlin or Gatling, scholarships available for Tupperware dealers and for the children of harness-race drivers; "Only 4% of the nation's scholarships are race-conscious—including, by the way, the ones for white kids who go to Virginia's two historically black campuses." In 1996 the University of California, Berkeley, was found to have been operating a special admissions program for students whose names were forwarded by VIPs ranging from a U.S. senator to the regent who is leading the effort to overturn the school's affirmative action policy; students who would not otherwise have been admitted were given undergraduate slots by a special committee set up to review the requests. Avida R. Lazo asks, "Who are all these black women that have all the advantages over, and at the expense of, white males? . . . White men make up 33% of the population but comprise 89% of the managers and professionals, and 368 of this country's 400 wealthiest people. Blacks make up only 4% of this nation's managers and 3% of its physicians and lawyers. Black women are an even smaller percentage of these already low percentages." Teepen says, "Where affirmative action sometimes creates specific white victims, the injustice must be redressed, but the policy deserves to be judged on its broad success, not by its rare missteps." *See also* racial preference.

afflicted with when speaking of people with disabilities, use instead *a person who has/a person with/a person living with a certain condition* (not an "affliction"). *See also* disability, "people first" rule, PWA/PWLA/ PLA.

Africa in the excellent *Guidelines for Creating Positive Sexual and Racial Images in Educational Materials* (Macmillan Publishing Company), writers are cautioned that Africa is not a homogeneous, underdeveloped "country," but rather a continent comprising many modern countries, each having a unique history, politics, culture, and economy. African nations should be described with the same complexity, attention to detail, respect, and imputed validity as European countries are. "When discussing Africa's past, be accurate and specific about tribal names, practices, artwork, and cultural artifacts. Generally, however, we should move away from depicting Africa only in terms of its past. (We do not, except in special circumstances, go to great lengths to describe the lifestyle of the Saxons or consider them typical of the British.)" *See also* darkest Africa/ the dark continent.

African of or pertaining to the continent of Africa or its people or languages, this term is not a synonym for "African American" nor is "black" a synonym for it (not all Africans are black). Whenever possible, use a specific national designation (Tanzanian, Moroccan, Ethiopian). *See also* Africa, African American, black, colored.

African American there has been much discussion of the appropriateness of "African American" versus "black/Black" (the latter is more popular); there are pros and cons for each term. Most people will accept either and use both themselves, but some individuals have a preference, which should be determined before writing about them. Most black publications still use "black," and the most commonly used strategy in all publications is to alternate the terms; there does not seem to be any resulting confusion. Like similar nouns ("Chinese American") "African American" is not hyphenated; the adjective can be ("African-American women"). *See also* African, Afro-American, black (noun), black/black-, black-and-white (adjective), colored, "hyphenated Americans," Negro.

Afro-American this is an acceptable term, although it has generally been superseded in recent years by African American and black. *See also* African American, black.

ageism defined as "a negative or prejudicial image of aging held by society or by individuals, ageism also exists when age is an influencing factor in situations where it is in fact inappropriate or irrelevant" *(Thesaurus of Aging Terminology).* Although age discrimination is prohibited in the workplace, our cultural preoccupation with youth results in keeping older people invisible and undervalued. Industrial designer and gerontologist Patricia Moore says we're the only country in the world that asks age-related questions by using the word "old" (in *Modern Maturity* magazine). In French the question and answer are: "What age have you?" "I have 53 years." In Italian: "How many years have you?" "I have 53 years." The concept of "old" is not included. When giving age, sometimes use "Rip Van Winkle, 78" instead of "78-year-old Rip Van Winkle." "A strange disparity exists. . . . In the news, we see active older persons as revered rulers, Nobel Prize winners, leading actors, explorers, educators, and thinkers, at the height of wisdom and ability. Yet we communicate a picture of waning physical and mental powers—people who are child-like, self-indulgent, helpless, and a bother to have around" (International Association of Business Communicators, *Without Bias*). Ageism (the term was coined by geriatric medicine specialist Robert Butler in 1969) is readily seen in the language. The disparaging sense of words like the following is intensified when used with "old": biddy, buzzard, codger, coot, dodderer, dotard, duffer, fogy, fool, fuddy-duddy, gaffer, geezer. Other offensive phrases include blue-haired, Geritol generation, has-been, over the hill. There is also a lack of respect for those who are too young; "adultism" is a form of ageism that discounts children and teenagers as too immature to know what's good for them and too inexperienced to do anything valuable. Some believe that adultism lays the foundation for accepting racism, sexism, and other oppressive relationships. *See also* adolescent, children, dirty old man, elderly, frail elderly, old, old lady/old man, old maid, old-timer, old woman, oldster, senior/senior citizen, teenager, youth.

agenda everybody has an agenda, i.e., priorities, but this term is often used accusatorially (with "hidden" or "secret") as though only the other side has one.

agent provocateur this specific and nearly irreplaceable term is used in French (where it is grammatically masculine) and in English for both sexes. If you must have a more inclusive- or English-sounding term consider *infiltrating agent, saboteur, instigator, disinformation agent, covert operative.*

aggressive "aggressive" and its more negative synonym "pushy" are often used disparagingly of women and Jews. Deborah Tannen *(Gender and Discourse)* suggests that the "stereotype of Jews as aggressive and pushy results in part from differences in conversational style." In the lead opinion in the court case of a woman who failed to be named a partner in a business because she was considered too aggressive, Walter Brennan wrote, "An employer who objects to aggressiveness in women but whose positions require this trait places women in an intolerable and impermissible Catch-22: out of a job if they behave aggressively and out of a job if they don't." Pollster Celinda Lake asked observers to rate women and men reading the same text at identical decibel levels. Invariably the women were described as louder, more aggressive, and shrill. *See also* feisty.

agribusinessman *farmer, agriculturist; agribusinesswoman and agribusinessman* (both terms have appeared in print). *See also* farmer, farm wife/farmer's wife.

ahistoricity *See* history.

aide (medical) *nursing assistant, nurse assistant, N.A.* Traditionally, aides and orderlies did the same work, but all aides were women and all orderlies were men. Most hospitals and nursing homes now use the inclusive terms.

aide de camp today both military and civilian aides can be women or men; historically an aide de camp was a man.

aidman *medical aide.*

AIDS "an equal opportunity pathogen," the AIDS (Acquired Immune Deficiency Syndrome) virus crosses all cultural, economic, ethnic, sex, sex-orientation, and social lines. It is not "a gay disease"; in some parts of the world it is found predominantly in heterosexuals. A person does not die from AIDS but from complications of AIDS. When disseminating information about AIDS, avoid vague, shortcut terms like "intimate sexual contact" and "bodily fluids"—tell exactly what kinds of sexual contact and exactly what kinds of bodily fluids can transmit AIDS. A person with AIDS is not "an AIDS victim" or "someone afflicted with/ suffering from AIDS." Use instead *person living with AIDS, someone with AIDS, person who has AIDS. See also* afflicted with, AIDS carrier, AIDS-related complex (ARC), AIDS victim, bodily fluids, disability/ disabilities, high-risk group, HIV, homophobia, innocent victim, "people first" rule, PWA/PWLA/PLA, victim.

AIDS carrier the Gay & Lesbian Alliance Against Defamation *(Media Guide to the Lesbian and Gay Community)* recommends not using this term as it is dehumanizing. It is acceptable and even recommended to educate people that someone who is HIV-infected/HIV-positive/seroposi-tive can infect others, but it should be made clear that transmission of the disease is effected only by means of high-risk activities (exchange of certain bodily fluids, sharing needles, etc.); one is not a "carrier" in the sense of a Typhoid Mary—"a person from whom something undesirable or deadly spread to those nearby" *(American Heritage Dictionary).*

AIDS-related complex (ARC) this term has been used by physicians since 1983 to characterize the intermediate stage of HIV infection—beyond asymptomatic, but short of meeting the criteria for AIDS determined by the Centers for Disease Control (Gay & Lesbian Alliance Against Defamation, *Media Guide to the Lesbian and Gay Community*).

AIDS victim individuals diagnosed with AIDS usually prefer to be identified as people with AIDS. They also prefer to be described as "living with AIDS" instead of "dying from AIDS." "Victim" implies a passive help-lessness—the opposite of the way many face the disease. *See also* AIDS, HIV, PWA/PWLA/PLA, victim.

airdox man *airdox fitter.*

airhead because this word, along with birdbrain, emptyhead, featherbrain, harebrain, and scatterbrain (and their adjectival forms), is used almost exclusively of girls/women, you may want sex-neutral alternatives: *out to lunch, space ranger, flake, out of it, on another planet, head in the clouds, not all there, missing some marbles, mind like a sieve, impractical, irresponsible, slaphappy, woolgathering, dreamy, mindless, brainless wonder, dense, muddleheaded, shallow, inane, foolish.*

airman *aviator, pilot, flier, airline/test pilot, co-pilot, navigator, flight/ aeronautical engineer, aerial navigator, flying officer, bombardier, air marshal, aeronaut, balloonist, aviation/aircraft worker, glider, skydiver, paratrooper, parachutist, airborne trooper, member of the U.S. Air Force.* The official U.S. Air Force publication is *The Airman* and the Air Force calls its members airmen, although all ranks are open to both sexes (16% of all officers and enlistees are women). You can also use *member of the U.S. Air Force.* Outside the Air Force, some 3% of all airplane pilots and navigators are women. *See also* birdman, wingman.

airman basic/airman first class man or woman. *See also* airman.

airmanship *aerial navigation/flying/piloting skills, flying ability, aeronauti-cal/flying/piloting expertise.*

airplane steward/airplane stewardess *See* steward/stewardess.

airport serviceman *airport attendant/servicer.*

alcoholic texts have customarily referred to a person addicted to alcohol as "he," but not all alcoholics are men; use inclusive pronouns. Because of the public perception that women rarely become alcoholic, many women have delayed recognizing and treating their problem. Using "he" also unfairly stereotypes men as alcoholics. Our cultural perceptions of "alcoholic" feature gutter drunks, "winos," and people whose lives are blatantly in ruins. But not all alcoholics are living on the streets; many are neatly dressed people who hold down jobs and who have good reputations in their communities. The false picture we have of an "alcoholic"— a down-and-out man on skid row—helps persuade people who have a problem to think that they don't. *See also* reformed alcoholic.

alderman *council/city council member, city/municipal councilor, chancellor, city/ward representative, commissioner, councilor, member of the council, municipal officer, ward manager; alderman and alderwoman.* In some areas they are officially called "alderpersons," but one doesn't have to like it.

alewife (fish) OK as is.

alewife (woman) *barkeep, barkeeper, bartender.*

alien *See* illegal alien.

alimony other terms are sometimes more appropriate: *back salary, reparations, permanent maintenance, permanent spousal maintenance, spousal support, rehabilitative/temporary alimony/maintenance.* The newer terms avoid the implication that one spouse is receiving unearned financial support from the other. Either sex may receive alimony or maintenance, although today only 15% of women are awarded alimony and most awards are temporary; men collect only when their wives earn markedly more (Jane Bryant Quinn, in *Newsweek*).

Allah the Arabic word for God. Note that because it means "God," Arab Christians also use the word "Allah."

all-American outside its use in sports, who or what in this diverse country could be truly "all-American"? When you picture, for example, an "all-American boy," is he black? gay? using a wheelchair? Probably not.

all boy/all girl/all man/all woman replace these vague, stereotypical expressions with specific descriptions. No two people will agree, for example, on what "He's all man!" means. What is fairly typical is that "all boy/all man" refers to action while "all girl/all woman" refers to physical appearance.

all chiefs and no Indians this phrase (or "too many chiefs and not enough braves") is disliked by most American Indians. You might construct substitutes of your own (*all queen bees and no drones, everybody wants to be the boss,* etc.).

alleyman *alley cleaner, bowling alley cleaner.*

all men are created equal *all women and men/men and women are created equal, all people/we are all/all of us are created equal.* "All men are created equal" is apparently one of the 10 most famous quotations in the world *(Time* magazine, cited in *Random House Dictionary of Popular Proverbs and Sayings);* its influence is undoubted, but when first written, "all men" meant "white adult males," not "all human beings." In 1790, when Frenchwomen observed that the liberty, equality, and fraternity won for Frenchmen in the 1789 French Revolution were just that (for French*men*), playwright and revolutionary Olympe de Gouges published "The Declaration of the Rights of Women," modeled on the "Declaration of the Rights of Man and the Citizen." (Three years later, after opposing Robespierre and the Jacobins, she went to the guillotine.) At the first American Woman's Rights Convention (1848), the proposed "Declaration of Sentiments" began: "We hold these truths to be self-evident: that all men and women are created equal; that they are endowed by their Creator with certain inalienable rights" (Susan B. Anthony, *History of Woman Suffrage).* Not only did "all men" not include women, but it did not include black men, and it took two amendments to the U.S. Constitution to establish just who "all men" rightly includes.

all the king's men *everybody, one and all, every last one, the whole world, everybody under the sun, all the monarch's soldiers. **See also** all the world and his wife; everybody and his grandmother/brother;* Tom, Dick, and Harry, every.

all the world and his wife *all the world and little Billing, everyone, everybody, the whole world, every last one of them, all the world and their offspring. **See also** all the king's men; everybody and his grandmother/ brother;* Tom, Dick, and Harry, every.

all work and no play makes Jack a dull boy *you know what they say about all work and no play; you know what they say, "all work and no play . . ."; all work and no play makes us pretty dull sorts; all work and no play makes Jill a dull girl/Jack a dull boy.*

alma mater this gender-specific term (from the Latin for "fostering/bounteous/nourishing mother") is not perceived as particularly biased. However, if you want a sex-neutral alternative consider *the university I (he/she/we/ they/you) attended, school attended, my (your/his/her/our/their) graduating institution, my (her/his/their/our/your) college or university. For the school song, use my school song/anthem/hymn, the school song, the University of Iowa school song.*

almsman *pauper, suppliant, mendicant, beggar, beneficiary, pensioner, recipient, welfare recipient.*

alphabetism this term, coined by Ian Stewart in 1987 (in *The New Scientist*), codifies the treatment people receive according to the position of their surnames in the alphabet. Although this is not one of the most serious problems in society today, it wouldn't hurt to be aware that people whose surnames fall near the end of the alphabet spend a lot of time waiting and often discover there are no supplies left when their turn comes.

altar boy *server, acolyte, attendant, helper; altar girl and altar boy.*

alterations woman *alterer, tailor. See also* dressmaker, seamstress, sewing woman.

alternative the use of this term implies the existence of a single norm and thus tends to marginalize the groups or "lifestyles" so described. Other uses of "alternative" (publications, library materials) have been debated as well. *See also* alternative lifestyle, normal.

alternative lifestyle most often used to refer to sexual orientation, this term implies there is "a" lifestyle to which one can be alternative. People don't have lifestyles, they have lives. *See also* lifestyle.

alto an alto is always a woman, although you will find both men and women singing in the alto range; the countertenor is the highest male voice and the contralto ("alto" is a contraction of contralto) is the lowest female voice.

alumna/alumnae/alumnus/alumni when used correctly to describe respectively a woman/women/a man/men, these Latin terms are gender-fair. The most common errors are the use of "alumnus" to refer to a woman and the use of "alumni" to describe both women and men. However, the trend is away from the more pedantic sex-linked Latin and toward pithier inclusive terms: *graduate(s), alum(s), member(s) of the class of 1996, postgraduate(s), former student(s), ex-student(s).* If you must for some reason use the Latin, write *alumna/us or alumnus/a and alumni/ae or alumnae/i.*

Alzheimer's disease named after German neurologist Alois Alzheimer, this disease is marked by progressive deterioration in cognitive skills and by behavioral and personality changes. The term always has an apostrophe. The condition can be referred to as "Alzheimer's" after a first mention as "Alzheimer's disease."

amaurotic family idiocy *Tay-Sachs disease.*

Amazon/amazon in Greek mythology, Amazons were fabulous female warriors, although recently archaeologists have discovered that a society of armed women existed nearly 2,500 years ago not far from where Herodotus first described seeing a race of Amazons. The 1970 edition of the *Encyclopaedia Britannica* explains (although a later edition deletes it): "The only plausible explanation of the story of the Amazons is that it is a variety of the familiar tale of a distant land where everything is done the wrong way about; thus the women fight, which is man's business." The word "amazon" is loaded with cultural and historical meanings; it has been used as a pejorative to describe certain women and certain kinds of women, but in other contexts it is a term of respect that women appropriate for themselves. (For example, The Amazon Bookstore, founded in 1970, is the oldest and one of the largest feminist bookstores in the U.S.) Use the term only if you understand its history and multiple connotations. For the casual use of "amazon" meaning a tall, strong, or belligerent woman, substitute those or other descriptive adjectives. *See also* combat, warrior.

ambassadress *ambassador. See also* "feminine" word endings.

Amerasian a person of Asian and U.S. parentage, especially the child of an Asian mother and a U.S. serviceman, "Amerasian" was coined during the Korean War but came into wider use during the Vietnam War. There is no specific racial connotation to the "Amer-" component of Amerasian, although it is implicit that one parent, usually the mother, is Asian or of Asian heritage. Most Amerasian children born in Vietnam were unacknowledged by their U.S. fathers and were discriminated against by the Vietnamese people and the government, who saw them as reminders of the U.S. presence in Vietnam (Lan Cao and Himilce Novas, *Everything You Need to Know About Asian-American History*). In 1987 the United States passed the Amerasian Homecoming Act to enable Vietnamese Amerasians born between January 1, 1962, and January 1, 1977, to relocate to the U.S. Some U.S. citizens of Asian American–U.S. American parentage also choose to call themselves "Amerasians."

America/American *the United States; U.S. national/citizen/resident.* Or, some people have been using "U.S. American" (Alex-Edmund S. DaHinten, Guatemalan Socio-Cultural Committee). The people of some 40 countries (those of North America, Central America and the Caribbean, and South America) can correctly call themselves "Americans." The terms "Asian," "African," and "European" properly refer to peoples in all the countries of their respective continents; it is puzzling to many outside the United States why "American" refers to only one of the American populations. Bernard E. Bobb, professor of history, emeritus, Washington State University, has one explanation: "We are the only nation in the world whose official name [United States of America] includes the word 'America.' Every other nation in the New World, from Canada to Argentina, has a specific name that doesn't include that word." Although the term "United Statesian" has been used occasionally by enterprising writers, there is no convenient shorthand term presently available comparable to Peruvian, Costa Rican, Canadian, etc.; only Spanish has a word

46

for "Americans"/"United Statesians": Estadounidenses." The American Political Science Association's style manual recommends the use of "United States, U.S., U.S. citizen, or citizen" instead of the ethnocentric "America/American" when the country is meant, reserving the use of "America/American" to refer to one or both continents. The use of "American" is ambiguous in many terms like "American history," "American heroes," and "American foreign policy," and on the grounds of clarity alone should be replaced. The exception to its use for U.S. citizens are the names used for immigrants and their descendants (Italian Americans, Japanese Americans); those terms are used only in the U.S. and are thus unlikely to be ambiguous. *See also* all-American, "hyphenated Americans."

American Indian *See* Indian.

Amerindian/Amerind the once-popular, cobbled-together "Amerindian" (and its shortened form "Amerind") has fallen out of favor and is no longer much used. "American Indian" is the preferred term. *See also* Indian.

amiga/amigo these are good sex-specific and parallel terms. For the inclusive plural use *friends*.

amputee avoid referring to a person by a surgical procedure or missing body part. Question the need to refer to the amputation (as with any disability). If relevant, the information can be conveyed without labeling the entire person by something that is only one part of their life. *See also* handicapped.

analysis girl *silver solution mixer.*

ancestress *ancestor. See also* fathers, "feminine" word endings, forefather.

anchoress retain despite the feminine ending. Julian of Norwich, the first English woman of letters and the first theologian of either sex to write originally in English, is widely, historically, and respectfully known as an anchoress. "Anchoress" is a strong, positive term that has not been discounted over time. For a man, use *anchorite*; in the broader sense, use *hermit*.

anchorman (black jack) *third base.*

anchorman (newscasting) *anchor, news anchor, newscaster, broadcaster, telecaster, sportscaster, announcer, reporter, TV reporter, commentator, communications artist, news analyst, narrator.*

ancient man *ancient people/peoples, ancient civilization, ancient humanity.*

androgynous/androgyny the ultimate in inclusive, these words contain the roots for both man ("andr") and woman ("gyne"). "Androgyny suggests a spirit of reconciliation between the sexes; it suggests, further, a full range of experience open to individuals who may, as women, be aggressive, as men, tender; it suggests a spectrum upon which human beings choose their places without regard to propriety or custom" (Carolyn G. Heilbrun, *Toward a Recognition of Androgyny*). According to *The Opposite Sex* (Anne Campbell), it is the androgynous person who shows the most satisfactory psychological and social adjustment. Gloria Steinem *(Outrageous Acts and Everyday Rebellions)* says the concept of androgyny "raised the hope that the female and male cultures could be perfectly blended in the ideal person; yet because the female side of the equation has yet to be affirmed, androgyny usually tilted toward the male. As a concept, it also raised anxiety levels by conjuring up a conformist, unisex vision, the very opposite of the individuality and uniqueness that feminism actually has in mind." John A. Sanford *(The Invisible Partners)* says, "Men are used to thinking of themselves only as men, and women think of themselves as women, but the psychological facts indicate that every human being is androgynous." And Samuel Taylor Coleridge said, "The truth is, a great mind must be androgynous."

angel in many cultures and for many men, women are either angels (perfect and innocent) or devils (evil tempters). Our ideas of both angels themselves and women-as-angels are highly mythic and in some cases insulting to real angels and real women. The association of women with angels is a little puzzling; in the Jewish and Christian scriptures, there were no female angels; angels were generally represented as men although in one case they appear to be neuter. They also must be fearsome; their first words are always, "Do not be afraid." Note that not all angels are Christian (there are Jewish, Muslim, and other angels) nor are they all white (when Oprah Winfrey mentioned that the black angels she collects are hard to find, she was inundated with them; her collection numbers nearly 600).

angel of the Lord *angel of God, angel. See also* Lord.

Anglo used as a generic synonym for "white," as it is in some parts of the U.S., "Anglo" is considered inaccurate (not all whites have an Anglo-Saxon heritage) and objectionable (those who have suffered from Anglo-Saxon oppression—the Irish, for example—resent being called Anglos). "Anglo" is slang for white non–Mexican Americans in the South and Southwest and for white non-Cubans in Miami. When combining terms, no hyphen is needed for lowercased words ("anglophone") but one is needed for capitalized terms ("Anglo-Saxon"). *See also* Anglo-American.

Anglo-American this refers to a U.S. citizen of English ancestry; it is not accurate to use it generically for every white person who speaks English. The hyphen is used in both the noun and the adjective because "Anglo-" is a prefix. *See also* Anglo.

anima/animus in Jungian psychology, "anima" (the feminine form of the Latin for "soul") refers to the female component in a man's personality, while "animus" (the masculine form) refers to the masculine component in a woman's personality. Use as they are.

animal/he if you know the animal's gender and it is important for your audience to know it also, use it; otherwise refer to animals of unknown or irrelevant gender as "it."

animal husbandman *animal scientist; farmer.*

animal (man) calling men "animals" carries with it a what-can-you-expect attitude and builds tolerance for behavior that is not particularly normative for men. *See also* animal names for people.

animal names for people using animal names to refer to people is generally insensitive and will not make you a lot of friends. In addition, most pejorative animal names are also sexist: ape, baboon, bat, beast, bird, brood mare, buck, bull, bunny, cat, chick/chicken/chickie-baby, cow, dog, dumb ox, filly, fox, gay dog, goose, gorilla, heifer, hellcat, hen, kitten, lapdog, mare, old bat, old goat, ox, pig, pussy, pussycat, quail, sex kitten, shark (card/financial/loan/pool shark), she-cat, sow, stag, swine, tigress, tomcat, top dog, turkey, vixen, weasel. A few terms seem descriptive without being derogatory; lamb is used affectionately for both sexes. Metaphors that compare people to animals in some particular way are seldom sexist and thus are acceptable, for example, merry as a cricket, wise as an owl, happy as a lark, feeling one's oats. To distinguish between pejorative and acceptable descriptions, determine whether a person is being labeled an animal or whether the person is being likened to some animal characteristic. Calling someone an eager beaver implies not so much that the person is a beaver but that the person is eager as a beaver is eager. Strong writing depends on metaphors—even metaphors based on animals—but there is a difference between labeling people and creating vivid word associations. *See also* animal (man), bitch, food names for people, fox/fox trap/foxy/foxy lady, hen party, lone wolf, stag line, stag movie, stag party, stud, wolf.

Anishinabe *See* Ojibwa/Ojibway.

anthropology the Greek word "anthropos" means "human being," although it has often been translated "man." In practice, "anthropos" words like anthropology, anthropocentric, anthropoid, anthropomorphism, misanthropic, philanthropic, philanthropist, and philanthropy are defined, used, and perceived as inclusive.

anti-choice *pro-life, anti-abortion. See also* abortion debate language, pro-life.

antifeminist man or woman.

anti-Semitic Semites are members of any of the peoples who speak a Semitic language, including Jews, Arabs, Assyrians, and Phoenicians. Most often, however, "anti-Semitism" refers to Jews and not to Arabs or others; it also is a much nicer-sounding word than "Jew-hating," which tends to obscure its hatefulness. It is more precise in most contexts to be specific: "anti-Arab hostility," "anti-Jewish publications."

any man's death diminishes me unless you are quoting John Donne, use *anyone's death diminishes me.*

ape-man *early human, prehuman, prehuman fossil, anthropoid ape.*

Apostolic Fathers leave as is; historically correct.

Appalachian "*Appalachians,* because of its identity with rural poverty and its largely uncomplimentary denotation of the quasi-ethnic group of the region, holds the potential of both an ethnic and a class slur. Better, more traditional terms are available: *Southern Highlanders* and *Appalachian Southerners* could serve" (Irving Lewis Allen, *Unkind Words*). Use "Appalachia" to refer to the area, not the people, thus "the rural populations of southern Appalachia." *See also* hillbilly.

apron strings, tied to someone's *dependent/overly dependent on, clinging, immature, timid, childish, youthful, pampered, protected, hang on the sleeve of, dance attendance on, can't make a move without, no mind of one's own.* Hugh Rawson *(Wicked Words)* defines the expression as being "unduly subject to one's wife or mother" and says it dates back to at least the 16th century when the legal term "apron-string hold/tenure" referred to tenure of an estate by virtue of one's wife or during her lifetime only. *See also* henpecked.

Arab Arabs are Semitic people who originated on the Arabian Peninsula. The 19 Arab countries on the west part of the Asian continent and the northern part of the Africa continent are: Lebanon, Palestine, Jordan, Syria, Kuwait, Saudi Arabia, Yemen, Oman, Bahrain, Tunisia, Algeria, Egypt, Sudan, Qatar, Mauritania, Iraq, Libya, Morocco, and the United Arab Emirates. The word Arab (pronouncing it as AY-rab is a slur) is not interchangeable with "Arab American," "Arab Canadian," or "Muslim." Not all Arabs are Muslims nor are all Muslims Arabs. Iranians are Persians, not Arabs. Watch for stereotypes: Arab women tend to be seen as either veiled or belly dancing; men are billionaires or bombers. *See also* Arab American, Middle East.

Arab American acceptable term for those who increasingly self-identify this way.

armed forces women make up 11% of the two-million-member armed forces, but fewer than 2% of the top officers are women, as are less than 1% in the ranks of brigadier general and above. Sexual harassment of women remains a significant problem in spite of clear policy guidelines, and facilities in some locations are not equal for women and men. *See also* combat, draft, serviceman.

army wife *See* service wife.

articulate the use of "articulate" is questionable when it is used only for certain ethnic groups, the implication being that "those people" are not normally well-spoken but that this individual is surprisingly so. *See also* qualified.

artificial insemination some people prefer *alternative insemination.*

artilleryman *artillery personnel, gunner.* "Artilleryman" is used in the U.S. Army to refer to either sex.

artiste woman or man.

Aryan although this term has a legitimate use in referring to the peoples speaking Indo-European languages, it is avoided otherwise because of its associations with Nazism, where it meant a white non-Jew of Nordic aspect, with the connotation that this type of human being was superior to all others and was meant to rule the world.

Asian this broad term refers to the continent, peoples, languages, and cultures of Asia. "Asian" is not interchangeable with Asian American or Amerasian; nor is "Asiatic" or "Oriental" acceptable. Whenever known, specify nationality (Laotian/Thai/Cambodian) in the same way you would distinguish between Italian/Spaniard/German and European. *See also* Asian American, Asiatic, Oriental.

Asian American writer Shirley Geok-Lin Lim says this homogenizing label includes "hundreds of tribes, language groups, a variety of immigration histories (from first-generation Chinese Americans, arriving from Taiwan or Hong Kong or the mainland, who have different stories to tell, to the Sansei, third-generation Japanese Americans whose American roots go back to the early nineteenth century)." There are times when "Asian American" may be appropriate, but in general use specific designations: Filipino American, Japanese American, Chinese American. Beware of the automatic use of certain terms to describe Americans of Asian descent: quiet, serene, industrious, reserved, smiling, intelligent, studious, philosophical. Even though these terms are "positive," they stereotype and make one-dimensional people from many different countries and widely varying cultures. "Asian American" is not interchangeable with "Asian" or "Amerasian." *Everything You Need to Know About Asian-American History* (Lan Cao and Himilce Novas) is a comprehensive, useful, and well-written reference book. *See also* Asian, Asiatic, Issei, Kibei, Nisei, Oriental, Pacific Islander, Sansei, Yonsei.

Asiatic *Asian, Asian American.* Or, be specific: Tibetan, Chinese, Korean; Japanese American, Vietnamese American. When referring to people, "Asiatic" is considered unacceptable for the same reasons "Oriental" is. *See also* Oriental.

as one man *See* man, as one.

asphalt-heater man *asphalt-heater tender.*

assemblyman (manufacturing) *assembler.*

assemblyman (politics) *assembly member, state assembly member, member of the assembly, legislator, representative.*

assembly-room foreman *assembly-room supervisor.*

assimilated sometimes this is used negatively to imply that an individual or a group has adopted the customs and attitudes of the prevailing culture to the detriment of their own, that they in effect assent to domination. The concept of assimilation goes to the heart of issues like diversity and national unity and issues like the dominant model of society—do those who traditionally have not had power in society become assimilated in order to become dominant or do they build a different culture?

assistant cameraman *dolly pusher.*

athlete there is great potential for nonparallel language in athletics: the practice of referring to women as "female athletes" while men are "athletes" is demeaning; using first names for women and surnames for men makes women appear childlike; if male athletes are tough and sweaty, so are female athletes. The importance of athletics to boys and men has always been a given; however, they appear to be equally important to girls and women: the Ms. Foundation found that girls and women who play sports have higher levels of self-esteem and lower levels of depression; the Institute for Athletics and Education found that high school girls who play sports are 80% less likely to be involved in an unwanted pregnancy, 92% less likely to be involved with drugs, and three times more likely to graduate from high school. To see if your treatment of male and female athletes is parallel, it is helpful to mentally substitute one sex for the other in what you have written to see if it reads sensibly.

Atlanta Braves *See* Redskins (sports team name).

at risk the *Publication Manual of the American Psychological Association,* 4th ed., says, "Broad clinical terms such as . . . 'people *at risk*' are loaded with innuendo unless properly explained. . . . Identify the risk and the people it involves (e.g., 'children at risk for early school dropout')." *See also* high-risk group.

attaboy/attagirl these terms seem to be used equally often and to be equally harmless, whether used of adults, children, or animals.

atypical *See* normal.

audism "Audism is the corporate institution for dealing with deaf people, dealing with them by making statements about them, authorizing views of them, describing them, teaching about them, governing where they go to school, and, in some cases, where they live; in short, audism is the hearing way of dominating, restructuring, and exercising authority over the deaf community" (Harlan Lane, *The Mask of Benevolence*).

augerman *rotary auger operator.*

aunt *See* avuncular.

au pair girl *au pair, live-in sitter/child-minder/family helper, family helper.* Male au pairs are not customary in the U.S., although in Great Britain the term "houseboy" was once used to denote a similar position ("au pair" is used there now for both sexes).

Australoid *See* -oid.

authoress *author. See also* "feminine" word endings.

automobile/she *automobile/it. See also* car/she.

automotive parts man *automotive stock clerk.*

auxiliary *See* ladies' auxiliary.

average man *average person/citizen/human being/voter, common person/ citizen/human being/voter, ordinary person/citizen/human being/voter, typical customer/consumer/reader/viewer, citizen, voter, layperson, taxpayer, resident, homeowner, landowner, passerby, nonspecialist, commoner, one of the people/masses, rank and file, people in general.*

aviation survivalman this Coast Guard title can refer to either sex. For non-official alternatives, consider *aviation survivalist/rescuer, aviation rescue equipment supervisor/manager/steward/chief/officer/clerk.*

aviatress/aviatrix *aviator. See also* airman, "feminine" word endings.

avuncular this is a useful term for men, but there is no equally tidy equivalent for a woman. "Auntly" and "auntlike" are possibilities, although they do not have the flavor of "avuncular"; "amitate" is a narrow term referring to a relationship in some cultures between a niece and her paternal aunt. Otherwise, consider adjectives with related meanings: indulgent, kindly, benevolent, genial, expansive, hearty, conspiratorial, friendly.

axman *axer.*

B

Few would suggest that sexual or racial inequality exists because of language use. Nor would many argue that banishing sexist and racist labeling would in itself result in a just society. At the same time, it is clear that language not only reflects social structures but, more important, sometimes serves to perpetuate existing differences in power; thus a serious concern with linguistic usage is fully warranted.

—Francine Wattman Frank and Paula A. Treichler

Communication provides the legs for bias, carrying it from person to person, from generation to generation. Eventually, however, communication will be the way to end discrimination.

—International Association of Business Communicators

babble not sexist per se, "babble" is generally used only for babies and women (originally it belonged only to babies) so you may need alternatives: *ramble, mutter, mumble, stutter, stammer, sputter, blather, splutter, gibber, blurt out, let slip, reveal foolishly, divulge secrets, spout/talk nonsense, talk through one's hat, run off at the mouth, talk idly, shoot the breeze, make chin music, rattle away, bend someone's ear. See also* bull session, chatter, chatterbox, gabby, gossip, gossipy, yenta.

babe/baby/baby doll (woman) picturing women as children and playthings has been highly damaging.

babysitter this inclusive word is sometimes used in a highly sexist manner: involved father Todd Melby says when he's out with his child, he's been "complimented" by people for babysitting. He says he is parenting, "not just giving Mom a few minutes away from the kids." Where mothers are never considered to be babysitting their children, fathers often are.

bachelor a single aspect of a person's life becomes the whole of the person when "bachelor" is used. If a reference to marital status is necessary (it rarely is), use an adjective instead of a noun: *single, unmarried, unwed.*

However, "unmarried" and "unwed" perpetuate a marriage-as-norm attitude. We write and speak as though marriage and parenthood somehow grant validity to a person when in fact a married person and an unmarried person often have more in common than not. Note the nonparallel connotations of the supposedly parallel "bachelor" and "spinster." Women go from single girl to spinster to old maid, but men are bachelors forever.

bachelor girl/bachelorette *woman.* If a reference to marital status is necessary (it rarely is), use *single woman. See* bachelor, spinster.

bachelor's button (flower) leave as is.

bachelor's degree *B.A., B.S., undergraduate degree, college degree, four-year degree, baccalaureate.* "Baccalaureate" means a college or university bachelor's degree and is therefore an exact synonym for "bachelor's degree" without gender-specific overtones (although its Latin roots are masculine).

backcourt man *backcourt player.*

backdoor man *backdoor lover/romance.*

backroom boys *power brokers, wheeler-dealers, politicos, strategists, movers and shakers.*

back-shoe girl *back-shoe worker.*

back-up man *back-up, back-up worker/player, backer-up.*

backward *See* primitive.

backwoodsman *settler, wilderness settler, backsettler, pioneer, woodlander, woodcutter; hermit, recluse; backwoodsman and backwoodswoman.*

bacon, bring home the both women and men bring home the bacon today and one of the purported derivations of the phrase is also egalitarian: according to ancient custom in Dunmow, England, a flitch of bacon was awarded "to any married couple who can take an oath that they have never once during the year wished themselves unmarried" (Charles Earle Funk, *A Hog on Ice*). *See also* provider.

bad guy *bad actor/news, villain.* There are few good alternatives because virtually all the "bad guy" words in our language are perceived as referring to men, even those that are not sexist per se. Although in theory the following words could be used of a woman, in practice they rarely are: *bounder, brigand, bully, cad, cheat, creep, crook, deviate, double-crosser/dealer, evildoer, fink, four-flusher, gangster, geek, goon, heel, hoodlum, hooligan, jerk, louse, lowlife, mobster, mountebank, mugger, outcast, outlaw, punk, racketeer, rascal, rat, ratfink, renegade, reprobate, rogue, rotter, ruffian, scalawag, scoundrel, scum/scumbag/scuzzbag/ scuzzbucket, sleaze/sleazebag/sleazeball, slimebag/slimeball/slime* *bucket, suspect, thug, turkey, two-timer, ugly customer.* Negative words for women focus on sexual promiscuity (there are 10 times as many words in English for "sexually promiscuous woman" as there are for "sexually promiscuous man"); negative words for men focus on moral vileness (almost all such terms are for men). Note that we traditionally personalize both "enemy" and "devil" as male. *See also* animal (man), animal names for people, bastard, deadbeat, devil/he, enemy/he, jackass, perpetrator, Satan/he.

badman *thief, robber, outlaw, gangster, desperado, bank robber, cattle/horse thief, rustler, villain. See also* bad guy, gunman, hit man, holdup man, triggerman.

bad workman quarrels with his tools, a *a bad worker quarrels with the tools, bad workers quarrel with their tools.*

baggageman *baggage checker/handler/agent.*

bag lady/bag man (homeless) *bag woman/bag man, street person.* The gender-fair use of "bag woman" and "bag man" (not the nonparallel lady/ man) is sometimes appropriate although we tend to hear more about bag women than we do about bag men even though more men than women are forced into trying to survive this way. *See also* homeless.

bagman (British) *traveling sales agent/representative.*

bagman (collector/distributor of illicit funds) *bagger, go-between, shark, racketeer, peculator, receiver.*

bailsman *bail agent, bond agent, bail bond agent/poster; provider, guarantor, bonding institution, underwriter.*

balcony man *platform worker.*

ball and chain (woman) although women being held back/enchained/ weighed down by men has been a predominant feature of society for centuries, no term like "ball and chain" for men ever got into the (male-dominated) language.

ball/bang these slang terms for sex convey a number of twisted and sexist attitudes: they are violent, they are non-reciprocal, and they make an object of the partner.

ball boy *tennis/basketball court attendant, ball/court attendant, ball tender/ fetcher.* "Ball kid" is used in some areas.

ballerina a ballerina is a principal (but not the principal) female dancer in a company, a soloist. Although the term is commonly used to refer to any female ballet dancer, this is not, strictly speaking, correct. The French word for a female solo dancer is "danseuse"; "ballerina" is the Italian equivalent and is the term most commonly used in the United States.

Retain "ballerina" for its narrow meaning within ballet companies, but describe anyone who dances ballet nonprofessionally as *ballet dancer.* *See also* danseur/danseuse, premier danseur, prima ballerina.

ballet master/ballet mistress these titles are standard within professional ballet companies; in other contexts use *ballet instructor/teacher.*

balls acceptable sex-specific word when it means testicles. For the inclusive metaphorical use substitute *guts, moxie, courage, nerve, bravery, self-assurance, confidence, determination, stamina, spunk.* Note that on occasion women have been congratulated with "That took balls!" or encouraged with "You have the balls for it." For "ballbreaker/ballbuster" meaning a difficult or complicated task or situation, use *gutbuster, bunbuster, backbreaker, tough row to hoe, killer, bad news, hell on wheels, no picnic, up a tree, hell of a note, tall/large order, tough grind/one, tough sledding, sticky business, stumper, uphill job, tight spot.* In a related expression, "testicular fortitude" can be rendered sex-neutral with "intestinal fortitude." For "ballbreaker" meaning a woman, *see* bitch, castrate/castrating, shrew. *See also* ballsy.

ballsy "a term that has slipped so far from its original mooring that it can be applied to females" (Hugh Rawson, *Wicked Words*). *See also* balls.

banana republic this derogatory term is used to refer to a small country (usually in Latin America) economically dependent on a single crop or product. It "trivializes the struggles that Latinas and Latinos have gone through, and still go through, to have stable sovereign governments in their own lands. The image of the so-called 'Banana Republic' continues to propagate the lie that Latinas and Latinos are hot-blooded, unstable, violent and incapable of competent self-rule, and it deflects attention away from Uncle Sam whose economic and political interests are almost always behind political upheavals and unrest in South and Central America, and the Caribbean" (Amoja Three Rivers, *Cultural Etiquette*).

bandsman *member of the band, band player/member/musician, player in the band.* Or, be specific: *trumpeter, drummer, saxophone player, pianist.*

banshee this female spirit has no male counterpart, but she plays an important part in Gaelic folklore; use as is.

Bantu "applied until recently to members of Bantu-speaking tribes. . . . Among linguists and anthropologists it is still in carefully controlled use but is otherwise taboo in most uses because of South African whites' use of it as an offensive name for black Africans" (Kenneth G. Wilson, *The Columbia Guide to Standard American English*). "Bantu" is still acceptable when referring to the group of over 400 closely related languages in the Niger-Congo language family.

baptismal name when you mean the name given at baptism, this is correct. For its generic meaning use instead *first/given name, forename.*

barbaric/barbarian *See* primitive.

barber almost half of all barbers are women, and the woman cutting your hair is not a "lady barber," "barberette," or "barberess." She is a barber.

bar boy *bartender/bar helper, bar assistant/server, waiter.*

bar girl with drinking age limits, the "girl" is obviously inappropriate, and the term has come to usually mean a prostitute who works out of bars. (Note the different path "bar boy" has taken.)

bard not itself sex-based, "bard" has acquired masculine overtones, probably from its close association with "the" bard, Shakespeare, and you may sometimes want more inclusive-sounding alternatives: *poet, poet-singer, epic/heroic poet, heroic versifier, minstrel, balladeer, ballad singer.*

bargeman *barge hand, deckhand.*

bargemaster *barge captain.*

barmaid *bartender/bar helper, bar assistant/server, waiter, cocktail server.*

barman *bartender, bar attendant, barkeeper, barkeep.* Half of U.S. bartenders are women.

bar mitzvah/bat mitzvah these terms refer both to the ceremony and to the young person initiated into adulthood in Judaism. Bar mitzvah is for boys and has been a part of classical Judaism. Bat mitzvah is for girls; first celebrated in 1922 and popular since 1960, it is found only in Conservative, Reform, and Reconstructionist Judaism.

barracuda (woman) directed at a forceful woman, this term penalizes one sex when it behaves as aggressively as the other. *See also* aggressive.

barren (referring to a woman) *sterile, infertile.* The alternatives are used for both sexes. "Barren," which is used only for women, carries an unwarranted stigma and many negative associations (synonyms include words like impoverished, desolate, arid, fruitless, unproductive, meager, ineffective, incompetent, useless, worthless, valueless, devoid, deficient). Saying that someone is "childless" or "has no children" is not recommended as those terms support a children-as-norm stereotype. *See also* childless, infertile, sterile.

baroness this title is used for a woman holding the title to a barony or for the wife or widow of a baron. Use "drug baron" for both sexes.

barrow boy *costermonger, street vendor.*

baseman (baseball) *base player, baser; first/second/third baser; first-base/ second-base/third-base player; first, second, third; first-base/second-base/third-base position; 1B, 2B, 3B* (baseball notation); *first/second/*

third sacker. There is good traditional support for the alternatives. According to Stuart Berg Flexner *(Listening to America),* "first base, second base, and third base" have referred to both the positions and the players since the 1840s, while "first," "second," "third," and "base player" were already being used in the 1860s. Note that other baseball terms use the common -er ending: outfielder, infielder, pitcher, catcher, batter. Base players may be girls/women or boys/men; Marcenia Toni Stone Alberga, the first woman to play professional baseball (not softball) on otherwise all-male teams, got a hit off pitcher Satchell Paige; in 1989 the first girl competed in a Little League World Series.

basketball Mariah Burton Nelson *(The Stronger Women Get the More Men Love Football)* notes that college basketball is still divided into "college basketball" and "women's college basketball" and that a facility's smaller gymnasium continues to be called the women's gym.

bassman (music) *bassist.*

bastard when you mean someone whose parents were not married to each other at the time of their birth, use *offspring/child/son/daughter of unmarried parents/of single parent/of unknown father.* Most often the status of a person's birth is gratuitous information; refer to it only when it is relevant and then relay it in a neutral way ("She never knew who her father was" or "His birth certificate was blank after 'father's name'"). When you mean "bastard" in the sense of "a wretched and repellent male" (Richard A. Spears, *NTC's Dictionary of American Slang and Colloquial Expressions*) you'll have to be creative—most alternatives are unacceptable on grounds of sexism, handicapism, ageism, or unprintable language. Try *ignoramus, saphead, stinker, ratfink, snake in the grass, creep, heel, jerk, bum, lowlife.* "Bastard" is sexist because it is used only for men and because the insult also slyly impugns the man's mother. *See also* bad guy, illegitimate.

batboy *batkeeper, bat attendant/tender/fetcher.*

bathing beauty *sunbather. See also* beauty queen.

batman *aide.*

bat mitzvah/bar mitzvah *See* bar mitzvah/bat mitzvah.

batsman (cricket) *batter.*

battered wife/woman retain the sex-specific terms: *battered wife or battered husband, battered man or battered woman.* When inclusive terms are needed use *battered spouse/partner, spouse/spousal/family abuse, marital/family violence.* Gender-neutral terms obscure the pattern of explicit violence perpetrated on overwhelming numbers of women compared with men. Some men's organizations claim more men than women are victims of domestic abuse. However, of cases taken through the courts, 95% result in conviction of men, 5% of women—most of whom are retaliating against abuse. The federal Centers for Disease Control reports that assaults involving people who are related, sharing a household, or otherwise intimate, are a major public health problem in which victims are predominantly female and perpetrators are predominantly male. (Battering is not, however, solely a male-female problem; partner-battering also occurs among gay men and lesbians.) The FBI estimates that one of every two women will be physically abused at some point in her life and says that 34% of all female homicide victims older than 15 are killed by their husbands or intimate partners. National studies have found battering to be the greatest single cause of injury to women, exceeding rapes, muggings, and even car accidents. Businesses lose $3 to $5 billion per year as a result of absenteeism due to spouse abuse, and medical costs reach $10 million per year (22% to 35% of women who visit emergency departments have abuse-related symptoms). For years the question has been: "Why doesn't she leave him?" We are beginning to ask: "Why is he violent?"

battle-ax (woman) *tyrant, grouch, bully, petty despot, ornery/quarrelsome/ domineering/strong-willed/high-handed/combative/hostile/battlesome/ hot-tempered person.*

battle of/between the sexes this adversarial approach to female-male relations legitimizes a certain hopelessness about women and men being able to coexist peaceably. Riane Eisler *(The Chalice and the Blade)* describes early partnership societies in which the sexes cooperated with each other on every social level. She says as long as there are imbalances of power between individual men and women, there will be imbalances of power in the larger society, leading to a dominator, warlike model of society. We still have the choice to be a partnership society or a dominator society; "battle of the sexes" (which also implies more equality of power than there is) would indicate there is no choice. *See also* opposite sex.

bawd/bawdy house *prostitute/house of prostitution.* For the rationale on avoiding euphemisms for prostitution, *see* prostitute.

bawdy despite the connection with "bawd," this adjective can be used of both sexes.

B.C. this common abbreviation for "before Christ" is sometimes replaced by B.C.E. (before the Common Era) to remove the Christian element from dating, although ironically B.C.E. has sometimes been taken to mean "before the Christian Era." *See also* A.D.

beach bum/beach bunny although "bum" and "bunny" carry some cultural pejoratives for their respective sexes, these terms are at least moderately parallel and will probably continue to be used.

beadsman/beadswoman (or bedesman/bedeswoman) *suppliant, licensed beggar, almshouse inmate, professional penitent.* "Beadswoman" or "beadsman" may sometimes be the correct choice, but avoid using "beadsmen" as a pseudogeneric.

be a man *See* man, act like a/be a/take it like a.

beau "beau" and "belle" are the masculine and feminine forms of the same French word, but the English meanings for the two words are nonparallel. For a sex-nonspecific word use *friend, lover, sweetheart. See also* belle, boyfriend.

beau idéal although inclusive, this term looks sexist because of the masculine "beau" (the French noun "idéal" is grammatically masculine in gender and thus takes a masculine adjective). If you prefer, use *perfect model/type/example, standard model/type/example, ideal, paradigm.*

beautician *hairdresser, hairstylist, hair designer, haircutter, cosmetologist.* Some people in the field still prefer "beautician," although that refers to someone who does only women's hair. *See also* barber.

beauty salon unless "beauty salon" is part of an establishment's name, use *hair salon.* The implication is that "beauty" is something definable and that it can be had for the asking (and paying).

bedesman/bedeswoman *See* beadsman/beadswoman.

bedfellow *bedmate, ally, partner, associate, cohort, companion, mate, pair, colleague, sidekick, chum, buddy.*

bedridden "bedridden," "bedfast," and "confined to bed" are more than simple descriptions; they almost beg for a "poor you!" response. Without euphemizing a situation that is far from desirable, you might consider rewording the sentence or using a less tragic-sounding (but perhaps less-than-ideal) alternative: *on bedrest, permanent/temporary bedrest, flat on one's back, laid up; needs to stay in bed for six months, is now on total bedrest. See also* disability/disabilities.

beefeater has always been a man.

bee in one's bonnet this is a fairly harmless phrase (except for the bee, of course), but alternatives are offered for the times it might sound silly to say "he's got a bee in his bonnet": *one-track mind, fixation, obsession, fixed idea/idée fixe, ruling passion.*

before you can say Jack Robinson *See* Jack Robinson, before you can say.

beget in the general sense of creating something, half the time use *give birth to. See also* father (verb).

beggarman/beggarwoman *beggar.*

belle/belle of the ball *charming/popular/attractive person, flirt, center of attention, success, stunner, head-turner.* The language never had a "beau of the ball," nor are many men described in "belle"-type terms—probably because women's successes have always been closely identified with the way they look and how they "behave" while men's successes correlate with what they have done and how they "perform."

bellboy *bellhop, attendant, hotel/passenger attendant, porter.*

bellman *bellhop, bell captain; bellringer, crier, herald.*

belly dancer in the Middle East, belly dancing is a traditional women's folk dance and there are no public performances by male dancers. In the United States, however, there are professional male belly dancers who perform publicly.

bench jockey/bench warmer may refer to either sex.

benchman *bench technician, bencher; sugar tester; bench baker.*

Benedict Arnold there is nothing wrong with using "a Benedict Arnold" to mean a traitor, but be aware of how many such expressions in the English language are male-based. It also sounds odd when used of a woman. Balance its use with female-based expressions, creative expressions of your own, or sex-neutral alternatives: *traitor, betrayer, double-dealer/-crosser, fifth columnist, informer.* **See also** sex-linked expressions.

benefactress *benefactor.* **See also** "feminine" word endings.

benjamin there is nothing wrong with using this word, but be aware of how many such expressions in the English language are male-based. Balance their use with female-based expressions, creative expressions of your own, or sex-neutral alternatives: *youngest/favorite child.* **See also** sex-linked expressions.

be one's own man/be your own man *stand on one's/your own two feet, be one's/your own person, be a do-it-yourselfer, be independent/inner-directed/self-ruling/self-reliant, self-regulated/individualistic/outspoken/self-confident, be a free-thinker/free spirit, be at one's own disposal, be nobody's lackey.*

best boy although this term is still seen today, alternatives are also being used: *best, gaffer's assistant; assistant to chief electrician, chief electrician's assistant; assistant, gofer.* The positions are held by both sexes.

best-laid schemes of mice and men, the unless quoting poet Robert Burns use simply *the best-laid schemes.*

best man "best man" is acceptable only if his partner is "best woman." Otherwise use *attendant, attendant of honor, honor/wedding/groom's* *attendant.* Use a parallel term for the female attendant. Male and female wedding attendants did not originally have the same duties, which is perhaps why nonparallel terms developed. Centuries ago, men enlisted the help of their friends to abduct a woman sought as a wife or to prevent her from being taken by someone else.

best man for the job *best choice/candidate/applicant/person/worker for the job.*

better half although in the past marriage has too often been portrayed as two half-people who were thus made whole, this particular use of "half" seems inclusive and loving: both women and men use it, and the speaker always allots the "better" portion to their mate. *See also* boyfriend, domestic partner, girlfriend, spouse.

bi slang for bisexual; the plural is bi's. As with any slang or shortened form, this term should be used only if you're sure of your context and audience. *See also* bisexual, shortened forms of words.

Bible language although there is often disagreement about inclusive-language translations of the Bible going too far or not going far enough, most individuals and churches can find something today to suit them. The degree of inclusiveness varies. The 1990 *New Revised Standard Version* has no "man" or "men" when the reference is to all people, but it retains male references to God. *An Inclusive Language Lectionary* eliminates all gender-specific words, including pronouns for God (or it refers to God as male and female). Among other publications are *The New Jerusalem* and *Psalms Anew: In Inclusive Language.* Although there is concern that "changing the language" means being unfaithful to the scriptures, there is much theological and linguistic support for the changes; in the introduction to the *Lectionary for the Christian People*, the editors say, "It is astounding how often masculine designations have entered the text in English translations and have no basis in the original language." Just as "thee" and "thou" are considered archaic and irrelevant and the products of translation, so are male-centered terms. Father Joseph Arackal says that going back to the original language of the scriptures eliminates 90% of the exclusive words in our English translations. The "newest" translations often turn out to be the "oldest," with their starting point ancient Greek and Hebrew texts rather than intermediate translations. Note that it is sometimes clearer to refer to the "Jewish Scriptures" and the "Christian Scriptures" rather than to the "Old Testament" and the "New Testament." Liturgical and prayer language is also being rendered inclusive in many temples, churches, and mosques in the U.S.; in Canada, the United Church of Canada and the Anglican Church of Canada have produced nonsexist guidelines, and the pastoral team of the Canadian Conference of Catholic Bishops has advocated a move from exclusive to inclusive language in official texts and also in the everyday language of the church. Works like Marcia Falk's *The Book of Blessings* offer prayers in English and Hebrew that avoid sexist language. *See also* hymn, Old Testament, Torah.

Bible thumper this pejorative term can sometimes be replaced by *fundamentalist*. However, while it is safe to say that all "Bible thumpers" are fundamentalists, not all fundamentalists are "Bible thumpers." It might be necessary to get past the quick label to show what behaviors or beliefs are involved.

bicker because "bicker" is generally reserved for women, you may want alternatives: *wrangle, argue, quarrel, have words, squabble, cross swords, disagree.*

big boss/cheese/enchilada/fish/gun/noise/shot/wheel/wig man or woman. Note that "big gun" and "big shot" are violent and rarely are needed with so many other choices available.

Big Brother unless referring to the Stalin-like figure watching everyone via television ("Big Brother is watching you") in George Orwell's 1949 novel *1984,* you might consider using alternatives: *mind police, dictator, omnipresent totalitarian authority, government spy, infiltrator, stakeout, monitor, watchdog, mole, surveillant, guard, someone who keeps tab on/ a sharp eye upon/a watchful eye upon.*

bigot woman or man.

bilingual French is the official language of the Canadian Province of Québec, so Québec is not "bilingual."

billionaire man or woman.

bimbette this word, apparently meaning "a young bimbo," enjoyed a Warholian 15 minutes of fame (in a well-publicized British libel suit). The case further featured "an aging bimbette," which may be more than a bimbette but not yet a regular bimbo. *See also* bimbo.

bimbo from the Italian for "little boy" or "little kid," this word now has a range of meanings: sexually loose woman, giddy woman, clown-like or klutzy person of either sex. It's been used chiefly to describe women involved with men involved with trouble (for example, Donna Rice, Fawn Hall, and Jessica Hahn with, respectively, Gary Hart, Oliver North, and Jim Bakker). Why the women get the label while the men who do the running around, arms dealing, and bilking remain just "guys" is a peculiarity of our values system. (William Safire has suggested that "stud muffin" is the male equivalent of bimbo, but the male term seems much more positive—which would you rather be called?)

bindle man *bindle stiff, hobo, wanderer, itinerant, migrant, harvest worker, lumberjack.*

biological father/mother/parent everybody has biological parents although not everyone is raised by them or even knows who they are. Biological parents are also called birth parents; they should never be called "real parents." "Mother" and "father" are the terms for the people who raise and nurture a child they have adopted. Describing birth parents as "real" implies that adoptive relationships are artificial, tentative, less important, and less enduring. *See also* adoption language, "real" father/mother/ parent.

biracial *See* multiracial.

birdbrain *See* airhead.

birdman *aviator.* If you use "birdman," use the equivalent "ladybird," which, even though it is nonparallel ("man/lady") and includes "lady," has a respectable history and associations. *See also* airman.

birth control this issue belongs to both men and women; avoid associating it solely with women. Other acceptable terms include *contraception, family planning, fertility control, reproductive freedom. See also* population control.

birth defect *congenital disability.* Or, *someone born with a congenital disability, someone disabled since birth, a disability that has existed since birth.* Or, be specific: *someone with a cleft palate, spina bifida,* etc. References to "abnormalities" are not recommended.

birth mother/father/parent *See* biological father/mother/parent.

bisexual a man or a woman who has affectionate, romantic, and erotic feelings for, fantasies of, and/or experiences with both men and women is a bisexual. The person does not need to have equal experiences with women and men, or even any experience at all; bisexuality is not behaviorally defined. The spelling "bi-sexual" is considered unacceptable by many bisexuals. The bisexual community reports antagonism from both the heterosexual and homosexual worlds; our binary-thinking society tends to think people are either gay or straight. "One thing that just about everybody agrees on is that 'bisexual' is a problematic word. To the disapproving or the disinclined it connotes promiscuity, immaturity, or wishy-washiness. To some lesbians and gay men it says 'passing,' 'false consciousness,' and a desire for 'heterosexual privilege.' To psychologists it may suggest adjustment problems; to psychoanalysts an unresolved Oedipus complex; to anthropologists, the narrowness of a Western . . . world view. Rock stars regard it as a dimension of the performing self. . . Bisexuality has sometimes been regarded as 'too queer' and at other times 'not queer enough'" (Marjorie Garber, *Vice Versa*).

bishop depending on the religious denomination, a bishop could be a man or a woman.

bitch (noun) when used of a woman, this is one of the most loaded of the sexist words. "'Bitch'—long a favorite linguistic weapon of those who yearn to put down uppity women—has become increasingly common" (Molly Hoben, *Minnesota Women's Press*, January 1995). Hoben notes that in pre-Christian Greek and Roman religions, one of the sacred titles of the goddess Artemis-Diana was "the Great Bitch," but like many other words that once had positive connotations for women, "bitch" has become a pejorative term used against strong women by those who feel threatened. Feminist theorist Mary Daly says "bitch" gets applied to women who are "active, direct, blunt, obnoxious, competent, loud-mouthed, independent, stubborn, demanding, achieving, overwhelming, lusty, strong-minded, scary, ambitious, tough, brassy, boisterous, turbulent, sprawling, strident, striding, and large (physically and/or psychically)." Attorney Rebecca Palmer says, "In the workplace setting, the label of 'bitch' is often accompanied by inappropriate, demeaning behavior. . . . A number of courts around the country have grappled with the issue of whether, from a legal standpoint, referring to a female employee as a 'bitch' is defamatory or discriminatory." Sometimes the correct alternative to "bitch" is simply *woman, person, individual.* Sometimes use an inclusive noun: *grumbler, grouch, griper, malcontent, sourpuss, sorehead, bellyacher, crab, crank, kvetcher.* Other times you may want an adjective: *hell on wheels, ruthless, aggressive, domineering, controlling, powerful, tyrannical, overwhelming, overpowering, spiteful, malicious, cruel, wicked, vicious, cold-hearted, hard-hearted, merciless.* In the sense of a complaint, use instead *gripe, complaint, problem, bone to pick, objection.* In the sense of something that is difficult, unpleasant, or problematic, use *tough row to hoe, tough nut to crack, heavy sledding, hornet's nest, between a rock and a hard place, bad news/one, tough grind/one, large order, predicament, no picnic, thorny/knotty problem, uphill job, backbreaker, gutbuster, bunbuster, dilemma, bind, tangle, mess, fine pickle, hell of a note.* ("Bitch" is the correct term for a female dog; the corresponding male term—"dog"—suggests that maleness is the norm for canines.)

bitch (verb) *complain, gripe, kvetch, grouse, grumble, badmouth, sound off, beef, bellyache, carp, crab, criticize, denounce, disapprove, dissent, object, protest, reproach, backbite, bawl out, call/dress down, call on the carpet/mat, call names, cuss, make cutting remarks/dirty digs/cracks, give someone hell/the devil/a going-over, lambaste, give someone lip, make it hot for, pick on, pitch into, put down, put someone in their place, tell someone where to get off.* When you mean "spoil or bungle" ("bitch something up") use *botch.*

bitch goddess Success unless quoting William James, avoid this term.

Consider the psychology involved in attributing one's successes and failures to a powerful, capricious, female Other. *See also* Dame Fortune.

bitch session *gripe session. See also* bitch (verb).

bitchy *grouchy, cranky, crabby, spiteful, moody, rude, ill-tempered, bad-tempered, irritable, surly, complaining, cantankerous, peevish, out of sorts.* This adjective is virtually never used of heterosexual men; it is leveled primarily at women and sometimes at gay men. *See also* bitch (noun).

black/Black (noun) this is still an acceptable and respected term, but do not refer to color or ethnicity when it is irrelevant to your material, as it most often is. Vivian Jenkins Nelsen *(New Voices in the Media)* says, "Persons of color are usually 'over-identified' as 'African American writers' or 'African American dentists,' when they would rather be identified as a dentist or a writer who is an African American. White people are 'under-identified' because most stories assume whiteness as the norm. . . . Write 'white' in front of every reference to a person who is not identified as a person of color, and you will see how artificial it feels." Identify people the way they identify themselves (black, African American, Afro-American, person of color) and accept that this may vary from group to group. There are strong, reasonable pros and cons for each term. Polls in the black community continue to show a preference for "black" (around 45%, compared with 28% for African American, and 10% for Afro-American). People of mixed ancestry, of which one is black, may or may not self-identify as black. Current style generally lowercases "black," but some writers and editors prefer it capitalized (*Jet*, for example, capitalizes both Black and White, while some publications capitalize only Black). *See also* African American, Afro-American, black/black-, black-and-white, denigrate, Negro, niggardly, nigger, niggling, nonwhite, people/person of color, white man's burden.

black/black- Martin Luther King Jr. pointed out that there are some 120 synonyms for "blackness," of which at least half have negative connotations. Almost all the 134 synonyms for "whiteness" are favorable. "The symbolism of white as positive and black as negative is pervasive in our culture" (Robert B. Moore, in Paula S. Rothenberg, *Racism and Sexism*). The good guys wear white hats and ride white horses, and everybody knows what the bad guys wear and ride. Dictionary definitions of black refer in part to evil, the devil, disaster, condemnation, dirt, sullenness, and darkness while definitions of white refer to innocence, purity, harmlessness, good fortune, and lightness. Avoiding words that reinforce the negative connotations of black will not of itself do away with racism, but we cannot unhorse racism while the language constantly tells us that black is anything but beautiful. The following terms can be replaced by those in parentheses: **blackball** (ostracize); **black comedy/black humor** (satire, sinister/morbid humor); **"black day in our nation's history"** ("bleak" or "sad"); **black deed** (evil deed); **blacken** (slander, defile, defame; smirch, soil, tarnish); **black eye** (mouse, shiner; bad name); **blackguard** (scoundrel, villain, ne'er-do-well); **blackhearted** (wicked); **blackjack** (bludgeon); **blackletter day** (evil/tragic day); **blacklist** (denounce, condemn, proscribe, ostracize); **blackly** (darkly, gloomily, hopelessly); **blackmail** (hush money, payola, extortion, shake-down; extort, bleed, put the arm on, shake down); **black mark** (mark against one, blot on one's copybook); **black market** (illegal market/trade/ trafficking); **black moment** (dark moment); **blackout** (lights out; moratorium; loss of memory/consciousness); **black outlook** (bleak outlook); **black sheep** (outcast, pariah, reprobate, renegade, idler, prodigal, born/ family loser, ne'er-do-well, bad apple in the barrel, family rebel). Other terms can be circumvented but with difficulty: black arts, black book, black hole, black ice, black lie (contrast with a white lie), black magic (contrast with white magic), Black Mass, Black Monday (stock market crash of October 19, 1987), Black Tuesday (October 29, 1929). And of course most of us are smart enough to cross the street when we see a black cat coming. In their excellent *Guidelines for Creating Positive Sexual and Racial Images in Educational Materials,* the Macmillan Publishing Company recommends not only avoiding the negative uses of black but applying the word's positive uses as often as possible: black pearls are the most valuable; ebony is used only on the finest guitars; oil is referred to as "black gold"; black diamonds are essential to industry; black soil is richest. They also suggest reinforcing positive attitudes toward blackness in descriptions of African Americans: too often references to "their beautiful white teeth" replace descriptions of the authentic attractions of black hair, skin, eyes. *See also* black-and-white (adjective), white.

black-and-white (adjective) *either-or, simple, all good or all bad, either here or there, binary, dogmatic, definite, unequivocal, absolute, positive, categorical, polar/diametric opposites, day and night, chalk and cheese.* This racist expression (dictionary definitions refer to things being sharply divided into good and evil groups, sides, or ideas) perpetuates the positive evaluation of white and the negative evaluation of black. One of its definitions is also "expressing, recognizing, or based on two mutually exclusive sets of ideas or values" (*American Heritage Dictionary*, 3rd ed.). *See also* black/black-, white.

Black English "contrary to the stereotypes, Black English is not substandard English; it is a separate linguistic system, although it shares much of its vocabulary, phonology, and syntax with standard English" (Francine Frank and Frank Anshen, *Language and the Sexes*). Judgments about individuals' intelligence and verbal skills based solely on their use of Black English (also known as Ebonics or ebonics, from a contraction of "ebony" and "phonics") have been found to be invalid.

Black Maria *patrol wagon, police van.* According to *Why Do We Say It?* the van was named in honor of Maria Lee, a black woman of great size and strength, who ran a sailors' boardinghouse in Boston; "The unruly stood in dread of her, and when the constables required help it was a common thing to send for Black Maria, who soon collared the culprits and led them to the lockup."

Black Muslims Muslims are Muslims; among the followers of Islam there is no color distinction. The members of the Nation of Islam, a 20th-century movement in the U.S. that has little in common with mainstream Islam, have been called Black Muslims, although they have never used the term for themselves (it was coined by the press in the 1950s). Members of the movement have always preferred "Muslim."

black tie this refers to men's attire for social occasions; for a sex-neutral alternative use *semiformal.*

blind this is an acceptable adjective to denote someone who is sightless or whose vision is so restricted as to be useless for ordinary purposes; "the substitution of a euphemistic expression for *blind* could itself be objectionable if perceived as implying that blindness is too piteous a condition to be stated in plain language" *(American Heritage Book of English Usage).* It is not used as a noun ("the blind"). "Visual impairment" implies a range of problems that stops short of total or legal blindness ("someone with a visual impairment"). Avoid once-I-was-blind-but-now-I-can-see metaphors, which associate physical loss of vision with negative personal characteristics. Instead of "blind" use *naive, unaware, ignorant, obtuse, dense, unreasoning, senseless, thoughtless, uncritical, undiscerning, insensitive, unfeeling, indifferent. See also* blindman's bluff, disability/disabilities, handicapism, handicapped, impairment, "people first" rule, "the."

blindman's bluff this game (also known as "blindman's buff") has been played for many centuries under different names, some neither sexist nor handicappist: *blufty, hoodwink play, the brazen fly* (Iona Opie and Peter Opie, *Children's Games in Street and Playground*). *See also* blind.

blonde *blond.* Use the shorter base word as an adjective for both sexes; historically both "blond" and "blonde" have been used to describe both women and men. However, the use of "blond" as a noun seems reserved for women, whereas equating a man with his hair color is uncommon (if someone refers to a "blond," the first assumption is that it's a woman). Use the adjective to modify hair rather than women (thus, "a woman with blond hair," not "a blond"). *See also* "feminine" word endings.

blood terms like "blue-blooded" and "royal blood," "full-blooded" and "mixed blood" have no validity or usefulness, and the last two are highly objectionable. Use instead *of mixed ancestry,* or one of the terms with which people self-identify *(métis, mestizo, mélange). See also* half-breed/half-caste, mulatto, multiracial.

blood brother "blood sister" is also used (although not nearly as often); in the plural use *blood brothers and blood sisters/blood sisters and blood brothers.*

blue long associated with boys, especially babies, this color was once thought to ward off the evil spirits that inhabited nurseries, perhaps because of its association with the sky (and thus with well-disposed heavenly spirits). According to David Feldman *(Imponderables),* boys were held to be very valuable by parents, so blue clothing was used as a cheap form of insurance. No such insurance was desired or apparently needed for girl babies. *See also* pink.

bluebeard the original Bluebeard, Gilles de Rais, abducted, raped, and murdered between 40 and 100 peasant boys: "The most amazing part of the Gilles de Rais story is that the legend of Bluebeard's Castle that we know today has metamorphosed from a terrifying account of a sex-murderer of small boys to a glorified fantasy of a devilish rake who killed seven wives for their 'curiosity'" (Susan Brownmiller, *Against Our Will).* According to Brownmiller, it is more palatable to men to accept women in the role of victim than themselves.

blue boys (police) *bluecoats, blues.*

blue-collar this imprecise term varies from somewhat to very classist and also carries a connotation of maleness; audiences will be better served by more specific designations (job descriptions, income ranges, education levels).

bluesman *blues musician/player/singer.*

bluestocking *intellectual, member of the literati, wit, artistic/learned person, egghead, dilettante, dabbler, amateur, culture vulture.* This derisory term for educated or literary women was originally used for both sexes, although no parallel term developed for men when this one became limited to women—even though the blue stockings worn at the small literary assemblies hosted by Elizabeth Montague, Portman Square, London, belonged to a certain Mr. Stillingfleet.

board boy/board girl *board maker.*

board man *board member.*

boatman *boater, boat worker/dealer/operator; sailor, merchant mariner. See also* seaman.

boat/she *boat/it. See also* car/she, ship/she.

boatswain "swain" refers to a servant or a boy, and boatswains have traditionally been men. However, "boatswain" could be used for a woman because its sex link is related more to the lack of female boatswains than to its etymology. More neutral-appearing alternatives might include *bosun, bosun's mate, ship's bosun, ship warrant officer/petty officer, deck crew/topside supervisor, hydraulic mate, rigging boss. See also* coxswain.

bobby (British) *police officer.* Sir Robert ("Bobby") Peel organized the London police force in the early 1800s and is also responsible for the other popular police nickname: "peeler." *See also* policeman.

bobsled not sex-linked; although its etymology is uncertain, this term does not appear to be based on a man's name.

Bob's your uncle there is nothing wrong with using this phrase, but be aware of how many such expressions in the English language are male-based. Balance their use with female-based expressions, creative expressions of your own, or sex-neutral alternatives: *there you are! there you have it! voilà! everything's great! See also* sex-linked expressions.

bodily fluids when used in reference to HIV or AIDS, clarify that semen, vaginal fluids, and blood are the only bodily fluids known to be capable of transmitting the virus. Sweat, saliva, and tears are also bodily fluids, but they do not carry a threat of HIV infection.

bodyguard because bodyguards historically were men only—and are primarily men today—you may sometimes need a term that sounds more inclusive: *personal protection agent/operative, personal security agent/ operative/consultant.*

body image we speak and write about men's bodies and women's bodies in very different ways. Writer Mary Morse Marti sees a direct association between a study showing that adolescent girls are almost twice as likely as boys to be depressed—primarily because of their poor body image—and, for example, media emphasis on women's swimsuit fashions that extol such virtues as "constructed bust lines" to "enhance smaller chests," "bottoms to flatter round stomachs and hips," and suits with "built-in shape" for women and girls unfortunate enough to have none. Morse Marti wonders if she can expect to see similar articles on men's swimwear that feature "size-enhancing groin pads, rear-end boning (for that all-important pert look), and retro 'Dad' full-cut boxer trunks (for men and boys with something to hide)." There are virtually no general-interest books telling teenage boys how to dress, how to control weight, how to feel more comfortable about their bodies; countless fiction and nonfiction books address these issues for teenage girls. Twice as many women ages 30–64 as men think they are "overweight"; 58% of 17-year-old girls said they were "overweight" when only 17% actually were according to the charts; some 90% to 95% of those with eating disorders are female. *See also* fat, looksism, overweight.

bogeyman *bogey/bogy/bogie, bogeymonster, goblin, hobgoblin, bugaboo, gremlin, phantom, spook, specter, ghost; nightmare.*

boilerman *boiler tender/operator.*

bomb disposal man *bomb disposal specialist, explosives expert/specialist.*

bombshell/blonde bombshell (woman) these terms are militaristic, violent, and sexist (there is no parallel for a man); they portray women as destructive to men, even though superficially they appear complimentary. The two-piece women's bathing suit was named after the island of Bikini, which was split in two during the first serial detonation of a hydrogen bomb on May 21, 1956; "the bomb dropped on Bikini was called Gilda [corresponding to the 1946 film *Gilda* starring Rita Hayworth] and had a picture of Rita Hayworth painted on it" (Michael Wood, *America in the Movies*). Although men conceived of and carried out the bomb project, it was symbolically linked to women; Rita Hayworth was henceforth known in France as the "Atomic Star" and attractive women have been called "bombshells" ever since (Jane Caputi, *The Age of Sex Crime*).

BOMFOG coined around 1960 by New York reporter Joe Shannon, BOMFOG came from a phrase repeatedly used by Nelson Rockefeller, "The brotherhood of man under the fatherhood of God." Used to indicate vague political rhetoric, the acronym has also been used by women (beginning with writer Eve Merriam) to describe the overwhelmingly male system under which they live.

bondman/bondwoman *bondslave, bond servant, slave, serf.*

bondsman (law) *bonding/bond/bail/bail bond agent, surety provider, guarantor, bonding institution, lender.*

bondsman/bondswoman (slave) *See* bondman/bondwoman.

bonhomie from the French for "good man," this is most often applied to men and groups of men, but there is nothing to say you can't use it for women and for groups of women, or for groups of women and men. For a more neutral-appearing alternative consider *good-naturedness, geniality, cheerfulness, light-heartedness, optimism, happiness, joy, liveliness, friendliness, affability.*

bon vivant the French is grammatically masculine and this term has become associated primarily with men over the years, but women are using it too: actor Catherine Deneuve—female and French—says, "I'm a bon vivant, a reveler." For times when you need something more neutral-looking try *connoisseur, hedonist, epicure, aesthete, sensualist, high-liver, sophisticate, enthusiast, someone with a great deal of joie de vivre.*

bookman *bookseller, publisher's representative, book dealer/collector/ salesclerk, bookstore clerk/owner; bibliophile, bookworm; librarian.*

boom man *log sorter.*

bordello *house of prostitution.* For the rationale on avoiding euphemisms for prostitution, *see* prostitute.

borderline/borderline personality "Broad clinical terms such as *borderline* . . . are loaded with innuendo unless properly explained" (*Publication Manual of the American Psychological Association*, 4th ed.). The term "borderline personality disorder . . . is frequently used with the mental health professions as little more than a sophisticated insult" (Louise Armstrong, *And They Call It Help*). Some clinicians argue that the term "borderline" has become so prejudicial that it should be abandoned altogether.

border patrolman *border guard/patrol, member of the border patrol.*

born out of wedlock this expression is outdated and judgmental. *See also* bastard, illegitimate, wedlock.

borrow from Peter to pay Paul there is nothing wrong with using this colorful and familiar phrase, but be aware of how many such expressions in the English language are male-based. Balance their use with female-based expressions, creative expressions of your own, or sex-neutral alternatives: *borrow from the left hand to pay the right, juggle the bills, keep one step ahead of the bailiff, indulge in creative accounting, six of one and half a dozen of the other. See also* sex-linked expressions.

bosom buddy despite its common associations with women, the noun "bosom" is defined as the human chest. The adjective "bosom," which is used here, means "close" or "intimate." The term is used of and by both sexes. *See also* buddy.

boss lady/boss man *boss, straw/job boss.* Note the nonparallel "lady/man." *See also* foreman, lady.

Boston Brahmin *See* Brahmin/Brahman.

boulevardier *See* man about town.

bouncer there may be exceptions, but for all practical purposes bouncers are men. Bouncing is associated primarily with bars, but similar work is done in other environments by women, who are then called *security officers/ guards/consultants, crowd controllers, patrols, bodyguards.*

bowman (boats) *bow paddler, rower, boater.*

bowman (weapons) *archer.*

box boy *carryout clerk, bagger.*

box man (gambling) *box boss/supervisor/collector.*

boy (referring to a man) *man, young man.* "Boy" usually refers to a male no more than 16 years of age and sometimes no more than 12 or 13, depending on the context and the individual. It is absolutely unacceptable when used of African American men. It is used sometimes in the phrase "good old boys," but they are always white. *See also* attaboy/attagirl.

boycott nonsexist; named after English land agent Charles Cunningham Boycott (1832–1897), who was so harsh on the Irish tenants of his employer, Lord Erne, during a period of crop failures and famines that his neighbors shunned him and the tenant farmers refused to pay rent, stopped harvesting, and formed the Irish Land League. They drove off his servants, intercepted his mail, and tried to cut off his food supplies.

boyfriend there is still no concise, appropriate, universally accepted term to describe the man or boy we are dating or with whom we live. Those in committed relationships (whether opposite-sex or same-sex) need a word with the corresponding weight and meaning of "husband" or "spouse" to denote their partners. Discussing the problem of introducing the woman she's lived with for seven years to her boss, syndicated columnist Deb Price concludes, "Who says the gay rights movement hasn't made a lot of progress? In just 100 years, we've gone from the love that dare not speak its name to the love that doesn't know its name." The increasing numbers of unmarried men and women living in stable, longterm relationships have the same problem. None of the following terms work in all situations; some of them hardly work in any situation. But until the right word comes along, you might want to consider some of them: *friend; man friend* (if "woman friend" is also used); *male friend* (if "female friend" is also used); *best friend; spouse* (this is becoming increasingly popular; E. J. Graff, in *Out* magazine, says "'Spouse' at least puts the pair in the same bed. Unlike 'lover,' 'spouse' knows the bedroom is just one of many rooms in the house"); *partner, domestic partner, or life partner* (despite its business associations, this is one of the most popular choices); *companion* (literally, the person with whom you share bread) or *longtime companion* (this is the second most popular choice); *the man I'm seeing; significant other; soulmate; constant/loving/live-in/intimate companion/ partner; partner of long standing; escort, date, datemate, steady, romantic interest, heartthrob; mate, housemate, roommate, bunkie; paramour, consort, lover, longtime love, live-in, live-in lover; fiancé, betrothed, sweetheart; sweetie, guy pal, main/major squeeze* (and for stars, *offscreen squeeze*); *my reason for living, the love/light of my life, alter ego, second self, mainstay, the man in my life.* Note that "girlfriend," meaning pal or buddy, has made a comeback and is acceptable where "boyfriend" in the same sense has not and is not. *See also* better half, domestic partner.

boyhood acceptable sex-specific word. If you want a generic, use *childhood, innocence, youth.*

boyish replace this vague word with specific inclusive adjectives: *ingenuous, naive, childlike, innocent, open, friendly, eager, youthful, immature, self-conscious, inept, bright-eyed, optimistic, cheerful, adolescent, childish, sophomoric, juvenile, kiddish, infantile, callow, unsophisticated.*

boys and girls half the time use "girls and boys."

Boy Scout Alan R. Brown says the Boy Scouts of America (BSA) and the Girl Scouts of the United States of America (GSUSA) "have done more than anybody else to break down stereotyped sex roles for young people. After all, who told girls that hiking and camping are for them too? The Girls Scouts! And what best-seller tells boys that a Scout helps keep his home and community clean (p. 8), that one of the requirements for the First Class award is to cook a certain number of meals (p. 16), and how to be a good baby-sitter (p. 506)? The *Boy Scout Handbook!* Page references are to the 1990 edition, but cooking and cleaning have been in the requirements all the way back to 1910." The issue of the Boy Scouts and Girls Scouts merging or of each of them fully integrating opposite-sex members is complicated and is being constantly reviewed. GSUSA's leadership believes girls need an organization of their own; BSA admits female members in limited ways but it is one of the last holdouts world-wide against full admission for girls and young women (the full Boy Scout program in other countries is open to both sexes). The BSA also explicitly excludes gay boys and men as well as those who are free-thinkers, humanists, atheists, or otherwise unable to subscribe to BSA religious beliefs. Although both organizations prefer Boy Scout and Girl Scout, there are generic terms: *scout, youth scout, scouter. See also* Girl Scout.

boys in blue (armed forces) the armed forces now consist of both girls and boys, so use instead *soldiers, members of the armed forces, armed forces personnel.*

boys in blue (Civil War) *Union soldiers, bluecoats, the Blue, Army blue.*

boys in gray (Civil War) *Confederate soldiers, graycoats, graybacks, the Gray.*

boys in the backroom *See* backroom boys.

boys will be boys *children will be children, kids will be kids.* Sometimes used archly of men when they indulge in games, adult "toys," or practical jokes, this expression has also served to excuse the inexcusable: a young woman at the U.S. Naval Academy was dragged from her dormitory room and handcuffed to a urinal by male classmates while others taunted her and took pictures, but the administration determined that the incident was "a good-natured exchange that got out of hand"; the Spur Posse, "the lowlife band of high school jocks who measured their own self-worth in terms of how many meaningless sexual encounters they'd had" (Anna Quindlen) were just boys being boys; three of the young men who sexually assaulted a young woman with mental retardation "were convicted but not before a theme emerged clearly in their defense: 'Boys will be boys,' according to one attorney." In *Boys Will Be Boys*, Myriam Miedzian says that many of the values of the "masculine mystique"—toughness, dominance, repression of empathy, extreme competitiveness, the win-at-all-costs sports world, eagerness to fight, war toys—play a major role in criminal and domestic violence and even underlie the thinking and policy decisions of many of our political leaders. From gangs to college hazings to members of the National Security Council showing how tough they are by advocating war, boys are busy being boys. "A lot of people just say it's testosterone," says Miedzian, "and throw up their hands. I take the opposite position, that because boys have potential for being this way, we have to create an environment that discourages violence." *See also* violence.

boy toy a man or a woman regarded as a sex object is a "boy toy." Madonna self-identifies this way and "Boy Toy" is the name of one of her companies. *See also* toyboy.

bozo since "bozo" almost invariably refers to men, you might sometimes want a more inclusive term: *clown, jerk, fool.*

bra burner women protesting at the 1968 Miss America Pageant in Atlantic City threw brassieres into a trash can, thereby shedding what they considered a symbol of female oppression. Although burning was in fact outlawed by a municipal fire ordinance and never did occur, newspapers mistakenly reported "bra burning." The use of this term generally indicates hostility toward feminists.

braggart technically inclusive, this word is more often associated with men. Alternatives are only slightly more inclusive-appearing: *bragger, boaster, show-off, loudmouth, windbag, blowhard.*

Brahmin/Brahman a member of the highest of the four Hindu castes (for which either spelling is correct), "Brahmin" came to be used for one of the social or cultural elite, especially in New England—thus, Boston Brahmin.

brainy in 1975 Robin Lakoff *(Language and Women's Place)* said, "the word *brainy* is seldom used of men; when used of women it suggests (1) that this intelligence is unexpected in a woman; (2) that it isn't really a good trait." Although "brainy" is seen less often today, it still seems to be reserved for women.

brakeman *braker, brake tender/holder/coupler/controller/operator, yard coupler; conductor's assistant.*

brass (high-ranking officers) man or woman.

brave (Indian) a Florida radio shock jock defending Atlanta's use of "Braves" for their baseball team demanded of an Ojibway caller if it wasn't true that Indian men had been called "braves." "Yes," she replied. "But not by us." *See also* Indian, Redskins (sports team name).

Braves (sports team name) *See* Redskins (sports team name).

brazen *fearless, dauntless, bold, daring, brash, defiant, audacious, plainspoken, outspoken, candid, frank.* "Brazen" is almost always ascribed to women (for example, "brazen hussy").

breadwinner woman or man. *See also* bacon, bring home the; provider.

brethren/brothers (pseudogeneric) *brothers and sisters/sisters and brothers, people, congregation, assembly, colleagues, friends, associates, peers, community, companions, family, kin, believers, the faithful, children of God, neighbors.* In direct address, use *my dear people, sisters and brothers/brothers and sisters, friends, dear friends, dearly beloved.* Nick Levinson suggests *sistren and brethren/brethren and sistren.* According to Jackie Graham (in the periodical *The Angelus*), in the biblical epistles, the Greek "adelphoi" was usually translated as "brothers," although the correct translation is "siblings" or "brothers and sisters."

brewmaster *brewing/brew director, head/chief brewer.*

bridal if not directly modifying the bride (e.g., "bridal gown" but not "bridal party"), use *wedding, nuptial, marital, connubial.*

bridal consultant *wedding consultant.*

bride and groom acceptable terms for the wedding couple, but *see also* bridal, bridegroom, give away the bride.

bride burning *See* suttee.

bridegroom *groom.*

bride of Christ one of the important titles of the Roman Catholic Church, this metaphor is used to characterize the church as loved by, but subordinate to, Christ. By strong implication, the image conveys the damaging idea that human brides are also subordinate to their god-like husbands. *See also* church/she, God.

bridesmaid *attendant. See also* best man, maid/matron of honor.

bring home the bacon *See* bacon, bring home the.

brinkmanship/brinksmanship *gamesplaying, gameplaying, courting catastrophe, risk-taking bluff, bluffing, savvy, gambling, playing chicken.*

Britain *See* Great Britain, United Kingdom.

British/Briton/Brit these terms refer to someone from the island of Great Britain (which includes England, Scotland, and Wales). They are not synonymous with "English" and they are not used to refer to someone from Northern Ireland. "Brit" is slang and can be mildly offensive in certain contexts. *See also* Englishman, Great Britain, United Kingdom.

bro the popular and affectionate "bro" is a nice addition to the language; the parallel term for women, "sis" has not enjoyed a parallel history.

broad (woman) no.

broad jump *long jump.* According to Hugh Rawson *(Wicked Words),* this jump was renamed by the Olympic Committee in the mid-1960s because of its connotations (for example, there were jokes based on the double entendre of "making the broad jump").

broken home *family, single-parent home/family.*

brothel *house of prostitution.* For the rationale on avoiding euphemisms for prostitution, *see* prostitute.

brother (religion) retain because of its narrow meaning and because all orders with brothers consist of men; religious orders with "brothers" and those with "sisters" both resemble and differ from each other.

brotherhood (pseudogeneric) *unity, unity among humans, humanity, world unity, compassion, peace, companionship, goodwill, amity, friendship, comradeship, camaraderie, esprit de corps, conviviality; family, the human family, kinship, shared/human kinship; community, society, association, organization, social organization, common-interest group, club, corporation, federation, union, group, partnership, society; brotherhood and sisterhood.* Protecting "brotherhood" from pseudogeneric use allows it to retain its strong original meaning; the word has been gaining new use as men find that other men can sometimes best understand, discuss, and reflect common joys and problems ("brotherhood" thus developing along the same lines that "sisterhood" developed as a description of a meaningful sex-specific bond). "Brotherhood" has been used since 1340 as a synonym for "guild" so we still see today, for example, the International Brotherhood of Electrical Workers. But another group calls itself the United Electrical Workers and "solidarity" is also useful in this context (for example, the Newspaper Union Solidarity Committee). When Katherine Lee Bates's "America the Beautiful" is sung at Macalester College, the lines referring to brotherhood have been replaced by "God shed full grace on thee, / Establish thee in unity," according to professors Joan Hutchinson and Stan Wagon.

brotherhood of man *human family/community/bond/solidarity, bond of humanity, humanity, humankind, global village.* **See also** BOMFOG.

brotherliness (pseudogeneric) *neighborliness, affection, concern, warmth, affability, camaraderie.* **See also** brotherly love.

brotherly this is a useful and accurate sex-specific word in most cases. Sometimes, however, it is used stereotypically when other words would be more descriptive: *affectionate, loving, caring, kindly, supportive, sympathetic, protective, indulgent, friendly, humane.*

brotherly love (pseudogeneric) *kindheartedness, goodwill, philanthropy, charity, good-naturedness, generosity, benevolence, loving kindness, geniality, human feeling, benignity, beneficence, humanity, compassion, unselfishness, friendship, amiability, tolerance, consideration, affectionate/human love, love of others/of neighbor, other love, love of people, agape.* **See also** City of Brotherly Love.

brothers (pseudogeneric) *See* brethren/brothers.

brother's keeper, I am not my use "my brother's keeper" for the biblical story (when God asks Cain where his brother is after Cain has killed Abel, Cain answers, "I do not know. Am I my brother's keeper?"). For alternatives to the contemporary meaning consider *don't look to me, it's none of my business, it's not my responsibility, I can't help what anyone else does, I'm not responsible for anyone but myself, I'm not her/his/my sister's/my brother's keeper.*

bruiser as this is by definition a big, rough, husky man, there are no inclusive alternatives or parallel terms for a woman.

brunette although the base (male) term is "brunet," it is rarely used, most likely because referring to people's hair color is largely reserved for women. Can you imagine calling a man a brunet? Question the labeling of women by facets of their appearance and the need to talk about their hair. **See also** blonde, "feminine" word endings.

brushman *brush seller.*

buccaneer *See* pirate.

buck (man) profoundly derogatory term when used for an African American or American Indian.

buckaroo *See* cowboy.

buck naked *stark naked, naked, nude, starkers, naked as a jaybird, without a stitch on, unclothed, in the altogether/raw/buff, in one's birthday suit, au naturel, unclad.* "Buck naked" refers either to the male animal or to the color of buckskin (which isn't everybody's shade); on either count the term is better replaced.

buddy woman/girl or man/boy. This word (from the word "brother") is a positive term denoting closeness and friendship, whereas its counterpart, "sissy" (from "sister"), is never used positively. In spite of its masculine associations, "buddy" can be used of either sex. "Buddy" (for either sex) is also used to describe someone working as part of a support organization who volunteers to give companionship, practical help, and moral support to those with AIDS or related medical problems.

bull *lies, exaggeration, tall tale/story, snow/snowjob, hot air, bunk, nonsense; police officer, private detective, guard; speculator.* **See also** bull session.

bull dyke (woman) this term, which is disliked by some lesbians but used by others, follows the "insider/outsider" rule: its use by non-lesbians is unacceptable. **See also** butch, dyke, femme/fem, homophobia, homosexual.

bullfighter most bullfighters are men. In 1996, Christina Sánchez became Spain's first female *matador de toros*—a bullfighter of the first rank. In Mexico, Raquel Martinez earned the "alternativa" certificate, but even after years of bullfighting she was discriminated against: very few other matadors would share a booking with her, and she was booed and had beer bottles thrown at her. A sports news director said, "the time, in Mexico, for women matadors has not come."

bullish/bullish on America/bull market stock market expressions using "bull" are some of the least problematic sex-linked terms in the language, and their inclusion here will be seen as nit-picking. However, given the cumulative and largely covert effect of the many such expressions in the language, some people may occasionally want sex-neutral alternatives: *escalating, rising, inflationary; strong on/optimistic about America; rising/improving/escalating/buy/favorable market.*

bull session "bull" does not refer to the male animal but to fraud or deceit, from the word "boule." However, for a more neutral-appearing term (since men seem to have "bull sessions" while women have "gabfests"), you could try *brainstorming/rap/buzz session, parley, talk, chat, free-for-all/informal discussion.*

bully boy/man or girl/woman. "Bully" is generally defined in terms of men and it has a masculine feel to it, but it can be used of both sexes. For a more inclusive-sounding noun, use *meanie, tormentor, browbeater, aggressor, terrorist, dictator, menace.* For the verb use *browbeat, mistreat, tyrannize, terrorize, threaten, domineer, bulldoze, intimidate, oppress, menace.* For "bully boy tactics," consider *bully tactics, browbeating, intimidation, bulldozing, badgering, harassing.*

bum although this theoretically inclusive term can refer to either sex, it tends to be reserved for men. Most synonyms for "bum" *(beggar, hobo, vaga-*

bond, sponger, scrounger, vagrant, parasite) also tend to have a male cast. You may want to use instead *street person, homeless person. See also* bad guy, homeless.

bumpkin *See* hayseed.

burgomaster *mayor.* Or, leave as is for European towns that use it.

busboy *busser, dining room attendant, kitchen helper, dish carrier, waiter's helper/assistant, serving/server's assistant; service worker; room service assistant/attendant; porter, runner.*

Bushman/Bushmen *San.* Library cataloger Sanford Berman says that Africanists, anthropologists, and other informed people avoid the racist, sexist, Eurocentric, and inauthentic "Bushman/Bushmen," terms that are unacceptable to the San. He cautions against replacing them with the ethnocentric and racist "native/natives" or "tribe/tribes."

businessman *executive, business executive/associate/professional, member of the business community, business leader/manager/owner, professional, merchant, shopkeeper, entrepreneur, industrialist, financier, manager, investor, speculator, buyer, trader, capitalist, retailer, wholesaler, mogul, magnate, tycoon; businesswoman and businessman* (if used in parallel ways). "Businessperson" is not recommended. Or, be specific: *stockbroker, advertising executive, chief executive officer, public relations officer, wholesaler, banker.* Plural: *people in business, businesspeople.* Richard A. Spears *(NTC's Dictionary of American Slang and Colloquial Expressions)* offers two colloquial alternatives for either sex: *pinstriper, vest. See also* career girl/career woman, entrepreneur.

businessman's lunch *business/working lunch.*

busman's holiday *bus driver's holiday, working vacation.* (About half of U.S. bus drivers are women.)

busy as a hen with one chick because most of our images of parenting emphasize mothers, you may occasionally want to alternate this expression with others: *never idle, going full tilt, have many irons in the fire, have one's hands full, not a moment to call one's own, in the thick of things, doesn't let the grass grow under one's feet, on the go/move/fly, tireless, up to one's eyebrows/ears in, not have a moment to spare, in full swing, not a minute to waste.*

butch (woman) use of "butch" follows the "insider/outsider" rule, that is, it is acceptable for lesbians who want to use the term; it is generally unacceptable for non-lesbians to use it.

butcher woman or man. (Some 7% of butchers are women.)

butler invariably a man.

butter-and-egg man *butter-and-egger, big spender, nouveau riche.* Coined by 1920s nightclub performer Texas Guinan for a shy, middle-aged man so flattered by her friendliness that he paid the steep cover charge for every guest in the house and pressed $50 bills on all the entertainers. When he said he was in the dairy business, she introduced him as "the big butter-and-egg man," which was then applied to anyone who liked to throw money around (Dorothy Herrmann, *With Malice Toward All*).

butterfly *See* social butterfly.

button man *button, button player/soldier, soldier, gangster, mobster. See also* hit man.

C

It is not too much to say that one of the really important functions of language
is to be constantly declaring to society
the psychological place held by all of its members.
—*Edward Sapir*

The fact that we are human beings is infinitely more important
than all the peculiarities that distinguish human beings from one another.
—*Simone de Beauvoir*

cabbages and kings if you are not quoting Lewis Carroll and you need
something sex-neutral, consider *this and that, odds and ends, threads and
thrums.*

cabin boy *cabin attendant/steward;* in some contexts, *merchant mariner,
sailor.*

cabinet member woman or man. However, before 1933, when Frances
Perkins was appointed, all U.S. cabinet members were men.

cabman *cabdriver.*

caddymaster *caddyboss, caddy supervisor/leader/director/captain.*

cad *See* bad guy.

cadet in the service academies, a cadet can be a woman or a man. Although
not used much in that sense anymore, a "cadet" can also refer to a
younger brother or son; there is no parallel for younger sister or daughter.
For the slang use of "cadet" referring to a pimp use "pimp."

cadette *cadet. See also* "feminine" word endings.

Caesar's wife if you need a gender-free substitute consider: *someone whose
conduct is impeccable, someone about whom there hovers the odor of
sanctity, someone who is beyond reproach/above suspicion/irreproach-
able/unimpeachable/innocent/blameless/sinless/clean-handed.*

Cajun/Cajan a Louisianian descended from French colonists originally exiled from Acadia ("Cajun" is a corruption of "Acadian") is called "Cajun," or occasionally "Cajan." "Cajan" usually refers to someone of mixed black, white, and American Indian descent living in Alabama or Mississippi.

calendar girl *calendar model.*

call a spade a spade *get to the point, speak plainly/straight from the shoulder/straight out, be up front/frank/on the up and up/aboveboard.* The expression is possibly based on, but at least related to, a racial slur and should be avoided.

call boy *page, caller; bellhop;* sometimes, *prostitute.*

call girl *prostitute.* Call girl services and call houses are thus prostitution services and houses of prostitution. *See also* prostitute.

camaraderie an inclusive term, although this feeling of unity and goodwill has most often been associated with men, particularly in team sports, bars, and wars. *See also* brotherhood, fellowship.

cameragirl/cameraman *camera operator/technician, cinematographer, camera crew; videographer; photographer.*

camp follower if you mean prostitute, use *prostitute.* If you mean a politician who switches parties for reasons of personal gain, the term can be used for either sex.

can-can dancer this has always been a woman; there is no equivalent for a man.

candy-striper *volunteer, junior/teen/hospital volunteer.* These volunteers include girls/young women and boys/young men.

canoness *canon.* Depending on the denomination, a canon might be a woman or a man. *See also* "feminine" word endings.

Canuck in the United States, this is offensive slang for a Canadian, especially for a French Canadian. In Canada, it is not considered derogatory; the Vancouver Canucks (hockey team) and Johnny Canuck (the personification of Canada) are positive terms.

carboy nonsexist; from the Persian "qaraba" for "large bottle."

car bra this close-fitting vinyl cover that protects the front end of an automobile from insects, gravel, and the elements is also called *front-end mask, sports-car snood.* When "car bra" is used to mean a radar-absorbing carbon filter on the front end of an automobile to resist and confuse police radar use *nose mask/cap.*

card boy *card doffer.*

career girl/career woman *professional, business executive, executive trainee, longtime/full-time employee, careerist.* Or, be specific: *sales rep,*

*paralegal, career scientist, industry representative, social worker,
professor, engineer, administrative assistant.* The only use for "career
man" seems to be in government service. When tempted to use "career
woman," consider how "career man" would sound and handle the
situation the way you would for a man. *See also* businessman.

car/she *car/it.* Referring to cars as "she" is part of the association of the
feminine with men's possessions. Everything that dominator societies
have traditionally run or overpowered has been imaged as female: church,
nations, nature, ships, cars, etc. *See also* fill 'er up (gas tank).

cart boy *cart attendant.*

Casanova if you need an inclusive alternative use *heartthrob, heartbreaker,
lover, great romantic, dashing lover, flirt, make-out artist, smooth operator.*

case the *Publication Manual of the American Psychological Association*
says, "Recognize the difference between *case*, which is an occurrence of
a disorder or illness, and *patient*, which is a person affected by the
disorder or illness and receiving a doctor's care." *See also* patient.

cash boy *cash messenger.*

Caspar Milquetoast *See* milquetoast/milksop.

Cassandra although this legendary prophet of doom was a woman, her name
has since been used to refer to both sexes.

castrate/castrating if you must use these terms metaphorically, be sure you
are on sound psychological ground. They blame women for something
that takes two to accomplish. It is not possible to "castrate" a secure,
independent person; the man is not an anesthetized patient in this type of
surgery. For "castrate" use *disarm, disable, incapacitate, undermine,
unhinge, unnerve, deprive of power/strength/courage/vigor, devitalize,
attenuate, shatter, exhaust, weaken, disqualify, invalidate, paralyze,
muzzle, enervate, take the wind out of one's sails, put a spoke in one's
wheels.* For "castrating": *ruthless, aggressive, domineering, controlling,
powerful, tyrannical, overwhelming, overpowering.*

catfight when women disagree with each other, the proceedings are sometimes stereotyped as a catfight, whereas men's disagreements are not
called catfights or dogfights or anything else; they are simply a *disagreement, debate, discussion, conflict, dispute.*

cathouse *house of prostitution. See also* prostitute.

cat may look at a king, a there is nothing wrong with using this expressive
phrase, but be aware of how many like it in the English language are
male-based. Balance their use with female-based expressions, creative
expressions of your own, or sex-neutral alternatives: *a person can dream,
someone who lives in a fool's paradise/has airy hopes/hopes against*

hope/catches at a straw/makes sheep's eyes at/eyes wistfully/longingly.
See also sex-linked expressions.

cattleman *cattle owner/raiser/buyer/grower/producer, rancher, farmer.*

catty *malicious, spiteful, snide, sly, underhanded, disingenuous, envious.* "Catty" is used exclusively of women; the alternatives can refer to either sex.

Caucasian arising from the old "racial" classifications, where it referred to peoples indigenous to Europe, western Asia, northern Africa, and much of the Indian subcontinent, "Caucasian" today is used infrequently (usually only by some police departments and hospitals) but erroneously as a synonym for "white" or "European." "Caucasian" is correct when used to refer to the region between the Black and Caspian seas that includes part of Russia, Georgia, Azerbaijan, and Armenia, but it may be ambiguous to call those peoples "Caucasians"; use instead "people in or from the Caucasus." **See also** -oid, race, white.

Caucasoid **See** -oid.

cavalryman *cavalry soldier/officer, horse soldier, trooper.* Or specifically, *Hussar, Lifeguard, Lancer,* etc.

caveman/cavewoman *cave dweller, early/ancient human, Neanderthal, Cro-Magnon.* Plural: *cave people.* The use of "cavemen" as a pseudogeneric and the cartoon image of a cavewoman being dragged away by her hair have obscured women's role in prehistory: researchers now say that, contrary to common assumptions, it was women who were probably responsible for making tools and pottery and for such major technological innovations as agriculture and textiles.

caveman (man who behaves boorishly toward women) *clod, slob, fumbler, boor, insensitive/ill-mannered person, masher.* It is difficult to render this concept inclusively since it refers by definition to a man, but you can use words that are less sexist-appearing and ethnocentric than "caveman."

celibate because this can mean either someone who abstains from sexual activity (especially because of religious vows), someone who is currently refraining from sexual activity, or someone who is unmarried, it can be ambiguous; you might want to be more specific if the term is not readily understood in context.

cellarman *cellarer, cellar clerk/worker/laborer, winery worker, wine officer/stocker.*

Celt/Celtic this is the most commonly seen spelling, but some people prefer Kelt/Keltic (see, for example, *The Keltic Fringe,* published by Maureen Williams). Use the spelling people use for themselves.

cenobite woman or man.

centerfold girl *centerfold model.*

CEO (chief executive officer) woman or man. *See also* chief.

cerebral palsied *someone with/who has cerebral palsy/C.P.* Cerebral palsy is a condition, not a disease. It is unacceptable to use palsied, cerebral palsied, spastic, or spaz. *See also* disability/disabilities, handicapped.

chainman *surveyor's assistant, chain surveyor helper; chain offbearer; pattern assembler.*

chairman (noun) *chair, moderator, committee/department head, presiding officer, presider, president, chairer, convener, coordinator, group coordinator, leader, discussion/group/committee leader, head, speaker, organizer, facilitator, officiator, director, supervisor, manager, overseer, administrator, monitor, clerk.* Some people use "chairwoman" and "chairman," but it is generally better to keep this term gender-free because "chairwoman" is perceived as a less weighty position; "chairperson" is an awkward and self-conscious term used mostly for women. There is much linguistic support for the short, simple "chair": it was, in fact, the original term (1647), with "chairman" coming into the language in 1654 and "chairwoman" in 1685. Using "chair" as both noun and verb nicely parallels the use of "head" for both noun and verb. (People who are upset about being called "a piece of furniture" apparently have no problem with the gruesome picture of a "head" directing a department, division, or group, nor is there evidence that anyone has actually confused people chairing meetings with their chairs.) The use of "chair" in this way is considered metonymy—a figure of speech in which a word or phrase is substituted for another with which it is closely associated (e.g., "the lands belonged to the crown"; "from an early age he had felt drawn to the pulpit"). *See also* chairman (verb), chairmanship.

chairman (verb) *chair, head, lead, moderate, direct, supervise, officiate, preside, convene, coordinate, facilitate, control, oversee, organize, govern.* The verb "chair" is highly preferred to "chairman" ("He chairmanned the committee").

chairmanship *chair, leadership, presidency. See also* chairman.

challenged the only "challenged" term that was ever seriously used (and not for long nor by everyone) was "physically challenged." That attempt to name one of the realities of disability innocently provoked the ridiculisms that were then charged to "political correctness." Even *Fowler's Modern English Usage*, 3rd ed., which ought to be able to distinguish between genuine and deliberately farcical uses of words, credits "the political correctness movement of the 1980s and 1990s" with "notorious formations" like "cerebrally challenged" (stupid) and "vertically challenged" (short). If it needs to be spelled out, the rash of simulated "challenged" words came not from the so-called PC "movement" but from the anti-PC "intelligentsia." *See also* disability/disabilities, physically challenged, politically correct.

chamberlain historically a man. If you need a similar, inclusive term, consider: *treasurer, chief officer/steward, household official.*

chambermaid *room/personal attendant, servant, cleaner, housekeeper.*

chancellor man or woman.

change, the this term predisposes women to expect more change than many of them actually experience. *See also* menopause.

change booth man *cashier.*

chanteuse this sex-specific term conveys a precise meaning; because there is no parallel for men you might sometimes need sex-neutral alternatives: *singer, nightclub singer, vocalist, balladeer. See also* torch singer.

Chanukah *See* Hanukkah.

chaperone *chaperon. See also* "feminine" word endings.

chaplain woman or man.

chapman *peddler.*

chargé d'affaires man or woman.

charley horse there is nothing wrong with using this popular and instantly grasped term, but be aware of how many such expressions in the English language are male-based. Balance their use with female-based expressions, creative expressions of your own, or sex-neutral alternatives: *strain, bruise, contusion, stiffness, muscular stiffness, cramp. See also* sex-linked expressions.

charwoman *char, charworker, cleaner, janitor, maintenance worker, custodian.* Plural: *chars, cleaning personnel/crews, commercial cleaners, building-service employees, clean-up workers, charworkers, charforce.*

Chasidim *See* Hasidim.

chaste/chastity these terms have been used almost entirely of women (often with the implied concept of virgin/virginity); except for priests and monks, men have not been held by society to any sexual standards. With the advent of AIDS, chastity has made a modest comeback as it is the only truly effective preventive. Use the terms for both sexes or not at all. *See also* celibate.

chatelaine retain in historical contexts where its companion word, "chatelain," is also used.

chatter this term tends to be reserved for women, children, birds, and squirrels, and, in the case of the humans at least, implies that the conversation is trivial and irrelevant. For the verb consider *shoot the breeze, talk* *idly, make small talk, bandy words, pass the time of day, make chin music, beat one's gums, jaw, talk one's arm/head off, be talkative/ loquacious/garrulous, ramble, run off at the mouth, rattle/ramble on, pour forth, talk oneself hoarse, talk at random, talk a donkey's hind leg off.* For the noun use *small/idle/empty talk, blather, palaver. See also* babble, bull session, chatterbox, gabby, gossip, gossipy, yenta.

chatterbox because this is almost always reserved for women, you may want alternatives: *windbag, blatherskite, excessive talker, jabberer, blabbermouth, motormouth, hot-air artist, magpie, palaverer. See also* chatter.

chauffeuse *chauffeur. See also* "feminine" word endings.

chauvinism although this term comes from a man's name (Nicolas Chauvin, known for his exaggerated patriotism and attachment to Napoleon), it seems male-associated not because of its etymology but because of its mid-20th-century use for men in such terms as "male chauvinist" and "male chauvinist pig." Both women and men can be chauvinists. *See also* male chauvinist/male chauvinist pig.

checkout girl/checkout man *checker, checkout/desk clerk, cashier.* Note the nonparallel "girl/man."

checkroom girl/checkroom woman *checkroom attendant.*

cheerleader man/boy or woman/girl.

cheesecake *See* food names for people.

chef until recently, men have been chefs and women have been cooks; not too long ago the idea of a woman chef was considered absurd. Today, however, women in the United States, France, and England wear the full title of chef. At the Culinary Institute of America, 25% of the students are women, and the American Culinary Federation has more than tripled its female membership since 1986.

cherchez la femme! a popular mystery story convention, implying that wherever there is dirty work afoot, unraveling it begins with locating the woman involved. This expression is either relatively harmless or so layered with sexist assumptions that it cannot be untangled here.

chessman *chess/game piece.* Or, be specific: *pawn, rook, bishop.*

Chicago Blackhawks *See* Redskins (sports team name).

Chicana/Chicano use these terms ("Chicana," female; "Chicano," male) for people who so label themselves. Some people of Mexican descent in the U.S. (it is not appropriate for Mexicans living in Mexico) prefer other terms (Mexican American, Latina/Latino, Hispanic). The terms "Chicana/ Chicano" (always capitalized) carry connotations of ethnic nationalism (Indian, African, and Spanish roots) and political activism, which means

89

they are often not preferred by those older, more conservative Mexican Americans who want middle-class respectability and assimilation. "Chicana/Chicano" is not used for other Spanish-language groups, for example Puerto Rican Americans or Cuban Americans, and the popularity of the term varies across the U.S. *See also* Hispanic, La Raza, Latina/Latino, mestiza/mestizo, Mexican American.

chick *See* animals names for people.

chief the use of "chief" as a generic for any American Indian man is highly offensive; when capitalized and part of a historic title of an Indian leader, it is retained. Other uses of "chief" to mean "head" are acceptable and not associated with Indians.

chief/chief justice/chief master sergeant/chief master sergeant of the Air Force/chief petty officer/chief warrant officer/chief of staff/chief of state/chief executive officer/chief financial officer man or woman.

childcare childcare issues do not belong uniquely to women; they are family, social, political, business issues (companies that have supportive policies on childcare and family-friendly benefits say they are not motivated by benevolence—their programs make good business sense).

child custody damaging stereotypes about both sexes play a role in child custody. While joint custody seems consistent with equal rights and equal responsibilities, it is often not in the child's best interest; when shared responsibility, equal rights, and cooperation do not exist pre-divorce it is almost impossible to legislate them during a custody suit and ensure compliance later. In some courts, women are almost automatically given custody simply because they are women, yet men might have been the more suitable custodial parent in some of the cases. With the growth of the fathers' rights movement, however, men are more often being given custody—but sometimes for the wrong reasons. Reviewing *Child Custody and the Politics of Gender* (Carol Smart and Selma Sevenhuijzen), Nancy D. Polikoff concludes that the book "presents devastating evidence that mothers are losing custody of their children because of economic disadvantage, because they are judged by a 'good mother' standard vastly different from the 'good father' standard, because women's nurturing of children (as opposed to men's) is profoundly undervalued, and because, more than anything, the rhetoric of equality has outdistanced the realities of parenting." When fathers act as individuals, their acts are not construed as conflicting with their children's interests, but mothers' interests as individuals (rather than as mothers) appear to courts as antagonistic to those of their children. Child custody issues are highly complex, and custody decisions have profound, longlasting, and sometimes devastating effects on all concerned. There are no simple, fair rules, but eliminating decisions based solely on sex might ensure that the child has the most suitable custodial parent. *See also* absent parent, alimony, courts (judicial), displaced homemaker, divorce, divorced father/mother, noncustodial parent, visitation.

child/he (pseudogeneric) there are several solutions when you need to use a pronoun with "child." Switch to the plural: "Children are remarkable for their intelligence and ardor . . ." (Aldous Huxley). Avoid the pronoun altogether: "One of the most obvious facts about grownups to a child, is that they have forgotten what it is like to be a child" (Randall Jarrell). Use "it": "Who will show a child, as it really is? Who will place it in its constellation and put the measure of distance in its hand?" (Rainer Maria Rilke). "People murder a child when they tell it to keep out of the dirt. In dirt is life" (George Washington Carver). "The finest inheritance you can give to a child is to allow it to make its own way, completely on its own feet" (Isadora Duncan).

child is father of the man, the unless quoting poet William Wordsworth, use *the child is parent to the adult, the child begets/gives birth to the adult, the oak tree sprouts from the acorn, the seeds of the future lie in the past/ present.*

childless this is a problematic term, both for those who are voluntarily without children (some of whom prefer the term "childfree") and for those for whom being involuntarily without children is profoundly tragic. Organizations such as Childless by Choice, Child-Free Network, and No Kidding say that nonparents are trying to win acceptance for a childfree lifestyle in an age defined by "family values." Those who want children but are unable to have them don't usually announce the details of their situation to the world, and so they are subjected to the same disapproving remarks as the voluntarily childfree: they are judged "selfish" and are asked hurtful questions about their attitudes. Anndee Hochman *(Everyday Acts and Small Subversions)* says the term is gender-weighted; "we don't refer, with quite the same sense of anomaly and pity, to 'childless' men." As with so many terms about people's personal lives, the fact of having or not having children usually needn't be mentioned at all.

children children are neither "little angels" nor "little devils"; name them in publications only when doing so will not harm them; let them speak for themselves when possible; although they are dependents of adults, they are not appendages. An "infant" is newborn up to approximately age 1; a "toddler" is usually ages 1 and 2 (when learning to crawl and walk); a "preschooler" is ages 2–5; "youngster" is appropriate from preschool to about 12; a "very young child" might be 3–6; "adolescent," "teenager," and "youth" include ages 13–20; "young adult" is sometimes used for older adolescents. *See also* adolescent, ageism, teenager, youth.

chimney sweep girls and women have not historically been chimney sweeps; today both men and women own, operate, and work for chimney cleaning companies, although neither actually climbs inside chimneys anymore.

China doll *See* doll.

Chinaman *Chinese.* The offensive "Chinaman" is racist as well as sexist; use "Chinese" (or, if correct and relevant, Chinese American) for both sexes. *See also* Chinese, ethnic slurs.

Chinaman's chance *not a prayer, not an earthly chance, no chance, no chance at all, not a hope in hell, fat/slim chance, a snowball's chance in hell, as much chance as a snowflake in hell, doomed, unlucky, ill-omened, ill-fated, unblessed.* "Chinaman's chance," which is both racist and sexist, arose from the years when Californians violently opposed the introduction of Chinese labor into the state; the chances of Chinese workers finding jobs were very slim, as were their chances of finding justice under the law.

Chinese referring to China, its peoples, languages, and cultures, this is not interchangeable with Chinese American. "Chinese" is used in a number of expressions, some of which are benign (Chinese checkers/puzzle, various plants and vegetables), and some of which are not. Most of the negative expressions have faded from view in the post–World War II years; a mildly pejorative one that is still heard is "Chinese fire drill"—to refer to a state of great confusion and chaos with everyone running about or to "a practical joke in which youngsters get out of a car that is stopped at a red light, run around it, and hop in and out of it even after the light changes, making other drivers think they will miss the green and then, presuming they have timed their movements correctly, all getting back into the car and speeding away just as the light changes to red again, leaving the other cars behind" (Hugh Rawson, *Wicked Words*). Alternatives for the first meaning include *hullabaloo, hubbub, commotion, ruckus, muddle, imbroglio, to-do, free-for-all, pandemonium, fracas. See also* Chinaman, Chinaman's chance.

chip off the old block both child and parent here could be either sex, but as this phrase is so often used for fathers and sons, you may want to use instead *the spit and image, the spitting image, following in the footsteps of, the very image/picture of, cast in the same mold, for all the world like, a carbon copy of, as alike as two peas in a pod.*

Chippewa *See* Ojibwa/Ojibway.

chit (girl/young woman) there is no parallel referring to a boy/young man for this outdated term.

chivalrous if you want the sense without the masculine overtones consider *courteous, considerate, protective, courtly, brave, civil, generous, honorable, kindly, heroic, mannerly, gracious, well-bred, upstanding.*

chivalry if you want the sense without the masculine overtones consider *courtesy, honor, high-mindedness, consideration, bravery, courage, civility, valor, fidelity, mannerliness.* Sexist attitudes underlie the concept of chivalry. The beliefs that women need protection ("for their own good"), special courtesies, and kid-glove treatment result in superficial pleasantness but deep-seated discrimination, paternalism, and oppression. "Protectiveness has often muffled the sound of doors closing against women" (Betty Friedan, *The Feminine Mystique*). What chivalry says is that women can't take care of themselves, are not the equals of men in most respects, and certainly cannot do certain heavy, dirty, dangerous (and high-paying) work. In 1915, Nellie L. McClung *(In Times Like These)* wrote, "Chivalry is a poor substitute for justice, if one cannot have both. Chivalry is something like the icing on the cake, sweet but not nourishing." *See also* lady.

choirboy *choir member/singer, member of the choir, singer, vocalist.* In the metaphorical sense, use adjectives for the traits you want to convey, or consider: *cherub, angel.*

choirmaster *choir/music/song director/leader/conductor, director of the choir.*

chorine *cabaret/nightclub dancer, chorus member, member of the chorus.*

chorus boy/chorus girl *chorus member/dancer/performer/singer, member of the chorus, singer, vocalist, dancer, musical cast member.*

Christ *See* Jesus of Nazareth.

christen *name, dedicate, identify, label, denote, designate, entitle.* (The term comes from "Christian.")

Christian "Christian" and "Judeo-Christian" are often used as inappropriate synonyms for morality. Use instead *ethical, moral, decent, upstanding, righteous, upright, high-minded, honorable, principled, conscientious, moralistic, right, good.* During the Middle East war of 1948, the U.S. ambassador to the United Nations urged the Arabs and Jews to resolve their disagreements "like good Christians." *See also* Judeo-Christian.

Christian name when you mean the name given at baptism, this is correct. For its generic meaning use instead *first/given name, forename.*

Christmas with the widespread commercialization and increasingly extended celebration of this religious (for some) holiday, those who are not Christian are involuntarily exposed to "pre-Christmas sales," "Merry Christmas," Christmas cards/decorations/lights/trees, and "after-Christmas sales." In any nonreligious sense, use instead *holiday, holiday season/sales/decorations/cards, Happy Holidays, Season's Greetings, year-end sales, New Year's greetings/cards.* This loose usage of "Christmas" also dilutes and perverts its original religious meaning. *See also* Hanukkah, Kwanzaa.

chronic disability *disability.*

church/she *church/it.* Everything that dominator societies have traditionally run or overpowered has been imaged as female: church, nations, nature, ships, cars. This is particularly inimical in religious matters because the image has the weight of moral "rightness" behind it. The longtime God-is-male, church-is-female metaphors have inspired the logical but untenable conclusion that male must be better than female. The National Council of Catholic Bishops' document on inclusive language advises using "it" or "they" for "church." Note that when you mention "churches," in most contexts you may also want to mention temples and mosques. *See also* bride of Christ, God, religion.

church father if you are referring to one of the Fathers of the Church, leave as is for historical accuracy. When referring to someone who was not acknowledged as one of the apostolic or patristic Fathers, use instead *fourth-century religious writer, bishop, great Christian teacher, early Christian philosopher, post-Nicene writer,* etc.

churchman *church member/worker, churchgoer, believer, member of a church, parishioner; churchwoman and churchman* if they are used gender-fairly. Also: *religious, clergy, ecclesiastic, priest, presbyter, pastor, imam, minister, confessor, elder, vicar, canon,* etc. *See also* clergyman.

Church of Jesus Christ of Latter-day Saints, The *See* Mormon.

cigarette girl *cigarette vendor.*

Cincinnati Reds *See* Redskins (sports team name).

circumcision for many Jews, circumcision of male infants is an important religious rite. Medically there is no clearcut and universal position on the advantages and disadvantages of routine circumcision, but some men oppose it, saying it is invasive, done without the consent of the person being circumcised, and more properly thought of as sexual mutilation. *See also* female genital mutilation.

city councilman *city councilor/council member.* The two alternatives are so widely used today that there should be minimal need for: *city councilwoman and city councilman.* If the sex of the council members is germane, it will be obvious from their names or the pronouns used to refer to them.

city fathers *city leaders/founders/councilors/elders/officials/legislators/ administrators/bureaucrats, the powers that be.* In some cases: *City Hall.*

city hostess *goodwill ambassador, city representative.*

City of Brotherly Love William Penn named Philadelphia after a city in Asia Minor that was the seat of one of the seven early Christian churches and known for its goodwill and generosity; "Philadelphia" comes from the Greek "phil-" ("love") and "adelphos" ("brother"). "The City of Love" and "The City of Human Love" are seen occasionally but they seem unlikely to replace the centuries-old term.

civilization our notions of "civilization" and "civilized peoples" are highly ethnocentric; a working definition would seem to be "people pretty much like us with lots of technology, television, and ATMs." There are other definitions: "To be civilized is to be incapable of giving unnecessary offense, it is to have some quality of consideration for all who cross our path" (Agnes Repplier).

claim (verb) some people "state" or "say," while other people "claim," and often the dividing line is whether the person has favored-group or non-favored-group status. At the very least "claim" implies dubiousness; at the most, dishonesty or guilt.

claim(s) man *claim(s) agent.*

clairvoyante *clairvoyant. See also* "feminine" word endings.

clansman *clan member, member of a clan.*

classism the United States believes itself to be a fundamentally classless society, yet the income gap between rich and poor (measured by the percentage of total income held by the wealthiest 20% of the population versus the poorest 20%) is approximately 11 to 1, one of the highest ratios in the industrialized world—Japan's is 4 to 1 (Paula S. Rothenberg, *Racism and Sexism*). According to a survey of 26 industrialized nations conducted by the Luxembourg Income Study, the gap between the wealthiest 10% and the poorest 10% is greater in the U.S. than in any country except Russia. Class differences affect educational opportunity and achievement, material well-being, employment, health, and death rates. According to Benjamin DeMott *(The Imperial Middle)*, the myth that upward mobility is available to everyone shapes our response to poverty; social programs pretend most needs are temporary (the stopgap welfare system) or narrow (nutritional supplements for pregnant women). Classist writing is subtle (for example, "welfare mother," "those people," "inner city") and difficult to weed out. It helps to imagine you are speaking of a well-dressed CEO in the same situation; barring the obvious differences, would the tone still be the same? *See also* blue-collar, poor, welfare, welfare mother.

classman *See* freshman, underclassman, upperclassman.

cleaning girl/cleaning lady/cleaning woman *cleaner, domestic/office cleaner, household/domestic/maintenance worker, housecleaner, houseworker, housekeeper, household helper, janitor, custodian, charworker. See also* charwoman.

cleft lip/cleft palate *See* harelip.

clergyman *clergy, cleric, member of the clergy, spiritual leader.* Or, be specific: *pastor, rabbi, minister, priest, deacon, presbyter, elder, ecclesiastic, confessor, bishop, prelate, rector, parson, dean, imam, vicar, chaplain, preacher, missionary,* etc. Some 84 Christian denominations ordain women; at least 82 do not. Among those religious bodies with female clergy are American Baptist, Christian (Disciples), Episcopal, Evangelical Lutheran, Presbyterian, United Church of Christ, United Methodist, and the Conservative, Reform, and Reconstructionist branches of Judaism. However, according to one study, women clergy are encountering a stained-glass ceiling. *See also* bishop, churchman, imam, man of God/of the cloth, minister, priest, rabbi.

cleric/clerical may refer to either sex.

Cleveland Indians *See* Redskins (sports team name).

clod/clodhopper *See* hayseed.

close shave this can be used of either sex as it does not refer to shaving whiskers but to removing a thin layer of anything and proceeding with difficulty, as in "scraping by" or "close scrape."

closet this term, which is defined in one of its meanings as "a state of secrecy or cautious privacy" (*American Heritage Dictionary*, 3rd ed.), is also used to refer to lesbians and gay men who prefer not to disclose their sexual orientation. *See also* coming out, outing.

clotheshorse *fancy/fashionable/sharp/conspicuous dresser, tailor's/sartorial dream, a person it pays to dress, one who keeps the tailor in business, clothes-conscious person.* "Clotheshorse" invariably refers to a woman, although there is another kind of clothes sexism: women today are free to borrow from what have traditionally been men's wardrobes (pants, suits, ties, hats, boxers) but men are still culturally discouraged from borrowing from women's wardrobes or accessories. *See also* dandy, looksism.

clothes make/don't make the man *clothes make/don't make the person/ individual, clothes can break/make a person, clothes aren't everything, dress for success, the right clothes make a difference, don't judge a book by its cover, appearances are deceptive, all that glitters is not gold, you can't make a silk purse out of a sow's ear, a monkey dressed in silk is still a monkey.*

clubman/clubwoman *club member, member of the club, enrollee, cardholder; clubber, joiner, belonger, social/gregarious person.*

coach woman or man.

coachman *coach driver, driver, chauffeur.* Retain "coachman" in some historical contexts.

coadjutress *coadjutor.* **See also** "feminine" word endings.

coastguardsman *coastguard, coastguarder, member of the coastguard.*

coatcheck girl *coatchecker, coatroom/cloakroom/checkroom attendant/clerk, coat attendant/checker.*

co-chairman *co-chair.* **See also** chairman.

cock Hugh Rawson *(Wicked Words)* says the cock, along with the bull, is one of the principal symbols of masculinity. Its slang meaning of "penis" ensures that most "cock" words carry some connotation of maleness. The barnyard cock is now a rooster; the weathercock is a weathervane. **See also** "cock" words below.

cock-a-hoop the maleness of this old-fashioned term has been blunted. If you need an alternative consider *feeling one's oats, flushed with victory, happy as a lark, merry as a cricket, lighthearted, jubilant, exultant, triumphant, jaunty; awry, out of shape, askew.*

cock-and-bull story "cock-and-cow" story would have provided a nice bit of sex-balance as well as alliteration, but as it is, this colorful expression isn't really prejudicial to either sex. (The original long, boring 17th-century tale featured a cock and a bull.) If you want a neutral-sounding alternative use *snow job, nonsense, a lot of nonsense, stuff and nonsense, tall tale, yarn, preposterous/improbable story, canard, moonshine, bunkum, poppycock, hot air, hogwash, banana oil, balderdash, not true, applesauce.*

cock of the roost for a sex-neutral alternative you might try *arrogant, conceited, careless, overbearing, in high feather, on a high horse, sitting pretty, riding tall in the saddle.*

cock of the walk for a sex-neutral alternative consider *crème de la crème, flower of the flock; tyrant, dictator, leader, ruler.* ("The walk" was the chicken yard.) **See also** high man on the totem pole.

cockpit (airplane) *flight deck.* **See also** cock.

cocksure/cocky this is used of both sexes although it comes from the male fowl and tends to be used more often of men. If you want a sex-neutral term use *self-confident, overconfident, arrogant, self-important, in love with oneself, pushy, overbearing, swaggering, aggressive, conceited, haughty, supercilious; jaunty, brash, cheeky, flippant, saucy, nervy, impertinent, insolent, careless.*

cockswain **See** coxswain.

cocktail there appear to be dozens of theories about the origins of this term; it is, however, functionally nonsexist. **See also** cock.

coed (noun) *student.* In theory a coed is a student at a coeducational school; in practice it is always a young woman. Several generations ago, Joe

College and Betty Coed were the popular generic couple on campus, but Joe got to be the whole college while Betty was the coed, the exception to the old rule that higher education was reserved for men. "In a plane-crash story we called one female victim a coed, bringing this well-taken protest: 'Coed carries with it the connotation of perky little female students in tight sweaters, or of women who have only recently been allowed to study with their more deserving male counterparts. Only men are students; women are just co-educated'" *(Wall Street Journal)*. Commented the paper: "'Tis truly sad to let go of such a headline-short word in newspapers, but let us put it on our list of sexist words to be avoided." *See also* feisty, perky/pert.

coffee girl/coffee man *coffee maker/server.* Note the nonparallel "girl/man."

coffee klatsch *See* kaffeeklatsch.

co-heiress *co-heir. See also* "feminine" word endings.

coiffeur/coiffeuse acceptable sex-specific terms. For a sex-neutral term consider *hairdresser. See also* barber, beautician.

college girl *college/university student.* The masculine equivalent is "college man," not "college boy." If necessary to specify sex, use "college man" and "college woman."

colonialization from The Power of Language Department: the United States has never had "colonies," only "territories and possessions."

colonist colonists have been both sexes and of diverse ancestry. Avoid using the word pseudogenerically (for example, "colonists, their wives and children") or implying that they were only white.

coloratura retain as is for the soprano who specializes in ornately figured vocal music.

colored as a description of African Americans, "colored" is unacceptable except in established titles (e.g., National Association for the Advancement of Colored People). One possible reason for the persistence of this term: "colored people" are perceived to "know their place" better than uppity blacks or African Americans. "People of color" (which is not at all the same) is used for groups who so name themselves. In South Africa, "colored" is "Coloured" and it refers to individuals of mixed black African and other ancestry. *See also* African American, black (noun), people of color.

colorism the prejudicial or preferential treatment or discrimination among persons of African descent because of skin shade (practiced by whites as well). "The upper echelons of black society in particular tended to rate beauty and merit on the basis of the lightness of the skin and the straightness of the hair and features. White features were often a more reliable ticket into this society than professional status or higher education. Interestingly enough, this was more true for women than it was for men" (Michele Wallace, *Black Macho and the Myth of the Superwoman*). Colorism compounds racism, both economically and socially.

coloured *See* colored.

colporteur although this French word is grammatically masculine, it is used in French and English to refer to both sexes. If you need an alternative, use *religious book peddler.*

combat in its narrowest sense, this term is sexist. It is still men only who must face the most dangerous military activities; women are not permitted to serve in direct ground combat units, although they fill jobs where the line between combat and combat-related is increasingly blurred: they train men for missions they can't carry out themselves; they command units in which they can't serve; in the Navy, they are barred from permanent assignment on combat ships such as carriers, destroyers, and submarines, but they can serve on repair and supply ships in the same waters. Although few enlisted women are demanding combat duty, the situation is different for female officers, who know that their exclusion from combat commands creates a glass ceiling; advancement to top ranks often depends on leading combat units. U.S. women who qualify for combat want to be allowed to fight, as women already do in some other Western countries (in 1989 Canada abolished laws barring women from combat and opened all military jobs, except on submarines, to women). Both women and men are wondering how fair it is to ask men to risk their lives while giving women special treatment—treatment that at least some of them do not want. While working toward a world in which neither men nor women need go to war, it seems reasonable to allow those women who want combat positions and who qualify for them to have them. The increasing number of women in the armed forces means that fewer men who don't want to be in the armed forces will end up there; it is largely women's making up for the shortfall in male volunteers that allows the suspension of the compulsory draft. It may be, too, that only when women are full participants in war will we rethink the way we have used men as pawns, cannon fodder, and "death objects." Former Secretary of Defense Caspar W. Weinberger said, "I think women are too valuable to be in combat." Does he then believe men are less valuable? Ellen Goodman writes: "Are Americans ready to see women come home in body bags? I hope not. But new risks and roles may force us to ask a deeper questions: Why are we ready to see men come home in body bags? . . . In the end, this must be said: Any war that isn't worth a woman's life isn't worth a man's life." *See also* armed forces, draft, serviceman.

combination girl/combination man *short-order cook*. Note the nonparallel "girl/man."

comedienne *comedian, comic, stand-up comic, comic actor, entertainer*. *See also* "feminine" word endings.

come-hither look this look often exists only in the eye of the beholder. Because advertisements constantly use the look, it is perhaps not surprising that some men see it when it isn't there. Rapists have claimed they were given the come-on although their victims denied it. In a survey on how men know when women don't want their advances, one man said the only way he would know if a woman didn't want to have sex with him was if she fought and screamed the whole time. *See also* provoke, "she asked for it."

come to man's estate *come of age, attain majority, settle down, become adult, mature, come into one's own*.

comfort women "The so-called 'comfort women' were, in actuality, women kidnapped and drafted into military sexual slavery by the Japanese government for the use of their troops during World War II" (peace activist Polly Mann). When referring to "comfort women," use quotation marks to indicate the dubiousness of the term and make clear the reality of their situation; they were essentially sex slaves. *See also* sexual slavery.

coming out the process of "coming out"—acknowledging and accepting one's lesbian or gay orientation—is a lifelong one. It involves accepting it within oneself, informing family, friends, and co-workers, and then perhaps the world at large, although publicly identifying oneself may or may not be a part of "coming out of the closet" (Gay & Lesbian Alliance Against Defamation, *Media Guide to the Lesbian and Gay Community*). GLAAD also says that to refer to those who have taken this step as "admitted," "avowed," or "declared" homosexuals is inappropriate because those terms imply something unsavory; "openly lesbian" and "openly gay" are preferable. *See also* openly lesbian/gay, outing.

commander-in-chief in the United States, this is the President, and thus gender depends on the person in office. *See also* chief.

committeeman/committeewoman *member of the committee, committee member; ward leader, precinct leader*. "Committeewoman" and "committeeman" are not as equal as they seem; "committeewoman" is a much less weighty term.

common-law husband/common-law wife *common-law spouse*, except when sex-specific terms are desirable. The woman in this household is often disparaged where the man is not. In a few states, common-law spouses are regarded as legally married; disapproval based on lack of marriage lines is misplaced.

common man *common citizen/person/human/human being/voter, average citizen/person/human/human being/voter, ordinary person/citizen/human/ human being/voter, everyday person, layperson, taxpayer, voter, resident, householder, homeowner, landowner, passerby, one of the people, citizen, the nonspecialist, commoner, rank and file.* "The common man" translates well to "ordinary people."

companion *See* boyfriend or girlfriend.

company man originally someone who led a company union and represented management's hope of keeping away outside unions, a company man today is someone who always sides with the boss or the company. It's a difficult term to replace as it says so much to us in two words. Today, however, there are company women, too, but "company woman" may not be understood in the same way. For both sexes use instead *loyal employee/worker, staunch supporter.* Or, use adjectives: *loyal, faithful, devoted, trustworthy, true-blue. See also* organization man, yes man.

comparable worth this term refers to pay schedules that give equal pay for jobs similar in education requirements, skill levels, work conditions, and other factors. "Equal pay" means people doing the same job receive equal pay, for example, female and male nurses of equal seniority working on the same hospital floor receive the same pay. "Comparable worth" means that a female clerk-typist might earn the same as a male warehouse employee. However, even the most carefully constructed comparable worth plans have serious difficulties weighting job dimensions. Marc S. Mentzer, associate professor of industrial relations and organizational behavior, gives an example: women historically have been concentrated in jobs requiring communication skills (secretaries, telephone operators, teachers) while men have historically been concentrated in jobs requiring physical skills (manual laborers, construction workers). In a job evaluation plan in which two of several dimensions might be communications skills and physical skills, how should these two be weighted? Are communication skills equal to, double, or half the weight of physical skills? In so subjective a judgment, a biased employer could tinker with the weights to produce the desired results. Thus, determining comparable worth is not an objective, scientific process. Another factor is a set of underlying attitudes so deeply entrenched that it will take more than legislation to arrive at comparable worth: "In just about every [society], whatever men do or produce is valued more highly than what women do or produce, even though what a man does in one society is done by women in another society. In most societies, it is not the thing done, nor the objects produced, but the sex of the doer that confers distinctions upon acts or products" (Marilyn French, *Beyond Power*). *See also* equal pay/equal pay for equal work, executive, glass ceiling, wage earner.

compatriot although "compatriot" has masculine roots (from the Latin for "land of my father"), the word is used in an inclusive manner today.

complain this is often used of women and members of minority groups to discount what they are saying. For example, "Women are more likely to complain of discrimination." Depending on the meaning, it should have read "to report discrimination" or "to experience discrimination." This usage may have come from legal terminology in which a complainant "complains," but using that word in everyday language for certain people and not others is ambiguous and biased. *See also* claim (verb).

conceive when you want the broader meaning of this term, as opposed to its narrow biological meaning, use alternatives that are not sex-linked: *imagine, dream up, think, invent, fashion, create, formulate, design, devise, contrive, concoct, hatch, form, originate, initiate, bring about. See also* beget, seminal.

concentration camp use "concentration camp" only in its primary meaning ("a camp where prisoners of war, enemy aliens, and political prisoners are detained and confined, typically under harsh conditions," *American Heritage Dictionary*, 3rd ed.). Using it casually or jokingly for a restrictive situation robs it of its needed power and discounts its horrors. *See also* "final solution," Gestapo/gestapo, Hitler/little Hitler, holocaust, Nazi/nazi.

concertmaster *concert leader/director, assistant conductor, first violinist.* Some concert directors, both women and men, prefer to retain "concertmaster."

concierge woman or man.

concubine this word, meaning "to lie with," refers to a woman who lives with a man outside marriage. The person she is presumably lying with has no label; he is simply a man. Perhaps she could simply be a woman. *See also* kept woman, loose woman, mistress, pickup.

conductress *conductor. See also* "feminine" word endings.

confessor the role of confessor originated with the development of the Celtic *anamchara* or "soul friend" (5th to 10th centuries) who could be female or male, single, married, or celibate. It was not until 1215 that the Fourth Lateran Council defined "confessor" in terms of a priest. Today we return to inclusive usage: *spiritual director, confidant, advisor, counselor, mentor, preceptor, therapist, mother confessor/father confessor.*

confidante *confidant. See also* "feminine" word endings.

confined to a wheelchair *wheelchair user, uses a wheelchair.* Also, but less recommended, *has a/in a wheelchair.* Wheelchairs are liberating, not confining. *See also* bedridden, disability/disabilities, wheelchair-bound.

confraternity as this is based on the Latin for "brother," you may sometimes need sex-neutral alternatives: *society, union, association, organization, group, club, religious society.*

confrere as this comes from the French (and before that, the Latin) for "brother," you may sometimes need sex-neutral alternatives: *colleague, associate, co-worker, teammate, collaborator, partner, companion, comrade, confederate, counterpart, accomplice.*

congressman *member of Congress, representative, congressional represen-tative, legislator, member of the United States House of Representatives, delegate, assembly member; congressman and congresswoman* if they are used fairly—and if "congressman" is not used as a false generic. "Congressperson" is not recommended, although it is seen from time to time. If "member of Congress" seems cumbersome, think of how often we have heard "member of Parliament" (nobody was ever a Parliamentman) and not only didn't wince but thought it sounded elegant. Although "congressman" or "congresswoman" is technically a correct title for senators and representatives, it is typically used to describe members of the House of Representatives; senators are always called "senator."

con man/confidence man *con artist, swindler, hustler, confidence operator, operator, chiseler, flimflammer, flimflam artist, fraud, cheat, faker, charlatan, mountebank, trickster, quack, shark, crook, dodger, defrauder, deceiver, sharpie, scoundrel, hoodwinker, phony, impostor, shortchange/ bunko artist, scammer, snollygoster.* Although all these terms are inclu-sive, many of them tend to be thought of first as male. *See also* bad guy.

conservative this word, from loose using, has become shapeless; it often means little more than "the other side." Try modifying it (*fiscal/social/ international/political conservative, ultra-conservative*) or occasionally replacing it: *traditionalist, fundamentalist, reactionary, Republican Conservative Party member, rightist, right winger.* The best solution is to indicate the person's beliefs, behavior, or voting record. "The develop-ment of society and culture depends upon a changing balance, maintained between those who innovate and those who conserve the status quo. Relentless, unchecked, and untested innovation would be a nightmare. . . . If repetition and rigidity are the dark side of the conservative coin, loyalty and stability are its bright side" (Judith Groch, *The Right to Create*). *See also* liberal.

constable depending on locale, a constable might be either a woman or a man.

construction worker 2% of construction workers are women; they earn 25% less than male hardhats. *See also* tradesman.

contact man *advance agent, song plugger.*

control man *control panel operator, control operator, controller.*

convent in almost all cases, it is religious women who live in convents, but historically mendicant friars also lived in convents. *See also* monastery.

conveyor belt man *conveyor belt repairer/tender/worker.*

cook *See* chef.

copy boy/copy girl *copy messenger/carrier/clerk/distributor, runner.*

copy man *copywriter; copy chief/editor.*

coquette *flirt.* All other coquette-type words are specific for women (tease, vamp, belle, hussy) or for men (playboy, masher, wolf, sheik).

Cornishman use also *Cornishwoman.* Plural: *the Cornish, inhabitants of Cornwall, Cornishfolk, Cornishwomen and Cornishmen* (but not "Cornishmen and women").

corporate welfare *See* welfare.

corpsman *medical aide; corps member.* "Corpsman" is still used by the Marine Corps but it may refer to either sex.

Cosa Nostra this U.S. crime syndicate is believed to be related to the Sicilian Mafia. Unless you are certain that you are referring to the Cosa Nostra itself, use *organized crime, crime syndicate. See also* Mafia.

costerman *costermonger, street vendor.*

costume clothing worn by indigenous peoples, native peoples, or people from other countries is often referred to as a costume when in fact it is simply clothing. Even when the clothing is more elaborate, as for rituals, ceremonies, or celebrations, it should no more be referred to as a costume than is a wedding dress or band uniform or graduation gown.

councilman *councilor, council member, member of the council/city council, city representative, municipal officer, ward manager, commissioner; councilwoman and councilman.* Beware of "councilman" as a false generic; "councilperson" is not recommended, although it is seen and heard from time to time.

countergirl/counterman *counter attendant/server, waiter.* Note the nonparallel "girl/man."

country bumpkin this term tends to be used more of a man than of a woman, although it is not in itself gender-specific. It supports a stereotype that rural people are provincial, ignorant, and have unpolished manners.

countryman *compatriot, citizen, inhabitant, native, resident, indigen; counterpart; country dweller, ruralist, farmer; countrywoman and countryman. See also* compatriot, fellow countrymen.

country/she *country/it.* *See also* car/she, ship/she.

couple in the sense of two people with emotional, domestic, or sexual ties to each other, do not assume a couple is a woman and a man; it might equally well be two men or two women. Instead of "married couple" try the inclusive "domestic partners." *See also* boyfriend, family, girlfriend, husband and wife.

courtesan *high-class prostitute.* A courtesan used to be the female equivalent of a courtier; "courtier" retains most of its former meaning, but "courtesan" has been completely devalued and there is no remaining parallel. *See also* prostitute.

courtesy boy (grocery store) *courtesy help, carry-out.*

courtesy titles *See* social titles.

courtier *attendant; flatterer. See also* courtesan.

courts (judicial) gender bias in the judicial system has been the subject of a number of court-sponsored studies in various states. The conclusion in New York was that unfairness and gender bias against women as litigants, attorneys, and court employees was a pervasive problem. In Minnesota, discrimination against women was found in areas such as divorce, domestic abuse, sexual assault, employment discrimination, and access to courts. The group also found examples of judges and lawyers addressing female litigants and witnesses by first names or by such terms as "dear" or "honey" while they did not do the same to men. In child custody cases, there was judicial bias against men and also against working women and poor women. One study found that other factors being equal, plaintiffs tend to receive higher awards for disfigurement if they are women and for loss of future earning capacity if they are men. The bias begins in law school. Carl Tobias (in the *Golden Gate University Law Review*) reported that a widely used torts casebook in U.S. law schools was overwhelmingly male: "All of the illustrations of people, including the legal heroes, torts scholars and judges, are males." The casebook relies almost exclusively on masculine pronouns (even when the litigants are women), it omits historical information useful in evaluating women's concerns before the law, and depicts "numerous female parties pursuing what appear to be frivolous, vindictive, or unsubstantiated litigation or otherwise seem to be crazy, inconsiderate or weak people." *See also* child custody, dear/dearie, divorce, honey/hon, lawyer.

couturière *high fashion designer, proprietor of a haute couture establishment; couturier/couturière.*

cover girl *cover model.*

cover that man (sports) *cover that receiver/player, cover them.*

coward/cowardly/cowardice nonsexist per se, these terms are almost entirely reserved for men/boys. From the Latin "cauda" for "tail," "coward" refers to a dog with its tail between its legs. According to Stuart Berg Flexner *(Listening to America),* "It doesn't seem to be until the 1850s that boys began to taunt each other with being timid, cowardly, or unmanly, perhaps because earlier frontier days had produced fewer such boys, or because now new diversity meant tough frontier and rural youths were meeting some milder boys." In one of the great social double standards, we hold boys/men to impossibly high and arbitrary standards of courage that we never hold women to—because of a cultural discounting that associates women with weakness and says women cannot and should not accept challenges that call for courage or risk-taking. Boys/ men are acculturated never to show fear, inadequacy, uncertainty, or weakness—and to be deeply stung by taunts of "coward." Variants on "coward" that are technically inclusive but that are generally applied to men: big baby, chicken, chicken-hearted, chicken-livered, creampuff, featherweight, fraidy cat, gutless, gutless wonder, jellyfish, lily-livered, Miss Nancy, nebbish, pantywaist, pussyfooter, quitter, rabbit, shirker, sissy pants, softie, spineless, traitor, twerp, weakling, weenie, wimp, worm, wuss/wussy. Especially for men is: are you a man or a mouse? *See also* crybaby; man, act like a/be a/take it like a; glass cellar; masculine mystique; milquetoast/milksop; sissy; weak sister; yellow/yellow-bellied/ yellow-bellied coward/yellow belly/yellow streak down one's back.

cowboy/cowgirl *cowhand, cowpuncher, ranch hand, hand, rancher, herder, cowpoke, wrangler, range rider, drover, buckaroo, rodeo rider/roper/ entrant, cowgirl and cowboy* (in some contexts, e.g., teenage rodeo participants). Although some of the terms in the list have a masculine flavor, there is nothing to contravene their use for girls/women. "While the cow*boy* is our favorite American hero—the quintessential man—most of us see the cow*girl* as a child who will grow up someday and be something else. The cowboy's female counterpart—who can ride and rope and wrangle, who understands land and stock and confronts the elements on a daily basis—is somehow missing from our folklore" (Teresa Jordan, *Cowgirls*).

cowboy hat *Stetson, ten-gallon/western-style/rodeo hat.*

cowboy shirt *western-style/buckskin/fringed/rodeo shirt.*

cowman *rancher, cattle owner/buyer/grower/producer, farmer, cowherd.*

coxswain "swain" refers to a servant or a boy, and most coxswains are and have been men. However, the term could be used for a woman as its sex link is related more to the lack of female coxswains than to its etymology. Or, use the more neutral-sounding *bosun,* derived from boatswain. (A "cock" was a small boat, so coxswain and boatswain are related.) Today most coxswains are found in the Navy, on small craft, and in racing shells. *See also* boatswain.

cracksman *safecracker, burglar, housebreaker.*

crafts "*Art* used to be definable as what men created. *Crafts* were made by women and 'natives.' Only recently have we discovered they are the same, thus bringing craft techniques into art, and art into everyday life" (Gloria Steinem, in *Ms.*).

craftsman *artisan, crafts worker, craftworker, skilled worker, skilled craft worker, handworker, handiworker, handicrafts worker, handicrafter, trade worker, artificer, technician, craftsperson* (use only as a last resort); *craftsman and craftswoman.* Plural: *craft workers, artisans, skilled workers, handworkers, handicrafts workers, handicrafters, trade workers, handiworkers, artificers, craftspeople, craftsmen and craftswomen.* Or, be specific: *potters, weavers, woodworkers.*

craftsmanship *artisanry, artisanship, craft, handiwork, skilled-craft work, expertise, handicraft, skill, artistry, quality, crafts skills, expertness, expertise.* Or, mention the characteristics that contribute to the piece's beauty or the specific skills that went into its making.

cragsman *climber, rock/cliff climber, mountaineer, alpinist.*

craneman *crane operator.*

crazy *See* mental illness.

Creatrix *Creator, Maker. See also* "feminine" word endings, God.

credit to her/his race once you have used this in print for a white person at least 10 times, you are entitled to use it for a person of color.

cretin *someone with congenital myxedema.*

crewman *crew member, member of the crew, hand, employee, personnel, staff member, worker; crew/deck hand, sailor, mariner.*

crime of passion this term usually refers to domestic violence/terrorism/murder, but "passion" makes it sound defensible and much more positive than it is.

criminal because only some individuals are labeled "criminals" while others go unlabeled, "criminal" and "poor" have become linked in people's mind, when in fact there are well-to-do criminals as well as "white-collar" crime. (None of those involved in the S&L "scandal"—a nicer word than "crime"—were called "criminals" although some had in fact broken the law.) This association between "poor" and "criminal" makes it difficult to get backing for anti-poverty programs; people think they're paying to support criminals (political scientist Mark Maggio). *See also* bad guy, juvenile delinquent, murderess, prisoner.

criminal class because those (principally white) people who underreport income to the IRS or who buy boats across state lines and falsify place of delivery to evade sales tax or who embezzle in the levels of upper management are never referred to as a "criminal class," it seems evident that this term has racist and classist dimensions.

cripple *person/individual with a disability/orthopedic disability/physical disability/functional limitation, someone who is mobility impaired, someone with paraplegia/arthritis.* Omit references to a disability if it is not strictly necessary to your material. "Cripple" (and "crip") follow the "insider/outsider" rule, that is, they are derogatory and unacceptable except when used by people with disabilities among themselves. "People—crippled or not—wince at the word *cripple*, as they do not at *handicapped* or *disabled*. Perhaps I want them to wince. I want them to see me as a tough customer, one to whom the fates/gods/viruses have not been kind, but who can face the brutal truth of her existence squarely. As a cripple, I swagger. But, to be fair to myself, a certain amount of honesty underlies my choice. *Cripple* seems to me a clean word, straightforward and precise. . . . As a lover of words, I like the accuracy with which it describes my condition: I have lost the full use of my limbs" (Nancy Mairs). Do not refer to a disease or a condition as a "crippler." *See also* disability/disabilities, handicapped, "insider/outsider" rule, wheelchair-bound.

Cro-Magnon man *Cro-Magnon(s), Homo sapiens, Neanderthal, prehistoric people.*

crone in other times, the crone was a wise, balanced, powerful elder honored by her society. Although this role is generally unacknowledged today, some women are reclaiming it, suggesting we invite some of our many wise older women to appear alongside our wise older men at public events, in newspaper columns, on speaker podiums, at society's head tables.

crooner this term tends to be associated with male singers, so either use it also for women or consider a more inclusive alternative: *pop singer, popular singer, vocalist, balladeer, warbler, blues singer. See also* torch singer.

crossbowman *crossbow archer, archer.*

cross-dresser "cross-dressers use attitude, clothing, and perhaps makeup to give the appearance of belonging to the other sex or to an androgynous middle ground. Most modern women may be considered cross-dressers since they often wear clothing normally intended for men. What is a new phenomenon is the rapidly rising number of men who wear women's clothing. Because a male-dominated society frowns on its members mimicking the 'inferior' female class, male cross-dressers are usually deep in the closet" (Martine Rothblatt, *The Apartheid of Sex*). It's true that when a woman wears slacks, a suit jacket, a button-down shirt, and an ultra-short haircut, she's considered "chic," not a cross-dresser. Kate Bornstein *(Gender Outlaw)* says most cross-dressers hold down mainstream jobs, careers, or professions, are married, and are practicing heterosexuals—the misconception is that they are gay or prostitutes. A female or male impersonator cross-dresses as a performing artist and/or as a stage personality but may or may not consider themselves to be transgendered. *See also* transgenderist.

crown prince/crown princess acceptable terms. Or, *heir apparent, heir to the throne*. However, a crown princess may also be the wife of a crown prince, whereas a man cannot become a crown prince by marrying a crown princess.

crybaby used as a taunt for children of either sex or as a criticism of a whiny adult, also of either sex, this disparagement carries a special sting for boys/men, who are perhaps allowed to cry, but only for extremely important things. *See also* coward.

cry uncle *See* uncle, say.

cubmaster *cub scout pack leader, pack leader.* Cubmaster is a title used by the Boy Scouts of America.

cuckold there is no inclusive alternative and no equivalent for a woman. "What do they call it when a woman is cuckolded? Or doesn't that matter enough to have its own word?" (Lisa Scottoline, *Running From the Law*). You might consider referring to one partner as being unfaithful while the other is betrayed.

culturally deprived/disadvantaged these terms imply being substandard in some vague hierarchy of cultures, whereas very often those so labeled are bicultural, bilingual, and rich in cultural traditions. Clyde W. Ford *(We Can All Get Along)* suggests substituting "culturally dispossessed." It would also clarify your material to describe the specific differences in traditions. If deprivations exist, relate them to their probable causes in social or economic conditions rather than implying there is a generic flaw in an entire people.

culture this broad and complex concept takes in, in one way or another, most of human life. When possible, narrow the term to fit your material and then define it. In the U.S. there is some perception that there is one culture when in fact there are many. Beware of assumptions of what is specific to U.S. culture. *See also* multiculturalism.

cureman *curer.*

curse, the this slang term for menstruation perpetuates the myth that women do not operate on all cylinders throughout the month, and it fosters incorrect and harmful attitudes in preadolescent and adolescent girls and boys.

curmudgeon because this is usually defined and used in reference to men, you may sometimes need more inclusive alternatives: *grouch, grumbler, bad-tempered/peevish/cranky/ petulant person, crosspatch, faultfinder, fire-eater, complainer, pain in the neck, nitpicker, troublemaker.*

currency man *currency dealer/broker, foreign exchange dealer/office.*

custodial parent some people find "custodial" a degrading adjective too evocative of prisons and guards, and would prefer to be simply a mother or a father or a parent. *See also* noncustodial parent.

customs man *customs agent/officer/inspector/official.*

cut the Gordian knot there is nothing wrong with using this phrase, but be aware of how many such expressions in the English language are male-based. Balance their use with female-based expressions, creative expressions of your own, or sex-neutral alternatives: *solve the riddle, solve an intricate/unsolvable problem, find the key, crack a hard nut, figure it out, find a way out, unravel something. See also* sex-linked expressions.

czarina correct term for the wife of a Russian czar. *See also* drug czar.

D

The music of difference, all alive.
The founders and this people, who set in diversity
The base of our living.

—*Muriel Rukeyser*

Diversity is the most basic principle of creation.
No two snowflakes, blades of grass or people are alike.

—*Lynn Maria Laitala*

daddy longlegs this term is correct for the arachnid; the slender-bodied, long-legged fly called daddy longlegs is also known by the more inclusive *crane fly.*

dairy husbandman *dairy scientist.*

dairymaid/dairyman *dairy worker/employee/milker/hand; dairy scientist.* The nonparallel "maid/man" goes more than skin deep; while dairymaids were appearing in entry-level jobs in fairy tales, dairymen were becoming scientists.

dalesman *dale inhabitant/dweller.*

damage controlman *damage controller; spin doctor.*

dame/damsel these terms are outdated and inappropriate and "dame" (except when capitalized and used for the official British title) is belittling. Alternatives include *woman, person, adult; young woman, teenager, adolescent.*

Dame Fortune this term is not grievously pejorative (presumably it refers to the "fickleness" of woman and the need to court her favors), but for those who need a sex-neutral alternative consider *fortune/Fortune, luck, chance, happy chance, wheels of fortune/chance, roll/throw of the dice, turn of the cards, luck of the draw, lucky stroke, the way things fall, how the cookie* *crumbles, the breaks, how the ball bounces, serendipity, happenstance, destiny, kismet, fate, fickle finger of fate, fortuity, whirligig of chance.*

dancing girl *dancer.*

dandy because only men are dandies (and because not many men like being called dandies), consider sex-neutral alternatives: *fashion plate, fancy/ sharp/conspicuous/fashionable dresser, tailor's/sartorial dream, a person it pays to dress, one who keeps the tailor in business, clothes-conscious person.*

danseur/danseuse a danseur is a principal (but not the principal) male dancer in a ballet company, a soloist, and a danseuse is a principal (but not the principal) female soloist. Retain "danseur" and "danseuse" for their specific meaning within ballet companies, but to describe a woman or a man who dances ballet nonprofessionally use *ballet dancer*. *See also* ballerina, premier danseur, prima ballerina.

darkest Africa/the dark continent these phrases are Eurocentric, ethnocentric, and inaccurate (on the literal level, only 20% of the African continent is wooded savanna; on the metaphorical level, Africa was "dark," i.e., unknown, only to those who didn't live there). *See also* Africa.

date inclusive term for someone of the same or opposite sex one makes arrangements to spend time with. For the person who pays for sex, use "prostitute user." *See also* prostitute.

date rape although this term is still not found in most dictionaries, it has appeared in print since 1985. Date rape may account for up to 80% of all sexual assaults. According to figures presented to the Senate Judiciary Committee in 1990, one in seven college women will be raped by the time she graduates, most often by someone she knows. One of the problems associated with date rape is that prosecutors and police investigators tend to give less credit to a charge of rape from someone who knew or who may even have had previous consensual sex with the rapist. However, taking something without permission is always wrong; the benefactor who often gives to a favorite charity will lodge a charge of theft if that charity decides to break into the benefactor's house one night to obtain additional funds. It is heterosexist to assume that date rape always involves a woman and a man. *See also* provoke, rape, rape victim, rapist, sexual harassment, "she asked for it," victim, violence.

daughter good sex-specific word for a female offspring. Inclusive alternatives: *child, descendant, offspring.*

daughterboard *board.* But retain "motherboard," q.v.

daughter cell leave as is; this is a biology term with specific meanings.

daughter track this media catchphrase describes women whose careers may be threatened because of time spent caring for elderly relatives; 11% of working caregivers (almost all of whom are women) quit or are fired. According to some figures, U.S. women spend an average of 19 years helping their parents or parents-in-law. Those men and women involved in both raising children and caring for parents are referred to as the sandwich generation.

David and Goliath there is nothing wrong with this phrase—it is in fact evocative and useful, but be aware of how many such expressions in the English language are male-based. Balance their use with female-based expressions, creative expressions of your own, or sex-neutral alternatives (which in this case are very much "second best" choices, but may be needed in a particular context): *unequal contest, unequal contestants, unexpected defeat. See also* sex-linked expressions.

Davy Jones's locker there is nothing wrong with using this colorful phrase, but be aware of how many such expressions in the English language are male-based. Balance their use with female-based expressions, creative expressions of your own, or sex-neutral alternatives: *ocean/sea bottom, the briny deep. See also* sex-linked expressions.

deaconess *deacon*, except when specific denominations designate "deaconess" as the office for women; in some churches "deaconess" is the functional equal of "deacon." Although most translations of the Bible use "deaconess," the original Greek used the same word—"diakonos"—for both sexes. And these women had the game as well as the name: in the early Church both men and women functioned as deacons. Whenever possible use the more authentic "deacon."

deadbeat dad "deadbeats" are people who don't pay their debts; if a noncustodial parent habitually fails to make timely court-ordered (or agreed-upon) support payments or ignores them altogether, it is hard to accept that "deadbeat dad/mom/parent" is unjustly pejorative and inappropriate, although a fine line separates labeling and describing. The biggest problem with the term is using it for people who don't fit the bill, for those who are making every effort to be faithful to their commitment but are dogged by unemployment or poor health, or for all noncustodial parents as a hostile stereotype.

dead man (empty liquor/beer bottle) *dead one.* ("Dead soldier" and "dead marine" are also seen listed as alternatives, but it is to be hoped they would be considered too ugly and morbid to be used.) According to the explanation in *Why Do We Say It?* in both empty liquor bottles and in the dead, the "spirits" are no longer present.

dead men tell no tales *the dead tell no tales.*

deaf/Deaf people born with a hearing loss, who can hear loud noises (like a jackhammer or an airplane) but cannot hear and/or understand speech, will function as and refer to themselves as "deaf." They will rely on visual more than auditory cues to understand spoken messages—whether through speech reading, sign language, or some other visual mode of communication; they will generally go to school with other people who are deaf and will probably use sign language and be a part of Deaf culture. (This scenario is not true for those who lose their hearing after living as a hearing person.) Use deaf only as an adjective ("deaf persons," not "the deaf"). According to the convention proposed by James Woodward in 1972, lowercase *deaf* refers to the audiological condition of not hearing; uppercase *Deaf* refers to a particular group of deaf people who share a culture and a language—American Sign Language (ASL), which is the native language of the Deaf in the United States. Members of this group live in the U.S. and Canada, have inherited their sign language, use it as a primary means of communication among themselves, and share beliefs about themselves and about their connection to the larger society. People who have lost their hearing because of illness, trauma, or age share the condition of not hearing, but they do not share the knowledge, beliefs, and practices that make up Deaf culture. Use "Deaf" for those who self-identify that way. Avoid terms like hearing-disabled/-impaired/-handicapped, auditorily handicapped, nonhearing. Because "hearing-impaired" can mean anything from hard of hearing to profoundly deaf, it is ambiguous and neither the profoundly deaf nor the hard of hearing think it means them; agencies using "hearing-impaired" in their titles or literature have been changing it. The International Federation of the Hard of Hearing, the World Federation of the Deaf, and other major organizations agree that "hearing-impaired" is no longer acceptable, and that "deaf" and "hard of hearing" are the terms of choice. Some Deaf people use "Deaf" to mean "a Deaf person" ("the Deafs I know don't think that way"). This usage is unacceptable from a hearing person and not liked by some Deaf people either. Some Deaf persons use "Deafie" as a term of affection; others dislike it. Expressions that use "deaf" metaphorically ("turned a deaf ear," "deaf to their request," "their story fell on deaf ears") associate negative personal qualities with deafness. Consider using instead: *unmoved, unwilling to listen, unconcerned, indifferent, inattentive, heedless, unswerving, insensitive.* **See also** disability/disabilities, handicapped, impaired, "inside/outsider" rule, "people first" rule, "the."

deaf and dumb/deaf-mute/dumb these offensive terms are also usually incorrect as they indicate an inability to speak or communicate; most deaf people have functioning vocal chords although they may choose not to use them (because of the difficulty of imitating sounds never heard) and they communicate fully and expressively by means of some form of sign language. For all three terms use simply *deaf*.

dear/dearie as long ago as 1687 playwright Aphra Behn wrote, "Dear me no Dears, Sir." These terms are patronizing and inappropriate when used by a man or a woman to someone (most often a woman) who has not given permission to be so addressed. These terms especially do not belong in the workplace or in social interactions with strangers where the lower-power person must tolerate an unwanted and insincere intimacy. Nearly 20 years ago, the Ford Motor Company advised its dealers, "Never call a would-be buyer 'honey' or 'dear.'" *See also* courts (judicial), honey/hon.

dear John letter, send a for a woman, use *send a dear Jane letter. If you mean in general to reject someone: jilt, brush someone off, show someone the door, give the gate to someone, swear off someone, give someone the air, whistle someone down the wind, send someone packing.*

Dear Sir *See* salutations (letters).

death the word is inclusive. However, death itself is sexist, racist, and classist; in the U.S., men in all age groups die earlier than women in the same age groups, and black men die even younger than white men. Depending on age, black men's rates of death are two and a half to nearly six times that of white women. In general, men die an average of eight years earlier than women. Those with the least economic resources have the highest rate of infant mortality, more maternal deaths, and a higher incidence of death from violent causes. *See also* violence.

deathsman *executioner.*

debonair because the usage of "debonair" seems limited to men (although it need not be—in *L'Allegro*, poet John Milton used it to describe a goddess) you may want alternatives: *jaunty, lighthearted, vivacious, breezy, nonchalant, free and easy, merry, cheery, sunny, sporty; well-mannered, well-bred, polite, refined, civil, charming, suave, courteous, urbane, gracious, graceful, obliging, affable.*

debutante *debutant,* except where "debutante" is still used for a young woman making her formal debut into society. *See also* "feminine" word endings.

deckman *log roller, deck worker; deckhand.*

defect/defective people are not "defective" and they do not have "defects"; they have disabilities. *See also* birth defect, disability/disabilities.

defenseman *defense, defensive/defense player.* Or, use specific term: *goalie, goalkeeper, goaltender, guard, linebacker. See also* lineman.

deformed/deformity people are not "deformed" and they do not have "deformities"; they are people with orthopedic or physical disabilities. *See also* disability/disabilities.

delivery boy/delivery man *deliverer, delivery driver/clerk, merchandise deliverer, porter, messenger, carrier, courier, runner; delivery truck/ system.*

dementia the *Publication Manual of the American Psychological Association,* 4th ed., says the term "dementia" is preferred to "senility"; "senile dementia of the Alzheimer's type" is an accepted term. *See also* ageism, Alzheimer's disease, senility.

demijohn leave as is because of its specific meaning and lack of alternatives. The word is actually a mistranslation of the French "dame-jeanne" meaning Lady Jane.

demimondaine if you mean prostitute, use *prostitute.* If you mean someone on the fringes of society, use *lowlife, riffraff, outcast, down-and-outer.*

demolitions man *demolitionist, demolitions expert.*

demure if there are any demure men, nobody is saying so. Consider more sex-neutral alternatives: *retiring, bashful, modest, diffident, reticent, taciturn.*

denigrate this word means to blacken someone metaphorically (the root word is "nigr-" for black). Consider using instead *disparage, defame, belittle, run down, revile, vilify, criticize, speak ill of, put down, do a hatchet job on, badmouth.*

den mother this term hearkens back to a brief era when mothers were responsible for the children's activities. Today, both men and women are den leaders; they do not necessarily even have children of their own. For a sex-neutral alternative use *den/group leader.*

dentist man or woman. Women are not particularly new to the profession: the School of Dentistry of Paris, founded in 1884, accepted students of both sexes from the beginning.

depot master *depot chief/supervisor.*

deskman *desk clerk/jockey. See also* newspaperman.

detail man *detailer, pharmaceutical sales agent, pharmaceutical company representative, representative, sales rep.*

deus ex machina this Latin phrase, "god from a machine" (because sometimes in Greek and Roman plays a god arrived onstage by means of a crane to produce a "providential" ending), is appropriate for either sex. However, since "deus" is in the masculine gender and since it is used most often in masculine contexts, occasionally you may want an alternative: *last-minute rescuer, eleventh-hour deliverer; contrived solution.*

developing nation/country *See* undeveloped/underdeveloped nation.

developmental disability although you can use the adjective "developmentally disabled" if space requires it, it is preferable to use "person/child with a developmental disability." *See also* disability/disabilities, "people first" rule.

deviant this is unacceptable when used for human beings, although there may be behavior that deviates from some statistical norms for human activity. It's an oddity of our perspective that we do not routinely refer to murderers or terrorists as deviants, but some of us refer that way to lesbians and gay men.

devil/he *devil/it.* Our idea of the devil is so male that we use a prefix ("she-devil") when we want to convey anything else. There is nothing but human imagination to account for the maleness of the devil; the same is true of the maleness of God. One could say, "win some, lose some," but both misattributions of maleness have been harmful to society, to women, and to men.

devotee woman or man. Unlike similar words borrowed from French— divorcé/divorcée, fiancé/fiancée, protégé/protégée—this one is used in the feminine form and without its accent for both sexes. Some have suggested using "-ee" for all such words, as is done in "employee."

diamond in the rough this has always been used for men, although there is no reason it couldn't also refer to women. If you want something less male-associated, use *rough/gauche/crude/ unpolished/untutored person, raw material, someone with rough edges/a little rough around the edges, someone with hidden talents/potential.*

diamonds are a girl's best friend at least consider the source of this inane and demeaning expression: a 1930s DeBeers ad campaign.

dick this slang term can mean (1) detective (if you want alternatives use *gumshoe, private eye, tail, shadow, flatfoot*); (2) penis (leave as is); (3) stupid person (*dork* is inclusive). Dick Hannasch adds, "Dick is also a nice name."

die man *die designer; die engraver/cutter.*

differently abled *See* disability/disabilities.

dike *See* dyke.

dingbat *kook, nitwit.* Thanks primarily to television's Archie Bunker, this technically inclusive word seems reserved for women.

directress *director. See also* "feminine" word endings, glass ceiling.

dirty old man ageist as well as sexist. This stereotype conveys very little real information. Describe instead what the person is doing, thinking, or saying. *See also* lech/lecher, satyr, pederast, pedophile, womanizer.

disability/disabilities when writing about a disability or disabilities (these are the preferred terms): (1) Mention a disability only when it bears directly on your material. (2) Complex human beings do not appreciate being defined solely in terms of a disability, so speak of the person first, then the disability (instead of "an arthritic," "an epileptic," or "a hemophiliac," use "someone with arthritis, epilepsy," etc.). Avoid also the construction, "is diabetic, autistic"; use instead "with/has diabetes, autism." In the same way, people are not their missing part or surgical procedure (instead of "amputee," "laryngectomee," "mastectomee," "ostomate," etc., use "someone who had an amputation, laryngectomy, mastectomy, ostomy"). Occasionally it is acceptable to use "disabled persons" (but never "the disabled") to alternate with "people with disabilities" or because of space limitations. (3) An illness is a disease; a disability is a condition. Cerebral palsy, epilepsy, arthritis, etc., are not diseases; they are conditions. (4) Emphasize abilities, not limitations (instead of "uses crutches/braces" say "walks with crutches/braces"), but not to the point of euphemism, of excessive or patronizing praise, or of portraying some people with disabilities as especially courageous or superhuman; this raises an unfair expectation that all people with disabilities should achieve at this level. (5) Do not use adjectives as nouns, as in "the disabled," "the blind," "the deaf." (6) Delete or replace such terms as abnormal; atypical; birth defect (congenital disability, someone born with...); burden/drain; crippled; defect/defective; deficient; deformed/deformity (orthopedic/physical disability); fit (seizure); gimp; harelip (cleft palate); invalid; lame; learning disabled (someone with/who has a learning disability); maimed; normal; patient (use only for someone in a hospital or under a healthcare specialist's immediate care); physical handicap (physical disability); plight; poor; spastic/spaz (someone who has cerebral palsy); stricken with (incurred); stutterer (person with speech impediment); unfit; unfortunate; withered. (7) The adjective is "disability," not "disabled," in such terms as the disability movement, the disability rights movement, disability activists, disability advocates, disability community. (8) Disability is not a fate worse than death; avoid giving the added emotional baggage of sensationalized words and phrases describing a disabling condition. Individuals with disabilities are increasingly insisting that the language used to describe them be emotionally neutral; avoid phrases that conjure up tragedy: suffers from, afflicted with, stricken with, bound, confined, sentenced to, prisoner, victim of, poor, unfortunate. Avoid referring to people with disabilities as a "drain" or a "burden" on family and friends, although they may represent "added/additional responsibilities." (9) Metaphors featuring disabilities ("deaf to our wishes," "blind to the truth") may be inappropriate or unintentionally offensive. (10) In the effort to find language to describe a reality that often had no positive descriptors, some terms have surfaced that tend to be trendy and euphemistic and are better avoided: differently abled, exceptional, handicapable, inconvenienced, mentally different, people with differing abilities, physically challenged, temporarily able-bodied. "Granted, some people with disabilities use the phrases. . . . But those of us who are active in the disability rights movement generally reject these terms as an insulting denial of our life experience, and of our hard-won community identity" (Laura Hershey, *RESIST Newsletter*). (11) When writing or speaking about people with disabilities, avoid portraying them as "other": "I felt permanently exiled from 'normality.' Whether imposed by self or society, this outsider status—and not the disability itself—constitutes the most daunting barrier for most people with physical impairments, because it, even more than flights of steps or elevators without braille, prevents them from participating fully in the ordinary world, where most of life's satisfactions dwell" (Nancy Mairs, *Waist-High in the World*). *See also* able-bodied, accessible, adjectives used as nouns, afflicted with, amputee, bedridden, blind, cerebral palsied, challenged, confined, cripple, deaf/Deaf, deaf and dumb/deaf-mute/ dumb, defect/defective, developmental disability, epileptic, exceptional, handicapism, handicapped, health appliance, idiot/idiocy, impaired, insane/insanity, learning disability, leper/leprosy, lip reading, mongolism/ mongoloid, paraplegic, "people first" rule, "physically challenged," quadriplegic, retard/retarded, schizophrenic, spastic, special, suffers from, "the," victim, wheelchair-bound.

disadvantaged *See* underprivileged.

discovery of America only from the most Eurocentric of perspectives can a continent inhabited by millions of people be "discovered." "'Discovery' terminology demeans and trivializes Third World and indigenous peoples" (library cataloger Sanford Berman). Oscar Wilde said, "It is a vulgar error to suppose that America was ever discovered. It was merely detected." The 40-year period following Columbus's arrival in the western hemisphere saw one of the greatest losses of human life in history. The "discoverers" had no interest in or respect for nature and human beings, but a high interest in and respect for gold and wealth—attitudes still seen today in the lack of respect society has for "nonproductive" individuals. Write, speak, and teach about American history and the origins of the U.S. from multiple perspectives. Instead of discovery, use terms like "arrival," "encounter," "colonization." *See also* savage.

discrimination when people's choices of and access to employment, education, housing, resources, and other public goods are limited by or dealt with differently because of their sex, ethnicity, age, religion, disability, sexual orientation, looks, or other class or category, discrimination exists.

diseur/diseuse *monologuist, soliloquist, professional reciter.* Or, use the base term, "diseur," for both sexes.

displaced homemaker this sex-specific term (defined as a woman whose principal job has been homemaking and who has lost her main source of income because of divorce, separation, widowhood, spousal disability, or loss of eligibility for public assistance) has no companion term for a man, although federal legislation and funding dictate that financial assistance for people in this situation be available to men as well as to women. An estimated 40% of homemakers fall into poverty following displacement; 58% are over 65; one in four is a minority woman. The first year after divorce, the standard of living for women and their children declines 73% while the standard of living for men rises 42% *(Congressional Caucus for Women's Issues)*. Approximately 60% of displaced homemakers are classified poor or near-poor; 45% do not have a high-school diploma. *See also* alimony, child custody, divorce, wage earner, working wife, working mother.

display man *displayer, merchandise displayer; window dresser; sign painter.*

dissemination although this word (meaning "scattering seed") is related to "semen" ("seed") it is not associated in ways that make it sexist; nor is it functionally sexist—anyone may disseminate information. Many words (e.g., "family" and "familiar," "guard" and "garden") derive from a common root but still have independent lives. *See also* seminal, seminar.

distaff side the female line or maternal branch of a family tree is called the "distaff side" because spinning (the distaff was used in spinning) was considered women's work. The male line or paternal branch is called the "spear side" (a term that doesn't appear in most dictionaries) because fighting was considered men's work. Less sexist terms include *female/ male line, maternal/paternal branch/line of descent.*

district lineman *district line maintainer. See also* lineman.

ditz/ditzy these terms seem used primarily of women, so you may want more inclusive-appearing alternatives: *out to lunch, space ranger, flake, out of it, on another planet, with one's head in the clouds, not all there, missing some marbles, with a mind like a sieve, mindless, brainless wonder, dense, muddleheaded, not bright, half-witted, dull-witted, dim-witted, thick-headed, thick-witted, inane. See also* airhead.

diversity at its simplest "diversity" means "variety": the makeup of the workforce, the student body, the organization reflects the diversity of the U.S. population. "The demands for diversity, for a government that 'looks like America,' go back over our history. What is different is our image of what America looks like. . . . When we talk about diversity now we are talking about race and gender and ethnicity. There was a time when geography was so important that the Constitution wouldn't allow a president and vice president from the same state. Diversity was a collection of white males from different places on the map. . . . Critics say that the claims of diversity are splintering America, dividing and subdividing us into our warring parts. Yet Americans have become less—not more—conscious of region, religion, nationality. It can happen with race and gender as well" (Ellen Goodman). Business leader Lawrence Perlman says, "Diversity is so important to companies not because it is the right thing to do, although it is, but because it is critical to competitiveness. I can't think of a worse fate for any organization than to become a place where everyone thinks the same and a place where everyone, in effect, is the same."

divorce avoid phrases like "he divorced her" or "she divorced him" unless you know this was the case and it is important to say so. Use instead they were divorced, they filed for divorce, they divorced. Divorce in the United States is often sexist and racist. When it first appeared over 20 years ago, the no-fault divorce was hailed as a quick and equitable solution to an unsalvageable marriage. However, according to Fred Moody (in *Seattle Weekly*), "Instead of reducing inequality between the sexes, no-fault divorce has widened the gap in status between men and women, and is the leading cause of the well-documented feminization of poverty in America." Lenore Weitzman *(The Divorce Revolution)* agrees: "No fault was taken to mean no responsibility," resulting in "a systematic impoverishment of women and children." (Over half the 18 million poor children in this country are living in single-parent homes caused by divorce.) Five years after a divorce, a woman's income is 30% of what it was during the marriage; a man's is 14% more. The lack of alimony and lax child-support enforcement in no-fault divorces contribute to the problem, with black women hurt the most: they are half again as likely as white women to be awarded alimony, and much less likely than white women to get property settlements. Weitzman suggests that husband and wife ought to "both share the burdens of divorce in America." *See also* child custody, courts (judicial), noncustodial parent.

divorcé/divorcée *divorced person, divorcé.* Or, *unmarried/unwed/formerly married person.* Or, nothing at all (a person's marital status is seldom relevant). It has usually been the woman who is called a divorcée (often with pejorative overtones), while a man is referred to as unmarried, a bachelor, or as someone who is divorced. Use parallel terms for both sexes. Casey Miller and Kate Swift *(The Handbook of Nonsexist Writing)* persuasively recommend the standard form of French words, that is, "divorcé" for both sexes. Note that "émigré" is used that way in English. This guideline can also be applied to such words as blond, brunet, chaperon, confidant, clairvoyant, debutant, fiancé, habitué, protégé.

divorced father/divorced mother *father/mother, single parent.*

dizzy with the exception of the nickname (Dizzy Dean, Dizzy Gillespie), which doesn't have the same connotations, this term is used only for women, especially for women with blond hair. For inclusive alternatives *see* ditz/ditzy, scatterbrained.

dockman *dockhand, dockworker, docker, stevedore, shoreworker, shorehand, longshore worker, longshorehand, wharfworker, wharfhand.*

dockmaster *dock supervisor/boss.*

doctoress *doctor.* Do use "woman doctor" where sex is irrelevant or where you would not use "man doctor." *See also* "feminine" word endings.

dogcatcher *animal control officer.* "Dogcatcher" is considered outdated and derogatory; it also seems to call to mind a man, whereas at least as many women as men work as animal control officers.

doll/dollie-bird/dolly-bird/China doll/Kewpie doll/dolled up/all dolled up these terms are patronizing, belittling, inaccurate, and objectifying. The terms "dolled up/all dolled up" are generally reserved for women, but can be, and have been, used of men. As long as we have Ken, men can be dolls too, although it is not perceived as quite so patronizing to call them "dolls." *See also* living doll.

domestic not sexist per se, "domestic" is sometimes used to further a sexist context—for example, the assumption that all domestic matters belong a priori to the nearest woman and are of no interest to any men.

domestic abuse/violence "domestic," with its connotations of coziness and warmth (one definition is "fond of homelife and household affairs"), tends to offset "violence" and "abuse"; "It makes the violence sound domesticated, and it makes it sound like a special category of violence that is somehow different from other kinds—less serious" (Ann Jones, in *Ms.*). The term "domestic violence" also conceals both the sexes of perpetrator and victim and the kinds of acts involved. Whenever possible, identify who is doing violence to whom, and what specifically, on the continuum of violent acts, they are doing. The latter could range from mind-games and put-downs to battering to attempted murder. It also includes other physical and emotional abuse, rape, threats, destroying property, threatening suicide, controlling finances and activities. Battering is the most prevalent cause of injury to women, exceeding rapes, muggings, and even auto accidents, and 95% of all assaults are committed by men on their spouses. *See also* rape, "she asked for it," violence.

domestic partner this is a useful and recognized term for someone of either sex in a committed relationship with someone of the opposite or same sex. *See also* boyfriend, domestic partnership, girlfriend, marriage.

domestic partnership this term is the one most often used in legal and business issues relating to unmarried people in a stable, committed relationship. Pioneered in San Francisco in 1991 and now available in several large cities and small towns, domestic partnership plans (some 35 states and municipalities officially recognize domestic partnerships) allow lesbians and gay men to register their relationships officially, just as heterosexual couples obtain a marriage license; some domestic partnerships allow city or corporate employees to be treated as married in terms of healthcare and other benefits. When American Express announced it was offering domestic partner benefits to employees, the stated reason was to "help us attract and retain outstanding people." Chair Harvey Golub said that although committed same-sex relationships involved probably only 1% of the corporation, domestic partner benefits were an important symbolic and equity issue. Denmark has recognized gay marriage since 1989; Spain adopted a national domestic partners policy, including same-sex partners; South Africa's new constitution protects against unfair discrimination on the basis of sexual orientation; Canada's House of Commons passed legal protections nationwide for gays and lesbians. "The world is telling the United States that we are behind the times in recognition of civil and human rights for gay people" (Bill Stosine, in the Minneapolis *Star Tribune*).

dominatrix *dominator, dominating partner. See also* "feminine" word endings.

dominie always a man. *See also* clergyman, schoolmaster.

don to mean a Spanish gentleman, grandee, or Mafia leader, "don" always refers to a man. Retain "don" as it is used at a college of Oxford or Cambridge, although you can sometimes replace it with *head, tutor, fellow.* For its (rare) use in the U.S., its meaning is simply *college/ university professor.*

Don Juan this term has no parallel for a woman and reinforces some stereotypes about men from Spanish-speaking countries, but it has no precise equivalent. For a sex-neutral term try *lover, dashing lover, great romantic, paramour, heartthrob, flirt, sexually aggressive/sexually active person, seducer, bedhopper, swinger.*

don't know from Adam *See* Adam, don't know from.

doorman *doorkeeper, porter, concierge, security guard, guard, caretaker, commissionaire, attendant, door attendant, doorkeep; warder, beadle; sentry, gatekeeper; bouncer.*

doubting Thomas there is nothing wrong with using this phrase, but be aware of how many such expressions in the English language are male-based. Balance their use with female-based expressions, creative expressions of your own, or sex-neutral alternatives: *skeptic, doubter, unbeliever, disbeliever, nonbeliever, cynic, questioner, pessimist, defeatist,* *someone from Missouri.* The tongue-in-cheek "doubting Thomasina" is sometimes seen. *See also* sex-linked expressions.

doughboy use as is in historical context. Or: *World War I soldier.*

dowager there is no parallel for a man. One definition of "dowager" reflects on a woman's marital status (widowed) while the other reflects mainly on her age. Decide if this information is relevant and then use descriptive terms that apply to both men and women. It should not be difficult to get along without the word; we have talked about men for centuries without using a similar term.

Down syndrome *See* mongolism/mongoloid.

down under this term referring to Australia or New Zealand is a good example of perspective; it's only "down under" if you're standing in the northern hemisphere. People from the southern hemisphere generally hear the term only when they're traveling in the United States and, so far, they tolerate it good-naturedly.

dowry death *See* suttee.

doyen/doyenne the French terms are functionally parallel; if you like the effect, *allez-y!* Otherwise consider *dean, senior/oldest member.*

draft "no form of sex discrimination, against either gender, has been as devastating and deadly as the military draft" (Mel Feit, in *University of Dayton Review*). Feit says, "We live in a strange society in which conscripted men have been deprived of their freedom and comfort, stripped of their dignity and civil rights, forced to leave their family and friends, compelled to interrupt their careers, brutally trained to kill or be killed, murdered and maimed in warfare, and where the public perception is that the victims of sex discrimination have been women." Whether it is of benefit to discuss who has been the most discriminated against, there is no denying the gender genocide in the males-only draft and centuries of males-only combat laws. The charge that "men make wars" and that therefore it is only right that they (and not women) fight the wars is indefensible. For one thing, there are the men who make the wars and the men who actually go to war; of the 56,886 Americans killed in the Vietnam War, there were 0 lawmakers. For another thing, women, from Queen Elizabeth I to Margaret Thatcher, have sent men into wars. *See also* armed forces, combat, coward, glass cellar, serviceman, sexism, warrior, weekend warrior.

draft dodger currently this can only be a young man/man because of the males-only draft. It is a values-laden, judgmental, sexist, and even classist term that is better replaced by a more neutral and specific term: *nonregistrant, conscientious objector/C.O., religious/moral/ethical/war objector, resister, refuser, noncombatant, noncooperator, draft exempt/*

deferred, medically unfit/exempt/deferred, passive resister, peace activist, organizer, antiwar organizer, pacifist. During certain periods of U.S. history, it was a common and legal practice to hire a substitute to fight in one's place. Grover Cleveland hired a substitute rather than fight in the Civil War but then had to worry that this would be held against him in the presidential campaign of 1884. But Cleveland was fortunate: his Republican opponent, James Blaine, had also hired a soldier substitute. One did, of course, need to be able to afford such a tactic; poor men did not have the option. This legacy continues today: the lawmakers who make the wars do not become foot soldiers in these wars; neither, generally, do their sons or the sons of other rich, powerful individuals. *See also* coward, draft.

draftsman *drafter, artist, copyist, landscape/technical artist, designer, architect, engineer, limner, drawer, sketcher, delineator.* If none of these terms work in your context and you cannot circumlocute, use *draftswoman/draftsman*; avoid the cumbersome "draftsperson."

draftsmanship *drafting expertise/skill.*

dragoman nonsexist; comes from an Arabic word for "interpreter" and the plural is either dragomans or dragomen. If the word's sexist appearance bothers you, use *interpreter, translator, travel agent, guide.*

drag/drag queen these terms usually refer to gay men, especially transvestites, cross-dressers, female impersonators. The terms are derogatory when used by those outside the gay community, usually acceptable when used within. *See also* "insider/outsider" rule, transgenderist.

drayman *dray driver.*

dredgemaster *dredge operator.*

dressmaker *tailor, custom tailor, clothier, garment designer/worker, mender, alterer, alterations expert, stitcher. See also* couturière, needlewoman.

drillmaster *drill sergeant/instructor.*

droit de seigneur a highly sexist concept that is no longer part of our vocabulary in the way it once was. However, the term may be useful (in quotation marks) to describe what happens in certain cases of sexual harassment of women where there is unequal power: professors and students, bosses and employees, political candidates and campaign workers. There is no parallel term for the absolute power of a woman over a subordinate man (possibly because this has been rare).

drug czar/drug lord/drug king *drug dealer/chief/boss/tycoon/ bigwig/ distributor.*

drugs one way in which the flourishing drug culture attracts young people is by establishing an insider vocabulary of colorful terms that make drugs and drug dealers seem harmless and fun. All drug-related street slang, including the following short list of sex-linked terms, ought to be replaced with words that reflect reality (in parentheses): Aunt Hazel (heroin); auntie (opium); Aunt Mary (marijuana); baglady/bagman (drug dealers); Barbies/Barbie doll (barbiturates); beeper boy (drug dealer); big Harry (heroin); blue johnnies (delirium tremens); boy (heroin); brother (heroin); businessman's lunch (amphetamines); candy man (drug pusher/dealer); Christinas (amphetamines); chick (cocaine); dollies (methadone); George smack (heroin); golden girl (cocaine); good-time man (drug dealer); Harry/Hazel/Henry (heroin); jane (marijuana); jug man/jug broad (drug user, but note grossly nonparallel "man/broad"); junker man or J-man (marijuana smoker); ken doll (barbiturates); kick man (drug dealer); Lady/Lady Snow/Lady White (cocaine); Lady H (heroin); Mary (morphine); Mary Jane/maryjane/Mary J. (marijuana); Mary Warner/Mary Werner/Mary Worner (marijuana); Miss Emma (morphine); pink ladies (barbiturates); schoolboy (codeine); simple simon (psilocybin); sister (morphine); swingman (drug connection/seller); tambourine man (drug dealer); white girl/white lady (cocaine); white goddess (morphine). In a somewhat related drug-euphemism issue, the Texas Longhorn Breeders Association of America has a list of "words that don't send a positive image to the general public" and on it is "drugs"; members are encouraged to call them compounds, health products, or pharmaceuticals.

drugstore cowboy there doesn't seem to be an equally pithy and colorful inclusive substitute for this phrase, especially as it's generally defined as a man who hangs around drugstores or other public places trying to impress women. If you need to describe a woman who hangs around drugstores, etc., "drugstore cowgirl" would probably be understood.

drum majorette *drum major, baton twirler.* **See also** "feminine" word endings.

drunk as a lord *drunk, intoxicated, tight, loaded, well-oiled, stewed to the gills, plastered, smashed, three/four sheets to the wind, half seas over, under the table, lit to the gills, pickled, high as a kite, out of it.* Consider the wisdom of dressing up something tied to numerous social problems; the plain word "drunk" may be the best choice here.

duchess retain for official title, which can refer either to the ruler of a duchy or to the wife or widow of a duke.

dude in the sense of a vacationer at a dude ranch, a dude can be either sex. The casual term, either as a form of address or to refer to a male friend, a boy/man, or an especially attractive man, is usually nonpejorative. There is no equivalent for a woman. For alternatives to "a fancy dresser," *see* dandy.

duenna this is always a woman. If you need a sex-neutral term use *chaperon.*

dukedom *duchy.*

dumb *See* deaf and dumb/deaf-mute/dumb.

dumb blond this cliché is overworked and inaccurate. *See also* blond/ blonde.

dumpman *dumper; dump truck.*

dustman *cleaner, sweeper, sweep, char; garbage collector/hauler, trash/ refuse collector, sanitation worker.*

Dutch the many disparaging phrases that include the word "Dutch" grew out of the bitter trade and marine rivalry that once existed between Great Britain and Holland. Although most of the more than 70 slurs listed in A. A. Roback's 1944 *A Dictionary of International Slurs (Ethnophaulisms)* are rarely used anymore, a few are still seen: "in Dutch" (in disgrace); "double Dutch" (nonsense); "Dutch cheer" (liquor); "Dutching" (according to the *Oxford Dictionary of New Words,* this is jargon in the British food industry for sending substandard food intended for the U.K. market for irradiation in the Netherlands—or other European country that permits irradiation—to mask any bacterial contamination before putting it on sale in British shops). *See also* Dutch courage; Dutchman; Dutch treat; Dutch uncle, talk to like a.

Dutch courage this term has probably not caused many people to think less of the Dutch. However, it is pejorative, and if you want to get around it use *sham courage, courage from a bottle.*

Dutchman *Hollander, Dutch citizen, Dutchwoman and Dutchman.* Plural: *Hollanders, Dutch people, Dutchfolk, Dutchwomen and Dutchmen* (but not "Dutchmen and women").

Dutch treat this term (or "go Dutch") has probably not caused many people to think less of the Dutch or to consider them cheapskates. However, it is pejorative, and if you want to get around it use *separate checks, I insist on paying for myself.*

Dutch uncle, talk to like a *talk to bluntly, rebuke, upbraid, admonish, chide, reprove, reprimand, reproach, scold, chew out, lecture, lay down the law, remonstrate, call on the carpet.*

dwarf although this term is still used in medical contexts, it is sometimes replaced with (when known) precise terminology: *someone who has/ person with achondroplasia.* Rarely does anyone self-identify as a "dwarf." Preferred alternatives include *Little Person/little person, short-statured person, person of short stature. See also* midget.

dyke (woman) this term, of obscure origins, is unacceptable to some lesbians, but it is used by others; it is always unacceptable when used by outsiders. Writer Denise Ohio says that dyke is "a word being reclaimed by the people it's normally used to denigrate. It was a total insult before; now it's showing power, solidarity." *See also* bull dyke, butch, femme/ fem, Gay Rights Movement, homophobia, homosexual, "insider/outsider" rule.

E

Exclusion is always dangerous. Inclusion is the only safety
if we are to have a peaceful world.

—*Pearl S. Buck*

Blessed are the inclusive for they shall be included.

—*Frances E. Willard*

each man for himself *See* every man for himself.

Eagle Scout young men only; this rank in the Boy Scouts of America is not available to young women.

early to bed, early to rise, makes a man healthy, wealthy, and wise *early to bed, early to rise, will make us all healthy, wealthy, and wise.*

earth mother there is no parallel term for a man and no inclusive term conveys quite the same idea of the wholesome, down-to-earth, back-to-nature woman. Despite the generally negative association of women with nature, this term seems positive and descriptive enough to retain. *See also* Mother Earth, Mother Nature, nature/she.

East Indian when applied to the people of India, this term is considered colonialist; they are properly called Indians. To avoid confusion with American Indians, use "Asian Indian." In the U.S., those from India or of Asian Indian descent are known as Asian Indian Americans. (The peoples of Burma, Bangladesh, Pakistan, and Sri Lanka are not Indians.) *See also* Asian American.

easy (referring to a woman) meaning "sexually willing," this adjective has been used only of women; the fact that sexually willing—and thus "easy"—men are doing the labeling and remaining unlabeled is one of the curiosities of our culture.

Ebonics *See* Black English.

ecofeminism coined by French writer Françoise d'Eaubonne in 1974, the term describes the synthesis of feminist and ecological concerns. According to Lindsy Van Gelder (in *Ms.*), "Ecofeminists believe that the domination of women and of nature comes from the same impulse. . . . In an ecofeminist society, no one would have power over anyone else, because there would be an understanding that we're all part of the interconnected web of life." Ecofeminists say environmental problems grow out of a logic of domination that oppresses and exploits women and nature, and that the best hope of saving the natural world lies in traditionally female (cooperation/partnership) values. "Some call it a philosophy, others find in it a spirituality, and most believe that it calls them to political action" (Greta Gaard, *Ecofeminism*). *See also* male hierarchy, Mother Earth, Mother Nature, nature/she.

economically disadvantaged the better term sometimes is *economically exploited.* "Many people of color have a painful history of being exploited for the benefit of European Americans. Blacks were enslaved as a cheap source of labor, Chinese were imported as cheap labor, Native American land was confiscated. 'Economically disadvantaged' sidesteps important issues, while 'economically exploited' more accurately represents the historical plight of people of color" (Clyde W. Ford, *We Can All Get Along*).

education education has not been and is still not an equal opportunity or parallel experience for both sexes and for various income, ability, and ethnic groups in the U.S. When writing about education, include students, teachers, and administrators from diverse backgrounds.

effeminate although this word could theoretically be used in a positive sense (and, in fact, there is a men's movement called Revolutionary Effeminism, which opposes the effects of masculinism), in its most commonly understood sense, it is pejorative and sexist, loaded with cultural stereotypes about what it means to be a man or a woman. Consider instead one of the following inclusive words, which are not synonyms but seem, rather, to be what most people are trying to convey with "effeminate": *passive, gentle, timid, weak, agreeable, docile, particular.*

effete when referring to people, "effete" is always pejorative; one of its meanings is "effeminate," and its roots are related to "giving birth." Consider using less sex-linked alternatives: *devitalized, exhausted; self-indulgent, decadent; overrefined. See also* effeminate.

elder/elderly "elder" in the sense of a respected religious, community, or other leader of either sex is acceptable; it is also used in the sense of "older" ("the elder of the two brothers"); it should not be used as a noun to mean "old person." It is also used as an adjective: Elderhostel, elder care, elder legal services. "Elderly" is unacceptable as a noun ("the elderly") and isn't too popular as an adjective—rarely does anyone self-identify as an elderly person, as it has connotations of diminished health and abilities; sometimes that sense is best conveyed by "frail elderly." The preferred term for most people is the adjective "older" ("as an older man, I think . . ." or "the older couple in front of us"). *See also* ageism, frail elderly, old, senior/senior citizen.

elder statesman *senior/longtime/career diplomat, skilled/career/experienced politician, foreign relations expert, power behind the throne.*

Electra complex acceptable sex-specific term; the parallel is "Oedipus complex."

Elks (Benevolent Protective Order of Elks) after 128 years of males-only membership, individual lodges across the U.S. have begun voting to admit women.

emancipate nonsexist; the Latin root means to free from ownership.

emasculate in the metaphorical sense, this may very occasionally be the word you mean, but too often it indicts something or someone (often a woman) for a process that depends just as importantly on a man's willingness to be emasculated, and unflatteringly implies that he is a passive victim. There are no parallel terms relating to women for "emasculate," "unman," and "castrate." For sex-neutral terms consider *disarm, disable, weaken, incapacitate, undermine, deprive of courage/strength/ vigor/power, unhinge, unnerve, devitalize, attenuate, shatter, exhaust, disqualify, invalidate, paralyze, undo, muzzle, enervate, tie the hands of, draw the teeth of, clip the wings of, spike the guns of, take the wind out of one's sails, put a spoke in one's wheels, render hors de combat. See also* castrate, unman.

emerging nation *See* underdeveloped/undeveloped nation.

emeritus "emeritus" is the male form, "emerita" is the female form. As fewer people learn Latin and are able to appreciate the distinction, "emeritus" may come to serve for both sexes, thus eliminating the reinforcement of woman as "other" by the less-common term.

émigré woman or man. Although you might expect to see a companion "émigrée," in English a single term is used for both sexes.

éminence grise the nickname of Père Joseph, French monk, diplomat, and confidant of Cardinal Richelieu, is used today to describe a confidential agent of either sex or, in popular usage, a renowned expert. "Grise" ("gray") was not the color of his hair, but of his habit.

emotional in our culture "emotional" is not an admired trait; the word is most often used as an antonym for "rational" or "intelligent." Largely because of changing social attitudes toward women, "emotional" is not used as often as it once was to rebut a woman's arguments or generally discount her as a thinking human being. The problem today, says M. Adam (in Francis Baumli, *Men Freeing Men*), is that "women can now wax logical while men look silly waxing emotional." Until men are free to wax emotional and "emotional" is a positive word for both sexes, use it cautiously. *See also* irrational.

empress acceptable official title. An empress may be an imperial titleholder in her own right or she may be the wife or widow of an emperor.

emptyheaded *See* airhead.

enchantress *enchanter. See also* "feminine" word endings.

endman this term has such a specific meaning that it is not easily rendered gender-free, the more so since historically minstrels were men; for a woman use *endwoman, end comic.*

enemy/he *enemy/it, enemy/they.*

enfant terrible although this French expression is grammatically masculine, "enfant" refers to both sexes and the term is used inclusively in English-speaking countries as well.

engagement ring this term, which refers to the custom of women wearing engagement rings while men rarely do, is a sexist holdover from the days when women were bargained-for commodities on the marriage market. According to syndicated columnist Diane Crowley, "When a girl's father struck a deal with the family of the groom-to-be, a ring on her finger (somewhat like a 'sold' sign on a TV or a washing machine) warned off other interested parties, and signaled her family's contract to turn her over to the groom. Men were transferors, not transferees, so they did not wear rings." This is not to belittle those who buy, give, or wear engagement rings, but to clarify the meaning of a custom few people question.

engineman *engine operator, engineer.*

England England is one of the countries of Great Britain, which also includes Scotland and Wales; "United Kingdom" refers to Great Britain plus Northern Ireland; "Britain" refers to the island of Great Britain in the period before the reign of Alfred the Great (A.D. 871–899). *See also* British/Briton/Brit, Englishman.

Englishman *Englishwoman and Englishman, English/British citizen/subject, Britisher, Briton, Brit (slang), Englander; the English, English people/ citizens, the British, Britons, Englishwomen and Englishmen* (but not "Englishmen and women"). "English" and "British" are not synonyms; use "English" for those living in England and for anyone of Anglo-Saxon descent in Great Britain and use "British" for those living in England, Scotland, Wales, and Northern Ireland. *See also* British/Briton/Brit, England.

enlisted man *enlistee, service member, recruit, enlisted member/person/ personnel/soldier/sailor, soldier, sailor; enlisted man and enlisted woman.*

entrepreneur in French the word is grammatically masculine, but it is functionally inclusive in both English and French. Almost 30% of sole proprietorships are owned by women.

entryman *entry miner.*

epileptic (noun) *someone with epilepsy.* Manifestations of the disorder are properly called seizures, not fits. *See also* disability/disabilities.

equal pay/equal pay for equal work the Equal Pay Act of 1963 requires that women and men receive equal pay for equal work. *See also* comparable worth.

Equal Rights Amendment (ERA) when writing or speaking about the ERA, it may be helpful to know its background: this proposed amendment to the U.S. Constitution, which failed to obtain ratification by two-thirds of the states, consists of three brief sections. The first says, "Equality of rights under the law shall not be denied or abridged by the United States or by any state on account of sex." The second states that Congress shall have the power to enforce the article, and the third says the amendment will take effect two years after ratification. This extremely simple amendment (different by only one word—"sex"—from the amendment ensuring racial equality) has been adamantly resisted for several reasons: many people have never read the simple, sensible words of the amendment; equal rights for women have been confused with androgyny, sameness of function, and a loss of certain rights specific to women (e.g., not having to register for the draft); and perhaps, as someone once pointed out, the equality of women means the eradication of a servant class—and this may be what fuels some fear. In 1915 President Theodore Roosevelt described a new world—one that has yet to arrive: "We have entered a new day in the great epic march of the ages. For good or for evil the old days have passed; and it rests with us, the men and women now alive, to decide whether in the new days the world is to be a better or a worse place to live in, for our descendants. In this new world women are to stand on an equal footing with men, in ways and to an extent never hitherto dreamed of."

equerry has always been a man.

equestrienne *equestrian. See also* "feminine" word endings.

eraism the assumption that earlier peoples were not our intellectual, moral, or emotional equals constitutes a sort of period chauvinism—the belief that earlier peoples and earlier times were inferior to us and our time. "For some strange reason, we believe that anyone who lived before we were born was in some peculiar way a different kind of human being from any we have come in contact with in our own lifetime. This concept must be changed; we must realize in our bones that almost everything in time and history has changed *except* the human being" (Uta Hagen, *Respect for Acting*, 1973).

errand boy/errand girl *errand runner, runner, messenger, courier, page, clerk, office helper, gofer.*

escape man *escape artist.*

escort service *prostitution service.* Programs that provide drivers or companions to assist older persons with their shopping, errands, and doctor appointments are sometimes called escort services. Because of the confusion with the more common meaning, alternatives might be useful: *transportation/dial-a-ride/chauffeur/elder/transportation services.*

Eskimo in 1977 at the Inuit Circumpolar Conference in Barrow, Alaska, the term "Inuit" ("the people") was officially adopted as a preferred designation for collectively referring to the group of peoples of northern Canada, Greenland, Alaska, and eastern Siberia known as Eskimos. "Eskimo" has long been considered (perhaps incorrectly) to come from a term meaning "raw meat eaters." Some Inuit, but not all, would rather it not be used. "Aleut" is the acceptable designation for the people of the western Alaska Peninsula, the Pribilof Islands, and the Aleutian island chain. Indians native to the Cook Inlet and interior regions of Alaska refer to themselves as "Athabaskans." Inuk (or Innuk) is the singular of Inuit (or Innuit). In Alaska, "Natives" and "Alaska Natives" are the accepted terms for the Inuit, Aleuts, and Athabaskans, when referring to the area's indigenous peoples in the aggregate.

Esquire/Esq. it is correct to address a letter to an attorney of either sex in the U.S. using this courtesy title, e.g., Marian Chernov, Esq. (In Great Britain "Esquire" signifies rank.)

-ess/-ette *See* "feminine" word endings.

ethnic/"ethnics" the adjective "ethnic" is acceptable, the noun "ethnics" is not; use instead *members of ethnic groups, ethnic-group members.* Although not everyone identifies strongly or consistently with an ethnic group, by definition everybody is ethnic; "Margaret Thatcher, Susan B. Anthony and Bach are just as 'ethnic' as Miriam Makeba, Indira Gandhi, and Johnny Colon" (Amoja Three Rivers, *Cultural Etiquette*). "In writing about a multicultural society, authors should take care not to imply that ethnic groups are defined by their departure from some spurious norm— to imply, that is, that *ethnic* means 'not of the mainstream.' Not all minority groups are ethnic, and not all ethnic groups are minorities" (Marilyn Schwartz and the Task Force on Bias-Free Language of the

Association of American University Presses, *Guidelines for Bias-Free Writing). See also* ethnicity, ethnic slurs, race.

ethnicity referring to a person's ethnic character, background, affiliation, or identification, this term is often more appropriate than the imprecise and disputed "race." Identify people by ethnic origin only when that information is central to your material and discuss all ethnic groups in parallel fashion. *See also* ethnic/"ethnics," ethnic slurs, race.

ethnic slurs epithets and slurs label people as less-than-human, which then makes them easier to discount, degrade, and destroy. In *Contreras v. Crown Zellerbach, Inc.,* the Washington Supreme Court held that "racial epithets which were once part of common usage may not now be looked upon as 'mere insulting language.'" They constitute instead a tort of outrage, or "intentional infliction of emotional distress." Richard Delgado (*Harvard Civil Rights–Civil Liberties Law Review*) says, "The racial insult remains one of the most pervasive channels through which discriminatory attitudes are imparted." According to Irving Lewis Allen in his excellent *Unkind Words: Ethnic Labeling from Redskin to WASP,* "Well over a thousand abusive nicknames aimed at more than one hundred different American ethnic groups have been recorded in dictionaries and other studies of our popular speech. Nearly every ethnic group—majority and minority alike—has slurred nearly every other group in the country. . . . If epithets were added for quasi-ethnic groups, such as the hundreds of terms for poor whites and rustics, mostly various white Protestant groups, the number of ethnic epithets in historical American slang and dialect would rise to nearly two thousand terms." In 1944 A. A. Roback collected 1,000 slurs in the English language alone against all nationalities in his *Dictionary of International Slurs (Ethnophaulisms).* Comparing the slurs pre-1940 with those of today provides a record of various immigrant groups' assimilation and acceptance by the wave of earlier immigrants. See also Hugh Rawson, *Wicked Words: A Treasury of Curses, Insults, Put-Downs, and Other Formerly Unprintable Terms From Anglo-Saxon Times to the Present,* and Vivian Jenkins Nelsen, *New Voices in the Media: The INTER-RACE Race & Media Guidebook.* Terms like the following range from moderately to deeply offensive: banana, camel jockey, chico, chink, coolie, coon, cracker, dago, flip, frog, gook, goy, greaser, gringo, guinea, honkie/ honky, jap, kike, kraut, limey, Mexican standoff, mick, oreo, paleface, Pancho, peon, pickaninny, Polack, sand nigger, sheeny, slant, slope, spade, spic/spick, spook, white trash, whitey, wop. (Note that there are no slurs for the British that compare in degree of disparagement to terms for other groups.) *See also* brave (Indian), Chinaman, Chinaman's chance, Chinese fire drill, Dutch treat, Finndian, half-breed/half-caste, hate speech, "Indian giver," Injun, jew boy, "jew down," Jewish American Princess/JAP, Jewish lightning, nigger, Nip, ofay, Oriental, redskin, Redskins (sports team name), shanghai, squaw, welsh (verb), wetback, Yid.

ethnocentrism this is the belief that the ways of one's own group are (1) natural, (2) right for everybody, (3) superior to others' ways. As it is most often used, "ethnocentrism" refers to white people seeing themselves as the center and norm, with everyone else being variations on the theme.

eunuch use this word only in the literal sense of a castrated man, in which case it is a legitimate sex-specific word. For its metaphorical sex-neutral use substitute *weakling, coward, wimp, pushover, doormat, lightweight, loser, craven*. *See also* castrate, emasculate, namby-pamby, sissy, unman.

Eurasian this can refer either to a person of mixed Asian and European descent or to someone who lives in "Eurasia" (the land mass comprising the continents of Europe and Asia). It is ambiguous in some contexts, too broad for precision in others, and considered derogatory in still others.

European American/Euro-American these terms, but most especially the first, are being seen more often, probably in response to the use of designations like Asian American and African American but also as a needed parallel for those designations (instead of the unparalleled default "American" for whites). *See also* "hyphenated Americans."

Eve Eve has traditionally symbolized the tempter, the one by whom evil came into the world; this incidentally leaves Adam looking suggestible, inept, and "belly-oriented," as one writer puts it. The story of the biblical Eve has underwritten highly negative attitudes toward women throughout history, largely because of misogynistic and patriarchal interpretations that labeled her evil, inferior, and seductive. Interpreters who argue Eve's inferiority and subordination to Adam because he was created first fail to apply the argument logically: in the story, God created light, water, land, plants, stars, animals, and finally man. According to this later-is-better hierarchy of creation, woman would be God's final, most glorious effort. (Note the story in the Jewish tradition about Lilith, the woman created simultaneously with Adam; when she wanted to be treated as an equal, Adam asked God to provide him with a more submissive mate, which turned out to be Eve.) *See also* Adam's rib.

even-steven few people perceive this as sex-linked, but it is one of many words based on men's names and you may occasionally want a sex-neutral equivalent: *equally divided, share and share alike, fifty-fifty, even, balanced, go halves, six of one and half a dozen of another.*

everybody and his grandmother/brother *everybody and their grand-mother/grandfather/brother/sister, all the world and their offspring, all* *the world and their dog, everybody and their second cousin, one and all, the whole world, everybody under the sun, every citizen of heaven and earth, everybody, everyone, crowd.* **See also** singular "they."

every dog has his day, and every man his hour *every dog has its day.* Also: *talent will out, cream will rise, to everything there is a season.* In Mexico it's "Every little chapel has its little fiesta" (Suzanne Brock, *Idiom's Delight*).

every inch a king leave as is when referring to a king, and for a queen use *every inch a queen;* otherwise use *a noble person, a regal bearing, an air of command.*

everyman/Everyman *the typical/ordinary person, the archetypical human being, Everyman and Everywoman* (always use together). **See also** average man, common man, man in the street.

every man a king *share the wealth.* From Huey Pierce Long's political campaign, this term referred to his share-the-wealth program.

every man for himself *everyone for themselves* (see singular "they"), *you're on your own, the devil take the hindmost, look out for number one, no time to be lost.* Or, if you like foreign expressions, there is the nonsexist French equivalent: *sauve qui peut!* ("Save yourself if you can!")

every man has his price *everyone has a price.*

every man is a king in his own castle **See** king in his own castle, every man is a.

every man jack *everyone, every single person, every last one of them.* **See also** everybody and his grandmother/brother.

every man's death diminishes me **See** any man's death diminishes me.

every mother's child/son *every last one of them.* **See also** all the world and his wife; everybody and his grandmother/brother; every Tom, Dick, and Harry.

every Tom, Dick, and Harry *every stranger off the street, every so-and-so, anybody at all, any old body, anyone, doesn't matter who it is.* **See also** all the world and his wife, everybody and his grandmother/brother.

evil men do, the *the evil we/people do.* **See also** man's inhumanity to man.

exceptional as used in reference to people with disabilities, this term tends to be vague and euphemistic. Imagine someone has said, "Just what do you mean by that?" and then use that instead. **See also** disability/disabilities, special.

exciseman *excise agent/officer/official/inspector/collector, tax/duty collector.*

exclusive language speech and writing that excludes, intentionally or unintentionally, certain groups of people and their experiences, which makes them invisible to others and less valuable in their own and others' eyes. They become symbolically annihilated. For years most of the advertising, writing, teaching, and speaking in our culture has been about, and directed toward, white, middle-class, Christian, heterosexual, able-bodied men. There is nothing wrong with this category of people; the problem is that there are many other members of society outside this category whose existence has been ignored by exclusive language.

executive almost 95% of the top executives at the largest companies in the U.S. are white and male.

executrix *executor, personal representative, administrator.* In some states "executrix" is still used in official legal matters; in others, the legal term is "personal representative." *See also* "feminine" word endings.

exotic avoid the double standard of using "exotic" to describe Chinese American New Year's dancers if you would not use the word to describe those dancing the Highland fling. Applied to human beings, "exotic" is ethnocentric and racist. "It implies a state of other-ness, or foreign origin, apart from the norm. It is not a compliment" (Amoja Three Rivers, *Cultural Etiquette*).

expatriate/ex-pat although based on the Latin for "country," "patria" (and thus on "pater," "father"), these words are functionally inclusive and their roots not as obtrusive as some "pater"-based words ("paternal," for example). If you prefer, use *American abroad, exile, displaced person, émigré.*

expert when journalists, producers, or writers need an opinion from an expert, they generally select from a rather narrow range of available humans, ending up with young or middle-aged white male experts, even when equally knowledgeable women, minorities, older people, lesbians and gay men, and people with disabilities are available. There is little good reason today not to be able to call upon an inclusive range of experts in any field.

ex-serviceman *ex-service member, ex-soldier, ex-member of the armed forces.*

F

Most of us do not use speech to express thought. We use it to express feelings.

—*Jennifer Stone*

Language is double-edged; through words a fuller view of reality emerges, but words can also serve to fragment reality.

—*Vera John-Steiner*

factory boy/girl/man/woman *factory worker.*

faculty wives *faculty spouses*; in some cases, *faculty guests.* Casey Miller and Kate Swift *(The Handbook of Nonsexist Writing)* say that tacking on identifiers like "faculty/Senate/service/corporate wives" makes women appendages of both a man and an institution while detracting from their own lives and roles. The terminology also assumes that all members of the institution are men.

fag/faggot (man) these terms are extremely derogatory when used by non-gays (with the diminutive regarded as the more pejorative) but are often acceptable when used positively among gay men. By reclaiming the terms for themselves, gay men defuse the words' hostility and power over them. *See also* "insider/outsider" rule, shortened forms of words.

fair-haired boy/fair-haired girl *the favorite, the apple of someone's eye, privileged person, someone with pull, front runner, person after one's own heart, in one's good graces, persona grata, teacher's pet.* "Fair-haired" is problematic because (1) making fair-haired the preferred coloring is racist; (2) the phrases are used of adults, which makes the boy/girl designation inappropriate; (3) "fair-haired boy" is common, while "fair-haired girl" is not.

fair sex, the this phrase has lost whatever meaning it ever had.

fairy (legend) fairies are both male and female, although they most often materialize in our culture as female (e.g., fairy godmother, Tinkerbell, the tooth fairy).

fairy (man) this highly derogatory term has fortunately pretty much died out; a few gay men might still want to use it in a friendly and positive way among themselves, but it's off limits to others. *See also* "insider/outsider" rule.

fairy godmother retain in traditional fairy tales and add fairy godfathers to modern tales. Also: *good fairy/genie/genius, guardian angel, benefactor, savior, hero.*

faith of our fathers *faith of our ancestors/forebears/mothers and fathers.*

fakir from the Arabic for "poor man," fakirs are generally men and the word is perceived as male. You may sometimes need a sex-neutral alternative: *wonder-worker, ascetic, mendicant; dervish; impostor, swindler.*

Falashas *Ethiopian Jews.* The unacceptable "Falashas" means "landless aliens" in Amharic.

fallen woman if you mean prostitute, use *prostitute.* Otherwise use for either sex *someone who is unfortunate/unlucky/sexually active/promiscuous, someone who has fallen on hard/evil times/from grace.* Note that there are no "fallen men" just as there are no "fall women" (*see* fall guy/fall man); judgments about sexual activity are reserved for women, while judgments about moral evil and foolishness are reserved for men.

fall guy/fall man *scapegoat, dupe, goat, sucker, victim, fool, laughingstock, loser, greenhorn, sitting duck, easy/soft mark, mark, target, pushover, sap, mug, nebbish.* Douglas R. Hofstadter *(Metamagical Themas)*: "You see it in animated cartoons, many of which feature some poor schlemiel—a sad 'fall guy,' a kind of schmoe with whom 'everyman' can identify—whose fate it is to be dumped on by the world, and we all laugh with him as he is dealt one cruel setback after another. But why aren't there women in this role more often? Why aren't there more 'schlemielesses'—more 'fall gals'?" *See also* fallen woman, whipping boy.

Fall of Man *fall of the human race, the Fall.*

family use "family" in ways that reflect contemporary realities; the family of nostalgia ("Father Knows Best," "Leave It to Beaver," "Ozzie and Harriet") that is still pictured as the "real" family was actually only an aberration (whose supposed perfection was not enjoyed by everybody even then; one-fourth of all Americans lived in poverty—without food stamps) that predominated for several decades following World War II. "The treasured belief that American families were once simpler and more innocent than they are today still exerts a powerful emotional pull on us" (Stephanie Coontz, *The Way We Never Were*). This is not a new thought;

in 1905 educator Frances E. Willard wrote, "The capacity of the human mind to resist knowledge is nowhere more painfully illustrated than in the postulate laid down by average minds that home is always to be just what it is now—forgetting that in no two consecutive generations has it remained the same." The legalistic definition of family is a group of people related by blood, marriage, or adoption, but the real-world definition is broader; in a Massachusetts Mutual Life Insurance Co. study, almost three-quarters of the respondents chose the description, "A group of people who love and care for each other." Real families include mother/father/children; mother or father and children; unmarried oppo-site-sex couples sharing a household, with or without children; same-sex couples living together, with or without children; children living with relatives who are not their parents; blended families in which some of the members are unrelated by blood to each other; widowed or unmarried siblings sharing a home. Anndee Hochman *(Everyday Acts and Small Subversions)* says, "The word 'family' itself is loaded. . . . No mere noun, it's a way of categorizing society, even allocating resources, with 'family' memberships and 'family' fares on airlines and trains." The term "family values" (political shorthand for, among other things, a narrow conceptualization of the family that includes a male breadwinner, a female homemaker, and a decent income, and excludes divorces, blended families, homosexuality, poverty, unwed or single parents) has been used to castigate single mothers and "atypical" families. Susan Ohanian *(Ms. Class)* points out that "from George Washington on, we are a nation led by the products of single-parent families." Among many U.S. leaders and heroes raised by one parent, an older sibling, grandparents, or non-relatives were George Washington, Thomas Jefferson, Andrew Jackson, Abraham Lincoln, Herbert Hoover, Sojourner Truth, Stonewall Jackson, Frances Hodgson Burnett, Herman Melville, Ralph Waldo Emerson, Eleanor Roosevelt, and Jacqueline Cochran. On a practical level, people often wonder how to distinguish between the family they grew up in and the family they presently live in. Although we do not yet have concise terms, consider some of these: *birth family, childhood family, family of origin, original family, first family; present family, adult family. **See also*** domestic partnership.

family man *homebody, stay-at-home, family head, home-lover, family-oriented/family-centered/home-centered person, someone devoted to the family.* Note the lack of parallel for women; all women are evidently "family women."

family name *See* surname.

family of man *the human family, humanity, humankind, the human family tree.*

family planning this sex-neutral term is too often discussed as the exclusive province/responsibility of women. *See also* birth control.

fancy girl/fancy lady/fancy woman *prostitute. See also* prostitute.

fancy man *prostitute's pimp. See also* prostitute.

farm boy (employee) *farm hand/worker.*

farmer approximately two-thirds of all farmers in the world are women; "And yet, of all the job descriptions in the English language, few jobs have a more masculine connotation than the title 'farmer.' . . . In most cultures, agriculture becomes 'men's work' when it progresses to the point of being a successful commercial industry" (Lee Egerstrom, *St. Paul Pioneer Press*). Casey Miller and Kate Swift *(The Handbook of Nonsexist Writing)* note that "most farmers in the developing world are women. According to United Nations estimates, women produce 60% to 80% of the food supply in Africa and Asia." Sign of progress: newspapers correctly referred to the Iowa woman who found missing parts of a crashed United Airlines DC-10 as a "farmer."

farmerette *farmer. See also* "feminine" word endings.

farm wife/farmer's wife most often, this woman is a farmer in all but name; give her the name. In one survey of farm women, nearly 95% were heavily involved in farm management, including basic farm labor and decision-making; 86% did the farm recordkeeping, 75% cared for the animals; 72% harvested crops. Sometimes farm wives have not only not been called farmers, they have not even been regarded as persons. In 1988 a federal judge had to rule against the U.S. Department of Agriculture, which claimed that a farm couple was only one person. Although a father and his son or a brother and a sister farming in partnership were regarded as two people, a husband and wife were counted as only one person for USDA purposes. U.S. District Court Judge Joyce Hens Green officially rejected "the archaic notion that husbands and wives are one 'person.'"

fast (referring to a woman) the use of "fast" to mean "promiscuous" came into the language around 1910 and gave rise to "fast house" (house of prostitution) in the late 1920s (Stuart Berg Flexner, *Listening to America*). Although it could have included both sexes (since its earlier meaning of "dissipated" applied to men), it's been used to label only women for (presumed) behavior that is found in both sexes. *See also* easy.

fat labeling people's appearance is usually unnecessary. When any type of description is required, says John Paschetto, "Most politicized fat people prefer the simple word 'fat' to describe their bodies. Such words as 'heavy,' 'big,' and 'large'—while less offensive than 'overweight'—are frowned upon both because they are unclear and because they suggest that 'fat' needs euphemisms. . . . the usage of 'fat,' 'overweight,' et al. is complicated by different preferences among the people being named. A lot of fat people accept the ruling group's opinion of their bodies and so are put off by the free use of 'fat.'" The principal activist organization, the National Association to Advance Fat Acceptance (NAAFA), prefers "fat." One woman asks, "When are we going to understand that fat is an adjective, not an epithet?" Useful considerations when referring to body size: like height, weight appears to be determined primarily by genes and can also be affected by a complex disorder of energy metabolism; it is possible to be fat and healthy at the same time; reducing diets are most often ineffective and unhealthy; statistically, being overweight has an associated economic disadvantage (one study found that businessmen sacrifice $1,000 in salary for every pound they are "overweight"); fat people endure open ridicule, lectures, and insults, yet studies show that fat people actually eat less than those of "average" weight, and dieters exhibit more willpower than those who do not need to worry about what they eat; the non-fat partners of fat people also experience societal disapproval; unlike people with other conditions or disabilities, fat people are doubly punished by being told they could be thin if they really wanted to. (Note that the average U.S. woman is 5'4", weighs 140 lbs., and wears a size 14 dress, whereas the "ideal" woman, as portrayed by models, actors, etc., is 5'7", weighs 100 lbs., and wears a size 8 dress; 75% of U.S. women are dissatisfied with their appearance.) Susan Wooley, director of an eating disorders clinic at the University of Cincinnati, says, "It has been clear in the scientific community that diets fail, yet scientists have been extremely reluctant to let go of diet programs. Why should we expect the general population to be any quicker than scientists in releasing prejudice?" *See also* looksism, obese/obesity, overweight, sizism.

father (pseudogeneric noun) *parent, progenitor, procreator, mother and father; source, ancestor, forebear; originator, founder, inventor, promoter. See also* forefather, mother and father.

father (verb) in the sense of "to beget a child" or "to carry out the childrearing functions of a father," this is the right word. When used pseudogenerically or metaphorically to refer to actions considered analogous to begetting, it is better replaced by terms such as *procreate, create, co-create, reproduce, breed, propagate, give life to, bring to life, bring into being, bring about, call into existence, cause to exist; produce, make, found, author, originate, generate, engender, establish, invent, introduce.* Or, alternate gender-specific words such as father/mother, beget/give birth to, conceive/beget. *See also* mother (verb).

father (parent) when writing about men as fathers, forgo stereotypes—that they are absent, inept, distant, or cold. Some may well be, but perpetuating these vague and oftentimes unfounded notions does a disservice to men who are committed, loving, and effective fathers. It also breeds social tolerance for second-rate fathering. When writing or speaking about fathers, give them a full range of behaviors, attitudes, and emotions. *See also* absent parent, advertising, parent.

father (clergy) leave as is in direct address ("Father Frank Friar") but when referring to someone use the inclusive *priest, minister, pastor. See also* clergyman, priest.

Father (God) some people believe the name "Father" and the concept of God as "Father" should be retained. Others, however, look back to the Gnostic and Semitic traditions from which the words "father" and "son" emerged, and say that these words have nothing to do with roles like father and son, or indeed with any familial roles, but that they were the closest worshipers could come to expressing in personal terms the concepts of Uncreated Source (God) and Reflected Image (Jesus). For these people, using metaphors for God (God as nurturing mother or loving father) is acceptable, but the idea of God having a gender is not. There is nothing wrong with thinking of God as Father—indeed, it is a strong, beautiful metaphor. The problem is that we have overused that metaphor until it has taken on a spurious life of its own. (Marcia Falk: "Dead metaphors make strong idols.") God is *like* a father; the metaphor does not mean God is a father or that God is male. New metaphors for God are needed and more emphasis can be given to the other ones that we have (God is also light, rock, potter, mother, bread, wind, water, sun, fire, wisdom, judge, homemaker, physician, warrior, midwife, lion, leopard, she-bear, mother eagle, and shepherd, for example). The question of God's gender or lack of it poses a dilemma for people who are equally sensitive to the Word of God, theological truth, sexist language, and the person in the pew. The latter often sees inclusive language (particularly the elimination of God as Father) as unconscionable tampering, and finds the challenge to faith overwhelming. Scripture scholar the Reverend Joseph J. Arackal says calling God "Father" has no tradition among the Hebrews and even the word "Abba" cannot be translated into the English word "Father" since *Abba* indicates "the spiritual source of being" rather than the male parent. In the Old Testament, where the issue is not so much the Fatherness of God as the Godness of God, the word "Father" can be replaced by one of the following: *Advocate, Almighty/the Almighty, Ancient of Days, Author, Being, Blessed One, Creator, Creator God, Creator of all things, Defender, the Deity, Divine Light/One, Elohim, the Eternal, Eternal One, Ever-Present God, Exalted One, First Cause, First and Last, Friend, Glory, God, Godhead, God in Heaven, God my Rock, God my Rock and my Redeemer, God of Abraham and Sarah (or God of Abraham and Sara, of Isaac and Rebecca, of Jacob,*

Leah, and Rachel), *God of Grace/Heaven/Hosts/Israel, God of our ancestors/forebears, God of the Nations, Good Parent, Ground of Being, Guide, Healer, Heavenly Creator/One/Parent, Helper, Holy One/the Holy One, Holy One of Blessing/Israel, the Infinite, Just One, Liberator, Living God, Maker, Majesty of the Universe, Merciful God, Mighty One, Most High/the Most High, Most Loving God, Nurturer, O God my God, O Gracious God, Omnipotent One, our Refuge and our Strength, Powerful One, Presence, Preserver, Protector of Sarah and Shield of Abraham, Providence, Redeemer, Rock, Rock of Refuge, Ruler, Savior, Shepherd, Shepherd of Israel, Source/the Source, Source of Life, Sovereign, Spirit, Supreme Being, Sustainer, the Truth, Wisdom.* When using the father metaphor, avoid as much as possible masculine pronouns in order to mitigate the strongly male orientation. *See also* Father, Son, and Holy Spirit; God; God/he; God/his; Holy Spirit; Lord; Son of Man.

father absence *See* absent parent.

father and mother *See* mother and father.

Father Christmas *See* Santa Claus.

father figure this term has a specific meaning and may need to be retained even though the potentially parallel term "mother figure" is not used very often (we have mother figures, but we are not so apt to label them). For sex-neutral alternatives consider *role model, mentor, idol, hero.*

fatherland *homeland, native land/country/soil, home, home/birth country, land of one's ancestors, natal place, the old country, country.*

fatherless (pseudogeneric) *orphaned, parentless.*

fatherly replace this vague adjective with precise ones: *warm, nurturing, loving, kind, kindly, protective, supportive, caring, solicitous, considerate, interested, benevolent, good-natured, fond, affectionate, devoted, tender, gentle, demonstrative, sympathetic, understanding, indulgent, obliging, forbearing, tolerant, well-meaning, sheltering, generous.* These adjectives also apply to women; they are not synonyms for "fatherly" but rather what the culture seems to understand by the word.

Father of Waters acceptable historic title for the Mississippi River.

fathers (pseudogeneric) *ancestors, forebears, progenitors, precursors, predecessors, forerunners, leaders, pioneers, founders, trailblazers, innovators, fathers and mothers.*

Father's Day first celebrated in Spokane in 1910, Father's Day was suggested by Mrs. John Bruce Dodd whose father, William Smart, had raised his children after his wife died. Prompted by Mrs. Dodd and by the new popularity of Mother's Day (1908), Spokane ministers, newspapers, and stores promoted acceptance of the idea. AT&T notes that Father's Day is the number-one day for collect phone calls, with 27% more collect calls than on Mother's Day. Dallas family psychologist Brenda Wall says, "We've always looked to Mom for love and nurturing. But when we look to Dad, it's usually a business transaction or something that relates to power, positioning, or money." *See also* Mother's Day.

Fathers of the Church leave as is; historically accurate. *See also* church father.

Father, Son, and Holy Spirit/Ghost *God, Jesus, and Holy Spirit; the God who created us, the God who redeemed us, and the God who continues to work through us to make us holy; Creator, Christ/Word, and Holy Spirit; Source of all Being, Eternal Word, and Holy Spirit; Maker, Jesus, and Holy Spirit; Creator, Savior, and Healer; Source, Servant, and Guide; Creator, Liberator, and Advocate; the grace of the Lord Jesus Christ and the love of God and the communion of the Holy Spirit; Creator, Redeemer, and Comforter/Sustainer/Sanctifier/Sanctifier God; Source of All Being, Eternal Word, Holy Spirit; the Holy Trinity; Three in One; One in Three; the Triune God.* When choosing alternatives note that some describe who God is ("God, Jesus, and Holy Spirit") while others describe what God does ("Creator, Savior, and Healer"). Some people object to the overuse of God-as-function terms.

Father Time alternatives, if you need them, include *time/Time, progress, ravages/march of time.*

father to the thought, the wish is *the wish gives birth to/begets/engenders/ brings forth/precedes/produces the thought.*

father upon *saddle with, lay at the door of, ascribe to, bring home to, charge with.*

favorite son candidate *state favorite, favorite candidate/citizen, favorite citizen candidate.* The alternatives aren't great, but the expression itself isn't seen much anymore.

featherbrain *See* airhead.

FBI agent woman or man. About 11% of the force are women.

feisty during her vice-presidential campaign, Geraldine Ferraro was referred to as "spunky" and "feisty"; Michael Geis *(The Language of Politics)* says both words are normally reserved for individuals and animals that are not inherently potent or powerful; "one can call a Pekinese dog spunky or feisty, but one would not, I think, call a Great Dane spunky or feisty." And the press would certainly not have labeled George Bush, then Ferraro's opponent, as spunky or feisty. "Numerous examples of the special or sexist treatment of female leaders include . . . use of the terms 'oppressive,' 'feisty,' and 'pushy' to describe behavior in women that would be called 'tough' and 'decisive' in men" (Thalia Zepatos and Elizabeth Kaufman, *Women for a Change*). *See also* perky/pert.

feller although "fellow" has some inclusive uses, "feller" does not; a feller's always going to be a feller. *See also* fellow.

fellow (noun/adjective) often considered to be used inclusively; women receiving academic fellowships are called fellows, for example, and among its dictionary definitions are many wonderfully inclusive concepts. However, because one definition is "a familiar synonym for man, male person" *(Oxford English Dictionary)*, it is difficult to determine whether "fellow" is being used in the inclusive or exclusive sense. A convincing argument for it being exclusive is the common perception of the word. If someone says, "Today I saw a fellow throwing away hundred-dollar bills," there is no doubt in anyone's mind that the distributor of largess was a man. The folksy "fella/feller" is also incontestably masculine. On the yet other hand, Casey Miller and Kate Swift (in Jane Mills, *Womanwords*, 2nd ed.) say, "Although *fellow* remains male-specific as it is most commonly used, the need for a term applicable to a comrade or associate of either sex may be leading it toward a wider application in which women as well as men are referred to as *fellows* in common parlance." If you want a substitute for the noun consider *person, partner, colleague, co-worker, companion, counterpart, associate, ally, comrade, friend, acquaintance, peer, affiliate, equal, mate, pair, double, twin, match.* For the adjective use *similar, alike, analogous, comparable, parallel, matching, corresponding, coinciding, like, something like, other, related, akin, equal, equivalent, associate(d), united, connected.* For the academic "fellow" you can sometimes use *scholar, recipient, postgraduate student.*

fellow countrymen *friends and neighbors, all of us, compatriots.* Reword the sentence to avoid this term if the alternatives don't work. *See also* compatriot, countryman, fellow man/men.

fellow feeling *sympathy, understanding, compassion, commiseration, empathy, rapport, link, bond, union, tie, closeness, affinity, friendship, agape, pity, walking in someone else's shoes, putting oneself in someone else's place.*

fellow man/men in most cases "fellow" is superfluous. We are so used to hearing this catch-all term in certain contexts that we don't question its necessity. Be specific: *other people, you, citizens, workers, another human being, all of us here, the average person,* etc. *See also* man/Man (pseudogeneric).

fellowship (social bond) *friendship, companionship, solidarity, communion, union, unity, unity of mind and spirit, association, camaraderie, comradeship, partnership, togetherness, collaboration, participation, esprit de corps, neighborliness, sharing, amity, goodwill, bonding, friendliness, conviviality, sodality, human community/kinship, kinship, humanity,* *family, the human family; society, assembly, community, organization, club, group, federation, corporation.* The substitute most often used for "fellowship" in religious materials is "communion." *See also* brotherhood, fellowship (scholarship).

fellowship (scholarship) when used officially, retain; otherwise consider *scholarship, assistantship, internship, stipend, subsidy, honorarium.*

fellow traveler *traveling companion, other traveler.*

fellow worker *co-worker, colleague, associate, teammate, partner.*

female (adjective) although it is preferable to use *woman* or *women* as adjectives (when it is necessary), there are times when "female" seems more appropriate. Use it, however, only when you would use "male" in a similar situation or when it is necessary for clarification; sex-specific adjectives are often gratuitous and belittling (one sees "female lawyer" but not "male doctor"). Watch especially for nonparallel usage ("two technicians and a female mechanic"). Note that *female* is not linguistically derived from, nor even related to, *male. See also* female (noun).

female (noun) "female" is used as a noun only in technical writing (medicine, statistics, police reports, sociology). It is most often reserved for biological or nonhuman references. When using "female," use the parallel "male," not "man." It is sometimes thought that "female" is sexist because it has "male" in it. Dennis Baron *(Grammar and Gender)* says, "Actually *female* derives from the Latin *femella*, a diminutive of *femina*, 'woman.' It is completely unrelated to *male*, which comes to us via Old French from Latin *masculus*, a diminutive of *ma*, 'male, masculine.'" *See also* female (adjective).

female genital mutilation this procedure, undergone by more than 80 million African women, is sometimes referred to as female circumcision, but it differs radically from male circumcision: it is always a sexual mutilation; it is performed without anesthesia by nonprofessionals, most often with unsterilized razor blades; it often leads to infection, life-threatening blood loss, painful intercourse, infertility, difficult childbirth, and even death. This mutilation of the external female genital organs (specifically, clitoridectomy, excision, and infibulation) is a centuries-old rite of passage, intended to ensure that young women become desirable wives. Not mandated by any particular religion, it is practiced by people of many faiths in some two dozen African nations, in Egypt, and in the Sudan. Although many organizations are working to educate about the problems caused by FGM, and laws have been passed in some countries to forbid it, observers fear the practice is spreading rather than waning. The issue is many-layered, from the heinous and nightmarish mangling and botching of women's bodies to issues involving people's rights to cultural self-determination. The U.S. has granted at least one woman political asylum based on the fact that if she were returned to her country she would be required to undergo female genital mutilation.

feminazi Rush Limbaugh has made himself a name (which isn't printable here—no, no, that's just a little feminist humor) by calling feminists fascists, and shortening it to feminazi. To be used only by Rush Limbaugh. *See also* Nazi/nazi.

feminine avoid this vague stereotype that conveys different meanings to different people according to their perceptions of what a woman ought or ought not do, say, think, wear, feel, look like. These subjective, cultural judgments have nothing to do with sex and everything to do with gender. Use instead specific descriptive adjectives: *gracious, warm, gentle, thoughtful, sensitive, loyal, receptive, supportive, compassionate, expressive, affectionate, tender, charming, nurturing, well-mannered, cooperative, neat, soft-spoken, considerate, kind.* These adjectives may be used equally appropriately of a man; they are not special characteristics of women but, rather, what most people seem to mean when they use "feminine." It can mean other things too: in *Thinking About Women,* Mary Ellmann notes that *"feminine* functions as an eight-letter word in the notorious Woodrow Wilson biography by [Sigmund] Freud and William Bullitt. At one heated point, Clemenceau calls Wilson feminine. Wilson calls Clemenceau feminine, then both Freud and Bullitt call Wilson feminine again. The word means that all four men thoroughly dislike each other."

feminine intuition *See* women's intuition.

feminine logic people who use "feminine logic" usually mean a woman is being "illogical," so they should save themselves a word and just say "illogical" if that's what they mean. Otherwise it's logic, period.

feminine/masculine (poetry, music) in poetry, rhyme with a stressed or strong final syllable is called masculine rhyme; rhyme with an unstressed or weak final syllable is feminine rhyme. In music, a masculine beginning (or ending) is a phrase that starts (or ends) on a strong beat; a feminine beginning (or ending) is a phrase that starts (or ends) on a weak beat. It would seem clearer (and use fewer syllables) to refer to stressed and unstressed rhymes and to strong and weak beats without bringing the sexes into it in this highly sexist manner.

feminine mystique from Betty Friedan's landmark 1963 book of the same title in which she exposed "the problem that has no name" (women's unhappiness with their role and status in society), this term refers to the then-narrow definition of women's "place" in the world.

feminine wiles *wiles.*

"feminine" word endings suffixes like *-ess, -ette,* and *-trix* (1) specify a person's sex when it is irrelevant; (2) carry a demeaning sense of littleness or triviality; (3) perpetuate the notion that the male is the norm and the female is a subset, a deviation, a secondary classification. A poet is defined as "one who writes poetry" while a poetess is defined as "a female poet"; men are thus "the real thing" and women are sort of like them. The recommended procedure is to use the base word for both sexes (thus, "waiter" instead of "waitress," "executor" instead of "executrix," "divorcé" instead of "divorcée"). For a complete discussion of "feminine" word endings and a list of examples, *see* the Writing Guidelines (pp. 13–14). *See also* divorcé/divorcée.

femininity notions of femininity are based on culturally defined roles and how closely a woman fulfills these expectations. Because the concept is so subjective, "femininity" may mean different things in Louisiana, Maine, Kansas, and California. Choose specific words for the qualities you want to describe: *warmth, graciousness, compassion, expressiveness, softness, self-confidence, strength, assurance, poise, charm, kindliness.* These words can also be applied to men; they do not describe the essence of women, but rather, what a particular culture takes it to be.

feminism the definition of "feminism" varies from person to person, although in general those who are identified with it advocate equal rights, opportunities, and responsibilities for both sexes; passage of the ERA; and support for comparable worth and other economic fairness programs. At its simplest, feminism is about leveling the playing field: working toward a just society that allows all individuals to live out their potential free from discrimination, physical harm, and inequitable economic policies. Although many people now accept it as a historical, enduring movement that has promoted changes beneficial to society as a whole, feminism still generates a certain amount of confusion and hostility: in a fundraising letter to voters during Iowa's ERA debate, Pat Robertson described feminism as "a socialist anti-family political movement that encourages women to leave their husbands, kill their children, practice witchcraft, destroy capitalism and become lesbians." So, yes, definitions vary. *See also* feminist, women's movement.

feminist a feminist is someone who believes in "the full humanity of women" (Gloria Steinem). In 1913, Rebecca West said, "People call me a feminist whenever I express sentiments that differentiate me from a doormat or a prostitute." Decades later, it is not always clear what the term means—to those who self-identify that way, to those who prefer not to use it ("I'm not a feminist, but . . ."), or to those who wield it like an epithet ("those blankety-blank feminists"). It is primarily women who identify themselves as feminists, but some men do too. In general, those who call themselves feminists are signaling their involvement in one or more social issues, their concern with the struggles of other people for justice, and their commitment to staying informed and compassionate. One of the principles of biased language is that labels are disabling; the label "feminist" has the shortcomings and disadvantages of all labels. However, until society reaches a point where no labels are needed, where we are all simply people, it will do. *See also* feminism, womanist.

feminization of poverty coined in 1978 by sociologist Diana Pearce, this term refers to the change that has taken place from the situation in the 1960s, when families with a female householder and no husband present constituted less than one-fourth of poor families, to the present when women and their families make up a clear majority of the American poor (Gertrude Schaffner Goldberg and Eleanor Kremen, eds., *The Feminization of Poverty: Only in America?*). "The millions of human beings that lamentable phrase hopes to describe will never agree that poverty is feminine or that they, themselves, participate in the invention of the tortures of poor women in America" (June Jordan, *Technical Difficulties*). Complex factors produce these numbers: much of the work that women do is unpaid; the rates of divorce, separation, and single motherhood (generally the result of relationships in which partners sooner or later disappeared) have risen; many women tried part-time work so they could be home and still make money, but they found they earned less and were also less likely to be promoted or to be covered by health insurance or pension plans. *See also* welfare.

fem lib *feminism, women's liberation movement, women's liberation, women's movement, female liberation movement. See also* shortened forms of words.

femme/fem these terms follow the "insider/outsider" rule: they are sometimes used positively among lesbians, but should not be used by non-lesbians.

femme fatale this term perpetuates the myth of woman as Eve/tempter/seducer and man as helpless prey. A rule of good writing is "show, don't tell"; instead of stating that someone is a "femme fatale," show how she affects others. The parallel for a man is probably the unfortunate term "lady-killer," q.v.

ferryman *ferry operator/pilot/captain/driver/boat operator;* sometimes simply *ferry boat.*

fetish (religious) this term is used to refer to the religious items of peoples of color when objects in other religions often serve similar purposes but are not called fetishes.

fiancé/fiancée these sex-specific terms are acceptable to most people and are still widely used. However, the trend is toward using only the base word (fiancé). According to Art Krug, quoted in the Portland *Oregonian*, "'Fiancée' is too stuffy in the '90s. I think I'll call her my 'intendo.'" *See also* divorcé/divorcée, "feminine" word endings.

fickle except for that notorious finger of fate, it is generally women who wear the "fickle" label, so you may want more neutral alternatives: *unpredictable, changeable, unaccountable, unreliable, impulsive, impetuous, indecisive, uncertain, unsteady, irresolute, vacillating, unfaithful, disloyal, inconstant, treacherous, tricky.*

fieldman *fielder, field player; canvasser, commercial traveler, fieldworker, field representative/technician/contractor/buyer.*

fighting man *fighter, soldier, pugilist, belligerent, belligerent/aggressive individual/person.*

figurine "figurine" (also, "statuette"), meaning small statue, illustrates how the suffix meaning "small" was originally (and correctly) used. It is only when this suffix is used for women that it is objectionable.

filial/filiation although these words come from the Latin for "son," they are defined and used inclusively in terms of children and offspring of both sexes.

Filipina/Filipino a woman/man native to or living in the Philippines; in the U.S. those from the Philippines are known as Filipino Americans. *See also* Pinay/Pinoy.

fill 'er up (gas tank) *fill it up. See also* car/she.

filterman *filter press tender, filter operator/tender, ripening room attendant.*

final solution this expression should be reserved for the Nazi program of exterminating Jews during the German Third Reich. Do not use it metaphorically or analogously. (An example given in Marilyn Schwartz et al., *Guidelines for Bias-Free Writing*, talked about an approach which "will not provide the hoped-for 'final solution' to pest problems.") *See also* concentration camp, Gestapo/gestapo, Hitler/little Hitler, holocaust, Jewish question, Nazi/nazi, problem.

Finndian derogatory vernacular from Michigan's Upper Peninsula for those of Finnish-American Indian ancestry.

finishing school *private school.* There are no finishing schools for boys; the cultural parallel has been the military school.

fireman *firefighter.* In some instances other terms are useful: *fire chief/ warden, fire/safety officer.*

fireman (locomotive/ship) *fire/furnace tender, firer, stoker, oil feeder.*

fire patrolman *fire patroller/ranger/guard.*

first baseman *See* baseman.

First Lady the wife of a U.S. president is often given this honorary and unofficial title. Thus, the "problem" of what to do with the husband of a U.S. president is moot; he will be known simply as "Mr. Last-Name." Presidents' wives were not always referred to as "first ladies"; in 1849 President Zachary Taylor eulogized Dolley Madison: "She will never be forgotten, because she was truly our First Lady for a half-century." But the term did not become part of the vocabulary until 1911, with the hit play about Dolley Madison titled, "The First Lady in the Land." The term is seen less and less often in print. Recent presidential spouses have preferred to be known by a name, rather than by a role. (Jacqueline Kennedy said, "The one thing I do not want to be called is 'First Lady.' It sounds like a saddle horse.")

fisherman *fisher, angler, fish catcher, fishing licensee* (for some legal purposes); *fisherman and fisherwoman* if used gender-fairly. Do not be afraid of "fisher." In the following series of -er words, "fisherman" would be the odd man out: camper, hunter, canoer, skier, runner, hiker, mountain climber, birdwatcher, biker, nature lover. "Fisher" is appearing more often in print; newspapers like its length for headlines. Author, library cataloger, and wordsmith Sanford Berman says some dictionaries give "a fisherman" as the primary definition of "fisher"; the Library of Congress has replaced the sexist catalog heading "fishermen" with "fishers"; and the Hennepin County Library (Minneapolis) has been using "fishers" since 1974. He adds that a venerable example of such usage appears in Matthew 4:19 and Mark 1:17: "I will make you fishers of men" (King James Version). (Incidentally, the "men" in that phrase were actually "human beings" in the original Greek. The phrase can be translated "fishers of souls.") The plurals "fisherfolk" and "fisherpeople" are seen in print.

fisherman's bend (knot) leave as is.

fishman *fishmonger, fish vendor/porter.*

fishwife *fishmonger, fish porter.* Avoid the word to mean an abusive, scolding woman; there is no parallel for a man (fishhusband?) and we tend to attribute those qualities to women. *See also* shrew.

fit *seizure.*

fit for a king *fit for royalty/for the best, magnificent, noble, magnificent, splendid, luxurious, sumptuous, one in ten thousand/in a million, of the best quality, first class/rate, top drawer, fit for a queen/king.*

fix-it man *fixer-upper, fix-it expert, fixer, repairer. See also* handyman.

flag girl *flag bearer.*

flagman *signaler, flagger, traffic controller, signal giver; flag waver/carrier.*

flagman ahead *construction/signal/signaler ahead, watch for signal.*

flapper use as is in historical context. Note, however, that before World War I a flapper was considered a sprightly, knowing, female teenager. Afterwards the term developed negative connotations, and flappers were thought to be promiscuous. There never was a male equivalent to the flapper.

flasher *exhibitionist.* You may use "flasher" to describe a woman if you want, but without any identifying pronouns, the word will be assumed to be male.

flaunt "For many gays, a trigger word has long been *flaunting*, as in 'I don't mind gay people as long as they don't flaunt their life-style.' . . . Many lesbians and gay men hear this as: Stay in your closet. Pass. And so long as you're invisible, I'll accept you. . . . heterosexuals . . . have little awareness of the way they 'flaunt' their life-style every time they mention a spouse or hold hands or kiss in public, on TV, and in the movies or magazines" (Joan Steinau Lester, *The Future of White Men and Other Diversity Dilemmas*). The "don't ask, don't tell" ruling in the U.S. military is another example of this double standard.

flesh (color) this could mean anything, unless it is taken in the ethnocentric way it was used for years to mean "pinky-beige." The Crayola company no longer labels a crayon with this "color."

flimflam man *flimflam artist, flimflammer.* **See also** con man/confidence man.

floor boy/floor girl *floor worker.*

floorlady/floorman *operator, supervisor, floor supervisor/worker, floorwalker.*

flower girl (vendor) *flower seller/vendor, florist.*

flower girl (wedding) *flower bearer/carrier.* Boys are flower bearers as well as ring bearers, and girls can be ring bearers.

flyboy *pilot, aviator, flier, high-flier, glamorous pilot, member of the Air Force.* **See also** airman.

flyman *flyhand, stagehand, flyworker.*

Flying Dutchman leave as is.

foeman *foe, enemy, opponent, rival, competitor.*

foilsman *fencer.*

food names for people while some food names for people are positive ("creampuff," "peach," "stud muffin"—if that belongs here), most are in some way belittling, trivializing, objectifying, or sexist: babycakes, beefcake, cheesecake, cookie, cupcake, cutie pie, dish, fruit, fruitcake, fruit salad, honeycakes, lambchop, marshmallow, pudding, pumpkin, sugar, sugar and spice, sweetie pie, sweet potato pie, tart, tomato, top banana. Metaphors are more acceptable than labels: "apple of my eye" can be said of either sex and it doesn't mean the person is an apple in the same way a woman is called a tomato—but rather that he or she is like the best apple from the tree. Strong writing depends on metaphors—even metaphors based on food—but there is a difference between labeling people and creating vivid word associations. *See also* animal names for people, honey.

fool and his money are soon parted, a *fools and their money are soon parted.*

footboy *page, attendant.*

footman leave as is in historical contexts; a footman was always a man. Or, *servant.* According to one source (Alvin Silverstein, *The Left-Hander's World*), the purpose of the footman in Roman households was to ensure that guests entered the home right-foot-first.

forefather *forebear, forerunner, ancestor, predecessor, precursor, pioneer; forefather and foremother.* Also, in some senses, *colonist, patriot, founder.* Note that because genes sort randomly, "It is possible for a female to end up with all her genes from male ancestors, and for a male to end up with all his genes from female ancestors" (Sally Slocum, *Toward an Anthropology of Women*).

forelady/foreman/forewoman *supervisor, lead/floor supervisor, team/floor/ work leader, line manager/supervisor, section head, manager, boss, job/ straw boss, chief, task sergeant, monitor, overseer, overlooker, superintendent, super, inspector, director, head, leader.* The British use *chargehand.*

foreman (jury) *head juror, jury designate/supervisor/chief/chair/representative/leader.* "Forewoman" and "foreperson," are seen and are acceptable enough if the pair is "forewoman and foreman" and not "foreman and foreperson," but they are not lovely constructions.

foremanship *supervisory duties/skills/ability, supervision.*

foremother while "forefather" is often used as a false generic, "foremother" may be valid to emphasize that there were indeed women before us even though they seldom appear in the history books, classrooms, or public halls. If you need a sex-inclusive term consider *forebear, forerunner, ancestor, predecessor, precursor, pioneer; forefather and foremother. See also* foresister.

foresister when a sex-specific term is useful, some people prefer this term to "foremother."

foretopman *foretopper, sailor, foretop sailor.*

forewoman *See* forelady/foreman/forewoman, foreman (jury).

fossil man *fossil human/remains/hominids, fossil, prehistoric human.*

foster mother/father/parent acceptable terms.

Founding Fathers *the Founders, writers of the Constitution; in some contexts, Founding Mothers and Founding Fathers; founders, pioneers, colonists, forebears, patriots.* An error sometimes seen is the assumption that these groups were male ("pioneers and their wives and children"). Although the term "founding fathers" (originally referring to the men who gathered at the constitutional convention in Philadelphia in 1787) has a venerable and ancient ring, it is of 20th-century origin; in 1918 and again in his 1920 presidential campaign Warren G. Harding used it: "I must utter my belief in the divine inspiration of the founding fathers." *See also* forefathers, pioneers.

fountain girl/fountain man *fountain/counter server, fountain attendant/ tender/waiter, lunchcounter waiter.* Note the nonparallel "girl/man."

fox/fox trap/foxy/foxy lady it is generally acceptable to use the adjective "foxy" but less acceptable to use the noun "fox" (the distinction lies in saying someone is like an animal or saying someone is an animal). "Foxy lady" is not acceptable because of "lady," and because "fox trap" (a customized car designed to attract women) perpetuates the man-the-hunter, woman-the-prey attitude. Note that while a man who is foxy is clever, a woman who is foxy is sexy. *See also* animal names for people, score, sex object.

frail elderly this term is acceptable, particularly in sociological or medical writing, to refer to those older persons who because of physical, mental, or economic problems need support from society. It is less acceptable when referring to a specific individual or when used casually. *See also* ageism, old.

frameman *framer, frame wirer.*

fraternal unless speaking of a brother, you may want a sex-neutral alternative: *warm, loving, friendly, kindly, teasing, protective, sympathetic, intimate.* In some contexts consider *sibling.* Because the feminine analog to "fraternal" ("sororal") is rarely seen—an example of the discounting of female words—even women's groups have used "fraternal." The Degree of Honor Protection Association, founded over 100 years ago, describes itself as "a fraternal insurance organization of women" and engages in "fraternal activities." "Fraternal" is used here as a synonym for "benevolent." *See also* fraternal order of, sororal.

fraternal order of *order of, benevolent order of. See also* fraternal.

fraternal organization *organization, society, association, common-interest group.*

fraternal twins *nonidentical/distinguishable/dizygotic twins.*

fraternity *organization, society, association, union, secret society, club, federation, fraternity and sorority, common-interest group; comradeship, unity, community, companionship, friendship, family, kinship.* **See also** brotherhood, fellowship, fraternity/frat (Greek).

fraternity/frat (Greek) these terms no longer refer strictly to male organizations: there are some fraternities that include women and some sororities are officially called fraternities. For sex-neutral alternatives use *Greek society/system, Greek-letter organization, Greek-letter society/group.* Although most fraternities have social service goals and almost all have nondiscriminatory membership codes, in practice they are often exclusionary. Robin Warshaw (in *The Nation*) says, "Universities across the country are proclaiming diversity—social, sexual, ethnic, racial, economic, and cultural—as the guiding spirit behind their pursuit of academic growth and excellence. At the same time, fraternities—whose members usually select one another on the basis of conformity to homogeneous group standards—are experiencing their highest membership levels ever. As a result, colleges find themselves trying to impart the bias-free goals of the 1990s to students who are clustering, in ever greater numbers, in the exclusionary communities of the 1950s . . . it's not the blood drives, charity fund-raiser, or improved résumé potential that brings in new members; it's an attraction to a culture that often seems to say, 'Become one of us and you'll get loaded, you'll get laid, you'll become a man.'" Referring to the "inherently destructive influence of fraternities," Warshaw says, "most fraternity cultures are still centered on proving manhood in accordance with three basic beliefs: that women are sex objects to be manipulated at will; that drinking and drug-taking are endurance sports; and that all non-members, be they other male students, professors, or college administrators, are deficient weenies. Because fraternities are essentially closed shops, both morally and intellectually, members are unlikely to have those beliefs disputed in any way they will find convincing."

fraternization *association, socialization, mingling, banding together, keeping company, hobnobbing, mixing, consorting, clubbing together, rubbing shoulders with.* There is no parallel based on the Latin for "sister," "soror."

fraternize *associate, socialize, mingle, band together, befriend, keep company, hobnob, mix, consort, club together, rub shoulders with.* There is no parallel based on the Latin for "sister," "soror."

fratricide although most dictionaries define this as the killing of a brother or sister, the word obviously comes from the Latin for "brother" and the correct sex-specific term, "sororicide," is rarely used. "Fratricide" is also used pseudogenerically when a better choice might be *internal struggle, internecine warfare, genocide.*

Frau there is nothing wrong with this word in German; the problem arises when it is used in English to convey a certain disdain for a narrowly defined role for women. There is no parallel English term for a man. *See also* hausfrau, Mademoiselle.

freedman *freed/former slave, ex-slave, free-issue black; freedman and freedwoman.*

Freedmen's Bureau, the/Freedmen's schools retain for historical accuracy.

freeman *citizen, citizen of a free country; freeman and freewoman.* "Freewoman" has had other connotations in the feminist movement; *The Freewoman,* one of the earliest feminist newspapers, was published in Great Britain as a weekly feminist review in 1911–1912.

Freemason "Freemason" (member of the Free and Accepted Masons or Ancient Free and Accepted Masons) always refers to a man. The Order of the Eastern Star is an affiliate, however, to which both women and men belong.

Frenchman *French native/citizen, French-born, Franco-, French person; Frenchman and Frenchwoman.* Too often "Frenchman/Frenchmen" are used as false generics. Plurals: *the French, French citizens/people/ persons, Frenchwomen and Frenchmen.*

freshman *first-year/first-semester/second-semester student, frosh, fresher, freshie, class of 1995, beginning/entering student, freshperson; beginner, novice, newcomer, greenhorn, tenderfoot.* Plurals: *first-year students, frosh, freshers, freshpeople, freshfolk.* "Freshman" has been eliminated from the *Yale Daily News,* also from *The Yale* (both now use "freshperson"); Harvard refers to "first years"; Princeton says "first-year students" is now the norm; "freshfolk" is used on the Oberlin campus; Cornell uses "Class of '99"; Stanford says "frosh" is increasingly sighted. A search of the Nexus database turned up 692 articles mentioning "frosh" between 1989 and 1993 (*Fortune* magazine). "Freshers" was commonly used earlier in the century (e.g., "when we were freshers" from Dorothy L. Sayers's 1936 *Gaudy Night*; "we were freshers together" in Margaret Kennedy's 1951 *Lucy Carmichael*). In "Here Come the Frosh" (*Atlantic Monthly,* February 1997), J. E. Lighter gives examples of the increasing use of "frosh" for the new members of Congress. According to Lighter, "frosh" does not appear to have come from "freshman" but rather from the 19th-century German use of *Frosch* (frog) for a student before entering the university. "That *frosh* has become the journalistic slang of choice for congressional freshmen seems inevitable in retrospect. It has a satisfying feel. It fits neatly in a headline. . . . Concise, familiar, associated with the sedulous world of academe, *frosh* is now respectful enough for members of any party."

freshman congressman *first-term member of Congress, frosh.* ***See also*** freshman.

frigid (referring to a woman's sexual response) *unaroused, unresponsive, uninterested, anorgasmic, nonorgasmic, preorgasmic.* "Frigid" is unscientific and sexist. Beware orgasm-as-norm thinking (contrary to cultural myth, it is possible to live a full life without being frequently orgasmic or, indeed, orgasmic at all). Men who cultivate reputations as high performers in the bedroom will be particularly careful not to label partners "frigid" as "frigidity" is most often traceable to an insensitive lover.

frivolous used almost exclusively of women and their interests and activities, this term should probably be replaced: *lighthearted, easygoing, trivial, insignificant, superficial, inane, vacuous, shallow, flimsy, idle, immature.*

frogman *military/deep-sea/scuba diver, skin-diver, underwater swimmer/ explorer, diver, frog; frogman and frogwoman.*

front-end bra *See* car bra.

front-end man *front-end mechanic.*

frontier this term often is ethnocentric. When used to mean the furthest reach of white settlement in the U.S., it is not much appreciated by American Indians; what for some represented the limits of known lands was for others their known, loved, and revered world.

frontiersman *frontier settler, pioneer, backsettler; frontierswoman and frontiersman.* ***See also*** frontier.

front man (industry) *stevedore, dockhand.* ***See also*** longshoreman, wharfman.

front man/frontman (music) *lead singer, vocalist, star, leader, front musician/player.*

front man *front, figurehead, nominal head, deputy, puppet, representative.*

front office man *manager, head, owner, upper-level manager, executive, policymaker;* sometimes, *front office, management.*

fruit *See* food names for people.

frump/frumpy because one of the two definitions of "frump" is an unattractive girl/woman, and because the terms are commonly reserved for women, you may need alternatives: *slob, sloven, unkempt person, stick-in-the-mud; dowdy, slovenly, unkempt, tacky, drab, old-fashioned, unfashionable, out-of-date, staid.*

fugleman *file leader, lead soldier, leader.*

full-blooded Tim Giago, objecting to the use of this term for American Indians (in *Indian Country Today*), says, "The day this same reporter writes 'full-blooded white man' or 'full-blooded African American,' then—and only then—will I know all races are being treated equally." *See also* half-breed/half-caste.

Fuller Brush man *Fuller Brush agent/distributor/independent distributor; Fuller Brush woman or Fuller Brush man.* About 85% of "Fuller Brush men" today are women.

fundamentalist reserve this for people and groups who self-identify as "fundamentalist." Otherwise, identify the characteristic you want to convey: *evangelical, militant, conservative, radical.* If you mean people who are very serious about their religion, *use devout, practicing, ortho-dox.* United Church of Christ minister Alexander Harper (in the *New York Times*) protested the increasing use of "fundamentalist" to describe those of strong religious convictions; where the meaning used to be "religiously conservative" it now often seems to mean "fanatical, potentially violent, possibly terroristic in political action." Harper says, "Within Christian fundamentalism, if the word can be used objectively anymore, there are biblical, doctrinal, and pietistic conservatives. The first typically stresses literal interpretation of the Scripture; the second, exclusive theories of salvation; the third, inner experiences of the spirit. They may or may not be political activists. One suspects that conservative Shiite Islam . . . admits to at least as many distinctions as those existing among Christian fundamentalists. I call for a moratorium on the use of 'fundamentalist' . . . the word only smears, casting no light but only heat, like ugly racial slurs."

funnyman *comedian, comic, humorist, wit, wisecracker, punster, satirist, comedist, clown, jokesmith, jokester, jester, mime; joker, practical joker, prankster.*

furnaceman *furnace installer/tender/stoker/repairer/cleaner.*

fuss (verb) this is almost exclusively reserved for women when in the same situation men would *object, argue, dispute, protest, quarrel, make a mountain out of a molehill*—or even *make a fuss*, which is different than fussing.

G

We believe the concern for words that are gender-tagged
is the most important shift in English usage in the last 400 years.

—*Anne Soukhanov*

Conventional English usage, including the generic use of masculine-gender words,
often obscures the actions, the contributions, and sometimes the very presence
of women. Turning our backs on that insight is an option, of course,
but it is an option like teaching children that the world is flat.

—*Casey Miller and Kate Swift*

Language is also a place of struggle.

—*bell hooks*

gabby nonsexist per se, "gabby" is functionally sexist and ageist because it is used exclusively for women and older men. Consider instead *talkative, loquacious, garrulous, voluble, fluent, glib, effusive, exuberant, talky, wordy, verbose, long-winded, windy, big-mouthed, talking a blue streak. See also* babble, bull session, chatter, chatterbox, gossip, gossipy, yenta.

gag man *gag writer, comedian.*

gal like many male-female word pairs, "gal" and "guy" have gone separate ways. "Gal" has few acceptable uses while "guy" is very common and in the plural can refer to both sexes. *See also* guy.

gal-boy this prison slang may have a certain limited legitimacy, although there is no parallel for women and no inclusive alternative.

gal Friday *See* girl Friday.

galley queen are there no lazy male flight attendants who hide out in the galley? Use instead *galley mouse.*

gamesman *gamesplayer, strategist, tactician; gamester, gambler, someone who sails suspiciously close to the wind/skates on thin ice/cuts corners/ squeaks home; risk-taker, high-flyer.*

gamesmanship *gamestership, expertise, skill, clever tactics, strategies; sailing close to the wind, sharp playing, cunning, suspiciously shrewd playing, dubious tactics, slight of hand, trickery.*

garageman *garage worker/attendant, gas station attendant/worker.*

garbageman *garbage collector/hauler, trash/refuse collector, sanitation worker;* sometimes, *garbage truck.*

gasman *gas fitter, gas pipe repairer/installer, gas appliance repairer/ installer.*

gateman *gatekeeper, gate tender/attendant.*

gathered to one's fathers *gathered to one's ancestors/forebears/mothers and fathers.*

gaucho always a man; there is no parallel for a woman and no inclusive term. *See also* cowboy.

gay (noun) using "gay" (or "Gay") as a noun to refer to individuals is not recommended; when referring to the general gay community in the plural, "Gays" is acceptable. *See also* gay (adjective), gay community, gay lifestyle, gay man, Gay Rights Movement, homophobia, homosexual, lesbian, queer.

gay (adjective) "gay," a term whose origins seem to be in 19th-century France and turn-of-the-century England, is used for issues, events, and places of relevance to gay men and lesbians. However, although "gay rights activists" work for the rights of both lesbians and gay men and other uses of "gay" are inclusive, the preference is to make women visible: "gay and lesbian activism," "lesbian and gay readership." Throughout the 1970s and 1980s, gay publications, gay bars, gay bookstores, etc., served men almost exclusively; to avoid confusion about who is included, use both adjectives. "Gay" is much preferred to "homosexual" because the latter emphasizes sexual practice whereas "gay" refers not just to sexual orientation but also to the cultural and social aspects of homosexuality. A person's sexual orientation is irrelevant in most situations; question the need to mention it. Some people feel they can no longer use the word "gay" in its meaning of merry, lively, or high-spirited. However, there is usually more anti-gay sentiment being expressed here than a legitimate linguistic grievance: most of us manage to deal with other homonyms—when we hear "the principal/principle was wrong," we decode it according to context, and for many years we insisted we could tell the difference between "man" (meaning adult male) and "man" (meaning humankind). *See also* gay (noun), gay community, gay lifestyle, gay man, Gay Rights Movement, homophobia, homosexual, lesbian, queer.

gay blade/gay dog these terms refer only to men and the use of "gay" (usually distinguishable in its different senses) could be ambiguous here. Consider using instead *high-flyer, fun-lover, high-spirited person; hedonist, sensualist, flirt, bedhopper, free spirit, swinger. See also* ladies' man, man about town, womanizer.

gay community this umbrella term, used like such phrases as "the Finnish American community" to describe groups with a shared trait or background, can refer to both men and women but "lesbian and gay communities" is preferred.

gay lifestyle Sonia Johnson says, "It's funny how heterosexuals have lives and the rest of us have 'lifestyles'" (*Going Out of Our Minds*). The fuzzy concept of a "lifestyle" has become code to convey "otherness" and "wrongness"; clear expression would demand that one specify what one is trying to say with "the homosexual lifestyle" or "the gay lifestyle." Most lesbians and gay men have as much or more in common with heterosexuals than they do with each other; they have jobs and library cards and dental appointments, they put money in parking meters, sprain their ankles, go to ballgames, and pay income taxes. There is no monolithic "lifestyle."

gay man this is the preferred term for a man with a same-sex emotional and sexual orientation. *See also* gay (adjective), Gay Rights Movement, homophobia, homosexual, queer.

Gay Rights Movement the beginnings of the movement, originally called the Gay Liberation Movement, can be traced to New York City's 1969 Stonewall Rebellion (also Stonewall Uprising or Stonewall riots) when gay men and lesbians fought back against a police raid on a gay bar. Goals of the movement include equal rights for lesbians and gay men, educating about AIDS and homosexuality, and working to eradicate hate crimes. PFLAG (Parents and Friends of Lesbians and Gays) is a well-organized and active organization within the movement. "Gay rights" are the same rights presently enjoyed by other citizens of the United States—particularly the right to live free from discrimination in employment, housing, education, etc. These rights are often referred to by anti-gay groups as "special rights," "special protections," "special-interest privileges," "special protected status," and "specialized legal perks"; they are portrayed as extra rights, rights the average person does not have, when in fact they are simply the same rights. In 1996, the passage of the federal Employment Non-Discrimination Act, a simple measure to outlaw discrimination against gay men and lesbians on the job, was defeated. *See also* gay (adjective), gay man, homophobia, homosexual, lesbian, queer.

geisha always a woman; there is no parallel for a man and no inclusive term. Use only in its narrowest definition, that is, a Japanese woman with special training in the art of providing lighthearted entertainment, especially for men.

gendarme when in France, use "gendarme" even though it is a masculine word (it means "men of arms"). There are, however, both female and male gendarmes with identical job descriptions. At one time the French experimented with the term "gendarmette" for its new female members, but the term was deemed profoundly sexist, was caricatured in a movie, and has since been retired.

gender understanding the difference between sex and gender is crucial to the appropriate use of language referring to women and men. Sex is biological: people with male genitals are male, and people with female genitals are female. Gender is cultural: our notions of "masculine" tell us how we expect men to behave and our notions of "feminine" tell us how we expect women to behave—but these may have nothing to do with biology. When deciding whether a word is restricted to one sex or the other, the only acceptable limitation is genetic sex. A woman cannot be a sperm donor because it's biologically impossible. It may be culturally unusual for a man to be a secretary, but it is not biologically impossible; to assume all secretaries are women is sexist because the issue is gender, not sex. Gender signifies a subjective cultural attitude while sex is an objective biological fact. Some people insist that "gender" be used to refer only to grammatical categories, but the term is currently being used widely for the meaning of sex-related roles. *See also* gender roles.

gender bender/gender changer this has nothing to do with people; it is an electronic device, which allows either changing electrical plugs or sockets to the opposite gender (male to female, female to male) or connecting cables with the same type of connector ends (male to male or female to female).

gender bias gender bias is behavior or decision-making that is based on or reveals: stereotypical attitudes about the nature and roles of men and women; perceptions of their relative worth; myths and misconceptions about the social and economic realities encountered by both sexes (*Judicial Council Advisory Committee on Gender Bias in the Courts Report*, 1990).

gender-fair language words that treat both sexes equally constitute gender-fair language. The words may or may not reveal the person's sex. For example, "girls and boys" specifies sex but because both are included, the phrase is gender-fair. Terms like "mail carrier," "firefighter," and "lawyer" are also gender-fair because they could be either sex.

gender-free language words that do not specify gender constitute gender-free language. "Students," "police officers," and "laypeople" are gender-free terms; "businessman" and "businesswoman" are not.

gender gap used in politics, economics, sociology, education, and other fields, this term gained prominence in 1982 when, for the first time in opinion-polling history, a significant sex difference in the job-approval rating surfaced during Ronald Reagan's first term; 61% of men thought he was doing a good job, but only 42% of women did. "Gender gap" has also been commonly used with respect to standardized test scores, where girls/young women used to score higher on verbal tests and boys/young men scored higher on math tests. In a discussion of these differences, a male director of math studies at Johns Hopkins said, "I wish the feminists would get busy and do careful longitudinal research on kids from kindergarten through high school." It was not clear why research in this area was the responsibility of "the feminists." Researchers of both sexes have since discovered that the gender gap has all but disappeared in verbal scores and has greatly narrowed in math scores. It is interesting that "gender gap" discussions are always phrased in terms of why women vote differently from men, why girls do better/worse than boys on tests/in school; the male is assumed to be the default.

gender roles gender roles (sometimes called sex roles) involve attitudes and behaviors that society expects *because* someone is a woman or *because* someone is a man. Roles traditionally assigned to men are "provider" and "protector." Women have been assigned "caregiver" and "sex object" roles. Biologically, both women and men can provide, protect, nurture, or be a sex object, but most often "cultural influences have been misrepresented as biological imperatives" (Deborah Rhode, *Theoretical Perspectives on Sexual Differences*). Lucile Duberman *(Gender and Sex in Society)* says "the truth is our gender roles are not innate and God-given, nor are they necessarily irrevocable. Society creates gender roles, and society can alter them." Biologist Robert Trivers and others suggest that there was a fairly reasonable perpetuation-of-the-species basis for these roles: to ensure that one of his many small and fragile gametes reproduced his kind, the man needed to fertilize as many women as possible—and they needed to be attractive to him and young enough to bear children, thus his emphasis on seeing women as "sex object"; a woman, on the other hand, with many fewer fertilization opportunities for her larger, less numerous gametes, needed quality rather than quantity—a partner with enough resources (a "provider") to maintain her and her child through the nine-month gestation and the growing-up period. This at least partly explains the stereotypical association of men focusing on women's bodies, and women focusing on men's money. Contemporary realities offer more flexibility to both sexes and freedom from rigid gender roles—if we can model this for upcoming generations of children. In 1993 some artists, parents, feminists, and antiwar activists claimed they "surgically altered" about 300 G.I. Joes and Barbies, switching their voice boxes, so that this "mutant colony of Barbies-on-steroids" (David Firestone, in the *New York Times*) roared things like "Attack!" "Vengeance is mine!" and "Eat lead, Cobra!" The altered G.I. Joes, meanwhile, twittered, "Will we ever have enough clothes?" and "Let's plan our dream wedding!" *See also* gender.

general population use only in its true sense, i.e., the population to which everyone belongs. The "general population" is sometimes contrasted with lesbians and gays, with those with disabilities, with the "welfare" population, or with other groups not very much in favor with whoever is writing or speaking.

gentile to Jews, a non-Jew; to Mormons, a non-Mormon.

gentleman except for the still-acceptable generic public address of "ladies and gentlemen" and for an occasional, "He is a real gentleman," this word ought to be retired. Its true mate, "gentlewoman," is long gone, and its other partner, "lady," has been retired in spite of herself. The word has lost its original meaning; Marjorie Luft collects published reports of such "gentle" men as the "gentleman" who beat his dog to death, the arsonists whose work resulted in the death of two women (Crime Stoppers asked the public to help bring "these gentlemen to justice"), or serial killer Ted Bundy—also referred to in news articles as a gentleman. Other examples quoted in the press: "the gentleman who shot President Reagan" and "the gentleman who raped the elderly woman." *See also* gentlewoman, lady.

gentleman farmer *hobby/Sunday/weekend/amateur farmer, farmer.*

gentleman friend *See* boyfriend.

gentlemanlike/gentlemanly this vague stereotype conveys different meanings to different people according to their perceptions of what a man ought or ought not do, say, think, wear, feel, look like. These words have nothing to do with sex and everything to do with gender. Use instead *courteous, civil, refined, polite, well-mannered, polished, mannerly, brave, thoughtful, considerate, agreeable, accommodating, decent, discreet, dependable, punctilious, civilized, cultivated, dignified.* These adjectives can be used equally well of women. They are not synonyms for "gentlemanlike/gentlemanly" but rather what society hears by those terms.

gentleman's agreement *unwritten/informal/oral/honorable/verbal agreement, verbal/oral promise/contract, handshake, your word, mutual understanding.*

gentlemen of the press *representatives of the press, press corps, journalists, reporters.* **See also** newsman/newspaperman.

gentle sex, the avoid; in its quiet way it discriminates against both women and men.

gentlewoman this would be appropriate when used with "gentleman" (although it never is), but it should especially not be used alone as it has developed along very different lines: We might say, "He's a real gentleman," while we would never say, "She's a real gentlewoman," or we might say, "That gentleman over there is waiting to speak to you," but not "That gentlewoman over there is waiting to speak to you."

gerontology this term, meaning the scientific study of old age and aging, comes from the Greek for "old man" but functions inclusively. Geriatrics, which is the branch of medicine that deals with diseases and problems specific to older people, is based on the Greek for "old age." The two words are not synonymous.

Gestapo/gestapo reserve these terms for their primary meanings (the terrorist German internal security police as organized under the Nazi regime or police organizations with very similar tactics). Using "Gestapo/gestapo" casually or "humorously" for high-handed people robs the words of their power and discounts their horrors. **See also** concentration camp, "final solution," Hitler/little Hitler, holocaust, Nazi/nazi.

ghetto because of the negative connotations of ghetto (crime, dilapidation, persecution, poverty, "otherness"), replace it when possible: *neighborhood, community, area, quarter, section of town/the city, district.* By adding descriptive or geographical adjectives to these general terms, you will give your audience a much more precise idea of your meaning. **See also** inner city.

ghetto blaster *boombox, portable stereo.* "Ghetto blaster" is unacceptable and offensive.

G.I. since this stands for "general issue" or "government issue," referring to everything in military life that is standardized, orderly, or regimented, including the soldiers themselves, it is inclusive.

giantess *giant.* **See also** "feminine" word endings.

gigolo there is no all-purpose word describing both men and women that conveys the same meaning. For women we use "kept woman"; French slang uses "gigolette" (a woman of "easy morals"). Gigolos have also been known as lounge lizards and taxi dancers. If you require a sex-neutral term try *lover, prostitute, parasite.* **See also** boy toy, gold digger, kept woman, toyboy.

G.I. Joe *G.I.* This nickname for U.S. armed forces personnel comes from "general issue" or "government issue" and thus without the "Joe" is not gender-specific.

gingerbread man *gingerbread cookie/figure, gingerbread man and gingerbread woman.*

gird (up) one's loins perceived as sexist because it is assumed to refer to men, this term comes from Proverbs 31:17 where the loins in question actually belong to a woman. If you want an alternative use *prepare, prepare for battle, buckle on one's armor, get the steam up, get in gear, batten down the hatches, grit one's teeth.*

girl (referring to a woman) *woman, young woman.* "Girl" is reserved for preteens or at the most for those 15 or under; it is objectionable and demeaning when used by men for young women or women. Some women have always referred to themselves and their women friends as "girls" either out of long habit, local custom, or because they continued to think of themselves that way—and this usage is enjoying a resurgence of popularity. With the mainstreaming of such well-liked African American expressions as "girlfriend" and "You go, girl!", "girl" is seen more often—on T-shirts and in terms like girl group, Cybergrrl, the Riot Grrrls, and the Guerrilla Girls. "No longer just a badge of youth or a sign of silliness, servitude, or class difference, 'Girl!' has almost become a mark of pride in one's gender, a sarcastic scoff at those who for centuries patronized females with its use" (Jessica B. Baker, in the periodical *Lilith*). However, for others to refer to women this way is unacceptable (and most particularly in the workplace) unless given tacit or explicit permission by them to use it. Mariah Burton Nelson notes the use of "girl" as an insult in sports, as in "you play/throw/catch like a girl." *See also* girl Friday, girlfriend, Guerrilla Girls, "insider/outsider" rule, office boy/office girl.

girl Friday *assistant, office assistant/specialist, administrative/executive/ program assistant, clerk, right hand, secretary, aide, office helper, gofer; man Friday and woman Friday* if used gender-fairly, although it is generally only "woman Friday" that is used, and even then there is reluctance to use "woman" instead of "girl." *See also* girl, office boy/ office girl.

girlfriend there is still no concise, appropriate, universally accepted term to describe the woman we love. Those in committed relationships (whether opposite-sex or same-sex) need a word with the corresponding weight and meaning of "wife" or "spouse" to denote their partners. Discussing the problem of introducing the woman she's lived with for seven years to her boss, syndicated columnist Deb Price concludes, "Who says the gay rights movement hasn't made a lot of progress? In just 100 years, we've gone from the love that dare not speak its name to the love that doesn't know its name." The increasing numbers of unmarried men and women living in stable, longterm relationships have the same problem. None of the following terms work in all situations; some of them hardly work in any situation. But until the right word comes along, you might want to consider some of them: *friend; woman friend* (if "man friend" is also used); *female friend* (if "male friend" is also used); *best friend; spouse* (this is becoming increasingly popular; E. J. Graff, in *Out* magazine, says "'Spouse' at least puts the pair in the same bed. Unlike 'lover,' 'spouse' knows the bedroom is just one of many rooms in the house"); *partner, domestic partner,* or *life partner* (despite its business associations, this is one of the most popular choices); *companion* (literally, the person with whom you share bread) or *longtime companion* (this is the second most popular choice); *the woman I'm seeing; significant other; soulmate; constant/loving/live-in/intimate companion/partner; partner of long standing; escort, date, datemate, steady, romantic interest, heartthrob; mate, housemate, roommate, bunkie; paramour, consort, lover, longtime love, live-in, live-in lover; fiancé, betrothed, sweetheart; sweetie, gal pal, main/major squeeze* (and for stars, *offscreen squeeze*); *my reason for living, the love/light of my life, alter ego, second self, mainstay, the woman in my life.* Note that "girlfriend," meaning pal or buddy, has made a comeback and is acceptable where "boyfriend" in the same sense has not and is not. *See also* better half, domestic partner.

girlhood acceptable sex-specific word. If you want a generic use *childhood, innocence, youth.*

girlie there are no circumstances in which this word is acceptable.

girlie magazine/movie *pornographic magazine/movie.*

girlie show *X-rated "entertainment" featuring women.*

girlish for this vague and almost always pejorative term consider alternatives: *ingenuous, naive, childlike, innocent, open, friendly, eager, youthful, immature, self-conscious, inept, bright-eyed, optimistic, cheerful, adolescent, childish, sophomoric, juvenile, kiddish, infantile, callow, unsophisticated.*

girls and boys *See* boys and girls.

Girl Scout the Girl Scouts of the United States of America (GSUSA) is a girls-only organization (although leaders include both men and women) with strong gender identity that promotes self-esteem, independence, and a variety of skills and interests among girls while also providing a supportive network for many members. Founded in 1912 by Juliette Gordon Low, membership is currently over 3 million. The correct term for adults is troop leaders. The Boy Scouts of America (BSA) and GSUSA prefer Boy Scout and Girl Scout, but there are generic terms for the rare occasion when you need one: *scout, youth scout, scouter. See also* Boy Scout.

give away the bride *escort the bride to the altar, accompany the bride down the aisle.* Women are no longer "given" by their fathers to their husbands.

give someone Harry there is nothing wrong with using this expression, but be aware of how many like it in the English language are male-based. Balance their use with female-based expressions, creative expressions of your own, or sex-neutral alternatives: *give someone hell, dress down, chew out, scold, reprimand, castigate, call someone on the carpet, read someone the riot act, tell someone where to get off. See also* sex-linked expressions.

glass ceiling the glass ceiling is a metaphor for all the barriers, overt and covert, that corporate, industry, military, academic, and professional women keep banging their heads against—they can see the top of the organization, but they can't get there. According to the corporate research firm Catalyst, 80% of CEOs admit that male managers stereotype and discriminate against women employees: women are excluded from the men's communication network where men who are still more comfortable with other men can maintain the status quo; women find it difficult to find mentors and role models; they are often harassed and must deal with stereotypical language and sexist behavior on the part of superiors and peers; in a Catch-22, women with family responsibilities are seen as lacking commitment to the organization, while women who are fully committed to the organization are often seen as abrasive, overly aggressive, and unfeminine. Mary Dingee Fillmore *(Women MBAs)* asked one woman what she would need to win a top slot in her corporation. The answer: "A sex-change operation." Anne Jardim (in *The New Yorker*) says, "The ceiling isn't glass; it's a very dense layer of men." And a woman quoted in Anne H. Soukhanov, *Word Watch*, says, "Looking through the glass darkly, one can define *glass ceiling* as 'what the men in the boardroom are standing on.'" *See also* executive, manageress, mommy track, wage earner.

glass cellar coined by Warren Farrell *(The Myth of Male Power),* this term refers to the ways in which men are more likely to die than women; "Just as the 'glass ceiling' describes the invisible barrier that keeps women out of jobs with the most pay, the 'glass cellar' describes the invisible barrier that keeps men in jobs with the most hazards. . . . Every day, almost as many men are killed at work as were killed during the average day in [the] Vietnam [war]." The death professions are men's biggest "glass cellar": 94% of occupational deaths occur to men; the U.S. has a worker death rate three to four times higher than Japan's; the U.S. has only one job safety inspector for every six fish and game inspectors; every workday hour, one male construction worker in the U.S. loses his life; the more hazardous the job, the greater the percentage of men in the field (firefighting is 99% male, logging 98%, heavy trucking 98%, construction 98%, coal mining 97%). Percentages of women are highest in the safest occupations (secretary is 99% female, receptionist 97%). The 10 "glass cellars" of male disposability identified by Farrell are: suicide (more than three out of every four suicides are men); imprisonment (more prisoners are men); homelessness (men are 85% of street homeless); the death (high-risk) professions; disease (men die earlier of all 15 of the major diseases and causes of accidents; assassinations and hostage-taking (women and children are more often released); executions (women are given the death penalty but generally only men are executed); the males-only draft; combat, which depends principally on men; early deaths (nondisease factors lead to men dying early more often than women). Farrell says, "We don't call male-killing sexism, we call it glory. We don't call it a slaughter when one million men are killed or maimed in the battles of the Somme in World War I; we call it serving the country. We don't call those who selected only men to die murderers, we call them voters. Our slogan for women is 'A woman's body, a woman's choice.' Our slogan for men is, 'A man's gotta do what a man's gotta do.'"

glassman *glassmaker, glass dealer/retailer/repairer.*

GLBT/glbt shorthand for gay, lesbian, bisexual, transgender, this convenient and inclusive adjective is useful in many contexts (don't bother pointing out that it sounds like a sandwich; that's already been done).

gloomy Gus *spoilsport, killjoy, crapehanger, party-pooper, prophet of doom and gloom, gloom and doomer, grinch, wet blanket.*

glowboy *radiation-control/nuclear power plant worker, jumper, fresh meat, radiation sponge, sponge* (terms from Anne H. Soukhanov, *Word Watch*). The male-linked term is used for yet another of the high-risk jobs usually held by men. *See also* glass cellar.

G-man *government/federal/FBI/plainclothes/secret/undercover agent, government investigative agent, intelligence officer, member of the FBI, spy.*

God although we have not assigned God an ethnic origin or an age, we have thought nothing of assigning a gender and a religion (God always belongs to the same one we do). Too often the default, the unmarked "God" is assumed to be Christian. And contrary to what most people understand, theology has never ruled that the Christian God is male. In the fourth century, St. Gregory of Nazianzus summed up traditional thought when he wrote that "Father" and "Son" as applied to the persons of the Trinity did not name their natures or their essences but rather were metaphors for their relationship to each other. John 4:24 says that God is pure Spirit (and thus is genderless), and the words for God in both Greek and Hebrew are sex-neutral. Sandra M. Schneiders *(Women and the Word)* lists some of the many metaphors we have for God (sun, rock, spring, fire, lion, leopard, she-bear, mother eagle, potter, builder, shepherd, hero, warrior, physician, midwife, homemaker, judge, king, mother, husband, father) and says, "While we are immediately aware that the personal God is not really a rock or a mother eagle, it is easy enough to imagine that God is really a king or a father. . . . We create the metaphor to say something about God; but then God seems to be saying something about the vehicle of the metaphor. Thus, if God is a king, there is a tendency to see kings as divine. If God is male, then males are divine and masculinity becomes normative of humanity." Theologian Mary Daly says simply, "If God is male, then male is God." God's presumed masculinity in Christianity has provided a religious legitimization of the social structures and attitudes that treat women as second-class, non-normative, derivative human beings. The key to inclusive God-language is to be conscious that we are using metaphors ("God is like a . . ." but not "God is a . . .") to make a pure Spirit more accessible to us. Therefore, use a variety of metaphors to enlarge our images of God, balance male and female metaphors, and use masculine or feminine pronouns only for specific, limited metaphorical uses (otherwise eliminate sex-specific pronouns). For an excellent discussion of the theology of metaphors for God, see Elizabeth A. Johnson, C.S.J., in *Commonweal,* 29 January 1993. When writing to Orthodox Jews, some people use "G-d" instead of "God"; in their tradition, anything with "God" written on it must be respectfully buried. *See also* Allah; Father (God); Father, Son, and Holy Spirit/Ghost; God/he; God/himself; God/his; God of our Fathers; Holy Spirit; Jehovah; Lord; Son of Man; Yahweh.

goddess religions in which people revered their supreme creator as female existed from approximately 7000 B.C. until about A.D. 500 (Merlin Stone, *When God Was a Woman*). Retain "goddess" in references to the goddess religions and to feminist spirituality that uses the term. When "goddess" indicates a lesser god, replace it with "god"; capitalize both or neither.

godfather/godmother acceptable terms. The use of "godfather" popularized by Mario Puzo's 1969 *The Godfather* has no comparable "godmother" partner, and alternatives are mostly male-oriented: *boss of bosses, head don, capo di tutti capi, don, capo.*

God/he avoid gender-specific pronouns by: (1) replacing "he" or "him" with "God" or another name for God; (2) recasting the sentence; (3) replacing the pronouns with "you/yours" or "who/whom/that." *See also* God, God/himself, God/his.

God/himself some people are using "Godself." "God himself" can sometimes be "that very God." Since the word "God" is sex-neutral, the correct pronoun should also be sex-neutral. You can often circumlocute to avoid the reflexive pronoun (sometimes this is best done by changing the verb that takes the pronoun). *See also* God, God/he, God/his.

God/his replace phrases like "his goodness," "his love," or "by his mercy" with sex-neutral expressions ("divine goodness," "eternal love," or "out of mercy") or with the second person: "Your Goodness," "Your Mercy." The proper possessive pronoun for God is "God's," for example, "God's goodness," "God's mercy." *See also* God, God/he, God/himself.

God of our Fathers *God of our ancestors/of all generations/of our forebears/of our mothers and fathers.*

go-go boy *go-go manager, go-go broker.* Fast-moving speculative funds called "go-go funds" were usually handled by an up-and-coming young man. Note the nonparallel "go-go boy" and "go-go girl."

go-go girl *go-go dancer.*

gold digger although theoretically this could be used of either sex, it is reserved for women. Parallel male terms in some cases might be "gigolo" or "toyboy," but try instead to describe the person you have in mind with inclusive adjectives: *greedy, grasping, avaricious, exploitive, self-seeking, rapacious, out for all one can get.*

Golden Ager *See* senior/senior citizen.

gondolier there are only about 320 gondolas left in Venice, and all of them are plied by men.

Good Humor man *Good Humor/ice cream vendor.*

good Joe *good sort, agreeable/good-natured/good-humored person.*

goodman/goodwife obsolete, but retain in historical material. Note the nonparallel "man/wife."

good old boy/good ole boy *loyal Southerner, Southern supporter, supporter, sidekick, crony, pal, goombah.* These terms were particularly popular in the mid-1960s when they referred to the Texas cronies of President Lyndon B. Johnson. Women don't often choose to play a "good ole boy" role; sometimes this might be the appropriate term for a particular man. *See also* old-boys' network, old-girls' network.

good old boys' network *See* old-boys' network.

good old girls' network *See* old-girls' network.

good Samaritan woman or man.

goody two shoes the original Little Goody Two Shoes from the nursery rhyme by Oliver Goldsmith was a girl who earned an undeserved reputation as a self-righteous, affected little do-gooder, but the phrase is scarcely perceived as sex-linked today. If you need strictly inclusive alternatives use *goody-goody, do-gooder.*

gook *See* ethnic slurs.

gossip not sexist per se (it originally meant "godparent"), "gossip" is functionally sexist because the term is reserved for women. For the verb use *talk, talk idly, talk over, talk up a storm, converse, discuss, shoot the breeze, pass the time of day, make small talk, jaw, make chin music, wag tongues, rattle away, run off at the mouth, beat one's gums, bend someone's ear, talk someone's arm/head off, talk the hind legs off a donkey; repeat everything one hears, tell secrets, spread rumors/stories, sling mud, dish the dirt.* For the noun use: *rumormonger, whisperer, talebearer, blabbermouth, big mouth, mudslinger, motormouth, jawsmith, loose tongue, chin wag, newsmonger, windbag, idle talker; palaver, idle/small/empty talk, scuttlebutt, hearsay, chin music, talkfest, an earful. See also* babble, bull session, chatter, chatterbox, gabby, gossipy, yenta.

gossipy *long-winded, big-mouthed, talkative, curious, loquacious, garrulous, gregarious, windy; rumormongering. See also* gossip.

governess to refer to a governor of either sex, use *governor.* For someone who teaches young children, use *tutor, private teacher, teacher, child mentor, instructor.* Note what happened to the formerly parallel word pair "governor/governess" over the years. As of 1997, 47 of the 50 U.S. governors are men; 48 are white.

gownsman *academic, academician, scholar.*

granddaddy/daddy of them all this is fairly harmless and it has the near relative "mother of all . . ." expression to balance it, but if you need something sex-neutral try *biggest/oldest/grandest/best of them all. See also* mother of all . . .

grand duchess retain for official title, which can refer either to the ruler of a grand duchy or to the wife or widow of a grand duke.

grande dame a complimentary sex-linked term, except that there is no precise equivalent for a man.

grandfather aid this legislative term must probably be left as is; those who have experimented with calling it "grandparent aid" find that others don't recognize it.

grandfather clause leave as is in legal and historical uses. Otherwise use *escape/existing-condition clause, exemption, retroactive exemption.*

grandfather clock/grandmother clock to the initiated, these terms indicate the size of the clock. The fact that all grandmothers are not shorter than all grandfathers is evidently irrelevant here; as is the case with many other male-female word pairs, the female term has all but disappeared. For an inclusive term you could consider *floor clock.*

grandfatherly/grandmotherly these vague adjectives have no universal meanings unless it is "kindly." The terms are especially useless in describing appearance. The fact of grandparenthood is often irrelevant; when it is relevant, recognize its important contributions and avoid outdated stereotypes.

Grandmaster the title "Grandmaster" for a member of the U.S. Chess Federation indicates a very specific level of ability and has no synonyms (Andy Sabl). Master, Candidate Master, National Master, and International Master are also specialized chess terms with no substitutes. Grandmaster is sometimes abbreviated GM (IGM for "International Grandmaster").

granny/grannie OK; "gramp/gramps" is for a man.

granny dress/gown use if you like; otherwise consider *old-fashioned/ Victorian/high-necked dress/gown.*

granny dumping *elderly abandonment, packed-suitcase syndrome.* "Granny dumping" was one of the American Dialect Society's New Words of the Year for 1991. Anne H. Soukhanov *(Word Watch)* defines it as offensive slang for the practice in which an elderly person is left in a hospital emergency room—usually by relatives, caregivers, or apartment manager—with a suitcase of essential personal effects.

granny knot this sexist term (it describes an insecure knot made inadvertently when one is trying to tie a square knot) has no "gramps" parallel and no good synonym.

grantsman *grantwriter, grantswriter.*

grantsmanship *the fine art of obtaining grants, grant-getting, the knack of attracting grants, grant-getting/grant-writing skills/ability.* There is no one-word substitute for this handy, but sexist, term.

grass widow/grass widower both terms refer to someone who is divorced, separated, or whose spouse is temporarily away, but "grass widow" has additional dictionary definitions (although they are rarely used) referring to a discarded mistress or an unmarried mother. "Grass widow" is also used more often than is "grass widower." Use the terms in parallel ways, or not at all. *See also* widow/widower.

Great Britain "Great Britain" refers to the island comprising England, Scotland, and Wales; "England" is one of the countries of Great Britain; "United Kingdom" refers to Great Britain plus Northern Ireland; "Britain" refers to the island of Great Britain in the period before the reign of Alfred the Great (A.D. 871–899). *See also* British/Briton/Brit, Englishman.

greater love than this has no man *greater love than this has no one.*

Green Mountain Boys leave as is (historical term).

greensman *greenskeeper.*

Griselda, patient *See* patient Griselda.

grisette if you mean a prostitute, use *prostitute.* There is no male parallel, so if you need a sex-neutral alternative for its other meaning, use *member of the working class, working-class person.*

groceryman *grocer, grocery store owner/worker.*

groomsman *best man, attendant.* Avoid "groomsman"; its opposite number ("bridesmaid") is nonparallel ("maid/man"). "Best man" is used with "best woman," and "attendant" is used when the bride's witness is also called an attendant.

groundsman *groundskeeper, grounds/yard worker, caretaker, landscaper, gardener, maintenance worker, parks worker.*

groupie although theoretically inclusive, "groupie" is used only for young women, and there is no parallel for young men. If you want something less sex-specific consider *admirer, fan, follower, worshiper at the throne.*

guardsman *guard, soldier, guardian, member of the guards, guard member/officer, National Guard member.*

Guerrilla Girls correct term for the group of art-world women who began papering sections of New York City with smartly designed black-and-white posters in 1985. Using sarcasm, statistics, and bold graphics, the posters charged galleries, museums, collectors, critics, and white male artists with sexism and racism. This term gives "girl" a new twist by associating it with the aggressive "guerrilla." *See also* artist, girl (woman).

Guatemalan American people from Guatemala dislike this term; it is like saying "Latin American American" because they already *are* Americans (Alex-Edmund S. DaHinten, Guatemalan Socio-Cultural Committee).

guildsman *guild member.*

guinea *See* ethnic slurs.

gumshoe this term, from the shoes with gum-rubber soles they wore, no longer belongs exclusively to male detectives like Dashiell Hammett's Sam Spade, Raymond Chandler's Phillip Marlowe, and Ross MacDonald's Lou Archer; we now have, among others, Marcia Muller's Sharon McCone, Sara Paretsky's V. I. Warshawski, Linda Barnes's Carlotta Carlyle, and Sue Grafton's Kinsey Millhone.

gunman *killer, armed/professional killer, assassin, robber, intruder, slayer, gun, trigger, hired gun/assassin, gunfighter, gunner, shooter, thug,* *gunslinger, gun-wielder, gun-toter, gunsel, sharpshooter, sniper, attacker, outlaw, bandit, terrorist, gangster, racketeer, mobster, hoodlum, liquidator, executioner, enforcer, croaker.*

gun moll *accomplice, gun-toting accomplice, sidekick, confederate in crime, gangster's companion.* **See also** girlfriend, gunman.

guru this term's original meaning (from the Hindu) is a personal spiritual teacher, and English uses it to also mean a trusted adviser or a recognized leader in a field. In the computer field, a guru is an expert, implying not only a wizard (someone highly skilled in a particular piece of hardware/ software) but also a knowledge resource for others (John A. Hobson). Use for both sexes. If you want something perceived as less masculine consider *spiritual guide/teacher/leader/adviser, sage, oracle, adviser, counselor; leader, authority.*

guy "*Guy* . . . may be undergoing a sea change. It has no history of common gender to support the vocative use of its plural form when addressed to an all-female or mixed male and female group, as in 'Hi guys.' But by the 1980s that salutation had become common . . . as had the usage exemplified by the nurse who, speaking to her Lamaze childbirth class, says, 'Now when you guys are going into labor . . .'" (Casey Miller and Kate Swift, in Jane Mills, *Womanwords*, 2nd ed.). When syndicated columnist Diane Crowley writes, "Does your husband know what you want from him? Do you know what he expects from you? Or is each of you assuming that the other guy is a mind reader?" the singular, inclusive use of "guy" is perfectly clear. Douglas Hofstadter (*Metamagical Themas*) used to be irritated by the inclusive use of "guys" but says now, "it appears to me that 'you guys' is indeed drifting—in fact, has already irretrievably drifted—over to being as close to generic as it could get." Miller and Swift equate the inclusive "you guys" with the word "child," which used to mean only a girl child and now means both; it lost its primary reference to one sex and became a term comfortably used of both, "a process we think *guys* is even now undergoing." They tell about the little girl at camp who asks her bunkmates, "Why am I the guy who always has to do the sweeping?" and the little boy who whispers shyly to the great-aunts he is visiting, "Do you guys have any candy?" "They are turning *guy* into a common-gender noun whether adults like it or not." Some people think that women use "guys" to appropriate for themselves the prestige that men enjoy in society. However, it is probably truer that the positive characteristics *guy* tends to evoke are not sex-related in the minds of those who use it; there is a need for an inclusive term to convey such qualities as confidence, mutuality, and camaraderie and "guy/guys" fills the bill.

guys and gals this phrase is acceptable for casual use with people you know. Otherwise consider *folks, people. See also* gal, guy.

gyp *cheat, defraud, rip off, soak, fleece, hoodwink, swindle, deceive, victimize, pull the wool over someone's eyes, take in, buffalo, con, sting, put across, put one over on, rig, fix, rook, gull, exploit, take advantage of, diddle.* The ethnocentric and pejorative "gyp" is considered unacceptable by most people.

Gypsy/Gypsies replace the singular noun with *Rom* or *Romani*; the plural is *Roma, Roms,* or *Romanies*; the adjective is *Romani* (as in the International Romani Union). If these terms are unfamiliar to your audience and you need to relate them to "Gypsy," capitalize the word. Whenever possible refer to specific Romani groups, e.g., Romanichal, Kalderash, Bashaldo. Although scattered among many countries, they share a history and have their own language and social hierarchy. For centuries the Roma have been severely oppressed and regarded as second-class citizens (and in some countries, not as citizens at all). Although there is virtually no mention of the Roma in references to the Holocaust and accurate figures are difficult to ascertain, it seems likely that one-fifth to one-fourth of the Romani population perished in Nazi death camps. An estimated 8 to 12 million Roma live in Europe today, where they are currently facing a surge of anti-Rom slogans and activities by neo-fascist groups in Eastern Europe. *See also* gyp.

H

Habit with him was all the test of truth,
It must be right: I've done it from my youth.
—*George Crabbe*

The perpetual obstacle to human advancement is custom.
—*John Stuart Mill*

There's nothing more innately human than the tendency to transmute what has become customary into what has been divinely ordained.
—*Suzanne La Follette*

habitué grammatically masculine in French (the feminine would be habituée) "habitué" is used for both sexes in English—a convention that has been suggested for other terms with "-ée" and "-é" endings. *See also* "feminine" word endings.

hackman *cabdriver.*

hag although there are attempts to reclaim this word's older meaning—a mature wise-woman—it is better avoided in its more widespread pejorative meaning.

hail-fellow-well-met *backslapping, hearty, jovial, breezy, extroverted, heartily informal, convivial, comradely, jocular, playful, full of life, in high spirits, glad hand.*

hair-do because this is used almost exclusively for women you may want to use *hairstyle.*

half-breed/half-caste these terms are unacceptable when referring to people of mixed ancestry or mixed descent. "*Half-breed* and *half-caste* are senseless. We're not half of anything. We are whole people" (Jaimie Markham, in *Colors*, 1994). Tim Giago, publisher of *Indian Country*

Today, the largest U.S. Indian weekly, says, "Two words . . . that create division and suggest a class status, almost like the caste system in India, are 'full blood' and 'mixed blood' or 'half-breed.' Research has shown that these terms were created by the federal bureaucracy to place Indian people into racial pigeon holes." They are equally offensive when used of the Aboriginal peoples of Australia. *See also* aborigine, Indian, mélange.

handicapism the attitudes, practices, and physical obstacles that lead to unequal and unfair treatment of people with disabilities constitute handicapism. A handicapist culture has a high tolerance for bias and discrimination against those with disabilities, sometimes seeming unaware of their presence in society and valuing the nondisabled more highly than the disabled. The term "ableism" is sometimes used as a synonym for "handicapism." *See also* ableism, handicapped.

handicapped *someone/person with a disability, the disability/disabilities* (not "disabled") *community, persons with disabilities* (not "the disabled"). Good example of correct usage: the 1990 Americans with Disabilities Act (which prohibits discrimination against individuals with disabilities in the areas of employment, public services, and public accommodations). Do not use "handicapped" as a noun or adjective referring to any of the 43 million Americans with disabilities. The difference between a "disability" and a "handicap" is crucial: a disability is a condition; a handicap is an obstacle. Someone with multiple sclerosis has a disability; the two flights of stairs leading to a classroom present a handicap to that person. Use "handicap" to describe a situation or barrier imposed by society, the environment, or oneself. Use "disability" for a functional limitation that interferes with a person's ability to see, walk, hear, talk, learn, etc. For a complete discussion of writing and speaking about disabilities, *see* disability/disabilities.

handicapped parking this term is used in state and federal laws. Although the Americans with Disabilities Act refers to it as "accessible parking," changing existing statutes and parking-lot language will probably take some time.

handmaid/handmaiden *servant, personal attendant, attendant; instrument, agent, tool, vehicle, facilitator, medium.*

handyman *odd/general jobber, repairer, fixer, fixer-upper, do-all, do-it-yourselfer, odd-job laborer, maintenance worker, carpenter, janitor, custodian, caretaker; handywoman and handyman* if used gender-fairly. People with a classics bent might like *homo habilis* (Latin for "handy human being") or *factotum*, Latin for "do everything" that means a person having many diverse activities or responsibilities. *See also* groundsman.

hangman *executioner, public executioner, lyncher.*

Hanukkah because of its calendar proximity to Christmas, Hanukkah is often referred to as though it is the most important Jewish holiday while the holidays that are in fact more important—Rosh Hashanah and Yom Kippur—are often overlooked by the media and non-Jews. Other major Jewish holidays include Purim, Sukkoth, Shevuoth, and Passover.

Hansen's patient/Hansen's disease *See* leper/leprosy.

harbor master *harbor chief/superintendent/officer/commander.*

hardhat man or woman. (See, for example, Molly Martin, ed., *Hard-Hatted Women*). *See also* tradesman.

hard master *tyrant, despot, dictator, iron hand/ruler, martinet, disciplinarian, oppressor, stickler.* For discussion of "master" words, *see* master.

harebrain *See* airhead.

harelip *cleft lip.* Cleft lip and cleft palate are distinct conditions; "harelip" is highly objectionable.

harem although the harem is negatively perceived in the West as a place of confinement for women, it is not always regarded this way by women in Middle Eastern cultures. "In the Middle East, the harem is the women's quarters for living and working protected by male members of the family from outside intrusion. It is the sphere of women, in many ways comparable to the ideal Victorian household where the modest wife creates a protected environment for family, children, and the domestic necessities of the household. The Victorian home, upheld as an ideal in the west, has been represented in countless sentimental songs, paintings, and novels. However, the equivalent women's environment in the Middle East, the harem, came to symbolize the opposite to eighteenth- and nineteenth-century Europeans" (Marsha J. Hamilton, in Joanna Kadi, ed., *Food for Our Grandmothers*). Use "harem" only if you understand its many culture-specific ramifications. The ethnocentric and incorrect use of "harem" to describe a man's several women friends is demeaning to women and, because of its connotations in the West, implies an inappropriate sense of men owning women. *See also* owner, purdah, sex object.

harlot/harlotry *prostitute/prostitution.* "Harlot" (from the Old French for "rogue") used to refer only to male vagabonds, rascals, vagrants, entertainers, etc. Later it was used for a person of either sex, and finally became restricted to women. *See also* prostitute.

harp (verb) this word is almost exclusively reserved for women; "men who are considered powerful protest, chew-out, or take action," but women harp (Susan Hoy Crawford, *Beyond Dolls & Guns*). When tempted to use "harp," determine what the same behavior in a man would be called.

harpy/harridan although "harpy" can mean a predatory person, it is usually used for "a shrewish woman"; the original Harpies of mythology were hideous, voracious monsters. A harridan is also a shrew, but vicious to boot. These terms have no male "equivalents"; even the stubborn and ill-tempered (not shrewish) curmudgeon, for example, is viewed with a certain fond tolerance. *See also* nag (noun), shrew, termagant, virago.

harvestman leave as is for the arachnid; for the machine used for harvesting or the person doing the harvesting, use *harvester.*

Hasidim members of the ultra-orthodox, alternative movement of popular mysticism founded in Eastern Europe in the 18th century are called Hasidim, Hassidim, or Chassidim in the plural; Hasid, Hassid, or Chassid in the singular.

hatcheck girl *hatchecker, hatcheck attendant/clerk, hat attendant/clerk, checkroom/coatroom/cloakroom attendant/clerk.*

hatcheryman *hatchery owner/worker.*

hatchet man *hatchet, hired hatchet/killer/attacker/assassin, killer, professional killer, murderer, slayer, executioner, mercenary, assassin, attacker, liquidator, terrorist, gangster, racketeer, mobster, hoodlum, cutthroat, thug; someone who gives you the axe or does a hatchet job on someone.* The term is much more difficult to replace in its sense of someone who carries out a disagreeable task or unscrupulous order for someone else. You can circumlocute, use "hatchet man" in quotation marks for a woman, or consider *character assassin, scandalmonger, head-roller, hireling, department of dirty works.*

hate crime terroristic and often violent acts that target individuals or groups because of their sex, race, color, religion, sexual orientation, disability, age, or national origin are called hate crimes. These acts include arson, bombings of homes and businesses, cross burnings, vandalism (like swastika drawings), personal assault, harassing or obscene phone calls, and threatening letters or packages. In some jurisdictions, hate crimes cannot be prosecuted independently; they need to be tried in conjunction with, for example, a crime against property.

hate radio *See* hate speech.

hate speech Brian E. Albrecht (in the Minneapolis *Star Tribune*) says, "Finding hate speech can be easier than defining it." The First Amendment right to free speech conflicts with the implied right of citizens to be free of verbal harassment, the latter often leading directly to hate crimes. (Stanley Fish, Duke University professor who teaches a course on First Amendment law and favors limited speech codes, says, "From what I know of college campuses, I don't think there's a thought police or a reign of terror, partly because every time I see somebody complaining that they've been silenced, the complaint is uttered before millions on a major television or talk show program.") Hate-speech monitoring groups such as Political Research Associates, the Anti-Defamation League, and the Southern Poverty Law Center, say hate speech is practiced by the National Alliance, Liberty Lobby, the Order, Aryan Nations/Brotherhood, Ku Klux Klan, the Patriot movement, John Birch, Posse Comitatus, Christian Identity, various White Aryan Nation people, neo-Nazis, skinheads, survivalists, conspiracy theorists, many private militias, and groups embracing racist, anti-Semitic, neo-Nazi, white-supremacist, antigay, and antifeminist philosophies. Chip Berlet, of Political Research Associates, says instantaneous communications technology lends impact to hate speech by delaying the checks and balances once brought to bear against it. This has led to the creation of social movements at unprecedented speed; processes that once took decades now occur in weeks. He says, "Hate speech is toxic to democracy. If democracy is based on informed consent, how does one really get informed consent? . . . Basically, truth emerges in vigorous if not chaotic, debate, but not when such debate is based on dehumanization, scapegoating, hate, lies, myths, and conspiracies. It's like running a sewer into your water supply and wondering why people get sick." Talk radio has been an important conduit. Patricia J. Williams (in *Ms.*, March/April 1994) says, "The polemics of right-wing radio are putting nothing less than hate onto the airwaves, into the marketplace, electing it to office, teaching it in schools, and exalting it as freedom." In the wake of the Oklahoma City bombing, President Bill Clinton lashed out against "purveyors of hatred" on the air waves who nurture an atmosphere than can foster such violence, people "whose sole goal seems to be try to keep some people as paranoid as possible and the rest of us all torn up and upset with each other." Although hate speech has been discussed mostly in terms of hate radio and freedom of speech issues on college campuses, it is also found on the Internet, in books, magazines and leaflets, and on shortwave radio (Radio for Peace International reports that one-third of the private shortwave broadcast stations in the U.S. have adopted "political far-right" programming featuring messages that deride ethnic and minority groups and espouse violence against them). In the end, hate speech is a problem that only those appalled by it can solve, says Berlet; "What we need is not more law enforcement, not more FBI infiltration, not more partisan politics. What we need is decent Americans standing up and saying, 'Enough.'" An interesting footnote to all the efforts to "protect free speech" by allowing hate speech: Robert D. Richards, associate professor of journalism and law at Pennsylvania State University (L.A. Times–Washington Post News Service), notes that 12 states have now passed laws providing a legal cause of action against anyone who disparages a perishable food product; vegetable libel bills are still on the table in several other states. Under the typical "anti-disparagement" or "fruit defamation" law, producers, marketers, and sometimes even sellers can collect damages for the disparagement of perishable food products or commodities. Richards says, "What interests me here is that we can have anti-disparagement laws about fruit but not about people, but of course in the case of fruit money is involved."

hats off to based on the male custom of doffing one's hat to indicate respect or appreciation, this term is used today without sex bias—perhaps because hat-wearing is no longer so closely associated with one sex.

hausfrau although this term means "housewife" for both the Germans and those English-speaking peoples who have borrowed it, its use is neutral-to-positive in Germany but largely pejorative in English-speaking countries. Use it only in Germany.

hautboy nonsexist; comes from the French "bois" for "wood."

Hawaiian although this term most strictly refers to the descendants of the original Polynesian inhabitants of the Hawaiian Islands, it is generally also used for those of Chinese, Filipino, Japanese, Korean, Portuguese, and Puerto Rican ancestry in Hawaii.

hayseed this term tends to be used more of a man than of a woman, although it is in itself not gender-specific. Along with such words as "bumpkin," "clod/clodhopper," and "plow jockey," it is pejorative and anti-rural. More sex-neutral and less pejorative terms include: *country cousin, tiller of the soil.*

he (pseudogeneric) never use "he" when you mean "he and she," or when you are referring to someone who could be either a man or a woman (for example, "the consumer/he"). Make your sentence plural, circumlocute, or use one of the suggestions given in the Writing Guidelines (pp. 6–9).

headman *head cager/worker; traditional chief; overseer, supervisor.*

headmaster/headmistress *private-school/school director/principal, principal, director, head administrator, head.* In some instances (e.g., a British boys'/girls' school) "headmaster" or "headmistress" might be correct.

head of family/head of household woman or man. In 1980 the U.S. Census Bureau broadened its "head of household" definition beyond the husband; almost 30% of households are headed by women. *See also* bring home the bacon, family man, housewife, provider.

head of state women have served or are serving as heads of state and government in Argentina, Barbados, Belize, Bolivia, Dominica, Iceland, India, Ireland, Israel, Nicaragua, Norway, Pakistan, the Philippines, Portugal, Sri Lanka, and the United Kingdom.

headsman *executioner, public executioner, beheader.*

headwaiter man or woman.

health appliance in material prior to 1991, this term is correct. Contemporary usage is *assistive device*. Assistive devices include equipment, aids, self-help devices, furniture, and other medical devices designed to facilitate living with disabilities.

hearing impaired *See* deaf.

heart disease heart disease death rates are higher among men than among women; for both sexes, death rates are higher among blacks than among whites. According to one study, many men see a heart attack as a sign that they have worked hard and done a good job, and so although they are more prone to heart attacks than women, they recover more quickly. A woman (along with the culture) tends to see her heart attack as a failure; she has not "coped" with her situation.

heathen defined as "one who adheres to the religion of a people or nation that does not acknowledge the God of Judaism, Christianity, or Islam" (*American Heritage Dictionary*, 3rd ed.), this term is better replaced by the name of the religion or belief system under discussion. "Heathen" resembles "nonwhite" in being a catchall term for everybody who isn't "us." It also describes those who are supposedly unenlightened and uncivilized, a vague and indefensible judgment. *See also* pagan, primitive, savage.

heavyweight in the sense of an important or successful person, a heavyweight could theoretically be either sex. There is, however, a male cast to the word (because of wrestlers and because it was used for so long only of men), and many people are acculturated to flinch from a word made up of "heavy" and "weight." You might consider instead *VIP, big wheel, bigwig, dignitary, personage, high-muck-a-muck.*

Hebrew this term is used principally to refer to the language of contemporary Israel and to the old Canaanite language of the Bible. *See also* Israeli, Jew.

hector although based on the Trojan champion slain by Achilles, this term is used inclusively and probably not one person in a million thinks of Hector while saying it.

Heidelberg man *Homo erectus, early human.* The physical remains are referred to as *the Heidelberg jaw* or *the Heidelberg fossil.*

heiress *heir. See also* "feminine" word endings.

heist man *armed robber, professional thief.*

hell hath no fury like a woman scorned from William Congreve's 1697 *The Mourning Bride,* the lines are "Heaven has no rage like love to hatred turned, / Nor hell a fury like a woman scorned." Not only does the senseless repetition of this phrase assume that women react in ways men wouldn't but it ignores the appalling statistical evidence that men are much more likely than women to express their fury by killing the women who have left or are leaving them.

helmsman *pilot, steerer, navigator.*

helpmate/helpmeet these terms are most often used for women and they imply a certain existential inferiority. While still in the White House, Louisa Adams wrote, "Man's interpretation of the word 'helpmate' as used in the Bible means this: Women made to cook his dinner, wash his clothes, gratify his sensual appetites, and thank him and love him for permission to drudge through life at the mercy of his caprices. Is this the interpretation intended by the Creator, the father of all mercy?" Probably not. Modern scholars say the original Hebrew that has been translated as "helpmate" (someone "to assist Adam in life") was actually "suitable partner," someone to walk side by side with him. *See also* Adam's rib, Eve.

he-man this term perpetuates stereotypes and expectations of men that are often false and damaging. Use instead precise adjectives: *aggressive, hardy, rugged, husky, hearty, robust, powerful, muscular, domineering, capable, dynamic, energetic, physical,* etc.

hemiplegic *someone with/who has hemiplegia.* If necessary to mention a disability, information can be conveyed without labeling the whole person by something that is only part of their life. Hemiplegia is a paralysis affecting only one side of the body. *See also* disability/disabilities, paraplegic, "people-first" rule, quadriplegic.

henchman *sidekick, hireling, underling, flunky, lackey, thug, hood, tool, puppet, accomplice, stooge, hanger-on, ward heeler, minion, myrmidon; follower, supporter, subordinate, helper, aide, right-hand, cohort; groom, attendant, page.* (William Safire notes that *henchman* is used only pejoratively; "nobody ever claims to be anybody else's henchman.")

henpeck/henpecked she henpecks; he is henpecked. When men have a problem, they are said to *protest, object, grumble, raise a fuss, grouse, beef, criticize, censure, deplore, disapprove, chew out, remind, take action, give a piece of their mind.* Use those terms for women too. Calling a man "henpecked" is as disparaging to him as it is to her; consider using instead terms that can apply to both sexes: *bossed around, bullied, browbeaten, soul not one's own, passive, submissive, dominated, subjugated, under someone's thumb, led by the nose, at one's beck and call, ruled with an iron hand, in leading strings. See also* castrate, nag (verb), unman.

herculean despite its obviously male provenance, "herculean" doesn't function as a sex-biased word. If you want something more neutral use *heroic, extraordinary, great-hearted, valiant, stalwart, invincible, unswerving.*

herdsman *herder, sheepherder, shepherd, swineherd, swineherder, cattle herder, herd breeder, livestock manager/breeder/tender, rancher.* "Herdsperson" has been seen, but it is not recommended.

hermaphrodite true hermaphroditism in human beings (someone with both male and female reproductive organs, also sometimes called "intersexed") is rare: only some 400 cases have been documented. Use "hermaphrodite" only in its scientific sense. John A. Hobson notes the use of the term in "hermaphrodite rig" (also known as a "jackass rig"), which is a nonstandard combination of square rig and fore-and-aft rig on a sailing ship with two or more masts.

hero/heroine use "hero" for both men and women even though it is the masculine form of the Greek word, while "heroine" is the feminine (although two of Greek mythology's best-known lovers were named Hero and Leander, and Hero was not the manly partner). In English, a heroine is defined as "a female hero"—that is, a subset of hero. Although theoretically it should be possible to use "hero" and "heroine" in a gender-fair manner, they are already subtly weighted in favor of the broader, more prestigious "hero" and, given the devaluation and discounting of woman-associated words in our language, it seems best to support one neutral term. "Heroine" is still useful when referring to the female main character in a literary work. Maya Angelou has suggested, and others have adopted, "sheroe." If you want alternatives to "hero" consider *protagonist, central/ main character, champion, celebrity, notable, rara avis, star, superstar, model, paragon, good example, demigod, saint, benefactor, salt of the earth, one in ten thousand, one of the best, winner, leader, ideal, shining example, luminary, dignitary, personage, figure, public/popular figure, social lion, big name, big cheese, idol, matinée idol, principal, principal character/role, title/starring/lead role, feature attraction.* **See also** unconventional spellings.

herstory coined by writer and former editor of *Ms.*, Robin Morgan, this term refers to all the parts of "her story" that have been left out of "his story." The word "history" itself is not sexist; the "his" in "history" is an English/American-language accident and has nothing to do with the male pronoun or with any male-based word. "Herstory" was never intended to replace or be a synonym for "history," but is used to "emphasize that women's lives, deeds, and participation in human affairs have been neglected or undervalued in standard histories" (Casey Miller and Kate Swift, *Words and Women*). Until recently, history was written by men about men. "Where women do appear in traditional accounts of the past, they emerge as adjuncts of the masculine world being recorded, as supporting players, seen only in their male-related roles as wife, mother, daughter, or mistress. History thus related occurs around them rather than with them" (Carol Ruth Berkin, in Thomas R. Frazier, ed., *The Underside of American History*). Eleanor S. Riemer and John C. Fout *(European Women)* describe the wealth of women's writings they found in "books, women's magazines, and periodicals written, edited, and sometimes typeset and printed by women, for women. . . . If historians until now have not used women's own sources to reconstruct women's past, it is only because they have not looked for them." *See also* history, unconventional spellings.

heterosexism the attitude that heterosexuality is the sole valid, "standard," or "normal" sexual orientation is called heterosexism; a heterosexist is a person who speaks or acts out of that attitude. On a milder level, heterosexism exists when people act as though everybody were heterosexual; for example, thinking that a "couple" is always a she and a he, forgetting that Valentine's Day is for all couples, not just opposite-sex ones, assuming that only married couples celebrate anniversaries. To include everybody in general statements, instead of husband or wife or spouse, use *partner, companion;* instead of marriage use *committed relationship;* for marriage counseling substitute *couples therapy* or *relationship counseling.* Do not compare the gay population to the "general" population.

heterosexual this is the acceptable term for a person of either sex whose primary emotional and physical attraction is to people of the other sex.

hetman (Cossack leader) leave this historical term as is.

he who hesitates is lost *they who hesitate are lost, once you hesitate you are lost.*

he who laughs last laughs best *they who laugh last laugh best, when you laugh last you laugh best.*

he who lies down with dogs rises with fleas *they who lie down with dogs rise with fleas.*

he who lives by the sword dies by the sword *they who live by the sword die by the sword, if you live by the sword you will die by the sword.*

he who seeks finds *they who seek find, seek and you shall find.*

hick this is derogatory and classist, as are the related hick town, hicksville, hick college. *See also* hillbilly, redneck, yokel.

highboy nonsexist; comes from French "bois" for "wood."

high man on the totem pole *See* totem pole, high man on the.

high priestess *high priest.* But retain "high priestess" when discussing ancient or present-day goddess religions; it has significance and weight as a sex-specific term. *See also* "feminine" word endings.

high-risk group *high-risk behavior.* It is not the group people belong to (needle-users, gay men, heterosexuals with multiple partners) that puts them at risk for AIDS, but rather their behavior: sharing needles, unprotected sex, etc. *See also* at risk.

highwayman *highway robber/bandit, robber, bandit, road agent, footpad, brigand, marauder, thug, outlaw, desperado, ruffian, rogue. See also* bad guy, gun man, holdup man.

highway patrolman *highway officer/patrol officer, motorcycle officer/police.*

high yellow Vivian Jenkins Nelsen *(New Voices in the Media)* labels this term objectionable when referring to lighter-colored African Americans and suggests avoiding any description of skin color or degrees of color. *See also* yellow.

hillbilly functionally nonsexist although it was originally based on a man's name, "hillbilly" is often classist and derogatory. It operates on the "insider/outsider" rule because some people good-humoredly self-identify as hillbillies. References to hillbilly music are acceptable.

him do not use "him" to mean "him and her," or when "him" might refer to either a man or a woman (for example, "the taxpayer/him"); replace with the plural, circumlocute, or *see* the Writing Guidelines (pp. 6–9) on pseudogeneric "he."

himself do not use "himself" to mean "herself and himself," or when it might refer to either a man or a woman (for example, "the priest/himself"); replace with the plural, circumlocute, or *see* the Writing Guidelines (pp. 6–9) on pseudogeneric "he."

hired man *farm hand/worker, hired/field hand, hand, helper.*

his do not use "his" to mean "his and hers," or when it might refer to either a man or a woman (for example, "the plumber/his"); replace with the plural, circumlocute, or *see* the Writing Guidelines on pseudogeneric "he" (pp. 6–9).

his bark is worse than his bite *her/their/its bark is worse than her/their/its bite, all clouds and no rain, all sound and no fury, empty threat, sham.*

his own man, be *See* man, be his own.

Hispanic used for people living in the United States who are of Mexican, Puerto Rican, Cuban, and other Spanish-speaking countries of Caribbean, Central and South American, and Spanish descent, the term "Hispanic" dates from a Nixon-administration attempt to refine its census classifications. Concise and useful, "Hispanic" is preferred by some of those so designated but considered unacceptable by others. "No one was brought up being told, 'You are Hispanic,'" says Lorenzo Cano, assistant director for the Mexican-American studies program at the University of Houston.

"That's just a term bureaucracies have used for filing and government purposes. Hispanic is offensive to some; no one wants to be associated with Spain and its history of colonization and oppression in the Americas; Hispanic is too broad and offers the perfect excuse for not exploring the diversity among people who are referred to by that term." Sandra Cisneros refuses to have her writings included in any anthology that uses the word "Hispanic." Critics of the term argue that it indifferently categorizes and thereby effectively camouflages the cultural, ethnic, class, religious, and historical realities of some 20 million Americans who share little more than varieties of the Spanish language, and sometimes not even that (the label can include Portuguese-speaking Brazilians, Europeans from Spain and Portugal who have settled in this country, French-speaking and English-speaking immigrants from Caribbean countries, and immigrant speakers of indigenous, South American Indian languages). However, Herman Badillo, then a member of Congress from New York and a founding member of the Congressional Hispanic Caucus, said that the move to "Hispanic" was cheered among the nation's various affected communities because they stood to gain more political representation and government services as a result of the designation. Chicana activist Elizabeth "Betita" Martínez (in *Teaching Tolerance*, Spring 1997), who prefers the term "La Raza," believes "that the advertising industry had a lot to do with 'Hispanic' becoming so established because of its desire to create a market that would encompass a single population. I don't use 'Hispanic' because it is Eurocentric and denies the fact that the people being labeled are not just of Spanish origin. Nor do they all speak Spanish. 'Hispanic' denies our indigenous, or Indian roots. It also denies our African roots, from the thousands of slaves that were brought to Latin America." Those who self-identify as Hispanics come from various backgrounds but in general tend to be politically conservative business or political leaders or professionals integrating themselves into the mainstream and corporate cultures; "Hispanic" is a term of pride for those who claim it. Before using "Hispanic" (1) make sure it is the term of choice of those you are describing; (2) if it is not, use the term preferred by the individual or group (e.g., Latina/Latino, Mexican Americans, Chicana/Chicano); (3) or, list all the specific groups being referred to (e.g., "Mexican Americans, Cuban Americans, and Puerto Rican Americans"). There is no question but that "Hispanic" is a convenient word; the problem lies with its inappropriate overuse or use for those who reject it. *See also* Chicana/Chicano, Latina/Latino, Mexican American, La Raza, Spanish.

history from the Greek "historia" meaning "inquiry/knowing/learning," the word "history" is not male-based and has nothing to do with the masculine possessive pronoun "his." However, the word "ahistoricity" has been coined to denote the ways in which the exclusion of women from history, as viewed and written by men, has been not just another exclusion, but women's most debilitating cultural deprivation (Gerda Lerner, *The Creation of Feminist Consciousness*). More than any other factor, the absence of a usable past explains why the subordination of women has persisted for so long; "Women, ignorant of their history," says Lerner, "had to reinvent the wheel over and over again." *See also* herstory.

Hitler/little Hitler using these terms metaphorically robs them of a horror they properly should retain; they are also painful for a Jew to hear. Either describe the person's actions or consider using *fanatic, tyrant, despot, bigot. See also* concentration camp, final solution, Gestapo/gestapo, holocaust, Nazi/nazi.

hit man *hired/professional/armed/contract killer, hired gun/assassin, assassin, killer, murderer, sniper, slayer, gunslinger, gunsel, executioner, liquidator, mercenary, thug, gangster, sharpshooter, attacker, outlaw, terrorist, mobster, racketeer, hoodlum, trigger, croaker, enforcer.*

HIV upon the first use of "HIV," it is helpful to spell out the meaning and explanation, thus: "Human immunodeficiency virus (HIV), the virus believed to lead to AIDS . . ." The word "virus" in "HIV virus" is redundant. The test is "HIV antibody test," not "AIDS test." And people test positive or negative for antibodies to HIV, so the acceptable terms are HIV-positive (or seropositive) and HIV-negative. HIV infection is not the same as AIDS or ARC (AIDS-related complex); hundreds of thousands of people who have been exposed to HIV have not developed, and may not develop, ARC or AIDS, particularly if their condition is monitored and treated.

hobo woman or man. *See also* knight of the road, road sister.

Hobson's choice there is nothing wrong with this phrase, but be aware of how many such expressions in the English language are male-based. Balance their use with female-based expressions, creative expressions of your own, or sex-neutral alternatives: *no choice, no choice at all, not a pin to choose between/from.* (Thomas Hobson, 17th-century livery stable owner, told customers they could take the horse nearest the stable door or none at all.) *See also* sex-linked expressions.

hoistman *hoist operator.*

hoity-toity because "hoity-toity" is invariably used of a woman (it is possibly related to "hoyden," a boisterous or high-spirited girl) you may want a more inclusive word: *pretentious, snobbish, pompous, highfalutin.*

holdup man *armed robber, thief, purse-snatcher, mugger, roller. See also* bad guy, gunman, highwayman.

holocaust/Holocaust use "Holocaust" to refer to the mass murder of European Jews and others by the Nazis. Although some regard "Holocaust" as unique to Jewish experience and limited to its World War II meaning, the word "holocaust," which has existed since the 14th century, is appropriately used in other contexts: Romanies were also part of the Holocaust—Nazis killed one-fifth to one-fourth of the total Rom population; the genocide of American Indians was a holocaust, as was the enslavement and murders of African peoples; the bombing of Hiroshima was a holocaust; "nuclear holocaust" is unfortunately a part of our vocabulary. The caution is to reserve "holocaust" for the most egregious cases of humans destroying humans. *See also* concentration camp, "final solution," Gestapo/gestapo, Hitler/little Hitler, Jewish question, Nazi/nazi.

Holy Spirit (Ghost)/he eliminate masculine pronouns for the Holy Spirit, replacing them with descriptive adjectives, or, in prayer, with direct address ("you" and "your"). At other times, circumlocution will be necessary. The Hebrew "ruah" or "ruach," meaning "wind, breath, spirit," is grammatically feminine, and the Greek word for "spirit," "pneuma," is neuter, which is why some writers and speakers refer to the Holy Spirit as "she" or "it." However, the most theologically and linguistically correct approach is to eliminate gender-specific pronouns.

Holy Roller instead of this disparaging term use the name of the particular denomination. *See also* fundamentalist.

homebody man or woman. *See also* family man, homemaker.

homeboy/homegirl all uses of these colloquial terms seem to be sex parallel; "homie" is also used.

home economics/home ec use this only for groups that so label their work. Despite a wide range of academic and professional pursuits, home economists are stuck with a gender stereotype: women in aprons. Preferred terms include *domestic science, human ecology.* "Human ecology" was the term used by ecologist Ellen Swallow, who pioneered the field, and "domestic science" indicates the field's professional, technical, and scientific aspects, which include healthcare and education, aging, nutrition, dietetics, AIDS, alcohol and drug abuse; food production, processing, supplies, and technology; design and textiles; family and social sciences, safety, housing; finance and planning, farm business development; consultation with government and industry. At least in some areas, the field is no longer so one-sexed: according to *Ms.* magazine (March/April 1994), in 1968 4.2% of the 2.2 million students enrolled in middle and high school home ec classes were boys; in 1993, 41.5% of an estimated 5.3 million home ec students were boys (state laws in many places require it for both sexes).

homeless stereotypes and misinformation plague this term, which is so often used to mean "shiftless." One in four persons reported as homeless is a child younger than 18 (Children's Defense Fund, *The State of America's Children Yearbook*, 1995). Of homeless mothers, nearly 90% have been physically and/or sexually abused (E. L. Bessuk, in *Scientific American*). There are many societal, economic, political, and medical reasons for homelessness; the rarest is laziness. In the case of homeless men, "Men are neither supposed nor allowed to be dependent. They are expected to take care of both others *and* themselves. And when they cannot do it, or 'will not' do it, the built-in assumption at the heart of the culture is that they are *less than men* and therefore unworthy of help. An irony asserts itself: Simply by being in need of help, men forfeit the right to it" (Peter Marin, in *The Nation*). *See also* bag lady/bag man, bum.

homemaker this unisex term is positive in itself. Use it to describe men as well as women, but examine the context in which you use it for hidden biases and prejudices that may tend to belittle homemakers.

homeowner this may become a classist term: 20 years ago it took less than one-fourth of the median income of young families to buy a home; today it takes over half. "The U.S. ranks only 29th in percentage of home ownership among 50 nations surveyed by the U.S." (David Wallechinsky, *Parade Magazine*, April 13, 1997). Another difference is that today nearly one-fourth of all homeowners are women.

homeroom mother *homeroom parent/aide/helper.*

homicide although this word comes from the Latin for "man," it is defined and used today inclusively.

hominid anthropologists use this word inclusively, and it is functionally fairly nonsexist. It is a problem only when it is defined or used as referring to "man" instead of to "human being," which is the meaning of its Latin root. For example, one dictionary defines it as "any of a family (Hominidae) of bipedal primate mammals comprising recent man, his immediate ancestors, and related forms" *(Webster's Ninth New Collegiate Dictionary)*. The unambiguous choice here would have been: "recent human beings, their immediate ancestors, and related forms."

homo- words beginning with "homo-" come from the Greek word meaning "same" or "equal" and are not sexist—for example, "homosexual" does not refer to a man but to someone whose sexual orientation is toward persons of the same sex.

homo (gay man) considered a highly objectionable, anti-gay slur. *See also* shortened forms of words.

Homo erectus this "homo" (see homo-) comes from the Latin for "human being." The ambiguity of the English "man" tars the Latin "homo," and gives it a sexist look. However, the term is well established—and used inclusively—in anthropology. The main problem with it is that it is so often followed by references to "man" and "mankind" when the correct references should be to "human being" and "humanity." When you see "Homo erectus" check the surrounding material for sexist language.

homoeroticism the "homo-" refers to "same," not to "man," so this term applies to both lesbian and gay love and desire.

homophobia defined as an irrational fear of gay and lesbian acts, persons, and sentiments, today this term includes hatred, prejudice, and discrimination and covers a range of anti-lesbian or anti-gay behavior and attitudes. (The "homo-" refers to "same" as in "same-sex," not to "man.") Surveys indicate that almost all lesbians and gay men have suffered some form of verbal abuse, while 25% of all gay men and 10% of all lesbians have been physically assaulted because of their sexual orientation. According to researchers, gay men and lesbians are the targets of more open and more intractable discrimination than that directed at any other group; abuse ranges from verbal harassment to physical assaults and murder. Many so-called gay bashings go unreported because victims fear retaliation, publicly identifying themselves, or being blamed for provoking the assault. There is a particularly high social tolerance for this abuse and discrimination. Unlike other groups, lesbians and gay men are still victims of legalized bias; they are, for example, barred from the armed services. In many states their sexual activities are illegal, and in some states it is expressly stated in the statutes that gay men and lesbians are not protected from discrimination. According to the Campaign to End Homophobia, homophobia comes in four types: personal, interpersonal, institutional, and cultural. Although there has been a great increase in anti-gay bias since the beginning of the AIDS epidemic, it appears that AIDS has not created the new level of hostility, but rather has given bigots an excuse to act out their hatred. Research indicates that some men use hostility and violence against gay men to reassure themselves about their own sexuality. Language is often used to express this fear and hostility (with epithets like "Miss Nancy," "pansy"). *See also* heterosexism, violence.

Homo sapiens this scientific name for the human species is based on the Latin word "homo" ("human being"). It is thus inclusive, although it tends to be heard as adult-male man rather than human-being man, especially when its common definition ("mankind") underlines the males-only flavor. When using this term in nonscientific material, it is less ambiguous to use short, direct English words: *human beings, humans, humanity, humankind, member of the human race, people. See also* mankind.

homosexual this term (from "homo," *same*, not "homo," *man*) refers to both women and men with same-sex emotional and sexual orientations and can be used with "heterosexual," "bisexual," or "transsexual," but in other uses it is seen as clinical, sexually objectifying, and limiting. Some of the aversion to "homosexual" comes from the emphasized syllable in the word, the implication being that all homosexuals are about is sex. Tim Campbell, publisher of the *GLC Voice,* says, "The word *homosexual* defines a person by sexual behavior whereas gayness does not necessarily include sexual behavior." For the cultural terms by which people choose to identify themselves use *lesbian* and *gay man.* "Homosexual" and "heterosexual," Gore Vidal says categorically, "are adjectives that describe acts but never people." The Association of American University Presses' *Guidelines for Bias-Free Writing* suggests that *"homosexual* is preferable in pre-World War II contexts and in references to some traditional or non-Western cultures, where *gay* would seem anachronistic or discordant." *See also* gay man, lesbian, same-sex.

honcho/head honcho a honcho can be either sex (it comes from the Japanese meaning "group leader") although it has generally been used for men. The semi-facetious "honcha" is incorrect. If you want a more neutral-sounding alternative, consider *big boss/wheel/cheese, leader, boss, person in charge.*

honest Injun *See* Injun.

honey/hon these terms are often acceptable to people in intimate relationships who have implicitly or explicitly approved their use. According to one study, "honey" was the overwhelming favorite term of endearment for both men and women. The second favorite, however, was no endearment at all; people just called their significant others by their names. "Honey" and "hon" are always demeaning, incorrect, and unwelcome when used for strangers or slight acquaintances. It is the person in the lower-power position in any relationship who gets called "hon," "honey," or "dear." The use of these terms by one person in an interaction implies that the other is inferior socially, intellectually, financially, or in some other way. If the second person wouldn't dare call the first one "honey," it is a sure indication of an inequality in the relationship. (Imagine responding in kind to a boss, professor, or customer who has just called you "hon.") *See also* courts (judicial), dear.

honky/honkie *See* ethnic slurs.

honor this term has traditionally meant different things for men and women and often has done neither sex any good. Russell Baker *(About Men)* says, "Honorable is peculiarly a man's word, as are its antonyms: dishonorable, ignoble, base, vile, swinish, caddish. Such words are rarely applied to women. Even the phrase 'a woman's honor,' referring to the high-toned sexual morality once demanded of the American female, sounds like a man's invention for burdening women with heavier moral luggage than men chose to bear. . . . They lay that honor business on you when you're just a little boy, long before you guess what it's leading up to, long before you can possibly know that if you don't live by that little-boy code someday a general may slap your face and call you a coward or order a firing squad to dispose of you as a disgrace to your sex and hence a menace to your country. So the idea of honor becomes a vital part of a man's boyhood experience." *See also* virtue.

honorary fraternity *honorary society/honorary Greek society.*

hoodlum *See* bad guy.

hooker *prostitute.* Although "hooker," whose exact origins are unclear, was already in use before the Civil War, it became identified with Union General "Fighting Joe" Hooker whose troops fought to defend the nation's capital and also frequented prostitutes in such numbers that the women were referred to as one of Hooker's Divisions. The area where the men were bivouacked was called "the plague spot of Washington" and included 109 houses of prostitution ("hook shops") and 50 saloons. *See also* prostitute.

Horatio Alger story based on the 120+ enormously successful boys' books written by Unitarian cleric Horatio Alger, this phrase refers to the poor but honest newsboys and bootblacks who by hard work and virtuous living overcame obstacles and achieved success. Because of the term's male orientation, you may sometimes need an inclusive alternative: *rags-to-riches story, personal success story; rise up/get on in the world, make one's fortune, work/make one's way up.* The Horatio Alger story has contributed greatly to the myth that anyone can be a financial success in the United States. *See also* classism.

horny despite its reference to the penis (horn), this term is used for both sexes.

horseman/horsewoman acceptable terms; they have not been used in sexist ways. If you want an alternative consider: *equestrian, horseback rider, horse rider/lover, rider, cavalier; trainer, handler, groom, jockey, horse breeder; hunter.*

horsemanship *equestrianship, riding/horseriding/equestrian/horse-handling skills/technique, equitation, equestrianism.*

hoseman *firefighter, hose carrier.*

hospitality industry this is preferred by makers and sellers of beer, liquor, and alcoholic beverages. The term has no racist, sexist, or any other bias; it is included here as an example of a suitably vague and warm euphe-mism used largely by white men that goes unchallenged, while preferred terms for people of color, people with disabilities, women, etc., are labeled ridiculous and euphemistic.

hostess *host.* Also, *social director, tour guide, attendant, receptionist.* There are no talk show "hostesses" (Oprah Winfrey and Rosie O'Donnell, for example, are hosts). There are also, it appears, very few guestesses: according to researcher Mark Harmon, the guest list on "Meet the Press" since the start of the program in 1947 has been dominated by white men, although slight progress has been made in inviting non-white guests. The percentage of women guests in any given decade held between 3% and 5%. *See also* "feminine" word endings.

hot-blooded this stereotypical description is used for Latin peoples when Poles or Swedes or Australians behaving the same way are termed *hot-headed, short-tempered, passionate, high-spirited, vehement, impetuous, ebullient, fervent, enthusiastic.*

hotelier woman or man.

hotelman *hotel proprietor/owner/manager/worker, hotelier.*

Hottentot *Khoikhoin/Khoi-Khoin.* The correct term is always the one by which a people refer to themselves.

houseboy/housegirl for "houseboy" use *servant*; for "housegirl" use *prostitute.* Note lack of parallel. *See also* prostitute.

househusband this term enjoyed a flurry of popularity, and while it will probably remain in the living language, it is not equivalent to housewife in either numbers of holders of the title or in the public's general perception of the person. Although some men care for children and home full-time from choice, for most it is not a primary career. It is either an involuntary change (because of unemployment or ill health) or they are involved in paid work done at home. And so far, it appears more socially acceptable to be a "workwife" than a "househusband." This reflects what has also happened in the workplace; while women go into male-intensive occupations (and generally enjoy higher status for doing so), men are not going in great numbers into female-intensive occupations (and they report raised eyebrows and lowered salaries when they do).

housekeeper not sexist per se, "housekeeper" is too often used as an all-purpose label for a woman. Professionals who manage others' homes call themselves *household technicians/workers/helpers, home managers.*

housemaid *servant, domestic worker, cleaner, house cleaner, household helper, housekeeper.*

housemaid's knee *inflammation of the kneecap.* This phrase is not a real problem in the language; use it if you like it.

houseman *caretaker, janitor, house cleaner, odd jobber, fixer-upper; intern, resident.*

housemother *houseparent, counselor, monitor, cottage parent, chaperon, resident assistant.* There has never been a "housefather."

housewife *homemaker, householder, homeowner, consumer, woman who works at home, woman, home/household manager, customer, shopper, parent.* Roseanne Barr refers to herself as a *domestic goddess.* "Housewife" marries a woman to her house, and is disliked by many women because it identifies them by gender and marital status (both often irrelevant in the context) and because of the practically endless possibilities for using it in sexist ways. Some women like the term and self-identify that way; their choice is also to be respected. *See also* househusband, housework, second shift, working mother, working wife, working woman.

housewifery *homemaking, housekeeping, home/household management.*

housework make no assumptions about the nature and ownership of housework. As the woman sings in the black musical *Don't Bother Me, I Can't Cope:* "Show me that special gene that says I was born to make the beds." Housework is a relatively recent invention, dating from the industrial revolution. In 1737 in England, for example, more than 98% of married women were employed outside the home. By 1911, more than 90% worked solely as housewives. This pattern was repeated throughout the industrialized world. Today housework "chore wars" are one of the commonest features of marriage. Ellen Goodman writes, "He is doing more than his father and feeling underappreciated. She is doing more than her husband and feeling undervalued. There is a friction between women whose lives have changed faster than the men they share them with. There is a stalemate over the household." Statistics proliferate on who does what around the house but they all come down to the same thing: women still have the primary responsibility for maintaining the home and caring for the children. Debbie Taylor (in *New International*), says, "Men perceive that equating love and domestic work is a trap. They fear that to get involved with housework would send them hurtling into the bottomless pit of self-sacrifice that is women's current caring role." In *The Handbook of Nonsexist Writing*, Casey Miller and Kate Swift (with credit to Marjorie Vogel for the insight), point out that "many women do not use the term *work* to describe their housekeeping or homemaking activities. Nor, in general, do members of their families. A woman 'stays home' rather than 'works at home.' She 'fixes dinner' rather than 'works in the kitchen.' In contrast, activities men traditionally undertake around the house are usually dignified by the name *work.* A man 'works on the car' or 'does his own electrical work.' He may have a 'workshop' in the basement." In summary: "Domestic work, is, after all, both tedious and repetitive, and it is not surprising that most women and all men avoid as much of it as possible" (Mary Stocks, *My Commonplace Book*); "The American home is getting dirtier. People have better things to do with their time than clean" (Mary Ellen Pinkham in the *New York Times*); "If your house is really a mess and a stranger comes to the door, greet him with, 'Who could have done this? We have no enemies'" (Phyllis Diller). *See also* housewife, man's work, moonlighter, second shift, working father, working mother, working wife, working woman.

hoyden (girl) this word used to refer to members of both sexes. Today it describes, with a disapproving cast, a boisterous, high-spirited girl. It may be more useful to your reader and constitute better writing to describe such a girl's actions rather than label them. *See also* tomboy.

hubby "hubby" came from "husband" just as "hussy" came from "wife" ("huswif") but with far different connotations. *See also* husband, husband and wife, hussy.

hula dancer woman or man.

human (noun) "human" refers to both sexes, although it's been a near thing for women at times. In 585 at the Council of Mâcon, 43 Catholic bishops and 20 men representing bishops debated the topic "Are Women Human?" After lengthy argument, the vote was 32 yes, 31 no; by one vote women were declared human. American Indians and African Americans have not fared any better. The early European settlers in the Americas "considered the original inhabitants of the continent as somewhat lower than human beings, a species of animal" (Ann H. Beuf, in Paula S. Rothenberg, *Racism and Sexism*). To maintain the institution of slavery, blacks were described as subhuman heathens, and in 1857 the U.S. Supreme Court labeled them "beings of an inferior order." "Human," which comes from the Latin "humanus" for "ground," has been used as a noun since 1533 and is used and perceived today as an inclusive term.

humanity/humankind these terms come from the Latin "humanus" ("ground") meaning "human being" and are used and understood today as inclusive terms.

humor humor that demeans others often masks hostility as well as a sense of inferiority. When others don't laugh at sexist, racist, or homophobic jokes/remarks, the jokester is quick to level the one accusation guaranteed to sting: "You don't have a sense of humor." But jokes about violence, rape, sexual harassment, and stereotyping provide a cultural tolerance for bias and give tacit permission to the name-caller, the gay-basher, the abuser, the rapist, even the murderer to rationalize their behavior because "everybody else" is down on "them" too.

hunk this sex-linked term tends to make sex objects of men and to support looksism, q.v. Some men will not mind being referred to this way, but many will definitely mind, and only you can know the difference. It is never appropriate in the workplace. If you want an inclusive alternative try *dreamboat, greatest thing since (fill in your own "sliced bread" equivalent), centerfold, pinup, smoothie. **See also** stud/studly/stud muffin.

huntress *hunter. **See also** "feminine"* word endings.

huntsman *hunter, hunt manager.*

hurricane now given both male and female names, hurricanes can be referred to as he/she or it. **See also** storms.

husband (noun) the "hus-band" was the Old English mate of the "hus-wif" ("hus" meaning "house"), although the word "husband" fared a great deal better than either "housewife" or "wife" in terms of prestige and accept-ability—possibly because "man" was used so often instead of "husband" (as in the egregious "man and wife"). Today, just as many men are redefining the husband role in positive ways, there is a subtle discounting of "husband"; advertisers portray the husband in stereotypical ways and more and more jokes and one-liners are putting down husbands. It's a pity; as Ouida wrote in 1884, "An easy-going husband is the one indis-pensable comfort of life." **See also** househusband, hubby, husband and wife, wife/husband.

husband (verb) *conserve, ration, measure, preserve, lay/put by, economize, store, reserve, accumulate, hoard, stockpile, stock, save, save for a rainy day, stow/squirrel/salt/sock/lay away.*

husband and wife vary this phrase half the time with "wife and husband." Male grammarians asserted centuries ago that the male was more impor-tant than the female, and should always be placed first, thus giving us husband and wife, Mr. and Mrs., boy and girl, he and she, etc. English jurist Sir William Blackstone was a man of their kidney: "Husband and wife are one, and that one is the husband."

husbandlike/husbandly these vague words leave us little the wiser about the person so described; there are as many kinds of husbands as there are husbands. Choose instead specific adjectives: *solicitous, gentle, support-ive, intimate, knowing, sensitive, protective.* These are not synonyms but rather what the culture understands by "husbandlike/husbandly."

husbandman *farmer, agriculturist, agronomist, farm scientist, vintager, horticulturist, citriculturist, gardener, florist, cultivator, tiller of the soil, sower, reaper, grower, forester, breeder. **See also** cattleman, herdsman, nurseryman.*

husbandry *household thrift, thrift, thriftiness, good housekeeping, frugality, frugalness, careful management, conservation, economizing, conserving; agriculture, agronomy, agronomics, agribusiness, farming, farm manage-*

ment, cultivation, tillage, forestry. Or, be specific: *arboriculture, floriculture, horticulture, landscape gardening, viniculture.*

hussy derived from "housewife," this word has taken the low road while its innocuous, affectionate mate, "hubby," has taken the high road. Consider replacing this word with adjectives that convey whatever meaning it has for you: *bold, brazen, seductive, shameless, immodest, immoral, indecent, bold-faced,* etc. *See also* femme fatale, Jezebel/jezebel, loose woman.

hustler used of either sex, although a male hustler is a man successful with women or, in some instances, a prostitute, while a female hustler is always a prostitute. In the sense of a go-getter or a con artist, a hustler is either sex.

hymn a number of religious groups are giving their hymns a more inclusive look. The United Church of Christ published its *New Century Hymnal,* a mixture of old and new hymns addressing God as Creator, Savior, Love, Spirit, Wisdom, Word, Shepherd, and more. The Presbyterian Church U.S.A. did likewise. The United Methodist Church, second largest U.S. Protestant denomination, revised its hymnal to reflect respect for women, blacks, and people with disabilities (although they retained "he" for God), changing such phrases as "his power and his love" to "God's power and God's love"; "pleased as man with men to dwell" to "pleased with us in flesh to dwell"; "sons of men and angels say" to "earth and heaven in chorus say"; "Good Christian Men Rejoice" to "Good Christian Friends Rejoice"; "God of our Fathers" to "God of the Ages." Washing people "whiter than snow" was eliminated, and hymns from African American, Latina/Latino, Asian, and Native American traditions were added.

"hyphenated Americans" this derogatory term arose from the earlier custom of joining national origin group to "American." Today noun forms are never hyphenated (Arab American, Chinese American) and adjectival forms generally are not (Irish American Cultural Institute, *The Finnish American Reporter*). There has been much conservative concern about these "hyphenated Americans," suggesting that they are not as fully American or loyal as the rest of us. "When people say we all ought to just call ourselves 'Americans,' they have in the back of their minds a norm which is the white American norm, and they're assuming that's the way things ought to be" (David R. Roediger, *Towards the Abolition of Whiteness*). Writer Lynn Laitala says that the supposedly endangered species, "just plain American," was always white, male, and privileged; "Our divergent histories do not confer special privileges. They give us special perspectives." Robert H. Scarlett says, "I can't understand why some people feel threatened by the fact that some people show interest and pride in their roots. As long as people include 'American' in their description of themselves, what's the big fuss?" Avoid the pejorative term "hyphenated Americans," but continue to use the ethnic designations themselves. When using "Cuban American," "German American," etc., use also "European American" rather than an unqualified "American," which would imply a standard against which others are contrasted.

hyphenated surnames hyphenated last names are not always ideal (computers sometimes don't recognize hyphens and some names are too long for most forms) but they have allowed couples to mark their relationships and children to carry their dual heritage. Even hyphenation doesn't assure gender fairness: the Nebraska Supreme Court ruled that the father's surname has to precede the mother's in hyphenated children's names. Hyphenation somewhat resembles the centuries-old custom in Spain, Portugal, and other Latin countries: children are given two fully functional surnames: the mother's and the father's (husbands and wives do not have the same last name after marriage). However, the father's name is the first surname (in between the first name and the mother's name) and it is this name that carries greater social weight and is passed on to the next generation. *See also* "hyphenated Americans," maiden name, matronym/matronymic, patronym/patronymic, surnames.

hysteria/hysterical based on the Greek for "womb" (hysteria was thought to be caused by disturbances in the womb), these terms are used almost entirely and often inappropriately of women. For the medical condition use *histrionic personality disorder.* For the noun use *terror, fear, frenzy, emotional excess, wildness, outburst, explosion, flare-up, seizure, eruption, delirium.* For the adjective use *terrified, angry, outraged, irate, incensed, enraged, furious, infuriated, livid, upset, agitated, delirious, beside oneself, carried away, raving, raging, seething, distracted, frantic, frenetic, frenzied, wild, berserk, uncontrollable.*

I

When once a social order is well established, no matter what injustice it involves, those who occupy a position of advantage are not long in coming to believe that it is the only possible and reasonable order.

—*Suzanne La Follette*

Language conveys a certain power. It is one of the instruments of domination. It is carefully guarded by the superior people because it is one of the means through which they conserve their supremacy.

—*Sheila Rowbotham*

I am not my brother's keeper *See* brother's keeper, I am not my.

ice-cream man *ice-cream vendor/seller; sometimes, ice-cream truck.*

iceman retain where necessary for historical accuracy. Otherwise consider *ice deliverer/carrier/seller, ice route driver.* For slang meaning "killer": *liquidator, hired gun, executioner, cutthroat, assassin, racketeer, butcher, mobster, thug, gangster, sharpshooter.*

idea man *idea machine, thinker, creative thinker, wizard, brain, brains, intellectual, genius, mental giant, think tank, sage, oracle, theorist, philosopher, savant, conceptualizer, visionary, daydreamer, expert, authority, ratiocinator, ideator.*

idiot/idiocy because the term "idiot" is unscientific, highly demeaning, and always unacceptable, use instead *someone with profound mental retardation/mental impairment/a mental disability; mental impairment/disability.* Also avoid abnormal, backward, feeble-minded, freak, imbecile, moron. For the casual insult consider using *blockhead, stupid, fool. **See also*** amaurotic family idiocy, disability, handicapped, normal, retard/retarded.

idiot savant *person/someone with savant syndrome.*

if you can't stand the heat, stay out of the kitchen despite the kitchen, this sentence is used for both men and women and carries no sexist sting.

I'll be a monkey's uncle *See* uncle, I'll be a monkey's.

illegal alien *undocumented worker/resident/immigrant/migrant/newcomer.* Most undocumented immigrants do not come to the U.S. by crossing a border illegally; 6 out of 10 enter legally—with student, tourist, or business visas—and become "illegal" by remaining here after their visas expire. The objection to "illegal" is that it applies to acts, not persons; "illegal immigration," might be the correct term in some cases. The objection to "alien" arises from its connotations of "strangeness" and "creature from outer space." Undocumented immigrants are not eligible for public assistance except emergency medical care and nutrition programs, but most do not use these programs because they fear detection by the Immigration and Naturalization Service. *See also* immigrant, wetback.

illegitimate/illegitimate child no human being is "illegitimate"; except for narrow legal uses, avoid these terms. Question the need to mention the circumstances of a person's birth; they are most often irrelevant. When necessary, use *child of unmarried parents.* Pejoratively labeling children is unhelpful in a situation with far-reaching social implications, and is sexist insofar as it is the mothers who, along with their children, usually suffer community disfavor and severe economic penalties.

illiterate "It is good to be able to read and write. It is good to have a culture that values literacy. It is also good to have cultures that value oral tradition, which is what some people have instead of written traditions. It is a more immediate and personal form of communication and transmission of culture, and it is just as 'good' and 'smart' as a literate culture. It does not denote 'backwardness.' It is simply indicative of a world-view that differs from that of the 20th century European" (Amoja Three Rivers, *Cultural Etiquette*). In discussing cultures with other communication traditions, describe those traditions factually or consider using *nonliterate. See also* culturally deprived/disadvantaged, primitive, savage.

imam this Muslim cleric is always a man.

I'm a monkey's uncle *See* uncle, I'll be a monkey's.

immigrant this term is sometimes used positively and sometimes negatively: surveys of U.S. public opinion as far back as the turn of the century show that earlier waves of immigrants were considered valuable citizens, but that the current wave is somehow "less desirable." Especially in today's climate of economic and social concerns, people are buying the inaccurate rhetoric from well-funded anti-immigrant groups that fuels the public perception that the foreign-born are flooding across U.S. borders and onto U.S. shores, draining welfare dollars, burdening public services, and taking jobs from citizens. Creditable studies to the contrary receive little attention. A *Business Week* editorial pointed out that immigrants earn

$240 billion, produce more than $90 billion in taxes, and receive approximately $5 billion in welfare; "We do not have an immigrant problem. We have a problem of right-wing xenophobes who skew statistics to create suspicion, fear, and hate between people." Another survey, by the Urban Institute, found that even when both legal and illegal immigrants were considered together, they paid some $70.3 billion in taxes while receiving $42.9 billion in services such as education and public assistance; more than 95% of immigrants (including refugees and the elderly) support themselves or are supported by family members. The total annual flow of legal and illegal immigration amounts to less than one-half of 1% of the total population; of the 100 million migrants worldwide, fewer than 1% come to the U.S. each year. *See also* illegal alien.

impaired most "impaired" terms have been the fabrications of lead-footed humorists. In their subsequent savage attacks on these silly words, they tend to forget who made them up. However, using the noun rather than the adjective produces one usable expression: "person/someone with a visual impairment." This is not a synonym for blind, but rather describes "conditions involving less than total loss of capacity" *(American Heritage Book of English Usage).* Some people will also accept "person with a hearing impairment," but generally that term is vague; "deaf" or "hard of hearing" is preferred. *See also* blind, deaf/Deaf, disability/disabilities, handicapped.

impersonator, male/female *See* cross-dresser, transvestite.

impotent use "impotent" only to describe a man unable to achieve erection; someone who is sterile or infertile may be potent, but unable to father children because of, for example, a low sperm count. Impotence in a man is not the same as "frigidity" in a woman. *See also* frigid, infertile, sterile.

impregnable there is nothing sexist about this term, but it does have a sex-specific base. In situations in which its actual meaning might overcome its metaphorical use consider *unassailable, invulnerable, impenetrable, safe, secure, invincible, indomitable, unyielding, irresistible, unconquerable, all-powerful.*

impregnate for metaphorical, non-sex-linked uses of the term consider *permeate, saturate, infiltrate, infuse, imbue, implant; fertilize, fecundate, generate, create. See also* impregnable.

impresario woman or man. For terms that may not appear as masculine as "impresario" consider *promoter, producer, director, manager, talent coordinator, talent agent, booker, advance agent.*

inamorata/inamorato meaning, respectively, a woman or a man with whom one is in love or with whom one has a relationship, these sex-specific terms are acceptable when used even-handedly. They have a faint, undeserved flavor of the immoral about them, which, given the linguistic emphasis on women's "promiscuity" (*see* prostitute), is perhaps why the female term is seen more often. *See also* boyfriend, girlfriend.

inclusive language inclusive language includes everyone. Nobody feels left out or thinks, "Where am *I* in all that?" Inclusive language is advocated by the Modern Language Association, has been used to revise government job titles, and is mandated in most publishing houses, newspapers, government offices, businesses, and higher educational institutions. *See also* the section on inclusive language in the Writing Guidelines, pp. 2–3.

incorrigible when referring to people, this is occasionally appropriate as an adjective, but it is unacceptable as a noun.

Indiaman *India trader, East India trading ship, merchant ship, trader;* or retain as is in historical context.

Indian (India) this is the correct term for people living in India. When there is a possibility of confusion with American Indians, use "Asian Indian": do not use the colonialist "East Indian." In the U.S., people of Asian Indian descent are called Asian Indian Americans. Burmese, Bangladeshis, Pakistanis, and Sri Lankans are not Indians.

Indian (United States) if necessary to identify someone by heritage, use the name of a specific people (Cherokee, Absaroke, Kiowa, Oneida). Otherwise, acceptable terms include *American Indian, Native American, Native peoples, Indian people, Indians, First Nations People, Indian Nations.* Because there are over 500 Indian nations, these blanket terms give no sense of the diversity of the various peoples; they are about as specific as "European" when speaking in generalities about people from Holland, Hungary, Portugal, Italy, Monaco, Switzerland, etc. "American Indian" is currently the most widely approved term; "Native American" is too easily confused with "native American" and is used by the federal government to include native Alaskans and Samoans, which makes it less acceptable to Native peoples. Inés Hernandez (in Patricia Riley, *Growing Up Native American*) says, "Native people know that the term 'Indian' is a misnomer, but we have made it our own, just as we have made 'American Indian' and . . . 'Native American' our own, even though in our original languages, each of our peoples had (and have) their own name for themselves and for this part of the earth that is now known as 'America.' We refer to each other by the tribe or nation that we are from—that is one of the first questions we ask each other, 'Who are your people?' and 'Where are you from?'" One may also ask, "What is your nation?" A few guidelines for writing and speaking about Indians: (1) it is redundant to use "Indian" following a tribe name (thus, "Lakota," not "Lakota Indian"); (2) make no assumptions about Indians' lives, dress, beliefs, or history without careful research—many myths and stereotypes are worked into the fabric of non-Indian "understandings"; (3) various peoples either have changed or are in the process of changing their names from those given them by others to the names they call themselves (from Nez Perce to Nimipu, from Crow to Absaroke, from Huron to Wyandot, from Gabrielino to Tongva, etc.)—be sure terms are current. And if they are hard to remember or difficult, persevere; Paul Chaat Smith, a Comanche writer and activist, points out that Mao Zedong and Beethoven are not translated from Chinese or German, but Indian names were usually translated into English in an attempt to make them "easy" and incidentally primitive, thus giving us "Sitting Bull" instead of his name in Lakota. The indigenous people of Hawaii prefer the terms "Hawaiians," "Hawaiian Natives," or "Native Hawaiians" to "Native Americans," the latter so offensive it is almost considered "fighting words." Not properly referred to as Indians, however, are the Inuit, Eskimo, and Aleut; Patagonians and Fuegians are also sometimes excluded from the term Indian. Indians in Latin America as a whole are often referred to as Latin American Indians, as opposed to American Indians. *See also* brave (Indian), chief, costume, half-breed/half-caste, "Indian giver," Indian summer, Injun, massacre, powwow, Redskins (sports team name), roaming, Sioux, squaw, tribe, warpath.

Indian file *single file.*

Indian giver this pejorative and highly resented term arose from a misreading of Indian customs. You may want to circumlocute, as alternatives are not wonderful: *half-hearted/two-faced/sorry/repentant giver, take-backer, wishy-washy giver, gives with the left hand and takes back with the right.*

Indian style, sitting *sitting cross-legged.*

Indian summer although the origins of this term are clearly pejorative ("Indian" was once used to indicate something sham or bogus, as in the "false summer" sometimes seen in the fall), today "Indian summer" has pleasant, positive associations. Dictionaries define it in terms of mild weather and tranquil days—altogether an agreeable period.

Indian time this term is pejorative only when it is meant to be. Mary Brave Bird writes, "There is Indian time and white man's time. Indian time means never looking at the clock. . . . There is not even a word for time in our language." From Indian and some non-Indian perspectives, it is a very positive concept: "Indian time conveys an old grasp of time and life, perceived and experienced collectively by Indian people. . . . From the edge of Indian time overlooking infinity, there is acute perception and perspective" (Anna Lee Walters, *Talking Indian*). In her poem "If Indians Are Coming It Won't Start on Time," Diane Glancy writes, "The unseen / Trails they follow / Take time."

indigenous peoples this is an acceptable term, always used in the plural. The World Council of Indigenous Peoples uses the following definition: "Indigenous peoples are such population groups as we are who from old-age time have inhabited the lands where we live, who are aware of having a character of our own, with social traditions and means of expression that are linked to the country inherited from our ancestors, with a language of our own, and having certain essential and unique characteristics which confer upon us the strong conviction of belonging to a people, who have an identity in ourselves and should be thus regarded by others."

Indochina the peninsula of southeast Asia that includes Vietnam, Laos, Kampuchea (Cambodia), Thailand, Myanmar (Burma), and the mainland territory of Malaysia is known as Indochina. The term also refers to the former French colonial empire, which included some, but not all, of the peninsula. To avoid confusion, you may want to use a more general term like "Southeast Asia" or name the specific countries you're discussing.

infantryman *infantry/enlisted soldier, footsoldier, member of the infantry, soldier, infantry; infantryman and infantrywoman* if used together.

infertile this term is used for both men and women, although most often it modifies "couple" ("an infertile couple"). "Infertile" refers to the lack of offspring in people who have been having unprotected intercourse for a certain length of time. "Sterile" usually indicates that a cause for the infertility has been found. Infertile people are not necessarily sterile. Sterile people are always infertile. Infertility is often treatable; sterility generally is not (unless, for example, a tubal ligation or vasectomy can be reversed). Do not confuse "sterile" with "impotent" or "frigid." *See also* barren, frigid, impotent, sterile.

informant in the sense of someone from another culture who works with an anthropologist, this has been replaced by *consultant.*

ingenue this well-established, narrowly defined role in the theater has no real male counterpart; "ingenu" is rarely seen. When using the term in its broader sense, consider *novice, amateur, beginner, tyro, neophyte, newcomer, innocent, greenhorn, tenderfoot, newcomer, initiate, fledgling, apprentice, trainee.*

inheritress/inheritrix *inheritor. See also* "feminine" word endings.

Injun along with "honest Injun" (which disparagingly implies the opposite), this term is derogatory and unacceptable, even when used "good-naturedly." Perhaps especially then.

inkman *inker.*

inner city Paul Kivel *(Uprooting Racism)* says, "The inner city is more a site in our minds than in our cities. For most white people 'inner city' means anywhere there are large concentrations of people of color, regardless of their economic status." Examine closely the use of "inner city" to describe the economic, ethnic, and business diversity found in urban areas. *See also* ghetto, underclass, urban.

inner man *inner person/self/core, soul, heart, psyche, private self; appetite, stomach.*

innocent women and children *civilians, innocent civilians.* In accounts of bombings, terrorism, guerrilla warfare, and other atrocities, one often finds references to "innocent women and children," the implication being that men somehow deserve what happens or that it is "natural" that they would be caught up in such death and destruction. Be aware of the language that underwrites this sexist view of the relative value of human life. *See also* draft.

innocent victim this phrase often implies that other victims are not innocent or at least not so innocent. This is sometimes defensible (in the casualties of gang warfare, the child who is caught in the crossfire is surely an innocent victim). However, the phrase is problematic when an infant or blood-transfusion patient dying of AIDS is referred to as an innocent victim, thus making other people with AIDS seem less "innocent" or when some rape victims are labeled "innocent victims" and others are not. *See also* victim.

insane/insanity when referring to people with a mental illness, use "has schizophrenia" or "with bipolar disorder." "Insanity" is a legal term, not a medical one. "Insane asylums" are psychiatric hospitals. *See also* mental illness.

inscrutable a fine word, but too often used stereotypically and unjustifiably of Asians and Asian Americans. This usage springs not so much from any notable characteristics of those so labeled but rather from an ignorance on the part of the labeler, i.e., "If I don't know anything about you (which I don't), you must be inscrutable."

inside man *accomplice, confederate, double/undercover agent, spy, insider; sometimes, inside job.*

"insider/outsider" rule certain terms used by people within a group would be considered derogatory and unacceptable when used by people outside that group. "Crip" (for "cripple") appears in *The Disability Rag* (now *Ragged Edge*); this does not mean that the word is available to anyone who wants to use it. "Big Fag" is printed on a gay man's T-shirt; a stranger may not call him a big fag. A group of women talk about "going out with the girls"; co-workers should not refer to them as "girls." People may call themselves whatever they like—terms that they reserve for use among themselves and terms by which they want to be known by others. Use only the latter. The rationale behind "insider" terms is the attempt to claim and rehabilitate offensive terms, using them often enough and positively among insiders to strip them of their power to wound. In any case, Miss Manners has decreed that "people are allowed more leeway in what they call themselves than in what they call others." *See also* the section on naming in the Writing Guidelines, pp. 15–18.

inspectress *inspector. See also* "feminine" word endings.

institutional racism *See* racism.

instructress *instructor. See also* "feminine" word endings.

insurance man *insurance agent/sales agent/representative/rep.*

intercourse *See* sexual intercourse.

internment *See* relocation.

interracial *See* multiracial.

in the arms of Morpheus there is nothing wrong with using this phrase, but be aware of how many such expressions in the English language are male-based. Balance their use with female-based expressions, creative expressions of your own, or sex-neutral alternatives: *fast/sound asleep, sawing wood, dead to the world, out like a light, sacked out. See also* sex-linked expressions.

intuition, women's/feminine *See* women's intuition.

Inuit this is the term preferred to "Eskimo" by Arctic and Canadian peoples. *Inuk* is the singular; plural is *Inuits, the Inuit.* The double-consonant forms *(Innuk, Innuit, Innuits)* are also acceptable. *See also* Eskimo.

invasion Paul Kivel *(Uprooting Racism)* notes the implications of our choice to use or not use this term; "Why don't we say that Europeans invaded North America? Or that settlers invaded the West? Most uses of the word *invasion* are about 'us'—white Americans—being invaded by Japanese investment, illegal aliens, people of color moving to the suburbs or Haitian refugees."

Iranian this term, along with "Persian," is acceptable to most Iranians. "Persian" is used to refer more to antiquity, to the pre-1920s era, or to ethnicity, where Iranian is used to indicate nationality.

Irishman *Irishwoman and Irishman, native of Ireland, inhabitant of Ireland.* Plurals: *Irishmen and Irishwomen/Irishwomen and Irishman* (but not "Irishmen and women"), *the Irish, Irishfolk, natives of Ireland, inhabitants of Ireland.*

Iron John "Iron John" has become a key term in the mythopoetic men's movement. In *Iron John,* poet and essayist Robert Bly reconfirms the power of ancient stories to guide and heal by using the Grimms' fairy tale about Iron John to examine a masculinity that goes beyond cultural stereotypes. He discusses male initiation, connecting with "the inner warrior," men's hunger for fathers and mentors, the missing or weak father-son bond in many men's lives, and the fashioning of a male identity that is "neither Rambo nor wimp." Although Bly's work has been much debated by both women and men, he offers an original perspective and is a source of inspiration and comfort to many men.

iron maiden historically, this is the term used, but contrast it with the positive term "iron man"; one wonders at the mentality that associated women, especially one as mild as a "maiden," with an instrument of torture.

iron man *iron woman/iron man.* Originally referring to a baseball pitcher of superior endurance, this term has come to mean anyone of unusual physical staying power. Except for roundabout phrases (someone "with the strength of ten," "with stamina"), there are no good alternatives for this pithy term.

The Ironman this triathlon championship event begun in 1978 has been open to women since 1979.

ironmaster *ironsmith, iron manufacturer/worker.*

interracial referring to the presence of different races in a certain defined area or group ("interracial neighborhood," "interracial gathering"), this term has lost its validity as the concept of "race" has lost its. When it has been used, it has often meant "blacks and whites," ignoring Asian Americans and other groups, or it has been code to signal the presence of blacks in the area. Replace the word with a precise, factual description of the makeup of the group you're describing.

irrational this term is too often used as a rebuttal of women's arguments or applied inaccurately to women as a catch-all condemnation; use carefully in reference to women. It is not used in the same way for men. *See also* emotional.

Islam this is the name of the religion founded by Muhammad; it embraces all the sects which are now found among his followers, who are known as Muslims; thus a Shiite and a Sunnite are both Muslims. "Islamic" is the adjective. *See also* Koran, Moslem, Muhammad.

Isle of Man "Man" is thought to come from a Celtic word meaning "mountain"; it has nothing to do with human beings. For the inhabitants, instead of Manxman/Manxmen use *someone from the Isle of Man; the Manx.*

Israeli this term originated with the creation of Israel in 1948 and should not be used to refer to people before that time. An Israeli is a citizen of Israel, but is not always a Jew; conversely, not all Jews are Israelis. The term for the biblical peoples is Israelites. *See also* Hebrew, Jew.

Issei literally "first generation," this acceptable term is used for a Japanese immigrant, especially to the United States. Plural is *Issei* or *Isseis*. *See also* Kibei, Nisei, Sansei, Yonsei.

Italian pronouncing it EYE-talian is taken as a slur.

it is a wise father that knows his own child leave as is. The old truth to this sex-specific proverb is that a mother can know with 100% certitude that a child is the child of her body, but a father has no such direct certainty.

it's a man's world this generalization is not true for men who are unemployed, homeless, or victims of street violence; for soldiers fighting wars of someone else's making; for divorced fathers who rarely see their children. Men also die an average of eight years earlier than women. The cliché has some use, however, as a means of expressing relative well-being: on average, men still earn more, have better jobs, and sit more often in the chairs of power. *See also* glass cellar, sexism.

it's not over 'til the fat lady sings *the game isn't over until it's over, it ain't over 'til it's over.* The sentences variously attributed to Yogi Berra are at least as succinct and colorful as the sexist, weightist, "The opera is never over until the fat lady sings."

Ivy Leaguer young woman/woman or young man/man.

J

"When will justice come to Athens?" they asked Thucydides.
And he answered, "Justice will not come to Athens until those who are not injured
are as indignant as those who are."

—*Thucydides*

I remember, we must remember
until justice be done among us.

—*Rosario Castellanos*

jack/jack-/-jack although the word, prefix, and suffix "jack" came from
Jacob and often meant a man/boy, they have come to refer without any
particular gender overtones to certain tools (e.g., bootjack, hydraulic jack,
jack, jackhammer, jackknife, jacklight, jackplane, jackscrew, and tire
jack), plants and animals (jackdaw, jackfish, jackfruit, jack-in-the-pulpit,
jack mackerel, jack pine, jacksnipe), other nouns (apple jack, blackjack,
cheap-jack, flapjack, jackboot, jackleg, jack-o-lantern, jackpot, jackstay,
jackstraw, jack-tar, jumping jack, lumberjack, steeplejack), verbs (ball the
jack, hijack, jack up prices, jack game), and adjectives (crackerjack,
jackleg). These can be used as they are, but one wonders: has any
woman's name ever influenced dozens of words? *See also* ball the jack;
every man jack; jackass; Jack Frost; jack-in-the-box; Jack Ketch; jackleg;
jackman; jack of all trades, master of none; jackrabbit; Jack Robinson,
before you can say; jacks; lumberjack/lumberman; Union Jack.

jackass although this word is defined as "a foolish or stupid person," it
means male donkey and is reserved for men. It's doubtful that people
shouting "jackass!" want alternatives, but more neutral-sounding terms
exist: *donkey, yo-yo, fool, nincompoop, blockhead, nitwit, dumbbell.*

Jack Frost there is nothing wrong with using this popular and familiar name, but be aware of how many such expressions in the English language are male-based. Balance their use with female-based expressions, creative expressions of your own, or sex-neutral alternatives: *the Frost Goblin, Jack and Jill Frost, the Frost Fairy.* Also: *frost, winter.* **See also** sex-linked expressions.

jack-in-the-box the clown that pops up in the box is generally male; the toy has no inclusive name.

Jack Ketch 17th-century Jack Ketch, who hung people for a living but whose occupation was listed as "civil servant," lives on in this phrase meaning someone whose job title hides their true and sinister task—a phrase for which there is no good gender-neutral equivalent.

jackman *printing-roller handler.*

jack of all trades, master of none this expression is nearly impossible to replace; it's familiar, pithy, and rhythmic. If the sex-specificity and the "master" are jarring, consider *good at everything, expert at nothing; good at all trades, expert at none; generalist; all-around expert; many-talented; someone who knows a little bit about a lot of things and not much about any of them.* Where appropriate, the shortened "jill of all trades" has been used. For discussion of "master" words, *see* master (noun). **See also** handyman.

jack rabbit leave as is to refer to several genuses of large hares. An adult male rabbit is called a buck.

Jack Robinson, before you can say there is nothing wrong with using this phrase, but be aware of how many such expressions in the English language are male-based. Balance their use with female-based expressions, creative expressions of your own, or sex-neutral alternatives: *in two shakes of a lamb's tail, on the double, in a jiffy, immediately if not sooner, before you can say "knife," right off the bat, in one fell swoop, in a pig's whisker, pronto, straightaway, lickety-split, in the same breath, in the wink/twinkling of an eye, at the drop of a hat, in double-quick time, on the spot, at once, immediately.* **See also** sex-linked expressions.

jacks (child's game) not sex-linked; originally called jackstones, the "jack" is from a corruption of "chuck" meaning "pebble."

jailbait (underage female sexual partner) the use of this term perpetuates the Eve-tempting-poor-Adam myth, implying a certain victimization and unwilling cooperation on the part of the man, and obscures the fact that the man is engaging in criminal activity (and laying the foundation for a statutory rape charge).

jailbird technically either sex, a jailbird is generally perceived as male, probably because men have always greatly outnumbered women in prison. *See also* bad guy, juvenile delinquent, prisoner.

Jane Crow attorney and educator Pauli Murray said this term "refers to the entire range of assumptions, attitudes, stereotypes, customs, and arrangements which have robbed women of a positive self-concept and prevented them from participating fully in society as equals with men. Traditionally racism and sexism in the United States have shared some common origins, displayed similar manifestations, reinforced one another, and are so deeply intertwined in the country's institutions that the successful outcome of the struggle against racism will depend in large part upon the simultaneous elimination of discrimination based upon sex." Shirley Chisholm says, "Of my two 'handicaps,' being female put many more obstacles in my path than being black." *See also* Jim Crow.

Jane Doe acceptable legal term; use with John Doe. *See also* John Doe.

Jane Q. Citizen/Jane Q. Public acceptable terms; use with John Q. Citizen/ John Q. Public. *See also* average man, common man, John Q. Citizen/ John Q. Public, man in the street.

janitress/janitrix *janitor. See also* "feminine" word endings, maintenance man.

JAP *See* Jewish American Princess/JAP.

Japanese this is not interchangeable with Japanese American, and it is never shortened to the offensive "Jap." *See also* shortened forms of words.

Japanese American acceptable term. *See also* Asian American, "hyphenated Americans," Issei, Kibei, Nisei, Sansei, Yonsei.

Java man *Homo erectus, early human, early human found in Java, prehistoric human, ancestral hominid, archaic homo sapiens.* Remains are called *Java fossil, Java skull.*

jazzman *jazz musician/player, member of jazz band.*

Jehovah this alteration of the Hebrew "Yahweh" is never used by Jews, is most often seen in Christian translations of the Old Testament, and is used by Jehovah's Witnesses. *See also* Yahweh.

Jekyll and Hyde there is nothing wrong with using this succinct and evocative term, but be aware of how many such expressions in the English language are male-based. Balance their use with female-based expressions, creative expressions of your own, or sex-neutral alternatives: *split personality, alter egos. See also* sex-linked expressions.

jerk technically available for both sexes, "jerk" seems to favor men. In a

Men's Rights, Inc. study of hundreds of advertisements in which both women and men appeared, every perceived "jerk" was a man. Since the advent of the women's movement, it has become much riskier to make women look feeble in advertisements, and since much lowbrow humor depends on putting someone down, men have become the targets. The problem is: some men are jerks. The problem with using this term for men is: many men are not jerks.

jerrican/jerry can "jerry" does not refer to a man's name but to the nickname for Germans (originally Gerry), to reflect the can's German design. Even though it involves an ethnic reference, the term is not functionally ethnocentric nor is it offensive to Germans.

jerry-built although its origins are unclear (either a builder named Jerry known for poor work or the apparently flimsy walls of Jericho), this term is functionally nonsexist. If a more neutral-looking term is needed consider *shoddy/flimsy/careless construction, cheaply/hastily/shoddily built.*

Jesus of Nazareth when writing about Jesus of Nazareth, the masculine pronouns are, of course, correct. However, some people suggest eliminating unnecessary ones because "theological tradition has virtually always maintained that the maleness of Jesus is theologically, christologically, soteriologically, and sacramentally irrelevant" (Sandra M. Schneiders, *Women and the Word*). There have been few individuals in history as completely androgynous and inclusive as Jesus, and it seems to do his message a disservice to overinsist on his maleness—or his usual whiteness. Theologian and biblical scholar Cain Hope Felder says the African origins of the people of the Holy Land have been ignored by European scholars. The image of Jesus as a white person was grafted onto the truth by European church leaders as a way of selling their theology to white people; "We're not saying he came from the Congo. But we are saying he was an average African-Asian man of his time."

Jew this is always a noun, never a verb, never an adjective. Author and scholar Osha Gray Davidson (*Des Moines Register*, March 12, 1996) notes people torturing their syntax to use "Jewish person/people" when "Jew/Jews" clearly would have fit the sentence structure better. He says people know that "Jew" is sometimes used as an epithet and so, with the best intentions, they reject that perversion; "But in the process they have cut out the word altogether, like a doctor who treats an infected finger by amputating the arm. The result: The perfectly acceptable name for a people with a 4,000-year history has, in certain circles, become the 'J-word.'" The *American Heritage Book of English Usage* says the "attributive use of the noun *Jew*, in phrases such as *Jew banker* or *Jew ethics*, is both vulgar and highly offensive. In such contexts *Jewish* is the only acceptable possibility. Some people, however, have become so wary of this construction that they have extended the stigma to any use of *Jew* as a noun, a practice that carries risks of its own. In a sentence such as *There are now several Jews on the council,* which is unobjectionable, the substitution of a circumlocution like *Jewish people* or *persons of Jewish background* may in itself cause offense for seeming to imply that *Jew* has a negative connotation when used as a noun." Irving Lewis Allen *(Unkind Words)* points out that the same thing has happen to "Poles" and "Swedes"; because of old derogatory uses that tainted these perfectly good proper names, they are replaced by circumlocutions. He says, "To some, *Jew* has a patent, even a harsh sound, which seems somehow softened by the adjectival *Jewish.* Perhaps *Jew* sounds too 'ethnic,' whereas *Jewish* sounds more 'assimilated.'" Catholics and Lutherans and Finns are not referred to as "a Catholic person" or "a Lutheran person" or "a Finnish person." Davidson adds that "Jewish" is an adjective; "It suggests an inessential quality, a trait cobbled on and easily dismissed. Worse, the '-ish' form is the 98-pound weakling of Grammar Beach; even other adjectives kick sand in its face. It denotes tendency rather than a full-blown characteristic, a wishy-washy retreat from beingness. She is tall*ish.* It is warm*ish* out. I am Jew*ish.* I grew angry as I noticed more people avoiding the J-word, picking their way through a sentence like fresh recruits crossing a minefield. I wanted to shout: The word is 'Jew!' Say it: 'Jew!' . . . One doesn't need to be a Holocaust scholar to grasp that once a society considers it uncouth to *say* 'Jew,' eventually— inevitably—it will become unsafe to *be* a Jew. What are words, after all, but the womb in which tomorrow's deeds slumber?" *See also* jew boy, jew down, Jewish American Princess/JAP, Jewish lightning, Jewish mother, Jewish question, Judeo-Christian.

Jew boy unbelievably offensive.

jew down this unacceptable expression is always derogatory and debasing to Judaism and to Jews. It is surprising how many people still use it unthink-ingly. Alternatives include: *talk down, bargain, deal, barter, haggle, dicker, negotiate, make an offer.*

Jewess *Jew. See also* "feminine" word endings.

Jewish American Princess/JAP this term, which portrays Jewish young women as self-centered, materialistic, and manipulative, appears in jokes and everyday conversation as well as in anti-Semitic graffiti. Many people use the term without realizing its powerfully damaging effects; tolerance of it has been puzzlingly strong. Some claim it is no coinci-dence that the term appeared when Jewish women were beginning to establish a place for themselves in Judaism, serving as rabbis and cantors, as well as in the commercial world.

Jewish lightning not acceptable; the use of it does not pass for wit.

Jewish mother the Macmillan Publishing Company's *Guidelines for Creating Positive Sexual and Racial Images in Educational Materials* says, "This has become a cliché used to describe the woman—Jewish or not—who tends to dominate the home, invest herself completely in her children and the preparation of food, and who views herself as a martyr. This image—a distortion of the traditionally strong role of Jewish women in the home—is degrading to Jews and women alike, and should be avoided." It seems possible, however, that the term still has some limited nonpejorative uses—when women use it in self-reference or when used in close relationships with the tacit permission of the women in question.

Jewish question Sanford Berman *(Prejudices and Antipathies)* writes, "On the face of it, 'Jewish Question' may seem a bland, neutral term. Yet it is just the opposite, masquerading ruthlessness and inhumanity—the age-old and altogether vicious practice of scapegoating—in a deceptive, leisurely abstraction. The phraseology is that of the oppressor, the ultimate murderer, not the victim. . . . The 'question' facing the soon-to-be-incinerated millions was not one to be calmly debated. It was fundamental: life or death." He says that Joseph Goebbels predicted in 1938, "The Jewish question will in a short time find a solution satisfying the sentiment of the German people." *See also* final solution, problem.

Jezebel/jezebel the biblical story of Jezebel depicts a murdering, controlling, rapacious person who is primarily an amoral manipulator and only secondarily a woman. Instead of focusing on Jezebel's viciousness, the common connotation of a jezebel is to her sexuality (dictionaries define her as a shameless or abandoned woman) when in fact she did not use sex to carry out her evil deeds. Consider using instead *evil influence, villain, murderer, bully, plotter, scourge of the human race, devil in human form/ shape.*

jiggerman *potter.*

Jim Crow from the obsolete derogatory name for a black man, "Jim Crow" came to be a synonym for practices that discriminate against blacks in the U.S., particularly segregation (as in "Jim Crow laws"). *See also* Jane Crow.

jim-dandy there is nothing wrong with using this phrase, but be aware of how many such expressions in the English language are male-based. Balance their use with female-based expressions, creative expressions of your own, or sex-neutral alternatives: *terrific, super, wonderful, marvelous, fantastic, sensational, fabulous, stupendous, out of this world, far out, extraordinary. See also* sex-linked expressions.

jimjams/jimmies/jimmy the origins of these terms are unclear, but because they appear sex-linked, alternatives may be needed on occasion. For "jimjams," use *jitters*. For "jimmies" use *candy sprinkles*. For "jimmy" (noun/verb) use *crowbar/burglar's crowbar; pry/pry up.*

Job, patient as/poor as *See* patient as Job, poor as Job/poor as Job's turkey.

jobmaster *supervisor, boss.*

job titles both statutory and administrative law now prohibit the use of sex- and age-referents in employment practices.

jock (athlete) although both sexes are referred to as jocks today, the tendency is still to think first of a man when one hears the word. And for good reason. The old "jock/jockum" meant "penis." Its meaning is particularly clear in "jockstrap." "Jock" usually has pejorative overtones, suggesting more brawn than brain. *See also* jockette.

jockette *jockey.* Some racing stewards have actually used the silly "jockette"—a pitiful thing to have done to a decent word like "jockey" and to the talented women who have made it into the ranks of professional jockeys. It has apparently also been used as the female "equivalent" of a jock. *See also* "feminine" word endings.

joe/Joe Blow "joe" and "Joe Blow" have long meant an average, typical, or ordinary man. They are sexist insofar as there are no parallel terms for women. Less casual inclusive synonyms for both sexes are *Jane Doe/ John Doe, Jane Q. Citizen/John Q. Citizen, and Jane Q. Public/John Q. Public.*

john (facility) *bathroom, restroom, toilet, washroom, privy, water closet, lavatory, W.C., comfort station, outhouse.*

john (person) our language is nowhere less descriptive of reality than when dealing with prostitution; there is currently no available term for the prostitute's sex partner equal to "prostitute" in weight, significance, and moral judgment. Consider employing the term *prostitute user*. Prostitutes carry the economic, psychological, physical, social, and linguistic burden for a system that could not exist without the participation of "users"; language ought to reflect the relationship. Instead there are scores and scores of pejorative terms for prostitutes, but only three relatively innocuous terms for prostitute users: john, date, and trick. While some people see the association of "john" with a toilet sufficiently evocative of the john's seedy activities, the fact remains that John is a nice name—too good for prostitution and certainly not parallel to the term "prostitute." *See also* prostitute.

John Bull (England) some countries are personified by men (the United States' Uncle Sam), while others are personified by women (France's Marianne). You can balance the male John Bull image with a female one:

Great Britain is personified by Britannia, a far more familiar and widely used national symbol that represents all of Great Britain, not just England.

John Doe acceptable legal term; the female form is Jane Doe. The only caution is not to use "John Doe" pseudogenerically to mean "average man." *See also* average man, common man, man in the street, John Q. Public.

John Hancock there is nothing wrong with using this expression, but be aware of how many like it in the English language are male-based. Balance their use with the use of female-based expressions, creative expressions of your own, or sex-neutral alternatives: *signature, name, moniker. See also* sex-linked expressions.

johnny *hospital gown.*

johnnycake nonsexist; the term seems to have come either from "journeycake" or from "Shawnee-cake" (originally made by the Shawnee). For more neutral-appearing words use *journeycake, cornbread, corncake, battercake, corn pone, hoecake, mush bread, ashcake.*

Johnny-come-lately there is nothing wrong with using this phrase, but be aware of how many such expressions in the English language are male-based. Balance their use with female-based expressions, creative expressions of your own, or sex-neutral alternatives: *newcomer, new arrival/ face, upstart, nouveau riche, arriviste, outsider, social climber, rookie, greenhorn. See also* sex-linked expressions.

Johnny-jump-up (flower) leave as is.

Johnny-on-the-spot there is nothing wrong with using this phrase, but be aware of how many such expressions in the English language are male-based. Balance their use with female-based expressions, creative expressions of your own, or sex-neutral alternatives: *friend in need, guardian angel, deus ex machina, right hand, at the ready, good Samaritan, benefactor, ministering angel, there when you need her/him. See also* sex-linked expressions.

Johnny Reb *confederate soldier.* Retain when used in historical material.

John Q. Citizen/John Q. Public acceptable when used with Jane Q. Citizen/ Jane Q. Public, these terms are sexist when used pseudogenerically to mean "the average citizen/person." *See also* average man, common man, man in the street.

jointress leave this very specific British legal term as is until it is changed or replaced.

journeyman in labor law or in the trades, "journeyman" has certain specific and so far irreplaceable meanings. It may be possible in some such cases to use *journeyman, journeywoman, journeyperson.* ("Journeyperson" is very much a last resort, but it may have limited usefulness while the term is in transition.) In the nontechnical sense, this word can be replaced by *journey worker, journeyed/trained/trade/craft worker, trainee, beginner, assistant, helper, subordinate; average performer; skilled craftworker; journey level* (adjective). Or, use a specific title, e.g., *iron worker.*

judas when using an expression like "judas" or one of its derivatives, be aware of how many figures of speech are male-based. Balance them sometimes with female-based expressions, creative expressions of your own, or alternatives. For "judas" *use false friend, betrayer, deceiver, traitor.* For "judas goat" use *bait, lure, decoy, trap, baited hook.* For "judas hole/judas window" use *peephole.* For "judas kiss" use *kiss of betrayal. See also* sex-linked expressions.

Judeo-Christian there are three problems with this term. (1) Along with "Christian," it is often used as an inappropriate synonym for morality. Use instead *ethical, moral, decent, upstanding, righteous, upright, high-minded, honorable, principled, conscientious, moralistic, right, good.* (2) The U.S. is often referred to as a "Judeo-Christian" culture. Rabbi Barry D. Cytron, of Adath Jeshurun Congregation in Minneapolis, says, "We are neither a 'Christian nation' nor a 'Judeo-Christian' one. We are not a land with one church, but of many—and of synagogues, mosques and sweat lodges, too. What makes us really unique is that we are not a nation of labels—but of people." (3) It overstates the homogeneity between the two groups. According to an editorial in the *Forward,* the term "Judeo-Christian" was first used in the late 19th century by Christian scholars wishing to emphasize the Jewish roots of early Christianity, but outside that narrow context it wasn't much seen until after World War II when it was part of a reaction to the Holocaust; "Only in the 1950s did it become a 'buzz word,' the function of which was to convey the notion that Jews and Christians, despite their historical antagonisms, have more beliefs and values in common than ones separating them." However, "For scholars of American religion, the idea of a single 'Judeo-Christian tradition' is a made-in-America myth that many of them no longer regard as valid" (*Newsweek,* December 7, 1992). Mark Silk says that, in addition, implicit in the idea of a common religious tradition is the image of Judaism as parent to a Christian offspring—implying that the child is the true spiritual heir, and the parent might as well retire. *See also* Christian.

judgette *judge.* "Judgette" was actually used to refer ("all in good fun") to Justice Sandra Day O'Connor. *See also* "feminine" word endings.

jumpmaster *jump director.*

junior/Jr. only boys/men are juniors; neither girls/women with feminized versions of their father's names nor girls/women named for their mothers are so tagged. The attitudes that underlie the use of "junior" have been more closely associated with boys/men (laws of primogeniture, the handing on of father-son farms, firms, businesses, etc.) but are slowly evolving to include girls/women. When versatile writer Alice B. Sheldon chose a male pseudonym, she made it really male: James Tiptree, Jr.

junior executive *executive trainee.* The "junior" makes the term mildly ageist and disparaging.

junior miss ageist, sexist (there is no parallel term for boys), coy, old-fashioned, and conveying certain cultural stereotypes, this term is better replaced with *young woman, high school student.*

junkman *junk dealer/collector, rag picker.*

jury foreman *See* foreman (jury).

juryman *juror.*

juvenile because of its associations (juvenile offender, juvenile behavior), you may want to consider using *young person/adult.* *See also* adolescent, teenager, youth.

juvenile delinquent *juvenile/youthful offender.* "Juvenile delinquent" is often used broadly of anyone who is in "trouble" (e.g., truants, runaways); it or "juvenile offender" is better reserved for someone who is guilty of criminal or antisocial behavior.

K

it is not that i am playing word games, it is that the word games are there,
being played, and i am calling attention to it.

—*Alice Molloy*

Language is neither innocent nor neutral. Linguistic habits
condition our view of the world and hinder social change.

—*Carmen Martínez Ten*

Language is *not* neutral. It is not merely a vehicle which carries ideas.
It is itself a shaper of ideas.

—*Dale Spender*

kaffeeklatsch/coffee klatsch in Germany this expression is sex-neutral,
referring to informal social gatherings of both sexes. In the United States,
however, it has been traditionally used to belittle gatherings of women
(U.S. men do not have kaffeeklatsches). The term seems much less
popular in recent years; people seem to be using instead *get together, tea,
coffee, coffee break, social hour, visit, talk, open house, party.*

Kaffir *Xhosa.* This offensive, derogatory slur for a black person, used
principally in South Africa but on occasion in the U.S., comes from the
Arabic for "infidel" and is roughly equivalent to the word "nigger"
(Sanford Berman, *Prejudices and Antipathies*).

kaiser roll there's nothing wrong with using "kaiser roll" for the crusty bread
with poppy seeds and distinctive crown-like appearance, but it is, strictly
speaking, a male-linked term; introduced at the 1873 World's Fair in
Vienna, it was named after the kaiser, Emperor Franz Joseph. If you want
an alternative use *Vienna roll; hard roll, hamburger roll.*

Kanakas this term, referring to South Sea Islanders or Hawaiians of Polynesian descent, is generally unacceptable and derogatory when used by outsiders.

Kansas City Chiefs *See* Redskins (sports team name).

kapellmeister *choir/orchestra conductor/director/leader.*

keelboatman *keelboater, keeler, keel/barge worker.*

keelsman *See* keelboatman.

keelson/kelson probably of Scandinavian origin, this word has nothing to do with male offspring.

keep a stiff upper lip *See* stiff upper lip, keep a.

Kelly Girl *office temporary.* In any case, "Kelly Girl" is a registered trademark; use only for someone who works for Kelly Services, Inc.

Kelt/Keltic *See* Celt/Celtic.

kennelman *kennel owner/operator/attendant, dog breeder.*

kept woman this term is offensive because of the woman's supposed passivity (she is "kept") and because of the lack of a parallel term to describe her partner ("sugar daddy" is sometimes used). (Anecdote: Estée Lauder president Leonard Lauder explained he wouldn't buy advertising space in *Ms.* because its readers weren't right for his product; Estée Lauder sells "a kept-woman mentality," he said. When Gloria Steinem pointed out that 60% of his customers worked, he said, Yes, but they would *like* to be kept. It is not known whether this insight into the female mind was based on market research or male fantasy.) *See also* gigolo.

key man *key person/individual/executive, linchpin, number one, numero uno, leading character, leader, chief, chief cook and bottle washer, pivotal person, cornerstone, focal point, axis, heart, prop, center, main ingredient, vital part.* Consider using "key" alone as an adjective or noun: *she's absolutely key to the project, he's the key to this transaction.* Or, choose an appropriate adjective: *crucial, critical, pivotal, essential, vital, indispensable.*

Kibei a Japanese American (usually born to immigrant parents in the U.S.) who is educated chiefly in Japan.

kid this widely used informal word is acceptable in certain contexts, but its use should be questioned in others because it is somewhat demeaning. "Despite their age, children are *people*" (Sanford Berman, *Prejudices and Antipathies*). For alternatives consider *child, girl/boy, young people, young women/young men, youth, youngster; student, pupil.*

kike *See* ethnic slurs.

kilnman *rotary-kiln operator, kiln worker/supervisor, annealer.*

Kinder, Küche, Kirche the "children, kitchen, and church" slogan used by the Nazis to reconfine women to their supposed biological roles has since been used to describe women's "rightful place" in the scheme of things. Many woman do, in fact, find deep satisfaction in children, kitchen, and spirituality. The problem arises when applying this "ideal" to every woman, just because and only because she is a woman.

king (noun) use when it is the correct formal title. For example, in 1644, Christina was proclaimed king, not queen, of Sweden. Otherwise, consider using *monarch, ruler, sovereign, crowned head, majesty, regent, chief of state, leader, governor, chieftain, potentate, commander, protector; autocrat, tyrant, despot, dictator; figurehead.* In religious writings, *Sovereign* is often used for God as King, while *ruler* is used for a human king. For its meaning as a superlative use *best, top, expert, superstar, boss, chief, leading light, dean, mogul, nabob, tycoon, high-muck-a-muck, big wheel, big cheese.*

king (adjective) *chief, main, top, leading; large, largest, outsize.*

kingcraft *statecraft, diplomacy, political savvy, leadership, politics, the art of governing, holding firmly to the reins of government, wielding the scepter.*

kingdom *realm, empire, land, country, reign, rule, monarchy, domain, dominion, nation, state, world, sovereignty, principality, territory, region, protectorate, fief, commonwealth, republic, world.* "Reign," "realm," and "dominion" are particularly good for references to the kingdom of God. "Kindom" is sometimes used to express the meaning of "kingdom" without the triumphal and male overtones. "World" can be used in quasi-scientific uses, for example, the animal, mineral, and plant worlds (but retain the biology term "kingdom" in scientific writing). Note that during the reigns of even the most powerful and influential queens (e.g., Queen Elizabeth I of England), no one ever used the word "queendom."

kingdom come *the next world, the world to come, paradise, eternity, the hereafter, eternal life, life after death; the end of the world, oblivion.* For the phrase "from here to kingdom come" use *from here to eternity.*

king in his own castle, every man is a *everyone wears a crown in their own castle* (see singular "they"); *we are all kings and queens in our own castles; in our own castle, each of us wears a crown; aboard our own ship each of us is captain; we are all rulers in our own castles; I am monarch of all I survey; home is where the heart is.*

kingliness *nobility, royalty, authority, dignity, gallantry, charisma, greatness.*

kingly *regal, dignified, majestic, imperial, aristocratic, autocratic, courtly, gallant, charismatic, sovereign, royal, dynastic, royalist, monarchical, imperialistic.*

kingmaker except when referring to Richard Neville, First Earl of Warwick (Warwick the Kingmaker) or in the very literal sense, consider using *power behind the throne/scenes, power broker, wheeler-dealer, a mover and a shaker, strategist, executive maker, earthshaker, someone with political clout, string-puller, operator.* Plural: *the powers that be.*

king of the hill/king of the mountain Or, *queen of the hill/mountain.* Other possibilities: *big wheel, bigwig, magnate, someone on the top of the heap, monarch of all they survey.*

king of the jungle although this term refers to the lion (also known as "king of the beasts"), you may want sex-neutral choices when referring to someone powerful: *star, superstar, mogul, nabob, boss, tycoon, high-muck-a-muck, leading light, luminary, chief, boss; "her nibs" or "his nibs"; wheel, big wheel.*

kingpin *linchpin. See also* key man.

kingpin (bowling) *head pin.*

king post specific architectural term with no substitute; leave as is.

king salmon *Chinook/quinnat salmon.*

King's Counsel when a queen is on the British throne, it's "Queen's Counsel."

King's English *standard/correct/accepted English, standard usage, correct speech.* When a queen is on the British throne, one ought to hear "the Queen's English," and one does hear it in Great Britain. In the United States "King's English" is used, although it has not been correct since early 1952, just before Elizabeth II acceded to the throne.

kingship *monarchy, majesty, royal position, royal office, dignity; statecraft, leadership, diplomacy.*

king-size terms like this give new meaning to the roles of kings and queens as "rulers." Retain as a specific description of bed sizes and bed linen (where the use of "single," "double," "queen," and "king" is standard). Whereas "queen-size" is relative, meaning "big, but less than king-size," "king-size" has a more objective meaning: it is the largest. Because it sings that old male-is-number-one/female-is-number-two song, you might want to use alternatives: *jumbo-size, jumbo, super-size, oversized, outsized, gigantic, enormous, huge, extra-large, of heroic proportions, larger than normal/life.* (But who says the king is always larger than the queen?)

king's ransom not a particularly damaging little cliché. If you want something that is not sex-linked, try for a colorful new expression of your own or consider *fortune, enormous/prodigious sum, priceless, beyond price, worth its weight in gold, above rubies, invaluable, matchless, peerless,* *inestimable, costly, of great price, precious, worth a pretty penny/a fortune.*

kinsman/kinswoman use as they are or, for gender-nonspecific terms: *relative, blood relative, relation, cousin, kin, kinsfolk, kith and kin, connection.* Plurals: *kinfolk, relatives, kin.*

knave historically this was a man or boy, in roughly the same pejorative sense that "boy" has been used in English for a man. For a tricky, deceitful person of either sex, use *mischief-maker, rascal, trickster, troublemaker, scoundrel, sneak; double-crosser, four-flusher, cheater; crook, villain, evildoer, traitor, betrayer.*

knavery *mischief, mischievousness, monkeyshines, shenanigans, hanky-panky, rascality; trickery, roguish trick; baseness, villainy, unscrupulousness, deviltry, wrongdoing.*

knight (noun) the knight of the Round Table was always a man, and there was no equivalent for a woman. Women members of British orders of knighthood are called ladies and addressed as dames (for example, Dame Agatha); men are called knights and addressed as sirs. For inclusive modern-day alternatives to the metaphorical use of "knight," use *champion, hero.* Full membership in groups with "knight" in their title (for example, the Knights of Columbus) is generally reserved for men. The word "knight" is not always a clue to noble deeds and high-mindedness; the most visible (so to speak) of the infamous kind are the Knights of the Ku Klux Klan. *See also* knight errant, knight in shining armor.

knight (verb) either a woman or a man may be knighted today, although this was not always the case. *See also* knight (noun).

knight errant *rescuer, champion, hero errant; dreamer, idealist, romantic; philanthropist, altruist, humanitarian. See also* knight in shining armor.

knight-errantry *gallantry, nobility, bravery, quixotism, generosity, altruism, philanthropy, kindheartedness.*

knighthood in the past, reserved for men; today both women and men may be raised to knighthood. *See also* knight (noun), knight (verb).

knight in shining armor this is still used, although there is no good parallel for a woman; perhaps the closest is "woman of my dreams." In the sense of rescuer, consider sex-neutral terms: *hero, deliverer, rescuer, lifesaver, savior, champion.*

knight of the road *vagabond, hitchhiker, hobo. See also* road sister.

knockout used colloquially to mean a wonderful thing or person, this word takes on new meaning in today's culture of violence: an ad for a woman's shelter asks, "Does your husband think you're a knockout?"; numerous men have been killed or severely injured as a result of knockouts in the "sport" of boxing. You may want to avoid this word. *See also* violence, violent language.

Koran *al-Qur'an* is the preferred term for the sacred text of Islam.

Korean American the correct term for those who self-identify this way.

Kwanzaa from the Swahili word for "first fruits," Kwanzaa (December 26 to January 1) is a celebration of African culture (not a religious holiday) that combines traditional African practices with African American ideals and centers on the seven principles of black culture (unity, self-pride, working together, helping the community, purpose, creativity, and faith).

L

Language is the common heritage of humans;
all humans must share in shaping and using it.

—*Francine Frank and Frank Anshen*

Our language is not the special private property of the language police,
or grammarians, or teachers, or even great writers. The genius of English is that
it has always been the tongue of the common people, literate or not.
English belongs to everybody . . . to those of us who wish to be careful with it
and those who don't care.

—*Robert MacNeil*

Real, live creatures are spinning the web of language all the time, making it as they use
it, without the slightest regard to the formulas of professors or the precepts of pedants.

—*Gamaliel Bradford*

We need a new language. The old language—with its prevalent male pronouns,
its color coding of light and dark for good and evil, its virtual absence
of language for gays, lesbians and people with disabilities—this language
doesn't describe the reality that is emerging.

—*Joan Steinau Lester*

lackey historically, lackeys were men. In today's sense of a servile follower,
servant, gofer, or toady, a lackey can be either sex.

lad use with "lass." Or: *child, youth.*

ladder man (firefighting) *firefighter.* An old synonym was "shepherd"
because of the staff-like rescue hooks carried up the ladders by these
firefighters.

ladder man (gambling) *ladder supervisor, overhead spotter/checker, supervisor, spotter, checker, guard, casino employee.*

ladies and gentlemen when used to address an audience, this will probably not set most teeth on edge although it is old-fashioned and the correct pair for "gentlemen" is "gentlewomen," not "ladies." Many speakers now use terms that are more generic, contemporary, and meaningful: *friends, family and friends, delegates, colleagues, members of the association, staff members.* Or, omit what is often a meaningless phrase and begin directly, "Welcome." *See also* gentlewoman, lady (noun).

ladies' auxiliary as ladies' auxiliaries become less common, so will this sexist term (women's auxiliary is slightly more acceptable and some groups use "alliance" instead of "auxiliary"). Concerns about the concept of ladies' auxiliaries are based on the secondary, helpmeet role played by women for so long and on the use of the term "ladies." In the U.S., these organizations have made numerous important contributions to society and to our communities. Use "ladies' auxiliary" for groups who so designate themselves. *See also* lady.

ladies' room *women's room.* The parallel term is men's room. *See also* potty parity.

ladies' man this term is problematic because there is no precise equivalent for women ("gentlemen's woman") and because of the use of "ladies." The lopsided and unattractive "parallels" for women would be the pejorative "femme fatale" and "man-eater." Some alternatives: *popular/ successful with the women/the men, heartbreaker, smooth operator, God's gift to men/women. See also* femme fatale, lady, man-eater, playboy, womanizer.

ladino this acceptable term is used for groups of Spanish-speaking or acculturated Indians from Guatemala or areas that were part of the former Kingdom of Guatemala. In Spanish, "ladina" is also used. Capitalized, Ladino is a Romance language with elements borrowed from Hebrew that is spoken by some Sephardic Jews.

lady (noun) *woman.* Many good people have trouble understanding the objections to "lady." "But isn't that a *nice* word?" they ask. "The concept of 'lady' goes far beyond a single word to a whole way of life" (Alette Olin Hill, *Mother Tongue, Father Time*). "Lady" defines women as ornaments or decorations rather than real people, as arbiters of both manners and morals, as members of a leisured class, as beings removed from any hint of sexuality, as needing protection from real life, as "too good" or "too special" to "dirty their hands"; it is classist, condescending, trivializing, and anachronistic. According to the unspoken operating instructions that come with a "lady," a "lady" doesn't go into combat, work on her car, organize a union, argue publicly with a co-worker, make more money than the men she knows (or even earn a salary at all), or sweat (she perspires). "To want 'equal pay for equal work' and at the same time to be treated 'like a lady' are inconsistent and incompatible objectives" (Laurel Richardson, *Feminist Frontiers*). "Lady" was once the female equivalent of "knight" in the social order, and it has also been paired with "gentleman," yet neither of these terms is used today in the way "lady" is. The objection to the term is not new or particularly radical, as a handful of the hundreds of opinions on it will show: "Ladies were ladies more by virtue of the things they didn't do than by the things they did. The other sort of woman had a different, more positive set of values" (Harriet Martineau, 1837); "Give us that grand word 'woman' once again, / And let's have done with 'lady'; one's a term / Full of fine force, strong, beautiful, and firm, / Fit for the noblest use of tongue or pen; / And one's a word for lackeys" (Ella Wheeler Wilcox, 1888); "There is a difference between women and ladies. The modern parasites made ladies, but God Almighty made women" (Mother Jones, 1912); "Ladies were ladies in those days; they did not do things themselves" (Gwen Raverat, 1952); "What restricts the use of the world 'lady' among the courteous is that it is intended to set a woman apart from ordinary humanity, and in the working world that is not a help, as women have discovered in many bitter ways" (Miss Manners, 1982); "Girls do what their mothers tell them. Ladies do what society tells them. Women make up their own minds" (Karen Kijewski, 1989); "Women are not ladies. The term connotes females who are simultaneously put on a pedestal and patronized" (Cynthia Heimel, 1993); "Ladies are just those of us who have been silenced" (Jennifer Stone, 1994). Note that "lady" is used sometimes to express annoyance where "woman" never is ("Hey, lady, I was here first!" or "Look, lady, we're sorry, okay?"). There are three times when the use of "lady" is unobjectionable: when referring to a female member of the House of Lords; when you want to convey a sense of breeding, delicacy, or graciousness ("she's a real lady"); when it is paired with "gentleman" ("Welcome, ladies and gentlemen"). *See also* chivalry, lady (adjective), ladylike.

lady (adjective) *woman.* A sex-identifying adjective is necessary in only rare cases; double-check phrases using one. *See also* lady (noun).

lady beetle/ladybird/ladybug leave as they are.

ladyfinger leave as is.

ladyfish leave as is.

lady friend/lady love avoid; for alternatives *see* girlfriend. *See also* lady.

lady-in-waiting *servant, attendant, personal attendant/servant.* Use "lady-in-waiting" when it is an official title.

lady-killer this violent term has moved from metaphor to ugly reality with increasing numbers of men murdering women, most often in the context of relationships (one said, "I just wanted her to like me"). One use of "lady killer" that is hard to quarrel with: the American Cancer Society has used it in anti-smoking ads as the cigarette industry targets women to boost sales in a shrinking market. For the usual meaning, use instead *popular/successful with the women/the men. See also* man-eater.

ladylike conveying different meanings according to people's perceptions of what a woman ought or ought not do, say, think, wear, feel, or look like, "ladylike" is a subjective cultural judgment that has nothing to do with sex and everything to do with stereotyped gender roles. Choose instead precise adjectives: *courteous, well-mannered, civil, polite, tender, cooperative, neat, soft-spoken, gentle, aristocratic, cultured, elegant, proper, correct, gracious, considerate, refined, well-bred, kind, well-spoken.* These adjectives may be used equally appropriately of a man; they are not synonyms for "ladylike" but rather what people seem to mean when they use it. *See also* lady.

lady luck *luck. See also* Dame Fortune.

lady of easy virtue/of pleasure/of the evening/of the night *prostitute.* These terms are sexist (there are no parallels for men), coy, and imprecise. Note the one-sidedness of the word "pleasure"; for the prostitute, the experience is most often one of degradation, pain, and fear. *See also* prostitute.

lady of the house *head of the house, householder, homeowner, registered voter, taxpayer, citizen, consumer. See also* housewife, man of the house.

ladyship used of a woman with the rank of lady; the equivalents for a man are "lord/lordship."

lady's maid *attendant, personal attendant/servant.*

lady's slipper/lady's smock/lady's thumb (plants) leave as they are.

laird *landed proprietor,* except where "laird" has specific use and meaning in Scotland.

lame some people who walk with difficulty report liking this word; it is not essentially derogatory nor is it generally used disparagingly. However "lame" is also used metaphorically to mean "weak," as in "a lame excuse," and in a small way this usage taints the physical condition. Use "lame" of those who self-identify that way but with caution otherwise.

landlady/landlord *proprietor, owner, land owner, property owner/manager, manager, leaseholder, lessor, manager, building/apartment manager, superintendent, rent collector, householder, real estate agent.* Note the differences in prestige conjured up by "landlord" versus "landlady."

landsman *landlubber; compatriot,* q.v.

Lapps/Lapland *Sami/Saamiland.* According to *Baiki: An American Journal of Sami Living* (1991), "The term Lapp is very dated, and is considered to be pejorative, in bad taste." "Lapp" means "outcast"; "Sami" means "the People."

La Raza this volatile term has two strong connotations for Mexican Americans: one is disparaging while the other is positive and a source of ethnic pride. "La Raza" (which means "the race," although it is not understood the way "race" is commonly understood in the U.S.) should be used only by those who are thoroughly familiar with the term, the context, and their audience.

lass use with "lad." Or: *child, youth.*

last name because not all cultures follow the same order of names, in some situations you may want to use instead *family name, surname.*

Latina/Latino these terms are generally preferred to "Hispanic," "Spanish-speaking," "Spanish-surnamed," or "Spanish." Those self-identifying as Latinas and Latinos are primarily people of Latin American descent living in the United States, although sometimes the terms may not include Mexican Americans and may or may not include Caribbeans; the caveat here is to use the terms for—and only for—those who prefer them. Standard American usage tends to be fairly evenly divided between "Latina/Latino" and the conveniently broad "Hispanic." The terms "Latino man" and "Latina woman" are redundant. Avoid using "Latino" or "Latinos" as generics; use instead "Latinas and Latinos," for example. The adjective "Latino" is a problem—is "Latino art" the work of only men? In such cases circumlocute or reword to make clear the presence of both women and men. *See also* Chicana/Chicano, Hispanic, hot-blooded, Mexican American.

Latin American when referring to those now living in Latin America (which includes South America, Central America, Mexico, and the islands of the Caribbean), use specific designations if possible: Uruguayan, Colombian, Panamanian, Bolivian. The term is also used to refer to U.S. residents of Latin American descent, but it implies an unrealistic homogeneity and lacks precision; use it primarily for those so identifying themselves. *See also* Chicana/Chicano, Hispanic, Latina/Latino, Mexican American.

laundress *launderer. See also* "feminine" word endings, laundryman/laundrywoman.

laundryman/laundrywoman *launderer, washer, clothes washer, laundry attendant/worker/hand/collector/deliverer, dry cleaner.*

lawman *lawmaker, lawgiver, law officer/enforcer, law enforcement officer/ agent, defender/upholder/arm/officer of the law.* Or, be specific: *sheriff, deputy, judge, attorney, officer, FBI agent, detective, marshal, police/ patrol/peace/traffic/highway officer, magistrate, justice, constable, warden, bailiff, guard.*

lay/easy lay/good lay (sex partner) of course nobody using this book would ever use these terms in print or in public speaking, but this is a good place to explain that referring to someone this way makes them an object, an incidental scratch for the speaker's itch. *See also* score.

layman *layperson, laic, member/one of the laity, lay Christian, congregation member, parishioner; amateur, nonprofessional, nonspecialist, nonexpert, the uninitiated, outsider, lay worker; civilian, secularist; average/ ordinary person.* Plurals: *laypeople, laity, the laity, layfolk, congregation members/membership, members of the congregation, the lay public.* Although "-person" words are generally not recommended, "layperson" has gained common acceptance and is one of the few "-person" words that does not seem to jar.

layman's terms *plain/nontechnical/ordinary/uncomplicated/informal language, common/simple/nontechnical/easy-to-understand/layperson's terms.*

layout man *layout artist/planner/worker, graphic artist, patternmaker, designer, typographer.*

lay-up man *lay-up worker, stocklayer.*

lazy usually an indefensible judgment on people (possibly only the one who says, "I am lazy" has a right to it), this word can be objectionable when used of persons of color (Vivian Jenkins Nelsen, 1994) or poor people. Bertha Damon says, "I have come to the conclusion that almost no one on earth is lazy. The truth is that the man you call lazy just doesn't want to do your kind of work; he wants to do his kind" *(A Sense of Humus).* Definitions of "success" and "ambition," as well as personal and financial resources, vary greatly from person to person.

lazy Susan if you want a sex-neutral expression consider *revolving/relish tray.*

leading lady/leading man these terms, with their nonparallel "lady/man," are deeply entrenched in the language. Sometimes you may be able to use *lead, principal, star, featured performer; leading woman/leading man.*

leading seaman "seaman" is still an official rank in the U.S. Navy—for both sexes.

leading the life of Reilly/Riley although "leading [or living] the life of Reilly" probably came from Pat Rooney's 1883 comic song, "Is That Mr.

Reilly?" (which tells what a suddenly rich Mr. Reilly would do, such as sleeping in the President's chair and buying up hotels), it has long since been used of both sexes.

leadman *group leader, supervisor; star, lead singer, lead guitar player.* **See** *also* foreman, frontman (music).

lead-off man *lead-off batter.*

leadsman *sounder, depth sounder/reader.*

learning disability this term is sometimes used unthinkingly and imprecisely. Although researchers and professionals do not agree on an exact definition, this broad one from the Learning Disabilities Association of Canada seems helpful: "a heterogeneous group of disorders due to identifiable or inferred central nervous system dysfunction. Such disorders may be manifested by delays in early development and/or difficulties in any of the following areas: attention, memory, reasoning, coordination, communication, reading, writing, spelling, calculation, social competence, and emotional maturation. Learning disabilities are intrinsic to the individual, and may affect learning and behavior in any individual, including those with potentially average, or above average intelligence. Learning disabilities are not due primarily to visual, hearing, or motor handicaps; to mental retardation, emotional disturbance, or environmental disadvantage; although they may occur concurrently with any of these. Learning disabilities may arise from genetic variation, biochemical factors, events in the pre- to perinatal period, or any other subsequent events resulting in neurological impairment." *See also* disability/disabilities.

leaseman *lease buyer, leaseholder.*

leatherneck (Marine) woman or man. The reference is not personal; the uniform once sported a leather neckband.

lecher/lecherous/lech by definition a man, "lecher" has no precise inclusive synonyms, and "lecherous" seems most associated with men, but "lech" is used casually for women and there are several sex-neutral related terms: *sex maniac/fiend, make-out artist, libertine, debaucher, swinger, bedhopper, seducer.*

lefthanded using "lefthanded" in its metaphoric sense perpetuates longtime adverse associations for those who are physically left-handed. The negative words "gauche" and "sinister" come from Germanic and Latin words also meaning "left." One of the new translations of the Bible omits the reference to "the right hand of God." Consider using instead *backhanded, offhanded, ambiguous, dubious, insincere, clumsy, awkward.* **See** *also* footman.

Legion of Honor/Legion of Merit all orders are awarded to both women and men.

legionnaire since the American Legion is open to both women and men who served in the U.S. armed forces during official conflicts as established by Congress, a legionnaire could be either sex. In historical and other contexts, a legionnaire is almost invariably male.

legislator *See* congressman.

legman *gofer, assistant, clerk, courier, runner, carrier, messenger, deliverer, page; reporter, correspondent.*

leman literally meaning "one who loves a man," this term is usually defined as a "mistress" (sexual sense). There's nothing to say it couldn't be used for a gay man too; it's an obscure enough word that nobody would probably argue with it. You may, however, want a more common, inclusive term: *sweetheart, lover.*

leopardess *leopard.*

leper/leprosy *person with Hansen's disease/Hansen's disease.* It is inaccurate to label the whole person by something that is only one part of their life, nor do we say someone is "suffering from" or "a victim of" Hansen's disease. A chronic, infectious, germ-caused disease, Hansen's is still one of the least contagious of all communicable diseases; only about 4.5% of the world's population is even susceptible to it. There are approximately 11 million instances of it in the world (about 5,000 in the United States). Underlying the stigma of Hansen's disease is the faulty association with biblical lepers—outcasts and undesirables. "Protestant, Catholic, and Jewish scholars are in remarkable agreement as to the biblical word *leprosy;* it was not a medical term designating Hansen's disease or any other specific disease. Rather it denoted an afflicted stigma or blemish which marked the victim as 'unclean' under Hebrew ritualistic law" (F. C. Lendrum). If we could truly free those with Hansen's disease from the association with "leprosy," we could once again use "leper" and "leprosy" as they were intended. Until then, many people will want to avoid even metaphorical uses of the term ("a social leper," "leprous wallpaper").

leprechaun these Irish elves ("leprechaun" means "small body") are traditionally referred to as male, but to have survived so long there are undoubtedly female leprechauns among them; use the term for both sexes.

leprosy *See* leper/leprosy.

lesbian (noun/adjective) this term, which is preferred by most of the estimated 6 to 13 million lesbians in the United States, refers to "a woman whose emotional and sexual energies are directed toward other women, and not toward men. We also extend its meaning to refer to ways of thinking and behaving that draw upon this primary identification, particularly when a Lesbian has become self-aware and consciously seeks out others like herself" (Julia Penelope and Susan J. Wolfe, *Lesbian Culture*). Examine the need to mention a person's sexual orientation; it is often gratuitous. Since "lesbian" includes the sense of "woman," the term "lesbian woman" is redundant. Respect the distinction between "gay" (men) and "lesbian" (women); when "gay" appears alone, you may generally assume it refers only to men. Occasionally "gay" is used as an adjective to include both women and men, but in general both "lesbian" and "gay" are used in adjectival form, for example, Lesbian and Gay People in Medicine, the Institute for the Protection of Lesbian and Gay Youth, the Lesbian/Gay Health Conference. *See also* butch, dyke, femme, gay (adjective), Gay Rights Movement, GLBT, homophobia, homosexual, lesbigay.

lesbie/lesbo/lezzie unacceptable terms except when used positively by lesbians among themselves. *See also* "insider/outsider" rule, shortened forms of words.

lesbigay/LesBiGay this term, since about 1993 fairly well established at least in the alternative press, has been called "a concise portmanteau word" as well as "an Orwellian butchery of language." Chris Dodge, Hennepin County Library in Minneapolis, has collected scores of examples of the term in print: "lesbigay economic boycott of Colorado"; "discrimination of lesbigays"; "lesbigay neuroscientists meet"; "integrating the military with lesbigays"; "LesBiGay bookstore," etc. Some feel that "queer" is a much more inclusive gay-positive term; others note that transgenders are not included in "lesbigay." *See also* GLBT/glbt.

let 'er rip *let it rip/go/roll/start! There's the signal! Time to start!* Maurice Sendak's contribution *(Where the Wild Things Are): Let the wild rumpus start!*

let George do it *let somebody else do it, pass the buck.*

letterman *letterholder, letter winner, letter, lettered athlete; letterwoman and letterman* if used fairly.

letters *See* salutations (letters).

leverman *lever operator.*

lib/libber *member of the women's liberation movement, liberationist, feminist.* "Lib" and "libber" are derogatory and generally indicate hostility on the part of those who use them. *See also* shortened forms of words.

liberal the use of this word as a pejorative by those who are not liberals has given it a meaning of "bleeding heart who is giving away all our tax money to deadbeats." Dictionary definitions of the political understanding of "liberal" include such concepts as freedom from bigotry, openness to new ideas for progress, and broad-mindedness. Liberals have historically worked to end slavery, institute child labor laws, fight anti-Semitism, support better working conditions, enact civil rights, establish open housing as well as openness in government, reduce military spending, allocate more money for education and good quality childcare, and protect the environment. It is not necessary to argue the relative merits of "liberals" and "conservatives," but it would be good to retain the meaning of the word "liberal" so that when it is used for communication, we will all know what is meant. For "a spendthrift legislator" or "a careless distributor of the nation's largess" or "an anti-hunger activist," use those words or others, but if you love language more than you need empty sound bites, avoid "liberal" and especially the trite "bleeding heart liberal." *See also* conservative.

liegeman *servant, subject, fiefholder, vassal.* Historically a liegeman was always a man; his wife and children were assumed to be part of him, not separate "liegemen."

lifemanship *put-down artistry, superiority complex.* This is a difficult term to replace with one word; circumlocution, elaboration of the characteristic, or showing the person's actions instead of just labeling them are possible solutions.

lifer this slang term is often acceptable, especially when used for self-identification. If you need alternatives consider *life sentence/life imprisonment prisoner; career soldier.* Although "lifer" is sometimes used to mean "right-to-lifer," both terms have a subtle pejorative cast. *See also* shortened forms of words.

lifestyle *See* gay lifestyle.

liftman (British) *lift operator/attendant.*

like a man *See* man, like a.

like father, like son this is a warm and positive (usually) phrase which can be used as is. Other variants are equally useful: *like father, like daughter; like mother, like daughter; like mother, like son.* If you want to convey the concept more sex-neutrally consider *the acorn doesn't fall far from the tree, a chip off/of the old block, spit and image, spitting image, birds of a feather, the very image of, for all the world like, as like as two peas, take after, follow in the parent's footsteps, take a leaf from the parent's book, like parent like child.*

lilywhite/lily-white this term is part of the problematic black/white dichotomy (one definition of "lilywhite" is "beyond reproach, blameless," which makes black . . . what?). It has layers of associations of "don't touch, don't dirty" that at some level have been transferred to people. One result is that "lilywhite" is used informally to mean excluding or seeking to exclude black people.

limp-wristed this stereotypical adjective is inaccurate most of the time and objectionable all of the time.

line foreman *line supervisor.*

lineman (job title) *lineworker, line installer/repairer/fixer/maintainer/ erector/installer-repairer/supervisor, line-service attendant, rigger, electrician.*

line man (sports) *line player, offensive/defensive tackle/guard/center; line umpire/judge/referee.* As long as football players continue to be boys or men, "line man" is acceptable; because some sports have female umpires, it is better to use "line umpire."

linesman *line judge/referee/tender, liner.*

linkboy/linkman *torch carrier, light attendant.* Or, retain in historical contexts as they were boys/men. For "linkman" as used chiefly in Great Britain, *see* anchorman.

linksman *golfer, golf player.*

lioness *lion.* By using the base word inclusively, terms like "lion's share" are also inclusive. *See also* "feminine" word endings.

lip reading because the person is also "reading" tongue, teeth, and related movements, the correct term is *speech reading.*

little Hitler *See* Hitler.

little lady it is never correct to refer to an adult woman this way; a useful alternative is *ma'am.* It is also inadvisable to refer to a girl this way because (1) a child is not an adult and should be allowed to be a child while she is a child and (2) telling a child she is a little lady almost without exception reinforces in her a limiting cultural stereotype for girls and women, e.g., sitting quietly and neatly in the background. There is nothing wrong per se with this behavior, but "little lady" tells the child this is the desired, best behavior for girls and women on all occasions.

Little League open to both boys and girls.

little man unlike "little woman," which can also be used to refer to an adult woman, "little man" is reserved for boys. Avoid it because (1) a child is not an adult and should be allowed to be a child while he is a child and (2) telling a child he is a little man almost without exception reinforces in him a limiting cultural stereotype for boys and men, e.g., not showing emotions. There is nothing wrong with suppressing fear or refraining from crying, for example, but "little man" tells the child that this is the desired, best behavior for boys and men in all circumstances.

little shaver although the origins of this expression may not be as masculine as they sound ("shaver" deriving perhaps from the chip-off-the-old-block kind of shaving rather than from whisker shaving), the term is defined either as a youngster or as a boy and it is perceived as masculine; girls were usually "little dolls." For inclusive alternatives consider *youngster, child, tyke.*

little woman, the some men use this expression with fondness and a happy ignorance of its implications; it is up to their spouses or partners to object to it. Wincing bystanders can take comfort in the fact that the expression seems to be on the wane.

liturgical language *See* Bible language.

liveryman *livery worker, vehicle-rental service operator; liveried retainer; livery company member.*

living doll unlike many other uses of "doll," this term refers to both sexes. Although it seems that there ought to be a general rule not to refer to people as dolls (because of all the implications of making objects of them), this particular expression has always been fairly benign, and there seems to be no difference in tone, intent, or significance between references to men and women.

lobsterman *lobster catcher/fisher/farmer/grower/cultivator/dealer.*

Lolita the Lolita myth ("myth" because it is not borne out very well by the book, *Lolita,* by Vladimir Nabokov) of a child who wants and can sustain a sexual relationship has been immeasurably harmful. It's not only beauty that's in the eye of the beholder; some people see desire where there is none. Several groups argue for "sexual freedom" for children, maintaining that children actually want and need sexual experience with an adult. Kiddie sex is a flourishing business in various parts of the country, but it is not the runaway street children who want sex (although they do want the money, food, or drugs it brings them), but the exploitative adults. There is no parallel to "Lolita" for a boy. If you need sex-neutral alternatives for the mythical Lolita consider *sexually precocious; underage and seductive. See also* jailbait, pornography.

lone wolf woman or man.

longbowman retain in historical contexts. Or: *archer, longbow archer.*

longjohns despite being based on the name John, this word is functionally nonsexist. If you need something more sex-neutral consider *woollies, winter underwear, BVDs.*

longshoreman *longshore worker, stevedore, dockhand, dockworker, shorehand, shoreworker, wharfworker, wharfhand, ship loader.*

looksism the subtle (and sometimes not-so-subtle) disparagement of and discrimination against people who are not physically attractive according to unstated but entrenched cultural definitions is called looksism. A study by economists Daniel Hamermesh and Jeff Biddle indicated that the earnings gap between "attractive" and "unattractive" people who share the same education and experience rivals the gap between black and white or male and female workers. Physically "unattractive" people are less likely than "attractive" ones to be hired for a job or to have their testimony accepted by jurors; they receive longer prison sentences, and people involved in service professions such as medicine and education give them less attention as patients and students. While "the latitude for a woman's appearance is generally narrower than for men" (employment discrimination consultant Freada Klein, *The Washington Post*), both men and women are spending more for plastic surgery, and, discounting for the exacerbating effects of sexism, fat or physically "unattractive" men suffer discrimination nearly as often as women. A study reported in *The New England Journal of Medicine* (1995) linked being overweight to being economically disadvantaged. Other studies have found that over-weight people make 10–20% less than their thinner colleagues. Only a smattering of state and local laws have "personal appearance" protec-tions. While federal civil rights laws bar discrimination based on race and sex, physical characteristics such as fatness, ugliness, and shortness are not protected. Lynn Romer, founder of the Pinocchio Plot to End Looksism, says childhood classics like Snow White, Beauty and the Beast, and Sleeping Beauty link beauty with goodness and homeliness with evil; "we need to get away from ugly ducklings and beautiful swans." Although it is sometimes referred to as "appearance discrimina-tion," the term "looksism" has much to recommend it: brevity; parallels with sexism, racism, ageism, etc.; and a fairly well-established foothold in the language. *See also* body image, fat.

loony *See* mental health.

loose woman if you mean *prostitute*, use it. If you mean a woman of ques-tionable morals (which is a questionable judgment), say exactly what you mean using inclusive words: *promiscuous, sexually active, undiscriminat-ing,* etc. The language has no such expression as "loose man," yet a "loose woman" must, by definition, have a partner; avoid judging one sex by criteria not applied to the other.

Lord retain "Lord" when referring to the Lord Jesus Christ, as that is part of who he is (although some churches prefer Redeemer, Comforter, Friend, Christ). However, when referring to the Godhead (not the person of

Christ), "Lord" can be replaced with one of the many inclusive names listed under Father (God). *See also* Father (God); Father, Son, and Holy Spirit; God; God/he; God/himself; God/his; Holy Spirit/Ghost (he); Jesus Christ; Lord's Prayer, the; Son of Man.

lord and master (husband) it's your choice, of course, but if nothing else, the phrase will date you even if used tongue-in-cheek.

lord it over someone *dominate, domineer, boss around, browbeat, bully, intimidate, tyrannize, overshadow, overpower, oppress, wear the crown, ride herd on, be hard upon, rule with a high hand, have the upper hand, deal hardly with, call the shots, run the show, keep a tight rein on, lay down the law, bend to one's will. See also* lord of the manor, play.

lordliness *stateliness, dignity, majesty, elegance, splendor; high-handedness, arrogance, haughtiness, imperiousness, insolence, overconfidence, conceit, condescension, pomposity.*

lordly *stately, imperial, imposing, dignified, noble, majestic, august; haughty, arrogant, insolent, overbearing, imperious, condescending, high-handed, domineering, arbitrary, peremptory, dictatorial, tyrannical, presumptuous, overconfident, snobbish, commanding, pushy, bossy.*

lord mayor leave as is where used officially (as in Great Britain).

lord of the manor, play *swagger, give oneself airs, act big, ride a high horse, act the high-and-mighty, be insolent/haughty/overbearing/pretentious/self-important/pushy/snobbish/pompous/high-handed. See also* lord it over.

Lord's Day for most Christians, this is *Sunday.*

lordship used of a man with the rank of lord; the equivalent for a woman is "ladyship."

Lord's Prayer, the some people feel that the two sex-linked words in this prayer ("Father" and "kingdom") are not sexist, but are instead theologically and scripturally sound and necessary. Others feel that the spirit of the prayer is in no way violated by replacing "Father" with "God," "Mother/Father," or another title, and "kingdom" with "dominion" or other synonym. That the word "Father" is even what was intended is doubtful. Neil Douglas-Klotz, who transliterates the "Our Father" from Syriac Aramaic, says that where we say "Father," the original was something like, "O Thou from whom comes the breath of life" or "O Thou, the Breath, the Light of All"; the words are neither male nor female.

Lothario for inclusive alternatives consider *heartbreaker, seducer, deceiver, libertine, lover, great/dashing lover, make-out artist, smooth operator, swinger, flame, admirer, flirt.*

242

lounge lizard because this term is used only of men, you may sometimes need a sex-neutral term: *barfly, social parasite.*

love, honor, and obey (wedding ceremony) the "obey," which was meant for women, has been replaced or removed in many wedding services: *love, honor, and cherish; love and honor; love, respect, and cherish; develop mutual love and respect; love, honor, and reverence; love, encourage, and accept; love and cherish.*

lover acceptable and useful term describing individuals of either sex and any sexual orientation. *See also* boyfriend, girlfriend, inamorata/inamorato, paramour, partner, significant other.

lowboy nonsexist; "boy" comes from the French for "wood," "bois."

lowerclassman *beginning student, first- or second-year student;* sometimes, *undergraduate. See also* freshman.

low-income question the use of this term; we tend to use it more often and with more meanings (some of them code) than we do "high-income."

low man on the totem pole *See* totem pole, low man on the.

lumberjack/lumberman *lumber worker/cutter, logger, tree cutter, woodcutter, log roller, timber worker, forester, sawyer, woodchopper.*

lust properly (or improperly) attributed to either sex. Craig Rice (pseudonym of Georgiana Ann Randolph), wrote in 1941, "'Tis better to have loved and lust than never to have loved at all."

M

"When you say Man," said Oedipus, "you include women too. Everyone knows that."
She said, "That's what you think."
—*Muriel Rukeyser*

According to the dictionary: "in modern apprehension man . . . primarily
denotes the male sex, though by implication referring also to women."
I am not sure that "by implication" fully expresses the degree
to which I wish to feel included in the human race.
—*Jane O'Reilly*

The important thing about any word is how you understand it.
—*Publilius Syrus*

All things tend to become specialized, except only words. . . . The word alone
grows not expert and special, but general and inexpert. It is obliged to do
more various things, and to do them with less directness.
—*Alice Meynell*

ma'am used in the same way "sir" is used for men, this contraction for
"madam" is practical and appropriate. *See also* madam.

macho/machismo by definition, only men are macho (the word is Spanish
meaning "male") or are associated with machismo; there is no parallel for
women ("macha" is incorrect). The word "machismo" has been used of
women (in *The Second Stage*, Betty Friedan says "female machismo . . .
hides the same inadmissible self-hate, weakness, sense of powerlessness
as machismo hides in men") and it is given a female spin in Grace
Lichtenstein's *Machisma*. As they are currently understood, the terms are
irreplaceable when describing certain behavior and a certain mindset in

some men and women, although you can approximate "macho" with sex-neutral alternatives: *overly aggressive, defensive, proud, swaggering, overbearing, overconfident, show-off, arrogant.*

madam used for a woman in the same way "sir" is used for a man, this term is convenient when addressing women you don't know or know only very slightly. At one time it appeared to be losing its respectability because of its other meaning (female head of a house of prostitution). Like other female words in male-female word pairs, in some uses it is deeply devalued (notice how nice "sir" has always been). For someone connected with prostitution, use *prostitute, owner/head of house of prostitution.* Use "madam" only for social address.

mad as a wet hen this sex-specific expression is both popular and useful, but if you need a sex-neutral term consider *mad as a hatter/hornet/rattler, mad as a bear with a sore head/as a striped adder/as blazes/as hops.*

Mademoiselle use only for a Frenchwoman who calls herself "Mademoiselle." In France, "Mademoiselle" is generally reserved for women in their teens or early to mid-20s while "Madame" is used for older women—in both cases irrespective of their marital status. This is also the case with "Frau" and "Fraülein," and it used to be true of "Miss" and "Mrs." *See also* Miss, Mrs., Ms.

madman/madwoman these terms are gender-fair but they are vague and inaccurate. If a person's mental condition must be mentioned, use correct medical terminology (e.g., "someone with obsessive-compulsive disorder"); avoid identifying the whole person with one aspect of their existence. *See also* insane/insanity, mental illness.

madness *See* mental illness.

maestro in some contexts, "maestro" is still considered irreplaceable and is used for both women and men. In other situations consider *conductor, orchestra leader; expert.*

Mafia *organized crime, the underworld.* In reference to non-Italian crime, "Mafia" is a misrepresentation and an ethnic slur, but even to use it "in reference to Italian criminals . . . implies that organized crime was begun by Italians and/or Italian-Americans, when, in fact, organized crime was thriving in the United States long before our grandparents arrived here. Although even the phrase 'organized crime' conjures up images of Italian-Americans for bigots, it's the only alternative I know" (Rose Romano, malafemmina press).

magsman *safecracker.*

maharaja/maharani acceptable sex-specific words.

maid/maidservant *household servant/worker/cleaner/helper, houseworker, servant, housekeeper, room attendant, attendant, cleaner, house cleaner/*

servant, custodian, janitor. ***See also*** charwoman, cleaning lady, handyman.

maid/matron of honor *attendant, best woman, attendant of honor, honor/ wedding/bride's attendant.* Whichever term you choose, be sure that the groom's attendant is referred to with a parallel term, for example, "best woman and best man" or "bride's attendant and groom's attendant." *See also* best man.

maiden (adjective) *first, inaugural, initial, premier, earliest, new, untried, untested, untapped, unused, fresh, intact, inexperienced; single, unmarried, unwed, unwedded, celibate.* Use terms like "single" and "unmarried," only if this information is necessary. *See also* maiden voyage.

maiden (noun) use only when quoting or in historical contexts.

maiden aunt *aunt.* Marital status is not specified in the same way for uncles, it is generally irrelevant, and in the use of "maiden" it carries stereotypical implications of fussiness, lack of attractiveness, and having been rejected by men.

maidenhead *hymen, virginity.* *See also* virgin/virginity.

maidenhood *youth, innocence, adolescence.* There is little reason to use the outdated and problematic "maidenhood." *See also* virgin/virginity.

maiden lady *See* spinster.

maidenly this is so vague that using it is poor communication; your audience will be no wiser. Decide what qualities you mean to convey and describe them.

maiden name *birth/given/birth family/family/former/original/premarital name, family of origin name, original surname.* "Birth name" is the most commonly used term, although in a few cases it will be inaccurate (e.g., when the woman's name before marriage is the name of the stepfather who adopted her). A Rhode Island probate court judge surprised a woman who thought her birth name was hers by ruling that a wife could not use her birth name without her husband's permission; the American Civil Liberties Union challenged the ruling. The usage is not as widespread as it is perceived to be: by the late 1990s, only some 10% of U.S. married women were choosing to use something other than their husband's last name. Since 1979, women in Québec legally retain their surname upon marriage unless they make a special application to change it (Ruth King, *Talking Gender*). In Sicily, many women have two names—their own "public" name and their married "private" name. *See also* hyphenated surnames, surnames.

maiden voyage *first/premier voyage, first trip/sailing; debut, initiation, premiere.*

maid of all work *general servant. See also* charwoman, cleaning woman, handyman, maid.

maidservant *See* maid.

mailboy *mail messenger.*

mailman *mail carrier, letter carrier, mail handler/deliverer/clerk, postal worker/clerk/officer.* Both the National Association of Letter Carriers and the National Postal Mail Handlers Union use inclusive terms.

mail-order bride there has never been anything parallel for men and thus there is no sex-neutral alternative. The practice still exists today.

main man (slang) this term has such a particular meaning that in most cases it is probably irreplaceable if you are writing or reporting street talk. If you need a sex-neutral alternative try *best friend, partner, hero, mentor.*

maintenance man *maintenance worker/engineer/mechanic/repairer/ specialist, maintainer, repairer, cleaner, office cleaner, custodian, janitor, porter, factotum, odd/general jobber, fixer, fixer-upper, troubleshooter.*

maître d'hôtel *dining room/restaurant host, host, head waiter, majordomo, hotel manager/steward/proprietor.*

majordomo nonsexist term (it comes from the Latin for "elder of the house") although almost all of them have been male stewards or butlers.

majorette *drum major, baton twirler, marching band leader, major. See also* "feminine" word endings.

make a man of *be the making of, do a world of good, improve, mature, toughen up.*

makeup girl/makeup man *makeup artist.* Note the nonparallel "girl/man."

malapropism from Mrs. Malaprop in Richard B. Sheridan's comedy *The Rivals* (1775), the word "malaprop" has passed into the language with no rival (although "spoonerism" is a near relative) and with no pithy substitute or alternative. In any case, it is not negatively sex-linked. *See also* spoonerism.

male (noun) "male" is used as a noun only in technical writing (medicine, statistics, police reports, sociology). It is most often reserved for biological or nonhuman references. When using "male" as a noun, beware of nonparallel constructions, for example, "three women and two males." *See also* male (adjective).

male (adjective) use only when you would use "female" or when it is necessary for clarification; this adjective is often inserted gratuitously, for example, "male nurse," "male secretary," "male model," "male prostitute." Watch particularly for nonparallel usage, for example, "three male dancers and one woman dancer." *See also* male (noun).

male bashing male bashing is so special and noticeable and new that it has its own term, whereas female bashing as a term appears in print here for the first time (it has always been "normal" to label women helpless, irrational, illogical, and inferior—"the weaker sex"). Although anger and criticism directed at all men simply because they are men has the defects and weaknesses inherent in stereotyping, there must be a way to discuss male-female relationships, from the societal to the personal, that is not labeled "male bashing." Contrast with "gay/queer bashing," which involves physical, sometimes murderous, attacks.

male bonding in *The New Republic,* Robert Wright says it's unclear "whether the intense bonds formed during war, and all the valor and sacrifice they inspire, result from 'male bonding' or simply 'person-under-fire bonding.'" The traditional meaning of male bonding (largely a matter of soldiering, drinking, and sports) is being replaced for some men by a new sense of what it means to be with other men as friends, brothers, and companions on the journey.

male chauvinist/male chauvinist pig *chauvinist, sex-chauvinist.* "Chauvinism" used to refer to the view that one's own country was vastly superior, right or wrong, to all other countries. Dictionaries now also define "chauvinism" as the view that one's own sex is vastly superior. Either a man or a woman can be a sex-chauvinist. *See also* chauvinism.

male-dominated society *dominator system, dominator model of society, hierarchy, hierarchical society.* The first two highly recommended alternatives are from Riane Eisler *(The Chalice and the Blade).* There are, however, good and logical reasons to speak of a male-dominated society and especially a male-dominated language, although not in terms of the actions of individual men but rather in terms of an ethic that has supported the supremacy of all things male: "inasmuch as the masculine sex is the superior and more excellent"; "the male being, according to our ideas, the nobler sex"; "in all languages, the masculine gender is considered the most worthy" (quoted in Francine Wattman Frank and Paula A. Treichler, *Language, Gender, and Professional Writing). See also* chivalry, matriarch/matriarchy, patriarch/patriarchy.

male ego *ego.* There is much food for thought and discussion here, but the principle involved is to make no generalizations about an entire sex.

male menopause by definition, menopause is the cessation of human egg production, and thus is specific to women. However, there is a corresponding period in men called the climacteric. Although levels of testosterone do not usually decline significantly until around age 70, some men in their 50s and 60s experience a gradual waning of the sex urge and occasional sleep problems, mood swings, depression, and anxiety—which could also be related to a mid-life crisis, q.v.

male privilege a few of the benefits men have traditionally enjoyed primarily because they are men include generally being paid more for comparable work; being able to ignore what women say and to interrupt them more frequently than women interrupt them; to be deferred to in group situations; to be called on more frequently in the classroom; within reason, to go where they like without fearing assault, rape, or sexual harassment; to do a disproportionately small share of housework and childcare; and even, in many cases and over centuries, to define reality. Along with this, however, has come the "privilege" today—simply because they are men—of registering for the draft, dying earlier than women, and living up to cultural expectations for them that include being strong, "virile," provident, and successful. Herb Goldberg *(The Hazards of Being Male)* says that "every critical statistic in the area of [early death], death, suicide, crime, accidents, childhood emotional disorders, alcoholism, and drug addiction shows a disproportionately higher male rate." Black men have the shortest average life span of any group and suffer proportionately more violence. Men in general tend to be more "privileged" in many ways than women; it is inadvisable, however, to refer stereotypically to "male privilege" as though it were given to everyone with the biological fact of maleness, especially since this "privilege" generally falls to those who are white and well-off as well as male.

males-only draft *See* draft.

male supremacy *See* male-dominated society, male privilege.

mama's boy *spoiled/immature/irresponsible person.* "Mama's boy" is an unfortunate cultural stereotype that keeps many parents from giving their sons the nurturing they need (and that they continue to seek, often in inappropriate ways, throughout life). Daughters, on the other hand, are more often encouraged (also with sometimes unfortunate results) to be "obedient" and dependent. *See also* apron strings, tied to one's.

mammal pioneer in men's studies Eugene R. August of the University of Dayton points out that "by categorizing animals according to the female's ability to suckle the young through her mammary glands, *mammal* clearly omits the male of the species."

mammy this term is sexist (there is no parallel term for a man), racist, and an objectionable stereotype that was probably always highly mythical.

man (adult male human being) this narrow definition is the only acceptable nonsexist usage for the noun. Dictionaries list two major definitions for "man": (1) adult male, (2) human being. However, studies have shown that people "hear" only the first meaning of the word. *See* Writing Guidelines for a complete discussion of pseudogeneric "man" (pp. 9–11). *See also* bad guy, coward, gender roles, males-only draft, male privilege, man/Man (pseudogeneric), provider, sex differences.

man/Man (pseudogeneric) *person/s, people, human/s, human being/s, the human race/family, civilization, society, individual/s, one, creature/s, creation, all creation, mortal/s, body, somebody, someone, anyone, soul/s, living soul/s, all living souls, society, all of us, ourselves, everyone, humankind, humanity, human society/nature/species/creatures/popula-tions, early peoples, we, us, mortality, flesh, all generations, folk/s, the public, the general public, the world, community, the larger community, nation, state, realm, commonweal, commonwealth, republic, body politic, population, resident/s, inhabitant/s, adult/s, citizen/s, taxpayer/s, worker/s, member/s, participant/s, hand/s, party/parties, earthling/s, worldling/s, our ancestors, figure (snow figure, underworld figure), women and men.* Or, be specific: *Neolithic peoples, early settlers, 15th-century Europe, civilization as we know it.* Although many people, including both women and men, insist that "man" is a generic term, that usage was declared obsolete in the 1970s by both the National Council for Teachers of English and the *Oxford English Dictionary,* and a close reading of books published before the 1970s shows that "man" never was truly generic. Erich Fromm wrote that "man" needs food, shelter, and access to fe-males. The "man/men" in our own Constitution couldn't have been generic since it took two amendments to give the vote to those who were not white men. For a complete discussion of pseudogeneric "man," *see* Writing Guidelines (pp. 9–11). *See also* Fall of Man, man (adult male human being), manhood.

man (chess, checkers, games) *piece, player, marker.*

man- many terms beginning with "man-" come from the Latin for "hand" and are not sexist: manacle, manager, mandate, maneuver, mangle, mangy, manicure, manifest/manifestation, maniple, manipulate, manners, mano a mano, mansion, mantel, mantis, manual, manufacture, manumis-sion, manure, manuscript. Other words that begin with "man-" have nonsexist roots: manciple (from Latin for "purchase"); mandate (from the Latin for "to command"); mandrake (from a Greek term for the plant); manege (from Italian for "horse training"); manes (from Greek for "spirit"); mangrove (from Spanish for the tree); "Manhattan" (from Algonquian word for "island"); mania (from Greek for "spirit"); Manichaeism (from Mani, the Iranian founder); manifold (from Old English for "many"); manor/mansion (from Latin for "dwell"); mantle (from Latin for "cloak"). *See also* Isle of Man, manageress, mandarin.

-man/-men not all words that end in "-man/-men" are sex-linked. For example, a Roman or a German may be either female or male; "whatman" is named after James Whatman; "amen" comes from Hebrew for "truly" or "certainly"; "dolman" from "dolama," a Turkish robe; "ottoman" from French for "Turk"; "talisman" from Greek for "consecration"; "catechumen" from Greek for "someone being instructed"; "tegmen" from Latin for "covering"; "gravamen" from Latin for "burden." When in doubt, check a dictionary. *See also* dragoman, Pullman car/ pullman porter.

man/manned for the verb use *operate, staff, run, supply a crew/personnel for, supply with/furnish with personnel/crew, people, populate, work, serve at/on, station, take stations at, control, cover, occupy, equip, hire, employ, outfit, arm, brace, fortify, garrison, fit out, prepare, protect.* For the adjective use *staffed, crewed, peopled, populated, operated, serviced, stationed, worked, ran, covered, handled. See also* manned space flight.

man!/oh man!/man alive! (interjections) nobody is complaining about these, but if you want alternatives, there is no end of them, beginning with *good grief! gee! gee whiz! gosh! golly! wow!*

man about town *sophisticate, socially active/worldly person, swinger, mover, high-liver, high-flier.* The foregoing can be used for either sex, whereas there is no phrase for women parallel to "man about town." A woman who has "been around" is not being complimented—au contraire. *See also* ladies' man, playboy, rake, womanizer.

man, act like a/be a/take it like a *be brave/bold, put on a bold face, defy, meet danger/trouble head on, bear up, meet/confront with courage/ bravery/valor/boldness, hold up one's head, screw one's courage to the sticking point, look in the face, nerve oneself, hold out against, take heart, have plenty of backbone, come up to scratch, face the music, act courageously/bravely/wisely/straightforwardly/honorably, show fortitude/ patience/determination/strength/vigor, stand up for oneself, be independent/resolute/unflinching/earnest, sit tall in the saddle, stand tall, keep one's chin up.* Expressions like these limit, bewilder, and oppress men while also implying that woman are not bold, courageous, straightforward, hardy, etc. (Alternatives are for both sexes.) Paul Theroux says that "be a man" really means "Be stupid, be unfeeling, obedient and soldierly, and stop thinking." Russell Baker *(About Men)* says, "Before you were old enough to think for yourself, they were preparing you for a lifetime of feeling like a disgrace to your sex. What was this 'man' you were supposed to take it like, to act like, to be?" He decided that these "men" were blessed with utter fearlessness, a zest for combat, and indifference to pain. "Men would rather have their eyes blackened and teeth loosened than let the whole world see that they hate being severely beaten." *See also* coward; manfully; man, like a; manlike/manly.

man after one's own heart, a *someone after one's own heart, someone for whom you have a soft spot, persona grata, favorite, general/personal favorite, apple of one's eye, my kind of person.*

man against man, man against himself, man against nature *the individual against self, other, and nature; literary characters may experience conflict within themselves, with others, or with nature.*

manageress *manager.* Although "manager" is not sexist (it comes from Latin, "hand"), many women say the word feels sexist to them because the "man" in the word is so reinforced by management practices, by the glass ceiling for women, and by the fact that management remains, in many areas, a male stronghold. Although the number of women holding middle-management jobs has been increasing, the percentage of women in senior management, as well as the number who are members of corporate boards, has changed very little. *See also* executive, "feminine" word endings, glass ceiling, wage earner.

man among men *one in a million, salt of the earth, one of the best, outstanding human being, ace, hero, champion, paragon, shining example, trump, marvel, a real lifesaver, a one-off.*

man and boy *always, since childhood, all one's life/natural life, all one's born days.*

man and wife never use this; it is a nonparallel construction. Use instead *man and woman/woman and man, wife and husband/husband and wife, spouses, mates, partners, married couple.*

man ape *See* ape-man.

man, as one *unanimously, simultaneously, as one person/body, without exception, of the same mind, of one accord, at one with each other, willing, agreed on all hands, in every mouth, in concert, carried unanimously/by acclamation, everyone, all.*

man-at-arms *warrior, soldier, combatant;* or, retain in historical senses.

man, be his own *stand on one's own two feet, someone who can't be bought, be inner-directed/self-governing/independent, be one's/your/her/his own person, be her own woman/his own man.*

man bites dog story there is currently no good gender-free substitute for this colorful phrase; it conveys something very particular that would be lost in translation. That doesn't mean, of course, that someone won't eventually come up with an equally pithy and evocative—but inclusive—phrase.

man-child use with "woman-child," not "girl-child," as is generally done. If "girl-child" is used, then "boy-child" is the equivalent, not "man-child."

mandarin when this term refers to a public official in the Chinese Empire, it is always male (but not because of the "man," which is part of the Sanskrit word for "counselor"). Its other uses are nonsexist.

man-days *worker-days, workdays, labor-days, average worker days, person-days. See also* man-hours.

man does not live by bread alone according to the New Revised Standard Version of the Bible, approved for use in the nation's major Protestant churches, this phrase is rendered, "One does not live by bread alone." You could also use: *we/you/people do not live by bread alone, not by bread alone do we/does one live.*

man-eater/man-eating *people-eater, human-eater, flesh-eater, carnivore, omnivore, cannibal; people-eating, human-eating, flesh-eating, carnivorous, omnivorous, cannibalistic, dangerous, deadly.* When referring to a woman considered dangerous or threatening to men, the term is offensive and says more about men's fears than women's powers. *See also* lady-killer.

man-for-man *player-for-player, one-on-one. See also* man-to-man defense.

man Friday *assistant, office/administrative/executive/program assistant, aide, clerk, right hand, secretary, gofer; man Friday and woman Friday* if used gender-fairly, although the convention generally remains limited to "woman Friday" and even then it seems difficult for people to use "woman Friday" instead of the familiar "girl Friday." Note the nonparallel "man/girl."

manfully for this vague cultural stereotype, substitute precise words: *strongly, resolutely, bravely, courageously, mightily, vigorously, robustly, sturdily, powerfully, potently, indomitably, huskily, energetically, boldly, defiantly, unflinchingly, inexorably, doggedly,* etc. These adverbs can be used for both sexes; they are not synonymous with "manfully" as much as they are what is most commonly meant by it. To replace the adjective "manful," use any of the foregoing words without its "-ly" form.

manhandle *abuse, mistreat, maltreat, mishandle, damage, maul, batter, push/kick/knock around, paw, maul, subdue, force, handle roughly, rough up, beat up, pummel, thrash, strike, injure.*

man-hater/woman-hater reserve these terms for the few cases in which they are authentic and meaningful; for too many years lesbians, for example, were assumed by some people to be man-haters (note that gay men were never, by the same token, assumed to be woman-haters). *See also* misanthrope/misogynist.

manhole *sewer hole, utility access hole.* Also, *utility/access hole, personnel access hole, sewer/service access/shaft, streethole, workhole, vent hole, utility tunnel, exit port, inspection chamber, sewer viewer, peephole, underground service access hole.*

manhole cover *sewer cover, street hole cover.* Also, *utility/utility-hole/ access/sewer-hole/access-hole/street/utility-access/sewer-access cover, sewer cover/top.* (People have been making fun of "person-hole cover" since at least 1978; we can stop now—it's not ever going to be a real word.)

manhood "manhood" has four dictionary definitions. (1) The first one is "the condition of being human"; do not use "manhood" as a synonym for "human"—this is a pseudogeneric. A useful and popular alternative is *personhood.* (2) Do not use "manhood" to mean "human beings"; this is also a pseudogeneric. (3) When you are referring to manly qualities in a man, its use is correct although your sentence will almost always benefit from more specific words: *pride, self-confidence, vigor, strength, courage, maturity,* etc. (4) Use "manhood" anytime to mean the condition of being an adult male human being ("womanhood" is the parallel term). *See also* man/Man ("generic"), man (adult male human being), mankind.

man-hours *total hours, hours, worker/work/working/staff/labor/operator/ employee hours, hours of work, hours worked, work/staff time, labor, time, labor time.* Or, be specific: *electrician hours, shop-hours, secretarial hours. See also* man-days.

manhunt *dragnet, chase, fugitive/person hunt, search for a fugitive, search, police search, hunt;* sometimes, *APB (all points bulletin).* "Manhunt" is one of the more difficult sexist words in that there currently exists no equally brief and descriptive inclusive term. When possible avoid it by circumlocution.

manic depression Kay Redfield Jamison *(An Unquiet Mind)* discusses "the current confusion over the use of the increasingly popular term 'bipolar disorder'—now firmly entrenched in the nomenclature of the *Diagnostic and Statistical Manual (DSM-IV),* the authoritative diagnostic system published by the American Psychiatric Association—instead of the historic term 'manic-depressive illness.'" She refers to herself as manic-depressive as she thinks that term captures both the nature and seriousness of her condition. "Most clinicians and many patients feel that 'bipolar disorder' is less stigmatizing than 'manic-depressive illness.' Perhaps so, but perhaps not." *See also* mental illness.

manikin "manikin" not only looks masculine, it means "little man." There is no parallel term for a woman. *See also* mannequin.

man-induced *artificially/humanly induced, human-caused, manufactured, of human genesis/origin(s).*

man in motion *player in motion.*

man in office *person in authority/office, official.*

man in the moon for a sex-neutral term consider *face in the moon.*

man in the street *average person/citizen/human/human being/voter, common person/citizen/human/human being/voter, ordinary person/citizen/ human/human being/voter, citizen, voter, layperson, taxpayer, resident, homeowner, householder, landowner, passerby, nonspecialist, commoner,* *one of the people/masses, rank and file, average/typical worker, Jane/ John Q. Citizen/Public; average woman and average man* if used gender-fairly.

man is known by the company he keeps, a *people/we/you are known by the company they/we/you keep, one is known by the company one keeps, birds of a feather flock together, we are judged by the company we keep, show me your company and I'll tell you who you are.*

man is only as good as his word, a *a person is only as good as their word.* **See also** singular "they."

man-killer *killer, murderer, slayer, assassin, cutthroat, sniper, silencer, dispatcher, liquidator, hired gun, bloodshedder.* **See also** gunman.

mankind *humanity, humankind, people, human beings, humans, human society/nature/species/creatures/populations, the human race/family, civilization, society, individuals, one, creatures, creation, all creation/ generations, mortals, body, somebody, someone, anyone, souls, living souls, all living souls, society, all of us, ourselves, everyone, early peoples, we, us, mortality, flesh, folks, persons, the public, the general public, the world, community, the larger community, nation, state, realm, commonweal, commonwealth, republic, body politic, population, residents, inhabitants, adults, citizens, taxpayers, workers, members, participants, hands, parties, earthlings, worldlings, our ancestors, women and men.* Or, be specific: *Neolithic peoples, early settlers, 15th-century Europe, civilization as we know it.* **See also** man/Man.

manlike/manly by definition, whatever a man does is manly or manlike because a man is doing it. Instead of these vague cultural stereotypes consider precise adjectives: *courageous, strong, brave, upright, honorable, mature, noble, resolute, straightforward, vigorous, adventurous, spirited, direct, competitive, physical, mechanical, logical, rude, active, self-confident,* etc. **See also** man, like a.

man, like a replace this vague cultural stereotype with the characteristics you have in mind: *with a high/strong hand, with a head for mechanics, resolutely, courageously, competitively, self-confidently, in a straightforward manner.* **See also** man, act like a/be a/take it like a; manlike/manly.

manly art of self defense self-defense is also a womanly art. If you want another cliché, use *the noble art of self defense* or, less classistly, *the art of self-defense.* The entry term came from 18th-century advertisements for boxing lessons taught in Great Britain by prizefighter Jack Broughton.

man-machine interface *user-system/human-machine interface.*

manmade *artificial, handmade, human-made, hand-built, synthetic, made, manufactured, fabricated, machine-made, homemade, produced, mass-*

produced, machine-produced, crafted, constructed, custom-made, simulated, machine-simulated; plastic, imitation, bogus, mock, spurious, counterfeit, fictitious, contrived; human-constructed, of human origin, result of human activity. "Manmade" can often be eliminated without affecting the meaning of the sentence; much of our resistance to avoiding or replacing it is habit—if you say "human-made" about 50 times it begins to sound quite natural and right.

manmade fibers industry *synthetic fibers industry.*

manned space flight this phrase currently has no equally pithy and inclusive description of space flight crewed by both women and men. Circumlocution is one solution ("the Columbia space flight with six astronauts aboard"). In print, "crewed space flight" works well, but in speech, "crude" will be heard. Other possibilities include: *piloted/staffed/live/astronaut-controlled space flight.* And, finally, it is possible, reasonable, and comprehensible to speak simply of *space flight. See also* man/manned, unmanned space flight.

mannequin although "mannequin" and "manikin" come from the Dutch word for "little man," a mannequin is often thought of as female. Should you need an alternative consider *model, dressmaker's/tailor's dummy, display figure, window display figure.*

mannish replace this meaningless term with adjectives that convey your precise meaning: *brusque, blunt, abrupt, direct, square-jawed, aggressive,* etc.

man of action *human dynamo, ball of fire, take-charge person, active/energetic/determined/ambitious/action-oriented person/individual, someone on their toes, woman of action and man of action.*

man of affairs avoid; the ersatz parallel for women doesn't sit well in polite society. Use instead *entrepreneur, operator, mover, wheeler-dealer, someone with fingers in many pies/many irons in the fire. See also* businessman.

man of all work *caretaker, odd-jobber. See also* groundsman, handyman, maintenance man.

man of business, one's *agent, factotum, caretaker, bailiff, factor, tax preparer, steward, clerk, attorney, broker, representative.*

man of distinction *important personage, person of distinction/note/mark/consequence/importance, prominent/high-ranking individual, nabob, man of distinction and woman of distinction.*

man of few words *strong, silent type; person of few words; close-mouthed individual.*

man of God/man of the cloth *See* churchman, clergyman.

man of his word/man of honor *honorable person, trustworthy individual, someone as good as their word, someone on the up and up/as honest as the day is long/tried and true, truth-speaker, truth-dealer, truth-lover, square-shooter, straight-dealer; woman of her word and man of his word.*

man of letters *writer, author, scholar, literary giant, one of the literati, pundit; woman of letters and man of letters.*

man of means *wealthy/rich/powerful/moneyed individual/person, plutocrat, capitalist, moneybags, nabob, millionaire, billionaire; woman of means and man of means.*

man of my kidney, a *my kind/sort/type of person, a person after my own heart.*

man of straw *See* straw man.

man of the hour *toast of the town, honored guest, star of the show, center of attention, star attraction, big name; woman of the hour and man of the hour.*

man of the house *homeowner, head of the household.* "Man of the house" and "woman of the house" have been so abused that even when they are used gender-fairly they still have a subtle sting. *See also* family man, homebody.

man of the world *sophisticate, person with wide experience, practical/sophisticated/worldly wise/well-rounded/well-traveled/experienced person, someone who gets around/who knows the ropes.*

man of the year *newsmaker/citizen/member/entertainer/ humanitarian of the year; man of the year and woman of the year.*

man-of-war retain in historical context. Otherwise use *warship, battleship, ship of war/of the line, war vessel.* Or, be specific: *cruiser, destroyer, gunboat.*

man on horseback *military leader, dictator, tyrant, despot.* (The controversial French general and minister Georges Ernest Jean Marie Boulanger made almost all his public appearances on horseback.)

man on the street *See* man in the street.

manor nonsexist; from the Latin for "to remain."

man or beast, not a fit night for *not a fit night to be out in/for two-legged creatures nor four-legged ones either/for humans or beasties, not a night to leave your fire by.*

man overboard! *overboard!, person/someone overboard!*

manpack *backpack, one-person pack.*

manpower (noun) *workforce, personnel, human resources, staff, available workers, workers, employees, labor, people, labor supply/force, staffing,* *human/people power/energy, staff time, payroll; muscle power, human power/energy.* "Womanpower" is seen occasionally ("the new womanpower in Japanese politics") but it is not parallel in meaning to "manpower."

manpower (adjective) *staffing, occupational, employee.* This term is so familiar it is difficult to think around it, but focusing on your meaning will help: manpower training programs (*occupational training*); manpower planning (*staff resources/human resources planning*); manpower levels (*employee/staffing levels*).

manpowered *muscle-/human-/people-powered.*

man proposes, but God disposes *creation proposes, but the Creator disposes; we/people/you/the world/the individual propose(s), but God disposes; the Missourians propose but the Kansans dispose.*

manrope *handrail.*

man's best friend there is no good substitute for this phrase because it is associated like none other with the dog, whereas we all know that a woman's best friend are diamonds, and the friend of the people could be anything from Smokey Bear to General Electric to Karl Marx. Consider using some of the time: *the devoted dog, our canine friend, our faithful canine friends, a human's best friend.*

manservant *servant, attendant, assistant.*

-manship when possible, replace words that use this suffix. *See* airmanship, brinkmanship, chairmanship, craftsmanship, gamesmanship, grantsmanship, horsemanship, marksmanship, salesmanship, sportsmanship, statesmanship, workmanship, yachtsmanship.

man's home is his castle, a *my home is my castle, a person's home is a/their castle, a woman's home is her castle/a man's home is his castle, the sanctity of the home, our home is our castle; home is where the heart is, there's no place like home.* This phrase is difficult to replace because of its familiarity, but finding alternatives is highly recommended: the phrase's sexism is underwritten by centuries of belief in male superiority; man's "kingship" in the home has been used to justify and tolerate behavior ranging from petty tyranny to domestic violence.

man's inhumanity to man *inhumanity, our inhumanity toward each other, cruelty; a house divided against itself.* Replacing this phrase with something both inclusive and elegant seems impossible, but your meaning may actually be made clearer by identifying the actions or conditions that bring this phrase to mind. *See also* evil men do, only man is vile.

man-size(d) *large-size(d), oversized, enormous, hefty, husky, big, ample, large, comfortably large, sizable, massive, weighty, impressive, considerable, capacious, towering, immense.*

man's job, a *an adult job, adult-sized job, a big job.*

manslaughter this term has a specific legal meaning—use it in that sense until a nonsexist legal term is developed; in its broader sense, use *murder, homicide, killing, butchery, wholesale killing/slaughter, assassination, bloodletting, slaughter, carnage, massacre, slaying.*

manslayer *slayer, murderer, assassin, killer, liquidator, dispatcher, blood-shedder, hired gun.* **See also** gunman, hitman, manslaughter.

man's work *work.* The only "work" biologically limited to men is the work they do in helping propagate the species and so far, it is rarely referred to as work. All other "men's work" is based on stereotypes. However, around the world and across centuries, men's work has been valued more highly than women's. Margaret Mead pointed out that there have been societies in which men fish and women weave, and societies in which women fish and men weave, but in both, the work done by men is valued more highly than the work done by women. This may be due to (1) the association of women with nature and men with culture (see Mother Nature); (2) women's reproductive activities keeping them closer to home where their activities are domestic and largely invisible, while men's activities are public and highly visible and thus command more cultural respect; (3) boys/men defining themselves by distancing themselves from and disdaining women and women's work. If men's work has been more highly valued it has also traditionally been very toxic. The responsibilities of the provider role, the lack of family or leisure time, and rigid and narrow expectations of what is "masculine" have denied men their full human range of expression and may be responsible for the sex difference in death rates. Today many women are also taking on toxic work loads. It would benefit both sexes to change our cultural norms for success and for what constitutes an appropriate work load. **See also** glass cellar, Mother Nature, provider, women's work.

man the barricades *mount/defend the barricades.*

man to man *one to one, heart to heart, person to person, one on one, face to face, straight from the shoulder, on the level, candidly, frankly, privately, confidentially.*

man-to-man combat *hand-to-hand/one-on-one/face-to-face combat.*

man-to-man defense *player-to-player/one-to-one/person-to-person/one-on-one/person-on-person (POP) defense.*

mantrap *booby/death trap, snare, trap.*

manup *personnel buildup; staff, increase personnel.*

manward *peopleward, toward/in relation to people/human beings, with respect to humans.* Many words that end in "-ward" with the meaning of "toward" are awkward and should probably be replaced anyway.

man who is his own doctor/lawyer has a fool for a patient/client, a *those who are their own doctors/lawyers have fools for patients/clients, if you insist on being your own doctor/lawyer, you have a fool for a patient/ client.*

manwise *humanwise, peoplewise* (if you must). Using the "-wise" suffix is Madison Avenue-ese (another example) that is better circumvented.

man without a country, a *a person without a country/with no roots.* **See** *also* expatriate/ex-pat.

marchioness or marquise/marquis (or marquess) retain these sex-specific titles.

mare's nest there's nothing particularly pejorative to women in this expression, but if you want a sex-neutral alternative consider *false alarm, hoax, delusion, great disappointment, worthless, much ado about nothing; chaos, mess.*

margrave/margravine retain these historic or hereditary sex-specific titles.

marine man or woman; 5% of those serving in the U.S. Marine Corps are women.

marketing man *marketer, marketing executive/associate/representative/rep, market researcher/executive; advertiser; copywriter.*

market man *market maker, stock market expert.*

marksman *sharpshooter, crack/good/dead/expert shot, first-class shot/aim; markswoman and marksman.* **See also** gunman, hitman, rifleman.

marksmanship *riflery skills, sharpshooting, shooting proficiency/ability/ expertise/skill.*

marry/marriage until recently it was not "correct" to say a woman married a man. He married her; she "was married" (Francine Wattman Frank and Paula A. Treichler, *Language, Gender, and Professional Writing*). When writing or speaking about marriage be aware that: she and he marry/get married/are married (there is no direct object); by using "couples" or "relationships" you can include unmarried and same-sex couples as well as married ones; the responsibility for the marriage is not the woman's alone (Gloria Steinem: "I have yet to hear a man ask for advice on how to combine marriage and a career"); marriage is not the end-all and be-all for everyone (cultural assumptions point to marriage-as-norm); the average married man is not trapped, henpecked, or unhappy (in fact, married men report a significantly higher level of well-being than those who are not married, earn an average of 30.6% more, and have lower death rates than unmarried men). The word "marriage" could be used to describe committed same-sex relationships, if the "legal union" aspect were emphasized over the "man and woman" aspect; we already use "marriage" in the sense of "a close union" ("the marriage of true minds"). *See also* divorce, domestic partnership, wedding.

married name *See* hyphenated surnames, maiden name, surnames.

martinet although this term is based on a man's name (Jean Martinet, a commander of the French infantry, instituted strict discipline based on severe punishment during the reign of Louis XIV), it is used for both sexes.

masculine avoid this vague stereotype that conveys different meanings to different people according to their perceptions of what a man ought or ought not do, say, think, wear, feel, look like. These judgments are subjective and influenced by culture; they have nothing to do with sex and everything to do with gender. Use instead precise adjectives: *strong, upright, charming, robust, hearty, direct, straightforward, deep-voiced, protective, nurturing, attentive,* etc. These are not synonyms for "masculine" but are rather some of the many qualities people mean by it.

masculine/feminine (poetry, music) *See* feminine/masculine (poetry, music).

masculine mystique where the feminine mystique referred to society's narrow definition of women as housewives whose primary competence lay in the domestic sphere, the masculine mystique refers to society's narrow definition of men as providers/protectors whose primary competence lies in the workplace. *See also* gender roles, glass cellar, provider.

masculinity what cultural (but not biological) truth is there in this old saying? "Women have their femininity as a birthright. Men have to prove their masculinity all their lives."

masculist/masculinist Nigel Rees defines these terms as referring to "a person who asserts the superiority of men over women." *The Oxford Dictionary of New Words* says a "masculinist" is someone who is anti-feminist or pro–men's rights. Use only for those who so identify themselves.

masher since a masher is a man who makes passes at women, there is no synonymous inclusive term. Today's masher is often found in sex harassment cases. For inclusive alternatives use *flirt, someone who comes on strong, sex harasser.*

Mason (member of fraternal organization) *See* Freemason.

massacre this word is often used to describe a battle won by Indians; when a battle was won by those moving onto Indian lands, it was called a "victory." Writers and historians have conveyed the idea that European Americans who protected their homelands were patriots whereas Indians who did so were murderers and savages. Jessamyn West's *The Massacre at Fall Creek* (1975) and Elliott Arnold's *The Camp Grant Massacre*

(1976) both use the word "massacre" to describe white killings of Indians that took place in 1824 and 1871. We do not usually label the 1945 atomic bombardment of Hiroshima or the 1940 aerial bombardment of Rotterdam, for example, "massacres," yet without our ethnocentric view, they would qualify.

masseur/masseuse these are acceptable sex-specific terms. If you need a sex-neutral term use *massager, massage therapist.*

master (noun) *owner, manager, chief, head, leader, governor, superior, director, supervisor, employer, boss, commander, captain, controller; sovereign, ruler, monarch, autocrat, dictator, potentate; expert, authority, artist, adept, proficient, specialist, connoisseur, professional, genius; mentor, teacher, trainer, instructor, educator, tutor; victor, conqueror, winner, champion; householder, proprietor, landholder.* "Master" has some inclusive meanings (owner, employer, teacher, scholar, artisan, victor, etc.) but because the principal meanings of the word are incontrovertibly masculine (e.g., "male head of household"), because there is no equivalent for a woman (in the once-parallel word pair "master/mistress" the prolific male word has spawned entire pages of "master"-based words in the dictionaries while the female word has shrunk to describe only the sexual function of the woman), and because of its association with slavery, "master" and its related words are not recommended. Because "master" is used as noun, verb, and adjective, as well as a compound in many other words, its overwhelmingly masculine, hierarchical, and slave-based flavor seasons a good bit of our language; from a racist and sexist perspective, "master" words have both reflected and helped shape grave social inequities. Except for its applications in trades where it has specific meaning and no currently acceptable substitutes, "master" and other forms of the word can be replaced with some of the many appropriate and easy-to-use alternatives. That said, there are times when nothing works quite as well and when the word seems to have gone beyond its associations with male dominance and slavery, for example, *master* (verb and adjective) and *mastery.* Casey Miller and Kate Swift (*The Handbook of Nonsexist Writing,* 2nd ed.) say, "The presence of *master* in many combinations like *masterful, mastery, masterpiece,* and *mastermind* assures its continuance as a useful sex-neutral term." *See also* discussion of "master" words in Writing Guidelines, pp. 18–19.

master (adjective) *expert, accomplished, proficient, skilled, excellent, competent, gifted, dexterous, adroit, deft, resourceful; controlling, main.* For discussion of "master" words, *see* master (noun).

master (verb) *excel in/at, grasp, learn, understand, comprehend, be successful at, be proficient in, acquire proficiency at, learn inside and out/ backwards and forwards, get a good grasp of, get a handle on, get the* *hang of, gain command of, be on top of; conquer, subdue, defeat, subject, vanquish, tame, subjugate, subordinate, suppress, get the upper hand, overcome, overpower, overwhelm, overthrow, surmount, humble, triumph over; rule, dominate, govern, control, command, dictate to, boss/order around.* For discussion of "master" words, *see* master (noun).

Master (Jesus) *Teacher.* For discussion of "master" words, *see* master (noun).

master/master mariner (sailing vessel) retain in official use; some marine occupational titles using "master" are used by the U.S. Employment and Training Administration. Otherwise use *captain.* For discussion of "master" words, *see* master (noun).

master bedroom/suite almost without exception these are the currently used terms. When real estate agents tried to use "owner's suite," buyers and sellers expressed confusion. You could, however, use that sometimes or *main bedroom, principal/largest bedroom, suite.* Or, refer to bedrooms by their location, as do some designers and architects ("the northeast bedroom"). For discussion of "master" words, *see* master (noun).

master builder *expert/award-winning/skilled/professional builder.* This may refer to either sex. For discussion of "master" words, *see* master (noun).

master class an advanced art, music, or dance seminar led by a recognized expert (of either sex), "master class" is difficult to replace with a term that is equally concise, descriptive, and meaningful in those fields. Sometimes it is possible to use *artist class* (it is not limited to the visual arts), *virtuoso class, expert tutorial.* For discussion of "master" words, *see* master (noun).

master copy *original, original copy.* For discussion of "master" words, *see* master (noun).

masterful *expert, skilled, articulate, authoritative, competent; powerful, commanding, domineering, sweeping, imperative, imperious, arbitrary, overbearing, arrogant, haughty.* For discussion of "master" words, *see* master (noun).

master hand *expert, genius, major talent, professional, authority, adept, proficient, whiz, dab hand.* For discussion of "master" words, *see* master (noun).

master key *skeleton/universal/all-purpose/pass/main/original/controlling key, passe partout.* For discussion of "master" words, *see* master (noun).

master list *overview, key, main/complete/primary/reference list.* For discussion of "master" words, *see* master (noun).

masterly *accomplished, skilled, knowledgeable, consummate, matchless, excellent, distinguished, experienced, crack, ingenious, able, felicitous, shrewd.* For discussion of "master" words, *see* master (noun).

mastermind (noun) *genius, brilliant thinker, intellectual/mental prodigy/ giant, inventor, originator, creator, brains; plotter, organizer, creative organizer, instigator, planner, leader, director, head, someone who pulls the strings.* For discussion of "master" words, *see* master (noun).

mastermind (verb) *oversee, direct, head, guide, lead, coordinate, plan, contrive, engineer, launch; originate, invent, devise, develop, have the bright idea.* For discussion of "master" words, *see* master (noun).

master of ceremonies/mistress of ceremonies *host, emcee, leader/coordinator of ceremonies, speaker, main/guest speaker, facilitator, moderator, introducer, announcer, marshal, parade marshal.* Although "emcee" comes from these sex-specific terms, it is used for both sexes and is perceived as neutral. For discussion of "master" words, *see* master (noun).

master of one's fate *captain of one's soul/fate.* For discussion of "master" words, *see* master (noun).

master of the situation *in charge, in control, on top of things, reins firmly in hand, finger on the pulse.* For discussion of "master" words, *see* master (noun).

masterpiece *great/greatest/best/classic work, work of art/genius, stroke of genius, consummate art, chef d'oeuvre, magnum opus, brainchild, cream of the crop, crème de la crème, pièce de résistance, museum piece, flower of the flock, nonpareil, acme of perfection, perfection, brilliant achievement, ne plus ultra, tour de force, coup de maître, model, monument, standard.* For discussion of "master" words, *see* master (noun).

master plan *overall/comprehensive/ground/working plan, blueprint, project design, overview.* For discussion of "master" words, *see* master (noun).

master print *original film, original.* For discussion of "master" words, *see* master (noun).

"master race" use this term only in its historical context and put it in quotation marks to indicate its lack of validity.

master's degree *M.A., graduate/advanced degree, first advanced/first graduate degree.* The spelled-out "master's degree" is still used in many cases; there is no current substitute for it. For discussion of "master" words, *see* master (noun).

master sergeant *See* serviceman.

masterstroke *trump card, clever/bright idea, good/brilliant move, bold/lucky stroke, checkmate, stroke of genius, coup, complete success, stunt, exploit, victory.* For discussion of "master" words, *see* master (noun).

master switch *control/lead/main switch, circuit breaker.* For discussion of "master" words, *see* master (noun).

master tape *pattern/final/original tape, template.* For discussion of "master" words, *see* master (noun).

master teacher leave as is where custom requires it. A substitute sometimes seen is *artist teacher* (not restricted to the visual arts). A master teacher can be either sex. For discussion of "master" words, *see* master (noun).

masterwork *See* masterpiece.

mastery *proficiency, understanding, knowledge, accomplishment, acquaintance with, competency, firm grasp, command, excellence, facility, advantage, adeptness, skill, dexterity, deftness, expertise, grip; rule, sovereignty; victory, ascendancy, supremacy, authority, subjugation, conquest, control, domination, dominance, upper hand, reins in one's hands, command, order, sway.* For discussion of "master" words, *see* master (noun).

matador used for both women and men. *See also* bullfighter.

mate (noun) used for both sexes in the sense of "partner," "spouse," or "lover" and also in navy and coast guard ranks. The popular Australian "mate" is used for both sexes.

mater/materfamilias acceptable sex-specific terms, although the Latin is more often replaced with "mother/matriarch." *See also* pater/paterfamilias.

maternal unless you mean motherlike or mother-related ("maternal grandfather"), use *parental, ancestral; kindly, kindhearted, loving, devoted, indulgent, solicitous, concerned, fond, protective, sympathetic.*

maternal deprivation *See* absent parent.

maternal instinct *nurturing/parental instinct.*

maternity leave *parental/family/childcare leave.*

materialman *material supplier, supplier.*

matman *wrestler.*

matriarch/matriarchy these correct sex-specific terms are sometimes used judgmentally. Because patriarchy is seen as the norm, a matriarchy tends to be viewed with suspicion, alarm, and disapproval; it doesn't seem "natural." In fact, the opposite of a patriarchy is not a matriarchy. Both matriarchies and patriarchies involve an imbalance of power between the sexes and are called dominator societies by Riane Eisler *(The Chalice and the Blade* and *The Partnership Way of Life).* The true opposite of a matriarchy or a patriarchy is a partnership society. Until we reach the point where neither sex needs to dominate the other, use "matriarchy/ patriarchy" terms cautiously. The word "matricentric" puts the mother at the center of the family or system without the hierarchical overtones of "matriarchal." Sex-neutral alternatives for "matriarch" include *ancestor/*

family elder, head of the family, family head. **See also** patriarch/patriarchy.

matricide correct sex-specific word. Inclusive alternative: *parricide.*

matrilineal refers to descent through the mother's line; its word pair is "patrilineal."

matrimony *marriage, union, nuptials, wedlock.* "Matrimony"—from Latin, "mother"—is sex-specific and is also part of the oddly nonparallel word pair "matrimony/patrimony" (which may not be so odd given that men have been able to inherit money while women marry it). "Marriage" is also sex-linked (from Latin for "a woman's dowry") but it is less obviously so than "matrimony." For the adjective "matrimonial" more sex-neutral alternatives include *marital, conjugal, wedded, wedding.*

matron *warden, attendant, police officer, deputy sheriff, bailiff, guard, prison/jail/custodial guard, superintendent, supervisor, overseer; principal, chief, director, head, manager.* In its narrow legal sense, "matron" must be used until a nonsexist legal term is developed. In the sense of a middle-aged woman, replace "matron" with words that more precisely describe the person. Note the widely different status and meaning of the word pair "matron/patron."

matronly replace this vague word with precise, inclusive terms: *dignified, gracious, ponderous, heavy-set, established, grave, comfortable-looking, serene, slow-moving, well-dressed, mature, sedate,* etc. There is no such word as "patronly."

matronym/matronymic referring to a name derived from the mother or a maternal ancestor, these are correct sex-specific terms. They also have a little-recognized historical accuracy: the practice of passing the father's name on to the children hasn't always been in force, nor is it universally practiced in the Western world. For example, Nelson is "Nell's son," Allison is "Alice's son," and Babson is "Barbara's son." Charles Panati *(Browser's Book of Beginnings)* says, "Seemingly, when surnames originated, few traces of male chauvinism historically were involved." **See also** hyphenated names, patronym/patronymic, surname.

matron of honor *See* maid/matron of honor.

maverick although this term comes from a man's name—a 19th-century Texas rancher named Samuel A. Maverick with a certain reputation for straying from the herd (he refused to brand his cattle)—its origins have been largely forgotten and it is perceived as sex-neutral.

mayoress *mayor. See also* "feminine" word endings.

may the best man win *may the best person win.*

meathead just as Archie Bunker linked "dingbat" to women, so he linked "meathead" to men.

meatman *butcher, meat vendor/cutter.*

mediatress/mediatrix *mediator.* *See also* "feminine" word endings.

medical man *doctor, physician, medical practitioner/specialist; medico* (informal). *See also* medicine man.

medicine man depending on the culture, alternatives might include *shaman, healer, faith healer; medicine woman and medicine man; magician.*

meistersinger "mastersingers," members of German middle-class guilds, flourished from the 14th to 16th centuries and were all men.

mélange speaking of the mélange nation (those with "racially" diverse heritages), Jaimie Markham writes (in *Colors*), "We name ourselves *mélange* to proclaim pride in our diverse origins and to be strong in a society that makes us an embodiment of its conflicted racial relations. . . . We are proud of our racial heritage, and we insist on respect for all our heritage cultures. We refuse to be forced to choose between one or the other. Our pride in both is a vitally important means for us as mélange people to deal with a racist social structure. Selecting one group over the other would require us to hate the white mother or the Filipino grand-mother, the black father or the white great-grandfather." *See also* multi-racial.

memsahib always a woman; the man is a "sahib."

men (pseudogeneric) for the military sense use *troops, soldiers, forces, armies.* For the sense of game pieces, use *players, pieces, markers.* For all other uses *see* man/Man, man (adult male human being), mankind.

men- most words that begin with "men-" are not sex-linked, for example, menace (from Latin, "threaten"); menagerie (from French, "household"); menarche (from Latin, "month"); mendacious/mendacity (from Latin, "lie"); mendicant (from Latin, "beg"); menhir (from Breton, "stone"); menial (from Latin, "dwelling"), menorah (from Hebrew, "candlestick"); mental (from Greek, "spirit"); mention (from Latin, "call to mind"); menu (from French, "small"). *See also* man-, -man/-men, mensch, menopause/menopausal, menses/menstrual/menstruation, mentor.

menfolk this term is interesting in that it is probably the only "man/men" word that has never been used pseudogenerically; "menfolk" and "wom-enfolk" truly refer to men and women.

men of goodwill *people/those of goodwill.*

menopause/menopausal the "men" comes from Latin for "month." "Meno-pause" is a neutral term describing a physical reality that is different for different women. Menopause does not appear to cause stress or depres-sion in most healthy women and may even improve mental health for some; avoid stereotyping menopause, and do not describe a woman as "menopausal" unless you are writing for a medical journal.

mensch this is Yiddish for "human being" or German for "person," although in English it is often reserved for men. Use it also to mean a purposeful, upright, honorable woman who stands up for the rights of others, as well as for her own.

menses/menstrual/menstruation these terms have nothing to do with men ("menses" is Latin for "months"). Throughout history, menstruating women have not had good press: in the Bible they were characterized as unclean; later they were thought to be diseased, animal-like, possessing supernatural powers, and responsible for rusted-out metal tools and weapons. Still later, they were thought to be subject to mood swings that affected their judgment and mental abilities. *See also* curse, the.

men's liberation/movement the women's movement's view of men as oppressors was not, naturally enough, received well by men—particularly by those who found themselves oppressed by the males-only draft, the provider role, rigid societal definitions of masculinity, unfair divorce and custody laws, and other biases in the culture. Men today report they are tired of criticism, frustrated with their limited roles compared with the options they see available to women, and confused about what it means to be a man or a father or a lover or a husband. Landmarks in the men's movement include: the 1970 formation of the Men's Center in Berkeley and subsequent creation of other men's centers around the country; founding of MEN International, Men's Rights Incorporated, Free Men, and other men's organizations; by the appearance of voices like those of poet Robert Bly, anthropologist Michael Meade, Warren Farrell *(Why Men Are the Way They Are)*, Herb Goldberg *(The Hazards of Being Male)*, Jungian psychologist James Hillman, and members of activist divorce reform and fathers' rights groups. Men are examining and challenging the traditional male sex role in the belief that "men, not women, must define what it means to be a man" (Tom Williamson in Francis Baumli, *Men Freeing Men*). Men's goals, attitudes, and organizations vary widely; generalizations are risky. *See also* draft, glass cellar, Iron John, male privilege, provider.

men's studies the first men's studies courses began in the early 1970s, and there are currently some 400 courses being taught in various disciplines. For further information see *The Journal of Men's Studies*, published by the Men's Studies Association, and *The New Men's Studies: A Selected and Annotated Interdisciplinary Bibliography* (2nd ed.) by Eugene R. August. *See also* women's studies.

mental illness this term is acceptable, although *mental disorder* is often preferred to describe any of the recognized forms of mental illness or several emotional disorders that result in the inability to function independently. The most acceptable construction is *people with mental* *disorders* or *a person with mental illness* or, best yet, the precise diagnosis: *someone with anorexia.* Avoid nouns like paranoiac, schizophrenic, manic-depressive, and anorexic that label the whole person by the disorder. "Mental illness" and "mental retardation" are separate conditions; one does not imply the other. "Mental institution" is rarely used anymore and "insane/lunatic asylum" is unacceptable; the correct term is *hospital/psychiatric hospital.* No one is a "mental patient" unless they are in the hospital, and then they are simply a "patient." Terms such as mentally deranged, mentally unbalanced, mentally diseased, deviant, and demented are not appropriate; terms such as neurotic and psychopathic should be reserved for technical and medical writing. Our everyday language is rife with words that reflect on mental illness: batty, certifiable, cracked, crazy, fruitcake, lunatic, loony, maniac, nuts, psycho, sicko, squirrel, wacko, weirdo, off the wall, off one's rocker, around the bend, a few apples short of a picnic, the funny farm, men in white coats. Few people actually use these terms to refer to those with a mental disorder; the problem is that the derision and ridicule they convey is carried over to our attitudes toward mental illness. Kay Redfield Jamison *(An Unquiet Mind)* writes that "allowing such language to go unchecked or uncorrected leads not only to personal pain, but contributes both directly and indirectly to discrimination in jobs, insurance, and society at large. On the other hand, the assumption that rigidly rejected words and phrases that have existed for centuries will have much impact on public attitudes is rather dubious. It gives an illusion of easy answers to impossibly difficult situations." Redfield thinks aggressive public education and not merely a change in the language is the answer. *See also* disability/ disabilities, idiot/idiocy, insane/insanity, manic depression, patient, "people first" rule, retarded, schizophrenic, "the."

mental retardation *See* retarded.

mentor this term, which is used for both sexes today, has an androgynous beginning: assistant professor of English Gayle Gaskill points out that the original Mentor was actually Athena, the female god of wisdom, who in response to the prayer of Odysseus's son Telemachos, came down from Olympus and appeared in the form and voice of Mentor, a male friend of Odysseus charged with Telemachos's education.

men working *work zone/crew, crew/people/workers working, crew at work, workers, working.*

mercenary this is still largely a male field, although you will occasionally find female mercenaries.

merchantman *merchant, merchant/commercial ship, merchant marine.*

merchant seaman *merchant mariner.*

mermaid/merman folklore and fantastic tradition have given us these creatures, along with nonparallel designations ("maid/man"). When possible use instead *merwoman/merman, sea creature, sea nymph, Nereid, sea god/sea goddess.*

mestiza/mestizo generally understood to be a person of Indian and Spanish ancestry, these terms (female/male) have no equivalents in English. Although the terms are nonpejorative in most Spanish-language countries, not everyone in the U.S. who meets the definition self-identifies that way; "La Raza" is preferred by many (Resource Center of the Americas). Jaimie Markham (in *Colors*), says, "Of all traditional words for us, *mestizo* comes closest to satisfying me, but only because the great Brazilian writer Jorge Amado so clearly articulated the culture of *mestizaje* in his novel *Tent of Miracles*. In the Brazilian context these words speak with conscious pride of diverse racial origins, but this pride is not conveyed by the literal translations: mixed blood and miscegenation." *See also* Hispanic, La Raza, Mexican American.

meter maid (parking) *meter reader/attendant/monitor/tender/ officer, parking monitor/officer/enforcer, parking enforcement officer.*

meter man (water/gas/electricity) *meter reader.*

métis/Métis from the French for "mixed," this refers to someone of French Canadian and American Indian ancestry; the capitalized form is used by some people to indicate that they are a distinct ethnic group. The term is analogous to mestiza/mestizo.

Mexican this is not interchangeable with Mexican American. *See also* Chicana/Chicano, Hispanic, Latina/Latino, Mexican American, Tejana/Tejano.

Mexican American this is an acceptable term for a U.S. resident with Mexican ancestry including those whose families lived in the territories taken from Mexico in the 1846–1848 war between the U.S. and Mexico. Use this for those who so self-identify. *See also* Chicana/Chicano, Hispanic, Latina/Latino, Tejana/Tejano.

Mickey Finn there is nothing wrong with using this term, but be aware of how many such expressions in the English language are male-based. Balance their use with female-based expressions, creative expressions of your own, or sex-neutral alternatives: *knockout drops. See also* sex-linked expressions.

Mickey Mouse (adjective) there is nothing wrong with using this term, but be aware of how many such expressions in the English language are male-based. Balance their use with female-based expressions, creative expressions of your own, or sex-neutral alternatives: *cheap, cheaply insincere, inferior, insignificant, worthless, petty, trivial, trifling, piddling,* *simple, easy, childish, flimsy, paltry, trite, nonsense, time-wasting, sentimental, corny.* **See also** sex-linked expressions.

Midas touch there is nothing wrong with using this term, but be aware of how many such expressions in the English language are male-based. Balance their use with female-based expressions, creative expressions of your own, or sex-neutral alternatives: *magic/golden touch, everything she/he touches turns to gold.* **See also** sex-linked expressions.

Middle East Joanna Kadi says "this term was given to the Arab world by Western (European) colonizers who named the region only as it related to their particular worldview. . . . It is offensive to me, and not at all affirming, to use such a term to describe my identity. Using the term 'Middle Eastern' feels very much like I am adopting the oppressor's language." In a culture that is generally weak in geography, it is probably in any case better to spell out exactly which countries you mean: the "Middle East" includes the 19 Arab countries on the west part of the Asian continent and the northern part of the Africa continent (Lebanon, Palestine, Jordan, Syria, Kuwait, Saudi Arabia, Yemen, Oman, Bahrain, Tunisia, Algeria, Egypt, Sudan, Qatar, Mauritania, Iraq, Libya, Morocco, and the United Arab Emirates) and the 3 non-Arab nations of Turkey, Armenia, and Iran. In some contexts, Somalia and Djibouti are also considered part of the Middle East.

middleman *go-between, agent, contact, third party, liaison, negotiator, intermediary, broker, mediator, arbiter, arbitrator, representative, messenger, factor, intercessor, intervener, umpire, referee, peacemaker, facilitator, contact, advocate, middle party; jobber, wholesaler, distributor, dealer, contract dealer, trader, reseller.*

midget use only for those extremely little but normally proportioned individuals who self-identify this way; the organization in the U.S. for short-statured people is called the Little People of America. Terms like "mental midget," while not reflecting directly on little people, indirectly disparage them. **See also** dwarf.

mid-life crisis somewhere between the ages of 35 and 50, individuals of both sexes tend to reorient themselves after reviewing where they have been and where they hope yet to go.

midshipman retain where this term is used officially; it can refer to either sex. Otherwise use *cadet, naval officer in training.* At the U.S. Naval Academy women are called "female midshipmen."

midwife (noun) this term is used for both women and men practitioners as the "wife" does not refer to the person assisting but to the person giving birth ("mid" means "with"). However, the "wife," and the fact that the vast majority of midwives have always been women, give it a feminine cast and you may sometimes want alternatives: *birth attendant, accoucheur.* The United States, Canada, and South Africa are the only industrialized nations in which midwives are not recognized and supported by the law and the medical community. In the five European countries with the lowest infant mortality rates, midwives supervise more than 70% of all births.

midwife (verb) *give birth to/beget, assist, facilitate, support, conceive of/beget (ideas), bring forth/about.*

mignonette (plant) leave as is.

migrant used as a noun, "migrant" is vague; it is better used to modify a specific noun (e.g., "migrant worker"; instead of "migrant children," use "children of migrant workers").

milady/milord sex-parallel historical terms.

militant the choice to use "militant" instead of "activist" may reveal bias; blacks are often called militants in situations in which whites are called activists.

militaristic language our language is shot through with the metaphors of war: we arm ourselves with information if we are not bombarded with it first, we take sides in the battle of the sexes, we work in the trenches or the front lines, we combat racism and sexism, poverty and injustice are the enemy. In hundreds of ways our language reveals a war mindset; being aware of it is probably an important step in working for global peace. Interestingly enough, our military language is intertwined with male imagery: Carol Cohn notes expressions such as vertical erector launchers, thrust-to-weight ratios, soft lay-downs, deep penetration, penetration aids, and protracted versus spasm attacks—or what one military advisor to the National Security Council called "releasing 70 to 80 percent of our megatonnage in one orgasmic whump . . ." *See also* violent language.

military draft *See* draft.

military man *soldier, member of the armed forces/the military, military officer. See also* armed forces, serviceman.

military wife *military/soldier's/service member's spouse.*

militiaman *militia member, member of the militia, soldier, citizen soldier, Revolutionary War soldier; if applicable, militiawoman and militiaman.*

milkmaid *milker, dairy worker/employee/hand/worker,* except for fairy tales or in historical contexts. A milkman sells or delivers milk while a milkmaid milks cows. (Note nonparallel ("maid/man"). *See also* milkman, dairymaid/dairyman.

milkman *milk route driver, milk/dairy deliverer; sometimes, milk truck. See also* dairymaid/dairyman, milkmaid.

milliner those who design, make, trim, and sell women's hats can be either sex.

millionairess *millionaire. See also* "feminine" word endings.

milquetoast/milksop (man) *timid soul, someone scared of their own shadow, someone with cold feet, timid/meek/poor-spirited/fearful/unassertive person.* ("The Timid Soul" was the name of H. T. Webster's newspaper cartoon featuring Caspar Milquetoast.) *See also* coward.

miner woman or man. The first woman miner in the U.S. coal industry was hired in 1973. *See also* glass cellar.

minister depending on the denomination, this might be a woman or a man. If you are unsure how to address a female minister, ask her; this varies from denomination to denomination and from person to person within a denomination. *See also* clergyman, imam, priest, rabbi.

minority "at least four-fifths of the world's population consists of people of color. Therefore, it is statistically incorrect as well as ethnocentric to refer to us as minorities. The term 'minority' is used to reinforce the idea of people of color as 'other'" (Amoja Three Rivers, *Cultural Etiquette*). Too often, "minority" is used today as code for poor black and Hispanic people. Alicia S. Jamerson says "minority" has come to be a catchword for any group being denied a full share of the American pie. However, the *American Heritage Book of English Usage* says that, despite some objections, "in the appropriate context, as when discussing a group from a social or demographic point of view, *minority* is a useful term that you need not avoid as offensive." The use of "minority" has troubled people for some time; as yet we have no good (i.e., instantly graspable and clearly defined) alternatives. Being aware of its shortcomings is a beginning; restricting its use to those instances in which nothing else will do also helps; sometimes it is useful to specify what kind of minority (linguistic/ethnic/religious); in general, reserve the term for groups defined by imbalances of power rather than for groups defined by a characteristic such as sex, ethnicity, income. *See also* people of color, nonwhite.

minstrel although most minstrels have been men, women belonged to some medieval troupes, juggling or acting out small parts. Troubadours, who flourished during the two centuries preceding the rise of the minstrels, also numbered some women among them (Meg Bodin, *The Women Troubadours*). At the height of the popularity of 19th-century minstrelsy, women were impersonated by men (for example, in the "wench performances"), so there appeared to be women on stage, but there rarely were.

minuteman retain for minutemen in the Revolutionary War or for minuteman rockets. Or, *soldier, citizen soldier, revolutionary soldier, Revolutionary War soldier.*

misanthrope/misogynist there's a strange imbalance here: although a
misogynist is a person who hates women, a misanthrope is not a person
who hates men, but a person who hates all humankind. A person who
hates men would be a misandrist (which you have probably never seen
before because it's not in any dictionary, although *The Oxford English
Dictionary* does list "misandry" to mean hatred of men). Related terms
show the difference: "androgyny" combines the Greek words for male
(andr-) and female (gyn-); "anthropology" means the study of humankind
(anthropo-). To be perfectly clear, you might want to use *misanthrope,
man-hater, woman-hater.*

Miss use "Miss" for those who prefer it; otherwise, especially in the workplace, use "Ms." Dale Spender *(Man Made Language)* says, "Contrary to
the belief of many people, the current usage of *Miss* and *Mrs.* is relatively
recent, for until the beginning of the nineteenth century the title *Miss* was
usually reserved for young females while *Mrs.* designated mature
women. Marital status played no role in the use of these terms." Calling
women "Miss" or "Mrs." labels them in relation to men although men
have never been labeled in relation to women. *See also* Frau, Mademoiselle, Mrs., Ms.

Miss America since 1921 this term, shorthand for the Miss America Beauty
Pageant in Atlantic City, has contributed to a competitive and unrealistic
idea of beauty for women. Although making it to the pageant is a dream-
come-true for many young women, as well as the result of years of hard
work, the pageant itself (as well as its other incarnations—Mrs. America,
Miss Vermont, Miss Indian America, pageants for toddlers and girls, etc.)
has much to answer for in its objectification of women and its unrelenting
emphasis on externals and physical perfection (which the tolerance of
injected, taped, and altered body parts falsely supports). There is nothing
of this scope and purpose for men.

missus/the missus this might be acceptable among an older generation to
refer to one's wife, if one is sure she doesn't object; it is unacceptable to
refer to other women this way, however.

mistress *lover.* Robin Lakoff *(Language and Women's Place)* points out the
possessiveness inherent in the term: "'mistress' requires a masculine noun
in the possessive to precede it. One cannot say 'Rhonda is a mistress.'
One must be *someone's* mistress." If you mean "mistress of the house,"
use *householder, homemaker, head of the household. See also* girlfriend,
kept woman, schoolmistress.

mistress of ceremonies *See* master of ceremonies/mistress of ceremonies.

mixed blood *mixed ancestry, multiracial. See also* blood, half-breed/half-
caste, mestiza/mestizo, métis/Métis, mulatto, multiracial.

mixerman *mixer tender.*

model used for both sexes.

modern man *modern people/peoples/humans/society/civilization/world, today's people, people today, modern/contemporary civilization, the modern age.* Use the term only for the Minnesotan who legally changed his name to Modern Man. *See also* man/Man ("pseudogeneric"), mankind.

modiste although a person who produces, designs, or deals in women's clothes can be either sex, this term is most associated with women. Sex-neutral alternatives include *clothier, clothing retailer, hatmaker, fashion/ high-fashion/garment designer.*

Mohammed *See* Muhammad.

Mohammedan as noun or adjective, this word is never correct and always highly objectionable. *See also* Moslem.

moldman *machine molder, mold mover/maker/worker, fiberglass laminator.*

mollycoddle (noun/verb) because of "molly" (from the woman's name) but even more because the noun is defined as "a pampered, spoiled, effeminate boy or man," this word is thoroughly sexist. For the noun use *spoiled/immature/irresponsible person, timid/gentle/sensitive person.* For the verb, use *indulge, spoil, pamper, dote on, overprotect. See also* mama's boy, sissy.

mommy track writing in the *Harvard Business Review* (January/February 1989), Felice N. Schwartz said "the cost of employing women in business is greater than the cost of employing men" (citing more career interruptions, plateauing, and turnovers for women). She asked employers to distinguish between "career-primary" and "career-and-family" women managers and to devise policies so that the latter could "trade some career growth and compensation for freedom from the constant pressures to work long hours." Although Schwartz added that "The costs of employing women pale beside the payoffs," the approach she proposed was labeled the "mommy track" (Schwartz herself never used the term). Schwartz and her work were criticized on a number of grounds: except for two unpublished studies by anonymous corporations, she offered no data to support her claim about the costs of employing women; she divided women into two groups while the diversity of men was ignored; her paper reinforced the assumptions that a woman can have either a family or a career but not both, and that it is always the woman's responsibility to care for children; her proposal tried to fit women into the existing culture instead of questioning the values of the culture; and her theory supported the contemporary situation in which women at upper levels of management mostly do not have children while their male colleagues do. Management consultant Audrey Freedman points out that in the aggregate, men cost corporations more than women; it is more often men who are involved in drug abuse, lawlessness, corporate takeover battles, incidents like the Valdez spill, and alcoholism, with its attendant loss of performance and productivity (43% of men are classified as moderate to heavy drinkers compared with 18% of women), but "the male-dominated corporate hierarchy most often chooses to ignore these 'good old boy' habits." It will probably be more profitable to abandon female-male cost comparisons (since both sexes are obviously needed) and to work to make the workplace less toxic and more user-friendly for both women and men. *See also* executive, glass ceiling, glass cellar, wage earner, working father, working man, working mother, working woman.

monastery most monasteries house or housed monks, but some abbeys and convents are also considered monasteries. Among others, Benedictine, Brigittine, Buddhist, Carmelite, Cistercian, and Visitandine nuns live in monasteries.

moneyman *financier, backer, sponsor, bankroller, benefactor, donor, angel.*

Mongolian acceptable term when referring to the central Asian region of Mongolia or its people.

mongolism/mongoloid *Down syndrome; someone with Down syndrome.* "Down's syndrome" is not pejorative, but it is less correct (Down is the physician who first reported it); "mongoloid" is objectionable but fortunately obsolete.

Mongoloid *See* -oid.

monk correct sex-specific term; the approximate equivalent for women is nun. There is no precise synonym that is sex-neutral but in some contexts you could use *religious, recluse, hermit, solitary.*

monkey's uncle *See* uncle, I'll be a monkey's.

monogamy either a woman or a man can enjoy monogamy. *See also* polyandry/polygyny, polygamy.

monsignor always a man; it means "my lord" or "my sir."

Montezuma's revenge there is nothing demeaning in this expression; most Mexicans find it humorous (it refers to the harm done Aztec peoples by the Spanish conquest). However, because it is male-based, you may want to balance its use with female-based expressions, creative expressions of your own, or sex-neutral alternatives: *dysentery, intestinal flu, travelers' tummy/scourge.* Liz Topete-Stonefield notes an expression that has surfaced recently to describe the discomfort suffered by some Mexican visitors to the U.S.: Pocahontas's revenge. She also points out that the correct spelling is Moctezuma; it has always, for some reason, been "Montezuma" in the U.S. *See also* sex-linked expressions.

Moonie instead of this disparaging term, use *member of the Unification Church.*

more bang for the buck although this probably refers more to a fireworks-type "bang" than to a sex-type "bang," it is an expression that makes many people wince. An alternative might be *get the most for your money/ your money's worth.*

Mormon member of The Church of Jesus Christ of Latter-day Saints. "'Mormon' is just a nickname (taken from *The Book of Mormon: Another Testament of Jesus Christ*). It is customary in our church to address someone of our faith as 'L.D.S.' (short for 'Latter-day Saint'), and so instead of 'Mormon Bishop,' it is more respectful and proper to write 'L.D.S. Bishop' (or 'LDS Bishop,' without the periods)" (Colleen D. Taylor). In the correct form of the name there is no "the" before "Latter-day," which is hyphenated; "-day" is lowercased.

Moslem *Muslim.* "Moslem" is an unacceptable westernized corruption of Muslim (which is both adjective and noun), referring to a follower of Islam or modifying anything of or pertaining to Islam. Never use "Mohammedan" or "Mohammedanism" since they imply worship of the prophet Muhammad, considered by Muslims to be a blasphemy against the absolute oneness of God. *See also* Black Muslims, Islam, Mohammedan, Muhammad.

mother (noun) mother is in most cases the word you want. However, "mother" should not be used for "parent" or "mother and father" (a breakfast cereal box has "kid-tested, mother-approved"); a woman expecting a child is a pregnant woman, not a mother (unless she has other children). Mothers can be adoptive, biological, birth, gestational, lesbian, ovarian, step-, surrogate, uterine—although the most popular word is still the unadorned "mother."

mother (verb) "To 'father' a child suggests above all to beget, to provide the sperm which fertilizes the ovum. To 'mother' a child implies a continuing presence, lasting at least nine months, more often for years" (Adrienne Rich, *Of Woman Born*). The differences in the verbs "to mother" and "to father" reveal much about our culture. When you need inclusive sex-neutral alternatives for the verb "mother" consider *parent, nurture, support, protect, take care of, look after, care for, be responsible for, rear children, caretake, supervise. See also* father (verb).

mother and father use "father and mother" half the time. Although there are inclusive alternatives (the best is "parents"), in this situation it seems important to make both sexes clearly visible; children need both fathers and mothers whenever possible. ***See also*** father (noun), mother (noun), parent (noun).

motherboard this is the most commonly used term. *System board* is also seen, and for some computers and in some contexts you may be able to use *analog/logic/CPU/primary circuit board*. ***See also*** daughterboard.

mother cell this biology term has a longstanding and specific meaning; leave as is. When mother cells split, they form daughter cells.

mother country *See* motherland.

mother deprivation *See* absent parent.

Mother Earth *Earth.* For the rationale on not feminizing nature, *see* Mother Nature.

mother hen *overprotective/indulgent/hovering person/parent.*

motherhouse correct sex-specific term for religious order headquarters, although there is no parallel "fatherhouse."

mother-in-law there are no father-in-law jokes and virtually no father-in-law put-downs.

motherland *homeland, native land/country/soil, home, home/birth country, land of one's ancestors, country of origin, natal place, birthplace, the old country.*

mother lode *main/principal lode.*

motherly replace this vague adjective with precise ones: *warm, nurturing, loving, kind, kindly, protective, supportive, caring, solicitous, considerate, interested, benevolent, good-natured, fond, affectionate, devoted, tender, gentle, demonstrative, sympathetic, understanding, indulgent, obliging, forbearing, tolerant, well-meaning, sheltering, generous.* These words also apply to men; they are not synonyms for "motherly" but rather what we seem to mean by it.

mother-naked *stark naked, naked, nude, bare, starkers, naked as a jaybird, without a stitch on, unclothed, in the altogether/raw/buff, in one's birthday suit, au naturel, unclad.* ***See also*** buck naked.

Mother Nature *Nature.* It is easier to rape, exploit, and subjugate Nature when it is considered female; "in our culture, words matter: The masculine dominates the feminine. To consider the Earth in terms wholly female implies that it is to be acted upon at our will. Plowing fields, cutting timber, mining ore, burning rain forests, and dumping our garbage into landfills and oceans are actions that characterize this view of the Earth as an entity we dominate" (Mary Morse, in *Utne Reader*). Elizabeth Dodson Gray (in *Creation*) says giving nature a traditional feminine image is reassuring to us for "surely a mother will always be loving toward us, continue to feed us, clothe us, and carry away our wastes, and never kill us no matter how much toxic waste we put into the soil or CFC's into the ozone." In the same way nature has been hurt by the association with the feminine, women have been discounted because of their association with nature. Sherry B. Ortner ("Is Female to Male as Nature Is to Culture?" *Woman, Culture, and Society,* eds., M. Z. Rosaldo and L. Lamphere) attributes the secondary status of woman in society ("one of the true universals, a pan-cultural fact") to the way every culture distinguishes between "nature" and "culture" and then associates women with nature and men with culture. Woman is perceived as being closer to nature because of (1) her body and its functions—which place her in (2) social roles that are considered to be at a lower order of the cultural process than man's and which lead to (3) a psychic structure which is seen as being closer to nature; "proportionately more of a woman's body space, for a greater percentage of her lifetime, and at some—sometimes great—cost to her personal health, strength, and general stability, is taken up with the natural processes surrounding the reproduction of the species." In contrast, man, lacking natural creative functions, asserts his creativity externally, "artificially," through technology and symbols. "In so doing, he creates relatively lasting, eternal, transcendent objects, while the woman creates only perishables—human beings." The association of women with second-class nature is reinforced by her association with incontinent, unsocialized children (who are, being "uncivilized," closer to nature) and by her traditional confinement to the domestic (originally because of bearing and nursing children); the domestic sphere is always considered less than the public sphere since society is logically at a higher level than the domestic units of which it is composed. "Since it is always culture's project to subsume and transcend nature, if women were considered part of nature, then culture would find it 'natural' to subordinate, not to say oppress, them."

mother of all . . . according to the American Dialect Society's journal, *American Speech,* neologists have recorded more than 70 variations of the phrase, including *mother of all victory parades, mother of all bagels,* and *mother of all mothers.* "All of the *mother of all* forms are joke uses, or at least playful allusions to Saddam Hussein's mauvais mot," says the journal. If you want alternatives consider *the ultimate . . ., the last word in . . ., the . . . to end all . . . See also* granddaddy/daddy of them all.

mother of pearl (British) rhyming slang for "girl" although it usually means wives or women friends; leave as is.

mother of pearl (mollusks) this term is acceptable but you can also use *nacre.*

mother of vinegar leave as is.

Mother's Day proposed by Anna Jarvis, Mother's Day was first observed on May 10, 1908, in Philadelphia. No florists, greeting card companies, or candy makers were involved at the time. *See also* Father's Day.

mother's helper *babysitter, childcare worker, family/parents' helper, live-in babysitter, child minder/monitor/attendant, housekeeper. See also* nanny.

mother ship *supply ship.*

mother superior retain when it is someone's title.

mother tongue if you want a sex-neutral alternative consider *native language/tongue, birth/first/original language.*

mother wit *native wit, natural wit/intelligence.*

motorman *driver, streetcar/railway/subway driver, dinkey/streetcar/motor operator, motor-power connector, engineer, motoreer* (a clever older word that was put together from motor + engineer), *railway/railroad conductor.*

moundsman *pitcher.*

mountain man/mountain woman acceptable if "mountain man" is not used as a pseudogeneric. Plural: *mountain people/folk.*

Mountie both men and women belong to the Royal Canadian Mounted Police Force.

movie man *projectionist, exhibitor.*

Mrs. some women prefer this title; respect their wishes. When their wishes or marital status are unknown, use "Ms." Dale Spender *(Man Made Language)* says, "Contrary to the belief of many people, the current usage of *Miss* and *Mrs.* is relatively recent, for until the beginning of the 19th century the title *Miss* was usually reserved for young females while *Mrs.* designated mature women. Marital status played no role in the use of these terms." (In French and German, Mademoiselle and Madame, Frau and Fraülein are still understood this way.) "Mrs." and "Miss" reflect a tradition of labeling women in relation to men although the converse has never been true. While some married women are moving away from the custom of calling themselves by their husbands' names, they account for only approximately 15% of married women. This practice may be preferred even less by African American women, "whose history denied them the legal right to that designation. What signifies bondage to one woman may mark freedom to another" (Francine Wattman Frank and Paula A. Treichler, *Language, Gender, and Professional Writing*). In the workplace this social title gives way to the more common "Ms." *See also* Frau, Mademoiselle, Miss, Ms.

Ms. pronounced "miz" and originating in secretarial manuals of the 1940s, this title is used for women where "Mr." is used for men. If you use "Mr.

Seifert," use "Ms. Ayallah"; if you call Seifert by his last name, do the same for Ayallah. "Ms." is generally acceptable when you don't know what social title (Ms., Mrs., Dr., Miss) the person uses; you may also omit the social title for both sexes ("Dear Cammie Farrell"; "Dear David Koskenmaki"). Where a woman indicates she prefers Miss or Mrs., use that instead. Using "Ms." for someone who lived before the 1970s will appear inappropriate. The greatest objection to "Ms." has been that you can't tell if she's married or not. The only sensible reply is that we have managed for centuries without knowing whether a "Mr." is married or not. According to the *American Heritage Book of English Usage*, "the term stands as a highly successful language reform—probably because people value its usefulness." The plural is "Mses." or "Mss." *See also* Mademoiselle, Miss, Mrs., salutations (letters).

muezzin always a man.

Muhammad this is the correct spelling of the name of the Muslim prophet of Allah. *See also* Islam, Moslem.

Muhammadan as noun or adjective, this word is never correct and always highly objectionable. *See also* Moslem.

mulatto *"Mulatto* is a slaveholder's word derived from the notion that, like mules, we were unable to have children. Racist pseudo-science said that since inter-species breeding produces infertile offspring, the children of whites (humans) and Africans (sub-humans) would be sterile. Hopefully, sensible people have abandoned the notion that human genetic pools— races—are different species and will therefore abandon this offensive word" (Jaimie Markham, in *Colors*). Use instead (if a reference is needed at all) *mixed ancestry, biracial, multiracial, mélange. See also* colorism, multiracial.

mullah this Muslim scholar is always a man.

multiculturalism the recognition in our writing and speaking that we come from, share the planet with, and are shaped by many cultures and individuals is called multiculturalism. Near synonyms include: cultural diversity, diversity, pluralism, cross-culturalism, ethnic inclusiveness. "None of us knows enough about the rest of us. . . . All of us, for the most part have been 'under-educated' about the history, lifestyles and contributions of groups different from our own" (Vivian Jenkins Nelsen, *New Voices in the Media*). "Multicultural education is, simply put, teaching and learning that effectively include the histories, contributions and perspectives of all groups and individuals who make up our national identity. . . . Genuine educational excellence recognizes multiple histories, cultural values and learning styles. . . . Partial or exclusive knowledge results in partial and exclusive truth" (Carol Miller, chair, Department of American Indian Studies, University of Minnesota). Sharon Bernstein (in the *Los Angeles Times*) says that within the multicultural movement, "two competing theories developed. One, called particularism, emphasized separate ethnic studies courses, such as Chicano Studies or Black Studies. The other, pluralism, recommended that information about each group be woven into traditional courses. . . . The new movement finds particularists and pluralists moving toward a middle ground, where instead of treating each ethnic group separately, elements from all their histories are woven into discussions of particular topics." "Multiculturalism is as American as apple pie. This is a nation of immigrants bound together, I hope, by a love of the U.S. Constitution—a constitution that enshrines and protects individual freedoms to an extent found nowhere else in the world" (Robert H. Scarlett). To determine if your materials exclude certain groups, read it as though you were the other sex, another race, 20 years older or younger, gay if you are straight, straight if you are gay, disabled if you are not, able-bodied if you are disabled. "Unity, not uniformity, must be our aim. We attain unity only through variety. Differences must be integrated, not annihilated, nor absorbed" (M. P. Follett, *The New State*).

multiracial "For the first time in U.S. history, birth data indicate that the number of children born to parents of different races is growing faster than the number born to single-race couples. . . . One point of contention is a move to have the U.S. Census add a 'multiracial' category to its survey forms" (Seth Schiesel and Robert L. Turner, *Boston Globe Sunday Magazine*). Since 1971 the U.S. Census has used five categories: black, white, Asian or Pacific Islander, American Indian or Alaskan native, and other. Proponents of the multiracial category say that there is discrimination (until some 30 years ago, biracial marriages were illegal in 16 states) and even virulent bigotry against "racial mixing" and you can't protect people if you don't acknowledge they exist; also, it avoids forcing people to choose on forms only one of their races ("To choose a single, monoracial category seemed as absurd as asking a child which parent she loves more"—Walter Hurdle, in the Minneapolis *Star Tribune*). Elliott Lewis (in the *Orlando Sentinel*) says, "You know how scholars talk about the black experience in America? I think there is also a biracial or multiracial experience in America." Opponents see it as a threat to the strength of racial identity and race-based organizations. They refer to the "one-drop rule": any black ancestor makes a person indelibly black. Although the concept of race itself is highly debatable today, terms like "biracial" and "multiracial" are still somewhat useful (when any such reference is necessary) and some people self-identify that way. Others prefer "mixed race," "mestiza/mestizo," "mélange," a specific reference to their ancestries (e.g., Korgentinian—from Korean and Argentinian, China-Latina, Blackanese), or no identification at all. *See also* mélange, métis/Métis, mulatto, race.

mumbo jumbo Mumbo Jumbo is an object of worship in parts of West Africa. For its borrowed, disrespectful, and ethnocentric use in English you may want alternatives: *nonsense, gibberish, twaddle, jargon, drivel.*

mum's the word this has nothing to do with "mum" ("mother") but with an old command to be quiet.

murderess murderer. *See also* "feminine" word endings.

muscleman *hired muscle, muscler, goon, thug, bully, menace, bruiser, ugly/ rough customer, enforcer, big tuna, hard case; powerhouse, weightlifter. See also* bad guy.

Muslim correct term for a follower of Islam or to modify something of or pertaining to Islam. *See also* Islam, Moslem, Muhammad.

mute this is acceptable in its sense of refraining from speaking ("when questioned, he remained unwaveringly mute"); it is less acceptable when referring to those who are incapable of speech or to those who are capable of producing vocal sounds but do not speak (usually because of deafness and the difficulty in reproducing sounds never heard). "Deaf-mute" is always unacceptable. The *American Heritage Book of English Usage* suggests "aphonic" as an adjective for someone who has lost the ability to speak; as for those who physiologically could speak but don't, "many deaf people today are brought up in a sign-oriented community that rejects the notion that speaking is necessary or, to some, even desirable; they are best referred to simply as *deaf*, or, if appropriate, *Deaf*." *See also* deaf/Deaf.

my brother's keeper *See* brother's keeper, I am not my.

my proud beauty/me proud beauty use only in melodramas where the villain has a particularly long and twirly mustache.

N

A stick or a stone only stings for a minute. A name seems to hurt forever.
—Barbara Park

Language is the road map of a culture.
It tells you where its people come from and where they are going.
—Rita Mae Brown

Language, as symbol, determines much of the nature and quality of our experience.
—Sonia Johnson

nabob historically the governor or deputy of a Mongol or Indian district or town was always a man, and there was no parallel term for a woman; in the broad sense of a wealthy, high-ranking, or prominent person, it can be used of both sexes.

nag (noun) because this is used to refer only to women (with no parallel word for men) you may want to consider *grouch, grump, grumbler, fussbudget, crosspatch, faultfinder, complainer, nitpicker, sorehead, crank, griper.*

nag (verb) although "nag" is not sexist per se, it has been used almost exclusively for women, while in the same situation men are said to bully, chew out, complain, or just plain talk. Consider using one of the many available alternatives: *complain, gripe, criticize, scold, kvetch, badger, pick on, find fault, pester, harass, grumble, grouse, irritate, drive up the wall, fuss, raise a fuss, have a bone to pick with; persist, lobby, push, press, ask again, tell, say, remind, repeat, reiterate. **See also** bitch, fuss, henpeck, whine.*

namby-pamby (noun/adjective) reserved almost exclusively for men, "namby-pamby" comes from a nickname given to the poet Ambrose (thus the rhyme with "Amby") Philips (1674–1749) whose poems were much parodied. Consider instead *softie, pushover, weakling, doormat, lightweight, featherweight; insipid, inane, shallow, flimsy, weak, indecisive, anemic, wishy-washy, colorless, milk and water, simpering. See also* baby, chicken, mama's boy, sissy, weak sister.

name *See* hyphenated names, junior/Jr., matronym/matronymic, patronym/ patronymic, surname. *See also* Writing Guidelines (pp. 15–18).

nanny this sexist term (because there are no biological, only cultural, reasons for its being limited to women) historically described a woman servant who had charge of young children. In Great Britain today it refers to a woman who has two or more years of formal training, has passed a national examination, and sometimes has served an internship. There are no certification boards or examinations for nannies in the United States, but a few programs offer nanny training. A U.S. nanny is usually someone who cares for children full-time in the home. Otherwise use inclusive terms: *babysitter, live-in babysitter, family/parents' helper, childcare worker/specialist, child minder/monitor/attendant, nursery worker, tutor. See also* au pair.

nation/she *nation/it.*

National Organization for Women (NOW) the "for" is often incorrectly replaced by "of."

native (noun) this term carries certain stereotypical connotations that make it offensive in many contexts. The first choice is always to call the people by the name they use for themselves. The second choice is to use "native" as an adjective (see below). Otherwise, possibilities—depending on context—might be *indigenous/original/aboriginal peoples. See also* aborigine/aboriginal.

native (adjective) the selective use of "native" as an adjective is generally acceptable. For example, Native American, native American, Native Alaskan/Hawaiian/Australian, native Indian (a Canadian term referring to indigenous peoples of Canada, excluding the Inuit), native peoples, peoples native to . . .

native American someone who was born in the United States. *See also* Native American.

Native American when both words are capitalized, this acceptable term refers to an American Indian. However, partly because of its imprecision (it could also mean a native American), the term has been largely replaced by "American Indian." *See also* Indian, native American.

"natural" father/mother/child *biological mother/father/child. See also* adoption language.

natural/nature because it is difficult to know (scientifically, psychologically, philosophically) whether something is indeed "natural" and, secondarily, whether being natural is good, it is better not to use these terms with respect to sex roles, age, race, sexual orientation, disabilities, or other human variables. These terms are often a substitute for informed thought, an opinion on what seems "right." "For centuries people have appealed to the 'natural' to back up their moral and social recommendations. . . . it is often taken for granted that if one persuades us that '"X" is natural,' he has also persuaded us that '"X" is good'" (Christine Pierce, in Vivian Gornick and Barbara K. Moran, eds., *Woman in Sexist Society*). Instead of "natural," consider using *automatic, instinctive, essential, idiosyncratic, usual, often-seen, common, habitual, accustomed, customary, established, time-honored, regulation, traditional, general, prevailing, frequent, popular, predictable, expected.* Instead of "nature," use *character, personality, individuality, essence, identity, quality, kind, type.* See *also* deviant, normal.

nature/she *nature/it.* For the rationale on not feminizing nature, *see* Mother Nature.

Navajo the Navajo Nation is considering a change to the name it has always called itself: *Dine* ("people of the earth"). They were named "Navajo" by outsiders (the Spanish), the word may mean "thief," and many older Navajos cannot even pronounce the word because there is no "v" sound in their language.

Nazi/nazi using this term for anything but a member of the National Socialist German Workers' Party robs it of an evil it properly should retain; it is also painful for a Jew to hear the word. There has been a recent outbreak of "humorous" -nazi forms, which desensitize us to a cruel piece of history. So far, standard dictionaries do not list this associative use of "nazi," but if the usage spreads, it will ultimately dilute and defuse the original term. The choice is always ours, but the implications of this spinoff usage should be acknowledged. For alternatives either describe the person's actions or consider using *fascist, neo-Nazi, fanatic, extremist, bigot, racist, supremacist.* See *also* concentration camp, final solution, Gestapo/gestapo, Hitler/little Hitler, holocaust.

Neanderthal man *Neanderthal, the Neanderthal, Neanderthals, early human, Pleistocene/Ice Age peoples, archaic human, Homo erectus.* The colloquial insult "Neanderthal" is sexist because it is reserved for men and ethnocentric because it represents early peoples unfairly. *See also* prehistoric man, primitive man, troglodyte.

necessity is the mother of invention if you need a sex-neutral expression try *necessity gives rise to/fosters/breeds/spawns/provokes/generates invention.* Or, instead of quoting Richard Franck, William Wycherly, or the anonymous Roman, you might consider using "Necessity does the work of courage" (George Eliot); "Sheer necessity—the proper parent of an art so nearly allied to invention" (Richard B. Sheridan); "The stomach is the teacher of the arts and the dispenser of invention" (Persius).

née because men don't change their names when they marry, the parallel French word meaning "born" for men ("né") is not used in English; he always is what he was "né." "Née" has outlived its usefulness, appearing only now and then in an obituary or society column. Use either "born Ella Gwendolen Rees Williams," "the former Virginia Stephen," or both the woman's names: Hillary Rodham Clinton.

needlewoman *needleworker, tailor, mender, alterer, stitcher, alterations expert, custom tailor, garment worker/designer.*

Negro except in established titles (e.g., United Negro College Fund), the term "Negro" is considered unacceptable, offensive, slavery-based, and contemptuous. Use instead *African American, Afro-American, black. See also* African American, Afro-American, black (noun).

Negroid *See* -oid.

neofeminist *See* feminist.

nerd male or female.

nervous Nellie this can be used to describe either a man or a woman, but it carries subtly different connotations for each. For a sex-nonspecific term, consider *fussbudget, worrywart, handwringer, terminal worrier.*

newsboy *newspaper carrier/vendor. See also* paperboy.

newshen this has been used to refer to a woman reporter where presumably a man would be a newshound. For alternatives *see* newsman/newspaper-man.

newsman/newspaperman *reporter, newspaper reporter, journalist, news representative/writer, correspondent, representative/member of the press/ media/Fourth Estate, newscaster; newsmonger.* Or, be specific: *war/ special/foreign correspondent, columnist, commentator, wire/roving/ investigative reporter, feature writer, sportswriter, stringer, editor, publisher, radio correspondent, television commentator, anchor, news anchor/director, announcer, reviewer, gossip columnist, photojournalist.* Newsroom staffs tend to be over 90% white and nearly three-fourths male; of newspaper executives approximately 15% are women and 4% are from minority groups. For a look at the intersection of news and bias, see Caryl Rivers, *Slick Spins and Fractured Facts: How Cultural Myths Distort the News. See also* anchorman.

New World this highly Eurocentric term disregards the fact that the world in question wasn't new at all to the people who had lived there for centuries. *See also* discovery of America.

niggardly although by definition and derivation "niggardly" and "nigger" are unrelated, the use of "niggardly" elicits uncomfortably negative reactions in many people. If you choose to replace it, there are many descriptive alternatives available: *stingy, miserly, parsimonious, skinflinty, cheeseparing, reluctant, ungenerous, grudging, begrudging, cheap, moneygrubbing, grasping; scanty, skimpy, piddling, measly, puny.*

nigger in 1933 Fannie Hurst *(Imitation of Life)* wrote, "Nigger is a tame-cat word when we uses it ourselves ag'in' ourselves, and a wild-cat word when it comes jumpin' in at us from the outside." It is still true that the word is used positively among some African Americans, but is off limits and considered deeply offensive when used by others. The term is much debated: some blacks believe that their open use of it among themselves will strip it of its racist meaning; others say that no matter who uses it, it is such a hideous pejorative that it should be stricken from the national vocabulary. Geneva Smitherman *(Talking and Testifyin)* says the division may be classist—"the bourgeoisie, the upper-class . . . may not want white folks to get the wrong impression. But among black folks in the plants and places like that, it's fine." Carla Hall *(Los Angeles Times)* writes, "As epithets go, it's a knife. It doesn't just cut, it slashes." Eugene Grigsby, director of UCLA's center for African American studies, says, "It's the ultimate way to remind someone you were once property, once chattel. To slip back into that terminology is to hurl an insult." Years after he made his 1974 comedy album, "That Nigger's Crazy," Richard Pryor returned from a visit to Africa and told audiences he would never use the word again as a performer because he never once saw a "nigger" in Africa. Public Enemy, one of rap's most respected and popular groups, has a song on its third album, "I Don't Wanna Be Called Yo' Nigga." The most common argument against use of it by blacks is that whites who hear it may think they too can use it. Rapper Q-Tip says, "The more and more hip-hop culture is being accepted into the white community, the more chances are greater for a white person to start saying it, and I'm really trying not to hear that." For the completely unacceptable phrase "nigger in the woodpile," substitute *fly in the ointment, catch, hitch, snag, drawback.* "Timber nigger," a highly offensive term describing American Indians involved in the fishing and hunting rights debate, has no good alternative except "American Indians involved in the fishing and hunting rights debate." *See also* "insider/outsider" rule.

niggling of possible Scandinavian origin, this term is unrelated to "nigger" and less questionable to the ear and eye than "niggardly," q.v. Although most people will find it unobjectionable, those who want to replace it can choose from among a number of alternatives: *petty, trivial, puny; piddling, trifling, fiddling; silly, inane, foolish, pointless.*

288

nightmare this sex-linked term with no inclusive alternative is not perceived today as disparaging to women.

night watchman *night guard/watch, security guard/officer, guard, building guard, watch, guardian, caretaker, gatekeeper, custodian, sentinel, sentry, lookout, patrol, patroller; the night watch.*

Nip a derogatory clipping of the word Nipponese (meaning Japanese, from "Nippon," another name for Japan), "Nip" is never acceptable. Note that although "nippy" is in no way related to "Nip," it falls unpleasantly on some ears. *See also* shortened forms of words.

Nisei literally, "second generation," this acceptable term is used for a U.S.-born Japanese American whose parents immigrated to the United States. It is sometimes used to refer to all Japanese Americans. Plural is Nisei or Niseis. *See also* Issei, Kibei, Sansei, Yonsei.

no better than she should be this phrase reeks of judgment, sexism (there is no parallel for a man), and a conception of virtue based solely on sexuality.

nobleman *noble, member of the nobility, aristocrat, peer; noblewoman and nobleman.* Or, be specific: *countess, duke, princess, earl, marquis, baroness.*

no man is an island unless quoting poet John Donne, *use no one is an island.*

no man is a prophet in his own country unless quoting the Bible (versions with the male pronouns range from "A prophet is not without honor, save in his own country" to "No prophet is without honor except in his native place, indeed in his own house"), consider alternatives: *we are slow to see the prophet in our midst; prophets are not without honor, save in their own country and among their own kind; prophets are seldom recognized in their own land; the prophet goes unrecognized at home; people rarely recognize the prophet in their midst; prophets are seldom recognized by their friends and neighbors; no one is a prophet in their own country.* **See also** "singular" they.

no-man's-land *limbo, wasteland, nowhere land, uninhabited/uninhabitable/uncharted/unclaimed/lawless/noncombatant/unclaimed land/zone/territory, demilitarized/buffer/dead zone, hostile country, nowheresville, gray area, vacuum, dead space/zone, in the crossfire, arid zone, the desert, the wild.* This is a difficult phrase to replace at times, not so much because there are no alternatives, but because we are seduced by its familiarity and by the ease with which it springs to mind. Randy Kloko points out that just as World War I gave us "no-man's land," the Vietnam War provided a modern equivalent: "free-fire zone."

nomenclature nonsexist; the "men" comes from "nomen," Latin for "name."

noncustodial parent it should not be assumed that this is always the father nor should a noncustodial mother be described judgmentally; our ideas of mothering and fathering are so narrow that we have difficulty imagining a mother who would give up custody of her children or of a father who is devastated when he fails to get custody of his. The force of these sexist attitudes is enough to pressure some women into taking custody of children who might be better off with their fathers. Then, too, it is not always a straightforward matter of do-I-want-the-kids-or-not. In *How Could You? Mothers Without Custody of Their Children,* Harriet Edwards reports that three-quarters of her survey respondents of noncustodial mothers left because of bad marriages (75% had been physically or emotionally abused) but economics prevented them from taking their children (only 5 of the 100 women earned over $10,000, only 17 had savings accounts—and 14 of those amounted to less than $400, and only 10 owned cars). They chose to avoid custody battles because they wanted to spare their children the conflict or because they were terrified of physical violence or of threats and harassment. One-quarter of them left because they didn't like mothering. This last group is often judged harshly, but there is nothing in the genes that says all women have a bent for nurturing. *See also* custodial parent, visitation.

nondisabled you could do worse than use this term, but you could also do better by being as specific as possible about the group you are referring to. Not everyone accepts or uses "nondisabled," but occasionally, given limited space and the need for something nonpejorative and succinct, this may be your best choice.

nonsexist language language that carries no cultural bias toward one sex or the other is nonsexist. It may or may not contain sex-specific words. "Businesswoman" and "businessman" are sex-specific but nonsexist. *See also* Bible language.

nontraditional career/employment *female-intensive occupation/career, male-intensive occupation/career.* Using "nontraditional" implies work that is unacceptable or abnormal for one sex. Statistics indicate that women's increasing interest in male-intensive occupations has not been matched by a comparable increase in men's interest in female-intensive occupations. And, despite decades of social change, women in male-intensive fields still describe inhospitable climates in which men ignore, discount, or sexually harass them—and advance more quickly to the more satisfying, higher-paid jobs. Men in female-intensive fields tend to average higher salaries. *See also* pink-collar worker.

nonwhite this ethnocentric, imprecise term assumes white is the standard and lumps everyone else together without any individual identity. Replace the term with specifics. "I wouldn't want to be a 'non-male'" (Joan Steinau Lester, *The Future of White Men and Other Diversity Dilemmas*).

noodle man *noodle-catalyst maker.*

normal referring to some people as "normal" automatically makes everyone else "abnormal" or "not normal." Although there are some appropriate uses (e.g., when referring to statistical human normalities), in general it is better replaced or circumvented: instead of "normal child" use "normally developing child" or "child with normal eyesight"; instead of "normal classroom" use "mainstream classroom"; the opposite of "persons with disabilities" is not "normal people" but "nondisabled people"; the opposite of gay men and lesbians is not "normal people" but "heterosexuals" (one man wrote, "As a gay man, I have waited a long time for the media to finally . . . limit the term *normal* to stories detailing automatic dryer cycle options"). "Abnormal" and "atypical" are equally suspect; who would claim to be an absolutely normal or typical individual? *See also* deviant, special.

normal man *normal individual/person.* The catch-all convention "normal man" is used, particularly in some medical and scientific writings, to designate a generic person; it is not a generic. *See also* normal.

Norseman *ancient/early Scandinavian, Scandinavian, peoples of old Scandinavia, Viking, Norseman/Norsewoman, Northwoman/Northman, Norsefolk.* Inhabitants of Scandinavia since the 10th century are properly called "Scandinavians." Before that they are "Northmen and Northwomen." Scandinavian sea-warriors from the 8th to the 10th centuries are "Vikings."

nosy this is too often used to describe women when men in the same situation are simply said to be curious. Consider using instead *curious, overcurious, supercurious, interested, interfering, intrusive, officious, snoopy, prying, spying, eavesdropping, tending/minding other people's business.*

nosy parker man or woman. From the word "parker" (park keeper), a "nosy parker" was someone who hung about London's Hyde Park around the turn of the century for the vicarious thrill of spying on lovemaking couples.

not a fit night for man or beast *See* man or beast, not a fit night for.

not by bread alone does man live *not by bread alone do we/do you/does one live.*

now is the time for all good men to come to the aid of their country/ party *now is the time for all good people to come to the aid of their country/party; the quick red fox jumps over the lazy brown dog.* The first alternative to the traditional (but sexist) typing drill is less partisan and the second is more effective (it contains all the letters of the alphabet).

nubile there is no parallel for a man. The main objection to this word is that it defines a woman primarily in terms of her readiness for a relationship with a man.

nude beach putting aside the issue of whether a beach can be nude, this expression is acceptable if you mean nothing but. If you want to convey the idea that all are welcome, use *clothing-optional beach.*

nudist camp/colony the preferred term is *nudist park.*

number-one man/number-two man *number one, boss, chief, head; number two, second in command, key/chief aide.* **See also** front man, high man on the totem pole, right-hand man.

nun acceptable sex-specific term.

nuncio so far, always a man.

nuptial/nuptials functionally nonsexist, these terms nevertheless come from the Latin meaning "to take a husband." Should you want something truly sex-nonspecific use *wedding, marriage.*

nurse man or woman, although only around 6% are male. Unless necessary for clarity, "male nurse" is not used.

nursemaid/nurserymaid *childcare worker, child minder/monitor/attendant, family/parents' helper, live-in babysitter, babysitter, nursery worker.*

nursery governess *teacher, private/in-home teacher, child minder/monitor.*

nurseryman *nursery owner/manager/operator/worker, tree farmer/grower, landscaper, gardener, horticulturist, florist, forester.*

nurture (verb) both men and woman can nurture. They can also mentor, encourage, train, reassure, motivate, support. You may sometimes want to zero in on the particular aspect of "nurture" you are describing.

nymph because this is a "beautiful maiden" and there is no parallel for a man, you may sometimes need a sex-neutral alternative: *nature god, sprite.*

nymphet the *American Heritage Dictionary*, 3rd ed., defines a nymphet as "a pubescent girl regarded as sexually desirable." How does it happen that the person who is doing nothing but breathing gets a label while the (usually older) man who is breathing heavily, metaphorically speaking at least, goes unlabeled, unremarked?

nymphomaniac defined as a woman with excessive sexual desire, "nymphomaniac" is, in theory, paired with "satyr," a man with abnormal or excessive sexual craving. In practice, we hear "nymphomaniac"—or "nympho"—much more often (and used much less precisely and with far less justification) than "satyr." Mignon McLaughlin *(The Neurotic's Notebook)* defined "nymphomaniac" as "A woman as obsessed with sex as an average man." Unless you use both terms gender-fairly choose inclusive terms: *indiscriminate lover, oversexed/promiscuous/sexually active/insatiable/sensuous/sensual person, "sex maniac/fiend," someone who sleeps around, bedhopper.*

O

Omissions are not accidents.

—*Marianne Moore*

If threatened by law that either they welcome the outsiders into their midst or be punished for failure to do so, the insiders can make their system work so as to avoid either outcome entirely. . . . Saying that a person cannot be kept out doesn't ensure that that person can get in, and more important, stay in.

—*Margaret Hennig and Anne Jardim*

oarsman *rower, competitive rower; boater, boathandler; paddler, canoer, canoeist, oar puller; punter, sculler.*

obese/obesity these terms have useful medical definitions and they are not discriminatory. However, they sound clinical and few people self-identify as "obese." *See also* fat.

oblate woman or man.

odd-job(s)-man *odd-jobber, odd-job laborer, general jobber, do-it-yourselfer, do-all, factotum, fixer, fixer-upper, repairer, maintenance worker, janitor, custodian, caretaker. See also* handyman.

odd man out *odd one out, loner, left out, third wheel, extra.*

Oedipus complex acceptable sex-specific term; the parallel is "Electra complex."

ofay this disparaging term for a white person seems to come from the pig Latin for "foe" (Stuart Berg Flexner, *I Hear America Talking*), although it may have older, African origins (*American Heritage Dictionary*, 3rd ed.).

offensive discussions about "offensive" language quickly bog down when it is discovered (surprise!) that the term in question doesn't offend everybody, especially not the person who has just used it. Some people are not moved by subjective arguments involving discomfort, offense, or even psychological pain. It is more helpful to focus objectively on the accuracy, precision, logic, or acceptability of language. For example, while "mailman" may be "offensive," it is also inaccurate: neither the national association nor the union speaks of "mailmen"; they use "mail carriers" or "mail handlers." Thus "mailman" may be "offensive" to some people because of its sexist construction and the fact that it is inappropriate for the 22% who are women, but it is above all inaccurate.

office boy/office girl *office worker/assistant/helper/staff member, staffer, assistant, right hand, aide, bureau assistant, co-worker, gofer.* Or, be specific: *secretary, clerk, bookkeeper, typist, receptionist, switchboard operator, messenger, courier, runner, deliverer, page. **See also** girl Friday.

ogress *ogre. **See also*** "feminine" word endings.

oh, boy! *wow! what a mess! whew! whoops!* "Oh, boy!" is not a dangerously sexist phrase; alternatives are included for those who want them.

-oid as "racial" categories, Australoid, Caucasoid, Mongoloid, and Negroid have no scientific validity; they are also considered pejorative and offensive.

oilman *oil company executive/sales representative, oil field worker, petroleum engineer, driller, wildcatter, wholesaler, retailer, refinery operator.*

Ojibwa/Ojibway some members of this American Indian people prefer to be known as "Chippewa"; others prefer "Anishinabe." All three are acceptable terms; to determine which is correct in the particular instance, use people's self-identification or ask for clarification. **See also** Indian.

old question the use of "old" in describing people; it is often irrelevant. Although "old" can be positive, connoting experience (an old pro/hand), its use as a pejorative intensifier (old bag, old bat, old biddy, old buzzard, old codger, old coot, old duffer, old fogy, old fuddy-duddy, old gaffer, old goat, old hat, old witch) makes it less than a neutral term. Sometimes, those terms are trying to convey non-age-related ideas like eccentric, character, card, odd duck, original, crackpot, oddball, fanatic; stick-in-the-mud, crank. If you need to mention advanced age, however, "old" is preferred to euphemisms. Consider using "older," which suggests a younger person than "old" (an old woman versus an older woman), for those beyond middle-age but not yet elderly. According to the *American Heritage Book of English Usage* (1996), "Where *old* expresses an absolute, an arrival at old age, *older* takes a more relative view of aging as a continuum—older, but not yet old. As such, *older* is not just a euphemism for the blunter *old* but rather a more precise term for someone between middle and advanced age." **See also** ageism, elderly, frail elderly, old lady/old man, old maid, old-timer, oldster, old woman.

old as Methuselah there is nothing wrong with this phrase, but be aware of how many such expressions in the English language are male-based. Balance their use with female-based expressions, creative expressions of your own, or sex-neutral alternatives: *old as the hills/as history/as time, an old chestnut. See also* sex-linked expressions.

old boy/old girl (British) parallel terms for public school graduates.

old-boys' network there may be times when this phrase is the one you want. However, to keep up with changing realities in the workplace, it is often appropriate to use *network, professional/career network, connections, business connections, contacts. See also* old-girls' network.

old-girls' network what began as a tongue-in-cheek takeoff on the powerful and long-established old-boys' networks today functions as a valuable means of sharing information for some women. However, to keep up with changing realities in the workplace, it is often appropriate to use *network, professional/career network, connections, business connections, contacts.*

old lady/old man these terms have been used for generations to refer—usually disrespectfully—to one's spouse, live-in partner, or parent. "Old man" has also been used to refer quasi-admiringly to one's boss or to a high-ranking male officer; "old lady" never was used this way. Note the nonparallel "lady/man." *See also* old woman.

old maid the correct alternative is *woman.* This term invariably appears in a negative context. Unless a person's marital status is relevant, avoid even such apparently benign expressions as "unmarried woman" and "single woman"; they perpetuate the marriage-as-norm stereotype. Why have unmarried women gone from bachelor girl to spinster to old maid, while unmarried men of all ages have simply been bachelors? *See also* bachelor, spinster.

Old Maid (card game) because commercial decks of cards for this child's game clearly mark the key card (which shows an old woman) as the "Old Maid," it is difficult to be anything but ageist and sexist when using a dedicated deck. The dreaded leftover card has not always been female; at times the game has been called Le Vieux Garçon (French for "the old boy") or Black Peter. Since the only known nonsexist name for the game is ageist (Old Miser), those who are passing it on to the next generation might want to rename it: remove three aces from a regular deck of cards (leaving the ace of hearts) and call it "Ace"; add a joker to the deck and call it "Joker," "Wild Card," or "The Cheese Stands Alone."

old-maidish replace this vague term with a more precise adjective depending on your meaning: *particular, fussy, finicky, fastidious, pernickety, set in one's ways, solitary, precise, old-fashioned, repressed, nervous, fearful.* These adjectives can be used for both men and women and are associated with unmarried older women only insofar as they convey the inaccurate, stereotypical meaning of "old-maidish."

old maids (popcorn) *unpopped corn/kernels, no-pops.*

Old Man River/Ol' Man River leave as is.

Old Man Winter there is a long poetic tradition of making a metaphorical man of winter: "Barren winter, with his wrathful nipping cold" (Shakespeare); "Lastly came Winter . . . [c]hattering his teeth" (Edmund Spenser); "winter [hath] his delights" (Thomas Campion); "Winter . . . [w]ears on his smiling face" (Coleridge); "O Winter, king of intimate delights" (William Cowper); "Winter . . . with all his rising train" (James Thomson). There is nothing untoward in this convention, but it is useful to be aware of it. What are the implications of personifying winter, time, and death as men?

old masters since the old masters were all men, and they were masters in the Western European system of master-apprentice relationships, this term is historically correct. When not referring to painters and works known as the old masters, use: *distinguished/great/classic painters/paintings, the classics, 13th/14th/15th/16th/17th-century artists/works.* Or, use specific names and painting styles. Note that the concept of "old masters" assumes a consensus on what constitutes great artists and artworks. "Master" and "mistress" illustrate what commonly happens to male-female word pairs: the male word takes on new and broader meanings while the female word shrinks to refer only to a woman's sexual function. Lord Beaverbrook underlined the absurdity of this word pair: "Buy Old Masters. They fetch a much better price than old mistresses." For discussion of "master" words, *see* master.

oldster does anyone self-identify as an "oldster"? Similar to "youngster" (which is also "good-humoredly" used of older people), "oldster" is a much less neutral term.

Old Testament reserve this for the first of the two main divisions of the Christian Bible; for the corresponding writings in Judaism, use *Hebrew Scriptures/Bible. See also* Bible language.

old-timer this is more of an affectionate term of respect than a negative reflection on age, and people sometimes self-identify this way. Although it has a masculine cast (associated forever with the grizzled old prospector of yore), it can be used of women too.

old wives' tale *superstitious belief/story/folklore, popular belief/folklore, common knowledge, ancestral wisdom, superstition, myth, silly myth, legend, folktale, tale, misconception.*

old woman this put-down does triple duty: it insults the man being so described, makes an epithet of "woman," and is also ageist. Use instead for both sexes *fussbudget, fuddy-duddy, weakling, worrywart,* *handwringer, worrier. **See also*** old lady/old man.

ombudsman *ombuds, ombud, ombudscommittee, ombudsteams, watchdog, investigator, referee, representative, surveillant, intermediary, go-between, censor, monitor, guardian of the public good, regulatory agent, protective services, complaints investigator, troubleshooter.* The Swedish word is inclusive—the "man" means "one"—but its English use is not. University campuses now have Student Ombuds Services, and at least one large metropolitan area has an "ombudscop" program under which police officers respond to neighborhood concerns.

one man, one vote *one person/citizen/member/legislator/voter, one vote; one vote per voter/person/citizen/member/legislator.*

one man's meat is another man's poison *one's meat is another's poison, one person's meat is another person's/another's poison.*

one-man/two-man/three-man, etc. (adjective) *one-person,* or substitutes such as *two-seater boat, two-way mayoral race, three-person tent, three-way contest, four-passenger plane.* Or use a noun: *two-seater, tent for two.* For "one-man" try: *individual, lone, solo, singlehanded, solitary.* For two-man/three-man block use *double/triple block.* Terms like 12-man jury can be *12-member jury.* Alternatives for "one-man show" include: *one-person/solo/individual/single-artist show/exhibition/exhibit/performance.* As there is no parallel nonsexist phrase for "one-man band" use *one-woman band or one-man band.*

one of the boys *one of the gang, a regular person.*

one small step for man, one giant leap for mankind unless quoting Neil Armstrong, use *one small step for a human being, one giant leap for the world/human race.*

one-upmanship *one-upping, one-upness, the art of one-upping, one-uppance, going one better, keeping a jump ahead, getting the jump on, trying to get the best of, competitiveness, competition, competitive skill, rivalry, outdoing someone, quest for superiority, keeping up with the Joneses, vying for top honors.* Stephen Potter, who popularized "one-upmanship" with his book *One-upmanship,* used "one-upping" and "one-upness" in the same book. With use, the shorter and punchier "one-upping" quickly begins to sound "right": "Keeping score of old scores and scars, getting even and one-upping, always makes you less than you are" (Malcolm Forbes).

only man is vile unless quoting Reginald Heber, use *only we/we mortals/ humans are vile, only humankind is vile. **See also*** sexist quotations.

openly lesbian/gay "openly" is an acceptable way of referring to someone who self-identifies as lesbian or gay in public and/or professional life. *See also* coming out, outing.

opera isn't over until the fat lady sings, the *See* it's not over 'til the fat lady sings.

opposite sex this phrase is sometimes used coyly in sexist contexts and also perpetuates an adversarial attitude toward female-male relationships. Give it a second look. Dorothy L. Sayers wonders why it has to be the "opposite" sex; why not the "neighboring" sex? *See also* battle of/ between the sexes.

orchardman *orchardist, tree grower/farmer, nursery owner/manager/ operator/worker, citriculturist, arborist, arboriculturist.*

orderly *nursing/nurse assistant, N.A.* Traditionally aides and orderlies did the same work, but all aides were women and all orderlies were men. Most hospitals and nursing homes now use the inclusive terms.

organization man "One of the interesting changes that has taken place in today's business climate is that many organization 'men' are now women" (Don Ethan Miller, *The Book of Jargon*). Until a more compact, inclusive term appears, use organization woman/women and organization man/men. Although they don't carry quite the same meaning you could also consider *team player, loyal employee. See also* company man.

Oriental *Asian, Asian American.* Or, be specific: *Japanese, Vietnamese, Chinese,* etc. The word "Oriental," which has been used for generations in the United States with increasingly negative connotations, is unacceptable as applied to individuals.

Our Father (prayer) *See* Lord's prayer, the.

outcall service *prostitution business. See also* prostitute.

outdoorsman *nature-lover, outdoors enthusiast/person, fresh-air lover/type, fan of the great outdoors; outdoorswoman and outdoorsman.* Or, be specific: *hunter, camper, fisher, hiker, birdwatcher, canoer, mountain climber.*

out-Herod Herod there is nothing wrong with this phrase in itself (if you don't mind its villainous origins), but be aware of how many such expressions in the English language are male-based. Balance their use with female-based expressions, creative expressions of your own, or sex-neutral alternatives: *outdo, outweigh, surpass, excel, exceed, transcend, outrank, get ahead of, be superior to, outstrip, beat one's own record, put into the shade, have the upper hand, go to any length. See also* sex-linked expressions.

outing in contrast to coming out, which is acknowledging one's sexuality to oneself and to others, outing is an aggressive act, informing the public that a person is lesbian or gay despite that person's desire to keep the information private. Although there have been some impassioned defenses of outing, most mainstream gay political groups oppose outing and support the right to privacy. Sexual orientation is nobody else's business, they say, and individuals have the right to "come out" (if they do) in their own idiosyncratic time, place, and manner. Outing, on the other hand, is a controlling, violent, and dominating act. Dragging unwilling victims to the sacrificial table went out of style a long time ago. *See also* coming out.

ovenman *oven tender/operator, malt roaster.*

overlord *supervisor, overseer, boss. See also* master.

overman (noun) *leader, arbitrator, referee. See also* foreman.

overman (verb) *overstaff, oversupply. See also* man (verb).

overmaster *overpower, overcome, overset, outwit, outflank, out-maneuver, defeat, conquer, vanquish, discomfit, confound.* For discussion of "master" words, *see* master.

overmastering *overpowering, overwhelming, all-powerful, irresistible, invincible, unconquerable, indomitable, unquenchable, incontestable.* For discussion of "master" words, *see* master.

overseas sometimes the correct term is foreign; in the U.S., "overseas" is not synonymous with "every country but us"; for example Mexico and Canada aren't "overseas markets," whereas Hawaii actually is but isn't likely to be so categorized.

oversensitive *sensitive, considerate, thoughtful; thin-skinned, touchy, easily hurt.* Nick Levinson points out that "oversensitive" is used to characterize outspoken minority folk. It has also been used as an epithet for people working on diversity, anti-discrimination, justice, and multicultural issues. It is not clear what the opposite of "oversensitive" would be; since even being "sensitive" is suspect, it must be "insensitive."

overweight this term implies that there is an objective, standard, "normal" weight for each person. It is also unhelpfully vague (a person could be from 2 to 200 pounds "overweight"). Most members of the National Association for the Advancement of Fat Acceptance dispute the term; they prefer "fat." Question the relevance of including "overweight" or rephrase your material in more meaningful terms ("he weighs more than he wants to"). *See also* body image, fat, looksism.

owner when referring to those who "owned" slaves, you may want to use terms that do not imply the legitimacy of "ownership": slaveholder, slaveholding master, slave master. The "ownership" of human beings has its most evil and incomparable expression in slavery. In a much different but also harmful way, men have often felt they "owned" women, children, and, sometimes, workers. *Esquire* magazine offered its readers a tear-out section entitled, "Your Wife: An Owner's Manual" (1990). A number of works have documented women's treatment as property, along with the consequences, which range from petty humiliation to murder. One study of women's deaths at the hands of lovers and husbands showed that the critical moment often occurred when the woman tried to leave. Chuck Niessen-Derry, who works with batterers through an intervention project, says, "It's like the ultimate expression of sexism, of ownership: 'If I can't have you, nobody can.'" There is only one person entitled to an owner's manual on a woman (an example of the proper use of this concept is The Diagram Group's publication, *Woman's Body: An Owner's Manual*). *See also* slave girl, violence.

oysterman *oyster farmer/grower/cultivator.*

P

Prejudice squints when it looks, and lies when it talks.
—*Laure Junot, Duchesse de Abrantès*

Beware how you contradict prejudices, even knowing them to be such,
for the generality of people are much more tenacious of their prejudices
than of anything belonging to them.
—*Susan Ferrier*

If prejudices belonged to the vegetable world they would be described under the
general heading of: "Hardy Perennials; will grow in any soil, and bloom without
ceasing; require no cultivation; will do better when left alone."
—*Nellie L. McClung*

Prejudice. A vagrant opinion without visible means of support.
—*Ambrose Bierce*

Pacific Islander this is an acceptable term to refer to a person from any of
the hundreds of Pacific Islands, which lie in the middle of the Pacific
Ocean in a region traditionally known as Oceania. It is always preferable,
however, to be as specific as possible (New Caledonian, Fijian).
Micronesia includes the Marshall Islands, the U.S. territory of Guam, and
Saipan in the Mariana Islands (peoples from Guam and Saipan are
collectively referred to as Chamorros); Polynesia includes the Hawaiian
Islands, Cook Islands, French Polynesia, American Samoa, Western
Samoa, and Tonga; Melanesia includes many countries, among them New
Caledonia, Papua New Guinea, Fiji, the Solomon Islands, and New
Hebrides. In the U.S., someone with Pacific Island ancestry is called
Asian Pacific American. *See also* Asian, Asian American.

packman *peddler.*

paddy wagon a derogatory shortening of "Patrick," "Paddy" is considered offensive by many Irish.

pagan a "pagan" is usually identified by negatives; the first three definitions in the *American Heritage Dictionary* (3rd ed.) are: one who is not a Christian, Muslim or Jew; one who has no religion; a non-Christian. The term also implies someone hedonistic and irreligious. Instead of the vague and negative "pagan," it is more helpful to identify the person by their belief system: polytheist, animist, Buddhist, atheist, etc. Only when someone self-identifies as a pagan is it acceptable. *See also* primitive, savage, uncivilized.

page boy *page.*

pageboy (hairstyle) this is not a particularly negative sex-linked term, but if you want something sex-neutral consider *bob, page-style hairdo, roll-under hairstyle.*

pal from the Romani for "brother" or "friend," "pal" is more often used of boys/men, but is also correctly used of girls/women.

paladin historically a man; for an outstanding champion of a cause, a paladin could be either sex.

palimony this court-ordered allowance may be made to either member of a former relationship.

pallbearer woman or man.

Pandora's box the majority of our sex-linked metaphors, expressions, and figures are male-based; female-based ones, like this one, are often negative. However, the familiar and evocative "Pandora's box" is probably the best choice for this meaning. If you need sex-neutral alternatives consider *opening a can of worms, the curiosity that killed the cat, unforeseen consequences, the unknown, mischief, the ills that flesh is heir to, machinations of the devil, all hell breaking loose.*

panjandrum man or woman.

pansy *See* homophobia.

pantryman *pantry worker/clerk.*

paperboy *newspaper/paper carrier/deliverer, news carrier, newspaper vendor; paperboy and papergirl* (if sex-specificity is necessary and if the carriers are preteens).

Papist derogatory term for Roman Catholics.

papoose this is unacceptable when used by non-Indians.

paramour from the French "par amour" (by or through love), "paramour" is used of either sex.

paraplegic *someone with/who has paraplegia.* If necessary to mention a disability, information can be conveyed neutrally without labeling the whole person by something that is only part of their life. Paraplegia is a complete paralysis of the lower half of the body. *See also* disability/disabilities, hemiplegic, "people-first" rule, quadriplegic.

parent (noun) three recommendations: (1) Whenever possible, use "fathers and mothers" or "mothers and fathers," rather than the inclusive "parents," in order to make both sexes visible in this important work. (2) Do not assume "parent" translates to "mother"; mail on infant care is addressed "Dear Mother" and an ad for an adhesive tape makes "diapering so easy, even Dad can do it." While the reality is that more women than men are active parents, it is also reality that many more men than before are becoming involved in parenting and should be given the name as well as the game. A step in the right direction: some stores now have diaper-changing counters in both the men's and the women's restrooms. (3) When working with children, do not assume that both parents live with the child; many children live with only one parent, with a parent and stepparent, with a guardian, in a foster home, or with two parents of the same sex. Teacher David Salmela asks his elementary-school pupils to take notes home to "the adults" at their house. *See also* babysitter, mother and father.

parent (verb) "to mother" a child is very different from "to father" a child, which is why "to parent" is such a useful and clear term.

parlormaid *servant. See also* cleaning woman, maid.

parson depending on the denomination, this may be either sex.

partner this word is used by many lesbian, gay, and unmarried heterosexual couples to denote the person with whom they are living or to whom they are romantically attached. "Partner" may suggest a business association, but until a better word is found, it is one of the more useful possibilities available today. Other terms in use are *companion, longtime companion, lover. See also* boyfriend, girlfriend.

parts man *stock clerk, parts clerk/worker.*

pasha retain as a male term in the context of Turkish or North African political life. However, there is nothing to say you can't use "pasha" metaphorically to describe a powerful or high-ranking official of either sex.

paste-up man *paste-up editor/copy editor, camera operator.*

past master *acknowledged expert, expert, adept, champion, genius; ex-champion; experienced/accomplished artist/writer/bricklayer,* etc. This may also refer to the holder of a Freemason office or to a specific title in a guild or society, in which case it should be used as it is. For discussion of "master" words, *see* master (noun).

pastor depending on the particular denomination, a pastor may be either sex.

pater/paterfamilias acceptable sex-specific terms, although the Latin is more often replaced with "father/patriarch." The original paterfamilias, head of the clan, tribe, or family, had unlimited power over his wives, concubines, children, slaves, servants, animals, and property. At times, his power extended even to deciding who would live and who would die (girl children, for example, or disobedient wives or slaves). Be sensitive to the history and legacy of this concept when using these terms. *See also* mater/materfamilias.

paternal unless you mean fatherlike or father-related ("paternal grand-mother"), use *parental, ancestral; kindly, kindhearted, loving, nurturing, devoted, indulgent, solicitous, concerned, fond, protective, sympathetic.* "Paternal" has been overused, and often the paternal verges on the patronizing.

paternalism (pseudogeneric) *parentalism, authoritarian parentalism, authoritarianism, protectionism, political intrusion/intervention, benevolent despotism.* "Paternalism" is entrenched in certain academic, philosophic, and political circles, and it is difficult (but not impossible) to replace with a commonly recognized one-word term. The concept of paternalism resonates negatively with many women and minorities; paternalistic societies, laws, churches, and husbands have been a fact of life throughout history. Former U.S. Supreme Court Justice William Brennan said, "Our nation has had a long and unfortunate history of sex discrimination . . . rationalized by an attitude of 'romantic paternalism' which, in practical effect, put women not on a pedestal, but in a cage." *See also* chivalry, male-dominated society.

patient use "patient" only if the person is under a doctor's or other healthcare provider's care or has a disease that requires such care. "For the 43 million people now designated as having a physical, mental or biological disability, only a tiny proportion are continually resident in and under medical supervision and are thus truly patients" (Irving Kenneth Zola, in Mark Nagler, *Perspectives on Disability*). The *Publication Manual of the American Psychological Association*, 4th ed., recommends reconsidering such terms as patient management and patient placement; "In most cases, it is treatment, not patients, that is managed; some alternatives are 'coordination of care,' 'supportive services,' 'assistance.'" *See also* case, disability/disabilities.

patient as Job there is nothing wrong with using this phrase, but be aware of how many such expressions in the English language are male-based.

Balance their use with female-based expressions, creative expressions of your own, or sex-neutral alternatives: *long-suffering, stoic, forbearing, uncomplaining, longanimous, abiding, patient, extraordinarily patient, patient as the grave, through fire and water, keeping the faith.* Job's opposite number is probably patient Griselda, but she does not, to put it mildly, provide a particularly acceptable or admirable model for today's woman, and it is better to avoid her. *See also* patient Griselda, sex-linked expressions.

patient Griselda *someone who is long-suffering/submissive/ humble/patient/ extraordinarily patient/patient as the grave/passive/abiding/stoical/ forbearing, someone who endures through thick and thin/through fire and water. See also* patient as Job.

patriarch/patriarchy the social systems traditionally referred to as patriar-chal form "the basic principle of all major relationship systems in the western world" (Sandra M. Schneiders, *Women and the Word*). Schneiders, theologian Rosemary Ruether, former president of the World Council of Churches Visser't Hooft, among others, say that this principle supports racism, colonialism, ageism, classism, and clericalism, as well as sexism. To clarify contemporary systems of oppression, replace "patriarchy" with *dominator system/society, dominator model of society, hierarchy, hierarchical/authoritarian society* (the first two terms from Riane Eisler *(The Chalice and the Blade, The Partnership Way of Life)*. While it is true that dominator models of society have been established and maintained almost entirely by men, it was not their maleness that was destructive and oppressive as much as their hierarchicalness and their abuse of power. In addition, not all men were involved in the dominator system; many men, especially those who did not conform, suffered under it. It is entirely possible to be a father (patriarch) without being oppres-sive; continuing to use terms like "patriarch" and "patriarchy" as syn-onyms for "oppressor" and "oppressor system" is not recommended. Note incidentally that the opposite of a patriarchy is not a matriarchy. Both matriarchies and patriarchies involve an imbalance of power between the sexes and are thus dominator societies; the true opposite of a matriarchy or a patriarchy is a partnership society (Riane Eisler). Until neither sex needs to dominate the other, use "matriarchy/patriarchy" terms cautiously. Sex-neutral alternatives for "patriarch" include *ances-tor/family elder, head of the family, family head.* The word "patricentric" puts the father at the center of the family or system without the hierarchi-cal overtones of "patriarchal." *See also* chivalry, male-dominated society, matriarch/matriarchy, paternalism.

patrician this word shares the same Latin root ("pater") as other "father" words, and there is no parallel "matrician." It is not functionally sexist, but it tends to be classist and you may sometimes want alternatives for the adjective: *elegant, well-bred, formal, stately, graceful, courtly, debonair, delicate, decorous, majestic, exquisite, polite, seemly, refined, genteel, cultivated, urbane, sophisticated, worldly, stylish, cosmopolitan, classy.* The best alternative for the noun is "aristocrat," although we tend not to use "patrician" in that sense, perhaps because of our democratic underpinnings.

patricide accurate sex-specific word. Inclusive alternative: *parricide.*

patrilineal refers to descent through the father's line; its word pair is "matrilineal."

patrimony *inheritance, estate, family estate, birthright, legacy, bequest, succession, inherited property, heirship, heritage, endowment, portion, share, lot.* Note the nonparallel "patrimony/matrimony." *See also* matrimony.

patriot/patriotic/patriotism from Latin for "land of my father," these terms function today as inclusive words. If you need alternatives without sex-linked roots, consider *nationalist, lover of one's country, loyalist, chauvinist, flag-waver, jingo, jingoist, hundred-percenter; nationalistic, loyal, allegiant, jingoistic, chauvinistic, flag-waving, public spirited, civic-minded; national loyalty, good citizenship, nationalism, allegiance, jingoism, chauvinism, love of country.* Note the use of "patriotic" to mean "thinks the way I do" or as a verbal club to convince people to do what is "right."

patrolman *patrol/highway/law enforcement/peace/police/traffic officer, patroller, state trooper, trooper, officer, police.*

patron both women and men are patrons today, and the word functions fairly inclusively, but it comes from the Latin for "father," it has been used more of men than of women, it is part of the exceedingly imbalanced word pair "matron/patron," and it has some fairly sexist relatives ("patronage," "patronize," "patronymic"). For those reasons you may want alternatives: *benefactor, sponsor, backer, donor, supporter, promoter, philanthropist, booster, champion, partisan, angel, guardian angel, bankroll, advocate, mentor, helper, protector; library user, customer, shopper, buyer, purchaser, subscriber, client. See also* matron.

patronage from the Latin for "father," this term has no female partner ("matronage"), is closely related to "patronize," and reflects centuries of "father"-inspired domination. These associations suggest you may want to consider alternatives: *sponsorship, support, auspices, advocacy, defense, championship, assistance, encouragement, promotion, protection, influence; business, trade, custom, customers, clientele, commerce, shopping, trading. See also* patron.

patroness *patron.* "Patron" may not always be the word of choice but it is far better than "patroness." *See also* "feminine" word endings, patron.

patronize "patronize" has highly sexist roots and associations (e.g., what some men did to some women for so long, but rarely vice versa) and can be easily replaced: *support, favor, uphold, promote, defend, sponsor, show favor to, defer to, tolerate; condescend to, treat condescendingly, underestimate, disparage, discount, look down on, talk down to, deign, stoop, be overbearing/arrogant; trade with, buy/purchase from, do business with, give business to, shop at, frequent. See also* patron.

patronizing *condescending, scornful, supercilious, overbearing, snobbish, superior-acting, offensive, humiliating, haughty, presumptuous, insulting, insolent. See also* patronize.

patron saint *namesake/guardian saint, special saint* (e.g., "Saint Appollonia, special saint of dentists"). *See also* patron.

patronym/patronymic referring to a name derived from the father or a paternal ancestor, these are correct sex-specific terms. If you mean the term in the generic sense use *surname, last name, birth name.* Una Stannard believes that giving children their fathers' surnames sprang from ignorance about the facts of life. Before the female ovum was discovered in 1827, people assumed that men contributed the seed of life while women's wombs simply provided the "soil" in which it grew. Stannard says, "Since the female role in generation was thought to be negligible, it seemed only logical that children would receive their names from their fathers, seen as their sole progenitors." *See also* hyphenated names, matronym/matronymic, surname.

patsy the origins of this word do not appear sex-linked and it is not perceived as particularly gender-specific. For a more neutral-appearing term use *scapegoat, goat, loser, born loser, dupe, nebbish, victim, mark, target, laughingstock, sad sack, doormat, sap, hard-luck story, pigeon, pushover, fool. See also* fall guy, whipping boy.

Paul Pry there is nothing wrong with using this expression, but be aware of how many like it in the English language are male-based. Balance their use with female-based expressions, creative expressions of your own, or sex-neutral alternatives: *snoop, busybody, stickybeak, eavesdropper, nosy parker. See also* nosy parker, sex-linked expressions.

pay equity *See* comparable worth, equal pay/equal pay for equal work.

paymaster *payroll agent/supervisor/manager, financial officer, treasurer, bursar, purser, receiver, accountant, cashier, teller, bookkeeper, controller, comptroller, steward.*

peace on earth, good will to men *peace on earth, good will to all.*

peacock/peafowl/peahen use the generic "peafowl" instead of the male "peacock" when referring to both males and females.

Peck's bad boy *enfant terrible, in the avant garde, innovative/unorthodox/ unconventional/nonconforming director/artist/musician,* etc., *heretic* (in nonreligious sense), *questioner; embarrassment; mischievous child. See also* enfant terrible.

Pecksniffian there is nothing wrong with using this word, but be aware of how many such expressions in the English language are male-based. Balance their use with female-based expressions, creative expressions of your own, or sex-neutral alternatives: *hypocritical, insincere, crocodilian, mealy-mouthed, double-dealing, two-faced, smooth-tongued, sanctimonious, self-righteous, unctuous, canting, pietistical. See also* sex-linked expressions.

pederast *child molester/abuser, habitual child molester.* The Greek root word means either "child" or "boy," but "pederast" is defined today as a man (usually someone over age 18) who uses boys (usually under age 16) as sex objects, and thus is sex-linked; there is no parallel for women/girls. Pederasts are not gay as such; they are unlikely to form relationships with men of their own age. Alternatives are given not to provide inclusive terms but to make clear exactly what a pederast does. *See also* pedophile.

pedophile *child molester/abuser, habitual child molester.* "Pedophile" is not sexist per se, but it is often associated with men since they are the principal abusers. Use alternatives because they appear more inclusive but, more important, they do not dress up an ugly practice with a fancy name. Child molesters are generally men attracted to prepubescent boys and girls; most abusers identify themselves as heterosexuals. *See also* pederast.

peeping Tom from the legendary tailor who tried to get a look at Lady Godiva as she rode naked through the streets of Coventry, this term can be replaced by sex-neutral alternatives if needed: *peeper, peeker, window peeper, voyeur, ogler, eavesdropper, breather, fetishist, pervert.* Although "peeping Thomasina" is seen occasionally, it is unnecessarily coy and not a good parallel for "peeping Tom." The male peeper is not the harmless voyeur he has been thought to be: statistics indicate that such individuals are usually involved or will be involved in more harmful deviant behavior, including rape and other sex crimes.

peeress *peer. See also* "feminine" word endings.

Peking man *early human, Peking fossil, Homo erectus.*

penman *writer, author, scribe, calligrapher.*

penwoman *writer, author, scribe, calligrapher.* But note the National League of American Penwomen, an organization of professional women writers and editors.

penmanship *handwriting, writing, longhand, hand, script, calligraphy, manuscription.*

"people-first" rule Haim Ginott taught us that labels are disabling; intuitively most of us recognize this and resist having labels put on us. The disability rights movement originated the "people first" rule, which says we don't call someone a "diabetic" but rather "a person with diabetes." Saying someone is "an AIDS victim" reduces the person to a disease, a label, a statistic; use instead "a person with/who has/who is living with AIDS." Instead of "crack babies," use "babies addicted to crack." The 1990 Americans with Disabilities Act is a good example of correct wording. "While this order of reference is more awkward, it is more respectful of persons with disabilities" (Joan Blaska, in Mark Nagler, *Perspectives on Disability*). Many disability groups and advocacy organizations encourage the public to use "person first" language. The "rule" is helpful not only in speaking and writing of those with disabilities. Readers of a magazine aimed at an older audience were asked what they wanted to be called (elderly? senior citizens? seniors? golden agers?). They rejected all the labels; one said, "How about just *people?*" When high school students objected to labels like kids, teens, teenagers, youth, adolescents, or juveniles, and were asked what they would like to be called, they said, "Could we just be people?" Name the person as a person first, and let qualifiers (age, sex, disability, ethnicity) follow, but (and this is crucial) only if they are relevant. *See also* disability/disabilities, handicapism, victim.

people of color/person of color use these terms when groups or individuals use them for themselves; when used by the dominant culture to label others from without, it is often problematic, masking people's individuality and diverse origins and functioning somewhat like the ethnocentric "nonwhite." Elizam Escobar (in *Prison News Service*) wonders if everybody doesn't have some color; "'people of color' has this fastidious 'picturesque' element so familiar to the vocabulary of tourism. It sounds like a color Polaroid photograph of 'nice' and 'cute' people; innocent, inoffensive, and domesticated people, where everyone is homogenized with this attribute of color. And who is this photographer who has so carefully taken this picture? A 'white' tourist with 'good intentions?' Or, in fact, is no one to be blamed but ideology itself?" On the other hand, the *American Heritage Book of English Usage* points out, "In effect, *person of color* stands *nonwhite* on its head, substituting a positive for a negative." On occasion, after a first full reference, some writers use "POCs."

perky/pert "No more stories describing women athletes or other women as 'perky,' please. It is demeaning" (editor Nancy Greiner). A similar caution might be applied to "pert." When did you last hear a boy or a man described as perky or pert? *See also* coed, feisty.

perpetrator "The words 'perpetrator' and 'male' are used interchangeably" (William Betcher and William Pollacks, *In a Time of Fallen Heroes*). Alternatives, like "criminal" or "rapist" or "assailant," are not any more inclusive. Because there is statistical support for the stereotype that perpetrators are mainly men, it is difficult to deal with this on the level of language. *See also* bad guy.

person/person-/-person not sexist; the Latin "persona" means "human being." In the plural "people" is preferred to "persons." Women-Are-Persons-Too Department: in 1988 a federal judge ruled against the U.S. Department of Agriculture, which claimed that a farm couple was only one person. Although a father and his son or a brother and a sister farming in partnership were regarded as two people, a husband and wife were counted as only one person for USDA purposes. U.S. District Court Judge Joyce Hens Green officially rejected "the archaic notion that husbands and wives are one 'person.'" For years African Americans were designated "nonpersons" in order to maintain the institution of slavery. Although using "person" as a suffix has been helpful in making the transition to inclusive language, it should be avoided whenever possible; it is awkward, contrived, unnecessary, and not always neutral. Except for "personhood," "person-" has been used as a prefix only by those who were making up words ("personhole cover") to ridicule nonsexist language. According to a story contributed by M. Larson in *Reader's Digest* (September 1982), when a male college friend said he was a freshperson, a puzzled bystander interrupted: "A freshperson? But I thought only women were 'persons.'" *See also* Writing Guidelines, p. 15, for a discussion of -man, -person, and -woman.

"person-first" rule *See* "people-first" rule.

person of color *See* people of color.

person of mixed ancestry *See* mixed blood.

pert *See* perky.

pervert defined as one who practices a sexual act considered abnormal or deviant, "pervert" is such a vague label that the only idea it conveys is that the speaker doesn't approve of the "pervert." Describe the behavior, including if necessary some sense of why it constitutes perversion. The word has most often been used of gay men and lesbians; however, although there are undoubtedly "perverted" homosexuals there are also undoubtedly "perverted" heterosexuals.

pet *See* speciesism.

peter/peter out (verb) because of the association of "peter" with "penis," you may sometimes want alternatives: *give/run out, become exhausted, dwindle, decline, shrink, shrivel, trail/drain off, dry/use up, dissipate.*

Peter Pan collar this term is so immediately evocative of a certain style that it is difficult to replace. Sometimes you can use *round collar.*

Peter's pence use this term when it refers to the annual papal collection in the Roman Catholic Church. Otherwise consider *church tax, donation, alms, honorarium, gratuity, offering.*

Peter to pay Paul, borrow from *See* borrow from Peter to pay Paul.

petite this is used only of women, and its masculine companion, "petit," has a rather important and meaningful life in the legal world—an example of yet another female-male word pair that bit the dust. If size is relevant use inclusive terms: *small, tiny, miniature, pint-sized, teeny, short, trim, slight, slender, thin, lean.*

pharaoh pharaohs were all men (the word means "king"); women married to a pharaoh or who served as regents were called queens. Christiane Desroches Noblecourt *(La femme au temps des pharaons)* notes that Egyptian women of the pharaonic periods had as many rights as men, being able to rule, teach, make their own decisions, and own property.

philanthropic/philanthropist/philanthropy *See* anthropology.

Philippines this is the correct name for the country in eastern Asia. *See also* Filipino, Pinoy/Pinay.

physically challenged/different *See* challenged, disability/disabilities.

pickup (woman) this not only says the woman is passive (she is "picked up") but it also implies (by giving her, but not her partner, a special derogatory label) that she is the guilty party. We pay lip service to the two-to-tango notion, but our language says that a man's actions are literally unremarkable while the woman's actions deserve a judgment. Eliminating words like "pickup" from the language will not also eliminate the double standard, but it is a necessary part of the process.

pied piper in the well-known fairy tale, the pied piper was a man, but the term is functionally gender-free.

pig *See* animal names for people.

pikeman *soldier; tollbooth operator; miner.*

Pilgrim Fathers *Pilgrims.*

pillar of society/of the community "Even when women occupy professional and community positions of great solidity and centrality, they are not called pillars of society: pillars, it seems, are male. Yet no society could contrive to function for even a day without the support of women, as the Greeks seemed to recognize when they used fully draped female figures as columns or pilasters supporting the entablatures of their buildings" (Marilyn French, *Beyond Power and Morals*).

pimp by definition a man. *See also* prostitute.

pink this color has traditionally been associated with girls/women from babyhood onward. Unlike blue, which can be worn by female infants, girls, and women with impunity, pink has remained largely associated with the feminine; men wear it only if it is called "salmon" or "magenta." According to European legend, girl babies were found inside pink roses (the same legend situated newborn boys in blue cabbages), thus giving rise to the pink-for-girls "rule" and reinforcing the blue-for-boys. *See also* blue, sexism.

pink collar job/worker "pink collar" refers to that small number of jobs into which some 80% of salaried women fit, e.g., secretaries, household/childcare workers, nurses, waiters, librarians, health technicians, elementary school teachers, bank tellers. Most women remain segregated in relatively low-paying, low-status, female-intensive occupations, and this clustering negatively affects earnings: a 1% increase in the proportion of female college graduates in an occupation reduces earnings by .42%; among women without college degrees, clustering accounts for 30% of the wage difference between the sexes. The few men in such pink-collar jobs as nursing, childcare, secretarial work, or teaching say "their hardest job is combating the poor image that society gives them for taking these jobs" (Mike Kelly, in Francis Baumli, *Men Freeing Men*). The men are perceived as unaggressive, unmasculine, and not career-oriented; they feel they have to perform better on the job than women; and they are constantly chided for doing "women's work." *See also* nontraditional career/employment.

pinko a person who holds moderately leftist views, a "pinko" is so labeled to contrast with a "Red" (Communist or revolutionary activist). Words that end in "-o" are generally derogatory (wacko, sicko, psycho, weirdo, chico, dago, gringo, homo, wino, fatso).

pin money an outdated term for an outdated concept whereby husbands gave their wives spending money (literally to buy pins). Use instead *pocket/mad/household/spending money, petty cash; loose change*.

Pinay/Pinoy these terms for a woman or a man from the Philippines are usually used by Filipinos only; they can be offensive when used by others. *See also* Filipina/Filipino.

pinup girl *model, photographic/calendar model*.

pioneer we too often incorrectly assume that all pioneers were not only male, but white.

pirate noted pirates (or buccaneers or freebooters) included Anne Bonney, Mary Read, and Grania O'Malley.

pitchman *sidewalk vendor/seller, barker; hawker, promoter, high-pressure seller, celebrity endorser.*

pitman (automobile) *connecting rod.* The "man" in "pitman" refers to the adult male, so the word's origins are sexist.

pitman (industry) *pit/underground miner/worker, miner.*

pivotman (basketball) *post/pivot player, pivot, center.*

placeman *political appointee, government official, bureaucrat, functionary, agent.*

plainclothesman *plainclothes/undercover officer/detective, detective, investigator, police officer.*

plainsman *plains dweller/inhabitant; plainswoman and plainsman.*

platform man *platform attendant/loader.*

playboy *swinger, bedhopper, philanderer, mover, hustler, free spirit, flirt, libertine, seducer, high-roller, high-liver, high-flier, hedonist, fun-seeker, pleasure-lover, good-timer, sport, gadabout, party animal, dissolute/ promiscuous/sexually active person, someone who sleeps around, make-out artist, lover. See also* ladies' man, man about town, rake, womanizer.

playfellow *playmate, friend.*

playgirl/playmate *centerfold, model, nude model.* If you mean "playgirl" in the same way "playboy" is used, *see* playboy for alternatives.

pleased as Punch in the standard "Punch and Judy" show, Punch carries a stick with which he "belabors" Judy—and then bursts into screams of laughter.

plowboy/plowman *plow driver/operator, farm worker, farmer, cultivator, sower.*

PMS *See* premenstrual syndrome.

poetess *poet.* Adrienne Rich said that whenever she was introduced as a poetess, she became a terroristress. *See also* "feminine" word endings.

poilu this World War I French soldier was always a man, with at least one known exception: Marie Marvingt, the Frenchwoman known as the Fiancée of Danger, disguised herself as a poilu and fought in the front lines for three weeks until she was discovered.

point man *high-scoring player/ballplayer, high-scorer, scorer.* "Pointperson" is used, but it looks awkward and self-conscious.

policeman *officer, police, police/peace/law/highway/patrol/law enforcement/ beat/traffic officer, officer/agent/arm of the law; policewoman and policeman.* Or, be specific: *sergeant, detective, sheriff, chief, deputy, lieutenant,* etc. There have been policewomen since 1910 when Alice Stebbins Wells was appointed to the Los Angeles Police Department. Invariably accused of using her husband's badge for the free streetcar rides offered police officers, she was issued "Policewoman's Badge No. 1." *See also* bobby, patrolman, stick man.

policeman of the world *watchdog/police officer of the world.* "Policeman of the world" has a specific and instantly recognizable sense in some disciplines. However, with a little effort one could get used to an alternative or construct a new one.

politically correct "There are few things more wearisome in a fairly fatiguing life than the monotonous repetition of a phrase which catches and holds the public fancy by virtue of its total lack of significance." Agnes Repplier wrote this in 1897, but surely she had some precognition of the term "political correctness" because she also wrote, in 1916, "People who pin their faith to a catchword never feel the necessity of understanding anything." The term "politically correct" is a loose term from much flabby living; its meanings run along the lines of "I hate what you're doing," "Stop it! Stop it right now!" and "For heaven's sake, why would we change anything?" Many people can no longer even identify what specifically they are decrying. Your writing and arguments will be much clearer if you drop "political correctness" altogether and state your objections: it is "bias-free language" or "multiculturalism" or "hate speech codes" or "affirmative action" or "diversity"—not "all that PC stuff."

politics makes strange bedfellows unless quoting Charles Dudley Warner, use *politics makes strange bedmates.*

Pollyanna if you need a sex-neutral term consider *irrepressible/eternal/ persistent/unflagging/perennial/cockeyed/foolish/incurable optimist, daydreamer, romantic, visionary, castlebuilder, utopian, idealist, victim of terminal cheerfulness, one who lives in a fool's paradise, wearer of rose-colored glasses.*

polyandry/polygyny correct sex-specific terms meaning, respectively, more than one husband, more than one wife. *See also* polygamy.

polygamy this term means a practice in which either spouse may have more than one mate at the same time. We tend to use it as though it means "several wives" instead of "several mates"; the correct term for "several wives" is "polygyny." Bring a different perspective to "polygyny" and instead of one man having many wives, it could also be defined as a group of women sharing one husband (Joan Steinau Lester, *The Future of White Men and Other Diversity Dilemmas*).

pom-pom girl *cheerleader, pom-pom twirler/artist.*

pontiff so far, always a man.

pontificate although this term comes from the Latin sex-neutral word for "bridge-building," its associations with the male papacy may suggest the need for alternatives in some cases: *orate, declaim, hold forth, harangue, expound, wax pompous, declaim; preach, lecture, sermonize, dogmatize.*

pooh-bah although the original character from *The Mikado* (1885) was a man, this term can be used to describe a self-important person of either sex who occupies a high position, holds several positions at once, or wields great influence.

poor when possible, be specific about the ways you mean "poor" (low income, substandard housing, illiteracy, without medical insurance, etc.). Do not use as a noun ("the poor") and watch that it is not code for "black" or other minority groups. Avoid classist assumptions about poor families' values, lives, and behavior. *See also* criminal, "the," welfare.

poor as Job/poor as Job's turkey there is nothing wrong with using these phrases, but be aware of how many such expressions in the English language are male-based. Balance their use with female-based expressions, creative expressions of your own, or sex-neutral alternatives: *poor as a church mouse, destitute, penniless, indigent, poverty-stricken, on one's uppers, down and out, out at the elbows, down at the heels. See also* sex-linked expressions.

population control *reproductive responsibility/freedom/rights/information, birth control, contraception, family planning, fertility control.* The term "population control" reveals a paternalistic, patronizing attitude (masculine terms are intended) toward people in general, toward peoples in nonaligned countries, and most particularly toward women. The alternatives shift the emphasis to the control people have over their own choices. *See also* birth control.

pornography most people have opinions on pornography: "Pornography is the attempt to insult sex, to do dirt on it" (D. H. Lawrence); "It is heartless and it is mindless and it is a lie" (John McGahern); "Pornography is the undiluted essence of anti-female propaganda" (Susan Brownmiller); Susan Sontag says it drives "a wedge between one's existence as a full human being and one's existence as a sexual being—while in ordinary life one hopes to prevent such a wedge from being driven." Pornography is often associated with the rising tide of sexual crime against both children and adults, the desensitization of individuals toward the horror of violence and rape, and the inability of many men to relate to women with any mutuality or respect because of their pornography-inspired but unrealistic expectations of women and of sex. Susan Griffin *(Pornography and Silence)* says pornography teaches men that sex has nothing to do with emotions. Child porn flourishes, and is even defended by a few well-organized political pressure groups (e.g., the North American Man-Boy Love Association and the Rene Guyon Society, whose motto is "Sex by Age 8 or It's Too Late"). As many as one million children have been used to create the child porn in some 275 monthly magazines (Carol Gorman, *Pornography*). Addiction is also a factor. (Harriet Beecher Stowe said years ago: "Whipping and abuse are like laudanum; you have to double the dose as the sensibilities decline.") Men may buy pornography but women pay for it—in terms of exploitation, rape, violence, and a society that sees them as disposable sexual objects. Pornography associates women with pain, inferiority, and humiliation; the assumption for the user is that this is real and normal. Good sex is also a victim; a graduate of The School of Pornography is a sex-illiterate. Erotica differs from pornography in celebrating rather than degrading human sexuality; it preserves the mutuality of sexual activity, is not exploitative, controlling, objectifying, addictive, a "using" activity, or effected for prurient interests; it also does not embarrass you if you are found reading it by a friend. Ann Simonton (in *Z Magazine*) says there "is a determined movement of millions of women and men nationally and internationally who are working on every level possible to help the public understand the consequences of our culture's addiction to pornographic images and to expose the fact that real people are being hurt through the making and distribution of pornography. Pornography, for many of us, is a form of hate propaganda designed to keep women subordinate to men; it is also a system of sexual exploitation for profit that targets women for rape, battery, and harassment." *See also* rape, sex object, violence.

portress *porter. See also* "feminine" word endings.

poseur this grammatically masculine French word is used (in French and English) for either sex. If you need a less masculine-appearing term try *pretentious person, mannerist, lump of affectation, charlatan, quack, humbug, pedant, pedagogue, pseudo-intellectual.*

postboy *postilion.*

postman *See* mailman.

postmaster/postmistress retain for titles in current use; otherwise use *postal chief/manager, post office supervisor/manager.* When the official title for men in the same position is "postmaster," use that (it is somewhat less sexist than "postmistress").

postmaster general retain for current titles; otherwise use *federal postal director/chief/supervisor.*

potboy retain in historical contexts. Otherwise use *barroom attendant, tavern helper, bar assistant.*

potentate in certain contexts today, this could be either sex; historically it was always a man.

potty parity after waiting in line to get into the women's restroom at a Houston concert, Denise Wells became increasingly desperate and finally used the men's room—for which she was ejected from the concert and fined. She was eventually found not guilty of illegally using a men's room, but her case highlighted what has since been called potty parity: the ratio of men's to women's rooms is 1:1, and there is often a higher combined total of urinals and toilets in men's rooms than toilets in women's rooms. This effectively discriminates against women who, for biological reasons, generally need more sanitary facilities. Men are more efficient, thanks to their particular physiology, while for women, more complicated clothing, pregnancy, menstruation, and caring for small children mean additional time. There is talk of more than doubling the number of toilets in women's rooms in convention halls and performing arts centers.

poultryman *poultry farmer/breeder, chicken farmer.*

poundmaster retain for official titles; otherwise use *poundkeeper, pound officer/chief/supervisor.*

pound of flesh *See* shylock.

poverty the term is inclusive; the issue is sexist, racist, and classist: a white male head of household has a one-in-nine chance of living in poverty; a black female head of household has a one-in-two chance; nearly one-third of urban-dwelling Native Americans and nearly one-half of those in rural areas live below the poverty line. More than one-third of all the nation's poor children, about 5.6 million of them, live in working-poor families, according to a state-by-state survey of children's well-being by the Annie E. Casey Foundation. Douglas Nelson, executive director of the foundation, says, "Although many factors put children at risk, nothing predicts bad outcomes for a kid more powerfully than growing up poor." After receiving tax breaks and social benefits, 21% of U.S. children still live in poverty, whereas the figures are 3.6% for Belgium, 3.8% for Germany, 3.7% for Sweden, 5.7% for France, 7.3% for the United Kingdom, and 7.6% for Ireland (Organization for Economic Cooperation and Development). Research at Syracuse University and Columbia University confirms that the U.S. has the highest child poverty rate of any major Western industrialized nation; it also has the widest gap between rich and poor families. In our welfare strategies we too often forget that "Poor people are not the enemy. Poverty is the enemy" (Pat Stave Helmberger). *See also* classism, poor, welfare.

powder room *restroom, washroom, lavatory, bathroom, lounge.* This word is sexist in an unexpected way: the "powder" in the phrase comes from the powder men used on their wigs in colonial times, yet today the powder room is reserved for women. The term is also coy and exclusive. *See also* john.

pow-wow "All too often the word 'pow-wow' is used out of context by writers. For those of us who are American Indian, a pow-wow is a dance and social gathering celebrating our traditions and cultures. It is a beautiful and powerful experience. I am offended by the co-opting of the word to describe a nonspiritual dialogue between two people" (Pauline Brunette). The use of "pow-wow" in other than Indian contexts is usually disparaging and offensive. For alternatives consider *talk, discussion, negotiation, dialogue, conversation, chat, confab, conference, parley, meeting.*

prattle "prattle" and most alternatives ("babble," "jabber") are used of women and children, and rarely of men. Examine your material to see if by choosing "prattle" you are making a subtle statement about women. For more inclusive-sounding alternatives use *rattle, rattle away, ramble, blabber, blather, spout, spout off, run off at the mouth, talk nonsense, talk through one's hat, talk idly, shoot the breeze, make chin music, bend someone's ear. See also* chatter, chatterbox.

preacher depending on the denomination, may be a woman or a man.

preadamite *prehuman.* In any case, the term "preadamite" is not a scientific anthropological term.

preceptress *preceptor. See also* "feminine" word endings.

pregnant nonsexist term, but sometimes found in sexist contexts. Is pregnancy treated as an illness, disability, misfortune, or inferior state of being? Is the pregnant woman assumed to be more moody and less capable than other people? Are expectant mothers penalized in the workplace? For sex-neutral terms for "pregnant" in its metaphorical sense, consider *meaningful, profound, momentous, ominous, expectant, suspenseful, waiting, teeming.*

prehistoric man *prehistoric/early peoples/humans, prehumans, fossil humans.* "Prehistoric" is imprecise; unless you mean to convey vagueness, indicate a specific period. Because history is defined as "a record of events," "prehistory" is correct because it refers, not to a time before history as we commonly think of it, but to a time before *recorded* history.

prehominid *See* hominid.

prelate so far, always a man.

premenstrual syndrome/PMS this term, which describes a recognized medical condition, is troublesome when it is either overidentified (using it as an explanation for anything a woman does that one doesn't like) or underidentified (discounted as a reality in the lives of some—but far from all—women). *See also* curse, the.

premier danseur a "premier danseur" is the principal male dancer in a ballet company; his opposite number is the "prima ballerina." Retain "premier danseur" for its narrow meaning within ballet companies, but describe a man who dances ballet nonprofessionally as *lead dancer, principal dancer, first dancer, ballet dancer. See also* ballerina, danseur/danseuse, prima ballerina.

prenuptial agreement "nuptial" has probably moved far enough from its roots ("to take a husband") to be functionally inclusive. Should you want alternatives consider *pre-marriage/pre-wedding agreement/arrangement/contract.*

pressman *press operator/tender/feeder/worker, printer, presser, compositor, typesetter, typographer. See also* newsman.

prick (man) the Title-Says-It-All Department: "'Pricks' and 'Chicks': A Plea for 'Persons,'" (Robert Baker, in Robert Baker and Frederick Elliston, eds., *Philosophy and Sex*).

priest in some faiths, a priest may be a man or a woman; in others they are always men. Knowing how to address a woman priest is not difficult; the most common practice seems to be the use of first names for both female and male clergy. Some women clergy are comfortable being called "Mother," while others say they are not disturbed when they are called "Father"; they accept it pro tem in the spirit in which it is meant. It is never in poor taste to ask a priest what she or he likes to be called. This is a time of transition and few people, including the clergy themselves, have hard and fast guidelines. (Neither male nor female priests are properly addressed orally as "Reverend," however.) *See also* clergyman, minister, priestess, rabbi.

priestess retain "priestess" in historical or present-day contexts where the term reflects a reality that is very positive for women, for example, in the goddess religions. In many instances the term is not second-best but one that offers a model of power and inspiration for women; when "priestess" is just a subset of "priest" use *priest.*

prima ballerina gender-specific terms are still used in professional ballet companies to distinguish between the female first dancer ("prima ballerina") and the male first dancer ("premier danseur"). Retain the narrow usage when referring to members of professional ballet companies, but use inclusive language for others: *ballet dancer, first dancer, star dancer, principal dancer. See also* ballerina, danseur/danseuse, premier danseur.

prima donna *lead, lead opera singer, opera star, leading role, opera/lead/ principal singer/performer.* There is no parallel for men. When describing an overly self-absorbed and temperamental person, it is used (in spite of its plainly feminine cast) for both sexes.

primitive referring to early peoples, indigenous peoples, or other cultures as "primitive" is unacceptable; anthropologists see the term as unhelpful and "loaded." Such a use of "primitive" depends on subjective judgments about such debatable concepts as civilization, intelligence, and social development. "Within the cultures of many people, more value is placed on relationships, and on the maintenance of tradition and spirituality, than on the development and acquisition of machines. It is ethnocentric and racist to apply words like backward, primitive, uncivilized, savage, barbaric, or undeveloped to people whose technology does not include plumbing, microwaves and micro-chips. Are people somehow more human or more humane if they have more technological toys?" (Amoja Three Rivers, *Cultural Etiquette*). "'Primitive' slurringly describes various forms and aspects of human life. No self-respecting social scientist is likely to use it" (Sanford Berman). He says the term "is heavily overlaid with notions of inferiority, childishness, barbarity, and 'state of nature' simplicity, whereas the societies, arts, economic modes, music, and religions it purportedly covers may be extremely complex, ingenious, creative, human, and—depending on taste and *Weltanschauung*—admirable." Replacing "primitive" will vary widely with context; some possible combinations include *folk/traditional/kin-organized/nonmechanized/early/indigenous society. See also* culturally deprived/disadvantaged, heathen, illiterate, pagan, savage, undeveloped/ underdeveloped nation.

primitive man *early people/peoples/societies/human being, cave-dweller, Cro-Magnon, Neanderthals. See also* caveman, prehistoric, primitive.

primogenitor because the "genitor" comes from the word for begetting, "primogenitor" refers to male ancestors. For a sex-neutral alternative use *ancestor, forebear.*

primogeniture in its narrowest sense (the inheritance rights of the firstborn son), "primogeniture" is the correct term to use, although the concept itself is very sexist. In the larger sense of being the firstborn of all the children of the same parents, use *firstborn, firstborn child, eldership, seniority, the rights of the firstborn.*

prince correct sex-specific term for royalty. In the generic sense, its sup- posed feminine parallel ("princess") has quite different connotations and there are no female equivalents for such expressions as "he's a prince," "a real prince," "a prince of a fellow," "a prince among men." For inclusive alternatives use *a real paragon, an ace, the acme of perfection, a trump, a* *marvel, a real lifesaver, a one-off, one in a million, salt of the earth, one of the best, outstanding human being, hero, champion, shining example.*

princely replace with precise, inclusive adjectives: *generous, liberal, bounteous, magnanimous, lavish, profuse, sumptuous, rich, abundant; luxurious, glorious, brilliant; noble, stately, grand, august, awesome, majestic, dignified.*

princess use only for royalty. *See also* prince.

princess dress this term is probably harmless enough in itself, although all the "princess" language has not been good for women. For alternatives describe the dress precisely or consider *flared/close-fitting/waistless dress.*

princess phone a small, lightweight phone introduced in 1959 and originally advertised as a private phone for teenage girls, this model was not produced after 1984 when its manufacturer, Western Electric, went out of business.

prioress this term denotes a woman with power and stature usually equal to that of a prior's. For the generic sense of "prioress" or "prior," you might use *religious, superior, administrator, director. See also* "feminine" word endings.

prisoner 95% of inmates in state prisons are men; more than 90% of those in jail are men. There is a disproportionate number of minority prisoners; several states are questioning whether statutes, rules, or practices in the court systems cause unfairness. Other groups are looking at social causes. *See also* bad guy, glass cellar.

prizeman *prizewinner, prizeholder.*

prizemaster *prize officer.* Retain in historical contexts.

PR man *PR agent.*

pro-abortion *pro-choice, abortion rights advocates.* Avoid "pro-abortion" as nobody views abortion as a good thing in itself; the "pro-choice" view is that it is sometimes better than the alternatives and always the decision of the woman concerned. "No one wants an abortion as she wants an ice-cream cone or a Porsche. She wants an abortion as an animal, caught in a trap, wants to gnaw off its own leg. Abortion is a tragic attempt to escape a desperate situation by an act of violence and self-loss" (Frederica Mathewes-Green, in *Policy Review*). *See also* abortion debate language, pro-choice.

problem expressions like "the Indian problem," "the black problem," and "the Jewish problem" have disgracefully associated victims with the results of their abuse. Where there is a problem, there must be a solution; Hitler's "final solution" to "the Jewish problem" illustrates how inappropriate "problem" terminology is. There was no "black problem" until four million people were brought to the U.S. as slaves (and without racism and discrimination it is possible there would be no "black problem" today); there was no "Indian problem" until virtually an entire people was killed, dispossessed, impoverished, and isolated; there was no "Jewish problem" until Nazi Germany needed a scapegoat. Identify instead the real issues: oppression, discrimination, racism, poverty, race relations, restitution for stolen lands, violence, etc. *See also* final solution, Jewish question.

pro-choice this is the term preferred by women and men who believe that each woman (not government, doctors, or clergy) should make the choice in her own case whether to have an abortion; the term "pro-abortion" is both inaccurate and highly offensive to this group. *See also* abortion debate language, abortionist, anti-choice, pro-abortion, pro-life.

proconsul Roman proconsuls were all men, as are almost all modern administrators of colonies, dependencies, and occupied areas.

procreate procreation is shared equally by men and woman. When speaking of it, sometimes use "beget" and sometimes use "give birth to."

procuress *procurer. See also* "feminine" word endings.

prodigal son *prodigal, returned prodigal, the prodigal one, the prodigal, one who returns to the fold, lost lamb; profligate, wastrel, squanderer, scattergood, waster, spendthrift, high liver.*

professional/pro while these terms have always been complimentary when referring to men, they were often synonymous with "prostitute" when referring to women. Although this usage is no longer so prevalent, occasionally the terms might be ambiguous (and their dichotomous usage reveals much about our sexism). Although the differences between "the professions" and "the trades" and between "white-collar" workers and "blue-collar" workers might occasionally be useful, many times the distinctions are gratuitous and classist. *See also* businessman, executive, glass ceiling.

Professional Secretaries Day/Week established with good intentions in 1952 by the National Secretaries Association (since 1981 Professional Secretaries International), these "holidays" have become problematic for many people. Some consider them a sexist (99% of secretaries are women) and exclusionary (leaves out other equally valued employees) substitute for a proper thank you for a job well done. Anne M. Dimock says, "Once we institutionalize gratitude, we lose the reason to distinguish and reward unique contributions made throughout the year." Professional groups suggest that if the tradition continues (broadened to "Staff Appreciation Day" to include everyone), lunch with the boss (a dubious pleasure in many cases) or flowers and candy could be replaced with a day off with pay, the chance to attend a seminar, or a special bonus to allow secretaries to buy professional handbooks or pay dues to a professional organization. Most bosses tend to think secretaries want flowers; few actually do.

professor emeritus *See* emeritus.

project *subsidized housing, public housing development.* "Project" has become a code word to connote poverty, crime, and dilapidation, all usually attributed to minority groups. *See also* ghetto.

pro-life this is the term preferred by men and women who oppose abortion, not only for themselves but for everyone else; they believe it should be outlawed in the United States. Pro-life stances range from opposing abortion for any reason whatsoever (and also opposing contraception) to favoring contraception and accepting abortion as a possibility in a few narrowly delimited instances. Some pro-life individuals are one-issue people (focused only on opposing abortion) while others define "pro-life" by a spectrum of issues (opposing the death penalty, fighting the causes and effects of poverty, and promoting justice and global peace). Some newspapers prefer "anti-abortion" because "pro-life" implies others are anti-life; it also focuses on the group's principal objective—where some people in the movement may be concerned about other issues, all pro-life individuals oppose abortion. "Pro-lifer" is sometimes derogatory. *See also* abortion debate language, abortionist, anti-choice, pro-abortion, pro-choice.

prolocutrix *prolocutor. See also* "feminine" word endings.

promiscuous this term tends to be judgmental and imprecise, referring to the lack of discrimination in the choice of (multiple) sexual partners. But it is difficult to know when to start labeling someone "promiscuous"—after 3 partners? 10? 20? if they choose partners who are unemployed, less educated than they, with bad reputations? Women are labeled promiscuous much more often than men; Julia Penelope Stanley found 220 terms in English that describe a sexually promiscuous woman, but only 22 for a sexually promiscuous man. She notes that there is no linguistic reason why the first set is large and the second set small. In its connotations of indiscriminate and irresponsible, it has some limited use.

pronouns for information on pseudogeneric "he," *see* pp. 6–9 of the Writing Guidelines. *See also* animal/he, automobile/she, church/she, devil/he, enemy/he, nature/she, singular "they."

propertyman/prop man *property/prop coordinator/attendant/handler/supervisor.*

prophet in his own country, no man is a *See* no man is a prophet in his own country.

prophetess *prophet. See also* "feminine" word endings.

proprietress *proprietor. See also* "feminine" word endings.

prostitute a prostitute may be either sex. Use the clear, simple word "prostitute" instead of the hundreds of slurs or euphemisms: baggage, bawd, B-girl, call girl, chippie/chippy, doxy, drab, fallen woman, fancy girl/ woman, floozie/floozy, hussy, lady of the night, magdalen, painted woman, pavement princess, piece, pro/pross/prossie/prostie/prosty, round heels, scarlet woman, sidewalk hostess, streetwalker, strumpet, tail, trollop, trull, woman of easy virtue/ill fame/ill repute, working woman. There are male prostitutes but the male-dominated language has been slow to name them, which is why all the foregoing words apply only to women. The words we use to describe those involved in prostitution are some of the most interesting and revealing in the language. Prostitution involving adults is a takes-two-to-tango operation and could not survive without the active and continued participation of both parties. Yet our language in no way treats prostitute and prostitute user equally. If there is an imbalance, if there is a victim, it is the prostitute who is often disadvantaged, compelled by poverty, a pimp, or a drug habit to maintain the system. The prostitute user does not suffer from similar life-and-death compulsions. Yet by naming prostitutes pejoratively, society apportions to them all the blame, all the "badness." Muriel R. Schulz reported finding roughly 1,000 words and phrases describing women in sexually derogatory ways; she cites a 1965 study (J. S. Farmer and W. E. Henley) that found over 500 synonyms for "prostitute" in English alone but only 65 synonyms for "whoremonger." We still have several hundred synonyms for "prostitute" today, but when it comes to the men who do with prostitutes that which supposedly makes the prostitutes bad women, we have only four generally used words for them: john, trick, score, date. "John" is a nice word. Many people name their sons John. "Trick" and "score" are not too shabby either; they are both used (although not in that sense) in polite society. And "date" is even more innocuous. Virtually none of the prostitute words have this double life; they live only on the streets. Until we find and use words for prostitute and prostitute user that are inclusive or symmetrical, we perpetuate a coverup for half the people involved in prostitution. A good start is to eliminate all terms for prostitutes except "prostitute"; this matter-of-fact word is as informative and descriptive as it needs to be and it can be used for both sexes. Tarting up the business with expressions like "lady of pleasure" and "pavement princess" is the worst kind of doublespeak. For want of a better term, call the prostitute's partner a "prostitute user." The user should be linguistically associated with the prostitute. Eliminate coverup terms like outcall service, escort service, red light district, call-girl service, brothel, bordello, call house; they are houses of prostitution or prostitution services. Before we can effectively discuss what prostitution is and what it does to those involved in it, we need an unbiased, forthright vocabulary. *See also* camp follower, courtesan, demimondaine, grisette, harlot/harlotry, hooker, houseboy/housegirl, Jezebel/jezebel, kept woman, lady of easy virtue/of pleasure/of the evening/of the night, loose woman, madam, sex worker, slattern, slut, tart, tramp (woman), wench, whore.

protectress *protector. See also* "feminine" word endings.

protégé/protégée *protégé* for both sexes. "Protégée" is defined in most dictionaries as "a female protégé," thus removing women one step from the real thing. Note that émigré, exactly parallel in construct, is used in English for both sexes. *See also* "feminine" word endings.

provider just as the caregiver role—as the primary work option—has limited, dehumanized, and oppressed some women, the provider role—as the primary work option—has limited, dehumanized, and oppressed some men. Men bring home more bacon than women, but many of them consider the economic benefits associated with their gender to be a mixed blessing. The notion that "it's a man's world" has obscured the fact that along with benefits have come severe lifestyle restrictions, stress, economic pressures and responsibilities, unrealistic social expectations, and being judged by criteria not applied to women. As more women providers join men in taking on toxic work loads, personal and societal goals may need to be reevaluated to help fashion a more lifegiving balance between work life and non-work life. The following words are theoretically inclusive, but we use them largely to penalize men for not being providers or "good enough" providers: also-ran, born loser, deadbeat, derelict, do-nothing, down-and-outer, dud, failure, freeloader, goldbricker, good-for-nothing, hard-luck case, idler, layabout, lazybones, lightweight, loafer, mooch, ne'er-do-well, nonstarter, parasite, piker, prodigal, schlemiel, shirker, skinflint, slacker, sponge, washout, wastrel. Traditionally a male "loser" is a financial failure—someone who can't "provide"; a woman who is a "loser" fails to be sexually attractive. *See also* breadwinner, bring home the bacon, bum, glass cellar, male privilege, masculine mystique, success object.

provocative when describing ideas or intellectual properties, "provocative" is nonsexist and meaningful. In a social or sexual situation, however, the word's connotations make it difficult to use fairly and factually. Too often it is women who are "provocative"—eternal Eves luring endless numbers of passive Adams. *See also* provoke.

provoke this word crops up frequently as a "reason" for beating, raping, and even killing women. A man in a domestic violence program explains, "I know I shouldn't hit her, but I can't seem to stop. The bitch really asks for it, you know. She really provokes me." When Carol S. Irons, the first female judge in Kent County, Michigan, was shot to death in her chambers by her estranged husband, the jury convicted him of a lesser crime (voluntary manslaughter instead of the first-degree murder charge) because, as one juror put it, "Everybody felt he was provoked by his wife to do this." A judge ruled that a 5-year-old girl was a "temptress" in "provoking" a sexual encounter with a 20-year-old man (Nijole V. Benokraitis and Joe R. Feagin, *Modern Sexism*). After Linda Simmons's husband, a hospital pathologist, killed her as she was walking out the door with their two young children, he told police, "She just wouldn't quit bugging me"—presumably about his severe and longstanding alcoholism. A man who strangled his woman friend after they had argued about Christmas toys said, "I did it, I did it. . . . I can't believe I killed her, I did it, I can't believe she made me that mad." *See also* "she asked for it."

prudent man (legal) *prudent person/individual. See also* reasonable man.

pseudogeneric words that purport to include everyone, but that in fact do not, are pseudogenerics. "A Muslim people of the northern Caucasus, the 1.3 million Chechens are dark-haired and tawny skinned, often with lush mustaches" (the *New York Times International*). "People" here is a pseudogeneric; it was intended to mean all Chechens, but "lush mustaches" betrays the writer's sense that the definitive people are men. *See also* he (pseudogeneric), man/Man (pseudogeneric), mankind (pseudogeneric).

public relations man *publicist, public relations/PR agent/practitioner/ director/executive/representative/specialist, promoter, publicity/press agent, booster, promoter, advance agent, propagandist, public information manager/officer, publicity writer. See also* adman, PR man, spokesman.

puerile the Latin "puer" means either boy or child. If you want a more strictly neutral alternative consider *juvenile, childish.*

Puerto Rican since Puerto Rico is an independent commonwealth of the United States, Puerto Ricans are U.S. citizens. José Cuello says many Puerto Ricans who live on the island, as well as Nuyoricans on the U.S. mainland, reject the image and heritage of being colonized by Europeans and use the term Boricua, derived from Boriquén, the Arawak Indian name of the island, instead of Puerto Rico (Wayne State University, for example, has a Center for Chicano-Boricua Studies).

Pullman car/pullman porter named after its inventor, George M. Pullman. You can avoid the masculine look of "pullman porter" with *porter, train attendant, red cap.*

pumpman *pumper.*

purdah purdah (literally, "curtain") is the pattern of veiled and secluded domesticity that characterizes the lives of certain Muslim, South Asian, and Hindu women. Emily C. Smith, member of Muslim Women of Minnesota, says, "Muslim women do not aspire to feminism on the Western model. Instead, they pursue the rights guaranteed to them in their own religious law, which 1,400 years ago granted them independent legal status and rights of voting, inheritance, and divorce. The adoption of Islamic dress is often a political statement by which the wearer rejects the sexual exploitation of women while reaffirming that she does not need to mimic customs and manners foreign to her own culture. To assume that the Muslim woman is universally oppressed is an insult which disregards the achievements of millions of our Muslim sisters worldwide." The Action Committee of Women Living Under Muslim Laws is involved in efforts to raise consciousness among Muslim women about what is really Islamic and what is being passed off as Islamic by religious and political vested interests to reinforce male political and social domination over women. *See also* harem.

purse strings despite the "purse," this isn't particularly sex-linked; historically both sexes carried purses and today the term is functionally nonsexist. Should you want alternatives consider *financial support/resources, control over financial support/resources; hold all the cards, lay down the law, run the place/show, call the shots/plays, be in the saddle/driver's seat, have under control, wear the crown, boss.*

pushy *See* aggressive.

pussy this vulgar slang for the vulva is also a derogatory term for a woman. For younger people it has come to be synonymous with "wimp," "loser," and other derogatory terms (Rosalyn Glorso).

pussy-whipped this is like "henpecked," only vulgar. For alternatives consider *bossed around, bullied, browbeaten, soul not one's own, passive, submissive, dominated, subjugated, under someone's thumb, led by the nose, at one's beck and call, ruled with an iron hand, in leading strings. See also* henpecked, pussy.

putty man *puttier.*

PWA/PWLA/PLA acceptable abbreviations for "person with AIDS" or "person living with AIDS." *See also* afflicted with, AIDS, AIDS victim, innocent victim, victim.

pygmy there are no peoples who call themselves "pygmies"; replace this ethnocentric, Eurocentric term with specific, authentic peoples' names (Mbuti, Twa, etc.).

Words set things in motion. I've seen them doing it.
Words set up atmospheres, electrical fields, charges.

—*Toni Cade Bambara*

In a ward on fire, we must
find words
or burn.

—*Olga Broumas*

quadriplegic *someone with/who has quadriplegia.* If necessary to mention a disability, information can be conveyed without labeling the whole person by something that is only part of their life. Quadriplegia is a paralysis of the body from the neck down. *See also* disability/disabilities, hemiplegic, paraplegic, "people-first" rule.

quail (girl/woman) *See* animal names for people.

Quakeress *Quaker.* Although the word "Quaker" was at one time used derogatorily, it was adopted early on by the members of the Religious Society of Friends. Today the word Quaker has a long and honorable history; it is used interchangeably with Friend. *See also* "feminine" word endings.

qualified this is a good word sometimes found in the wrong places, i.e., "qualifying" people whose qualifications would be taken for granted if they were, for example, white, male, young, and able-bodied. "Why is the word 'qualified' applied only to those who have to be more so?" (Gloria Steinem, *Moving Beyond Words*). Use cautiously.

quality-control man *quality controller, quality-control engineer/inspector/ supervisor/evaluator.*

quarryman *quarrier, quarry worker.*

quartermaster in the Army this term refers to a field of specialization, not to an individual; members of this branch include supply sergeants, supply officers, and supply NCOs. In the Navy and Coast Guard, "quartermaster" is a job title or rank used for both women and men involved in navigation. Civilian equivalents might include: *petty officer, quarterdeck; commissary, provisioner, storekeeper, victualer; navigator, small craft/ large ship operator.* The Air Force and the Marine Corps do not use the term "quartermaster"; they call their supply branches "individual equipment" (Air Force) or "supply" (Marines).

queen (royalty) acceptable sex-specific word. If you need a gender-free term try *ruler, monarch, sovereign, crowned head, leader.*

queen (verb) women "queen it over" others while men "lord it over." While somewhat asymmetric, the terms are functionally benign. Should you need inclusive alternatives consider: *have the upper hand, hold something over someone's head, wear the crown, hold court, have/get it all one's own way, have the game in one's own hand/corner/court.*

queen (gay man) this term is unacceptable when used by non-gays. Gay men might use it among themselves. *See also* "insider/outsider" rule.

queen bee correct when referring to the inhabitant of a hive. If you want a less sex-specific expression for its metaphorical use consider *big wheel.* For additional terms, *see also* high man on the totem pole, prima donna.

queen consort in referring to the wife of a reigning king, it is acceptable to drop the word "consort" except in some narrow circumstances (legal or historical references and official titles).

queenlike/queenly there is nothing particularly biased about these sex-specific words, but, like most stereotypes, they are vague. If you want more precise adjectives consider: *regal, imperial, noble, dignified, imposing, impressive, stately, majestic, commanding, haughty.*

queen-size terms like this give new meaning to the roles of kings and queens as "rulers." The term is irreplaceable because of its specific descriptions of beds and bed linen (where the use of "single," "double," "queen," and "king" is standard) and its euphemistic use for such items as queen-size pantyhose. However, it undergirds the female-as-lesser/smaller perspective, and if you simply mean "very large," you might consider one of the many synonyms of huge. *See also* king-size.

queer "For decades the term 'queer' was used pejoratively. In recent years, thanks to groups like ACT UP and Queer Nation, many gay people have reclaimed 'queer,' using it to describe the many and sometimes outrageous facets of our gay selves and communities. 'Queer' is sometimes used as shorthand for 'l/g/b/t,' and some people even use the word 'queer' to describe those straight people who have a cutting-edge attitude toward their own sexuality" (Lynn Witt, Sherry Thomas, Eric Marcus, eds., *Out in All Directions*). The Gay and Lesbian Alliance Against Defamation (GLAAD) says the term has been appropriated by some gay men and lesbians to describe themselves; "Some value the term for its defiance and because it is inclusive—not only of lesbians and gay men but of bisexuals and transgendered people as well. Nevertheless, it is not universally accepted within our communities, and used out of context it is still derogatory." The use of the term by Queer Nation, which emerged in August 1990, "most often sets up queerness as something different from gay, lesbian, and bisexual assimilationism. In this case, to identify as a queer means to be politically radical and 'in-your-face': to paradoxically demand recognition by straight culture while at the same time rejecting this culture" (Alexander Doty, *Making Things Perfectly Queer*). ACT UP's slogan is, "We're here. We're queer. Get used to it." Not all gay men and lesbians like the term; Internet postings show that some love it, some hate it, and some only tolerate it. Some feel it is emblematic of self-hatred and internalized homophobia; others think it portrays lesbians and gay men as other than normal, everyday people; some feel it is overly inclusive; and one person wanted to know why it should be reclaimed: "Garbage is garbage." The use of "queer" has given rise to a word for the violence against gay men and lesbians: queer bashing. Use "queer" with gay abandon when you so self-identify or when you might expect your readership to appreciate it. Otherwise, avoid it and others based on it ("queer beer," "queer as a three-dollar bill"). *See also* homosexual.

quizmaster *quiz show host.* Use for both women and men.

quotas *See* affirmative action.

quotation marks quotation marks are used to question the legitimacy of a word or phrase, e.g., "Indian giver," "all-American," "Yellow Peril." Sometimes they impute dubiousness where there is none. Journalist Susan Berkson writes, "George Will came up with another boffo idea: To silence any radical feminist criticism, put basic facts—'sexual violence,' 'survivors,' 'silencing'—in quotation marks, calling into question their very existence." Use quotation marks to imply that something is "so-called" or "alleged" or to express your disagreement with a concept; be wary of using them to disparage other people's realities.

al-Qur'an this is the preferred term (instead of Koran) for the sacred text of Islam.

R

They say that there is no reality before it has been given shape by words rules
regulations. They say that in what concerns them everything has to be remade
starting from basic principles. They say that in the first place the vocabulary of
every language is to be examined, modified, turned upside down,
that every word must be screened.

—Monique Wittig

Nowadays a word is a deed whose consequences cannot be measured.

—Heinrich Heine

rabbi women are rabbis in the Conservative, Reform, and Reconstructionist
branches of Judaism, and they are addressed like men rabbis: "rabbi."
There are no women rabbis in the Orthodox branch.

race the use of this word "to refer to a group of persons who share common
physical characteristics and form a discrete and separable population unit
has no scientific validity, since evolutionary theory and physical anthropology have long since demonstrated that there are not fixed or discrete
groups in human populations. . . . However as a folk concept in Western
and non-Western societies the concept of race is a powerful and important one, which is employed in order to classify and systematically
exclude members of given groups from fully participating in the social
system controlled by the dominant group" *(Macmillan Dictionary of
Anthropology)*. "There are no pure races in any meaningful sense, only
large geographical groupings whose genetic histories can never be fully
known. . . . the terminology of race has shifted in recent years from
anthropological classifications toward a more flexible language of
geography, culture, and color" *(American Heritage Book of English
Usage)*. Amoja Three Rivers *(Cultural Etiquette)* says, "If there ever was
any such thing as race (which there isn't), there has been so much
constant criss-crossing of genes for the last 500,000 years, that it would

have lost all meaning anyway." Clyde W. Ford *(We Can All Get Along)* suggests discarding "this outmoded term" and replacing it "with another term like ethnic group, ethnicity, cultural background, nationality, or human variation when speaking about differences among human beings. The term race is loaded with a history of fiction, conflict, violence, and racism." In *The Idea of Race,* Ashley Montagu says, "The idea of 'race' as a widespread secular belief is, in fact, no older than the nineteenth century. . . . In part because of that phrase, 'All men are created equal,' and, of course, because of all those other conditions that bound them to support the institution, the defenders of slavery felt it necessary to show that the Negro was biologically unequal to the white man, both in his physical traits and in his mental capacities. . . . it was in this way that the doctrine of racism was born." As long ago as 1936 biologist Julian Huxley and anthropologist Alfred Cort Haddon found the biological concept of race wanting; "It is very desirable that the term *race* as applied to human groups should be dropped from the vocabulary of science" *(We Europeans: A Survey of "Racial" Problems).* Although terms like "racism" are necessary to a discussion of these issues and to denote the entrenched bias that the false concept of "race" has underwritten, the word "race" itself is best avoided or used very carefully. *See also* multiracial, racism.

racial preference the National Association of Black Journalists advises against using "racial preference"; they recommend terms such as "race-based remedies," "affirmative action programs," and "policies designed to benefit women and racial minorities," which they say are more accurate and neutral. *See also* affirmative action.

racism any attitude, action, social policy, or institutional structure that discriminates against a person or a group because of their color constitutes racism (a term Nigel Rees dates from 1936). More specifically, racism is the subordination of people of color by white people. "While an individual person of color may discriminate against white people or even hate them, his or her behavior or attitude cannot be called 'racist.' He or she may be considered *prejudiced* against whites and we may all agree that the person acts unfairly and unjustly, but *racism* requires something more than anger, hatred, or prejudice; at the very least, it requires *prejudice plus power*. The history of the world provides us with a long record of white people holding power and using it to maintain that power and privilege over people of color, not the reverse" (Paula S. Rothenberg, *Racism and Sexism*). "Racism is not just the sum total of all the individual acts in which white people discriminate, harass, stereotype or otherwise mistreat people of color. The accumulated effects of centuries of white racism have given it an institutional nature which is more entrenched than racial prejudice. In fact, it is barely touched by changes in individual white consciousness. We often find it difficult to see or to know how to challenge institutional racism because we are so used to focusing on individual actions and attitudes" (Paul Kivel, *Uprooting Racism*). Johnetta B. Cole (in *McCall's*) says poverty alone will not explain why more college-age African American men are in prison, jail, or on parole than in college, that poverty and sexism alone will not explain why a black woman has only one chance in 21,000 of receiving a doctorate in mathematics, engineering, or the physical sciences. Only racism can explain why a young African American woman has one chance in five of dropping out of high school, and three chances in five of becoming pregnant before age twenty, why a black baby has a nearly one in two chance of being born poor, and why a black infant is twice as likely as a white baby to die before its first birthday. Zora Neale Hurston *(Dust Tracks on a Road)* wrote, "Light came to me when I realized that I did not have to consider any racial group as a whole. God made them duck by duck and that was the only way I could see them." *See also* race.

racketeer functionally sexist; although women may be involved in racketeering, there are not many of them and they are rarely called racketeers. *See also* bad guy.

raconteur this French word is grammatically masculine (and its partner, "raconteuse," evidently stayed in France) but is used in English for both sexes. If you want a more inclusive-sounding alternative consider *storyteller, anecdotist, teller of tales, taleteller, talespinner, spinner of yarns, romancer, monologuist, narrator. See also* diseur/diseuse.

radarman *radar operator.*

radioman *radio technician/operator/repairer/engineer.*

raftsman *rafter.*

ragman *ragpicker, rag collector, junk dealer/collector.*

raise Cain there is nothing wrong with using this phrase, but be aware of how many such expressions in the English language are male-based. Balance their use with female-based expressions, creative expressions of your own, or sex-neutral alternatives: *make mischief/a fuss, carry on, lose one's temper, fly off the handle, flare up, run amok, raise a rumpus/a storm/a hue and cry/the devil/hell, castigate, lecture, rail, fulminate, find fault; be boisterous/loud/rowdy/disorderly, disturb the peace. See also* sex-linked expressions.

rajah always a man; the woman is a "rani."

rake because this term is used only for men and there is no true parallel for women, consider *libertine, swinger, bedhopper, free spirit, high-roller, dissolute person. See also* ladies' man, man about town, womanizer.

rallymaster *rally director/organizer.*

ranchman *rancher. **See also** cattleman, cowboy.*

randy this adjective has no connection with a male name (it most likely comes from "to rant"). ***See also*** horny.

rape 99% of all victims of rape are women; figures indicate that a woman is raped every 3.5–5 minutes in the United States, that one of four women is raped during her lifetime, that 25% of college women have been victims of rape or attempted rape, that the rape rate is increasing four times as fast as the overall crime rate, and that only about one rape in six is reported to the police. Insights into the alarming increase in rape: one of eight Hollywood films has rape scenes; men who watch R-rated films are less likely to think a woman is being brutalized during a re-enactment of a rape than those who haven't seen the movies; discussing a TV scene, actor Michael Paré said, "It's not going to be a violent rape, where the guy rapes her and kills her. It's going to be a friendly rape"; in one study, one of 12 men surveyed admitted to acts that met the legal definition of rape; in another study, a majority of children surveyed thought rape was acceptable; New York City rape arrests of 13-year-old boys increased 200% in a recent two-year period; less than 3% of charged rapists go to prison; one man who admitted raping a woman was given no prison time (despite guidelines and a plea agreement for at least four years in prison) because the judge knew the woman from a divorce case he handled several years earlier and thought she was "pitiful" (the judge advised the man to be more careful in choosing women); police departments are either ill-equipped or ill-motivated to pursue rapists—a few years ago the Oakland, California, police department had to reopen 203 rape cases that had been dropped without even minimal investigation; less than half the states have laws allowing charges of spousal rape. Obstacles to dealing effectively with rape include the myths surrounding it. One says that nobody can be sexually assaulted against their will; in fact, 87% of all adult rape victims are faced with weapons, death threats, or threats of bodily harm, and nearly one-fifth of all rapes involve two or more assailants. In almost 90% of the cases, victims attempt self-protective measures such as physical force, threats, or calling for help. Rape victims range from infants to people over 80; about one-fifth of all rape victims are aged 12–15. Although another myth says women "ask for it" by dressing or behaving seductively or by being in the wrong place at the wrong time, studies indicate that 60%–70% of rapes are planned in advance; victims' actions have little effect on the outcome. Since rape does not involve sexual desire, but rather violence and power, "seductiveness" is not a factor. We tend to react differently to property crimes than to crimes against persons. A prosperous-looking man who is robbed is

rarely accused of "asking for it" by the way he was dressed (rape victims'
attire and manner are often a big issue in court); when a woman gives
frequently to charity, we don't fail to call it a crime if someone robs her
on the theory that she doesn't appear to mind "giving it away" (women's
sex lives are often cited against them in rape cases, on the theory that this
wasn't anything they hadn't done before); if a man gives money to
members of his family, it is still wrong for his wife and children to steal
from him (women who report date rape or husband rape are told that
since they have previously been willing to have sex, they have no recourse when sex is forced on them). The racist twist to rape is not the one
of myth: "the rape of black women by white males has been far more
commonplace than the white fantasy about black men raping white
women suggests" and it is "still a serious problem for black women in
some parts of the United States" (Nijole V. Benokraitis and Joe R.
Feagin, *Modern Sexism*). Some cautions in using the term "rape": (1)
consider using the construction "men raping women" rather than "women
are being raped"; Sonia Johnson *(Going Out of Our Minds)* says that
when we say "'women are raped,' the syntax helps convey the impression
that *women* do the acting, that *women* are responsible. But when I say
instead, 'Today, men in this country raped over 2000 women,' I lay the
responsibility exactly where it belongs. Rape is *not* passive. Women are
not raped. *Men rape women.*" (2) Avoid using "rape" in the figurative
sense ("rape of the taxpayers")—it devalues the original meaning. *See
also* date rape, provoke, rape victim, rapist, sexual harassment, "she
asked for it," victim, violence.

rape victim there is an increasing tendency for a person to self-identify as
rape survivor. Discussing the language of rape of women, Tami Spry
(*Women and Language*, Fall 1995), says, "the agency of a woman as
meaning maker of her own experience is denied in having to choose
between the categories of victim or survivor. The pain and confusion
following the assault is further complicated by having to structure and
make sense of her experience within the assailant's language. . . . How
can one tell a story of sexual violence from a woman's bodily narrative
point of view? . . . The language of victor or survivor defines the meaning
of the assault in relation to *his* action rather than her experience; she
survived *it* or was a victim of *it*. . . . the narrative focus, the *primary*
experiential focus is on the male perpetrator, what *he* did and why *he* did
it." The most important caution in writing or speaking of rape victims is
to avoid blaming them; although this is usually done indirectly, it is
damaging and indefensible. The myth is that most sexual assaults are
provoked by, or preventable by, the victim, when in fact 60% to 70% of
all rapes are planned in advance; nothing the victim does or doesn't do

can avert it. There is no agreement on the pros and cons of publicly identifying survivors of rape; use someone's name only with their express permission as there are good reasons not to further expose the person at such a vulnerable time. But not using a name so that nobody will know about it seems to imply that there is something shameful about having been raped, when in fact the shame—and the crime—belong to the man who committed the rape. Suzette Haden Elgin (*The Lonesome Node*, 1991) says the ugly truth about not publicizing rape victims' names "is because most of our society looks upon them as *damaged goods.*" Although nearly all reported rape victims are women, the fact remains that men are raped, particularly in prisons where rape is a common way of maintaining an inmate power structure; be careful of excluding men from the term "rape victim" or assuming that victim and violator are of different sexes. *See also* date rape, rape, rapist, "she asked for it," survivor, victim, violence.

rapist in a letter to the St. Paul *Pioneer Press*, Naomi Lifejoy writes, "Why isn't it called a raper? It seems that some words that describe what people do have an 'ist' at the end, and they command a certain degree of respectability, such as scientist, archeologist, biologist, balloonist. Rapist sounds like too soft a word to me. We say robber, not robbist; killer, not killist; abuser, not abusist. Why then do we not say raper, rather than rapist?" A comparison of prestigious "-ist" words (dentist, scientist, therapist, geneticist, ophthalmologist, gynecologist, metallurgist, etc.) with criminal "-er" words (murderer, slayer, poisoner, strangler, sniper, knifer, slaughterer, destroyer, bloodshedder, shoplifter, mugger, etc.) would support Lifejoy's concern. (There may be others, but "arsonist" was the only exception found.) *See also* man-hater/woman-hater, rape, rape victim, violence.

Rastafarian not all Jamaicans are Rastafarians; not all Rastafarians are Jamaicans; not all people with dreadlocks are Rastafarians (Amoja Three Rivers, *Cultural Etiquette*). Use only for those who self-identify this way.

Raza, La *See* La Raza.

real father/mother/parent *biological mother/father/parent, birth father/ mother/parent.* Describing birth or biological parents as "real" implies that adoptive relationships are artificial, tentative, less important, and less enduring. *See also* adoption language, biological father/mother/parent.

real McCoy, the this is used of men, women, and objects, even though the original was a man: according to *Why Do We Say It?* a prize fighter by name of McCoy was being annoyed by a drunk whose friends tried to tell him that this was the great McCoy. McCoy eventually fought the man who, when he came to, said, "You're right. He's the real McCoy."

reasonable and prudent man (law) *reasonable and prudent person/*

individual; reasonable, prudent person; reasonable person; the ordinary, reasonable, prudent person (ORP person); the average person; objective standard of reasonableness. See also reasonable woman (law).

reasonable woman (law) "In determining whether conduct or statements are sufficiently severe to rise to the level of unlawful sexual harassment, some state courts have relied upon a 'reasonable woman' standard. Under federal law, however, an objective standard, the 'reasonable person' standard, as well as the victim's subjective perception are applied to determine whether a hostile or abusive work environment exists" (N. Elizabeth Fried, *Sex, Laws and Stereotypes*). The "reasonable man" does not always agree with the "reasonable woman" about exactly what constitutes sexual harassment. *See also* reasonable and prudent man.

rector depending on the denomination or educational institution, this may be either a woman or a man.

redhead this is much more likely to be used of a woman than of a man. It's not offensive in itself and has its uses but, in general, question the labeling of people by facets of their appearance and the need to talk about women's hair.

red light district *prostitution district.* (One explanation for the term is that train crews left their red lanterns outside the house of prostitution so they could be located in case of an emergency. When those who ran the houses realized this was an excellent way to advertise, the custom spread.)

red man *American Indian, Native American, first American.* Or, use specific name (Chippewa, Anishinabe). *See also* Indian, Native American, redskin, Redskins (sports team name).

redneck this classist, judgmental, and inflammatory term is used mostly of men. If you mean "bigot" or "racist" or "conservative," use those terms instead of the vague "redneck"; all it conveys is that you don't much like the person.

redskin this reference to American Indians is always unacceptable. *See also* Redskins (sports team name).

Redskins (sports team name) the use of Indian names for sports teams (e.g., Atlanta Braves, Cleveland Indians, Kansas City Chiefs, and Washington Redskins) is considered by various dictionaries, groups, and individuals to be derogatory, demeaning, disparaging, defamatory, racist, offensive, and insensitive. *Indian Country Today,* the largest Indian weekly in the U.S.; the National Indian Education Association; the National Congress of American Indians (NCAI); as well as other national and regional Indian and non-Indian organizations have long advocated the end of Indian-oriented mascots and nicknames for sports teams. NCAI says, "Our sacred songs, dances, ceremonies, languages and religions are precious to us as a people." In a letter to the editor of the St. Paul *Pioneer Press*, Bill Pensoneau writes, "The bottom line is that only Indians can say what is offensive, regardless of the intent. If we say 'Redskins' reminds us of massacres, believe us." In 1992, the Portland *Oregonian* discontinued use of sports teams' names and nicknames such as "Redskins, Redmen, Indians, and Braves." In 1994, the Minneapolis *Star Tribune* announced a policy of eliminating offensive Indian nicknames; they refer to the "Redskins," for example, as "the Washington football team" or simply "Washington." (Note the analogous and reprehensible practice of using American Indian names for weapons and equipment in the U.S. military; Daniel A. Buford, in *Conscience*, lists the H-13 Sioux, CH-21 Shawnee, UH-1A Iroquois, H-19B Chickasaw, OH-58A Kiowa, T-41 Mescalero, CH-47A Chinook, Chief, AH-64A Apache, OV-1 Mohawk, Tomahawk, U-8F Seminole.)

reformed alcoholic *recovering alcoholic. See also* alcoholic.

refugee by definition, a refugee is fleeing war, political oppression, or religious persecution; "refugee" is not interchangeable with "immigrant" (someone who chooses to relocate) and it is not used for people who have been in a country long enough to be settled. *See also* illegal alien.

regal/regalia/regent these words are based on the Latin "rex" for king, but they no longer have any strong male associations, except perhaps for those who know Latin. Either a woman or a man may be regal or a regent.

Reilly/Riley, leading the life of *See* leading the life of Reilly/Riley.

reinsman *driver, coach/sulky driver, horse racer.*

relocation Executive Order 9066, signed by President Franklin D. Roosevelt on February 19, 1942, empowered the Secretary of War to carry out a mass internment policy involving anyone of Japanese descent. West-coast Japanese Americans (two-thirds of whom were U.S. citizens) were forced into hastily built prisons in western desert regions. Among violated Constitutional rights were freedom of speech, freedom from unreasonable searches and seizures, the right to be informed by charges, the right to a speedy and public trial, the right to legal counsel, the right to a trial by jury, and the right to equal protection under the law. In an article in *Rethinking Schools* (Fall 1996), Mark Sweeting writes, "Fifty years ago the term used to describe the internment was 'relocation.' That it is still used in textbooks to describe the internment is discouraging."

remainderman *remainderer, remainder agent, reversioner.* "Remainderperson" has been seen, but is not recommended.

Renaissance man the *American Heritage Dictionary*, 3rd ed., gives identical definitions for "Renaissance woman" and "Renaissance man."

repairman *repairer, service rep/technician, servicer, adjuster, technician, mechanic, fixer, troubleshooter, restorer, custodian.* Or, be specific: *plumber, electrician, carpenter, roofer,* etc. In England a "repairman" is a "fitter," a neat, useful -er word.

repo man *repossessor, the repo.*

representative *See* congressman.

restaurateur woman or man.

retarded *person with mental disability/impairment/retardation, someone with developmental delays.* "Mental illness" and "mental retardation" are separate conditions; one does not imply the other. Labels such as feeble-minded, idiot, imbecile, mental defective, mentally deficient, moron, and retard are highly offensive and inaccurate. *See also* disability/disabilities, handicapped, idiot/idiocy, "people first" rule.

retreat master *retreat director.*

reverend (adjective) depending on the denomination, this title may be used for a woman or a man. Use "The Reverend Dinah Morris" when writing, but in general do not use "reverend" as a noun, as in "How are you today, Reverend?" Use instead the person's first name, "Father" or "Mother," or the title the person prefers. Clergy today welcome a question like "What shall I call you?" *See also* clergyman, minister, priest.

reverse discrimination although this term now has its own dictionary definition, its linguistic and real-life legitimacy is still debated. On the level of language, the "reverse" is questioned: discrimination is discrimination; why is discrimination somehow different, needing a special label, if it is leveled against traditionally dominant groups? The arguments about whether or when policies established to correct discrimination against members of minority groups discriminate against members of majority groups are many and impassioned; if you use this term, you should probably be able to justify it. *See also* affirmative action.

rewrite man *rewriter. See also* newspaperman.

Rhodesian man *the Rhodesian, archaic/early human, Homo erectus.*

rhyme, feminine/masculine *See* feminine/masculine (poetry, music).

rich as Croesus there is nothing wrong with using this phrase, but be aware of how many such expressions in the English language are male-based. Balance their use with female-based expressions, creative expressions of your own, or sex-neutral alternatives: *well-to-do, made of money, worth a bundle/a pretty penny, rolling in money, on Easy Street, has a goldmine, has money to burn, flush, someone whose ship has come in. See also* sex-linked expressions.

rifleman *sharpshooter, carabineer, crack shot, sniper, sharpshooter, shooter, gunner, soldier.* **See also** gunman, hit man, marksman.

right-hand man *right hand, deputy, lieutenant, assistant, right-hand/chief/ invaluable assistant, aide, key aide, helper, attendant, co-worker, side- kick, subordinate.*

right to die a study by Steven Miles of "right-to-die" cases showed that men are more likely to be granted the right to die than women, largely because courts usually characterized men as rational and mature, while character- izing women as immature, emotional, and needing protection. When patients could not communicate their own healthcare preferences, the court reconstructed them from the memories and insights of family and friends 75% of the time for men, 14% of the time for women. In Miles's study, no man's treatment decision was ever made by the state (families or doctors made it); 21% of the women's cases were. Men's views were frequently accepted as "deeply held," "intelligent," and "very serious." Women's views were often rejected as "offhand remarks," "speculation," or "spontaneous." A 23-year-old man who two years before his accident said "he would want to die" rather than live like the people in the nursing home where his woman friend worked was determined to be "exercising his right to control the course of medical care." An 84-year-old woman who spent her life as a hospital administrator repeatedly discussed right- to-die issues in the context of her work and again after suffering a series of strokes. Yet the court concluded that "there is nothing other than speculation . . . her expressions were no more than immediate reaction to the unsettling experience of seeing or hearing of another unnecessarily prolonged death."

right to life acceptable synonym for pro-life. "Right-to-lifer" and "pro-lifer," however, are not always taken as positive.

ringman *bettor, gambler, gamester.*

ringmaster this term is entrenched in the language and has high meaning for most people; it almost invariably refers to a man, thus justifying its male character; and the "master" is overlooked by many people. If you want an alternative consider *ringleader, ring supervisor, circus announcer/leader/ producer, announcer, host, leader.* **See also** master of ceremonies/mistress of ceremonies.

risk **See** at risk, high-risk group.

riverman *river logger/jobber.*

road sister this colorful term was used for girls/women when they first became hoboes in the 1930s. If you need a sex-neutral term use *hobo*. **See also** knight of the road.

roaming indigenous or native peoples are often described as "roaming" or "wandering," which is defined as moving without purpose or direction, whereas in fact their movements had both; describe instead what they were actually doing: moving between winter and summer homes, going on religious pilgrimages, following sources of food.

rob Peter to pay Paul *See* borrow from Peter to pay Paul.

rob the cradle in the case of a partner below the age of consent, there are legal terms with associated criminal penalties that are more accurate. In the case of adult couples with an age difference, both women and men marry or date younger people, so the phrase isn't sexist, but it is ageist, judgmental, and unwelcome. *See also* toyboy.

rodman *See* gunman.

roger although based on a man's name (from the old communications code for the letter "r"), this term meaning, "OK," "that's right," or "over and out" is not functionally sexist.

Romeo this evocative name conveys a whole story and complex understandings to those familiar with its origins. Should you need a less specific but inclusive term consider *lover, doomed/young/dashing lover.*

roommate inclusive term describing someone you share quarters with; so far, it is not generally used as a euphemism for lover.

roscoe although based on a man's name, "roscoe" is a fairly harmless sex-linked term. What is not harmless is the roscoe itself; while countries in other respects similar to the United States have at most several dozen handgun deaths per year, the yearly total in the United States is around 10,000 deaths; according to a 1996 study, of the total homicides among children in the world, 73% occurred among U.S. children. For sex-neutral alternatives consider *handgun, revolver.*

roughhouse/roughneck although culturally reserved for men, particularly because one meaning of "roughneck" is "oilfield worker" (traditionally an all-male occupation), this term may also be used for women when appropriate.

roundsman *deliverer; inspector, police officer, watch, patrol; relief cook.*

roustabout a roustabout has invariably been a man, but inclusive alternatives are available: *deckhand, wharfhand; circus worker/laborer; oilfield worker/laborer.*

routeman *route worker/supervisor, driver, newspaper carriers' supervisor, delivery person, deliverer.*

rowdy can be said of women/girls or boys/men, although girls have often been reproached for being rowdy, while in boys it was considered "natural." *See also* boys will be boys.

royal/royalty although these terms are based on "roy" ("king"), they no longer have perceived male associations.

rubbing noses Eskimos don't rub noses and they object to the characterization; also, most of them aren't called Eskimos. *See also* Eskimo.

rube based on a man's name and used more of a man than of a woman, this term is also a derogatory anti-rural stereotype. More sex-neutral and less pejorative terms include: *country cousin, rustic, tiller of the soil, provincial.*

rule of thumb there has been much debate about this term and its association with the right of a man to chastise his wife with a switch no thicker than his thumb. It is probably beyond dispute that the original "rule of thumb" had nothing to do with wife-beating (among the etymologies: the last joint of the thumb is about an inch in width and so was commonly used as a measure; artists used a thumb to gauge perspective; the thumb was used to test the degree of fermentation of malt in making beer in 19th-century England; the thumb was used as a tiny writing pad to calculate the exchange of Spanish dollars for French francs by French contractors in the early 1800s in southern France). However, it is also probably beyond dispute that wife-beating has been associated or identified with the "rule of thumb" for a long time: in 1881, Harriet H. Robinson *(Massachusetts in the Woman Suffrage Movement)* wrote, "Thirty years ago, when the Woman's Rights Movement began, the status of a married woman was little better than that of a domestic servant. By the English common law, her husband was her lord and master. He had the sole custody of her person, and of her minor children. He could 'punish her with a stick no bigger than his thumb,' and she could not complain against him"; in Margaret Deland's 1924 *New Friends in Old Chester,* a woman said to the man who had "jokingly" threatened to beat her, "Let's see . . . you can use a stick no bigger than your thumb, can't you?" In *"Rule of Thumb* and the Folklaw of the Husband's Stick," *Journal of Legal Education* (September 1994), Henry Ansgar Kelly points out that printed references to "rule of thumb" as a guideline antedate references to it in the context of wife-beating by almost several hundred years. An 1868 case, *State* v. *Rhodes*, appears to be the only case on record in which a husband was let off because "His Honor was of opinion that the defendant had a right to whip his wife with a switch no larger than his thumb," but the principle was ridiculed on appeal the next year. It was also rejected in another case, *State* v. *Oliver* (1874), in which the judge said, "We may assume that the old doctrine, that a husband had a right to whip his wife, provided he used a switch no larger than his thumb, is not law in North Carolina. Indeed, the Courts have advanced from that barbarism until they have reached the position, that the husband has no right to chastise his wife, under any circumstances." "Rule of thumb" has unpleasant associations for many women, not because the phrase arose from wife-beating, but because references to the supposed thumb-measurement principle for beating wives are associated with it. For those who prefer alternatives consider *general rule, rough guideline, commonsense/ballpark/approximate measure.*

rule the roost this phrase is sexist because, although the roost is invariably "manned" by a rooster, the expression refers to a woman who dominates her family. The expression developed from the nonsexist British variant "rule the roast" where "roast" refers either to a governing body or to the roasted beef served for Sunday dinner (and it is moot who ruled it: the woman who roasted it or the man who carved it). If you want an alternative consider *call the shots/the tune/the plays, wear the crown, sit on the throne, wield the scepter, have it all one's way, lay down the law, be in the saddle/driver's seat, hold all the cards.*

S

What is repugnant to every human being is to be reckoned always as
a member of a class and not as an individual person.

—*Dorothy L. Sayers*

We all know we are unique individuals, but we tend to see others
as representatives of groups.

—*Deborah Tannen*

Stereotypes are based on assumptions that run deep in our culture—so deep that they
can slip by unnoticed unless our awareness is continually sharpened and refined.

—*Matina S. Horner*

saboteur this grammatically masculine French word is used for both sexes in
French and in English.

sacristan depending on the denomination, a sacristan may be either sex.

safe sex this ought to be "safer sex," since the only 100% safe sex is no sex
at all. When using "safe sex," define terms and spell out relative margins
of "safety."

safety man *safety inspector/engineer.*

sahib always a man; the woman is a "memsahib."

salad girl/salad man *salad maker.* Note the nonparallel "girl/man."

salesgirl/saleslady/salesman/saleswoman *salesclerk, clerk, sales associate/
rep/agent/representative/broker/manager, agent, seller, door-to-door
seller, canvasser, commercial traveler, vendor, dealer, marketer, merchant,
retailer, wholesaler, trader, estimator, driver, solicitor, shop assistant,
peddler.* These terms are not interchangeable: "salesclerk" is appropriate
for a retail store employee, while "sales representative" describes someone employed by a large manufacturing company who is a combination

business manager, product specialist, and sales trainer. For "salesmen" use plurals of the alternatives given, as well as *sales force/staff/personnel, salespeople.*

salesmanship *sales ability/expertise/technique/skill, high sales potential, selling ability; vendorship, sales record; hucksterism.*

salutations (letters) when you know the person's name but not their sex or social title, write Dear Lane Busby; when you don't have a name, either address yourself to the company (Dear Gates-Porter) or to a job title (Dear Credit Manager) or to a role (Dear Neighbor). The trend in non-personal letters is toward replacing the salutation with a subject line ("Re: enclosed contract"). For more information and lists of salutation possibilities *see* the Writing Guidelines, pp. 19–20.

salvage man *salvage worker/inspector/repairer, salvager, parts salvager.*

Samaritan, good man or woman.

same-sex this adjective is used (1) to refer to situations that include only one sex (same-sex school, same-sex friends) and (2) as an inclusive adjective meaning lesbian or gay (same-sex couples, same-sex marriage).

sampleman *sampler, sample collector/worker/reworker, raw sampler.*

samurai this member of the historical Japanese warrior class was always a man.

sandboy *sand/beach flea.* Or, leave as is.

Sandman, the derived from an old European tale, the Sandman is harmless enough in himself; the problem is that so many of his ilk are male (Santa Claus, Jack Frost), and small children are especially susceptible to the subliminal messages about maleness and femaleness in a world overrun with "he"s. If you're interested in establishing your own terms, consider *Sandy Eyes, the sleep/sand fairy, sand sprinkler, the sleep genie.*

sandwich man *sandwich board advertiser.*

sandwich girl/sandwich man *sandwich maker.* Note the nonparallel "girl/ man."

sanitation man *sanitation worker/engineer.*

San Quentin quail (underage female sexual partner) labeling the girl/young woman this way (while failing to label the man) incorrectly places the onus for the relationship on her, perpetuates the Eve-as-tempter/helpless-Adam stereotype, and implies a certain victimization of the man, obscuring the fact that he is engaging in criminal activity (and laying the foundation for a statutory rape charge).

Sansei literally, "third generation," this acceptable term is used for the U.S.-born grandchild of Japanese immigrants to the U.S. Plural is Sansei or Sanseis. *See also* Issei, Kibei, Nisei, Yonsei.

Santa Claus Father Christmas, Père Noel, Saint Nicholas, Kris Kringle, and Santa Claus are better left as they are, even with the acknowledgment that these male figures reinforce the cultural male-as-norm system. Mrs. Claus goes largely unrecognized; she doesn't even have a first name. There is nothing inherently wrong with a male Santa Claus; the problem is that nearly every cultural icon of this magnitude is male. (The Santa Claus World Union is currently debating opening its membership to female Santas—Mrs. Claus or Mother Christmas.) Those interested in promoting female as well as male heroes could introduce Befana, or La Befana, the Italian version of Santa Claus, who carries a cane and a bell and traditionally drops down the chimney on the twelfth night of Christmas.

sapphic acceptable term meaning "of, or relating to, lesbianism."

sassy/saucy because these are used primarily for girls and women, you may want to consider instead *impudent, insolent, mouthy, bold, nervy, forward.*

Satan/he *Satan/it.*

satyr by definition a satyr is male. If you want sex-neutral alternatives consider *libertine, bedhopper, swinger, lover, seducer. See also* nymphomaniac.

saucy *See* sassy/saucy.

savage this highly ethnocentric term has been used to justify invading, dispossessing, and subjugating entire populations. In the case of American Indians, their manner of defending themselves was called "savage," and Indian victories were called "massacres," (while unprovoked attacks and indiscriminate killings of Indians were called simply "victories"); "any attempt to evaluate war as 'civilized' or 'savage' usually depends on which side one is on" (Thomas R. Frazier, ed., *The Underside of American History*). Slavery was made possible by labeling kidnapped Africans "savages." *See also* "discovery" of America, heathen, illiterate, massacre, pagan, primitive, uncivilized.

savant the French word is grammatically masculine but is used in French and English for both sexes. *See also* idiot savant.

say uncle *See* uncle, say.

scalper (tickets) the first meaning of "scalper" is "one (esp. an American Indian) who removes scalps" (*The Oxford English Dictionary*, 2nd ed.). The second meaning refers to selling tickets (or stocks) for higher (or lower) prices than usual. The term is objectionable, even though everybody may not associate it consciously with Indians. There is currently no easily recognized equivalent. Write when you find one. Until then, experiment with combinations like *ticket shark/sharp/hustler/runner, stock rustler* (probably related to the cattle rustler).

scarlet woman there is no parallel term—nor any expressed condemnation—for the men who are the "partners in crime" of scarlet women.

scatterbrained *See* airhead.

schizophrenic *person who has/with schizophrenia.* "Schizophrenic" is often erroneously used to refer to a state of being divided, torn in two, of two minds, etc. "Schizophrenia" means incoherent, hallucinatory, delusional thinking, not "having two personalities," which is termed multiple personality disorder. *See also* disability/disabilities, handicapped, mental illness.

schlemiel woman or man.

schmuck this term and its lesser-known euphemism, "schmo," are reserved for men; they are from the Yiddish for "penis," which is why Yiddish-speaking individuals don't use them in polite company. To non-Yiddish-speakers, "schmuck" means something like "stupid jerk." It might be better to use that.

scold (noun) a common scold was legally defined as a troublesome, angry woman who broke the public peace (and the law) with her brawling and wrangling and was punished by public ducking (Abby Adams, *An Uncommon Scold*); a U.S. woman was booked (but not convicted) on a common scold charge as recently as 1971.

scold (verb) instead of this, use for a woman the term you would use for a man in the same situation: *chide, reprimand, lecture, admonish, criticize, remonstrate, upbraid, chew out, rebuke, chastise, give a piece of one's mind, read the riot act, lay down the law.*

schoolboy/schoolfellow/schoolgirl *schoolchild, schoolmate, classmate, peer, youngster, elementary school child, child.*

schoolman/Schoolman *scholastic, academic, teacher, school administrator, pedagogue, academician, academist, professor, scholar, savant.* "Schoolman" is historically correct for a Scholastic.

schoolmarm/schoolmaster/schoolmistress *schoolteacher, teacher, educator, instructor, tutor, principal.*

score the concept of scoring (a man "getting" or "having" a woman sexually) underlies much that is skewed with female-male relations. Thinking of a woman in this way makes her a notch on the bedpost—she is not a partner in any meaningful sense. Lack of mutuality underlies a "score" (e.g., "Man is the hunter; woman is his game," wrote Alfred, Lord Tennyson in *The Princess*). "Score" is also an inclusive term for the client of either sex of a male or female prostitute. *See also* "lay"/"easy lay"/ "good lay," sex object, sexual conquest.

Scotch a contraction of "Scottish," this term is not in high favor although it is accepted in certain fixed expressions (e.g., "Scotch whisky"). It is always avoided in reference to people. *See also* Scotsman, Scottish.

Scotchman *See* Scotsman, Scottish. *See also* Scotch.

Scotsman *Scot, Scotlander, inhabitant of Scotland, Scotsman/Scotswoman.* Plural: *Scots, Scotlanders, inhabitants of Scotland, Scotswomen and Scotsmen.* This form is preferred to "Scotchman/Scotchwoman." *See also* Scotch, Scottish.

Scottish this adjective is acceptable for referring to Scotland or its people, language, or culture. "Scots" is the Scottish shortened form; "Scotch" the English form (and thus less acceptable). Whether to use "Scots" (informal) or "Scottish" (formal) depends on your style.

scout girl or boy. *See also* Boy Scout, Girl Scout.

scoutmaster *scoutleader.*

scowman *scow hand/worker.*

scrapman *scrap worker/separator/collector.*

script girl/script man *script supervisor; continuity, continuity supervisor.* Note the nonparallel "girl/man."

Scrooge there is nothing wrong with using this colorful and highly meaningful term, but be aware of how many such expressions in the English language are male-based. Balance their use with female-based expressions, creative expressions of your own, or sex-neutral alternatives: *tightwad, money-grubber, penny pincher, pinchpenny, miser, skinflint, cheapskate, piker, cheeseparer. See also* sex-linked expressions.

scrubwoman *janitor, cleaner, office cleaner, household helper, custodian, domestic worker, char, charworker, maintenance worker.*

scullery maid retain in historical context. Or, *scullery worker.*

sculptress *sculptor. See also* "feminine" word endings.

seamaid *See* mermaid.

seamstress *seamster, sewer, tailor, mender, alterer, stitcher, alterations expert, custom tailor, clothier, dressmaker, fashion sewer, garment worker/maker/designer, needleworker.*

seafaring man *seafarer.*

seaman *seafarer, sailor, enlisted sailor, naval recruit, mariner, merchant mariner, marine, navigator, pilot, argonaut, tar, salt, gob, captain, skipper, mate, first mate, crew member, deck hand, boater, yachter.* "Seaman" and "seaman recruit" are official U.S. Navy terms, but refer to either sex.

seaman apprentice *apprentice sailor/crew member, marine apprentice.* "Seaman apprentice" is an official Navy term used for both sexes.

seamanlike/seamanly *shipshape, sailor-like.* Or, be specific: *tidy, orderly, skilled.*

seamanship *navigation/ship-handling skills, marine strategy, navigational/ ship-handling/sailing expertise/techniques.*

second baseman *See* baseman.

second shift, the from Arlie Hochschild's *The Second Shift,* this term refers to the unpaid job a woman comes home to each day after 8 hours of paid work. Hochschild says that because husbands generally do little more housework or childcare than their fathers did, even though wives now work outside the home, wives spend 15 fewer hours at leisure each week than their husbands and, over the course of a year, work the equivalent of an extra month of 24-hour days. Most men in two-career marriages are not significantly involved in childrearing, cooking, cleaning, food shopping, or other chores, although they "help out"—an expression that identifies whose job it really is. One of the couples in Hochschild's book devised an equal "division of labor": he took care of the dog and the garage; she took care of the child and the house. Couples who did share housework equally were found to be the happiest, although it's unknown whether they were already happier and thus shared more, or whether the sharing made them happier. However, men who "win" the argument about housework, whose wives work that extra month, lose a good deal to exhaustion and resentment: the second most common reason women cited for wanting to divorce (after "mental cruelty") was their husbands' "neglect of home or children." This was mentioned more often than financial problems, physical abuse, drinking, or infidelity. The idea that women work two—or three—shifts is not new. In 1918, Alexandra Kollontai wrote, "The wife, the mother, who is a worker, sweats blood to fill three tasks at the same time: to give the necessary working hours as her husband does, in some industry or commercial establishment, then to devote herself as well as she can to her household and then also to take care of her children. Capitalism has placed on the shoulders of the woman a burden which crushes her: It has made her a wage earner without having lessened her cares as a housekeeper and mother" (in Eleanor S. Riemer and John C. Fout, *European Women*). *See also* housewife, housework, working father, working mother, working wife, working woman.

second-story man *cat burglar, burglar, housebreaker, professional thief.*

secretary although the number of men in this "pink-collar" occupation has increased, 98.5% of all secretaries are women—which is a switch: until the 1870s, when the typewriter was introduced, the secretarial profession was considered strictly men's work. From the Middle Ages onward, a "secretarius" (from the Latin for "secret") was a confidential male officer who could be trusted with state secrets. When the YWCA hired eight women to be "typewriters" in 1873, physicians were brought in to certify that the women's physical and mental abilities could withstand the pressure; many people predicted the women's minds would snap. In 1880, the all-male First Congress of Shorthand Writers issued a statement saying, "Some day women will be smart enough to write shorthand." According to an article in *New Woman,* "Many secretaries feel the title [secretary] is so pejorative and deficient in conveying their responsibilities (which have shifted from clerical positions toward those of middle management) that it should be amended or replaced." Preferred titles include executive secretary, executive assistant, administrative assistant/coordinator, and office administrator/professional/manager. The largest professional association for secretaries, Professional Secretaries International, is thinking of changing the title "secretary," as well as its own name, and predicts that "secretary" will probably be replaced by office administrator. Legal secretaries have discussed changing to "legal support professionals." Some judges' secretaries are now called "judicial assistants" or "administrative assistants." *See also* girl Friday, Professional Secretaries Day/Week, pink-collar job/worker.

Secret Service man *Secret Service agent, member of the Secret Service, bodyguard, intelligence agent/officer, plainclothes officer.* The Secret Service has nearly 200 female agents.

seductive both men and women can be seductive; don't limit the word to women.

seductress *seducer. See also* "feminine" word endings.

see a man about a dog/horse *see somebody about a dog/horse.* Or, replace the phrase with whatever you really mean. This Victorian circumlocution was designed to avoid mentioning anything inconvenient or embarrassing: visiting the restroom, going to a bar or tavern for a drink, seeing a prostitute. (Dorothy Parker once said, "Excuse me, everybody, I have to go to the bathroom. I really have to telephone, but I'm too embarrassed to say so.")

seedsman *sower, seed dealer, seed store owner, seed company representative.*

seeress *seer. See also* "feminine" word endings.

seigneur/seigneury retain in historical context. Alternatives: *member of the landed gentry, feudal property owner, elder, local authority; landed estate, manor house.*

selectman *representative, city representative, commissioner, council member, member of the council, councilor, municipal/board officer, board member, chancellor, ward manager; selectwoman and selectman.*

self-made man *self-made individual/person, entrepreneur, go-getter, hardworker, rags to riches story; self-made woman and self-made man.*

self-mastery *self-control, self-discipline.* For discussion of "master" words, *see* master.

seminal because "seminal" is the adjectival form of "semen," than which nothing could be more male, the use of the word is not only sex-linked etymologically but the way it's been used historically tends to underscore the notion that only men have important, "seminal" ideas. Many people are unaffected by these associations and use the word in its functional sense of *originative.* If you want alternatives consider *germinal, germinative, creative, original, inventive, innovative, primary, primal, primordial, prototypal, prototypical, exemplary, fresh, novel, unprecedented, precedent-setting, pivotal, first of its kind, initial, earliest, unorthodox, nonconforming, unconventional, rudimentary, inceptive, fundamental, source, productive, catalytic, influential, far-reaching, potential, possible, probable, likely, unrealized.*

seminar although "seminar" is related to "semen" by the back door (it comes from the word for "seed plot"), it is a nonsexist term, etymologically and functionally. If women anywhere have held "ovulars" because of their objection to "seminars," it was probably done in fun, and reports of real sightings are rare. In *The Official Politically Correct Dictionary and Handbook,* Henry Beard and Christopher Cerf give "ovular" as "a nonphallogeneric term for 'seminar,'" but their footnote cites an unnamed professor cited by Christina Hoff Sommers in an unpublished manuscript quoted in Dinesh D'Souza.

seminary both sexes have attended seminaries in the past, but their experiences have not been parallel: seminaries for women enrolled high school–aged girls while seminaries for men trained clergy. The former is now a rarity, while the latter include women, depending on the denomination. *See also* clergyman.

senator *See* congressman.

senility *dementia.* The *Publication Manual of the American Psychological Association,* 4th ed., says the term "dementia" is preferred to "senility"; "senile dementia of the Alzheimer's type" is an accepted term. Avoid the casual use of "senile/senility" as a synonym for "forgetful/forgetfulness" or "old/old age," and do not use it as though it is something inevitable for everyone. *See also* Alzheimer's disease.

senior airman this official U.S. Air Force term is used for both sexes.

senior/senior citizen although not universally liked, these terms are probably here to stay when referring to people 65 or older. A possible alternative: *older adult/person.* Or, use the person's age or age group ("those over 65," "patients aged 75–90"). References to age are often irrelevant or used in nonparallel ways (we see "elderly man dies" but not "middle-aged man dies" and "robs elderly woman" but not "robs young woman"). Avoid euphemisms like "golden agers" or the term "retirees" when not all the group are retired, and probably not idle either. The "citizen" in senior citizen at least acknowledges that age is not the only relevant characteristic of people over 65, although the National Gray Panthers, the American Association of Retired Persons, and the National Retired Teachers Association all prefer "older person/people/American" to "senior citizen." *See also* ageism, elderly, old, old man/old woman, oldster, old-timer.

separate the men from the boys *separate the sheep from the goats/wheat from the chaff/professionals from the amateurs/strong from the weak/ good from the bad/able from the incompetent/mature from the immature.*

serf man or woman.

seropositive *See* HIV.

serve two masters *serve God and mammon, have divided loyalties, be torn in two.* For discussion of "master" words, *see* master (noun).

serviceman (armed forces) *service member, member of the service/armed forces, enlistee, recruit, officer, sailor, soldier, Marine, flyer; service personnel, servicewoman and serviceman.* Or, use specific service titles—all of which may now refer to either a woman or a man. Some of the following sample titles still appear "masculine" as we are unused to women in these ranks—and women may not, to date, have filled all of them—but they may potentially be held by either sex: adjutant, admiral, brigadier general, captain, colonel, commandant, commander, command sergeant major, commodore, corporal, ensign, field marshal, first lieutenant/sergeant, fleet admiral, general, gunnery sergeant, lance corporal, lieutenant/lieutenant colonel/lieutenant commander/lieutenant general/ lieutenant junior grade, major, major general, master sergeant, military police, NCO (noncommissioned officer), paratrooper, petty officer, private/private first class, rear admiral, second lieutenant, senior naval officer, sergeant/sergeant at arms/sergeant first class/sergeant major, squadron commander/squadron leader, staff officer/staff sergeant/staff sergeant major, subaltern, technical/top sergeant, vice admiral, warrant officer, wing commander. *See also* airman, armed forces, aviation survivalman, combat, corpsman, draft, midshipman, wingman.

serviceman (repair) *servicer, service contractor, repairer, technician, maintenance/repair worker, troubleshooter, fixer, mender, adjuster; gas station/service station attendant, mechanic.*

service wife *military/soldier's/service member's spouse.* Casey Miller and Kate Swift *(The Handbook of Nonsexist Writing)* say that tacking on identifiers like "service wives" makes women appendages of both a man and an institution while detracting from their own lives and roles. The terminology also assumes that all members of the institution are men, whereas today a number of service spouses are men.

session man (music recording session) *session player/musician, studio musician/player; session man and session woman; free-lance musician.*

settler those who moved onto Indian homelands have generally been referred to by historians as "settlers," whereas to Indians they were trespassers or invaders.

set-up man *set-up mechanic/operator, setter, preparer, press/kick press/ machine setter, setter mechanic/worker; denture mounter.*

sewer-bottom man *trench trimmer.*

sewing woman *sewer, tailor, mender, alterer, alterations expert, stitcher, garment worker/maker/designer, fashion sewer, custom tailor, clothier, dressmaker, needleworker.*

sex understanding the difference between sex and gender is crucial to the appropriate use of language referring to women and men. Sex is biological: people with male genitals are male, and people with female genitals are female. Gender is cultural: our notions of "masculine" tell us how we expect men to behave and our notions of "feminine" tell us how we expect women to behave—but these may have nothing to do with biology. When deciding whether a word is restricted to one sex or the other, the only acceptable limitation is genetic sex. A woman cannot be a sperm donor because it's biologically impossible. It may be culturally unusual for a man to be a secretary, but it is not biologically impossible; to assume all secretaries are women is sexist because the issue is gender, not sex. Gender signifies a subjective cultural attitude while sex is an objective biological fact.

sex change operations of the operations since 1979, approximately one-half have been male-to-female and one-half female-to-male. Often preferred is the term *gender reassignment.*

sex differences in 1947, Dorothy Sayers wrote, "The first thing that strikes the careless observer is that women are unlike men. . . . But the fundamental thing is that women are more like men than anything else in the world." In 1955, Ivy Compton-Burnett *(Mother and Son)* observed,

"There is more difference within the sexes than between them." Thirty-five years later, a *Newsweek* article concurs: "Social scientists agree that the sexes are much more alike than they are different, and that variations within each sex are far greater than variations between the sexes." According to *The Opposite Sex* (Anne Campbell), "As soon as we finish with sexual anatomy and move on to questions about behavior, abilities and social roles, 'obvious' differences [between the sexes] turn out to be not nearly as obvious as we may have thought at first." Patricia McBroom *(The Third Sex)* writes, "Few sex differences survive the test of crosscultural analysis. Martin and Voorhies examined aggression, intelligence, dependency, ambitiousness, and nurturance, finding all these traits to be culturally variable. Anthropologists do, however, recognize that endemic warfare is a virtually exclusive male activity. Crosscultural patterns in gender personality do exist, but they are neither innate nor universal." The differences between the sexes can be examined along three axes: (1) anatomy, or how we are physically different from each other; (2) biology, or how we behave innately differently from each other because we are male or because we are female; (3) culture, or how we live out certain social roles as women/girls and men/boys. A sperm donor is always a man, not because of the culture, but because of anatomy and biology. A CEO today is far more likely to be a man than a woman, not because of anatomy or biology, but because of culture. It is easy to see when anatomy determines behavior (only women give birth, only men can produce sperm). It is not quite so easy to see when culture determines behavior and when biology determines it. Are girls innately better at verbal tasks and boys innately better at spatial tasks? Or is it the culture that determines the small statistical test-score variations between the sexes? (Sex differences in abilities are only averages, which means that men/boys can do as well on verbal abilities as the best women/girls, and girls/women can do as well as the best boys/men on spatial abilities.) Is it biology or culture that determines who is "the weaker sex"? Research shows that when adults are told a baby is a girl, they view the child as delicate, fragile, or small in size. But when told the *same* child is a boy, they think of him as strong, alert, and large. Increasingly, social scientists emphasize that society as much as nature turns girls into women and boys into men. James M. Dubik (in *Newsweek*) explains how he came to see, via his two daughters and his experiences teaching male and female cadets at West Point, that "Many of the characteristics I thought were 'male' are, in fact, 'human.'" Infant psychiatrist Taghi Modarressi says, "When we talk about inborn, intrinsic maleness and femaleness, we really don't know what we're talking about." Our western, hierarchical thinking says that if two things are different, one must necessarily be better or worse, higher or lower, than the other. Applied to the differences between the sexes, this attitude has been particularly malignant. (Which is "better," an apple or an orange, a lake or a river, geology or astronomy, the way women think or the way men think?) Deborah Rhode *(Theoretical Perspectives on Sexual Differences)* says we can deny sex differences, we can celebrate them, or we can "dislodge difference as the exclusive focus of gender-related questions." Anatomically, there are great differences between the sexes; biologically, there are some interesting differences (among the possibilities are that men generally appear to have greater muscle mass, cardiovascular capacity, more lefthandedness, and a higher concentration of red blood cells while women generally have more "good" cholesterol, handle stress better, sing better, have a keener sense of smell, and live longer—in addition, neurobiologists report structural differences in at least two regions of the human brain); culturally, there remain great differences in attitudes, behaviors, opportunities, and expected roles for women and men. Anatomy and biology may be immutable; culture is not. *See also* gender roles.

sex discrimination *See* sexism.

sex industry the multi-billion-dollar sex industry is blatantly sexist: those who profit from it financially are almost all male; the majority of victims are female, although boys/young men are also victims. One of the most vicious and appalling aspects of this "industry" is the large number of children involved. According to an insider, "The word on the street is johns prefer chickens—kids." There are upwards of 25,000 street kids in New York City alone. The most common scenario involves a middle-class suburban male who pays for sex with underagers. Abuse, degradation, drugs, disease, poverty, and death are facts of life for the young victims of this man's idea of "consensual sex." *See also* sex worker.

sexism both boys/men and girls/women are objects of discrimination based on their sex; "sexism" is an inclusive term when viewed primarily as discrimination. However, sexism is often defined specifically as the subordination of women by men; "While some women may dislike men intensely and treat them unfairly and while some women may be equally guilty of prejudice toward other women, the balance of power throughout most, if not all, of recorded history has allowed men to subordinate women in order to maintain their own privilege" (Paula S. Rothenberg, *Racism and Sexism*). Unequal, discriminatory treatment of the sexes touches almost every aspect of society, from large issues like the males-only draft, the feminization of poverty, the disparity in income between women and men, and the glass ceiling for many working women, to everyday issues like lifestyle ("work wives" are more socially acceptable and admired than "house husbands"), clothing (women wear just about anything men wear, while men aren't culturally approved for skirts, dresses, or most women's wear), colors (women can wear blue, but men rarely wear pink unless it is called "salmon"), activity (girls can be "tomboys" but boys better not be "sissies"). Nijole V. Benokraitis and Joe R. Feagin *(Modern Sexism)* say, "Although both men and women can be targets and victims of sex discrimination, a vast literature indicates that being a woman is frequently a better predictor of inequality than such variables as age, race, religion, intelligence, achievements, or socioeconomic status." In all but two respects that is true: today people with same-sex orientations are likely to be more discriminated against than any other group; the males-only draft provides a stunning inequality for men. *See also* blue, combat, glass ceiling, glass cellar, draft, pink, wage earner.

sexist (adjective) this is used to describe attitudes, practices, behavior, language, codes, laws, cultures, etc., but generally not people. Instead of "Dale is so sexist," say, "she uses sexist language" or "he encourages sexist practices in the office" or "your attitude seems very sexist to me."

sexist language sexist language promotes and maintains attitudes that stereotype people according to gender; it favors one sex, demeans or excludes one sex, or portrays members of one sex as all alike. Writing for members of the Foreign Service Institute, Mortimer D. Goldstein sums up the status of sexist language in his chapter title, "Sexist Language Is Yesterday's Style: Besides, It's Against the Policy" *(Disciplined Writing and Career Development). See* Writing Guidelines, beginning on page 1, for more information on identifying and dealing with sexist language.

sexist quotations it is standard practice not to rewrite quotations, even ones with sexist language. However, for reasons of space or sense, we often paraphrase or use only parts of quotations—even those without sexist language. Especially when using quotations in educational settings, it may be important to call attention to the sexism so that it is not absorbed unthinkingly; journalist and educator Ann Daly Goodwin used to write quotations on the chalkboard, but place—without comment—an "X" under any sexist terms. It did not take her students long to figure it out. When you need to work around sexist language (e.g., Wendell Phillips, "The best use of laws is to teach men to trample bad laws under their feet"), there are several possibilities. (1) Omit the quotation marks and paraphrase the remark (still attributing it to the author): Wendell Phillips suggested that the best use of laws is to teach people to trample bad ones underfoot. (2) Replace the sexist words or phrases with ellipsis dots and/ or bracketed substitutes: "The best use for laws is to teach [people] to trample bad laws under their feet" (Wendell Phillips). (3) Use "[sic]" to show that the sexist words come from the original quotation and to call attention to the fact that they are not inclusive: "The best use of laws is to teach men [sic] to trample bad ones under their feet" (Wendell Phillips). (4) Quote only part of it: Wendell Phillips said the best use for laws was to teach people "to trample bad laws under their feet." (5) Replace the quotation with one that isn't sexist.

sex-linked expressions our rich and colorful language contains hundreds of striking, evocative, and useful metaphors, expressions, and figures of speech. As is true of the rest of the language, the sex-linked among these phrases are dominated by male images. There is nothing wrong with any of them per se, but this guidebook lists several dozen expressions with comments and possible alternatives, *not so that they can be removed from the language,* but so that you will be aware of how many such expressions there are. It is the story of Lilliput again: one Lilliputian is harmless enough, but an army of them can overtake a Gulliver (nonsexist language authority Marie Shear). Each individual male-based expression is acceptable; to use only or principally male metaphors is not. Aware of their weight, you can then use only the most dynamic and appropriate of the male-based expressions, otherwise creating original ones of your own, using neutral or female-based expressions, or choosing from among alternatives for the less important terms. In the end, this attention to literary expressions improves our writing; many of the old phrases have become clichés; readers and audiences are sparked by fresh, new uses of language. And when we do use the time-tested expressions, we will have first given them a good sharp look to make sure they are exactly what we need.

sex object for centuries women have been treated as sex objects ("piece of ass"), things ("skirt," "doll"), possessions ("my woman"), and commodities ("birds," "chicks"). Heavily reinforced by advertising, which uses women's sexuality to sell everything from razor blades to cars, this concept has had invidious results: prostitution, rape, laws and societies that "protect" women and relegate them to the status of children, words and attitudes that label women solely by their sexuality, even murder when the mythic cultural promise that women exist for the sexual pleasure of men goes unfulfilled. An article on male friendship before marriage (*Esquire,* June 1990) says, "You compete for women"—as if women were passive things for the having. *See also* gender roles, owner, score, success object.

sexpot used only for women, "sexpot" supports the stereotype of woman as tempter and narrows her entire personhood to her sexuality.

sex roles *See* gender roles.

sexton woman or man.

sexual assault *See* rape.

sexual conquest whether by one sex or the other, is "conquest" an appropriate term? *See also* battle of/between the sexes, score, sex object.

sexual harassment sexual harassment consists of unwelcome, unsolicited, nonreciprocated sexual advances, requests for sexual favors, sexually motivated physical contact, or communication of a sexual nature, usually by someone who has power over another; it includes comments, jokes, looks, innuendos, and physical contact, and emphasizes a person's sex role over their function as a worker or student. A government report puts the annual cost of sexual harassment among federal workers at $95 million—not including legal fees or settlements. In one report, more than 80% of students surveyed said they had been sexually harassed at least once during their school years. However, most sexual harassment is unreported, and fewer than 5% of victims seek institutional remedies. Almost worse than the harassment are responses to it: the person "asked for it"; they should have been flattered; it wasn't such a big deal; victims are oversensitive—it was all in fun; "can't you take a little joke/a little teasing?"; the person is "imagining" it or "too uptight"; in the case of sexual harassment by fraternities and male sports teams, "boys will be boys" and "it's just youthful highjinks." In a stunning flight of fancy, Phyllis Schlafly says, "For the virtuous woman, sexual harassment is not a problem, except in the rarest of cases." She also says, "If it is perfectly clear that the answer is 'no,' the man doesn't ask. A man doesn't need to be told more than once." In case he does, however, there is now a remedy: sexual harassment is against the law. To a woman whose boss had been sexually harassing her, Miss Manners wrote, "he will undoubtedly claim that he didn't see anything wrong with what he was doing. He was only (he will protest) joking, or complimenting you, or helping you with your image, or being friendly. How was he to know that you would take it amiss? The answer is that his mother, his wife, his daughter, and in fact, the entire society has been trying to teach him that a gentleman does not make indecent gestures to a lady. . . . it has also been made abundantly clear that any romantic overtures, even when they are the polite sort that might be acceptable in social circumstances (where the lady could decline further acquaintance without imperiling her livelihood), violate office etiquette." A note on the pronunciation from Nick Levinson: although the emphasis falls on the first syllable of "harass" (thus, HARass) in some dictionaries (e.g., *American Heritage Dictionary*, 3rd ed.), the preferred emphasis in "harassment" is haRASSment. Language maven Richard Lederer points out that the first-syllable stress was the exclusive pronunciation in the 19th century. So although many authorities, including National Public Radio's pronunciation guidelines, recommend haRASSment, Levinson points out that those who would prefer to hear it HARassment have a strong linguistic precedent for it. *See also* battered wife, date rape, provoke, rape, rape victim, "she asked for it," victim, violence.

sexual intercourse when discussing sexual activity inclusively replace this heterosexist term with *sex, sexual activity, had sex with someone.*

sexual preference *sexual orientation/identity.* "Preference" implies that homosexuality, bisexuality, transsexuality, and heterosexuality are casually chosen rather than crucial, given, inextricable aspects of one's identity. Sexual orientation is not synonymous with sexual behavior; one's sexual identity is just that—who one is, not what one does.

sexual revolution "In the 1960s, any sex outside marriage was called the Sexual Revolution, a nonfeminist phrase that simply meant women's increased availability on men's terms. By the end of the seventies, feminism had brought more understanding that real liberation meant the power to make a choice; that sexuality, for women or men, should be neither forbidden nor forced" (Gloria Steinem, *Outrageous Acts and Everyday Rebellions*).

sexual slavery this is not yet history; it still exists in many parts of the world. For example, prostitution in Thailand often amounts to slavery; "children cannot give consent, and many others are held in captivity or debt bondage . . . in Thailand, sexual slavery, for the most part, has been internationally ignored" (Gayle Reaves, in *St. Paul Pioneer Press*). *See also* comfort women, white slavery.

sex worker this term for a women or a man who works in the sex industry is being seen more often; it is sometimes useful as a generic (with, however, the attendant vagueness of a generic). "A sex worker might work on a pay-telephone fantasy line, dance topless, strip, perform in simulated or real sex shows, sell sexual services to individuals, be a sexual surrogate, or work as an explicit sex demonstrator" (Sallie Tisdale, *Talk Dirty to Me*). "A sex worker might do all manner of things: massage, exotic dance, out-call, Lesbian videos, hard-core magazines" (Sue Grafton, *"K" Is for Killer*). It is debatable whether "sex worker" confers dignity on people who do in fact work hard to make a living or whether it is a euphemism disguising the nature and effects of such work. *See also* sex industry.

Shaker this term for a member of the United Society of Believers in Christ's Second Appearing has come to be respected and respectable even though it was originally a pejorative. The name "Shaker" referring to styles and furniture is a prestigious one.

shaman woman or man.

shamus although this could refer to either sex, it tends to be heard as masculine, and so do its equally "neutral" alternatives: *cop, copper, flatfoot, gumshoe, private eye, shadow, sleuth, tail.* With the advent of good fictional female gumshoes (*see* gumshoe), these words are beginning to seem more inclusive.

shanghai it's not easy to replace this compact, instantly comprehensible term, but its negative—and unmerited—reflection on the Chinese city should at least be acknowledged: English sailors were kidnapped (often after being drugged) to work the ships sailing to Shanghai. Possible alternatives might include *impress, conscript, kidnap, abduct, commandeer, force, trick.*

shantyman *shanty dweller.*

"she asked for it" this corrupt and specious "explanation" has been used to excuse everything from unwanted sexual attentions to rape. No woman ever asks to be harassed, abused, or violated. *See also* battered wife, date rape, domestic abuse/violence, provoke, rape, rape victim, victim, violence.

sheikh/sheik always a man.

shepherdess *shepherd. See also* "feminine" word endings.

sheroe *See* hero, unconventional spellings.

shiftless when used of African Americans, this word is highly objectionable because it has been reserved almost solely for them. If you need to convey this idea, instead of using a label, describe the specific behavior.

shipman *sailor. See also* seaman, shipmaster, yachtsman.

shipmaster *ship captain/commander/officer, sea captain, merchant marine officer/captain.* For discussion of "master" words, *see* master (noun).

ship/she *ship/it.* In the early days of sailing, a new ship was customarily dedicated to a goddess, under whose protection it sailed. Today, referring to ships and boats as "she" is outdated, unnecessary, and unacceptable because of the association of the feminine with men's possessions. Everything that dominator societies have traditionally run or overpowered has been imaged as female: church, nations, nature, ships, cars, etc.

shoeshine boy *shoeshiner.*

shogun always a man; no parallel for women.

shoot the bull this phrase doesn't refer to the male animal, but probably comes from "boule" meaning "fraud/deceit." To avoid its masculine orientation (it is almost always used of men rather than women) use *shoot the breeze. See also* gossip.

shop girl *shop clerk/assistant/employee/manager/owner, salesclerk, clerk.*

shoreman *shorehand, dockworker, dockhand, stevedore, shoreworker, longshore worker, wharfworker, wharfhand.*

shortened forms of words while personal names are shortened as an expression of affection (Liz, Pat, Jack), shortening of names of groups usually indicates hostility: abo (for "Aborigine"), lib, libber, women's lib, fag (even more hostile than "faggot"), Yid, jap, nip, bi, homo, lezzie, spic (from "Hispanic"). Marc Wolinsky and Kenneth Sherrill *(Gays and the Military)* note the further derogation of shortened words like "homo" that end in "-o." Other examples: chico, dago, fatso, gringo, lesbo, psycho, sicko, wacko, weirdo, wino.

shovelbill/shovelman *shoveler, shovel hand.*

showgirl *dancer, performer, performing artist.* **See also** showman.

showman *performer, entertainer, limelighter, razzle-dazzle/stage artist, theatrical person, exhibitionist, someone with a flair for the dramatic, ham, show-off, actor, theatrician, show manager/producer/stager.* Note the nonparallel "man/girl" and the differences in prestige and type of work between a showgirl and a showman. **See also** impresario.

showmanship *showcraft, stagecraft, razzle-dazzle, performing/staging skills, production genius, virtuosity, dramatics, theatercraft, theatrics, showiness, flair for the dramatic, dramatic flair.* None of these terms may feel as satisfactory as "showmanship." Try showing what you mean (by examples, description) rather than just telling.

shrew in theory nonsexist, in practice "shrew" is reserved for women. Consider using instead *grouch, grumbler, crosspatch, faultfinder, fire-eater, complainer, pain in the neck, nitpicker, troublemaker, bad-tempered/peevish/cranky/petulant person.* Ethel Strainchamps has pointed out the root of "shrew" is the same as that of "shrewd," which is more commonly used of men.

shrill **See** strident.

shylock this term, from Shakespeare's usurer of the same name in *The Merchant of Venice*, is sexist and anti-Semitic. Use instead *loan shark, usurer, extortionist, moneylender, parasite.* Shylock demanded the original "pound of flesh" (meaning today *spiteful penalty, harsh demand*).

shyster although the roots of this word are not very nice, they are not related in any way to "shylock." There may be lawyers who are shysters, but for every shyster there are a thousand honest, effective lawyers who are our neighbors, serving on community and charitable organizations, donating their time, talents, and money to local fine arts groups, school boards, food shelves, zoos, educational activities, and in general contributing to the larger good as well as practicing good law (attorney Patrick J. Maggio). Shun the loose use of "shyster."

Siamese twins the preferred term is *conjoined twins.*

Siberia Nick Levinson points out that "Siberia" (which is often used to indicate banishment—as when someone is sent to the branch office) is home to the Siberians; the forced labor camps did not constitute all of Siberia. In objecting to this misuse of "Siberia"—a "region of good-natured and proud people"—Russian professor and author Viktor K. Kabakchi cites a mention in *Newsweek* (August 8, 1994): "Once or twice every decade, a kid phenomenon sweeps the country. . . . Now it's Power Rangers, as any parent not living in Siberia knows."

sibyl retain in historical contexts and in those present-day contexts where the term finds validation among women. If you need an inclusive alternative use *prophet, fortuneteller.*

sideman *musician, instrumentalist, member of the band, band member.* Or, be specific: *bassist, drummer, clarinetist.*

sight-effects man *sight-effects coordinator/specialist/technician/crew.*

signalman *signaler, signal operator.*

significant other used for a woman or a man in a same-sex or opposite-sex relationship, this is still occasionally seen, but it is a little too arch and cumbersome for most people. *See also* boyfriend, girlfriend.

silk stocking district *posh neighborhood, wealthy/aristocratic area, deluxe section/fashionable part of town, the Gold Coast.*

Simon Legree "Simon Legree" and its common synonym "slave driver" have negative associations and no equivalent for women, but in certain contexts they may be the words you need. They are not easily replaced with terms as familiar and evocative, but sometimes you can reword or use an alternative: *hard/brutal taskmaster, ogre, tough/strict boss, martinet, stickler, severe disciplinarian.*

simon-pure there is nothing wrong with using this term (from the character Simon Pure in Susanna Centlivre's 1718 play, "A Bold Stroke for a Wife"), but be aware of how many such expressions in the English language are male-based. Balance their use with female-based expressions, creative expressions of your own, or sex-neutral alternatives: *pure, genuine, untainted, sterling, honest, truthful, pure-hearted, flawless, upright, highminded, reliable, real, veritable, authentic, exact, precise, credible, worthy; clean as a whistle. See also* sex-linked expressions.

single "singles sometimes find themselves outside the cultural loop in a society that considers marriage the natural state for healthy adults. People are expected to grow up, get married and stay married—or risk the wrath of politicians who brandish spouses and children like banners of morality" (Barbara Yost, in the *Arizona Republic*). Yost points out that with Americans increasingly delaying marriage (in 1992, the median age of first marriage reached an all-time high of 24.4 for women and 26.5 for men, up from 20 for women and 22.5 for men in the 1950s) and half of all marriages ending in divorce, singles constitute a growing segment of the population. Despite this, our language often reflects a Noah's ark view of society, where singles are overlooked, ignored, or excluded. For example, at company events, employees' "guests," not "spouses and families" can be welcomed. (People in committed relationships are not considered to be "single" even though they are not married.)

single mother/single father there are times when it may be necessary to specify "single"; most of the time it is not. It is better to use "single father" or "single mother," as "single parent" is too often thought to refer to a woman. The inclusive term may also obscure the gender breakdown: 13,700,000 children under 18 live with a single mother; 1,793,000 children under 18 live with a single father. In Great Britain "lone parent" or "solo parent" is used, to avoid the connotation of "unmarried" in single. However, in the U.S. "single" has long been used without pejoration for unmarried, divorced, separated, or widowed parents.

single-sex colleges "Historically, the reason for placing boys and girls in separate learning environments was to ensure that boys were better educated. Today, the justification for such grouping strategies is enhanced achievement levels for both groups. While there is no convincing evidence to suggest that one sex benefits more than the other from instruction in single-sex classes, girls are more likely to enjoy greater advantages. This is particularly true among certain age groups and with regard to specific subject areas" (Thomas J. Brown, *Toward a Rebirth of Common Sense in Education*). There are over 90 women's colleges (down from 224 in 1969) and some half-dozen males-only private educational institutions. Private institutions justify single-sex status by their specific alternative missions, lack of federal support, and, in the case of women's colleges, an affirmative action rationale. Single-sex colleges appear to be highly advantageous for women: compared to students enrolled in coeducational institutions, women in single-sex colleges participate more fully in and out of class, develop measurably higher levels of self-esteem, score higher on standardized achievement tests, choose more male-intensive majors, and are more are likely to graduate. Afterward they are more successful in their careers (e.g., hold higher positions, are happier, earn more money), are twice as likely to receive a doctoral degree, six times more likely to be on the boards of Fortune 500 companies, seven times more likely to be named a *Good Housekeeping* outstanding woman graduate, and even appear to have lower divorce rates. While graduates of women's colleges constitute only 5% of all college-educated women, they make up 44% of female members of Congress. *See also* education.

singular "they" since medieval times "they," "their," and "them" have been used as singular pronouns (for example, Jill Ruckelshaus's "No one should have to dance backward all their lives"). "'They' has been in continuous use as a singular pronoun in English for over 600 years. Two centuries of vigorous opposition, including concerted efforts by the education and publishing industries and an 1850 Act of Parliament declaring the masculine pronoun to be the proper third singular generic pronoun, have not eradicated it" (communications professor Miriam Meyers). Singular "they" is now accepted or endorsed by many authorities: *Oxford English Dictionary* ("The pronoun referring to everyone is often plural"); *Chicago Manual of Style*, 14th ed.; *American Heritage Dictionary of the English Language*, 3d ed. ("may be the only sensible choice in informal style"); *American Heritage Book of English Usage* ("The alternative to the masculine generic with the longest and most distinguished history in English is the third-person plural pronoun"); the National Council of Teachers of English ("In all but strictly formal usage, plural pronouns have become acceptable substitutes for the masculine singular"; *Random House Dictionary II; Webster's Third New International Dictionary* (their definition of *everyone* reads in part, "Usually referred to by the third person singular . . . but sometimes by a plural personal pronoun," and they give the example of "Everyone had made up their minds"); Randolph Quirk et al., *A Grammar of Contemporary English*. "However negatively one may react to this recourse, it is of long-established use" (Robert N. Mory, Assistant Research Editor, *Middle English Dictionary*). Singular "they" was proscribed in 1746 on the theory that the masculine gender was "more comprehensive" (whatever that means) than the feminine. But it wasn't until the 19th century that prescriptive grammarians tried to enforce it; many writers continued to use singular "they." Casey Miller and Kate Swift *(The Handbook of Nonsexist Writing)* say that "the continued and increased use of singular *they* in writing as well as speech—and the restitution of the status it enjoyed before grammarians arbitrarily proscribed it—now seems inevitable." Among the many writers who have used singular "they" are Jane Austen, Samuel Johnson, Anaïs Nin, Shakespeare, Elizabeth Gaskell, Agatha Christie, George Eliot, Charles Dickens, Anthony Trolloppe, George Bernard Shaw, William Congreve, Thomas Malory, William Thackeray, L. E. Landon, Anne Morrow Lindbergh, W. H. Auden, F. Scott Fitzgerald, Jonathan Swift, Lawrence Durrell, and Doris Lessing. You can find it today in the *Christian Science Monitor, Washington Post, New York Times*, and *Wall Street Journal*. (Note that "you" is also used as both singular and plural, and people seem able to understand when it is singular and when it is plural.)

sins of the fathers are visited on the children, the unless quoting Euripides (in which case it is "The gods visit the sins of the fathers upon the children), use *the sins of the parents are visited on the children* (if you can stand this expression in the first place).

Sioux "most of the people once called 'Sioux' by the white man now call themselves by their traditional name, Lakota, Dakota or Nakota, which means 'allies' rather than 'little snake'" (Tim Giago, in *Indian Country Today*).

sir "sir" and "dame" are parallel sex-specific titles for those raised to knighthood. "Sir" and "madam" are parallel and useful sex-specific terms for everyday social exchanges.

siren the definition of a siren sounds flattering (a woman seen as beautiful and seductive), but the stereotype of a woman luring a man to his destruction belittles both sexes.

sissy from "sister," this pejorative word denotes excessive timidity. "Buddy," from "brother," is a positive term describing a good friend. "Tomboy" is often paired with "sissy," but since it has the masculine connotation, society is more tolerant of so-called tomboy behavior than it is of so-called sissy behavior. Eugene R. August points out that our language lacks "a favorable or even neutral term to describe the boy who is quiet, gentle, and emotional." Instead of "sissy" consider using nothing at all with this connotation. If you must, try *timid, gentle, sensitive; weakling, pushover, wimp, doormat, easy mark, weak stick. See also* coward, mama's boy.

sister (adjective) the use of "sister" in such constructions as "sister cities/plants/companies" is not pejorative to women or to men ("brother" doesn't operate similarly). However, it introduces sex where it is superfluous. If you prefer something else try *related, twin, cousin, co-, companion, neighboring, paired, partnered, affiliated, allied, associated.* None of these feel as comfortable as "sister," but you can also circumlocute ("both magazines are published by . . .").

sisterhood unlike "brotherhood," which has been overused as a pseudogeneric, "sisterhood" has meaning for women as a description of a sex-specific, unique bond and should be retained in most instances. When you want an inclusive alternative consider *unity, unity among humans, humanity, compassion, peace, companionship, goodwill, amity, friendship, comradeship, camaraderie, conviviality; family, the human family, kinship, shared/human kinship; community, society, association, organization, social organization, common-interest group, club, corporation,* *federation, union, group, partnership, society; sisterhood and brother-hood. See also* brotherhood.

sisterly this is a useful and accurate sex-specific word in most cases. If you need a sex-neutral substitute consider *affectionate, loving, caring, kindly, supportive, sympathetic, protective, indulgent, friendly.*

sizism this term is used to describe discrimination based on body size (especially fatness or shortness). *See also* fat, looksism.

skinhead when using "skinhead" to convey more than physical description, qualify it: some skinheads are neo-Nazi white supremacists/racists, while other skinheads are anti-racist.

skirt/a bit of skirt (woman) these terms make of a woman an object, by inference a sex object, and there is no parallel for men. *See also* suit.

slagman *slag worker.*

slattern for prostitute, use *prostitute.* If you need a sex-neutral alternative for the meaning of an unkempt, slovenly woman consider *sloven, slob, unkempt person. See also* frump/frumpy, prostitute.

slave/slavery "Next time you read the word slaves substitute Africans forcefully removed from their families and homes, or African people held in captivity" (Clyde W. Ford, *We Can All Get Along*). In discussing slavery include the black point of view instead of discussing slavery merely as a boon, and later a problem, for whites (Macmillan Publishing Company, *Guidelines for Creating Positive Sexual and Racial Images in Educational Materials*). The two main problems with the terms "slave" and "slavery" are that they have generally been discussed from a non-slave point of view and that we have discounted the horror of slavery by the casual use of the words (slave of fashion, slavish imitator, work like a slave, work for slave wages, etc.).

slave girl in addition to its association with slavery, this sexist, racist term perpetuates the false notion that most women secretly enjoy being enslaved.

slaveholders historically these were both men and women.

slumlord *slum boss, slumholder, slum owner/manager, absentee slum owner, absentee fat cat slum owner.*

slut a 1996 survey of teenagers *(USA Weekend)* indicated that "when people find out that a boy and a girl have had sex, he is a 'stud,' but she is a 'slut.'" Only 22% of boys and 15% of girls say sex hurts a boy's reputation, while 70% of boys and 87% of girls say a girl's reputation is damaged. Both sexes conclude it's not fair, but that's the way it is. *See also* prostitute.

small step for man, giant leap for mankind *See* one small step for man, one giant leap for mankind.

smart aleck this expression comes from the man's name Alexander, but it is used for both sexes. Should you need a more sex-neutral alternative consider *know-it-all, blowhard, egomaniac, braggart, big/swelled head, arrogant/conceited/mouthy person/individual.*

sneaky Pete there is nothing wrong with this, but be aware of how many such expressions in the English language are male-based. Balance their use with female-based expressions, creative expressions of your own, or a sex-neutral alternative: *cheap wine. See also* sex-linked expressions.

snowman *snow figure/sculpture/creature/statue, snowwoman or snowman.* Yes, it seems bad-tempered to question the venerable "snowman," but as it is children who are primarily exposed to it, it's an important term in painting their world more male than it actually is and establishing the primacy of the male; on another level, it limits their creativity: if they hear "snowman," that is what they are mostly likely to make—instead of dragons and snow castles and huge birthday cakes.

snow man (job title) *defroster.*

sob sister *sob story writer/journalist, yellow journalist; bleeding heart, pushover.*

social butterfly this phrase generally refers to a woman, but there are no equally good inclusive alternatives for it. "Social butterfly" conveys a sense of light-mindedness along with the sociable, gregarious character of the person. Either use "social butterfly" for men too, or consider sex-neutral adjectives and nouns: *gregarious, outgoing, social, sociable, socially active, convivial, extroverted; joiner, gadabout, socialite.*

social titles use the titles people use for themselves. If you don't know, ask or omit the title, referring to them by first and last names. In work situations, "Ms." is generally acceptable. *See also* Esquire/Esq., Miss, Mrs., Ms., salutations (letters).

socman *See* sokeman.

socmanry *socage.*

sodomite from the inhabitants of the biblical city of Sodom, this term is often taken to be synonymous with "homosexual," when in fact it refers to anyone of either sex and any sexual orientation who performs, according to the wording of most laws, an "unnatural act" (anal or oral sex or bestiality).

sokeman *tenant, landholder.* Use "sokeman" in historical contexts to refer to an individual male landholder by socage.

soldier *See* armed forces, combat, draft dodger, draft, serviceman, sexism, warrior.

soldier of fortune generally a man.

soldier-statesman *soldier-politician/-diplomat/-lawmaker.*

solicitor (British) man or woman.

solon although this derives from Solon, the Athenian lawgiver (560 B.C.), it can be used for wise legislators of both sexes.

"some of my best friends are . . ." there is nothing wrong with this phrase if you don't mind betraying your bias against the group you are about to mention. Ironically, it's often used to defend oneself: "I'm not prejudiced! Why, some of my best friends. . ."

sommelier traditionally sommeliers have been men, but today a handful of the world's top sommeliers (known as "master sommeliers") are women. You can also use *wine steward/waiter* for both women and men.

sonarman *sonar technician.*

songbird *singer. See also* songstress.

songstress *songster, singer, vocalist, balladeer. See also* bluesman, crooner, chorus girl/chorus boy, prima donna, torch singer.

son of a bitch this insult, aimed at a man, ricochets off a woman—his mother. When you need an interjection or exclamation, use *doggone! doggone it! rats! shoot! damn! good grief!* There is generally no dearth of good swear words; replacing this expression is a matter of choice. When you want to refer to a person this way, use *so-and-so, ignoramus, saphead, stinker, ratfink, snake in the grass, creep, heel, jerk, bum, lowlife.* When using the term to describe a difficult job or situation, use instead *a tough one, uphill job.*

son of a gun most often a meaningless interjection or a cheery backslapping greeting between two men (preceded by "you old"), this relative of "son of a bitch" is genial and unobjectionable most of the time. Finding an alternative that women could use is difficult, mainly because women have their own ways of greeting each other in similar circumstances, few of which resemble the male scenario. Vive la différence. For the rather meaningless interjection, you could use *good grief! doggone! See also* son of a bitch.

Son of God (Jesus) *Beloved of God, Only Begotten, God's Own, Eternally Begotten, Chosen One.*

Son of Man (Jesus) the original phrase, translated simply "member of the human race," emphasized the humanity as well as the divinity of Jesus.

Jesus describes himself often with this phrase, underscoring its profound significance, and those rendering "Son of Man" inclusive will want to express "member of the human race" in a way that is theologically correct, scripturally sound, and acceptable both to congregations and hierarchies. This is a difficult phrase to retranslate, but there are several possibilities: *the Incarnate One, the One who became human/flesh, the One made human/flesh, Son/Child of Humanity/Humankind/the People, one like you, one of you.* You can also reword, for example: *Jesus, who was flesh and blood even as you and I are flesh and blood.*

sons (pseudogeneric) *children, heirs, offspring, progeny, daughters and sons/ sons and daughters.*

sonship *parent-child relationship.* There is no inclusive alternative for "sonship" that captures the fullness (or would-be fullness if it were inclusive) of this word. Until some creative mind comes up with a pithy inclusive word, circumlocute. (There is no "daughtership.")

sons of God *daughters and sons/sons and daughters of God, children of God, believers, the faithful.* Because of its brevity and familiarity, "children of God" is a good choice although it doesn't work in all contexts because of the difference between "children" and "adult children."

sons of man *children/daughters and sons of humanity/humankind, daughters and sons/children of the earth, our children/sons and daughters.*

sorceress *sorcerer.* See also "feminine" word endings.

sororal from the Latin for "sister," this is the little-known companion to "fraternal." Forms of it are seen principally only in "sorority" and Soroptimist International of the Americas (SIA), a service organization of professional women. "Sororal" could be used to describe all-women groups, activities, and friendships. Like other female-male word pairs, "sororal" and "fraternal" have developed along very different lines, with "fraternal" taking on many meanings, associations, and uses—some of them pseudogeneric. *See also* fraternal, fraternal order of, fraternal organization, fraternal twins, fraternization/fraternize.

sorority unlike "fraternity," which in the case of the Greek society is sometimes coed or which as a pseudogeneric refers to groups including both women and men, "sorority" refers strictly to women. If you want an inclusive alternative for the Greek society use *Greek society/system, Greek-letter organization, Greek-letter society/group.* Otherwise use *organization, society, association, union, secret society, club, federation, fraternity and sorority, common-interest group.* See also fraternity, fraternity/frat (Greek), sororal.

soubrette retain for the well-defined stage and opera role; there is no precise synonym and no parallel for a man.

sound-effects man *sound-effects coordinator/specialist/technician/crew; sometimes circumlocuted with simply sound effects.*

sound man *sound controller/technician/specialist/coordinator; sound mixer.*

soul brother/soul sister acceptable, parallel sex-specific terms.

Southeast Asian American this refers to ethnically, culturally, and geographically diverse peoples: the Vietnamese; the ethnic Lao, Mien, and Hmong of Laos; the Khmer of Cambodia, the Thai, and the various ethnic groups of Indonesia, Myanmar, Brunei, Singapore, and Malaysia. The majority of Southeast Asians in the U.S. are Vietnamese, Laotian, and Cambodian. Whenever possible (and the reference is necessary) use the more precise terms.

Soviet someone from or something pertaining to the former U.S.S.R. Not interchangeable with "Russian."

sow wild oats both young men and young women do this while their parents pray for crop failure.

spaceman *astronaut, cosmonaut, astronavigator, celestial navigator, member of the space program/space exploration team, space explorer/traveler/ aviator/pilot/ranger/walker, rocketeer, spacewoman and spaceman; extra-terrestrial, person from outer space.*

Spanish of or relating to Spain or its people or culture, this term is not interchangeable with Mexican, Chicana/Chicano, Latina/Latino, Hispanic, Cuban American, Puerto Rican, Latin American, or any other peoples not specifically from Spain. "Spaniard" is used for a person from Spain.

spastic *someone with spasticity/spastic muscles.* "Spaz" is also unacceptable. *See also* disability/disabilities.

spearman *spear thrower.*

special in referring to disabilities, use "special" only when it is part of a title (Special Olympics, Department of Special Education). "Special" acts to set apart those with disabilities, implying that they are not just different, as we are all different from each other, but of a different species; it is considered by the disability rights community to have definite negative connotations. It's hard to hear the word "special" with all its wonderful ordinary meanings when it is used to label you, exclude you from full participation, and keep you on the sidelines of life. Instead of "special buses," for example, use "separate buses" or "specially equipped buses" or "accessible buses," depending on what you mean. *See also* disability/ disabilities, exceptional.

special-effects man *special-effects coordinator/technician/crew.*

speciesism "Philosopher Peter Singer, one of the prime movers in the growing animal rights movement, has coined the term speciesism to denote a prejudice toward the members of one's own species as against the interest of members of other species. While admitting that it is an unattractive word, he nonetheless feels that it gets across the point he is trying to make: speciesism is analogous to racism and sexism and is as morally unacceptable" (Timothy J. Madigan, in *Free Inquiry*). Tad Clements says, however, "If by 'speciesism' is meant favoring one's own species above others, then speciesism is universal in nature. Natural selection through evolutionary mechanism leads to decline or extinction of any species if its population fails to promote the long-range success of that species. Whatever the mechanism employed—parasitism, predation, symbiosis, or whatever—the bottom line for every species is success as a species. So speciesism—preferring, whether consciously or not, one's own species—is the natural state of affairs throughout the biotic world." Because of the growing visibility of the animal rights movement and the awareness of speciesism, there have been some changes in language: the preferred term for "pet" is *companion animal, animal companion.* The first has been the term of choice for years for groups such as the Humane Society of the United States and the American Society for the Prevention of Cruelty to Animals. Instead of owner/master recommended terms are *caretaker, guardian, steward.*

spend money like a drunken sailor this phrase perpetuates an outdated stereotype and is sexist in that the "drunken sailor" is never visualized as a woman. Consider instead *spend money like water, throw money around, squander one's money, spend foolishly/ extravagantly/outrageously/ lavishly/imprudently/immoderately.*

spin-cast-pipe man *centrifugal spinner.*

spinning jenny this generally refers to a specific machine; sometimes you can use the generic "spinning machine."

spinmeister the "meister" gives this a masculine flavor, although it could be used for either sex. The sex-neutral alternative is the more common *spin-doctor.*

spinster something that is only one part of a person's life (being single) becomes the whole of the person when "spinster" is used; references to marital status are also usually unnecessary. When they are necessary, use an adjective instead of a noun: *single, unmarried, unwed.* Even such terms as "unmarried" and "unwed," however, perpetuate the marriage-as-norm stereotype. We act as though marriage and parenthood grant validity to a person when in fact married and unmarried often have more in common than not. Historically, single women enjoyed more civil powers than married women who were dependent upon and secondary to their husbands. Note the nonparallel connotations of the two supposedly parallel terms, "spinster" and "bachelor" (and was there ever an "eligible spinster" as there are "eligible bachelors"?). Women go from bachelor girl to spinster to old maid, but men are bachelors forever. *See also* celibate, maiden aunt, old maid, spinsterhood.

spinsterhood *singleness.*

spoilsman *spoils advocate, supporter of the spoils system.*

spokesman *official, representative, speaker, source, company/union/White House official, publicist, prolocutor, company/White House/union representative, advocate, proponent, voice, agent, press/publicity agent, PR coordinator, proxy, stand-in, intermediary, mediator, medium, go-between, negotiator, arbitrator, speechmaker, keynoter, promoter, aide, deputy, diplomat, mouthpiece, spokester, public information manager/ officer, public relations director, news bureau manager.* "Spokesman" (first used in 1540) and "spokeswoman" (first used in 1654) are acceptable if used gender-fairly. "Spokesperson" (1972) is not only awkward and contrived, but is generally reserved for women; it is not recommended. There are some excellent (and more descriptive) terms in the list of alternatives; "prolocutor," for example, is an exact synonym meaning "speaker for." You can also use *speaking for the group/in behalf of, representing,* or *"the company/firm/department said."*

spoonerism switching the initial sounds of two or more words ("it is kisstomary to cuss the bride," "one swell foop," or "the queer old dean," in a reference to Queen Victoria) results in a spoonerism, named after Oxford educator William A. Spooner. Retain the term; some linguistic sex balance is provided by Mrs. Malaprop and the term that describes her own brand of confusion. *See also* malapropism.

sportfisherman *sportfishing boat.*

sporting gentleman *gambler.*

sport of kings this expression has been associated for centuries with horseracing.

sportsman *sports lover, sport, sportster, sports/outdoor enthusiast, athlete, gamester, hobbyist, competitor; gambler; honorable competitor, good sport, honest/fair player; sportswoman and sportsman.* Or, be specific: *angler, hunter, fisher, tennis player, canoer, ballplayer, golfer.*

sportsmanlike/sportsmanly *sporting, fair, fair-minded.*

sportsmanship *sporting behavior, fair play, fairness, fair-mindedness, playing fair, sense of fair play, being a good sport/good loser, sportslike behavior, honor, honorable competition, competing honorably. See also* sportsman, sportsmanlike/sportsmanly, unsportsmanlike.

sportsman's license *sports license.*

spot man *spotter.*

spouse "spouse" has had a straightforward, nonpejorative history; it has always referred to the marriage partner of either sex. It is also used sometimes in same-sex or nonmarried heterosexual relationships. "Spousal equivalent"—which may sound either officious or tongue-in-cheek—has been sighted.

spry this hackneyed, ageist term is almost always used of older people to indicate that they are livelier than you would expect. As Mary Pettibone Poole *(A Glass Eye at a Keyhole)* said, "There are no old people nowadays; they are either 'wonderful for their age' or dead."

spunky *See* feisty.

squaw this racist, sexist, demeaning term from a word meaning "vagina" has long been considered unacceptable by American Indians. A campaign against the term begun by high school students Angelene Losh and Dawn Litzau resulted in a 1995 Minnesota state law requiring name changes for the 119 Minnesota lakes, creeks, islands, and other geographic features using the word "squaw" in their name. There appear to be some 921 uses of "squaw" throughout the U.S. (at least five of them are the incredibly offensive "Squaw's Tits"); the U.S. Geological Survey identifies 73 locations in Arizona alone that begin with the word. Ontario has 50 such names and is cooperating in changing the name of Squaw Narrows, which it shares with Minnesota. "Changing place names, maps, and documents will be a bother and it will take time. But the bother of changing a word is small when compared to the daily bother, the daily reminder to the Native Americans in our midst that they are seen through eyes of contempt and derogation. When we insult one among us we insult ourselves" (Robert Treuer).

squire (noun) always a man; there is no parallel for a woman.

squire (verb) *accompany, escort* (used of either sex).

stableboy/stableman *stable hand/worker/attendant, groom, handler.*

stage man *stagehand, stage manager.*

stag line a group of dateless, danceless men at a dance, the stag line is rarely seen today. It was, however, a terrifically sexist concept, burdening men with the social duty of requesting dances of women, and restricting women to a passive object status. Compare "wallflower," applied to groups of dateless, danceless women, to "stag line."

stag movie *pornographic movie.*

stag party for men only, a stag party can mean simply a gathering of men unaccompanied by women (perhaps a parallel for "hen party") or it can mean a raunchy party where prostitutes perform, pornographic movies are shown, or less publicly acceptable behavior occurs. If you mean the party for a man about to be married (which can be either of the above), you could also use *pre-wedding/bachelor party.* "Going stag" (that is, attending a party or event without a partner) used to be applied only to men; women also use it now.

stand pat nonsexist; the "pat" is not a person.

starlet *aspiring/promising young actor, neophyte/novice/beginning/young/ inexperienced/rookie actor, rookie/young performer, tyro screen star, newcomer to the stage/screen, young/future/minor star.* Or, use whatever term you would use for a male actor at the same level of professional experience.

statesman *diplomat, world/government/political leader, politician, legislator, lawmaker, public figure, political/government strategist, public servant/ official; stateswoman and statesman.* Do not use "statesperson"—it's not only awkward, but so far it's been used only for women.

statesmanlike/statesmanly *diplomatic, politically savvy.*

statesmanship *statecraft, diplomacy, government/world leadership, leader- ship, political savvy.*

stationmaster *station manager/head/chief.*

steersman *pilot, navigator, steersmate, steerer, guide.*

stepfather/stepmother these are acceptable terms, although some people prefer "mother/father by marriage." *See also* stepmother, wicked.

stepmother, wicked leave this phrase in the old fairy tales but do not write any new ones using it. It is sexist because there is no equally developed wicked stepfather persona; its mythic influence has unnecessarily compli- cated many blended family situations.

stereotype a stereotype (the word comes from the process of duplicating printing plates made from set type) is a shorthand method of labeling and cataloging people. "We might define a stereotype as the continual portrayal of a group of people with the same narrow set of characteristics. . . . It shows a cultural bias toward the characteristics of one's own culture, painting characters outside that culture in limiting and sometimes dehumanizing ways" (Linda Seger, *Creating Unforgettable Characters*). Stereotypes are quick and convenient because they require no thought. For the same reason, they are often inaccurate—and racist, sexist, homophobic, ageist, handicappist, or ethnocentric. "The holder of a stereotype will accept any information, no matter how improbable, which reinforces the image. Conversely, the holder will discard as irrelevant any data which does not confirm the stereotype" (Marsha J. Hamilton, in Joanna Kadi, *Food for Our Grandmothers: Writings by Arab-American and Arab-Canadian Feminists*).

sterile this term is used for both women and men. "Infertile" refers to the lack of offspring in people who have been having unprotected intercourse for a certain length of time. "Sterile" usually indicates that a cause for the infertility has been found. Infertile people are not necessarily sterile. Sterile people are always infertile. Infertility is often treatable; sterility generally is not (unless, for example, a tubal ligation or vasectomy can be reversed). Do not confuse "sterile" with "impotent" or "frigid." *See also* barren, frigid, impotent, infertile.

sternson nonsexist; from a Scandinavian word that has nothing to do with a male offspring.

stevedore nonsexist; from the Spanish for "to pack."

steward (manager) the word itself is nonsexist and can be used for both sexes, but stewards have traditionally been men so it will seem to have a male cast to it.

steward/stewardess (flight crew member) *flight/cabin attendant, attendant, crew member.* Plural: *flight crew.* In spite of the attempt to equalize the job label, sexist, ageist terms for flight attendants still pop up in the popular culture: skygirl, senior mama, gold winger, galley queen.

stickman (gambling) *casino employee, stick/craps boss.*

stick man (police) *stick officer, police patrol officer, beat officer/patrol.*

stickman (sports) *stick player.* There is no substitute for this term in some games.

stickup man *armed robber, thief, mugger, purse-snatcher, roller. See also* gunman; holdup man.

stiff upper lip, keep a although a woman may occasionally be given this advice, it is something of a cultural imperative for men. It's never been clear why repressing feelings and putting a false face on things is desirable; it is far more likely to be unhealthful. *See also* man, act like a/be a/ take it like a.

stillman (liquor) *distiller.*

stillman (oil) *refinery operator.*

stock boy/stock girl/stock man *stockkeeper, stock/stockroom clerk/assistant, stock gatherer.*

stockman *rancher, cattle owner/raiser/breeder, sheep farmer/owner/raiser/ breeder.*

Stone Age this is the correct term for the earliest known period of human culture. It is questionable when used to refer to non-Stone Age cultures and people, implying that they are somehow inferior, backward, or unchanging.

storageman *storage agent.*

storeman *storekeeper.*

storms in 1979 the National Weather Service stopped naming storms exclusively with women's names; half are now given men's names. *See also* hurricanes.

straight (adjective) "straight" and "gay" is an adjective pair referring to people who have respectively other-sex and same-sex attractional orientations. Despite its dictionary definitions ("exhibiting no deviation from what is established or accepted as usual, normal, or proper," *Webster's Ninth New Collegiate Dictionary*; "right; correct . . . not deviating from what is considered socially normal, usual, or acceptable," *American Heritage Dictionary*, 3rd ed.), the term "straight" is acceptable to lesbians and gay men. There are a number of gay-straight school alliances and student organizations. "Straight" is almost always used in informal contexts, unlike the broader "gay." The even more informal "het" is sometimes used instead of "straight."

straight man *comedian, stooge, entertainer, the straight, comic's partner, comedy partner, feeder of straight lines.* None of these work as well for meaning and conciseness as "straight man," but as it's not a widely used term today the issue may not arise.

straw man *straw argument/figure, nonexistent problem, diversionary tactic, hoax, imaginary/weak opposition, carefully set up just to be knocked down, front, cover; red herring; nonentity, hot air, ineffectual person, weakling; sitting duck.* Bankers use the term "straw borrower" for a nonoccupying co-borrower.

street people *See* bag lady/bag man, homeless.

strident used primarily to describe women (especially feminists) indiscriminately and discriminatingly, "strident" (as well as "shrill") has become devalued and stereotypical. Alternatives include: *harsh, jarring, raucous, dissonant, discordant, unharmonious, clashing, sharp.*

strongarm man *strongarm guard, bodyguard, the muscle; enforcer, goon, ugly/rough customer, bully, hard case.*

strongman *dictator, tyrant, military dictator; weightlifter, iron pumper, powerhouse.*

stud/studly/stud muffin (man) these colloquial terms for a man can have several meanings: a man who is successful sexually with women, someone who is macho and muscular, an athlete, a competent, strong man, a good-looking man with more brawn than brain. Because their connotations can be either positive or negative (labeling men as sex objects, animalizing them, tending toward lookism), use these terms cautiously—and of course they don't belong in the workplace. *See also* animal names for people, hunk, ladies' man, man about town, playboy, rake, slut, womanizer.

stuffed shirt this term is appropriate for both sexes, but if you need a more neutral-sounding alternative consider *big head, prig, someone who is stuffy/stuck-up/conceited/smug/self-important/parochial/provincial/ supercilious/snobbish/puffed-up/complacent/self-satisfied/pleased with themselves.*

strumpet *See* prostitute.

stuntman "stuntwoman" is an equally acceptable sex-specific word. If you need inclusive alternatives consider *stunt performer/driver/actor, professional acrobat, daredevil, breakneck, acrobat, aerialist, contortionist, gymnast.*

suave technically inclusive, this term is curiously reserved for men. There is nothing to say it can't be used of women. You could also consider sex-neutral alternatives: *sophisticated, smooth, worldly, polite, diplomatic, civil.*

subassemblyman *subassembler.*

subjects terms like "subjects" and "sample" are acceptable when discussing statistics, but the *Publication Manual of the American Psychological Association*, 4th ed., suggests replacing the impersonal term *subjects* with a more descriptive term: *participants, individuals, college students, children, respondents.* "Scientists who refer to people as *subjects*, businessmen who refer to people as *personnel*, teachers who refer to people as *culturally disadvantaged* are not merely describing; they are committing themselves to a point of view" (Neil Postman, *Crazy Talk, Stupid Talk*). *See also* case, patient.

subkingdom retain this biology term as it is.

submissive promoting submissiveness as a "natural" attitude for women has often been based on the biblical injunction for wives to be submissive to their husbands. That this use of "submissive" may have arisen from factors in the mid-Eastern culture of the first centuries A.D. or from subsequent translations is not taken into account.

success object (man) if women have traditionally been viewed as sex objects, men have traditionally been viewed as success objects; both roles are artificial, highly limiting, and destructive. For men, economic success is still the crucial criterion of self-worth—witness the bumper sticker "He who dies with the most toys wins." Avoid writing and speaking of men solely in terms of their achievements, finances, possessions, and social rank. This is not to belittle accomplishment, hard work, or success, but to say that men are more than machines that endlessly crank out "product" for the boss, the family, the neighborhood, and the IRS. *See also* provider.

suffers from (a condition) *someone who has (a condition), someone with (a condition).* In referring to people with disabilities avoid all forms of the afflicted with/suffers from/victim of construction. Use instead, for example, *has diabetes, has multiple sclerosis. See also* disability/disabilities, handicapped.

suffragette *suffragist.* Although women in Great Britain chose to call themselves "suffragettes," U.S. women did not want the demeaning "-ette" ending ("majorette," "usherette," "farmerette") and were called "suffragettes" only by those periodicals and speakers hostile to the women's goals. *See also* suffragist.

suffragist this term describes anyone of either sex who works for the voting rights of others, especially women's, but it most often refers to a woman. In 1912, Mark Twain wrote of suffragists: "For forty years they have swept an imposingly large number of unfair laws from the statute books of America. In this brief time these serfs have set themselves free— essentially. Men could not have done as much for themselves in that time without bloodshed, at least they never have, and that is an argument that they didn't know how." *See also* suffragette.

sugar daddy there is no parallel word to describe a woman who supports a younger man, but if you really need to convey this concept, a possible inclusive alternative might be *meal ticket.*

suicide *See* glass cellar.

suit this jargon for "manager" or "boss" can be used of either sex (women wear suits too) although at present it tends to be more male-associated.

suitor in affairs of the heart, this term has traditionally been reserved for men. Today, it is not so much the case that women may also be suitors as that the term is no longer necessary because forming a relationship tends to be a mutual activity. No longer is one person the supplicant, the pursuer, while the other is the "sued."

sultan/sultana acceptable sex-specific terms.

superhero/superheroine these denizens of popular comic book/strip genres might seem to be equals, but as long as "heroine" is defined as "a female hero," she is a subset and thus the lesser of the two. Call all such characters "superheroes." *See also* hero.

superman/superwoman these are fairly equivalent gender-specific terms and they can be used as they are. The inclusive alternative is superhero.

superstition every religion requires faith for at least some of its beliefs, but "superstition" is applied (and negatively at that) only to other people's beliefs. Many religious beliefs not so labeled fit the dictionary definitions of "superstition."

surname there are three issues here: (1) Male surnames prevail in that in the U.S., wives traditionally take their husbands' names, and children take their fathers' names. The custom has been slowly changing and there is currently no law that requires a child's birth certificate to bear the father's last name. In 1988 in Nebraska, however, a couple were stopped, first by state bureaucrats and then by a three-judge panel of an appeals court, from giving their daughter a last name different from either the father's or the mother's. According to the ruling, parents have no fundamental right to choose their children's names. A dissenting judge wrote, however, that "a person's name is, in a sense, her identity, her personality, her being. There is something sacred about a name. It is our own business, not the government's." To solve the surname problem, some people are renaming themselves and their children, making up a new family name when they marry, or hyphenating names. Sharon Lebell *(Naming Ourselves, Naming Our Children)* proposes the "bilineal solution" whereby boys are named after their fathers, girls after their mothers, or vice versa, thus ensuring that both names get passed on. (2) Do women have names of their own? "The argument that 'women have no names' is selectively lopsided logic," says Marilyn Vos Savant (in *Parade Magazine*). "If a woman doesn't have a name (because it's 'her father's'), then a man doesn't have one either (because it's *his* father's). And you can say the same thing about the fathers themselves. So, if a male gets a name when he's born that becomes his own at that point, then a female gets a name when she's born that becomes her own at that point too." (3) Use parallel treatment for men's and women's surnames: if you use his surname alone (Tascher), don't add a social title to hers (Ms. Demeter); if you call her Magnolia, don't call him Mr. Bartleby. In dealing with married couples, too often he is the main Primrose while she is Mrs. Primrose, Deborah, or Deborah Primrose; they should be referred to as Charles Primrose and Deborah Primrose, Mr. Primrose and Ms. Primrose, or Deborah and Charles. *See also* baptismal name, Christian name, hyphenated surnames, maiden name, matronym/matronymic, patronym/patronymic.

surrogate mother a legitimate sex-specific word, although other terms are being advocated: *biological/gestational/ovarian/uterine mother, egg donor.*

survivor *See* rape victim.

suttee "It was once a common practice in many parts of the world to kill the wives, concubines, and female (and sometimes male) servants of deceased patriarchs, perhaps in the hope that they would continue to serve their masters in the next world. Widow-sacrifice has existed not only in India, but in Scandinavia, Slavia, Greece, Thrace, Scythia, Ancient Egypt, among the Tongans, Balinese, Fijians and Maoris, in some African and Native American tribes, and in China. India is unusual only in that there the practice has continued into modern times" (Mary Anne Warren, *Gendercide*). Although the practice of suttee, in which widows were burned alive on their husbands' funeral pyres, was outlawed in India in 1829, immolations still continued. In recent years, brides who bring an insufficient dowry into their marriage have also faced a fiery death for disappointing their in-laws. More than 20,000 women have been killed in "bride burnings" (or "dowry deaths") since 1988. Human rights groups have suggested sanctions against countries that practice gender apartheid and tolerate violence against women.

swagman *swagger, swaggie, vagrant, vagrant worker.*

swain *admirer.* "Swain" comes from "swein" meaning "boy" or "servant." *See also* boyfriend, suitor.

swami from the Hindi for "owner, lord," this word is perceived as male. Unless you are using it in its narrowest sense, you may substitute *teacher, religious teacher, ascetic, pundit, seer, mentor, leader, guide, spiritual guide, guru.*

swarthy although references to complexions are not in themselves unaccept-able, "swarthy" always seems to convey a little something negative; "dark-complexioned" says the same thing without also implying that this person is possibly someone to keep an eye on.

swashbuckler this term seems ineradicably associated with men, although there have been women who have behaved like swashbucklers, among them pirates Anne Bonney, Mary Read, and Grania O'Malley and the French daredevil Marie Marvingt. More neutral-appearing words include *daredevil, adventurer, sensation-seeker, thrill-seeker, show-off, exhibition-ist, fire-eater.*

swear like a trooper troopers and soldiers include both sexes now, but if you want something else try *turn the air blue, cuss a blue streak, curse up hill and down dale, curse up one side and down the other, badmouth.*

sweater girl if it is truly necessary to describe a woman in terms of her voluptuousness, use adjectives ("curvaceous," "buxom," "voluptuous") instead of a noun so that a piece of clothing (emphasizing one part of her) does not become the whole woman. "Sweater girl" implies a great deal more than what the woman looks like: it also hints at her lifestyle and her intelligence. Even though some men look wonderful in body shirts, we don't have a term like "body shirt guy"; rarely is man's appearance treated as woman's is. *See also* body image.

sweet sixteen (and never been kissed) as this always refers to a young woman, it is sexist. No 16-year-old wants to hear it anyway.

sweet william leave as is.

swingman (basketball) *swingplayer.*

switchman *switcher, switch/switchyard operator, technical equipment operator/technician, switching equipment technician/operator.*

swordsman *fencer, dueler, duelist, blade, swashbuckler, sword fighter; swordswoman and swordsman.*

swordsmanship *fencing/sword fighting skills/expertise/ability, sword-handling skills.*

T

Words are name tags which save us the trouble of thinking about the objects or ideas which they represent. Here exactly lies their capacity for mischief.

—*Judith Groch*

If you are a thinker, you will change the language. You will not use words the way others do.

—*Gertrude Stein*

Most people wish to be consoled, confirmed. They want their prejudices reinforced and their structured belief systems validated. After all, it hurts to think, and it's absolute agony to think twice.

—*Jennifer Stone*

tailor woman or man.

take it like a man *See* man, act like a/be a/take it like a.

take off one's hat to this formerly male custom has all but disappeared; the term is used today inclusively.

talesman *substitute juror.*

talisman nonsexist; the "man" is not sex-linked but comes from a Greek word for "consecration ceremony." The plural is talismans.

talk to like a Dutch uncle *See* Dutch uncle, talk to like a.

tallboy nonsexist; "boy" is from the French for wood, "bois."

tallyman *tallykeeper.*

tapman *taproom attendant.*

tart if you mean prostitute, use *prostitute*. If you mean a woman considered to be sexually promiscuous, consider describing her behavior factually rather than labeling her judgmentally. (Originally "tart" was used as an endearment, much as "honey" or "sugar" is used.) *See also* prostitute.

taskmaster/taskmistress *supervisor, boss, job boss, task sergeant, disciplinarian, inspector, instructor, overseer, monitor, martinet, surveyor, superintendent, director, manager, employer.* For discussion of "master" words, *see* master.

taximan *taxi driver.*

taxman *tax collector/inspector/agent/preparer/consultant.*

teacher 98% of preschool and kindergarten teachers and 85% of elementary school teachers are women, while 96% of public school superintendents are men, and 97% are white.

teach one's grandmother to suck eggs *teach a bird to fly/fish to swim, reinvent the wheel, carry coals to Newcastle.* In Italian it's *teach a dolphin to swim.*

tease (woman) the dangerous myth that women are teasing when they say "no" to a man's advances has been responsible for much grief, criminal behavior, and even murder. The notion of woman-as-tease is often in the eye (and elsewhere) of the beholder.

teen/teenager acceptable age-specific terms, although less acceptable in generalizations; young people (the preferred term) reject a one-size-fits-all label and particularly dislike being called kids, girls and boys/boys and girls, youths, adolescents, juveniles, or teenyboppers (which is also sexist, as it's reserved for girls). Older teens can be called *young adults*, and secondary students can be called *high schoolers*. Career teacher Richard Demers addresses his high school students as "scholars." *See also* adolescent, ageism, juvenile, youth.

teen moms the majority of babies born to teenage mothers are fathered by adult men an average of four to six years older than the young women, according to a 1996 California study by Mike Males, and the younger the mother, the greater the age gap: high-schoolers had babies with men an average 4.2 years older, junior-high girls with men an average of 6.7 years older (13% of those men were at least 25 years old), and among 10-to 14-year-old girls, some 27% of the fathers were 20–24. Males said the study raises questions about whether girls' early sexual experiences are truly consensual. There is also much societal disapproval and anger (expressed concretely by "reforms" in welfare programs) against "teen moms" (there is no corresponding label for the man), but very little is said or done about the men who are equally (or perhaps a little more, in view of their greater age) responsible.

Tejana/Tejano Chicana/Chicano (or someone of Mexican descent) from Texas; use for those who self-identify this way.

teleman *communications officer; petty officer in charge of communications or petty officer, communications; sparks.*

telephone man *telephone installer/repairer/worker.*

telephone operator man or woman.

television largely sexist, racist, homophobic, ageist, handicapist, and violent, television is not an equal opportunity medium—not perhaps surprising considering that over three-quarters of television writers are white men. Men are featured much more often, in more lead roles, and for a wider range of roles. While men are shown more often at work, women are usually presented in family roles and given explicit marital status (most female characters are married, about to be married, or in a serious relationship with a man, while most male characters are single). Men are more likely to dominate women than vice versa, and even when they have equal status, men are more likely to assume control, both physically and emotionally. Men are the movers and shakers who earn the money; women are responsible for the well-being and cleanliness of the family. Despite exceptions, women are often shown as half-clad and half-witted, needing to be rescued by quick-thinking, fully clothed men. On the other side of the camera, women make up approximately 25% of writers, 15% of producers, and 9% of directors. *See also* advertising.

tell it to the marines nonsexist since marines are now both women and men. Or use: *pull the other one.*

temp short for temporary worker/employee, this informal term applies to both men and woman, although since women make up the majority of temporary office workers, it is likely to be perceived as female.

temporarily able-bodied *See* able-bodied.

temptress *tempter. See also* "feminine" word endings.

termagant since this term is reserved for women and there is no parallel for men, you may want to consider sex-neutral alternatives: *faultfinder, grouch, grumbler, crosspatch, fire-eater, loud/overbearing person. See also* shrew.

terrorist terrorism is the act of causing terror, usually for political purposes and usually directed at innocents (people not involved in the disputed issue). Outside blatantly terroristic acts like the bombing of a civilian airliner, the use of "terrorist" often varies according to the writer's perspective; a terrorist in one case might be a freedom fighter, guerrilla, resister, or commando in another. "This has become a code word for Arabs. When using it we can mask anti-Arab statements and politics while ignoring the terrorist acts of white people and European and U.S. governments, such as the bombings of civilian areas in Panama and Iraq" (Paul Kivel, *Uprooting Racism*). Sanford Berman *(Prejudices and*

Antipathies) gives examples of terrorism as practiced by the Minutemen, Ku Klux Klan, saturation bombing during World War II, the atomic bomb dropped on Japan, search-and-destroy missions together with massive defoliation and the use of Napalm in Vietnam. Reserve "terrorist" only for those who fit the definition, and use it of all those who practice it.

testatrix *testator.* "Testatrix" is still used for certain legal matters. *See also* "feminine" word endings.

testimony nonsexist; terms like "testimony," "protest," "New Testament," and "testicles" all come from the Latin "testari" meaning to testify or to witness (the word "testes" developed as a supposed "witness" to virility). The connection between testes and testimony was reinforced by the old Roman custom whereby men swore oaths by laying a hand on their genitals while women swore by their breast. (Freud was puzzled as to how women, not fearing castration, developed a conscience.)

testosterone testosterone circulates in both sexes but is much more abundant in males; post-pubertal men have testosterone levels about 10 times higher than in women. Some studies have indicated that testosterone is a likely source of aggression and that men who dominate in social situations have higher testosterone levels than their peers. While the presence of high levels of testosterone may have some behavioral consequences, scientists warn against generalizations and are skeptical that testosterone is a strong, direct cause of specific human activity when so many other social factors determine if and how testosterone translates into such behavior as aggression, dominance, or competitiveness. It appears, for example, that women can be as competitive as men, even with much lower testosterone levels. To imply that the violence men commit is inherent and unavoidable is not only unscientific but dangerous insofar as it gives a kind of permission to male acting out. With so little factual evidence, it is indefensible to accuse men ("jokingly" or not) of "testosterone poisoning." Just as menstrual cycles and menopause have been blamed for unrelated behavior in women, men are beginning to hear more unscientific remarks about their testosterone levels. Restrain yourself.

testy this comes from Latin for "head" and has nothing to do with testicles or testosterone.

"the" when used before adjectives to make a noun phrase (the elderly, the poor, the blind), "the" is disparaging and objectifying; it also often betrays the writer or speaker as an outsider. Put the adjective with an accurate and specific noun (elderly residents, poor taxpayers, blind students). This use of "the" is acceptable when used with nationalities (the Swiss, the Japanese, the French). *See also* adjectives as nouns.

thealogy *See* unconventional spellings.

their/them/they *See* singular "they."

thinking man *thinker, thinking/reflective/intelligent/learned person, thinking/intelligent being, intellectual, philosopher, sage, scholar, brain, highbrow.*

third baseman *See* baseman.

Third World introduced in 1952 by French demographer Alfred Sauvy, the term describes countries that are marginalized economically and politically in the international system. It is also used sometimes to refer to minority groups as a whole within a larger culture. Today there is dissatisfaction with the term as being imprecise (definitions vary), simplistic (the countries differ widely), antagonistic (like "nonwhite," it's a catchall way of marking "us" and "them"), and demeaning (no matter how you look at it, being third is not as good as being first or second). "The Third World is gone. . . . the countries once assigned to the Third World are still there, but the concept of the Third World is no longer connected to any reality" (Robert J. Samuelson, *Newsweek*, July 23, 1990). Alternatives suffer from some of the same problems as "Third World," but you might consider in some contexts *nonindustrialized/developing/emerging/ overexploited/economically exploited countries/nations.* ("Nonaligned" and "unaligned" are political rather than economic concepts.) But as Mary Beth Protomastro *(Copy Editor)* points out, "Third World" is succinct and everybody knows what it means. Until an equally useful term surfaces, "Third World" will still be used.

those people *See* you people.

three-man (adjective) *See* one-man/two-man/three-man, etc.

thresherman *thresher.*

thug the original thugs were members of a professional gang of thieves and murderers in India who strangled victims, and the term still seems male although there is nothing to prohibit it being used for women too. *See also* bad guy.

ticket girl *ticket taker, pricing clerk.*

tied to someone's apron strings *See* apron strings, tied to someone's.

tigress *tiger.* By using the base word inclusively, terms like "tiger's eye," "tiger lily," and "have a tiger by the tail" are not sex-specific either. In its meaning as a daring, protective, or fierce woman, "tigress" is a judgment call. *See also* "feminine" word endings.

tillerman *tiller, tiller operator.*

timberman *timber cutter/worker, logger, tree cutter, forester, woodcutter, log roller.*

time-study man *time-study engineer.*

time waits for no man *time waits for no one.*

timothy grass leave as is.

tin lizzie *Model T.* The innocent-sounding "tin lizzie" comes from the name Elizabeth (also Liza or Lizzie), which was such a common name for black women (H. L. Mencken posited that its popularity came arose from Eliza in *Uncle Tom's Cabin*) that it was used from the 1880s until the late 1920s as a generic name for any black woman, but especially a servant, maid, or cook (Stuart Berg Flexner, *I Hear America Talking*). Flexner says the name was given the car because it, like the maid, "worked hard all week and prettied up on Sundays." (Henry Ford said the car was available in "any color you choose as long as it's black.")

tinman *tinsmith, tin manufacturer.*

tirewoman *personal attendant.*

T-man *Treasury agent.*

to a man *without exception, unanimously, of one mind/accord, with one voice, at one with each other, willingly, agreed on all hands, in every mouth, carried by acclamation/unanimously, to a one/person; like-minded; every last one of them, everyone.*

toastmaster/toastmistress these terms are difficult to replace as they have specific meanings and are deeply entrenched in the language, particularly because of the many toastmasters clubs around the country. When possible replace with *emcee, host, speaker, announcer, introducer, lecturer, talker, guest lecturer, orator, declaimer, speechmaker, rhetorician, elocutionist, preacher, interlocutor.*

to boldly go where no man has gone before in the first "Star Trek" TV series in the 1960s, this phrase was used; in the late 1980s, "Star Trek: The Next Generation" used *to boldly go where no one has gone before* (Ruth King, *Talking Gender*).

to each his own *to each their own, there's no accounting for tastes, it takes all kinds, chacun à son goût, to each her own/his own.* **See also** singular "they."

toff refers to men only; there is no parallel for women.

token defined as someone hired to deflect accusations of discrimination against the employer, this implies the person was unqualified for the job; use cautiously.

tollman *toll collector, toll booth operator.*

tomato *See* food names for people.

tomboy *active/agile/athletic/boisterous/adventurous/physically courageous/*

competitive child, live wire, one of the gang, strong/vigorous/direct/ spirited/self-confident child, rude/blunt/messy/rough/tough child, logical/ mechanically minded child, etc. "Tomboy" used to refer only to boys, then to both girls and boys, and now only to girls. In *Women of the World,* Julia Edwards says of foreign correspondent Dickey Chapelle: "Although she called herself a tomboy, she was better described as a tomgirl, for she didn't want to be a boy. She just wanted to do the things boys get to do." Sociologists and behavior experts suggest that the concept of tomboy (along with the term) is obsolete; behavior that another generation found tomboyish is considered normal today. Sociologist Barrie Thorne spent 11 months observing boys and girls on a playground; only twice did she hear them use the word "tomboy" although adults did so fairly commonly. Many children were clearly unfamiliar with the term and several said they'd never heard of it. She predicts the word will disappear within the next decade. *See also* sissy.

tomcat Hugh Rawson *(Wicked Words)* says this originated from the hero's name in a 1760 bestseller, *The Life and Adventures of a Cat.* In reference to a cat, use only for male cats. To mean a man who is sexually active with more than one partner, it may be clearer to describe rather than label the behavior.

Tom, Dick, and Harry, every *See* every Tom, Dick, and Harry.

tomfool (adjective/noun) if the connection with the man's name is a problem in your context consider *foolish, imprudent, irresponsible, unwise, hasty, shortsighted, foolhardy, reckless, pointless, nonsensical, ridiculous, silly, crazy, daft, simpleminded, stupid, mindless, thick-witted; fool.*

tomfoolery/tommyrot if the connection with the man's name is a problem in your context consider *foolishness, nonsense, rubbish, shenanigans, monkeyshines, monkey business, mischief, hanky-panky, trick, buffoonery, silliness, malarkey, baloney, poppycock, balderdash, moonshine, gobbledygook, garbage, stuff and nonsense, hogwash, bunkum, craziness, goofiness.*

Tommy retain in historical contexts. Or, *British soldier.*

tommy gun nonsexist; named after John T. Thompson.

tommyrot *See* tomfoolery.

Tom Thumb this is the hero of English folklore; if you should ever need a sex-neutral expression like it, he was known in some accounts as *Hop-o'-My-Thumb.*

tom-tom nonsexist; from the Hindi word "tamtam."

tonto this unacceptable term is borrowed from the Lone Ranger's loyal Indian companion.

too big for one's britches said of both sexes.

top banana/top brass/top dog use for both sexes.

Torah, the consisting of the five books of Moses (Genesis, Exodus, Leviticus, Numbers, and Deuteronomy), the Torah is only part of—not synonymous with—the Hebrew Bible or Scriptures. (The other two parts are The Prophets and The Writings). *See also* Bible.

torch singer this has always been a female singer with a husky, passionate voice who has generally lost her man. The term may include in the future male singers in gay bars. An inclusive alternative (although it is not an exact synonym) is *blues singer. See also* bluesman, crooner, songster/ songstress.

totem pole, high man on the *number one, second to none, front-runner, star, the favorite, person on top, high-ranking individual, someone with seniority, winner, top scorer, cream of the crop, influential person, big boss/wheel/cheese, hotshot, bigwig, someone at the top of the ladder/ heap/tree.* The phrase is ethnocentric as well as sexist. *See also* lord it over.

totem pole, low man on the *lowest ranking individual, new kid on the street, someone with no seniority/clout, the last one in, washout, loser, three-time loser, hard-luck case, defeatee, the low scorer, also-ran, plebeian, neophyte, proletarian, rookie, beginner, tyro, gofer.* The phrase is ethnocentric as well as sexist.

tough cookie/tough guy although of typically nonparallel construction ("cookie/guy"), these terms for a woman and a man mean roughly the same thing. Sex-neutral alternatives include *toughy/toughie, tough, bully, someone who is hard as nails, hard-nosed, callous, unsympathetic, hard-boiled, unfeeling. See also* hard-boiled.

tough titty *tough luck/toenails, tough, too bad, that's the breaks.* Its origins are unclear, but its association with the slang for a woman's breast makes this a term to avoid.

towerman *tower tender/operator/attendant.*

townsman *town-dweller, local, native, resident, citizen, neighbor, member of the community; townie, city slicker; urbane person.* Plural: *townspeople, townsfolk.*

toyboy defined as a young man, more handsome than intelligent, who dates older female celebrities, this term is ageist, highly judgmental, and as sexist as "kept woman." Our national obsession with other people's lives and our willingness to judge those we don't know encourages the popularity of quick-fix stereotypes fashioned to sound-bite dimensions. *See also* boy toy.

trackman *track layer/inspector, trackwalker; track athlete, runner, sprinter, relay/distance runner, track event entrant, member of the track team, athlete who competes in track events; discus thrower, high-jumper, hurdler, long-jumper, shot-putter.*

tradesman *shopkeeper, storekeeper, small business owner, merchant, retailer, dealer, store owner/manager/worker/employee, tradeswoman and tradesman; trades worker, skilled/construction worker.* Or, be specific: *electrician, mason, machinist, sub-contractor.* Plural: *tradespeople, people in the trades. See also* hardhat.

tradevman *training devices personnel.*

tragedienne *tragedian. See also* "feminine" word endings.

trailing spouse *See* two-person single career.

trainman *train worker/operator/crew member, railroad employee; rail worker; conductor; track layer; train buff.*

traitress *traitor. See also* "feminine" word endings.

tramp (hobo) woman or man. *See also* bum, hobo, road sister.

tramp (woman) for prostitute, use *prostitute.* For someone with questionable morals (a questionable judgment) consider inclusive terms: *promiscuous/ sexually active/undiscriminating person/individual.* Women are often judged by criteria not applied to men; "tramp" is used for men only in the original meaning of a vagrant or hobo. *See also* prostitute.

transgenderist "A grass-roots movement called transgenderism developed during the 1980s. The guiding principle of the movement is that people should be free to change, either temporarily or permanently, the sex type to which they were assigned since infancy. Transgenderism makes manifest the continuum nature of sex types. . . . There are two main types of persons in the movement: transsexuals and cross-dressers" (Martine Rothblatt, *The Apartheid of Sex*). *See also* cross-dresser, transsexual, transvestite.

transsexual a transsexual is a man or a woman who feels that the gender into which they were born is not right for them and that they were intended to be the opposite sex. They may choose to simply live as a member of the opposite sex in as complete a way as possible or they may undergo sex-reassignment surgery. Most often, the direction of the change is male to female. "Transsexuals use sex hormones and sometimes plastic surgery to change their anatomy toward the other sex type. The results are so persuasive that rarely can a 'new man' or 'new woman' be distinguished from a biological original. Over a thousand persons a year actually have sex change surgery, and many more than this number simply use hormones to change their facial hair, voice, and physique" (Martine Rothblatt, *The Apartheid of Sex*). In the sexual identity that feels natural to them, transsexuals can be romantically and emotionally attached to the opposite sex, the same sex, or both sexes. "I think the name transsexualism is what throws a lot of people off. They seem to take the 'sex' part as referring to the sex act (an act many of us on hormones would find difficult to perform anyway) rather than to gender. I prefer to talk about gender dysphoria. It sounds more clinical and is more accurate" (Terri Main, in *Grace and Lace Letter*). *See also* cross-dresser, transgenderist.

transvestite according to the Gay & Lesbian Alliance Against Defamation *(Media Guide to the Lesbian and Gay Community)*, a transvestite is "an individual who regularly or occasionally prefers wearing the clothing socially assigned to the opposite gender. Contrary to popular belief, many male transvestites are heterosexual. The term applies to women as well as to men, but the greater variety of clothing options accorded women in our society has made female transvestism less noticeable." Transvestism is sometimes also called cross-dressing. *See also* cross-dressing, transgenderist.

trash *See* poor white trash.

trashman *trash collector.*

traveling salesman *traveling sales agent/rep, commercial traveler. See also* salesgirl/saleslady/salesman/saleswoman.

trawlerman *trawler, trawler owner/operator.*

trencherman *hearty/heavy/serious eater.*

tribal warfare "Conflicts among diverse peoples within African nations are often referred to as 'tribal warfare,' while conflicts among the diverse peoples within European countries are never described in such terms. If the rivalries between the Ibo and the Hausa and Yoruba in Nigeria are described as 'tribal,' why not the rivalries between Serbs and Slavs in Yugoslavia, or Scots and English in Great Britain, Protestants and Catholics in Ireland, or the Basques and the Southern Spaniards in Spain?" (Robert B. Moore, in Paula S. Rothenberg, *Racism and Sexism*). In the same way, "We hear about 'black on black' violence in Africa, but Eastern European warfare is called an 'ethnic clash'; we never hear about 'white on white' violence. It's just people from 'ethnic' groups clashing. How much more understandable than those enigmatic 'tribal bloodbaths'" (Joan Steinau Lester, *The Future of White Men and Other Diversity Dilemmas*).

tribe *nation, people.* Or, use specific designation (Cheyenne, Ibo, San). For an excellent analysis of the issues involved in the use of "tribe" for

American Indians, see Ward Churchill, "Naming Our Destiny: Towards a Language of Indian Liberation," *Global Justice,* 1992, vol. 3. He says, "Words such as 'nation' and 'tribe' are not, all protestations of government officials and 'responsible tribal leaders' notwithstanding, 'interchangeable' in either political or legal contexts. To the contrary, phrases such as 'tribal sovereignty' add up to near-perfect politicojudicial oxymorons. . . . No native language in North America . . . contains a word which translates accurately as 'tribe.' The literal translation of most American Indian people's names for themselves was, traditionally, exactly that: 'people.'" Originally, Indian peoples were treated as nations, complete with ambassadors and treaties. In the 1860s and 1870s "tribe" began completely displacing "nation" in the legal discourse leading to congressional termination of treaty-making with Indians and full and absolute power over Indians' property and affairs. The use of "tribe" for African peoples is also rejected. "How an ethnic group with two or ten million people in East or West Africa, with a parliamentary government, can be described as a tribe and not the Irish, the Scot, the Welsh, the French or the English, still baffles the non-European" (Sanford Berman, *Prejudices and Antipathies*). *See also* Indian, tribal warfare, tribesman.

tribesman *tribe/tribal member, member of a tribe.* However, the use of "tribe" is generally considered ethnocentric or racist; it is particularly inaccurate and inadmissible with respect to African ethnology (use "people"). For American Indians, use "nation," "people," or a specific group name. *See also* savage, tribal warfare, tribe.

trick *prostitute user. See also* john, prostitute.

trickmaster *trickster, magician, conjurer, illusionist, sleight-of-hand artist; hoodwinker, faker, cheat, impostor, swindler, fraud, bunko artist, charlatan, quack, sharpie.* For discussion of "master" words, *see* master.

triggerman *professional/armed killer, killer, gangster, gun, hired gun, gunner, gunfighter, gunslinger, assassin, slayer, gun-wielder/-toter, sharpshooter, sniper, attacker, outlaw, bank robber, bandit, terrorist, racketeer, mobster, hoodlum, liquidator. See also* gunman, holdup man, marksman, rifleman.

Trinity, the *See* Father, Son, and Holy Spirit.

troglodyte this term for the very early or mythical peoples who lived caves or dens is now used to denote someone who is thought to be reactionary, out of date, reclusive, boorish, or backward. It is used inclusively (unlike its near relative, "Neanderthal").

trooper/trouper all meanings of these words are inclusive.

troop sergeant historically, it was undoubtedly a man; if used today, it could refer to either sex.

trophy wife introduced in *Fortune* magazine's 1989 article, "The CEO's Second Wife," this term describes an (apparently) growing trend among chief executives to discard longtime spouses for women typically younger, "sometimes several inches taller, beautiful and very often accomplished." (There are so far no trophy husbands, although the "toyboy" may represent an intermediate stage.)

troubadour woman or man. For information on the little-known women troubadours, see Meg Bogin, *The Women Troubadours.*

truck driver statistics vary, but it appears that from 2% to 10% are women.

truckman *driver, truck driver, trucker; ladder truck firefighter.*

truckmaster historically always a man.

turfman *racetrack regular, horseracing/track fan, devotee of horseracing.*

tutoress *tutor. See also* "feminine" word endings.

twinkie although this could refer to both sexes, it's generally reserved for teenage girls/young women. If you want a more neutral-sounding alternative consider *space ranger, flake, brainless wonder. See also* airhead.

twit man/boy or woman/girl.

two-man (adjective) *See* one-man/two-man/three-man, etc.

two-person single career introduced by Hanna Papanek in 1972, this term describes women's vicarious achievement through their husbands' jobs. Formal and informal institutional demands made of both members of a married couple (of whom only the man is employed by the institution) were prevalent for many years in middle-class occupations in the United States, and still exist in some ways today. These wives' contributions to their husbands' work include status maintenance, intellectual contributions, and public performance. Their rewards consist of raises in salary and perquisites granted to the husband; open acknowledgment of collaboration was infrequent. Although this phenomenon was problematic when it was unquestionably assumed that all women would be willing to be supporter, comforter, backstage manager, home maintainer, and main rearer of children, today it is a valid, satisfying, and practical choice for the couples who freely choose it. Anne H. Soukhanov *(Word Watch)* also notes the phrase "trailing spouse": the partner in a two-career marriage who relinquishes employment in order to follow to a new locale where the other has obtained employment.

tycoon woman or man.

typist man or woman.

tzarina *See* czarina.

U

Unity, not uniformity, must be our aim. We attain unity only through variety.
Differences must be integrated, not annihilated, nor absorbed.

—*M. P. Follett*

All people are made alike.
They are made of bones, flesh and dinners.
Only the dinners are different.

—*Gertrude Louise Cheney*

umpire/ump Pam Postema appears to have been the only woman umpire in professional baseball, but there are umpires of both sexes at other levels of baseball and in other sports.

unbrotherly replace this vague term with more precise words: *unkind, cold, uncaring, unfriendly, unfeeling, uncharitable, mean-spirited, hostile, distant,* etc.

uncivilized *See* primitive.

uncle, I'll be a monkey's this term could be reduced to "Well, I'll be!" although anyone who wants to be a monkey's uncle is probably not a threat to the language. (Correspondent par excellence Bob Considine wrote of female war correspondents: "In Korea, they landed with both feet, and if they aren't in war to stay, I'm a monkey's aunt.")

Uncle Sam while some countries are personified by men, others are personified by women (for example, France's Marianne and Great Britain's Britannia). If you need a sex-neutral replacement for "Uncle Sam" use: *the United States, the United States of America, the U.S., the U.S.A., the U.S. government, the armed forces, the military.*

uncle, say *surrender, give up, throw in the towel/sponge, knuckle under, raise the white flag, draw in one's horns, cry quits/barley, strike sail, throw* *oneself on the mercy of, pack it in, throw up one's hands, capitulate, eat one's words.*

Uncle Tom it is problematic and objectionable to attempt to evaluate another person's behavior and motivation; this judgmental term is better left alone unless you are confident of your usage and your audience. As well as being racist, it is sexist (there is no equivalent for a woman). Possible alternatives include: *collaborator, traitor to one's race, toady, sycophant, stooge, backscratcher, bootlicker, puppet, rubber stamp, dupe, doormat, flunky, subservient/obsequious person.* Today we would speak of someone who has been co-opted.

unconventional spellings to highlight social and linguistic inequities, certain words (for example, herstory, sheroe, thealogy, wimmin, womyn) are spelled unconventionally. None of these terms has replaced the standard term; their use is optional and specific to certain types of material and certain goals of consciousness-raising. In the case of "wimmin" and "womyn," follow the alternative spelling to identify groups that use it. *See also* herstory.

underclass this term is often used as code for poor African Americans. "It suggests that they are a separate group from other poor people, a class by themselves which is 'below' the rest of us. It connotes hopelessness, desperation and violence, and implies that this group lives by values which are different from ours and is therefore immune to efforts to change their economic circumstances" (Paul Kivel, *Uprooting Racism*). He points out that African Americans have no monopoly on poverty; there are over twice as many poor whites as poor blacks in the U.S.; "Nor is there a special 'culture of poverty' (another racially coded phrase). There are certainly negative effects of poverty, but well-paying jobs, access to decent housing and schooling would mitigate most of these."

underclassman *undergraduate.* Or, be specific: *first-year student, second-year student; class of 2005. See also* freshman.

underdeveloped *See* undeveloped/underdeveloped nation.

undercover man *undercover agent/officer, private eye, eye, plainclothes detective, sleuthhound;* sometimes, *spy. See also* G-man, gumshoe, plainclothesman.

underlord *second in command, subordinate, subaltern, underling.*

undermanned *understaffed.*

underprivileged this term, along with "disadvantaged," tends to refer most often to poor black and Spanish-speaking Americans. Instead of using this code word, detail in what specific way advantages are lacking (education, financial resources, housing, access to healthcare, etc.). *See also* culturally deprived/disadvantaged.

undeveloped/underdeveloped nation labeling is always an iffy business; in the case of countries with economic systems and values that differ from those in the U.S., it is especially problematic. Terms that are used, in order of apparent use and acceptability, include: *developing nation, newly industrializing country (NIC), emerging/overexploited nation. See also* culturally deprived/disadvantaged, illiterate, primitive, savage, Third World.

undomestic domesticity is a talent found in both women and men; either may also be "undomestic" without an implied criticism being leveled at undomestic women, which used to be the case. Note that the term itself is vague; spell out what you mean.

unfeminine avoid this vague, self-contradictory cultural stereotype. A woman's clothes, behavior, words, feelings, and thoughts are, by definition, "feminine" because a woman is wearing them, saying them, feeling them, etc. Words like "womanly/unwomanly," "manly/unmanly," "feminine/unfeminine," "masculine/unmasculine," "ladylike/unladylike," and "gentlemanly/ungentlemanly" are based on cultural, not biological, expectations. Language should not underwrite this sort of illogic. The only truly unfeminine things are those things biologically reserved to men. Replace the unhelpful and inexact word "unfeminine" with descriptive adjectives: *cold, hard, selfish, abrupt, analytical, direct, competent, logical,* etc. Note that these adjectives can apply equally well to a man, and that they are not synonyms for "unfeminine" but rather reflect the cultural spin on this word.

ungentlemanly try to define what you mean by "ungentlemanly" and choose precise terms: *impolite, crude, rude, insensitive, thoughtless, discourteous, poorly behaved, ill-mannered, uncivil, disagreeable, inconsiderate.* These adjectives (which can apply equally well to women) are not true synonyms for "ungentlemanly" but rather reflect the way this word is most often used. *See also* unmasculine.

Union Jack the correct term for the normal-sized flag of the United Kingdom (flown on land, or at sea from the starboard yardarm) is Union Flag (or Union Flag of 1801). The Union Jack is a flag smaller than usual flown from a jackstaff at the stern of a British ship. By definition, a "jack" is a small flag, usually indicating nationality, located at the bow of a ship.

union man *union member, labor/trade unionist, unionist, union backer, member of a union, organized worker.*

United Kingdom the full title is the United Kingdom of Great Britain and Northern Ireland; it is commonly called Britain or Great Britain; it is abbreviated U.K. or UK; it includes England, Scotland, Wales, and

Northern Ireland. *See also* British/Briton/Brit, Englishman, Great Britain, Irishman, Scotsman, Welshman.

Unknown Soldier, the this World War I soldier is a man.

unladylike for the vague and often inappropriate "unladylike," substitute *insensitive, indelicate, awkward, uncharming, unkind, rude, undignified, ill-mannered, ungracious, impolite, abrupt,* etc. Note that these adjectives apply equally well to a man, and that they are not synonyms for "unladylike" but rather reflections of what society tends to understand by the word. *See also* unfeminine.

unman *unnerve, disarm, weaken, devitalize, incapacitate, disable, unhinge, undermine, frighten, paralyze, petrify, terrorize, appall, horrify, deprive of courage/strength/vigor/power, render hors de combat, attenuate, shatter, exhaust, disqualify, invalidate, muzzle, enervate, take the wind out of one's sails, put a spoke in one's wheel, undo.* In the narrower sense of emasculate or castrate, use "unman" sparingly as it implies, unflatteringly, that the man is a passive victim. There are no parallel terms referring to women for "unman," "emasculate," and "castrate." *See also* castrate, emasculate.

unmanliness/unmanly replace these limp terms with descriptive adjectives: *dishonesty/dishonest, cowardice/cowardly, deviousness/crooked, weakness/weak, fearfulness/fearful, timidity/timid,* etc. Note that these words can be applied equally well to a woman, and that they are not synonyms for "unmanliness/unmanly" but simply the stereotypical and unreflected notions of a sexist society on what it means to be a man. *See also* unmasculine.

unmanned *unstaffed, having no staff aboard, unpeopled, unpopulated, uninhabited, lacking crew, crewless, remote control, on automatic pilot; frightened, undone. See also* unman.

unmanned space flight *remote-controlled/mission-controlled/control-operated/unpiloted/crewless/automatic space flight.*

unmarried mother *See* unwed mother.

unmasculine avoid this vague, self-contradictory cultural stereotype. A man's clothes, behavior, words, feelings, and thoughts are, by definition, masculine because a man is wearing them, saying them, feeling them, etc. Words like "womanly/unwomanly," "manly/unmanly," "feminine/unfeminine," "masculine/unmasculine," "ladylike/unladylike," and "gentlemanly/ungentlemanly" are based on cultural, not biological, expectations. Language should not underwrite this sort of illogic. The only truly unmasculine things are those things biologically reserved to women. Replace the unhelpful and inexact word "unmasculine" with descriptive adjectives: *timid, craven, weak, indirect, fearful, soft, faint-hearted, gentle, overemotional, comfort-loving,* etc. Note that all these adjectives can apply equally well to a woman, and that they are not synonyms for "unmasculine," but stereotypical cultural notions of what society tends to understand by the word.

unsalaried *See* unwaged.

unsportsmanlike *unsporting, unfair, unfair play/playing, unsporting behavior, dishonorable, underhanded, unprincipled, behavior of a poor loser.*

unstatesmanlike *undiplomatic, impolitic, imprudent, lacking stature/grace and diplomacy, showing poor political strategy/ineffective government leadership.*

Untouchables *Dalits.* "Dalits" (literally, "the oppressed") is preferred; "Untouchables" is approximately the equivalent of "nigger."

unwaged/unsalaried not a synonym for "unemployed," this term recognizes the contributions and economic issues of groups whose work is unpaid (full-time mothers, community volunteers, activists, etc.).

unwanted child in some instances the more precise term is unwanted pregnancy; with those wishing to adopt children outnumbering adoptable babies, the child may be wanted, but by someone other than the birth parents.

unwed mother *mother, woman, head of household, single parent.* Or use whenever possible: *unwed parents.* The term "unwed mother" disregards the also unwed (at least to this woman) father. In addition to not getting the label, the father also avoids getting the child, the poverty, and the social disapproval that come with it. According to a radio news item, "More women than ever before are living with men without being married to them. And more unmarried women than ever before are having babies." A more accurate and inclusive report would have said: "More men and women than ever before are living together without being married. And more unmarried couples than ever before are having babies." If it's not possible to speak of "parents" (perhaps because the father is no longer in the picture), at least do not linguistically stigmatize the woman who has accepted the consequences of her actions. An "unwed father" shows no external signs of his fatherhood—and thus does not make a good target for society's strictures and moralizations. "Unwed mothers" and their children, on the other hand, are all too visible. *See also* teen moms.

unwomanly use instead *cold, hostile, sharp, unloving, ungentle, uncharming, ungiving, unsupportive, ill-mannered, unmannerly, ungracious, undignified, indecorous, unattractive, unappealing.* Note that these adjectives apply equally well to a man, and that they are not synonyms for "unwomanly," but rather reflections of what society tends to understand by the word. *See also* unfeminine.

unworkmanlike *unprofessional, unskillful, slipshod, unskilled, inexpert, inexperienced, untrained, inefficient, unsystematic, unbusinesslike, incompetent, sloppy, careless, unsuitable, irresponsible, unhandy, imprecise, unproficient.*

up and Adam *up and at 'em.* "Adam" was a mistake.

upperclassman *upperclass student.* Or, be precise: *third-year student, fourth-year student; junior, senior; class of 2005.*

urban see Irving Lewis Allen, *Unkind Words,* for an excellent discussion of "urban" as a code word for ethnic minorities and their problems while "suburban" signals white, middle-class, wholesomeness. *See also* inner city.

usherette *usher. See also* "feminine" word endings.

utility girl/utility man *utility worker/hand/cleaner, typewriter repairer.* Note the nonparallel "girl/man."

uxoricide although this term, meaning the killing of a wife by her husband, is not commonly seen, its parallel ("mariticide," the killing of a husband by a wife) does not appear in any dictionaries although "mariticidal" (*wanting* to kill one's husband) appears in a few.

V

A very great part of the mischiefs that vex this world arises from words.

—*Edmund Burke*

Words are seductive and dangerous material, to be used with caution.

—*Barbara W. Tuchman*

It is well that we should become aware of what we are doing when we speak, of the ancient, fragile, and (well used) immensely potent instruments that words are.

—*C. S. Lewis*

Valentino this evocative name is usually just what you want. For inclusive alternatives use *heartthrob, great/dashing lover.*

valet/valet de chambre *personal/room attendant.*

valley girl the valley girl seems to be history now, and as such the term is correct; there never was a "valley boy."

vamp (woman) short for "vampire," this word posits hypnotic power for women and helplessness for men, which disserves both. "Vamp" was popularized by Theda ("Kiss me, my fool") Bara in the 1914 *A Fool There Was.* She and Pola Negri played many other vamps, strongly identifying the role with women.

vampire if there are vampires, they are both women and men; in the metaphorical sense the word is also used of both.

varlet historically varlets were always young men. If an alternative is needed, consider *attendant, menial, page.*

vassal although taken to mean a man, this word is defined as "a servant, slave, dependent, or subordinate," and historically it included all members of the household of the feudal tenant, male and female.

vegetable man *vegetable peddler/vendor.*

venireman *venire/potential juror.*

verger man or woman.

verseman *versifier, rhymester, maker of verses; poet.*

vestryman *vestry member, member of the vestry, parish council member.*

veteran man or woman, for the meaning of both a person who has served in the armed services and an experienced person.

vicar depending on the Protestant denomination, a vicar may be either sex.

vice-chairman *vice-chair, second in command, deputy, deputy director, vice-president.*

vicereine/viceroy these sex-specific titles (literally, "vice-queen" and "vice-king") denote the governor of a country, province, or colony, ruling as the representative of a sovereign. "Vicereine" can mean either a ruler in her own right or the wife of a viceroy. For unofficial uses consider *deputy, ruler, sovereign, governor, regional governor, vice-consul.*

victim the use of this word is problematic in two instances. (1) There appears to be unanimous disapproval of its use to describe people with disabilities (instead of "polio victim" or "victim of multiple sclerosis" say "someone who has polio" or "someone with multiple sclerosis"). According to *The Disability Rag* (now *Ragged Edge*), "'Victim' sensationalizes a person's disability. Instead, avoid emotional language by using 'has': 'has AIDS,' 'had polio.'" (2) Avoid blaming crime or rape victims in subtle ways; "We all want injustice to be the victim's fault" (Hortense Calisher). This is seen in reflections like "what was she doing at a bar at one o'clock in the morning?" or "why did he leave his car unlocked?" Sometimes people can be called, or want to be known as, survivors rather than victims. *See also* date rape; disability; handicapped; provoke; rape; rape victim; "she asked for it"; victimization, culture of; violence.

victimization, culture of commenting on the "recent spate of letters, books, and columns blaming feminism for creating a 'culture of victimization' in which women are supposedly wallowing every time they stand up for their right not to be raped, beaten, sexually harassed, or denied employment or a promotion on the basis of their gender," Brian Ashley says, "It would seem rather obvious that when a person fights back when *others* attempt to make her a victim that she is not 'wallowing in victimhood'; she is, in fact, fighting against it. [The very people] who are having such fun castigating women are the ones who've consistently promoted attitudes, lifestyles, and even laws that not only victimize women but establish barriers preventing women from being able to speak against their oppressors. This 'culture of victimization' baloney is nothing more than another such barrier created by these people in their attempt to recreate a 'natural order' in society. A 'natural order' in which white men are on top and everyone else, especially women, is on the bottom." Those complaining about the "culture of victimization" say that when women resort to the law for redress in sexual harassment or other such suits, it only shows they are weak and need to be protected. But Jodie L. Ahern says we don't think that way when men go to the law. "When a man sues his neighbor for a tree overhanging his property, is he weak and needing protection? Why doesn't he just go *tell* the guy to cut down his tree? And if there is a 'frivolous' lawsuit *(if)* does it diminish the claims of women who have been forced into court as a last resort? Men also file frivolous suits and it doesn't seem to diminish similar but serious suits."

victory for mankind *victory for the world, victory for humankind/all peoples/everyone, our common victory.* **See also** one small step for man, one giant leap for mankind.

victress *victor.* **See also** "feminine" word endings.

Vietnam War note that among Vietnamese, this is often called the American War to distinguish it from other wars, against the Chinese and the French, for example.

vigilante woman or man.

villainess *villain.* **See also** "feminine" word endings.

violence violence has sexist and racist implications: men are more likely than women to be perpetrators of a wide range of violent activities; of all those arrested for violence in any year, the great majority (for the U.S. the figure is around 90%) are men. They are also more liable than women to be victims of violence, while black men are victims more often than white men; in his lifetime an African American man has a 1 in 21 chance of being murdered by an unlicensed gun, compared to a 1 in 131 chance for a white man. Although most violence is not sex-biased in that the sex of the offender or victim is not a contributing factor in the violence, there are two exceptions. (1) Men have died in wars solely because of their sex. While civilians of both sexes also die in wars, and while some women have died in combat, particularly in recent years, their deaths were not institutionalized and their sex was not a factor in their deaths. Young men still face prison and fines for failing to register for the draft; young women do not. (2) Women suffer disproportionately from violence by men, primarily because they are women. According to the Justice Department, three out of four women can expect to be victims of at least one violent attack in their lifetime. There is a high societal tolerance for abusing women; a nationwide Louis Harris Poll found that 25% of the men in the sample approved of a husband slapping his spouse. "Men are raised with a sense of entitlement, privilege and expectation that women can and should do what we want them to do," says Edward Gondolf, a researcher on male violence. "And if they don't we resolve the problem with aggression and force." The violence continuum includes sexist language, anti-woman jokes, abusive rap lyrics, film and TV violence against women, sexual harassment, pornography, wife beating, rape, and murder. Chuck Niessen-Derry of BrotherPeace says men need to "start making the connection between the rape joke on Tuesday and the rape on Thursday." And Myriam Miedzian *(Boys Will Be Boys)* says, "At least 235 studies of the effects of showing violence in films and on television have overwhelmingly shown that watching violence increases violent behavior." Tolerance for the "milder" forms of violence permits the more serious forms. Men are also abused by their wives and murdered by them, although in far smaller numbers. Many of the more serious assaults by wives have been reported as self-defense in response to abuse. This is not to discount the reality of abused men, but to give it perspective: when was the last time a man feared for his physical safety when he passed a group of women on the street? (However, gay men, as well as women, may experience fear when approaching a group of men standing on a corner.) One of the most serious indications of the violence in our culture is the violent death rate of our children. According to a 1996 study by the Centers for Disease Control and Prevention, the U.S. has the highest rates of childhood homicide, suicide, and firearms-related deaths of any of the world's 26 richest nations; nearly three-quarters of all the murders of children in the industrialized world occur in the United States; statistics show that the epidemic of violence that has hit younger and younger children in recent years is confined almost exclusively to the U.S. Some U.S. cities have violence rates higher than some foreign cities in the midst of civil war, like Belfast. *See also* battered wife, date rape, knock-out, lady-killer, provoke, rape, sexual harassment, "she asked for it," victim.

violent language our language reflects our violent ways; it also helps perpetuate them. If you aren't already aware of the frequency of violent language in our speech, consider the following randomly selected common expressions: kill two birds with one stone, big gun/shot, shoot from the hip, shoot down the idea, straight shooter, quick on the draw, smash hit, hit below the belt, on target, kick an idea around, crack the whip, hitting on someone, how does that strike/hit you, knock someone dead/for a loop/out, take a beating, sock it to 'em, give a black eye to, rake someone over the coals, hit someone up for something, slap on the wrist, skin someone alive, knock heads together, beat the tar/stuffing/ living daylights out of someone, pin someone's ears back, give a tongue lashing to, going great guns, one thing triggers another, hair-trigger, blow one's top, blow somebody away, skin someone alive, bite/snap/take someone's head off, shoot full of holes, blast them out of the water, explode onto the scene, twist someone's arm, shoot oneself in the foot, loose cannon, dead meat, hit them where it hurts, take a stab at it, hit or miss, pack a wallop, wipe somebody out, beat one's brains out, knock one's head against a wall, knock oneself out, kill oneself with work, shooting one's mouth off, this'll kill you, this'll knock 'em flat, fight the good fight, hold the fort, hit the [computer] key, make a killing, magic bullet, get someone in the crosshairs, attack someone's argument, deep-six something, heads roll, people are terminated, shot down. *See also* knockout, militaristic language, violence, violently.

violently examine the use of "violently" (as in "objected violently") when what you really mean is *intensely, severely, excessively, virulently, stringently, urgently.*

virago the first dictionary definition of "virago" is "a loud, overbearing woman: termagant." The second is "a woman of great stature, strength, and courage" *(Webster's Ninth New Collegiate Dictionary)* and as such is being reclaimed by some members of the women's movement.

virgin/virginity if you must use these terms for some logical reason, do so for both sexes with equal weight and meaning. The double standard still expects virginity or at least some measure of virginal behavior from women while rewarding men in subtle and unsubtle ways for being experienced. The concept of virginity is also heterosexist, euphemistic, and difficult to define with any precision.

virgin forest/virgin fiber, etc. use only when necessary because of specific designations. Otherwise consider *unspoiled, untouched, pristine, unused, untainted, uncharted, undeveloped, unprocessed, pure.* "Virgin paper" is "nonrecycled paper." John A. Hobson points out that in the computer field, "virgin" means "unused, pristine; in a known initial state" ("Let's try writing it on a virgin diskette and see if it gets corrupted"). In reference to things of nature, "virgin" alludes to their being unused by man (sex-specific word intended). *See also* Mother Nature.

virile this is a properly sex-specific word when it refers to a man's ability to function sexually. In its broader sense, you may want inclusive alternatives: *energetic, vigorous, forceful, strong, powerful, dynamic, spirited, daring, fearless, venturesome, courageous, intrepid, tough, audacious, dashing, potent, hardy, hearty, rugged, bold.*

virtue/virtuous these terms, which come from the Latin *vir* for "man," have two general connotations: the first involves high-minded traits of morality, honor, integrity, and uprightness and is applied generally to men; the second deals with sexual purity (closest synonyms for this sense are chastity, virginity, and purity) and is almost always used for women. Today we rarely refer to a man as virtuous, and if we hear of "a virtuous woman," we "know" two things: she is chaste and her eyes are probably cast modestly down.

visitation (child custody) for some people, this is a common, unambiguous word (it is also the legal term); others find it too closely associated with visits to prisoners, and prefer *access, parenting time.* (The term "access" was used instead of "visitation" in the 1988 Family Support Act.)

visiting fireman *visiting firefighter/colleague.*

visual-effects man *visual-effects coordinator/supervisor/specialist/technician.*

visual impairment *See* blind, impaired.

vivacious as Francine Frank and Frank Anshen point out *(Language and the Sexes),* both girls and boys may have lively personalities, but when did you ever meet a "vivacious" boy? Two-thirds of the *American Heritage Book of English Usage*'s panel on usage felt that "vivacious" could be used only of a female subject. If this interests you, you could either begin trying to present men as vivacious or use more inclusive substitutes: *spirited, high-spirited, full of pep, breezy, animated.*

vizier has always been a man.

volunteer a volunteer can be either a woman or a man, of course, but volunteer work has traditionally been apportioned along sexist lines: "For men it usually means serving in prestigious policymaking or advisory capacities, with the encouragement of the employer to take time off from work to serve as the company's 'goodwill ambassador' to the community. For women, volunteerism means providing direct services at their own expense (transportation, lunch). Second, because women volunteers work almost exclusively at the lowest levels of the volunteer hierarchy, they obtain little valuable work experience or training. Popular mythologies to the contrary, displaced homemakers have been continuously frustrated to find that their résumés, which have meticulously translated 15 to 25 years of volunteer activities into marketable skills, elicit . . . negative responses from prospective employers . . . " (Nijole V. Benokraitis and Joe R. Feagin, *Modern Sexism*).

voodoo as used in expressions like "voodoo economics," the word disparages someone else's religion.

votaress *votary.* **See also** "feminine" word endings.

voyageur history records only male voyageurs.

voyeur although the term is inclusive, factually voyeurs are much more likely to be male, and recent studies indicate that far from being the relatively harmless fellows they were once thought to be, many voyeurs "graduate" to rape and other sex crimes. Use of "voyeur" should reflect the gravity of the behavior.

Words can destroy. What we call each other ultimately becomes
what we think of each other, and it matters.

—*Jeane J. Kirkpatrick*

A broken bone can heal, but the wound a word opens can fester forever.

—*Jessamyn West*

There are worse words than cuss words, there are words that hurt.

—*Tillie Olsen*

Words have their genealogy, their history, their economy, their literature,
their art and music, as too they have their weddings and divorces, their successes
and defeats, their fevers, their undiagnosable ailments, their sudden deaths.
They also have their moral and social distinctions.

—*Virgilia Peterson*

wage earner although the term itself is inclusive, what it means in dollars
and cents reveals societal sexism and racism: female college graduates
generally make less than male high school graduates, with the average
black female college graduate often earning the same as the average
white male high school dropout; more than two-thirds of all minimum-
wage workers are women; disproportionate numbers of women and
members of minority groups lack employment-related benefits such as
health and pension coverage. The situation in Canada is similar, where
women generally must work eight days to earn what men earn in five.
The statistics vary in specifics, but when using the term "wage earner,"
make no assumptions about its current homogeneity.

waiter woman or man. This is the preferred term for both sexes. *See also* waitress.

waitress *waiter, server, attendant, table/restaurant server; serving staff.* Also being used in some areas: *wait, waitron, waitperson; waitstaff.*

Walkman unless referring to Sony's trademarked "Walkman personal stereo," use *headset/headphone radio/tape player, stereo/radio headset/ headphones, walkabout radio/cassette player.*

wallflower although it theoretically could refer to either sex, it's reserved for women/girls and it reflects outdated customs and attitudes.

Walter Mitty there is nothing wrong with evoking Mr. Mitty to convey a ready-made picture of someone like James Thurber's character, but be aware of how many such expressions in the English language are male-based. Balance their use with female-based expressions, creative expressions of your own, or sex-neutral alternatives: *daydreamer, escapist, secret adventurer. See also* sex-linked expressions.

wandering *See* roaming.

wanton this tends to be used only for women, holding them to a higher arbitrary moral standard than men. If you must use it, do so gender-fairly to describe behavior but not people ("they behaved wantonly," not "they were wanton").

war bride were there ever any war grooms? Retain in historical contexts.

wardrobe mistress *wardrobe supervisor/manager/clerk/handler/department/ coordinator.*

wardress *warden. See also* "feminine" word endings.

warehouseman *warehouse laborer; warehouser.*

war hawk/warmaker/warmonger although studies show that the tendency toward warfare is characteristic of men across many cultures (the only nonbiological characteristic that can be attributed consistently to one sex), distrust generalizations: many men have devoted their lives to peace issues and some women are hawkish. *See also* combat, draft.

warlock "witch" (female) and "warlock" (male) are strong, evenly balanced words. If you want sex-neutral alternatives consider *conjurer, sorcerer, magician.*

warlord because of the sex-linked "lord," consider using *military commander/leader, supreme military leader, militarist, warmonger, jingoist.* Another caution is using the term fairly; Joan Steinau Lester *(The Future of White Men and Other Diversity Dilemmas)*, says "*Warlords?* This is a term reserved exclusively for Asians and Africans abroad, and African American or Latino gang leaders at home. Europeans in a similar feudal spot were 'lords of the manor'—or, if they were especially warlike, 'knights.'"

war of/between the sexes *See* battle of/war between the sexes.

warpaint (woman's makeup) probably not.

warpath this is considered objectionable and disparaging. In any case, it's an overworked cliché that wants to be retired.

warrior both women and men have been and are "warriors"—whether this means fighting in battles or living out the warrior archetype. In *The Warrior Queens,* Antonia Fraser describes female warrior-rulers who have often been the focus for what a country afterward perceives to have been its golden age, for example, Queen Elizabeth I of England, 12th-century Queen Tamara of Georgia, or 15th-century Queen Isabella of Spain. In more recent times, women have taken part in every American military crisis since the Revolutionary War. Harriet Tubman planned and led a military campaign for the Union Army in South Carolina in 1863. At least some men—the traditional warriors—are becoming "new warriors" today. Acknowledging and coming to terms with the warrior within, the new warrior is ideally without guilt, shame, or apology about being a man; both fierce and compassionate, he holds himself accountable for his actions. Feeling truly powerful, he does not need to dominate anyone. He directs his considerable energy in constructive, nonthreatening ways and is able to renew connections with self, others, and the world. *See also* Amazon/amazon, combat, warrior (Indian).

warrior (Indian) Indians have typically been called warriors when under other circumstances, living in other lands, they would have been called soldiers. Consider the implications of the words "soldier" and "warrior" as they are used for various conflicts.

washerman/washerwoman/washwoman *launderer, laundry worker, cleaner, drycleaner.*

Washington Redskins *See* Redskins (sports team name).

WASP this acronym for White Anglo-Saxon Protestant has become a simplistic synonym for oppression, discrimination, and spurious superiority. Irving Lewis Allen devotes chapter 10 of *Unkind Words* to WASP, "one of the most ingenious codewords, with several layers of covert meaning."

watchman *security guard, watch, night guard/watch, guard, building guard, security officer/consultant, gatekeeper, guardian, sentry, sentinel, lookout, caretaker, custodian, patrol, patroller; guardian; crossing tender/guard.*

watchman's rattle *sentry's/lookout's rattle, alarm, warning, distress/danger signal.*

waterboatman (bug) leave as is.

water boy *water carrier.*

waterman *boater, ferry/watercraft operator.*

watermanship *swimming/boating/rowing/sailing/water sports skills, canoeing expertise,* etc. Or, reword to describe the person with these skills: *competent swimmer, professional boater, skilled canoeist, veteran rower, proficient/expert/talented/knowledgeable/skillful swimmer/boater,* etc.

water witch *water dowser.*

way to a man's heart is through his stomach, the *the way to a person's heart is through their stomach* (see singular "they"); *the quickest way to the heart is through the stomach, the way to the heart is through the stomach.*

weaker sex, the this is, with justification, rarely heard anymore.

weak sister although this term is used to refer unflatteringly to both men and women (leaning more toward putting down men), the underlying assumption is extremely prejudicial to women. Alternatives include *weakling, weak link in the chain, weak reed to lean on, weak spot, one who blows hot and cold, unreliable/untrustworthy/half-hearted/wishy-washy/fickle person, someone who is weak as a child/weak as water.*

wear the pants (woman assuming "masculine" role) unfashionable term, in both form and content.

weatherman *weathercaster, meteorologist, weather reporter/forecaster/ prophet, forecaster, climatologist.*

wedding although this has also been used for same-sex couples, the more common term is "commitment ceremony." A wedding band/ring is a commitment band/ring.

wedlock far from the imagined imprisonment of facile wit, the "lock" in this word is from the Anglo-Saxon for "gift." "Wed" means "promise." Marriage, or wedlock, is thus the promised gift of happiness.

weekend warrior this is an inaccurate and derogatory way to refer to military reservists. Activated during times of war and at other times engaged in humanitarian services, reservists work hard, live with disrupted lives, and contribute to the common good.

weighmaster *public weigher, licensed public weigher.* Sometimes the official job title "weighmaster" must be used.

weight man *thrower, throw, weight thrower.* Or, be specific: *shot-putter, discus/hammer/javelin thrower.* Both women and men are throwers.

welder man or woman. Approximately 5% are women.

welfare this term is overused in some cases, underused in others, misused much of the time, and often used in discriminatory ways. Material containing the word "welfare" needs to be carefully checked for bias and inaccuracies. "Welfare" includes government moneys that go to individuals and government moneys that go to corporations. In the first type of welfare, the myth is that typical welfare recipients are unemployed, inner-city minorities whose families have received public assistance for generations. However, according to the independent research organization Population Reference Bureau, the average welfare recipient is white and lives in a suburb or rural area; "While many Americans believe that those who are poor will remain for years on public assistance, the study found that one of three people living below the poverty line will be out of poverty within 12 months. While it is often assumed that the poor live primarily off welfare benefits, the study found that less than half the poor receive cash from the government; furthermore, those people would find it difficult to survive on the amount they receive; a typical Georgia AFDC family (one parent, two children), for example, receives $250/month in benefits. While many believe that AFDC takes up an increasingly larger chunk of the federal budget, AFDC costs have been relatively constant— about 2% of the budget—over the past 20 years." According to government estimates, total expenses for AFDC are typically one-fourth what the Pentagon wastes each year; it's not those on AFDC who spend $435 for an $8 hammer, $2,103 for a 13¢ nut, or $640 for a toilet seat (Women, Work & Welfare Task Force). The other kind of welfare, corporate welfare, includes all the federal spending and tax measures that benefit the business community. The Cato Institute reports that in 1994 "corporate wealthfare" included $2 billion in subsidies to electric utilities designed to hold down utility rates in affluent communities like Aspen, Colorado, and Hilton Head, South Carolina; $140 million spent by the Forest Service to build roads providing access to national forests so timber companies can go in and cut them down (over the past 20 years, the Forest Service has built—at public expense—240,000 miles of roads for logging companies); $500 million to prop up the ethanol industry" (Kevin Clarke, in *Salt of the Earth*). From *Humanist News and Views* (July 1996): "U.S. tax dollars support a cartel of the 14 biggest computer chip manufacturers, putting all the smaller companies at a disadvantage. Taxpayers support major companies like Pillsbury, M&M and Sunkist with $110 million per year to help them promote their products abroad. Special interest subsidies and tax laws actually encourage U.S. companies to ship jobs overseas while cutting them here. Big mining companies and many ranchers pay a pittance for the use (and depletion) of federal lands, enriching a few at the expense of many." From *Network* (1995):

billions of dollars of federal lands are sold to mining companies, who are allowed to purchase land for $2.50 to $3.00 per acre and pay no royalties on the minerals they extract. From *Nonviolent Action* (Summer 1996): "The nation's largest corporations and richest citizens receive more welfare money than our social welfare programs. In 1994, the U.S. spent $104.3 billion on corporate welfare and $619 billion on the military, while spending only $14.4 billion on Aid to Families with Dependent Children (AFDC). Federal aid to corporations and wealthy individuals includes bailouts, export promotions, loans, loan guarantees, debt forgiveness, below cost sales, interest free financing and other benefits." Stephen L. Carter (*Utne Reader,* July/August 1996) says, "A central theme of the argument against treating government assistance as an entitlement is that reliance on aid supposedly cripples self-reliance. . . . If welfare programs have bad effects on individuals, they must also have bad effects on corporations, and corporate welfare should receive the same scrutiny—and be subject to the same dismissive rhetoric—as welfare for individuals. The Progressive Policy Institute has pointed out that corporate subsidies are deeply regressive, providing benefits to a relatively small group of upper-income Americans, largely with money taxed from those earning far less. In other words, corporate welfare programs are like individual welfare programs except that they transfer tax dollars from low- and middle-income people to upper-income people." Paul Kivel *(Uprooting Racism)* says, "By 1994, the 1986 tax 'reform' alone had transferred over $200 billion to about 150,000 individuals and families with annual incomes over a half-million dollars. We have corporate welfare policies, such as unlimited deduction for interest on corporate debt, intangible asset write-offs, foreign tax credits and write-offs for banks for foreign debt losses, costing us over $160 millions a year." The *Wall Street Journal* estimates corporate welfare has reached $140 billion a year, including subsidies, grants, bailouts, giveaways, inflated government contracts, tax loopholes, and forgiveness of corporate debt; "Aid to Dependent Corporations" (Robert Reich's term) swamps the mere $23 billion spent by all the states and federal government for AFDC. In 1997 both Democrats and Republicans launched a broad attack on corporate welfare, saying that the elderly and the poor must not be alone in bearing the brunt of government budget cuts. For further information see Theresa Funiciello, *Tyranny of Kindness;* Mark Zepezauer and Arthur Naiman, *Take the Rich Off Welfare;* Fred Strobel, *Upward Dreams, Downward Mobility. See also* welfare mother.

welfare mother *welfare/public assistance client/recipient.* Myths, stereotypes, misinformation, and unjustified hostility surround "the welfare mother." For example, although the prevailing public notion is that welfare families are larger than most, women on welfare actually have fewer children than other women (45.8 per 1,000 welfare recipients give birth each year compared to 71.1 for women in general). "Being a mother is a noble status, right? Right. So why does it change when you put 'unwed' or 'welfare' in front of it?" (attorney Florynce Kennedy). *See also* welfare.

welsh (verb) *renege, default, backpedal, back/pull out, weasel/worm out of, cheat, swindle.* Although this term may or may not have anything to do with the people of Wales, it is considered a slur by them; the Welsh American Legal Defense and Development Foundation has persuaded several news organizations to avoid the terms "welshing" and "welsher."

Welshman *inhabitant/native of Wales, someone from Wales, Welshman and Welshwoman.* Plural: *the Welsh, people of Wales, Welshfolk, Welshwomen and Welshmen* (but never "Welshmen and women").

wench retain in the earlier, historical sense ("young woman" or "female servant"). In its contemporary use (always for a young woman), it could mean "promiscuous," but more often it is a negative reflection on the order of "jerk."

werewolf although this term comes from the word *wer* for "man" and is most often perceived as male, the *American Heritage Dictionary* defines it as "a person transformed into a wolf or capable of assuming the form of a wolf"; use it of either sex (there is no parallel for a woman).

wetback *undocumented resident/worker.* This term, for someone from Mexico in the U.S. without a visa, is derogatory and unacceptable. *See also* ethnic slurs, illegal alien, immigrant.

wet nurse legitimate gender-specific word.

whaleman/whalerman *whaler.* A whaler can also refer to a whaling ship.

wharfman *wharfworker, wharfhand, dockhand, dockworker, stevedore, shoreworker, shorehand, longshore worker.*

wharfmaster *wharfinger, harbor manager.* The nonsexist "wharfinger" is actually the older term (1552); "wharfmaster" came into the language in 1618. For discussion of "master" words, *see* master.

what evil lurks in the hearts of men? *what evil lurks in our/people's/human hearts? what evil lurks in the hearts of humans?*

what in (the) Sam Hill! *what in the heck/hell/world!*

whatsoever a man sows, that shall he also reap *whatsoever you sow, that too shall you reap; whatever we sow we will also reap.*

wheelchair-bound *wheelchair user, someone who uses a wheelchair.* Considered completely unacceptable: wheelchair-bound, confined/bound/restricted to a wheelchair. A wheelchair is a tool, not a prison, something

that frees rather than restricts. *See also* confined, crip/cripple/crippled/
crippler, disability/disabilities, handicapped.

wheelman *cyclist; getaway driver.*

wheelsman *pilot, steerer, navigator.*

whine this word is functionally sexist since it is used primarily of women
and children, while in similar circumstances men are said to ask, tell,
repeat, complain, criticize, or just plain talk. Use instead *complain,
grumble, grouse, gripe, criticize, fume, find fault, be dissatisfied, pester,
harass, fuss, raise a fuss. See also* bitch (verb), complain, fuss, nag.

whipping boy *whipping post, scapegoat, goat, victim, target, dupe, tool.*
Although the most precise synonym, "whipping post" is violent and
might be rejected for that reason. In the historical sense of whipping a
substitute for the prince, it was always a boy. *See also* violent language.

whirling dervish although a dervish is the Muslim equivalent of a monk or a
friar (some of whom whirled), the metaphorical sense is used of both
women and men.

white (noun, referring to people) this is the generally accepted term for all
those who are not people of color, sometimes including, sometimes
excluding, those of Latin ancestry. The tendency is to underuse, not
overuse, "white"; if skin color or ethnicity is pertinent to your material,
check for parallel usage across named groups and include references to
"white" if you have included, for example, references to "black." "White"
is usually spelled lowercase, although the style for some publications and
writers is uppercase. It is not a synonym for Caucasian or Caucasoid
("white" refers to light-skinned peoples of Europe and parts of Asia;
"Caucasian" and "Caucasoid" refer to a now-discounted racial categori-
zation that included Europeans, North Africans, Middle Easterners, and
some people of the Indian subcontinent). "European American" and
"Euro-American" are used instead of "white" to parallel other "-Ameri-
can" usages. The problem with "white" isn't so much with the word itself
as with what it stands for; "The word 'white,' which has been used to
describe European Americans, does not reflect anyone's skin color so
much as a concept of racial purity which has never existed" (Paul Kivel,
Uprooting Racism). *See also* black/black-, Caucasian, -oid, white
(adjective).

white (adjective) whenever possible avoid the metaphorical use of "white"
for purity, goodness, rightness (the opposite of all this being, of course,
black). Do not use "that's white of you" (that's good of you), replace
terms like "white lie" (social/innocent lie), and circumvent others like
"white knight," "white hope," and "white list." *See also* black/black-,
white (noun, referring to people).

White House, the could we at least be aware of the implications of calling the most important house in the country White? This is not a suggestion to rename it (although a woman who called a Boston radio show said she likes to refer to it as the House for the People) but, rather, a signaling of one more way in which we in the U.S. equate "white" with all things superior, and vice versa.

white man's burden one of the most egregious expressions in the language (from Rudyard Kipling's 1899 poem of the same name), this refers to the alleged duty of white peoples to manage the affairs of "less developed" nonwhite peoples; it has served to justify immeasurable horror and injustice, and lingering colonial/domineering/protectionistic/patriarchal attitudes stemming from this phrase still color much Western thought.

white slavery *female sexual slavery.* The use of "white slavery" implies that the unmarked term ("slavery") does not refer to whites, that a special modifier is needed to indicate when it is. In the 19th century, the racist term was used because it was the only form of slavery to which whites were subjected.

whore *prostitute.* "Whore" used to be a nonjudgmental term describing a lover of either sex; now it is a profoundly derogatory term describing a woman. *See also* prostitute.

whorehouse *house of prostitution. See also* prostitute.

whoremonger this ambiguous term can mean both a pimp and a prostitute user; it is rarely seen anymore, which is just as well since it is based on the highly pejorative "whore."

wicked stepmother *See* stepmother, wicked.

widow/widower these are acceptable sex-specific words. If you need an inclusive term use *surviving spouse.* "Widow" and "widower" are also used by lesbian and gay couples when one dies. "Widower" is one of the only male words that is the marked term—that is, the female "widow" is the unmarked or default word and the male word is based on it. Notice how often a woman is referred to as someone's widow—and how very seldom a man is referred to as someone's widower.

widow burning *See* suttee.

widowhood there is such a word as "widowerhood," but you have probably never seen it.

widow lady *widow, surviving spouse. See also* lady; widow/widower.

widow's mite *one's last cent/dime, giving of one's all, giving out of one's need, giving 'til it hurts.* Retain the term sometimes to balance the many male expressions in the language.

widow's peak there appears to be no good inclusive alternative to this recognizable and concise term. Either a man or a woman may have a widow's peak, although the term arose from the superstition that it heralded early widowhood.

widow's walk leave as is. Or, *railed observatory platform.*

wife an acceptable word in itself (from a general Germanic term meaning "female human being"), "wife" is sometimes used gratuitously or in highly sexist ways. An effective test is to see if you would use "husband" in a similar context. Casey Miller and Kate Swift *(The Handbook of Nonsexist Writing)* point out that in the traditional marriage service provided in the Book of Common Prayer, the couple was initially referred to as "the Man and the Woman"; it was not until the words of marriage were pronounced that they were referred to henceforth as "Man and Wife"; "Symbolically, two have been made one, but also symbolically the man's status as a person remains intact whereas the woman's is changed from person to role." This language is history now in many churches, but we have inherited much of its spirit in the use of "wife" today. When *Esquire* offered its readers a special tear-out section entitled "Your Wife: An Owner's Manual," editor-in-chief Lee Eisenberg introduced it: "We are gathered together in the sight of our readers to come to grips with the subject of a man's wife, his partner, the little woman, the missus. . . ." The issue included a list of synonyms for "wife," some of which were positive or neutral and some, acknowledged as offensive, that illustrated what some men and some husbands think of wives: bitch, hussy, old lady, the gadget, Darth Vader, the hag, the nag, the rag, the bag, the spandex monster, my little piranha fish, the war department, twitface, the mouse queen, Evita, the terminator, the queen, the princess, Her Majesty, the boss, the worse half, exec-u-wife, the fishwife, the shrew, the mouth, the ballbuster, the creature, squaw, the powers that be, the ball and chain. *See also* farm wife/farmer's wife, husband and wife, owner, wife/husband, working wife.

wife/husband in Old English, the "hus-wif" and the "hus-band" ("hus" means "house") were parallel terms, titles of respect and honor in the community, descriptors of the couple's partnership as householders. The connotation for both terms was that of "a substantial person." Since that time, the words have taken different roads and were gradually replaced by one of the most glaringly unbalanced gender pairs in the language: "man and wife." Use instead man and woman/woman and man, wife and husband/husband and wife. Use "wife" and "husband" in parallel ways; should you need a word to include both consider *spouse, mate, partner. See also* boyfriend, couple, girlfriend, housewife, hubby, husband, husband and wife, hussy, wife.

wifehood/wifelike/wifeliness/wifely our ideas of "wifelike," "wifely," "wifeliness," and "wifehood" depend entirely on subjective cultural stereotypes. Replace these terms with words that are gender-nonspecific, precise, and descriptive. For example, for "wifely" use *companionable, helpful, supportive, sympathetic, sensitive, affectionate, intimate, loving, approving, admonishing,* etc. These words would do equally well for "husbandly." *See also* wife, woman, womanly.

wife-swapping *spouse-swapping, swinging.* Why don't we have the term "husband-swapping"?

wilderness European Americans generally referred to the lands they settled as "wilderness." American Indians called these same lands their "home-lands" or "sacred geography" (Arlene B. Hirschfelder, in *Library Trends*).

wild Indians most often used to tell children what not to behave like, this term is objected to by American Indians.

wild man *"wild" human.*

willy-nilly this term is male-based, but not because of a man's name; the original expression was "will he or nill he." Even so, it functions inclusively and it would be a rare individual who perceived it as sexist.

wimmin/wimyn/womon/womyn some women favor spellings for "woman/women" that leave out "man/men." These terms should be used for groups and individuals that so name themselves. *See also* unconventional spellings, woman.

winchman *wincher.*

wingman *wingmate, flying partner.* "Wingman" is used in the Air Force for either a woman or a man. *See also* airman.

wingmanship *flying skills/expertise.* *See also* airmanship.

win one's spurs the strong masculine overtones probably come from knights being given golden spurs for their exploits. You can use the expression for both sexes or you could consider an alternative: *earn one's wings, come of age, triumph, succeed, arrive, make a hit, pull it off, carry the day, come off with flying colors, have it all one's own way, have the world at one's feet, turn up trumps, have one's star in the ascendant.*

wireman *wirer, electrician; wiretapper.*

wise as Balaam's ass/Solomon there is nothing wrong with using these phrases, but be aware of how many such expressions in the English language are male-based (or at least in this case, we know Balaam and Solomon were men; the sex of the ass is unknown). Balance their use with female-based expressions, creative expressions of your own, or sex-neutral alternatives: *wise as an owl/a serpent/a judge.* *See also* sex-linked expressions.

wise man *wise person/one, elder, leader, sage, philosopher, oracle, mentor, luminary, learned person, pundit, scholar, savant, authority, expert, guru, thinker.* "Wise man" or "wise woman," which are currently used gender-fairly, will sometimes be the terms of choice. The biblical "Wise Men" remain as they were.

wish is father to the thought, the *See* father to the thought, the wish is.

witch woman or man. Although "witch" has undeservedly negative connotations for many people, it is being reclaimed with pride by the estimated 150,000 witches in the U.S. who tend to be gentle people who believe in responsibility toward self, others, and the world. Write or speak about today's witches only if you are knowledgeable about their beliefs and activities. Genuine benevolent witchcraft does not in any way include, let alone worship, Satan.

wizard in the sense of a sorcerer, magician, conjurer, or witch, we tend to picture a wizard as a man. However, a computer wizard or someone who is a wizard (expert) in some field could be either sex.

wolf (man) there is no inclusive alternative for this term. However, if you want a sex-neutral approximation consider *flirt, seducer, predator, someone who comes on strong.* The distinctive "wolf whistle" is by definition sounded by a man, but women have also used it to tease male friends. (Ruth Weston said, "A fox is a wolf who brings flowers.") *See also* lone wolf, womanizer.

woman the Old English word from which "woman" is taken ("wif-man") came from "wif" ("female") plus "man" ("human being"). Women continued to be "female human beings," which is fairly decent, but the word for "male human beings" ("wer-man") was gradually lost (it survives only in "werewolf") and men got to be human beings, period, full stop, no qualifications for sex. Although suggestions are made from time to time to replace the word "woman," it appears to be solidly positioned in the language. In any case, the problem with "woman" is really "man" (used as a generic). When "human being" is used for everyone, "man" for adult males, and "woman" for adult females, the word "woman" is a respected, acceptable, sex-specific term. Women haven't always been regarded as individuals (*see* farm wife/farmer's wife) or even as human beings (*see* human), and in such roles as lovers, wives, sex partners, and wage earners (*see* girlfriend, prostitute, wage earner, wife) the average woman has not been equal in status to the average man; without the illogical counterweight of pseudogeneric "man"; the word "woman" is in every way equal to the word "man." A neat if perhaps facile summary of female-male history might be Theodor Reik's statement, "In our civilization, men are afraid that they will not be men enough and women are afraid that they might be considered only women." Avoid using "woman" attributively when you would not use "man" in a parallel situation ("woman driver," "woman scientist"). If it is necessary to specify sex, "woman" is preferred to "female" or "lady" ("women candidates"). *See also* female, lady (adjective), lady (noun), wimmin/wimyn/womon/womyn.

woman-hater *See* man-hater/woman-hater.

womanhood both definitions of this word are acceptable—"the state of being a woman" and "women or womankind." "Manhood" (q.v.) has four definitions, two of which are falsely generic, the other two of which correspond to the two definitions for "womanhood." If you want a broader, sex-neutral term use *personhood, selfhood, adulthood, majority, maturity.*

womanish replace this vague and pejorative stereotype with descriptive words: *fussy, particular, overparticular, choosy, fastidious, anxious, overanxious, worried, nervous, timid, weak, indecisive, unathletic, vapid,* etc. "Womanish" uses "like a woman" as an insult to put down men, thus disparaging both sexes with a single word.

womanist used by some black feminists, this term was coined by Alice Walker, who says, "Womanist is to feminist as purple is to lavender" *(In Search of Our Mothers' Gardens). See also* feminist.

womanize/womanizer *philander, bedhop, sleep around, seduce, be promiscuous/sexually active/sexually aggressive/indiscriminate, have many love affairs; swinger, philanderer, seducer, bedhopper, sensualist, free-lover, flirt, freethinker, free spirit, voluptuary, sybarite, hedonist, lover, big-time operator.* It's difficult to find appropriate inclusive substitutes for "womanize" and "womanizer" because we so rarely need that exact word for anything except a man who pursues or courts women habitually or illicitly. Women who philander are either "man crazy" or "promiscuous." Gay men who have many affairs are also "promiscuous" or they have "one-night stands." Ellen Goodman says "manize" hasn't made it into the language because women have always associated sex with danger (rape, pregnancy, the double standard), because getting men on their backs isn't a power trip for most women, and because so far the power of successful older women does not seem to act as an aphrodisiac on younger, good-looking men. There have been too few highly public and powerful women to know if "manizing" is something women would do (Golda Meir? Indira Gandhi? Margaret Thatcher? probably not). *See also* ladies' man, man about town, playboy, rake.

womankind there is a legitimate use for the word "womankind," where "mankind" is problematic since it has been misused for so long as a pseudogeneric.

womanlike/womanliness/womanly these vague and subjective cultural stereotypes convey different meanings to different people according to their perceptions of what a woman ought or ought not do, say, think, feel, and look like. They have nothing to do with sex and everything to do with gender. Choose words instead that express precise characteristics: *gracious/graciousness, warm/warmth, gentle/gentleness, receptive/ receptivity, supportive/supportiveness, tender/tenderness, charming/ charm, sympathetic/sympathy, nurturing/nurturance, well-mannered/ good breeding, considerate/consideration, kind/kindness, intuitive/ intuition, strong/gentle strength,* etc. All these words may be used equally appropriately of a man. They are not synonymous with the sexist terms, but are rather what people generally seem to mean by them. *See also* gender.

woman's place is in the home, a when a man's "place" is also in the home and when the woman truly wants to be there, this is a powerful sentiment. It also rings true if we substitute "heart" for "place" and apply it to both sexes. Unfortunately, this dictum has been used with all the finesse of a sledgehammer and promulgated as a "natural" law, as well as a test of patriotism, "femininity," conjugal love, and right-thinking. Working at home is an excellent choice for many women and one that society ought to value and support with positive attitudes and practical assistance. This expression becomes a problem when it is used as a mandate for all women, ignoring a man's involvement with the home.

woman suffrage movement this is the term used most often by historians.

woman's work except for what goes on during childbirth, there is no work biologically specific only to women. "[I]t is a retrogressive idea to call any particular sphere of work 'Women's'. We do not know what women's work will be, we only know what it has been" (Caroline Boord, *The Freewoman*, 1911). *See also* man's work.

women and children pairing women with children is illogical, belittling to women, and a paternalistic attempt to perpetuate the subordination and powerlessness of women. The Napoleonic Code (1804) did much to legitimize the second-class status of European women. Among other things, the code grouped women and children with "persons of unsound mind," judging them all equally incapable of entering into contracts. *See also* innocent victim, women and children first.

women and children first *those who need extra assistance first.* This expression probably arose not so much from some medieval idea of chivalry as from a more ancient fact of life: an early society's main chance for survival rested on its being able to reproduce itself. Men can father children every day, but women need nine months to produce a child, and a child represents a considerable investment in the future. Thus in times of crisis, women and children were protected so as to ensure the future of the society. Today the future of our society depends on both sexes. *See also* innocent victim, women and children.

womenfolk *See* menfolk.

women's intuition *intuition, sixth sense, hunch, perspicacity, insight.* As a concept, "women's intuition" doesn't do much for either sex; underneath the implied compliment it imputes a certain insensitivity to men and a certain erratic reasoning to women.

women's issues by using this vague label, politicians and others are able to discount and stereotype issues such as abortion rights, ageism, childcare, comparable worth, divorce, domestic violence, the Equal Rights Amendment, flextime, parental leave, poverty, rape, and sexual harassment, when they are in fact family, political, social, ethical, and human issues.

women's lib/women's libber *women's liberation movement, women's movement, feminism, feminist movement; feminist, supporter/member of the women's movement.* "Women's lib" and "women's libber" may be used sometimes positively among women, but in general, the terms are considered derogatory, patronizing, trivializing, and condescending when used by people who are feeling hostile. *See also* shortened forms of words.

women's movement/women's liberation movement/women's rights movement in 1838, Adelaide Anne Procter wrote to her friend Anna Jameson, "The men are much alarmed by certain speculations about women; and well they may be, for when the horse and ass begin to think and argue, adieu to riding and driving." In the same year, Sarah M. Grimké wrote, "I ask no favors for my sex. All I ask of our brethren is, that they will take their feet from off our necks." In 1739 it was Sophia, identified only as "A Person of Quality": "What a wretched circle this poor way of reasoning among the Men draws them insensibly into. Why is learning useless to us? Because we have no share in public offices. And why have we no share in public offices? Because we have no learning." Or Mary Astell in 1694: "Women are from their very infancy debarred those advantages with the want of which they are afterwards reproached. . . . So partial are men as to expect bricks when they afford no straw." Choose almost any year and you will find women writing, agitating, outlining arguments we are still using today. In that sense, there has always been a women's movement. However, the "women's rights movement" as a formal movement commonly dates from 1848 when women met in Seneca Falls, New York, to draw up the first public protest in the U.S. against the political, social, and economic repression of women. The "women's liberation movement," which grew out of leftist politics in the 1960s, was never a monolithic group, but its proponents generally espoused more radical issues than those of the women's movement; they were also the first to promote consciousness raising. The feminist movement, which has been around for several centuries at least, has had different focuses and is generally more politicized and radicalized than the women's movement—a general term that covers most of the activities defined as women working for equality of opportunity and access.

women's studies there are approximately 650 women's studies programs in the U.S. and nearly 400 women's centers and research institutes. There are also numerous professional journals, and over 100 feminist bookstores. *See also* men's studies.

Wonder Woman Wonder Woman is not a female parallel for Superman, Batman, or Tarzan. Cheris Kramarae *(Women and Men Speaking)* points out that, without belittling her strength, magic, courage, and independence, it must be said that Wonder Woman is an aberration rather than a super specimen of her gender: "She lives in a community that is dominated by women; however, there are no men living on her island. Even on the island, the queen is given insight, wisdom, and knowledge by two men from another world. All the women except Wonder Woman are spectators to the action of the story."

wonk this new anti-intellectual term, of unknown origin meaning an industrious student or grind, seems to function inclusively; both President Bill Clinton and Hillary Rodham Clinton have been referred to as wonks.

woodsman in the sense of someone who lives and works in the woods or who enjoys the outdoors, "woodsman" has few good sex-neutral alternatives. Fortunately, "woodswoman" is a functional, independent term (although not in most dictionaries yet), thanks to Woodswomen, an organization for outdoorswomen who like outdoor sports and adventure travel. Rebecca A. Hinton writes in *Women's Outdoor Journal,* "Women have been enjoying the outdoors since the beginning of time, but if we'd all been wearing camouflage we couldn't be more invisible." In some contexts you can use: *woodlander, forest dweller, backsettler; woodworker, carver, woodcrafter, carpenter; forester, logger, woodchopper, woodcutter, woods worker.*

working father according to the Bureau of National Affairs, fathers still define themselves primarily as providers and continue to face traditional pressure to be good workers, but they are increasingly torn between work and family, wanting to connect with their children in stronger ways than their own fathers did. In one study 36% of fathers and 37% of mothers reported "a lot of stress" in balancing work and family. Men often keep quiet about their family interests because of workplace attitudes, but fear of reproducing their fathers' absence and detachment sets up conflicts for them as they move through their careers; 58% of the male workforce are men with children under 18. Companies are beginning to recognize this need and to consider benefits (time off, childcare facilities, flexible benefit programs, etc.) for both fathers and mothers. *See also* childcare, parent, provider.

working girl *worker, employee, jobholder, wage earner, laborer.* Or, be specific: *typist, programmer, mechanic, librarian, pipefitter, teacher, physician, electrician.* "Working girl" is sexist (we have no "working boys"), inaccurate (if she's old enough to work, she's not a girl), and has unpleasant overtones; in the late 1940s it was synonymous with prostitute. *See also* businessman, career girl/career woman, working mother, working wife, working woman.

working man *worker, employee, jobholder, wage earner, laborer, day laborer, average/typical worker, blue-collar/industrial worker, professional.* Or, be specific: *programmer, mechanic, librarian, pipefitter, teacher, physician, electrician.* *See also* wage earner, working father, working girl, working mother, working wife, workman.

working mother using this term to describe mothers who work outside the home implies that mothers who work inside the home do not really work. For those who work outside the home, use *wage-earning/jobholding/ salaried woman/mother, woman/mother employed outside the home/in the paid workforce, working-for-pay mother,* or her specific job title. For those who work inside the home, use *nonsalaried/unsalaried woman/ mother, woman/mother working/employed inside the home/at home, at-home parent, home-working mother, home-employed mother, woman who works as a homemaker, woman who is her own child-care giver* (the last two are used by the U.S. Department of Labor). Question the need to specify gender and the existence of offspring; most of the time your meaning will be served by a neutral term like "jobholder." (At work, too often men with children are men, and women with children are mothers.) If both partners work, use inclusive terms like *working parents, a two-income/two-paycheck family, two-earner/dual-career/dual-income couple.* Mothers who work inside the home and those who work outside it both have their hands full; William Safire points out that "motherhood begins with *labor,* and the work does not end when the little job product is brought home." Although working mothers have been criticized for destroying the traditional family, they have, on the contrary, kept millions of children from sinking below the poverty line; two-thirds of the women in the workforce today are either the sole support of their children or have husbands who earn less than $15,000 a year. *See also* housewife, housework, maternity leave, second shift, woman's work, working wife, working woman.

working wife using this term to describe married women who work outside the home implies that married women who work inside the home do not really work. To describe the former, use *wage-earning/job-holding/salaried woman, woman employed outside the home/in the paid workforce,* or her specific job title. To describe the latter, use *nonsalaried/unsalaried woman, woman working/employed inside the home/at home.* If both partners work, avoid gender-specific distinctions and describe the couple as *a working couple, a two-income/two-paycheck family, two-earner/dual-career/dual-income couple/household.* There is sometimes a hint of disapproval in discussing the working wife; the subtext is: "She has a husband—why is she working?" *See also* housewife, housework, second shift, woman's work, working mother, working woman.

working woman *worker, employee, jobholder, wage earner, laborer, day laborer, average/typical worker, blue-collar/industrial worker, professional;* "working woman" also includes those who work inside the home. Or, be specific: *programmer, mechanic, librarian, pipefitter, teacher, physician, electrician.* From a 1919 *Smith College Weekly:* "We cannot believe that it is fixed in the nature of things that a woman must choose between a home and her work, when a man may have both." *See also* career girl/career woman, housewife, housework, second shift, working girl, working mother, working wife, workman.

workman *worker, artisan, crafter, employee, laborer, operator, hand, staff.* Or, be specific: *repairer, landscaper, electrician. See also* handyman, odd-job(s)-man, repairman, working man.

workmanlike/workmanly *skillful, skilled, expert, professional, businesslike, competent, efficient, careful, precise, proficient, first-rate, top-flight.*

workman quarrels with his tools, a bad *See* bad workman quarrels with his tools, a.

workmanship *artisanship, work, construction, handiwork, handicraft, artisanry, skilled-craft work, skill, technique, style, expertness, expertise, competence, proficiency, finish, quality, polish, execution, technique, performance.* "Workmanship" may need to be retained in the legal sense as case law often uses it.

workmen's compensation *workers' compensation.*

worth a king's ransom *See* king's ransom.

writing guidelines for guidelines on using fair and accurate people language, *see* the Writing Guidelines, pp. 1–27, where you will find definition of terms, issues on naming, information on pseudogeneric "he" and "man/

men/mankind," and special problems. ***See also*** entries in the main part of this guidebook: adjectival forms as nouns, exclusive language, "feminine" word endings, inclusive language, "insider/outsider" rule, offensive, "people first" rule, prostitute, pseudogeneric, salutations (letters), sexist language, sexist quotations, sex-linked expressions, shortened forms of words, singular "they," "the," unconventional spellings.

wuss/wussy *See* coward.

Y

It always seemed to me that white people were judged as individuals. But if a Negro did something stupid or wrong, it was held against *all* of us.

—Bessie Delany

If a man does something silly, people say, "Isn't he silly?"
If a woman does something silly, people say, "Aren't women silly?"

—Doris Day

It is sad, very sad, that once more, for the umpteenth time, the old truth is confirmed: "What *one* Christian does is his own responsibility, what *one* Jew does is thrown back at all Jews."

—Anne Frank

yachtsman *yacht owner/captain/racer/sailor, yachter; yacht club member; yachtswoman and yachtsman.* **See also** seaman.

yachtsmanship *yachting skills/techniques/proficiency, yacht sailing techniques.*

Yahweh (YHWH) because this personal name for God is not gender-specific, it has been used by groups seeking inclusive terms. However, observant Jews neither use nor speak this sacred word, and out of respect for this belief system, many non-Jews have chosen to forego its use also. Jews use instead "Ha-Shem" ("The Name"). Jews also refer to God as "Adonai," "Lord," and "Eloheino"—but never "Jehovah." **See also** Father (God), God, Jehovah, Lord.

yammer nobody yammers very much, but apparently men absolutely never do. For alternatives to this functionally sexist word, *see* babble, chatter, and gossip (verb).

Yankee/Yank/Yanqui a positive term today when used to refer to New Englanders, "Yankee" was originally derogatory and is still occasionally used that way in other countries to refer to the United States ("Yankee, go home"). During the Civil War, it referred to any Northerner; traces of this antagonism can sometimes be heard in it today. Like all shortened forms, "Yank" is disparaging; "Yanqui" is the Spanish-language term sometimes used as an epithet. "Yankee" also has some negative overtones of cleverness verging on sharp practices.

yardman *yard worker/laborer, caretaker, odd-job laborer; gardener, landscaper; yard supervisor/chief; stockyard handler/laborer; railroad worker.*

yardmaster *yard manager/supervisor, railroad yard operations supervisor.*

yellow according to the *American Heritage Book of English Usage* (1996), "Of the color terms used as racial labels, *yellow*, referring to Asians, is perhaps the least used and the most clearly offensive." Yellow has also been used to single out Jews: in some countries during the Holocaust, Jews were forced to wear a yellow badge; the Nazis required yellow stars. The color has also been associated with cowardice. *See also* high yellow, yellow/yellow-bellied, etc., yellow peril.

yellow/yellow-bellied/yellow-bellied coward/yellow belly/yellow streak down one's back wholly reserved for boys/men, these insults indirectly discount girls/women (who have not been expected—or allowed—to accept challenges that call for courage, bravery, or risk-taking) and hold men/boys to impossibly high, dubious, and constantly shifting standards of courage. Boys/men are acculturated to be sensitive to taunts of "coward." Most people would not use these terms; they are included here to show the cultural bias that expects too much of men and too little of women. *See also* coward.

yellow peril this term, expressing turn-of-the-century fear of being "overrun" by peoples from Asia, is rarely seen today. In discussing it historically you may want to use quotation marks to show the dubiousness of the concept.

yente/yenta this Yiddish word for a constantly talking, gossiping, meddling, or scolding woman is defined fairly negatively (synonyms include "gossip" and "blabbermouth"), yet few people hear it that way today—partly because it's not commonly used as an epithet and perhaps partly because of the Barbra Streisand movie *Yentl*. For inclusive alternatives, *see* gossip (noun).

yeoman/Yeoman of the Guard/yeomanry/yeoman's service some of these terms have historical (yeoman, yeomanry, yeoman's service) or official

(Yeoman of the Guard, yeoman) meanings that defy substitution, but others can be variously replaced: *retainer, attendant; military corps personnel attached to the British royal household; smallholding/ freeholding farmer, smallholder, freeholder; petty officer, clerical officer; clerk, paralegal, typist, copyist, transcriber; helper; beefeater, warden, bodyguard. See also* yeomanly, yeoman's job.

yeomanly there isn't a great call for this adjective so it is not overwhelming us with its manly presence. If you should need a sex-neutral term consider *loyal, faithful, courageous, stalwart, staunch, steadfast, true, true-hearted; unwavering, unswerving, firm, stable, solid.*

yeoman's job this is a difficult term to replace; consider making up your own metaphor or using *impressive/remarkable/extraordinary/outstanding/valiant/heroic/superexcellent/first-class/bang-up/A-number-one job, massive/enormous effort.*

yes man *yea-sayer, toady, rubber stamp, sycophant, flunky, puppet, stooge, dupe, brown-noser, apple polisher, bootlicker, backscratcher, flatterer, hanger-on, follower, doormat, tool, minion, myrmidon; an obsequious underling.* (Hugh Rawson, *Wicked Words,* says that earlier, such people were known as *amen* men, and even earlier as *yea-forsooth* types.) *See also* company man, organization man.

yessiree, Bob! *Yes indeed! Yessiree!* But feel free to use this harmless expression. Abbott and Costello would have said if Bob don't mind, why should we?

Yid offensive slang, from "Yiddish," but one that is sometimes used by Jews themselves. *See also* shortened forms of words.

yogi woman or man. Indians call the woman a "yogini."

yokefellow *yokemate, partner, sidekick, helpmate, right hand, comrade, co-partner, co-worker, companion, opposite number.*

yokel this disparaging, anti-rural, usually classist term is also functionally sexist as it is almost always used for a man.

Yonsei this is an acceptable term for fourth-generation Japanese Americans. *See also* Issei, Kibei, Nisei, Sansei.

Yorkshireman *inhabitant/native of Yorkshire, someone from Yorkshire, Yorkshirewoman/Yorkshireman.* Plural: *Yorkshirewomen and Yorkshiremen* (but never "Yorkshiremen and women").

young lady *young woman.* For discussion, *see* lady.

youngster female or male. When used of a child, it is respectful and correct, if somewhat less common today than it used to be. When used jocularly to refer to or address older people, it is in questionable taste.

you people this phrase is not so much objectionable—although it is that too—as it is a glaring betrayal of the speaker's feelings (generally hostile, disparaging, and shaming) about "those people" (a companion term).

You've come a long way, baby! although this phrase looks gender-free, it has been so profoundly associated with a cigarette advertisement aimed at helping women catch up to men's lung cancer and cardiac death rates that "baby" is assumed to be female. In addition, it is generally women who have been called by "endearments" that make of them babies, babes, girls, and other young, helpless dependents. If you want to defeminize it, men's groups have been known to use: "You've come a long way, Bubba!" It's also being used simply without the "baby."

yuppie/Yuppie from "young urban professional," "yuppie" has the usual defects of a facile label: imprecision, thoughtless and unsupported usage, and a distancing from the reality and humanity of those being tagged. Although the term sounds flattering, it implies a materialistic, egocentric approach to life and fails the self-naming test: rarely has anyone announced with genuine pride, "I am a yuppie." You may want to set it in quotations.

Z

No dictionary of a living tongue ever can be perfect, since while it is hastening to publication, some words are budding and some falling away.

—Samuel Johnson

The dictionary is . . . only a rough draft.

—Monique Wittig and Sande Zeig

zoo apparently because of the colloquial association of "zoo" with confusion and disorder, the New York Zoological Society decided to rename its zoos "wildlife conservation parks." Stanley Park Zoo in Vancouver was considering calling itself Stanley Park Wildlife Biology Centre for the same reason. Using "zoo" metaphorically also makes certain assumptions about the people involved in the confusion and disorder. Although this is the last and probably the "least" entry in the book, it offers another opportunity to think about word choices.

Bibliography

The books and articles listed here have been selected to provide a working knowledge of the principles, research, and theory underlying the fair and accurate use of language. Some offer extensive bibliographies if you are interested in further reading. The majority of the titles deal with sex-bias in language because to date more work has been done in that area, but the principles and understandings are useful in dealing with all biased language.

Allen, Irving Lewis. *Unkind Words: Ethnic Labeling from Redskin to WASP* (New York: Bergin & Garvey, 1990).
>   Highly recommended. See also his *The Language of Ethnic Conflict.*

American Heritage Book of English Usage (Boston: Houghton Mifflin Company, 1996).
>   Useful, authoritative sections on "Gender" and "Names and Labels."

American Psychological Association. *Publication Manual of the American Psychological Association,* 4th ed. (Washington, DC: APA, 1994).
>   See "Expression of Ideas: Guidelines to Reduce Bias in Language," pages 46–60.

Baron, Dennis. *Grammar and Gender* (New Haven: Yale University Press, 1986).
>   Highly recommended; a classic.

Berman, Sanford. *Prejudices and Antipathies: A Tract on the LC Subject Heads Concerning People* (Jefferson, NC: McFarland, 1993).
>   Although this update of the 1971 edition is oriented toward librarians, Berman's principles and examples make it a "must read" for anyone interested in biased language.

Bodine, Ann. "Androcentrism in Prescriptive Grammar: Singular 'They,' Sex-Indefinite 'He,' and 'He or She'," *Language in Society* 4 (1975): 129–46.
>   This classic work on the topic is also reprinted in Deborah Cameron's *The Feminist Critique of Language* (London: Routledge, 1990).

Bosmajian, Haig A. *The Language of Oppression* (Lanham, MD: University Press of America, 1974, 1983).
>   This excellent, groundbreaking work covers the language of anti-Semitism, white racism, Indian derision, sexism, war.

Clausen, Jan. *Beyond Gay or Straight* (Philadelphia: Chelsea House Publishers, 1997).
Good definitions of terms like "gender identity," "transsexual," "heterosexism."

Frank, Francine, and Frank Anshen. *Language and the Sexes* (Albany: State University of New York Press, 1983).
Readable, highly recommended.

Frank, Francine Wattman, and Paula A. Treichler. *Language, Gender, and Professional Writing: Theoretical Approaches and Guidelines for Nonsexist Usage* (New York: The Modern Language Association of America, 1989).
Highly recommended.

GLAAD (Gay & Lesbian Alliance Against Defamation). *Media Guide to the Lesbian and Gay Community* (New York: GLAAD, 1995).
This handbook contains a glossary of terms and usages as well as background information on lesbian and gay issues. Available from GLAAD, 150 West 26th Street, Suite 503, New York, NY 10001, 212-807-1700.

Hardman, M. J. "The Sexist Circuits of English," *The Humanist* 56, no. 2 (March/April 1996): 25–32.
The author makes the connection between the structures of language and the social order; she details the sexist concepts that are built into the English language and describes her work with the Jaqi people, whose language has a very different conceptual framework.

Hill, Alette Olin. *Mother Tongue, Father Time: A Decade of Linguistic Revolt* (Bloomington: Indiana University Press, 1986).
A review of language changes in the years 1975–1984.

Hofstadter, Douglas R. "Changes in Default Words and Images, Engendered by Rising Consciousness," and "A Person Paper on Purity in Language," *Metamagical Themas: Questing for the Essence of Mind and Pattern* (New York: Basic Books, 1985).

International Association of Business Communicators. *Without Bias: A Guidebook for Nondiscriminatory Communication* (New York: John Wiley & Sons, Inc., 1977, 1982).
One of the earliest and most useful, this guidebook treats all forms of bias, using clear, helpful examples.

Kay, Mary Ritchie. *Male/Female Language* (Metuchen, NJ: Scarecrow, 1975).
By a linguist who pioneered the subject, this is one of the earliest books on sexist language; includes a comprehensive bibliography.

King, Ruth, et al. *Talking Gender: A Guide to Nonsexist Communication* (Toronto: Copp Clark Pitman Ltd., 1991).
Presents rationale for language reform in both English and French and offers recommendations for rendering language nonsexist.

Kramarae, Cheris, ed. *The Voices and Words of Women and Men* (Oxford: Pergamon Press, 1980).
An excellent collection that includes Jeanette Silveira, "Generic Masculine Words and Thinking" and Donald G. McKay, "The Pronoun Problem." See also Cheris Kramarae, *Women and Men Speaking: Frameworks for Analysis* (Rowley, MA: Newbury House, 1981).

Kramarae, Cheris, and Paula Treichler. *Amazons, Bluestockings and Crones: A Feminist Dictionary* (London: Pandora Press, 1992; first published as *A Feminist Dictionary*, 1985).
This classic includes an extensive bibliography.

Kramarae, Cheris, Muriel Schulz, and William M. O'Barr, eds. *Language and Power* (Beverly Hills, CA: Sage Publications, 1984).

Lakoff, Robin. *Language and Women's Place* (New York: Harper & Row, 1975).
   An early and influential discussion of language and gender, this monograph has been widely discussed and debated, and has provided the impetus for much subsequent work. See also Robin Tolmach Lakoff, *Talking Power: The Politics of Language in Our Lives* (New York: Basic Books, 1990).

Macmillan Publishing Company. *Guidelines for Creating Positive Sexual and Racial Images in Educational Materials* (New York: Macmillan, 1975).
   This 96-page booklet is a pioneering work that still makes good sense today. Available from Macmillan, 866 Third Avenue, New York, NY 10022.

Miller, Casey, and Kate Swift. *The Handbook of Nonsexist Writing: For Writers, Editors and Speakers*, 2nd ed. (New York: Harper & Row, 1980, 1988).
   This is to nonsexist usage what Strunk and White's *Elements of Style* is to writers in general—a "must read." See also their groundbreaking *Words and Women: New Language in New Times* (New York: Anchor/Doubleday, 1976, updated 1991).

Mills, Jane. *Womanwords: A Dictionary of Words About Women* (New York: The Free Press, 1989, updated 1996).

Nelsen, Vivian Jenkins, and Dan Olson. *New Voices in the Media: The INTER-RACE Race & Media Guidebook,* 2nd ed. (Minneapolis: Inter-Race, 1997).
   Highly recommended. Available from Inter-Race, The International Institute for Interracial Interaction, 600 21st Avenue South, Box 212, Augsburg College, Minneapolis, MN 55454, 612-339-0820.

Nilsen, Alleen Pace, Haig Bosmajian, H. Lee Gershuny, and Julia P. Stanley. *Sexism and Language* (Urbana, IL: National Council of Teachers of English, 1977).
   Highly recommended.

Pauwels, Anne, ed. *Women and Language in Australian and New Zealand Society* (Mosman, N.S.W.: Australian Professional Publications, 1987).
   A good overview of research in this area.

Rawson, Hugh. *Wicked Words: A Treasury of Curses, Insults, Put-Downs, and Other Formerly Unprintable Terms from Anglo-Saxon Times to the Present* (New York: Crown, 1989).
   Offers interesting background on many terms.

Schwartz, Marilyn, and the Task Force on Bias-Free Language of the Association of American University Presses. *Guidelines for Bias-Free Writing* (Bloomington: Indiana University Press, 1995).
   Concise, practical chapters on usage in gender, race, ethnicity, citizenship and nationality, religion, disabilities, sexual orientation, and age.

Shear, Marie. "Solving the Great Pronoun Problem: 14 Ways to Avoid the Sexist Singular" and "Equal Writes" (a review of guidebooks on unbiased communication).
   For copies of these articles, send a #10 self-addressed stamped envelope and $5 for each article to: Marie Shear, 282 East 35th Street, #7N, Brooklyn, NY 11203-3925.

Smith, Philip M. *Language, the Sexes and Society* (Oxford: Blackwell, 1985).
   Includes an extensive bibliography.

Sorrels, Bobbye D. *The Nonsexist Communicator: Solving the Problems of Gender and Awkwardness in Modern English* (Englewood Cliffs, NJ: Prentice Hall, 1983).
> An excellent guide with practical suggestions.

Spender, Dale. *Man Made Language* (London: Routledge & Kegan Paul, 1980, 1985).
> One of the early, influential works on sexist language; highly recommended.

Stedman, Raymond William. *Shadows of the Indian: Stereotypes in American Culture* (Norman, OK: University of Oklahoma Press, 1982).
> An excellent exposition of the image of American Indians in U.S. culture; while there is little specifically on language, it is useful in avoiding bias that is content/context-based rather than word-based.

Thorne, Barrie, Cheris Kramarae, and Nancy Henley, eds. *Language, Gender and Society* (Rowley, MA: Newbury House Publishers, Inc., 1983).
> This important collection of key essays includes Wendy Martyna, "Beyond the He/Man Approach: The Case for Nonsexist Language"; Donald G. MacKay, "Prescriptive Grammar and the Pronoun Problem"; and a 187-page annotated bibliography.

Thorne, Barrie, and Nancy Henley, eds. *Language and Sex: Difference and Dominance* (Rowley, MA: Newbury House, 1975).
> This landmark collection includes Alma Graham, "How to Make Trouble: The Making of a Non-Sexist Dictionary," Muriel Schulz, "The Semantic Derogation of Women," Cheris Kramer, "Women's Speech: Separate But Unequal?" and Barrie Thorne and Nancy Henley, "Difference and Dominance: An Overview of Language, Gender, and Society."

Three Rivers, Amoja. *Cultural Etiquette: A Guide for the Well-Intentioned* (Indian Valley, VA: Market Wimmin, 1991).
> Excellent overview of issues.

Todasco, Ruth, and the Feminist Writers Workshop, *An Intelligent Woman's Guide to Dirty Words: English Words and Phrases Reflecting Sexist Attitudes Toward Women in Patriarchal Society, Arranged According to Usage and Idea* (Chicago: Loop Center YWCA, 1973).
> List and analysis of the pejorative words referring to women—e.g., Woman as Whore, Woman as Whorish, Woman as Body, Woman as Animal, Woman as *-ess,* Woman as *-ette.*

Vetterling-Braggin, Mary, ed. *Sexist Language* (Totowa, NJ: Littlefield, Adams and Co., 1981).
> These 23 essays include philosophical positions as well as practical issues: courtesy titles, terms for sexual activity, pseudogenerics, parallels with racist language.